Dictio

Latin and Greek

Quotations, proverbs, maxims, and mottos, classical and mediaeval, including law terms and phrases

Editor

H. T. Riley

Alpha Editions

This edition published in 2020

ISBN : 9789354031489

Design and Setting By
Alpha Editions
email - alphaedis@gmail.com

A DICTIONARY

OF

LATIN AND GREEK

QUOTATIONS, PROVERBS, MAXIMS AND MOTTOS,

CLASSICAL AND MEDIÆVAL.

INCLUDING LAW TERMS AND PHRASES.

EDITED BY

H. T. RILEY, B.A.,

LATE OF CLARE HALL, CAMBRIDGE.

LONDON: GEORGE BELL AND SONS, YORK STREET,
COVENT GARDEN.

1891.

PREFACE.

A Dictionary of Latin Quotations more copious, correct, and complete than any hitherto published had long been a cherished idea of the publisher, and awaited only time and circumstance for its development. Finding in the present editor a gentleman well qualified both by reading and industry to carry out his views, he placed the materials in his hands, and these with large additions, the fruit of further researches, are now laid before the reader.

The present collection differs from its predecessors in being limited exclusively to Latin and Greek quotations, the publisher intending, at a later period, to give French, Italian, Spanish, and German, in a separate volume. This arrangement has enabled him to nearly quadruple the number of Latin quotations given heretofore, and to extend the number of Greek from about twenty to upwards of five hundred; amounting in all to an aggregate of more than eight thousand.

The translations are throughout either new or carefully revised, and as literal as is consistent with neatness and point. It would have been easy to make many of them more epigrammatic, but it was thought better to leave this to the reader's own taste.

Authorities are adjoined wherever it has been found possible to discover them, and in a vast many instances they appear for the first time in a Dictionary of Quotations.

Many of the nonsensical commentaries have been dispensed with, as in almost every instance, where the translation is correct, the quotation is more intelligible without them. Our only fear is that we have adopted too many.

One new, and it is hoped valuable, feature in the present volume, is the marking of the metrical quantities, which has been done in all cases where their absence might lead to mispronunciation. A quotation, however appropriate, would entirely lose its effect with those who are best able to appreciate its force, if blemished by false delivery. It has been thought unnecessary to mark the final *e*, because, as the classical reader will know, it is never silent.

The publisher claims little merit for himself in what concerns this volume, save the plan and a diligent reading of the proofs; but he thinks it right to avow the assistance of his eldest son, William Simpkin Bohn, who has been a useful coadjutor throughout, particularly in the Greek portion. The printer, too, richly deserves his meed of praise for watchfulness and scholarship.

It remains only to speak of previous collections of the same character. The first and principal is Macdonnel's, originally published in 1796, and repeatedly reprinted, with gradual improvements, up to a ninth edition in 1826. This is the work of a scholar, and praiseworthy as a first attempt, but much too imperfect to satisfy the wants of the present day. The next was Moore's, which, though as recent as 1831, is little more than an amplification of Macdonnel's, avoiding as much as possible, for copyright considerations, the very words of his translations, but seldom improving them.

The Dictionary of Quotations which passes under the name of Blagdon (we say this advisedly, as the work was posthumous) differs so entirely from the plan of the present, as scarcely to be cited as a precursor. It is arranged under English 'common-places,' which are illustrated by lengthy quotations from a few of the Greek and Latin poets, each accompanied by metrical versions selected chiefly from Pope, Dryden, Francis, and Creech. It is a small volume of limited contents, but executed up to its pretensions.

After thus much had been written, and on the very eve of publication, we are unexpectedly greeted with a small "Manual of Quotations," by Mr. Michelsen, 308 pages, published at 6*s*. The basis of this work is Macdonnel's, which is incorporated almost verbatim from an early edition, the editor adding some little from other sources. It can in no way interfere with the present volume, and we rather hail it as showing that there must have been an evident want of what we have undertaken to supply.

H. G. B.

York Street, Covent Garden,
April 18, 1866.

DICTIONARY

OF

LATIN QUOTATIONS, PROVERBS, AND PHRASES.

A bove majōri discit arāre minor. *Prov.*—"The young ox learns to plough from the older." See *Ne sus*, &c.

A căpĭte ad calcem.—"From head to heel." From top to toe.

A fonte puro pura dēflŭit aqua. *Prov.*—"From a clear spring clear water flows." A man is generally estimated by the company he keeps, as his habits are probably similar to those of his companions.

A fortĭōri.—"From stronger reasoning." With much greater probability. If a pound of gunpowder can blow up a house, *a fortiori* a hundredweight must be able to do it.

A fronte præcipitium, a tergo lupus.—"A precipice before, a wolf behind." Said of a person between the horns of a dilemma.

A lătĕre.—"From the side." A legate *a latere* is a pope's envoy, so called because sent from his *side*, from among his counsellors.

A mensâ et toro.—"From table and bed," or, as we say, "from bed and board." A sentence of separation of man and wife, issuing from the ecclesiastical courts, on account of acts of adultery which have been substantiated against either party. It is not of so decisive a nature as the divorce *A vinculo matrimonii*; which see.

A postĕrĭōri. See *A priori.*

A priōri; a postĕriōri.—"From the former; from the latter." "Phrases used in logical argument, to denote a reference to its different modes. The schoolmen distinguished them into the *propter quod*, wherein an effect is proved from the next cause, as, when it is proved that the moon is eclipsed, because the earth is then between the sun and the moon. The second is, the *quia*, wherein the cause is proved from a remote effect; as, that plants do not breathe, because they are not animals; or, that there is a God, from the works of the creation. The former argument is called demonstration *a priori*; the latter, demonstration *a posteriori*."

A re decēdunt.—"They wander from the point."

A tĕnĕris unguĭcŭlis. Cic.—"From your tender little nails." From your very earliest boyhood. See *Sed præsta*, &c., and *Amores de*, &c.

A verbis legis non est recedendum. Coke.—"There must be no departure from the words of the law." The judge must not give to a statute a forced interpretation contrary to the reasonable meaning of the words.

A vincŭlo matrimōnii.—"From the bonds of matrimony." See *A mensâ*, &c.

Ab actu ad posse valet illātio.—"From what has happened we may infer what will happen."

Ab alio spectes altĕri quod fĕcĕris. Syr.—"As you do to another, expect another to do to you."

Ab amīcis honesta petāmus. Cic.—"We must ask what is proper from our friends."

Ab honesto virum bonum nihil deterret. Sen.—"Nothing deters a good man from the performance of his duties."

Ab inconvenienti.—"From the inconvenience." The *Argumentum ab inconvenienti*, is an argument to show that a proposition will be unlikely to meet the expected end, and will therefore be inexpedient.

Ab inĭtio.—"From the beginning."

Ab ovo usque ad mala. Hor.—"From the egg to the apples." From the commencement to the end; eggs being the first, and apples the last, dish served at the Roman entertainments.

Ab Urbe condĭtâ, more usually denoted in the Latin writers by the initials A. U. C., signifies, "from the building of the city" of Rome, B. C. 753.

Abeunt studia in mores. OVID.—"Pursuits become habits." Use is second nature.

Abi in pace.—"Depart in peace."

Abiit nemine salutato.—"He went away without bidding any one farewell."

Abite nummi, ego vos mergam, ne mergar a vobis.—"Away with you, money, I will sink you, that I may not be sunk by you."

Abiturus illuc quo priores abierunt,
Quid mente cæca miserum torques spiritum?
Tibi dico, avare—— PHÆD.

—"As you must go to that place to which others have gone before, why in the blindness of your mind do you torment your wretched existence? To you I address myself, miser."

Abnormis sapiens. HOR.—"Wise without instruction." Naturally gifted with a sound understanding.

Abracadabra.—A cabalistic word, the name of a deity formerly worshipped by the Syrians. The letters of his name, written on paper, in the form of an inverted triangle, were recommended as an antidote against various diseases.

Absens hæres non erit. *Prov.*—"He who is at a distance will not be the heir." "Out of sight out of mind."

Absentem lædit cum ebrio qui litigat. SYR.—"He who disputes with a drunken man, offends one who is absent." The senses of a drunken man may be considered as absent.

——*Absentem qui rodit amicum,*
Qui non defendit alio culpante; solutos
Qui captat risus hominum, famamque dicacis;
Fingere qui non visa potest, commissa tacere
Qui nequit, hic niger est, hunc tu, Romane, caveto. HOR.

—"He who backbites an absent friend, who does not defend him when another censures him, who affects to raise loud laughs in company and the reputation of a funny fellow, who can feign things he never saw, who cannot keep secrets, he is a dangerous man; against him, Roman, be on your guard."

Absque argento omnia vana.—"Without money all is in vain."

Absque hoc, &c. *Law term.*—"Without this," &c. The technical words of exception used in pleading a traverse.

Absque sudōre et labōre nullum opus perfectum est.—"Without sweat and toil no work is made perfect." Without exertion and diligence success is rarely attained.

Absque tali causâ. Law Term.—"Without such cause."

Abstinēto a fabis.—"Abstain from beans." An admonition of Pythagoras. Equivalent to saying, "Have nothing to do with elections." The Athenians, at the election of their public magistrates, balloted with beans. It is also worthy of remark that the Pythagoreans had a superstitious belief that the souls of the dead were harboured in the centre of the bean.

Absurdum est ut alios regat, qui seipsum regere nescit. Law Maxim.—"It is absurd that he should govern others, who knows not how to govern himself." Quoted by Rabelais, B. i. c. 52.

Abundans cautēla non nocet. COKE.—"Excess of precaution can do no harm."

Abundat dulcĭbus vitĭis. QUINT.—"He abounds with alluring faults." Said in allusion to an author the very faults of whose style are fascinating.

Ac velŭti magno in popŭlo cum sæpe coorta est
Seditio; sævitque anĭmis ignōbile vulgus,
Jamque faces et saxa volant, furor arma ministrat. VIRG.
—"And as when a sedition has arisen amongst a mighty multitude, as often happens, and the minds of the ignoble vulgar are excited; now stones, now firebrands fly; fury supplies arms."

Accēdas ad curĭam. Law Term.—"You may come to the court." A writ issued out of Chancery when a man had received false judgment in a hundred court or court baron, was so called.

Accēde ad ignem hunc, jam calesces plus satis. TER.—"Approach this fire, and you will soon be too warm." Said in allusion to the seductive beauty of the courtesan Thais.

Accensâ domo proxĭmi, tua quoque periclitātur. Prov.—"When the house of your neighbour is in flames, your own is in danger." See *Proximus ardet*, &c.

——*Acceptissima semper*
Munĕra sunt, auctor quæ pretiōsa facit. OVID.
"Those gifts are always the most acceptable which our love for the donor makes precious."

Accĭdit in puncto, et toto contingit in anno.—"It happens in an instant, and occurs throughout the whole year." Said in reference to those occurrences which are ruled by the uniform laws of nature.

Accĭdit in puncto, quod non contingit in anno.—"That may happen in a moment, which does not occur in a whole year."

Accĭpe nunc, victus tenuis quid quantăque secum
Affĕrat. In primis valeas bene—— Hor.
—"Now learn what and how great benefits a temperate diet will bring along with it. In the first place, you will enjoy good health."

——*Accĭpe, si vis,*
Accĭpiam tabŭlas; detur nōbis locus, hora,
Custōdes: vĭdĕāmus uter plus scrībĕre possit. Hor.
—"Take, if you like, your tablets, I will take mine: let there be a place, a time, and persons appointed to see fair play; let us see who can write the most."

Accĭpe, sume, cape, sunt verba placentia papæ.—"Take, have, and keep, are pleasant words from a pope." A mediæval saying. It may also be translated, "to a pope."

Accĭpĕre quam făcĕre præstat injuriam. Cic.—"It is better to receive than to do an injury."

Accĭpio revocāmen—— Ovid.—"I accept the recall."

Acclīnis falsis anĭmus meliōra recūsat. Hor.—"The mind intent upon false appearances refuses to admit better things."

Accusāre nemo se debet nisi coram Deo. Law Maxim.—"No man is bound to accuse himself except before God." It is a maxim of our law, that no man can be forced to become his own accuser.

Acer et vehĕmens bonus orātor. Cic.—"A good orator is pointed and forcible."

Acerrĭma proximōrum odia. Tacit.—"The hatred of those most nearly connected is the bitterest of all."

Acerrĭmus ex omnĭbus nostris sensĭbus est sensus videndi. Cic.—"The keenest of all our senses is the sense of sight."

Acrĭbus initiis, incuriōso fine. Tacit.—"Zealous at the commencement, careless towards the conclusion." Said of those who commence an undertaking with more zeal than perseverance or discretion.

Acriōra orexim excĭtant embammata. COLUM.—"Savoury seasonings stimulate the appetite."

Acta exteriōra indĭcant interiōra secrēta. COKE.—"The outward conduct indicates the secrets of the heart."

Actio personālis morĭtur cum personâ. *Law Maxim.*—"A personal action dies with the person."

Actum est de republicâ.—"It is all over with the republic." The constitution is overthrown.

Actum ne agas. CIC.—"What has been done do not over again."

Actus Dei nēmĭni facit injuriam. *Law Maxim.*—"The act of God does wrong to no man." The word *injury* is here used in its primary sense. God, who is the author of justice, cannot do that which is unjust.

Actus legis nulli facit injuriam. *Law Maxim.*—"The act of the law does wrong to no man."

Actus me invĭto factus, non est meus actus. *Law Maxim.*—"An act done by me against my will, is not my act." According to the principles of law, acts done under duress are void.

Actus non facit reum, nisi mens sit rea. *Law Maxim.*—"The act does not make the crime, unless the intention is criminal." The law requires that evil intention, or malice prepense, should be reasonably proved against the person accused, before he can be pronounced guilty.

Acum in metâ fœni quærĕre.—"To seek a needle in a bundle of hay." A mediæval saying.

Ad calamitātem quilĭbet rumor valet. SYR.—"Every rumour is believed when directed against the unfortunate." To the same purpose as the English proverb, "Give a dog a bad name and hang him."

Ad Calendas Græcas.—"At the Greek Calends." As the Greeks, in their division of the months, had no calends, (which were used by the Romans only,) this phrase was used in reference to a thing that could never take place. "To-morrow come never," as we say.

Ad captandum vulgus.—"To catch the mob." Said of a specious argument "for the nonce."

Ad connectendas amicitias, tenacissimum vincŭlum est morum similitūdo. PLINY *the Younger.*—"For cementing friendship, resemblance of manners is the strongest tie."

Ad consilium ne accessĕris, antĕquam vocĕris. *Prov.*—"Go not to the council-chamber before you are summoned." "Speak when you are spoken to, and come when you are called."

Ad ĕundem.—"To the same (rank or class)." Graduates of one university, when admitted to the same degree in another, but not incorporated as members, are said to be admitted *ad eundem.*

Ad intĕrim.—"For," or "during the meanwhile." A temporary substitute is appointed to act *ad interim.*

Ad lĭbĭtum.—"At pleasure." In music this term is used to show that the passage may be played at the discretion of the performer.

Ad mala quisque anĭmum refĕrat sua—— OVID.—"Let each person recall to mind his own mishaps."

Ad mensūram aquam bibit.—"He drinks water by measure."

Ad minōra me demittĕre non recusābo. QUINT.—"I will not refuse to descend to the most minute details." I will sift the matter to the bottom.

——***Ad mores natūra recurrit***
Damnātos, fixa et mutāri nescia—— JUV.
—"Human nature ever reverts to its depraved courses, fixed and immutable."

Ad nomen vultus sustŭlit illa suos. OVID.—"On hearing her name she raised her eyes."

Ad nullum consurgit opus, cum corpŏre languet. GALL.—"The mind cannot grapple with any task when the body is languid."

Ad omnem libīdĭnem projectus homo.—"A man disposed to every species of dissipation."

Ad perdĭtam secūrim manubrium adjĭcĕre.—"To throw the helve after the lost hatchet." To give way to despair.

Ad perniciem solet agi sincĕritas. PHÆD.—"Sincerity is frequently impelled to its own destruction."

Ad pœnitendum propĕrat, cito qui judĭcat. SYR.—"He hastens to repentance, who judges hastily."

Ad popŭlum phalĕras, ego te intus et in cŭtĕ novi. PERS.—"Display thy trappings to the vulgar, I know thee inside and out."

Ad præsens ova cras pullis sunt meliōra.—"Eggs to-day are better than chickens to-morrow." A mediæval proverb, in defective verse, similar to ours—"A bird in the hand," &c.

Ad quæstiōnem juris respondĕant judĭces, ad quæstiōnem facti respondĕant juratōres. *Law Maxim.*—"It is the duty of the judge to decide as to the point of law, of the jurors to decide as to the matter of fact."

Ad quod damnum. *Law Term.*—"To what damage." A writ issued to inquire into the damage that may be sustained before the grant of certain liberties.

Ad referendum.—"To be referred," or, "to await further consideration."

Ad respondendum quæstiōni.—"To answer the question." Students at the university of Cambridge, who are about to be examined for their degree in Arts, or in other words, admitted *ad respondendum quæstioni*, are thence called *questionists.*

Ad suum quemque æquum est quæstum esse callĭdum. Plaut.—"It is only right that every one should be alive to his own advantage."

Ad tristem partem strenua suspĭcio. Syr.—"The minds of men who have been unfortunate are prone to suspicion." Much to the same purpose as our proverb, "A burnt child dreads the fire."

Ad turpia virum bonum nulla spes invītat. Sen.—"No expectation can allure a good man to the commission of evil."

Ad unum corpus humānum supplĭcia plura quam membra. St. Cyprian.—"One human body is liable to more pains than the members of which it is composed."

Ad utrumque parātus.—"Prepared for either alternative."

Ad valōrem.—"According to the value." Duties are imposed on certain articles of merchandise, *ad valorem*, or according to their value.

Ad vivum.—"To the life."

Adæquārunt judĭces.—"The judges were equally divided."

Adde parum parvo, magnus acervus erit.—"Add a little to a little, and there will be a great heap." An adaptation from Ovid.

Adde, quod injustum rigĭdo jus dicĭtur ense,
Dantur et in mĕdio vulnĕra sæpe foro. Ovid.
—"Besides, iniquitous retaliation is dealt with the cruel

sword, and wounds are often inflicted in the midst of the court of justice."

——*Adeo in tenĕris consuescĕre multum est.* VIRG.—"Of such importance is it to be well trained in youth." "Train up a child in the way he should go," says Solomon, *Prov.* xxii. 6.

——*Adeōne homĭnem immutāri*
Ex amōre, ut non cognoscas ĕundem esse? TER.
—"Is it possible that a man can be so changed by love, that you could not recognise him to be the same?"

Adeste, si quid mihi restat agendum.—"If aught remains to be done by me, despatch." The words of the emperor Severus, just before his death, according to Lord Bacon; but they are not to be found in Dio Cassius or Spartianus.

Adhibenda est in jocando moderatio. CIC.—"Moderation should be used in joking." A joke should never be carried too far.

Adhibenda est munditia, non odiosa, neque exquisīta nimis, tantum quæ fugiat agrestem ac inhumanam negligentiam. CIC.—"We should exhibit a certain degree of neatness, not too exquisite or affected, and equally remote from rustic and unbecoming carelessness."

——*Adhuc sub jūdice lis est.* HOR.—"The point is still in dispute before the judge." The controversy is yet undecided.

Adĭtus est ipsi ad omnes facĭlis et pervius. CIC.—"He has free and ready access to every one."

——*Adjūro numquam eam me desertūrum,*
Non si capiendos mihi sciam esse inimīcos omnes homines;
Hanc mihi expetīvi, contingit; convĕniunt mores; valeant
Qui inter nos discidium volunt; hanc, nisi mors, mi adĭmet nemo. TER.
—"I swear that I will never desert her, even though I were sure that I should make all men my enemies. Her have I desired above all things, her have I obtained. Our humours agree; farewell to those who would set us at variance. Nothing but death shall deprive me of her."

Adolescentem verecundum esse decet. PLAUT.—"A young man ought to be modest."

Adornāre verbis benefacta. PLINY *the Younger*.—"To enhance the value of a favour by kind expressions." The best of actions is liable to be undervalued, if done with a bad grace.

Adscriptus glebæ.—"Belonging to the soil." Attached to the soil, like the *serfs* and *neifs* in England so late as the reign of Edward VI., and the greater part of the peasantry of the Russian empire at the present day.

——*Adsit*
Regŭla, peccatis quæ pœnas irrŏget æquas. HOR.
—"Let a law be made which shall inflict punishment commensurate with the crime."

——*Adulandi gens prudentissima laudat*
Sermōnem indocti, faciem deformis, amīci. JUV.
—"The crafty race of flatterers praise the conversation of an unlearned, the features of an ugly friend." See the Fable of the Fox and the Crow, in ÆSOP.

Adversus solem ne loquĭtor. *Prov.*—"Speak not against the sun." Do not argue against that which is as clear as the sun at mid-day.

Æăcus in pœnas ingeniōsus erit. OVID.—"Æacus shall refine in devising tortures for you."

Ædificāre in tuo proprio solo non licet quod altĕri nocеat. *Law Maxim.*—"You may not build on your own land that which may injure another." See the same principle in *Sic utere*, &c.

——*Ægrescitque medendo.* VIRG.—"He destroys his health by his very anxiety to preserve it."

——*Ægri somnia vana.* HOR.—"The delusive dreams of the sick man."

Ægritudĭnem laudāre, unam rem maxime detestabilem, quorum est tandem philosophōrum? CIC.—"What kind of philosophy is it, pray, to extol melancholy, a thing the most detestable of all?"

Ægrōtat dæmon, monăchus tunc esse volēbat;
Dæmon convălnit, dæmon ut ante fuit.
"The devil was sick, the devil a monk would be;
The devil got well, the devil a monk was he."
Lines composed in the middle ages.

Ægrōtatiōnes animi, qualis est avaritia, ex eo quod magni æstimētur ea res, ex qua anĭmus ægrōtat, oriuntur. CIC.—"Diseases of the mind, such as avarice, spring from too high a value set upon the things by which the mind becomes corrupted."

Ægrōto dum anĭma est, spes est. CIC—"So long as the

sick man has life, there is hope." A common saying with us, "While there is life there is hope."

Æmulatio æmulationem parit.—"Emulation begets emulation." A spirit of emulation excites others to similar exertions.

Æmŭlus studiōrum et labōrum. Cic.—"The rival of his pursuits and of his labours."

——*Æquâ lege necessitas*
Sortītur insignes et imos. Hor.
—"Fate, by an impartial law, is allotted both to the conspicuous and the obscure."

Æquam memento rebus in arduis
Servāre mentem, non secus in bonis
Ab insolenti temperātam
Lætitiâ—— Hor.
—"In arduous circumstances remember to preserve equanimity, and equally in prosperous moments restrain excessive joy."

——*Æqua tellus*
Paupĕri recludĭtur,
Regumque puĕris. Hor.
—"The impartial earth is opened alike for the pauper and the children of kings."

Æquĭtas enim lucet ipsa per se. Cic.—"Equity shines by her own light."

Æquĭtas est correctio legis generaliter latæ quâ parte defĭcit. Plowden.—"Equity is the correction of the law laid down in general terms, in those parts in which it is deficient." It modifies the rigour of the law, and takes into consideration the *circumstances* of the case.

Æquo animo parātōque morĭar. Cic.—"May I meet death with a mind prepared and calm."

——*Æquum est*
Peccātis vĕniam poscentem reddĕre rursus. Hor.
—"It is fair that he who expects forgiveness should, in his turn, extend it to others." We are also taught by a higher sanction, that, as we forgive them that trespass against us, so may we hope to be forgiven.

Æra nitent usu; vestis bona quærit habĕri;
Canescunt turpi tecta relicta situ. Ovid.
—"Brass grows bright by use; good clothes require to be

worn; uninhabited buildings grow white with nasty mould."

Ærūgo anĭmi, rubīgo ingenii. SEN.—"The rust of the mind is the blight of genius." Said of idleness.

Ærumnābilis experientia me docuit.—"Sorrowful experience has taught me."

Æs debĭtōrem leve, gravius inimīcum facit. LABER.—"A trifling debt makes a man your debtor; a more weighty one, your enemy."

Æs erat in pretio; chalybēia massa latebat;
Heu! quam perpetuo debuit illa tegi. OVID.
—"Copper became valuable; the iron ore still lay hid. Alas! would that it had ever remained concealed."

Æsōpo ingentem statuam posuēre Attici,
Servumque collocārunt æternā in basi,
Patēre honōris scirent ut cuncti viam. PHÆDR.
—"The Athenians erected a lofty statue to Æsop, and placed him, though a slave, upon an everlasting pedestal, that all might know that the way to fame is open to every one."

Æstimatio delicti prætertĭti ex post facto non crescit. Law Maxim.—"The delinquency attaching to a crime that has been committed, is not increased by anything that has happened since."

——*Æstuat ingens*
Imo in corde pudor, mixtoque insānia luctu,
Et Furiis agitātus amor, et conscia virtus. VIRG.
—"Deep in his heart boils overwhelming shame, and frantic rage, with intermingled grief, and love racked with furious despair, and conscious worth."

Ætas parentum, pejor avis, tulit
Nos nequiōres, mox daturos
Progĕniem vitiosiōrem. HOR.
—"The days of our parents, more dissolute than those of our forefathers, produced us more wicked than they; we, who are destined to produce a more vicious progeny still."—Horace is here a *laudator temporis acti*, a praiser of the "good old times."

Ætātem non tegunt tempŏra.—"Our temples do not conceal our age." The wrinkled forehead betrays the hand of time.

Ætātem Priămi Nestŏrisque
Longam qui putat esse, Martiāne,
Multum decĭpĭtur fallĭturque,
Non est vīvĕre sed vita. MAR.
—"He, Martianus, is much mistaken and deceived, who thinks that the life of Priam and of Nestor was long: not existence, but health, is life."

Ætātis cujusque notandi sunt tibi mores. HOR.—"You must carefully observe the manners of every age." By inattention to this rule, even Shakspeare has committed anachronisms.

Æternum inter se discordant. TER.—"They are everlastingly at variance with each other."

Æthiŏpem dealbāre. *Prov.*—"To wash a blackamoor white."

——*Ævo rarissima nostro*
Simplicitas—— OVID.
—"Simplicity, a thing most rare in our age." Ovid, like Seneca, sometimes praises a simplicity and self-denial, which he himself failed to practise.

Affectum dantis pensat censura Tonantis.—"The judgment of the Thunderer weighs the intention of the giver." A mediæval line.

Afflāvit Deus et dissipantur.—"God has sent forth his breath, and they are dispersed." In the reign of Queen Elizabeth, a medal with the above inscription was struck, to record the destruction of the Spanish Armada.

——*Age, libertate Decembri,*
Quando ita majōres voluĕrunt, utĕre—— HOR.
—"Come, since our forefathers would have it so, use the freedom of December." Said in allusion to the Saturnalia, during which the slaves at Rome were allowed a greater latitude than usual.

Age quod agis.—"Attend to what you are about"—or, as the clock at the Inner Temple formerly had it, "Begone about your business."

Agĕre considerate pluris est quam cogitāre prudenter. CIC. —"It is better to act considerately than to think wisely." Very similar in meaning to the maxim, *Paulum sepultæ, &c.*, which see.

——*Agnosco vĕtĕris vestīgia flammæ.* VIRG.—"I recognise

the remains of my former attachment." A somewhat similar expression to that of Gray,

"E'en in our ashes live their wonted fires."

Agnus Dei.—"The Lamb of God." A cake of wax stamped with the figure supporting the banner of the cross. It is supposed by the Romish Church to have miraculous powers for preserving the faithful. A part of the mass for the dead is also so called, from the circumstance of its beginning with these words.

***Agrĭcŏla** incurvo terram dimōvit aratro;*
Hinc anni labor; hinc patriam parvosque nepōtes
Sustĭnet: hinc armenta boum, meritosque juvencos.

VIRG.

—"The husbandman cleaves the earth with his crooked plough: hence the labours of the year: hence he supports his country and his little offspring: hence his herds of kine and the steers which have earned his sustenance."

***Agri** non omnes frugiferi sunt*. CIC.—"All fields are not fruitful." So too all men are not equally susceptible of improvement.

——*Ah miser!*
Quantâ labōras in Charybdi,
Digne puer meliōre flammâ! HOR.

—"Into what an abyss hast thou fallen, unhappy youth! deserving of a more happy flame!" A parallel case to that of Samson and Delilah.

***Ah!** nimium facĭles, qui tristia crimina cædis*
Fluminĕâ tolli posse putētis aquâ. OVID.

—"Ah! too credulous mortals, who imagine that the guilt of bloodshed can be removed by the waters of the stream."

***Albæ** gallīnæ filius*. *Prov*.—"The son of a white hen." Said of a person extremely fortunate. An eagle is said to have dropped a white hen, with a sprig of laurel, into the lap of Livia, the wife of the Emperor Augustus.

***Album** calcŭlum addĕre*.—"To give a white stone." In voting, among the ancients, approval was signified by putting into the urn a white stone; disapproval, or censure, by a black one.

***Alea** judiciōrum*.—"Chance judiciary." "The uncertainty of judgments;" which too often, as it were, depend on the throw of a die. "The glorious uncertainty of the law."

Aleātor, quanto in arte est mělior, tanto est nequior. SYR.—"The gambler, the more skilful he is in his art, the more wicked is he."

Alexander victor tot regum atque populorum iræ succubuit. SEN.—"Alexander, the conqueror of so many kings and nations, was himself subdued by anger."

Aliam quercum excŭte.—"Go, shake some other oak." Said by a person who has already shown his liberality to an applicant.

Alia res sceptrum, alia plectrum.—"A sceptre is one thing, a fiddlestick another."

Alĭas.—"Otherwise." Applied to persons who assume two or more names; as A, *alias* B. It also means a second writ, issued after a first writ has been issued to no purpose.

Alĭbi.—"Elsewhere." *Law Term.* When a person accused of an offence endeavours to prove that he was absent from the place at the time when the crime was committed, he is said to set up an *alibi.*

——*Aliēna negotia centum*
Per caput, et circa sălient latus—— HOR.
—"A hundred affairs of other people come into my head, and beset me on every side."

——*Aliēna negotia curo,*
Excussus propriis.—— HOR.
—"I attend to the business of other men, regardless of my own." This quotation may be aptly applied to such busy-bodies as Æsop met, when carrying his lantern at mid-day. See *Phædrus*, B. iii. F. 19.

Aliēna nobis, nostra plus aliis placent. SYR.—"That which belongs to others pleases us most, while that which belongs to us is most valued by others." Few men are content with their station: so true it is that—

"Men would be angels, angels would be gods;
Aspiring to be gods, if angels fell,
Aspiring to be angels, men rebel." POPE'S *Essay on Man*

——*Aliena opprobria sæpe*
Abstĕrrent vitiis—— HOR.
—"The disgrace of others often deters us from crime."

Aliēnâ optĭmum insaniâ frui.—"It is best to profit by the madness of others." A proverb quoted by the Elder Pliny. See *Optĭmum est aliēnâ, &c.*

Aliēna vitia in ocŭlis habēmus—a tergo nostra sunt. SEN.—"We have the vices of others always before our eyes—our own behind our backs." See *Ut nemo in sese, &c.*

Aliēnâ vivĕre quadrâ. JUV.—"To eat off another man's trencher." To live at another's expense.

Aliēni appĕtens, sui profusus. SALL.—"Covetous of another's, lavish of his own." Catiline is here described by the historian.

Aliēni tempŏris flores.—"Blossoms of a time gone by." Flowers that bloomed in other days.

——*Aliēno in loco*
Haud stabĭle regnum est. SEN.
—"Over a distant realm sovereignty is insecure."

Aliēnos agros irrĭgas tuis sitientibus. *Prov.*—"You are watering your neighbours' fields, while your own are parched with drought." Said to an interfering busy-body.

Alii sementem făciunt, alii metent. *Prov.*—"The one sows, the other will reap."

Alio patriam quærunt sub sole jacentem. VIRG.—"They seek a country situate beneath another sun."

Aliōrum mĕdĭcus, ipse ulcĕribus scates.—"The physician of others, you are full of ulcers yourself."

Aliquando gratius est quod făcili quam quod plenâ manu datur.—"Sometimes that is more acceptable which is given with a kindly, than that which is received from a full hand." Presents are acceptable according to the spirit in which they are given.

Alĭquem fortūnæ filium reverentissimè colĕre ac venerāri. AUST.—"To treat with the greatest reverence and respect a man who is the darling of fortune." To

—"follow that false plan,
That money only makes the man."

Alĭquis non debet esse judex in propriâ causâ. COKE.—"No man ought to be judge in his own cause."

Alis volat propriis.—"He flies with his own wings." He is able to take care of himself. Motto of the Earl of Thanet.

Aliter cătŭli longe olent, ălĭter sues. PLAUT.—"Puppies have one smell, pigs quite another." All animals have an instinct by which they recognise their young.

Alĭtur vĭtium, vīvitque tegendo. VIRG.—"Vice is nourished and lives by concealment."

Alium silēre quod văleas, primus sile. SEN.—"That you may impose silence upon another, first be silent yourself."

Alma mater.—"A kind," or "benign, mother." A term originally used in reference to the earth, but employed by students to designate the university in which they were educated. It is said to have been first applied to Cambridge.

——*Alta sedent civīlis vulnĕra dextræ.* LUCAN.—"The wounds inflicted by civil war are deeply seated."

Altĕrâ manu fert lăpĭdem, altĕrâ panem ostentat. PLAUT.—"In one hand he carries a stone, while in the other he shows bread." So our proverb, "He carries fire in one hand, and water in the other."

Altĕrâ manu scabunt, altĕrâ fĕriunt. *Prov.*—"They scratch you with one hand, and strike you with the other." Said of treacherous and deceitful persons.

Alter idem. CIC.—"Another self." See *Verus amicus.*

Alter ipse amīcus. *Prov.*—"A friend is a second self." The thought occurs more than once in the works of Aristotle.

Altĕrĭus non sit qui suus esse potest.—"Let no man be the servant of another, who can be his own master."

——*Alterĭus sic*
Altĕra poscit opem, res et conjūrat amīcè. HOR.
—"Thus does one thing require the co-operation of another, and they join in mutual aid."

Alter remus aquas, alter mihi radat arēnas. PROP.—"Let one of my oars skim the water, the other touch the sands." By acting thus, we shall not find ourselves out of our depth.

Alter rixatur de lanâ sæpe caprīnâ,
Propugnat nugis armātus.— HOR.
—"Another raises a dispute about a lock of goat's wool, and has recourse to arms for trifles." Potentates, as well as wolves, have often acted upon this principle, when they have deemed it to their interest to "pick a quarrel"

Altissĭma quæque flumĭna mĭnĭmo sono labuntur. CURT.—"The deepest rivers flow with the least noise." Of similar application to our proverb, "Empty vessels make the greatest sound."

A. M. for *Artium Magister.*—"Master of Arts." The highest University degree in Arts. See also ***Anno Mundi***, *Ante meridiem.*

Ama tanquam osūrus. Odĕris tanquam amatūrus. **Prov.**—"Love as though you might hate. Hate as though you might love." Be prepared in either case for a change of circumstances; and neither make your friend acquainted with your failings and weak points, nor make it impossible that your enemy can ever become reconciled to you. Cicero, with considerable reason, dissents from the first part of this adage. See *Amicum ita,* &c.

Amantium iræ amōris integratio est. Ter.—"The quarrels of lovers are the renewal of love." So our old proverb, "Old pottage is sooner heated than new made."

Amāre et sapĕre vix deo concēditur. Laber.—"It is hardly granted to a god to be in love and to act wisely."

Amāre juvĕni fructus est, crimen seni. Syr.—"It is proper for a young man to be in love, a crime for an old one."

Ambĭgŭas in vulgum spargĕre voces. Adapted from Virgil.—"To spread ambiguous reports among the populace."

Ambĭgŭum pactum contra vendĭtōrem interpretandum est. Law Maxim.—"A doubtful agreement is to be interpreted against the vendor."

Amīci probantur rebus adversis. Cic.—"Friends are proved by adversity."

Amīci vitium ni feras, prodis tuum. Syr.—"Unless you can put up with the faults of your friend, you betray your own;" you show that either the ties of friendship are easily relaxed, or that you are put out of temper by trifles.

Amicitia semper prodest, amor et nocet. Laber.—"Friendship is always productive of advantage, and love of injury." This *dictum* seems to be stated in rather too general terms.

Amicōrum, magis quàm tuam ipsius laudem, prædīca.—Enlarge upon the praises of your friends rather than on your own."

Amīcos res opīmæ parĭunt, adversæ probant. Syr.—"Prosperity begets friends, adversity proves them."

Amīcum ita hăbĕas posse ut fiĕri hunc inimīcum scias. Laber.

—"Live with your friend as if you knew that he might become your enemy." This maxim, though inculcating caution, a considerable virtue, is better adapted to the political world than to the sphere of private friendship. See *Ama tanquam*, &c.

——*Amīcum*
Mancipium dŏmĭno et frugi. HOR.
—"A servant faithful to his master, and true."

Amīcum perdĕre est damnōrum maxĭmum. SYR.—"To lose a friend is the greatest of losses."

Amīcus certus in re incertâ cernĭtur. ENNIUS.—"An undoubted friend shows himself in doubtful circumstances." Very similar to our proverb, "A friend in need is a friend indeed."

Amīcus curiæ. *Law Term.*—"A friend of the court." A member of the bar who makes a suggestion on any point of practice as to which the judge is in doubt is so called.

Amīcus magis necessārius quam ignis aut aqua.—"A friend is more needful than fire or water."

Amīcus Plato, amīcus Socrates, sed magis amīca verĭtas. CIC. —"Plato is my friend, Socrates is my friend, but truth is a friend I prize above both."

Amīcus usque ad aras.—"A friend to the very altar."

Amissum quod nescĭtur non amittĭtur. SYR.—"The loss that is not known is no loss." Similar to our saying, "What the eye don't see the heart don't grieve." So also Gray's line, "Where ignorance is bliss 'tis folly to be wise."

Amittit merĭtò proprĭum qui aliēnum appĕtit. PHÆD.—"He who covets that which belongs to another, deservedly loses his own." Covetous men not unfrequently fall into the pit which they have dug for others.

——*Amor omnĭbus īdem.* VIRG.—"Love is in all the same."

Amor et melle et felle est fecundissĭmus. PLAUT.—"Love is most fruitful both in honey and in gall."

Amor tussisque non celantur.—"Love and a cough cannot be concealed." A proverbial saying.

Amōre nihil mollius, nihil violentius.—"Nothing is more tender, nothing more violent than love."

——*Amōres*
De tenĕro meditātur ungui. HOR.

—"She plans amours from her tenderest years."

——*Amōto quærāmus sēria ludo.* Hor.—"Joking apart, let us give our attention to serious matters."

——*Amphŏra cœpit*
Institui: currente rotâ cur urceus exit? Hor.
—"A fine jar is intended to be made; why, when the wheel goes round, does it come out a humble pitcher?" A figure taken from the potter's wheel. It has the same application as the Fable of the Mountain in Labour.

Ampliat ætātis spatĭum sibi vir bonus; hoc est
Vivĕre bis vitâ posse priōre frui. Mar.
—"The good man extends the period of his life; it is to live twice, to enjoy with satisfaction the retrospect of our past life."

An boni quid usquam est, quod quisquam uti possit
Sine malo omni; aut, ne labōrem capĭas, cum illo uti velles. Plaut.
—"Is there any good whatever that we can enjoy wholly without evil, or where you must not endure labour when you would enjoy it?"

An dives sit omnes quærunt, nemo an bonus.—"All inquire whether a man is rich, no one whether he is good." A translation from Euripides.

——*An erit qui velle recūset*
Os populi meruisse, et cedro digna locūtus
Linquĕre?—— Pers.
—"Will there be any one to disown a wish to deserve the people's praise, and to leave words worthy to be preserved in cedar?" Presses for books were made of cedar, and the paper was steeped in oil of cedar, that wood being esteemed for its antiseptic qualities.

An nescis longas rēgĭbus esse manus? Ovid.—"Knowest thou not that kings have long arms?" that they can reach you at a distance even?

An potest quidquam esse absurdius, quam quo minus viæ restat, eo plus viatĭci quærĕre? Cic.—"Can there be anything more absurd, than to be making all the greater provision, in proportion as the less of your journey remains to be performed?" A reproof of covetousness in old age.

An quisquam est alĭus liber, nisi ducĕre vitam
Cui licet, ut voluit?—— Pers.

—"Is any man free, but he who is at liberty to spend his life in whatever manner he may please?"

Anceps remĕdium est mĕlius quam nullum.—"A doubtful remedy is better than none."

Anguillam caudâ tenes. Prov.—"You hold an eel by the tail." You have got to deal with a slippery fellow, and if you do not hold him fast, he will slip through your fingers.

Anĭma est amĭca amanti. PLAUT.—"His mistress is the very life of a lover."

Anĭma magis est ubi amat quam ubi anĭmat. AUST.—"The soul is more where it loves than where it lives."

——*Anĭmasque in vulnĕre ponunt.* VIRG.—"And they leave their lives in the wound."

Anĭmi cultus quasi quidam humanitātis cibus. CIC.—"Cultivation is to the mind what food is to the body."

Anĭmo ægrotanti medĭcus est orātio. Prov.—"Words are as a physician to an afflicted spirit." See *Sunt verba*, &c.

——*Anĭmoque supersunt*
Jam prope post animam. SIDON. APOLL.

—"They display spirit even though they have all but breathed forth their spirit." There is a play upon the resemblance of the words *animus*, "courage," and *anima*, "soul."

——*Animōrum*
Impulsu, et cæcâ magnâque cupĭdine ducti. JUV.

—"Led on by the impulse of our minds, by blind and headstrong passions."

Animŭla, vagŭla, blandŭla!—
Hospes, comesque corpŏris—

—"Dear, fluttering, fleeting soul of mine, thou guest and companion of the body." The beginning of the address of the emperor Adrian to his soul, composed in his last moments, and preserved by the historian Spartianus, as expressive of his uncertainty as to a future existence. The idea of Pope's "Dying Christian's Address to his Soul," was suggested by these lines, which are replete with exquisite beauty.

——*Anĭmum nunc huc celĕrem, nunc divĭdit illuc.* VIRG.—"Now this way, now that, he turns his wavering mind."

Anĭmum pictūrâ pascit ināni. VIRG.—"He feeds his mind

with an empty picture." He amuses himself with unsubstantial anticipations. See the stories of the Barmecide's Feast, and of Alnaschar and his brittle ware, in the *Arabian Nights.*

——*Anĭmum rĕgĕ, qui nisi paret*
Impĕrat.—— Hor.
—"Control your temper, for if it does not obey you, it will govern you."

Anĭmus æquus optĭmum est ærumnæ condimentum. Plaut.—"A patient mind is the best remedy for affliction."

Anĭmus est in patĭnis. Ter.—"My thoughts are among the saucepans." I am thinking of something to eat.

Anĭmus furandi. *Law Term.*—"The intention of stealing." It is the *animus*, and not the act, that constitutes an offence.

Anĭmus homĭni, quicquid sibi impĕrat, obtĭnet.—"Whatever it resolves on the human mind can effect."

Anĭmus hŏmĭnis semper appĕtit agĕre aliquid. Cic.—"The mind of man is always longing to do something."

Anĭmus memĭnit prœterĭtōrum, prœsentia cernit, futūra prœvĭdet. Cic.—"The mind remembers past events, scans the present, foresees the future."

——*Anĭmus quod perdĭdit optat,*
Atque in prœterĭtā se totus imăgine versat. Petron.
—"The mind still longs for what it has lost, and is wholly intent upon the past." The contemplation of lost opportunities has a kind of fascination, which at the same moment both invites and repels.

——*Anĭmus si te non defĭcit æquus.* Hor.—"If your equanimity does not fail you."

Anno Domĭni.—"In the year of our Lord;" for brevity, A. D.

Anno Mundi.—"In the year of the world;" for brevity, A. M.

Anno Urbis condĭtæ.—"In the year from the building of the city." See *Ab urbe*, &c.

Annōsam arbŏrem transplantāre.—"To transplant an aged tree." Said of a person late in life quitting an employment in which he has been long engaged, for a new one.

Annōsa vulpes haud capĭtur laqueo. *Prov.*—"An old fox is not to be caught with a springe." "Old birds are not to be caught with chaff."

Annus mirābĭlis.—"The year of wonders."

Ante barbam doces senes. *Prov.*—"Before you have got a beard you are for teaching the aged."

Ante diem clauso compōnet Vesper Olympo. VIRG.—"The evening star will first shut the gates of heaven upon the day."

Ante mare, et tellus, et quod tegit omnia cœlum,
Unus erat toto natūræ vultus in orbe,
Quem dixēre Chaos; rudis indigestaque moles. OVID.
—"At first the sea, the earth, and the heaven which covers all things, were the only face of nature through the whole universe, which men have named Chaos; a rude and undigested mass.

Ante meridiem.—"Before noon," or "mid-day," generally denoted by the initials A. M.

Ante ocŭlos errant domus, urbs, et forma locōrum;
Succēduntque suis singŭla facta locis. OVID.
—"Before my eyes flit my home, the city, and each well-known spot: and then follows, in order, each thing, as it happens, in its appropriate place."

Ante senectūtem curāvi, ut bene vivĕrem; in senectūte, ut bene moriar. SEN.—"Before old age, I made it my care to live well; in old age, to die well." St. Jerome ranked Seneca among the writers of Christianity.

Ante tubam trepĭdat.—"He trembles before the trumpet sounds."

Ante victōriam canĕre triumphum.—"To celebrate the triumph before victory." Similar in meaning to our expression, "To count our chickens before they are hatched."

Ante victōriam ne canas triumphum.—"Don't sing your triumph before you have conquered." So we say, "Don't halloo before you are out of the wood."

Ante vidēmus fulgurātiōnem quam sonum audiāmus. SEN.—"We see the lightning before we hear the thunder."

Antehac putābam te habēre cornua. *Prov.*—"Till now I thought you had horns." Said to a blusterer, who, at the last moment, is found defective in courage.

Antequam incĭpias consulto, et ubi consulu ĕris facto opus est. CIC.—"Before you begin, consider, and when you have considered, act."

Antīquâ homo virtūte ac fide. TER.—"A man of the virtue and fidelity of the olden time."

Antiquĭtas sæcŭli juventus mundi.—"Ancient time was the youth of the world." An aphorism of Lord Bacon, for which, according to Hallam and Whewell, he is indebted to Giordano Bruno.

Anus sīmia sero quidem. *Prov.*—"The old ape is taken at last." Of the same meaning as our saying, "The old fox is caught at last."

——*Apĕrit præcordia Liber.* HOR.—"Bacchus opens the heart."

Apertè mala cum est mulier, tum demum est bona. SYR.—"When a woman is openly bad, then she is good." This paradoxical expression implies that less injury results to the world from open dissoluteness, than from the hypocrisy of those who conceal profligacy under the guise of sanctity and virtue.

——*Aperto vivĕre voto.* PERS.—"To live with every wish revealed." The motto of the Earl of Aylesford.

Apio opus est. *Prov.*—"There is need of parsley." Said when a sick person was past all hope of recovery. The Grecians sowed the graves of the dead with this herb.

Apparātus belli.—"The matériel of war."

Appārent rari nantes in gurgĭte vasto. VIRG.—"A few are seen here and there, swimming in the boundless ocean." Virgil here describes the shipwrecked sailors of the Trojan fleet.

Appetitus ratiōni parĕat. CIC.—"Let your passions be obedient to reason." Employed as the motto of Earl Fitzwilliam.

Aquam perdo.—"I lose my time." Time was measured by the ancients by means of water running in the clepsydra, as in more modern days by sand. A certain portion of time was allotted to each orator to plead his cause; whence the present expression, which literally means, "I am losing the water."

Aquam plorat cum lavat fundĕre. PLAUT.—"He weeps at throwing away the water in which he was washed." Said of a miser.

Aquĭla non capit muscas. *Prov.*—"The eagle does not stoop to catch flies."

Aquĭlæ senecta. *Prov.*—"The old age of an eagle." Applied to aged topers—as the eagle was supposed, in its latter years, to live by suction only.

Aquĭlam volāre doces. *Prov.*—"You are for teaching an eagle how to fly." "You are teaching your grandam," &c.

Aquōsus languor.—"The watery weakness." The dropsy.

Araneārum telas texĕre.—"To weave a spider's web." Meaning, to support an argument by fine-spun sophistry, or to engage in a frivolous pursuit.

Arbĭter bibendi.—"The arbitrator of drinking." The master of the feast among the ancients gave directions when to fill the cups. See the *Stichus of Plautus*, A. iv. sc. 4.

Arbĭter elegantiārum.—"The arbitrator of politeness." Commonly used in reference to the person whose duty it is to decide on any matter of taste or form; a master of the ceremonies.

——*Arbĭter hic sumtus de lite jocōsâ.* Ovid.—"He was chosen umpire in this sportive contest." Said of Tiresias, who was chosen umpire in the contest between Jupiter and Juno.

Arbŏre dejectâ qui vult ligna collĭgit. *Prov.*—"When the tree is thrown down, every one who pleases gathers the wood." The meanest may, and often do, triumph over fallen majesty. See the fable of "The aged Lion and the Ass," in *Phædrus*, B. i. F. 21.

Arbŏres magnæ diu crescunt, unâ horâ extirpantur. Curt.—"Great trees are long in growing, but are rooted up in a single hour."

Arbŏres serit dilĭgens agricŏla, quarum aspiciet nunquam ipse baccam. Cic.—"The industrious husbandman plants trees, of which he himself will never see a berry." In imitation of him, we must not confine ourselves to good works, the fruit of which is to be *immediately* gathered.

——*Arcădes ambo*
Et cantāre pares, et respondĕre parāti. Virg.
—"Both Arcadians, equally skilled in the song and ready for the response."

Arcāna impĕrii.—"The mysteries of governing." State secrets.

Arcānum demens detĕgit ebriĕtas.—"Frantic drunkenness reveals every secret."

Arcānum neque tu scrutābĕris ullius unquam,
Commissumque teges et vino tortus et irâ. Hor.
—"Enquire not into the secrets of others, and conceal

what is intrusted to you, even though racked by wine and anger."

Arctum annŭlum ne gestāto. *Prov.*—"Do not wear too tight a ring." Do not by imprudence waste your property.

Arcum intensio frangit, animum remissio. Syr.—"Straining injures the bow, relaxation the mind." This maxim is in words not unlike that taught in the Fable of "Æsop at Play," except that he warns us against giving, not too much, but too little, relaxation to the mind. See *Phædrus*, B. iv. F. 14.

Ardĕat ipsa licet, tormentis gaudet amantis. Juv.—"Although she herself may burn, she delights in the torments of her lover."

Ardentia verba.—"Words that glow." Expressions full of warmth and ardour.

——*Ardua cervix*
Argūtumque caput, brevis alvŭs, obĕsaque terga,
Luxuriatque toris animōsum pectus—— Virg.

—"Lofty is his neck, and his head slender, his belly short, his back plump, while his proud chest swells luxuriant, with brawny muscles." A fine description of what a horse should be.

Ardua molimur; sed nulla nisi ardua virtus. Ovid.—"I attempt an arduous task; but there is no merit but what is to be secured by arduous means."

Arēna sine calce. *Prov.*—"Sand without lime." If sand is used too plentifully, the mortar will not adhere. This saying was used by the emperor Caligula with reference to the desultory works of the philosopher Seneca.

Arēnæ mandas sĕmina. *Prov.*—"You are sowing your grain in the sand." You are labouring at an impossibility.

Arescit gramen veniente autumno.—"The grass withers as autumn comes on." Applicable to the sear and yellow leaf of old age.

Argentum accĕpi, dote impĕrium vendĭdi. Plaut.—"I received money with her, and for the dowry have sold my authority."

Argillâ quidvis imitabĕris udâ. Hor.—"With moist clay you may imitate anything you please." Early impressions are most indelibly fixed.

Argumentum ad hŏmĭnem.—"An argument direct to the man." An argument which admits of a personal application.

Argumentum ad ignorantiam.—"An argument to ignorance." An argument founded on the ignorance of your adversary.

Argumentum ad judicium.—"An argument by appeal to the judgment."

Argumentum ad verecundiam.—"An argument to decency."

Argumentum baculīnum.—"The argument of the stick." Club law.

——*Argūtos inter strepit anser olōres.* VIRG.—"He gabbles like a goose among the tuneful swans."

Arma cereālia.—"The arms of Ceres." Implements of husbandry, of which Ceres was the goddess.

——*Arma tenenti*

Omnia dat, qui justa negat.— LUCAN.

—"He who refuses what is just, grants everything to his opponent when armed." Consciousness of rectitude inspires us with that confidence which so greatly conduces to success.

Ars est celāre artem.—"The great object of art is to conceal art." The perfection of art is attained when no traces of the artist are to be seen.

Ars est sine arte, cujus principium est mentīri, medium laborāre, et finis mendicāre.—"The art is devoid of art, whose beginning is falsehood, its middle labour, and its end beggary." The character of the delusive science of alchemy.

Ars longa, vita brevis.—"Art is long, life is short." A translation of the first of Hippocrates' Aphorisms.

——*Ars mihi non tanti est.* OVID.—"The art is not worth so great a penalty to me."

Ars varia vulpis, ast una echīno maxĭma. *Prov.*—The fox has many tricks; the hedgehog only one, and that greater than all." The hedgehog effectually defends himself by rolling himself up in a ball. See *Multa novit*, &c.

Artem quævis alit terra.—"Every country nurtures some art."

Artis magistra necessĭtas. PLINY *the Younger.*—"Necessity is the mistress of the arts."

Asĭnum sub fræno currĕre docēre. *Prov.*—"To teach an

ass to obey the rein." A task which was considered by the ancients to be "labour in vain." See *At si cognātos*, &c.

Asĭnus asĭno, et sus sui pulcher.—"An ass to ass is a beauty, a swine to a swine." Somewhat similar to our saying, "Every Jack has his Jill." A fortunate feature in the harmonious system of nature.

Asĭnus inter simias. *Prov.*—"An ass among apes." Said of a fool among ill-natured persons who make a butt of him.

Asĭnus in unguento. *Prov.*—"An ass among perfumes." Said of a person "out of his element."

Aspĕræ facetiæ, ubi nimis ex vero traxēre, acrem sui memŏriam relinquunt. TACIT.—"Cutting jokes, especially when based too much upon truth, leave a bitter remembrance." The truth of this is experienced by those who prefer to *have* their joke, and *lose* their friend.

Aspĕrĭtas agrestis et inconcinna gravisque. HOR.—"A clownish roughness, churlish and ill at ease."

Aspĕrius nihil est humili cum surgit in altum. CLAUD.—"Nothing is more unendurable than a low-bred man, when he attains an elevated station." We have a proverb to the same effect, "Set a beggar on horseback, and he will ride to the devil."

Aspĭce curvātos pomōrum pondĕre ramos. OVID.—"Behold the branches bending beneath the weight of apples."

——*Assiduo labuntur tempŏra motu*——
Non secus ac flumen. Neque enim consistĕre flumen,
Nec levis hora potest——

—"Time glides on with a constant progress, no otherwise than as a flowing stream. For neither can the stream nor the fleeting hour stop in its course."

Assumpsit. *Law Term.*—"He engaged to pay." An action of *assumpsit* lies on the promise to pay, which the law implies on the part of every man who buys of another.

——*Ast alii sex*
Et plures, uno conclāmant ore—— JUV.

—"Six others, ay more, with one voice assent."

Astra regunt hŏmĭnes, sed regit astra Deus.—"The stars govern man, but God governs the stars." The belief of the astrologers.

Astūtior coccȳge. *Prov.*—"More crafty than the cuckoo," who lays her eggs in the nest of another bird.

At dæmon hŏmĭni quum struit alĭquid malum,
Pervertit illi primĭtus mentem suam.
EURIPIDES, *as quoted by Athenagoras.*
—"But the dæmon, when he devises any mischief against a man, first perverts his mind." See *Quem Deus*, &c., and *Quem Jupiter*, &c.

At hæc etiam servis semper lībĕra fuĕrunt, timĕrent, gaudērent, dolērent, suo potiùs quam altĕrīus arbitrio. CIC.—"Slaves, even, have always been at liberty to fear, to rejoice, to grieve, at their own pleasure, and not at the will of another."—The body may be "cribb'd, cabin'd, and confin'd," but the mind cannot be chained.

At jam non domus accipiet te læta; neque uxor
Optima, nec dulces occurrent oscŭla nati
Præripĕre, et tacĭtâ pectus dulcēdĭne tangent. LUCR.
—"No longer shall thy joyous home receive thee, nor yet thy best of wives, nor shall thy sweet children run to be the first to snatch thy kisses, and thrill thy breast with silent delight." See the similar lines in Gray's Elegy.

At pulchrum est digito monstrāri et dīcier, Hic est. PERS.—"It is a gratifying thing to be pointed at with the finger, and to have it said, That is he." Of course this applies to a man who has become *famous*, not *notorious*.

At redĭtus jam quisque suos amat, et sibi quid sit
Utĭle, solicitis suppŭtat artĭcŭlis—— OVID.
—"Now-a-days every one loves his own interests, and reckons, on his anxious fingers, what may turn out useful for himself."

——***At scio, quo vos soleātis pacto perplexarĭer;***
Pactum non pactum est; non pactum pactum est, quod vobis lubet. PLAUT.
—"But I understand the fashion in which you are wont to equivocate; an agreement is no agreement, no agreement is an agreement, just as it pleases you."

At si cognātos, nullo natūra labōre
Quos tibi dat, retinĕre velis, servāreque amīcos,
Infēlix opĕram perdas, ut si quis asellum
In campo docĕat parentem currĕre frænis. HOR.
—"If you think to retain and preserve as friends the rela-

tives whom nature gives you, without taking any pains, wretched man! you lose your pains just as much as if a person were to train an ass to be obedient to the rein, and run along the plain." See *Asinum sub*, &c.

At vindicta bonum vitâ jucundius ipsâ,——
Nempe hoc indocti.— JUV.
—"But revenge is a blessing more sweet than life itself. Yes, fools think so."

Atque deos atque astra vocat crudelia mater. VIRG.—"Both gods and stars his mother charges with cruelty." A description of the grief of Daphnis on hearing of the death of her son.

Atque utĭnam his potius nugis tota illa dedisset
Tempŏra sævitiæ—— JUV.
—"And would that he had devoted to such trifles as these all those days of cruelty." Said of Domitian.

Atqui vultus erat multa et præclara minantis. HOR.—"But you had the look of one that threatened many and excellent things."

Atria regum homĭnibus plena sunt, amicis vacua. SEN.—"The halls of kings are full of men, empty of friends." Kings have many followers, but few real friends.

——*Audācem fecĕrat ipse timor.* OVID.—"Fear itself had made her bold."

Auctor pretiosa facit. OVID. "The giver enhances the value of the gift." See *Acceptissima*, &c.

Audāces fortūna juvat timidosque repellit. —"Fortune favours the bold, and repels the timid."

Audax ad omnia fœmina, quæ vel amat vel odit.—"A woman, when inflamed by love or by hatred, will dare everything."

——*Audax omnia perpĕti*
Gens humāna ruit per vĕtĭtum et nefas. HOR.
—"Bold to perpetrate every species of crime, mankind rushes into everything that is wicked and forbidden." These words may be appropriately applied to vice and refined dissoluteness, but they were used by Horace as a censure upon what we should now call "the march of progress."

Aude alĭquid brĕvibus Gyăris et carcĕre dignum
Si vis esse alĭquis. Probĭtas laudātur et alget. JUV.

—"Dare to commit some act worthy of the little Gyara or the gaol, if you wish to be somebody. Virtue is praised and shivers with cold." The Romans used the island of Gyara in the Ægean Sea as a place of transportation for criminals.

Audendo magnus tegĭtur timor. LUCAN.—"Great fear is concealed under a show of courage."

Audendum est, ut illustrāta verĭtas patĕat multique a perjurio liberentur. LACTANT.—"We must make the attempt to set forth the truth, that it may be seen, and so be rescued from the mischiefs of perjury."

——*Audentem Forsque Venusque juvant.* OVID.—"Fortune and Venus befriend the bold."

Audentes fortūna juvat. VIRG.—"Fortune favours the brave."

Audi altĕram partem. *Prov.*—"Hear the other side." Listen to what each party has to allege, before you give your decision.

——*Audi,*
Nulla unquam de morte hŏmĭnis cunctātio longa est. JUV.
—"Listen! when a man's life is at stake no delay can be too long."

Audi, vide, tace, si vis vīvĕre in pace.—"Listen, look on, and hold your tongue, if you would live in peace." A Leonine line of the middle ages.

Audiet pugnas, vitio parentum,
Rara juventus—— HOR.
—"Our youth, thinned by the vices of their fathers, shall hear of these battles."

Audīre, atque togam jubeo componĕre quisquis
Ambitiōne malā, aut argenti pallet amōre,
Quisquis luxuriā—— HOR.
—"Whoever is pale through foul ambition, or the love of money, or luxurious living, him I bid sit still and listen."

Audīre est opĕræ pretium. HOR.—"It is worth your while to listen."

Audītā querēlā. *Law Phrase.*—"The complaint of the defendant having been heard." The name of a writ by which a defendant appealed against a judgment given against him.

——*Auditque vocātus Apollo.* VIRG.—"And Apollo hears when invoked."

——*Auferĭmur cultu.* Ovid.—"We are captivated by dress."

Auguriis patrum et priscâ formidĭne sacrum. Tacit.—"(A grove) hallowed by the auguries of our forefathers, and by ancient awe." Like a fly in clouded amber, this hexameter lies concealed in the prose of the historian. It is probably a quotation from some Latin poet, but has been overlooked as such.

Augurium ratio est, et conjectūra futūri:
Hâc divīnāvi, notĭtiamque tuli. Ovid.
—"Reason is my augury, and my estimate of the future; from it have I made my prediction and derived my knowledge."

Aula regis.—"The court of the king." A court which, in the middle ages, accompanied the king wherever he went, and in which originated the present Court of King's Bench.

Aura populāris.—"The breeze of popularity." A man who has the populace upon his side, is for the moment wafted on by the *aura popularis.* See *Virtus repulsæ,* &c.

Aurea ne credas quæcunque nitescĕre cernis.—"Think not that everything that shines is gold." "All is not gold that glitters." Trust not to outside appearances.

Aurea nunc vere sunt sæcŭla, plurĭmus auro
Venit honos: auro conciliātur amor. Ovid.
—"Truly this is the *golden age*: the chief honours accrue through gold; with gold love is purchased."

Aurea prima sata est ætas, quæ vindĭce nullo,
Sponte suâ, sine lege, fidem rectumque colēbat.
Pœna metusque abĕrant—— Ovid.
—"The golden age was first founded, which without any avenger, of its own accord, and without laws, practised faith and rectitude. Punishment, and the fear of it, did not yet exist."

Auream quisquis mediocritātem
Dilĭgit, tutus caret obsolēti
Sordĭbus tecti, caret invidendâ
Sobrius aulâ. Hor.
—"Whoever loves the golden mean, avoids in safety the squalor of an old house, while, in the enjoyment of moderation, he escapes the cares of splendour."

Aureo piscāri hamo. *Prov.*—"To fish with a golden hook."

To spare no sum however large in obtaining the object of our pursuit. A saying much used by Augustus Cæsar.

Auri sacra fames—— VIRG.—"The cursed greed of gold." See *Quid non mortalia*, &c.

Aurĭbus tĕnĕo lupum. TER.—"I hold a wolf by the ears." If I leave go he will destroy me, yet I shall not be able long to retain him. Somewhat similar to our English phrase of "catching a Tartar." An Irish soldier, under Prince Eugene, called out to his comrade, in a battle against the Turks, that he had caught a Tartar. "Bring him along then," said the other. "He won't come," was the reply. "Then come yourself." "But he won't let me," was the answer.

Auro contra cedo modestum amatōrem. PLAUT.—"Find me a reasonable lover against his weight in gold."

Auro loquente nihil pollet quævis rătio. Prov.—"When gold speaks, no reason is of the slightest avail."

Auro pulsa fides, auro venālia jura,
Aurum lex sĕquĭtur, mox sine lege pudor. PROP.
—"By gold good faith is banished, the laws are put up to sale for gold, the law follows gold, and before long will modesty lose the protection of the laws."

Aurum e stercŏre.—"Gold from a dunghill;" said of a thing which lies concealed where least expected.

Aurum in fortūnâ invĕnĭtur, natūrâ ingĕnium bonum. PLAUT.—"Gold is met with by luck, a good disposition is found by nature."

Aurum omnes, victâ jam pietāte, volunt. PROP.—"All men now long for gold, piety being overcome;" in other words, "Money now only makes the man."

Aurum per mĕdios ire satellĭtes
Et perrumpĕre amat saxa, potentius
Ictu fulmĭnĕo—— HOR.
—"Gold delights to make its way through the midst of guards, and to break through stone walls, more powerful than the thunderbolt." The poet alludes to the story of Jupiter and Danaë.

Aut amat, aut odit mulĭer; nil est tertium. SYR.—"A woman either loves or hates; there is no third part."

Aut bĭbat, aut ăbĕat.—"Let each one drink or begone." The man who passes the bottle without helping himself may possibly take advantage of the unguarded expressions of those who are drinking more freely.

Aut Cæsar aut nullus.—"Either Cæsar or nobody." I will attain supreme eminence, or perish in the attempt. A saying of Julius Cæsar.

Aut hoc quod produxi testium satis est, aut nihil satis.—"Either this testimony which I have brought is sufficient, or nothing will suffice."

Aut insānit homo, aut versus facit. HOR.—"Either the man is mad, or is making verses."

Aut non tentāris, aut perfice. OVID.—"Either try not, or persevere."

"Fain would I climb, but that I fear to fall,"

were the words written by Sir W. Raleigh on a pane of glass:

"If thy heart fails thee, why then climb at all?"

was Queen Elizabeth's rejoinder.

Aut pĕtis, aut urges ruitūrum Sisyphe, saxum. OVID.—"You, Sisyphus, either pursue or push forward the stone that is destined to fall back again."

Aut potentior te, aut imbecillior læsit: si imbecillior parce illi; si potentior tibi. SEN.—"He who injured thee was either stronger or weaker: if weaker, spare him; if stronger, spare thyself."

Aut prodesse volunt aut delectāre poētæ,
Aut simul et jūcunda et idonea dicere vitæ. HOR.
—"It is the wish of poets either to instruct or to amuse at the same time to inculcate what is agreeable and what is conducive to living well."

Aut regem aut fatuum nasci oportuit. Prov.—"A man ought to be born a king or a fool." Idiots were in former times, and still are, in the East, held in the highest respect. The fools, or jesters, of kings and nobles, both in ancient times and the middle ages, were allowed the utmost licence; and it was a common saying, that "Fools are fortunate."

——*Aut virtus nomen ināne est,*
Aut decus et pretium rectè petit experiens vir. HOR.
"Either virtue is an empty name, or the wise man rightly seeks it as his glory and reward."

***Autumnus**—Libitīnæ questus acerbæ.* HOR.—"Autumn—th

harvest of the direful Libitina." Autumn was in ancient times, as now, accounted a sickly season, and Libitina was the patron goddess of the *pollinctores*, or undertakers.

Auxilia humilia firma consensus facit. LABER.—"Concord gives strength to humble aids." Union imparts strength.

Avārus, nisi cum morĭtur, nil rectè facit.—"A miser, until he dies, does nothing right." His heir, at all events, is apt to think, that his dying was the best action of his life.

Avia Piĕrĭdum perăgro loca, nullius antè
Trita solo, juvat intĕgros accedĕre fonteis
Atque haurīre.—— LUCRET.

—"I wander through the retired retreats of the Muses, untrodden before by another foot; I delight to approach their untouched fountain, and to drink thereof."

Avĭda est perīcŭli Virtus, et quo tendat non quid passūra sit cogĭtat. SEN.—"Virtue courts danger, and considers what it may accomplish, not what it may suffer."

Avĭdis natūra parum est. SEN.—"The bounty of nature is too little for the greedy man."

——*Avītus apto*
Cum lare fundus. HOR.

—"A farm inherited from my ancestors, with a suitable dwelling." Horace here describes his Sabine farm.

B.

Balnea, vina, Venus corrumpunt corpŏra nostra;
Sed vitam faciunt balnea, vina, Venus.
Epitaph in Gruter's Monumenta.

—"Baths, wine, and Venus cause our bodies to decay: but baths, wine, and Venus make up the sum of life."

"Wine, women, warmth, against our lives combine,
But what were life without warmth, women, wine?"

Barbæ tenus săpientes. Prov.—"Philosophers as far as beard." Ironically said of persons who, by assuming grave manners, wish to pass themselves off for men of learning.

Bastardus nullius est filius, aut fīlius pŏpŭli. Law Maxim.—"A bastard is the son of no man, in other words, the son of the public." A bastard, not being born in wedlock, his father is not recognised as such by the law; but, as an individual, the public laws protect his life and property.

Beāti immaculāti in viâ.—"Blessed are the undefiled in the way." The commencing words of the 119th Psalm.

Beāti monŏcŭli in regiōne cæcōrum.—"Happy are the one-eyed in the country of the blind." All things ought to be judged of *comparatively;* and, whatever may be the extent of our misfortunes, there will still be found something for consolation.

Beātissĭmus is est, qui est aptus ex sese, quique in se uno sua ponit omnia. Cic.—"He is the most happy who is self-prepared, and who centres all his resources in himself."

Beātus ille qui procul negōtiis,
Ut prisca gens mortālium,
Paterna rura bobus exercet suis,
Solūtus omni fœnŏre. Hor.

—"Happy the man who, remote from business, after the manner of the ancient race of mortals, cultivates his paternal lands with his own oxen, disengaged from all usury."

Beātus qui est, non intellĭgo quid requīrat ut sit beātior. Cic.—"I do not see why he who is already happy, needs seek to be happier."

Bella! horrĭda bella! Virg.—"War! horrid war!"

Bella matrĭbus detestāta. Hor.—"War, so detested by mothers."

Bella—nullos habitūra triumphos. Lucan.—"Wars which will leave no cause for triumph." Most truly said of civil war.

Bella suscipienda sunt ob eam causam, ut sine injūriâ in pace vivātur. Cic.—"Wars are to be undertaken in order that we may live in peace without suffering wrong."

Bellè narras.—"You tell a very pretty story." Said ironically.

Bellua multōrum capĭtum.—"The many-headed monster." The mob.

Bellum ita suscipiātur, ut nihil ălīud nisi pax quæsīta videātur. Cic.—"War should be so engaged in, that nothing but peace should appear to be aimed at."

Bellum nec timendum nec provocandum. PLINY *the Younger.*—"War ought neither to be dreaded, nor provoked."

Bene dormit, qui non sentit quam male dormiat. SYRUS.—"He sleeps well who does not perceive how badly he has slept."

——*Benè est cui Deus obtŭlit*
Parcâ quod satis est manu. HOR.
—"Happy for him, to whom God has given enough with a sparing hand."

Bene ferre magnam
Disce fortūnam. HOR.
—"Learn to support your good fortune with moderation."

Bene merenti bene profuĕrit, male merenti par erit. PLAUT.—"To the well-deserving God will show favour, to the ill-deserving will he give like for like."

Benè nummatum decŏrat Suadēla Venusque. HOR.—"Love and compliance* favour the wealthy suitor."

Bene si amīco fēcĕris, ne pĭgeat fecisse,
Ut pŏtius pudeat si non fēceris. PLAUT.
—"If you have conferred a favour upon your friend, repent not of having done so; rather feel that you would have been ashamed had you not done so."

Benefacta malè locāta, malefacta arbĭtror. CIC.—"Favours injudiciously conferred I consider injuries." Nothing is more injurious to the common good, than indiscriminate charity, or profuse indulgence.

Beneficia dare qui nescit injustè petit. SYR.—"He who knows not how to bestow a benefit, is unreasonable if he expects one."

Beneficia plura rĕcĭpit qui scit reddĕre. SYR.—"He receives most favours, who knows how to make a proper return."

Beneficia usque eo læta sunt dum videntur exsolvi posse; ubi multum antevenêre, pro gratiâ odium reddĭtur. TACIT.—"Benefits are only acceptable so long as we think we may requite them; but when they exceed the possibility of so doing, hatred is returned instead of gratitude." This maxim, it is to be hoped, is not of general acceptation, but applies to the exception, and not the rule. If universally acted on, the world would soon be a dreary wilderness. See *Æs debitorem*, &c.

* *Suadela*, or *Suada*, the goddess of persuasion.

Beneficium accipĕre libertātem vendĕre est. LABER.—"To accept an obligation is to barter your liberty."

Beneficium dignis ubi des, omnes oblĭges. SYR.—"Where you confer a benefit, worthy of it, the obligation is extended to all."

Beneficium invito non datur. *Prov.*—"A benefit conferred on a churl is no benefit." The phrase may also mean that a benefit conferred with an ill grace is no benefit.

Beneficium meminisse debet is, in quem collocāta sunt; non commemorāre qui contŭlit. CIC.—"He ought to remember benefits on whom they are conferred; he who confers them ought not to mention them."

Beneficium non in eo quod fit aut datur constĭtit, sed in ipso facientis aut dantis anĭmo: anĭmus est enim qui beneficiis dat pretium. SEN.—"A benefit consists not in that which is done or given, but in the spirit in which it is done or given; for it is the spirit which gives all the value to the benefit."

Beneficium sæpe dare, docēre est reddĕre. SYR.—"Often to confer a benefit is to teach how to make a return." In giving to others, we teach them to be charitable.

Benefĭcus est qui non sui, sed altĕrius causâ benignè facit. CIC.—"He is beneficent who acts kindly, not for his own sake, but to serve another." Disinterestedness is the soul of benevolence.

Benignior sententia in verbis generālibus seu dubiis est præferenda. COKE.—"In cases where general or doubtful words are employed, the more merciful construction is to be preferred."

Benignĭtas quæ constat ex ŏpĕrâ et industriâ honestior est, et latius patet, et prodesse potest plurĭbus. CIC.—"That bounty, the essence of which is works and industry, is more honourable and more extended in its results, and has the power of benefiting more largely." The distinction between active charity and the mere bestowal of money.

Benignus etiam dandi causam cogĭtat. *Prov.*—"Even the benignant man takes into consideration the grounds of his liberality." Indiscriminate bounty is as baneful as avarice. See *Benefacta male*, &c.

Bibĕre papāliter.—"To drink like a pope." A mediæval expression.

Bis dat qui citò dat. Alciatus.—"He gives twice who gives in time." The value of a service depends very much upon the grace and promptness with which it is done. See *Inopi beneficium*, &c., *Gratia ab*, &c.

Bis est gratum quod opus est, si ultro offĕras. Syr.—"That is doubly acceptable, which is spontaneously offered when we stand in need." "A friend in need is a friend indeed."

Bis interĭmĭtur qui suis armis perit. Syr.—"He dies twice who perishes by his own arms." Misfortunes are doubly bitter when caused by ourselves.

Bis peccāre in bello non licet. *Prov.*—"It is not permitted to err twice in war." Errors in war are often irretrievable, and leave no opportunity for a repetition.

Bis pueri senes. *Prov.*—"Old men are twice children." Said in reference to the years of dotage. "Once a man, twice a child."

Bis vincit qui se vincit in victoriâ. Syr.—"He conquers twice, who, when a conqueror, conquers himself."

Blandæ mendacia linguæ.—"The lies of a flattering tongue."

Bœōtum in crasso jurāres aĕre natum. Hor.—"You would swear he was born in the dense atmosphere of Bœotia." The inhabitants of Bœotia, in Greece, were said to be remarkable for extraordinary stupidity. Their country, however, produced Pindar and Epaminondas.

Bombălio, clangor, stridor, taratantăra, murmur.—Words descriptive of a hubbub, or *charivari*.—"Oh what a row, what a rumpus, and a rioting!" as the song says.

Bona bonis contingunt.—"Blessings befall the good."

Bonâ fide.—"In good faith."

Bona malis parĭa non sunt, etiam pari numĕro; nec lætĭtia ulla mĭnĭmo mœrōre pensanda. Pliny *the Elder*.—"The blessings of life do not equal its ills, although even in number; nor can any pleasure compensate for even the slightest pain." The sentiment of a melancholy mind, which looks on the dark side of things.

Bona nĕmĭni hora est, ut non alĭcui sit mala. Syr.—"There is no hour good for one man but that it is bad for another." "One man's loss is another man's gain."

Bona notabĭlia. *Law Term.*—"Known goods." Goods beyond the value of five pounds left by a person deceased, in any other diocese than that in which he died.

Bonæ leges malis ex mōribus procreantur. Macrob.—"Good laws grow out of evil acts."

Bonārum rerum consuetūdo pessĭma est. Syr.—"The constant enjoyment of good things is most hurtful." Habitual indulgence in luxuries is prejudicial; by constant repetition the taste becomes cloyed, and all sense of enjoyment lost.

Boni nullo emolumento impelluntur in fraudem, imprŏbi sæpe parvo. Cic.—"Good men are never induced to commit fraud by any gain whatsoever; the bad often by a very little."

Boni pastōris est tondĕre pecus non deglubĕre. Sueton.—"It is the duty of a good shepherd to shear his sheep, not to flay them." A saying of Tiberius Cæsar, in reference to excessive taxation.

Boni vēnātōris est plures feras căpĕre non omnes.—"It is the business of a good sportsman to take much game, not all." From Notes to Horace, by Nannius.

Boni viri omnes æquitātem ipsam amant. Cic.—"All good men love justice for its own sake."

Bonis avibus.—"With good omens."

Bonis inter bonos quasi necessaria est benevolentia. Cic.—"Between good men there is a necessary interchange, as it were, of good feeling."

Bonis nŏcet quisquis pepercĕrit malis. Syr.—"He injures the good, who spares the wicked." Misplaced sympathy is an injury committed against society.

Bonis quod bĕnĕfit haud perit. Plaut.—"A kindness done to the good is never lost." Good deeds are never ill-bestowed.

Bono ingĕnio me esse ornātam, quam auro multo mavŏlo. Plaut.—"I had much rather that I was adorned with a good disposition than with gold."

Bonum ego quam beātum me esse nimio dici mavŏlo. Plaut.—"I would much rather be called good than fortunate."

Bonum est fugienda aspicĕre in aliēno malo. Syr.—"It is well to see what to avoid in the misfortunes of others."

Bonum est, pauxillum amāre sane, insāne non bonum est. Plaut.—"It is good to love in a moderate degree; to love to distraction is not good."

Bonum magis carendo quam fruendo sentĭtur. Prov.—"A

good is more valued when we are in want of it, than when we enjoy it." The value of good health is only truly estimated by the sick man.

——*Bonum summum quo tendĭmus omnes.* LUCRET.—"That ultimate good at which we all aim."

Bonus anĭmus in malâ re dimidĭum est mali. PLAUT.—"Good courage in a bad case is half of the evil got over."

Bonus arātor agricultiōne se oblectat, cultu sæpe defatigātur, cultūrâ ditescit. CIC.—"A good husbandman takes delight in agriculture; he is often wearied with his labours, but by culture he gets rich."

——*Bonus atque fidus*
Judex honestum prætŭlit utĭli. HOR.
—"A good and faithful judge prefers the honest to the expedient."

Bonus dux bonum reddit mīlĭtem. *Prov.*—"A good general makes good soldiers."

Bonus judex secundum æquum et bonum judĭcat, et æquitātem strictæ legi præfert. COKE.—"A good judge gives judgment according to what is equitable and right, and prefers an equitable construction to the strict letter of the law."

Bos aliēnus subinde prospectat foras. *Prov.*—"The strange ox repeatedly looks to the door." Significant of that love of home which pervades the animated creation.

Bos fortius fatigātus figit pedem. *Prov.*—"The wearied ox treads the surest."

Bos in linguâ.—"An ox on his tongue." Said of a man who had been bribed, as the Athenians had money stamped with the figure of an ox.

Breve tempus ætātis satis est longum ad bene honestēque vivendum. CIC.—"A short life is long enough for us to live well and honestly."

Brevi manu.—"With a short hand." Off-hand, in a summary manner.

——*Brevis esse labōro,*
Obscūrus fio.—— HOR.
—"While I endeavour to be brief, I become obscure." Said of authors who, aiming at conciseness, give their readers credit for knowing too much. The exclamation of Thomas Warton, on accidentally snuffing out a candle.

Brevis ipsa vita est, sed malis sit longior. SYR.—"Life itself is short, but it may last longer than your misfortunes." Somewhat similar to our proverb, "It is a long lane that has no turning."

Brevis voluptas mox dolŏris est parens.—"Short-lived pleasure is the parent of speedy sorrow."

Brutum fulmen.—"A harmless thunderbolt." Big words; the groans of the mountains when they were delivered of the mouse.

C.

Cacoëthes.—"A bad habit." This is a Greek word Latinized, which has been adopted in other languages.

Cacoëthes carpendi.—"An itch for finding fault," or "carping at."

Cacoëthes scribendi.—"An itch for scribbling."

Cadit quæstio. A phrase in Logic.—"There is an end of the question." The matter requires no further investigation. See *Casus quæstionis.*

Cæca invidia est, nec quidquam aliud scit quam detrectāre virtutes. LIVY.—"Envy is blind, and knows not how to do aught but detract from the virtues of others."

Cæci sunt ŏcŭli, cum anĭmus res ălias agit. SYR.—"The eyes are blind, when the mind is intent upon something else."

Cæcus non judĭcat de colōre.—"A blind man is no judge of colours."

Cæsărem portas, et fortūnas ejus.—"Thou carriest Cæsar and his fortune." Said by Cæsar to the pilot in the tempest.

Cætĕra desunt.—"The rest is wanting."

Cætĕra quis nescit? OVID.—"The rest who knows not?"

Calamĭtas quĕrŭla est et superba felicĭtas. CURT.—"Adversity is complaining, and prosperity proud."

Calamitōsus est anĭmus futūri anxius. SEN.—"The mind that is anxious about future events, is miserable."

——*Campos ubi Troja fuit.* LUCAN.—"The fields where Troy once stood."

Callĭdos eos appello, quorum tanquam manus ŏpĕre sic anĭmus usu concalluit. CIC.—"I call those experienced, whose minds become strengthened just as the hands are hardened by labour."

Calumniāre fortĭter, aliquid adhærēbit."—"Slander stoutly; some of it will stick."

Calumniāri si quis autem voluerit,
Quod arbŏres loquantur, non tantum feræ;
Fictis jocāri nos memĭnĕrit făbŭlis. PHÆD.
—"But if any one shall think fit to cavil, because not only wild beasts, but even trees speak, let him remember that we are disporting in the language of fable."
"'Tis clear that birds were always able
To hold discourse, at least in fable." COWPER.

Camēlus desīdĕrans cornua etiam aures perdĭdit. Prov.—"The camel begging for horns lost its ears as well." We should be thankful for the faculties with which Providence has endowed us, and not wish for those which are inconsistent with our condition.

Camēlus saltat. Prov.—"The camel is dancing." Said of a person doing something quite repugnant to his ordinary habits.

Candĭda me capiet, capiet me flava puella. OVID.—"The blonde will charm me, the brunette will charm me too."

Candĭda pax homĭnes, trux decet ira feras. OVID.—"Fair peace becomes human beings, savage fury wild beasts."

Candĭda, perpetuo rĕsĭde, concordia, lecto,
Jamque pari semper sit Venus æqua jugo:
Dilĭgat illa senem quondam; sed et ipsa marīto,
Tunc quoque cum fuerit, non videatur anus. MAR.
—"Fair concord, ever attend their bed, and may Venus ever prove auspicious to the well-matched pair; may she at a future day love her old man; and may she, even when she is so, not appear to her husband to be aged."

Candĭdus in nautâ turpis color: æquŏris undâ
Debet et a rădiis sīdĕris esse niger. OVID.
—"A fair complexion is unbecoming in a sailor; he ought to be swarthy, from the spray of the sea and the rays of the sun."

Candor dat vīrĭbus alas.—"Candour imparts wings to strength."

Canes socium in culīnâ nullum amant. Prov.—"Dogs love no companion in the kitchen." See *Figulus*, &c., and *Una domus*, &c.

Canes tĭmĭdi vehementiùs latrant qùam mordent. Q. CURT. "With cowardly dogs, the bark is worse than the bite."

Canīna facundia.—"Dog eloquence." Mentioned by Quintilian as that kind of eloquence which distinguished itself in snarling at others. See *Littera canina.*

Canis festinans cæcos parit cătŭlos. *Prov.*—"The bitch, in making too much haste, brings forth her whelps blind." Said of persons who are in too great a hurry to put the finishing stroke to what they have undertaken.

Cantābit vacuus coram latrōne viātor. JUV.—"The traveller with empty pockets, will sing in presence of the robber." He who has nothing to lose is in no fear of being robbed.

Cantantes licet usque (minus via lædet) ēāmus. VIRG.—"Let us sing as we travel on, the journey will be all the less tedious."

Cantat, et ad nautas ēbria verba jacit. OVID.—"He sings aloud and cracks his drunken jokes upon the sailors."

Cantat vinctus quoque compĕde fossor,
Indŏcĭli nŭmero cum grave mollit opus.
Cantat et innītens līmōsæ pronus arēnæ,
Adverso tardam qui trahit amne ratem. OVID.
—"The miner, chained with the fetter, sings as he lightens his heavy labours with his untaught numbers; and the man sings, who strives as he bends forward on the oozy sand, while he drags the slow barge against the tide."

Cantāte Domĭno.—"O sing unto the Lord (a new song)." Beginning of the 98th Psalm.

Cantilēnam eandem canis. TER.—"You are singing the same tune." Like our expression, "You are always harping on one string."

Căpĭas. Law Term.—"You may take" the body of the defendant, under either a

Căpĭas ad respondendum. Law Term.—"You may take him to make answer." A writ issued to take the defendant and make him answer to the complaint,—or a

Căpias ad satisfaciendum. Law Term.—"You may take him to satisfy." "A writ of execution on a judgment obtained, commanding the officer to imprison the defendant until satisfaction is made for the debt recovered against him."

Captantes capti sumus.—"We catchers are caught." "The biter is bitten."

Capistrum maritāle. Juv.—"The noose matrimonial."

Capĭta aut navem ?—"Head or ship ?" Or as we say, "Head or tail." "Cross or pile ?" The copper coins of Rome had on one side the double head of Janus, on the other the figure of a ship.

Căpĭtis nives. Hor.—"The snows of the head." White hair.

Captum te nidōre suæ putat ille culīnæ. Juv.—"He thinks he has caught you with the fumes of his kitchen." He thinks that you will submit to anything for a good dinner.

Caput artis est, decēre quod făcias. *Prov.*—"It is the perfection of good management, to let all that you do be becoming." Every one should endeavour to act in a manner becoming to his age and position.

Caput mortuum.—"The dead head." A term used in chemistry, meaning the residuum of a substance that has been acted on by heat. By punsters the term has been applied to a blockhead.

Caput mundi.—"The head of the world." The designation of ancient Rome in the days of her splendour. It is still applied, by Roman Catholics, to modern Rome, as the see of the head of their religion.

Cara fuit, conjux, primæ mihi cura juventæ
Cognĭta ; nunc ubi sit quærĭtis ? Urna tegit. Ovid.
—"I once had a dear wife, known as the choice of my early youth. Do you ask where she is now ? The urn covers her." Lines full of pathos.

Carbōne notāre.—"To mark with charcoal." To place a black line against the name of a person was to signify disapproval.

——*Caret insĭdiis homĭnum, quia mitis, hĭrundo.* Ovid.—"The swallow is exempt from the snares of men, because it is gentle."

Caret perīcŭlo, qui etiam cum est tutus cavet. Syr.—"He is secure against danger who, even when in safety, is on his guard." This caution must however be used, without being over anxious about the future. See "*Calamitosus est,*" &c.

Cari sunt parentes, cari lībĕri, propinqui, familiāres ; sed omnes omnium carĭtātes patria una complexa est. Cic.—"Dear are our parents, dear our children, our relatives, our friends; but our country in itself embraces all of these affections."

Caritāte benevolentiāque sublāta, omnis est e vitâ sublāta jucunditas. Cic.—"Charity and benevolence removed, all the delights of life are withdrawn."

Carmen triumphāle.—"A song of triumph."

Carmĭna nil prosunt; nocuerunt carmĭna quondam. Ovid.—"Verses are of no use; verses once did me harm."

Carmĭne fit vivax virtus; expersque sepulcri,
Notitiam seræ posteritātis habet. Ovid.
—"By verse is virtue made immortal; and, secure from death, it thereby obtains the notice of late posterity."

Carni vale.—"Adieu to flesh." Hence the Carnival of the Romish Church, the beginning of Lent.

Carpe diem quàm minĭmè credŭla postĕro. Hor.—"Seize upon to-day, trusting as little as possible in the morrow." The poet says this in conformity with the Epicurean maxim, "Eat, drink, and be merry, for to-morrow we die;" but it may admit of a more extended and more useful application, and teach us not to put off till to-morrow what may be done to-day.

Caseus est nequam quia concŏquit omnia secum. *Med. Aphor.*—"Cheese is injurious, because it digests all things with itself." The saying is at the present day, that cheese digests all things *but* itself.

Caseus est sanus quem dat avāra manus. *Aphorism of the School of Health at Saleeno.*—"Cheese, when given with a sparing hand, is wholesome."

Cassis tutissĭma virtus.—"Virtue is the safest helmet." Motto of the Marquis of Cholmondeley.

Casta ad virum matrōna parendo impĕrat. Syr.—"A virtuous wife, by obeying her husband, gains the command over him."

Castor gaudet equis, ovo prognatus eodem
——*Pugnis.*— Hor.
—"Castor delights in horses, he that was born from the same egg, in boxing." All men have their own peculiar tastes.

Casus belli—"A cause for war."

Casus in eventu est. Ovid.—"The result is doubtful."

Casus omissus. *Law Term.*—"A case omitted." A case for which provision was not made in the statute under consideration, either from neglect, or from the fact of its antecedent improbability.

Casus quæstiōnis.—"Loss of question." In Logic, this means the failure to maintain a position. This is most probably what is alluded to in a passage of Shakspeare, which has so puzzled his commentators,

"As I subscribe not these nor any other,
But in the loss of question."

Measure for Measure, A. ii. s. 4.

Casus quem sæpe transit, aliquando invĕnit. SYR.—"He whom misfortune has often passed by, is by it at last assailed." Good fortune, however long continued, is no pledge of future security. "The pitcher that goes oft to the well gets broken at last."

Casus ubīque valet; semper tibi pendeat hamus.
Quo minĭmè credas gurgĭte, piscis erit. OVID.
—"Chance is powerful everywhere; let your hook be always hanging ready. In waters where you least think it, there will be a fish."

Cato mirāri se aiēbat, quod non ridēret aruspex aruspĭcem cum vidēret. CIC.—"Cato used to say that he was surprised that one soothsayer could keep his countenance when he saw another." In allusion to the barefaced manner in which they imposed upon the credulity of the multitude.

Cătŭlæ domĭnas imitantes. Prov.—"Puppies imitating their mistresses." Said of servants affecting the state and grandeur of their masters, and acting "high life below stairs."

Catus amat pisces, sed non vult tingĕre plantas.—"Puss loves fish, but is loth to wet her feet." It wisely "lets 'I dare not' wait upon 'I would.'" A mediæval adage.

Caudæ pilos equīno paulātim oportet evellĕre. Prov.—"You must pluck out the hairs of a horse's tail one by one." Many things can be effected by patience and perseverance, which are proof against the efforts of violence and precipitation.

Causa latet, vis est notissĭma. OVID.—"The cause lies hid, the power is most evident." The evil is unseen, but its mischievous effects cannot be overlooked.

——*Causam hanc justam esse in animum inducite,*
Ut aliqua pars laboris minuatur mihi. Ter.
—"For my sake come to the conclusion that this request is fair, that so some portion of my labour may be abridged."

Cautus enim metuit foveam lupus, accipiterque
Suspectos laqueos, et opertum miluus hamum. Hor.
—"For the cautious wolf dreads the pit, the hawk the suspected snare, and the fish the concealed hook."

Cave a signatis.—"Beware of those who are branded." Avoid bad company.

Cave ne quid stultè, ne quid temerè, dicas aut facias contra potentes. Cic.—"Beware that you neither say nor do anything rashly against the powerful."

Cave sis te superare servum siris faciendo bene. Plaut.—"Take care that you do not let your servant excel you in doing well."

Cave tibi a cane muto et aquâ silenti. *Prov.*—"Have a care of a silent dog and a still water."

Caveat emptor; qui ignorare non debuit quod jus alienum emit. *Law Maxim.*—"Let the buyer be on his guard: for he ought not to plead ignorance that he is buying the right of another." He is bound to take all reasonable precautions in such a case, and will be supposed to have seen all patent defects.

Cavendum est ne assentatoribus patefaciamus aures. Cic.—"We must be careful not to give ear to flatterers."

Cavendum est ne major pœna, quam culpa, sit; et ne iisdem de causis alii plectantur, alii ne appellentur quidem. Cic.—"Care must be taken that the penalty does not exceed the fault, and that some are not punished for the same offences for which others are not so much as called upon to answer."

Cedant arma togæ, concedat laurea linguæ. Cic.—"Let the sword give place to the gown, the laurel yield to the tongue." Let violence give place to law and justice, the sword of the conqueror to the eloquence of the orator.

Cedant carminibus reges, regumque triumphi. Ovid.—"Let kings, and the triumphs of kings, yield to verse."

——*Cedat uti conviva satur*— Hor.—"Like a well-filled guest, let him depart (from life)." See *Cur non, &c.*

Cede *Deo.* VIRG.—"Yield to God." Submit to the decrees of Providence.

Cede *repugnanti; cedendo victor abībis.* OVID.—"Give way to your opponent; by yielding you will come off victorious." A prudent concession will often secure for us greater advantages than an obstinate assertion of our rights.

Cēdite Romāni scriptōres, cēdite Graii. PROP.—"Yield, ye Roman writers; give way, ye Greeks:" ironically applied to a conceited scribbler, such for instance as Zoilus, the sour critic of Homer.

Cedunt grammatici, vincuntur rhetōres. JUV.—"The grammarians give way, the rhetoricians are vanquished."

——*Celsæ graviōre casu*
Decĭdunt turres. HOR.
—"Lofty towers fall down with the greatest crash." The greater the elevation, the heavier the fall.

Centum doctûm homĭnum consĭlia sola hæc devincit dea Fortūna. PLAUT.—"This goddess, Fortune, unaided, prevails over the plans of a hundred learned men."

——*Centum solātia curæ*
Et rus, et cŏmĭtes, et via longa dabunt. OVID.
—"The country, and companions, and the length of the journey, will afford a thousand solaces for your cares."

Cepi *corpus.* *Law Term.*—"I have taken the body." The return made by the sheriff upon a *capias*, or other similar process.

Cĕrĕrem pro frugĭbus, Lībĕrum pro vino, Neptūnum pro mari, Curĭam pro senātu, Campum pro comĭtiis, togam pro pace, arma ac tela pro bello appellāre solent. CIC.—"They are in the habit of using the word 'Ceres' for fruits, 'Bacchus' for wine, 'Neptune' for the sea, 'Curia' for the senate, 'Campus' (Martius) for civic elections, 'Toga' for peace, and 'arms' and 'weapons' for war." Examples of the figure Metonymy.

Cēreus in vitium flecti, monitōribus asper. HOR.—"(Youth), pliable as wax to the bent of vice, rough to its reprovers."

Cernis, *ut ignāvum corrumpant ōtia corpus;*
Ut căpiant vĭtium, ni moveantur, aquæ. OVID.
—"You see how ease enervates the slothful body; how water contracts a taint if it remains unmoved."

Cernĭte sim qualis; qui modo qualis eram. Ovid.—"Behold what I am; and what I was but a little while ago!"

Cernuntur in agendo virtūtes. Cic.—"The virtues of a man are seen in his actions."

Certa amittĭmus, dum incerta petĭmus. Plaut.—"We lose what is certain, while we are seeking what is uncertain."

Certa sunt paucis. Prov.—"There is certainty in few words." This, however, may admit of some doubt.

Certe ego fecissem, nec sum sapientior illo. Ovid.—"At all events I should have done so, and I am no wiser than he."

Certe ignorātio futurōrum malorum utilior est quam scientia. Cic.—"Assuredly the ignorance of future evils is preferable to the knowledge of them." To much the same effect as our proverb, "What the eye don't see the heart don't grieve." "Where ignorance is bliss," &c.

Certiorāri. Law Term.—"To be made more certain." A writ from the Court of Chancery, or Queen's Bench, commanding the judges of the inferior courts to certify or to return the records of a cause pending before them.

Certis rebus certa signa præcurrunt. Cic.—"Certain signs precede certain events." This reminds us of Campbell's line, "Coming events cast their shadow before."

Certum est quod certum reddi potest. Coke.—"That is certain which is capable of being made certain."

——*Certum voto pete finem.* Hor.—"To your wishes fix a certain end."

Cervi, lupōrum præda rapācium,
Sectāmur ultro, quos opimus
Fallĕre et effugĕre est triumphus. Hor.

—"We, like stags, the prey of rapacious wolves, follow of our own accord those, whom to deceive and escape would be a signal triumph."

Cessante causâ, cessat et effectus. Coke.—"The cause removed, the effect ceases also."

Chius dŏmĭnum emit." Prov.—"The Chian buys himself a master." This adage was used in reference to those who bring calamities on themselves. When Chios was conquered by Mithridates, he delivered the inhabitants into the hands of the slaves, whom they themselves had imported.

Christe eleison.—"Christ have mercy upon us." Latinized

Greek, used in the service of the Romish Church. See *Kyrie eleison*.

Chronĭca si penses, cum pugnant Oxonienses,
Post paucos menses, volat ira per Angliginenses.
—"If you examine the chronicles, when the Oxford men fall out, within a few months the strife will fly throughout all England." A monkish Leonine proverb in reference to the numerous strifes and dissensions which arose at Oxford during the middle ages.

Circuitus verbōrum.—"A round-about expression." A rambling story.

Cĭtius quam aspărăgi coquuntur. *Prov.*—"Quicker than you could cook asparagus." A proverb frequently used by the emperor Augustus, when he wanted anything to be done instantly.

Cĭtius venit perīcŭlum cum contemnĭtur. SYR.—"When danger is despised, it overtakes us all the sooner." An enemy despised is the most dangerous enemy of all.

Cito matūrum cito putrĭdum.—"Soon ripe, soon rotten." A proverb in dispraise of precocity. See *Odi puerulos*, &c.

Cĭtò scribendo non fit ut bene scribātur, benè scribendo fit ut citò. QUINTIL.—"In writing readily, it does not follow that you write well, but in writing well, you must be able to write readily." See *Sat cito*, &c.

Citra pulvĕrem.—"Without dust," i. e. "without labour." The ancient wrestlers, after anointing themselves, sprinkled their bodies with fine dust, to stop the pores and prevent exhaustion by too great perspiration.

Cives magistrătibus pāreant, magistrătus lĕgibus.—"Let the citizens obey the magistrates, the magistrates the laws."

Cīvĭtas ea autem in libertāte est posĭta, quæ suis stat virĭbus, non ex aliēno arbitrio pendet. LIVY.—"That nation is in the enjoyment of liberty which stands by its own strength, and does not depend on the will of another."

Clamăto, Meus est hic ager, ille tuus. OVID.—"Cry aloud, 'This is my land, that is yours.'"

——*Clarum et venerābile nomen*
Gentibus, et multum nostræ quod prōdĕrat urbi. LUCAN.
—"A name illustrious and revered by nations, and one that has advantaged our city much." Said of Cato of Utica.

Claudicantis conversatiōne utens, ipse quoque claudicare disces.

Prov.—"Associate with the lame and you will learn to limp." To the same effect as the line quoted by St. Paul from the Greek, "Evil communications corrupt good manners." We have a very similar proverb, "Tell me your company, and I will tell you what you are."

Claudite jam rivos, sat prata bibērunt. VIRG.—"Now close your streams, the meadows have imbibed enough." Alluding to irrigation of the fields, but figuratively meaning, "Cease the song," or "conversation," as the case may be.

Clausum fregit. *Law Term.*—"He broke into my enclosure." An action of trespass committed on lands or tenements.

Clavam extorquēre Hercŭli. *Prov.*—"To wrest his club from Hercules." To attempt to do a thing which is far beyond our capacity.

Clericus, vel addiscens.—"Either a clerk, or learning to be one." A mediaeval expression, used with reference to a man who wishes to appear very knowing.

Clodius accūsat mœchos. *Prov.*—"Clodius accuses the adulterers." Clodius himself was one of the greatest profligates of his age. Hence these words became a proverb, like our saying, "The devil rebukes sin."

Cœlo tĕgitur qui non habet urnam.—"He is covered by the heavens who has no urn."

Cœlum ipsum petĭmus stultitiā. HOR.—"We aim at heaven even in our folly." Said in allusion to the Fable of the Giants attempting to seize heaven, and the restless spirit of man.

Cœlum non animum mutant qui trans mare currunt. HOR. —"Those who cross the sea, change their clime but not their character."

Cœpisti mĕlius quam desĭnis; ultĭma primis
Cedunt: dissimiles hic vir, et ille puer. OVID.
—"With more honour didst thou begin, than thou dost close; the last scene falls short of the first: how unlike the present man and the child of that day!"

Cœtus dulces, valēte!— CATUL.—"Happy meetings, fare ye well!"

Cogenda mens est ut incipiat. SEN.—"The mind must be excited to make a beginning." The great difficulty in most things is how to make a beginning, hence the saying, "A thing begun, is half done."

Cogi qui potest nescit mori. SEN.—"He who can be compelled knows not how to die." A man who, upon compulsion, will do that which is dishonourable, is afraid to meet death, the other alternative.

Cogitāto, mus pusillus quam sit săpiens bestia,
Ætātem qui uni cubīli nunquam committit suam. PLAUT.
—"Consider the little mouse, what a sagacious animal it is, for it never intrusts its life to one hole only."

Cognātio movet invĭdiam. *Prov.*—"Relationship gives rise to envy." We are more apt to envy the good fortune of our relatives than that of strangers.

Cognōvit actiōnem. *Law Term.*—"He has confessed the action." The case is so called where a defendant confesses the plaintiff's cause against him to be true, and suffers judgment to be entered against him without trial.

Collectumque fremens volvit sub nāribus ignem. VIRG.—"And snorting, rolls the volumes of fire beneath his nostrils."

Colŭbram in sinu fovēre.—"To cherish a serpent in one's bosom." To admit into your confidence a false friend, or as we call him, "a snake in the grass."

Comes jucundus in viâ pro vehicŭlo est. SYR.—"A pleasant companion, upon a journey, is as good as a carriage." Because he will shorten the journey by beguiling the time.

Comis et humānus erga alios. CIC.—"One courteous and humane towards others."

Comis in uxōrem—— HOR.—"A man attentive to his wife."

Comĭtas inter gentes.—"Comity between nations." Courtesy in their intercourse, and consideration for the interests and feelings of each other. It is this *comity* that renders sacred between belligerents the flag of truce.

Commŏdum ex injuriâ suâ nemo habēre dēbet. *Law Maxim.*—"No man ought to derive advantage from his own wrong."

—— *Commōtâ fervet plebēcŭla bile.* PERS.—"Its anger moved, the rabble is excited."

Commūne bonum.—"A common good."

Commūne pericŭlum concordiam parit.—"A common danger produces unanimity."

Commūne naufragium omnĭbus est consolātio.—"A general

shipwreck is a consolation to all." A general calamity, when all row in the same boat, is borne with more firmness of mind, by each individual, than a similar misfortune would have been, had it happened to himself alone.

Commūne vitium in magnis lībĕrisque civitātibus ut invidia comes gloriæ sit. CORN. NEP.—"It is a common vice in great and free states, for envy to be the attendant upon glory,"—especially in Athens, where Aristides became hated, because he had deserved to be called "the Just."

Commūnia propriè dicere. *Adapted from* HORACE, *De Arte Poet.*—"To express common-place things with propriety."

Commūnibus annis.—"One year with another."

Commūnis utilitas societātis maximum vincŭlum est. LIVY.—"The common good is the great chain which binds men together in society."

Commūniter neglĭgitur, quod commūniter possidētur.—"That is neglected by all, which is possessed by all." "Every man's business is nobody's business."

——*Compōnĭtur orbis*
Rēgis ad exemplum; nec sic inflectĕre sensus
Humānos edicta valent, quam vita regentis. CLAUD.
—"The manners of the world are formed after the example of the king; nor can edicts influence the human understanding, so much as the life of the ruler."

Compŏsitum miracŭli causā. TACIT.—"A story trumped up for the sake of exciting wonder." Much like what we call a "cock and bull story."

Compos mentis. *Law Lat.*—"In the enjoyment of his understanding."

Conciliat anĭmos comĭtas affabilitasque sermōnis. CIC.—"Courtesy and affability of address conciliate the feelings."

Concordia discors. LUCAN *and* OVID.—"A discordant concord." Expressive of a harmonious union of things of different natures.

Concordiā res parvæ crescunt, discordiā maxĭmæ dilabuntur. SALL.—"With concord, from small beginnings things increase: with discord, the greatest advantages are frittered away." The former part of this quotation is the motto of the corporation of the Merchant Tailors.

Condo et compōno quæ mox deprom ĕre possim. HOR.—"I

store and lay by things which I may be enabled one day to draw upon." In my hours of study I gain knowledge, which is to be useful to me in after-life.

Confirmat usum qui tollit abūsum. *Law Maxim.*—"He confirms the use of a thing, who takes away the abuse."

Confiteor, si quid prodest delicta fatēri. OVID.—"I confess my errors, if it is of any use to acknowledge them."

Conjugium vocat, hoc prætexit nōmĭne culpam. VIRG.—"She calls it wedlock, by this name she glosses over her fault." The unfortunate Dido is not the only one who on such an occasion has laid the same "flattering unction to her soul."

Conscia mens recti famæ mendācia risit;
Sed nos in vitium crēdŭla turba sumus. OVID.
—"Her mind, conscious of integrity, laughed to scorn the falsehoods of report; but we are, all of us, a set too ready to believe ill."

Conscientia mille testes. *Prov.*—"The conscience is as good as a thousand witnesses."

Conscientia rectæ voluntātis maxĭma consolātio est rerum incommodārum. CIC.—"A consciousness of good intentions is a very great consolation in misfortunes."

Consensus facit lēgem. *Law Maxim.*—"Consent makes the law." Two parties having made an agreement with their eyes open, and without fraud, the law will insist on its being carried out.

Consentientes et agentes pari pœnâ plectentur. COKE.—"Those who consent to the act, and those who commit it, should be visited with equal punishment." See *Qui facit*, &c.

Consentīre non vidētur qui errat. *Law Maxim.*—"He who is under a mistake is not considered to consent." No one, in law, is deemed to consent to that of which he had not a previous knowledge. But every man is supposed to know the law, and "*ignorantia legis non excusat.*" See *Nil volitum*, &c.

Consĭlia firmiōra sunt de divīnis locis. PLAUT.—"Advice is given with higher sanction from holy places."

Consĭlia qui dant prava cautis homĭnibus,
Et perdunt ŏpĕram et dērīdentur turpĭter. PHÆD.
—"Those who give bad advice to discreet persons, both lose their pains and, to their disgrace, are laughed to scorn."

Consilium Pompeii plane Themistoclēum est; putat enim, qui mari potitur, eum rerum potiri. CIC.—"The plan of Pompey is clearly that of Themistocles; for he thinks that he who gains the command of the sea, must obtain the supreme power."

—— *Conspicit arcem,*
Ingĕniis, opibusque, et festâ pace virentem. OVID.
—"She looks upon the citadel, flourishing in arts, in wealth, and joyous peace."

Constans et lenis, ut res expostŭlet, esto. CATO.—"Be firm or mild, as circumstances may require."

—— *Constitĕrant hinc Thisbe, Pyrămus illinc,*
Inque vicem fuĕrat captatus anhēlitus oris. OVID.
—"They took their stations, Thisbe on the one side, and Pyramus on the other, and the breath of their mouths was mutually caught by turns."

Constructio legis non facit injuriam. COKE.—"The construction of the law does no injury."

Consuefacĕre alĭquem suâ sponte rectè facĕre quam aliēno metu. TER.—"To teach a person to act correctly of his own accord, rather than through fear of another."

Consuetūdine anĭmus rursus te huc inducet. PLAUT.—"Through habit your inclination will be leading you to do it again."

Consuetūdĭnem benignitātis, largitiōni munĕrum antepōno. Hæc est gravium homĭnum atque magnōrum; illa quasi assentatōrum popŭli, multitudĭnis levitātem voluptāte quasi titillantium. CIC.—"I prefer much the habit of courtesy, to the bestowing of contributions. The one is in the power of men of eminence and high character; the other belongs to the flatterers of the populace, who in a manner tickle and delight the multitude thereby."

Consuetūdo est altĕra natūra. CIC.—"Use is second nature."

Consuetūdo est altĕra lex. COKE.—"Usage is a second law."

Consuetūdo est optĭmus interpres legum. COKE.—"Custom is the best interpreter of the laws."

Consuetūdo pro lege servātur. *Law Max.*—"Custom is held as law." Usage from time immemorial is the basis of our common law.

Consŭle de gemmis, de tinctâ mūrice lanâ,
Consŭle de făcie corpŏrĭbusque diem. OVID.

—"Consult the daylight about gems, about wool dyed in purple; consult it about the face and the figure as well."

Consummātum est.—"It is finished."

Contemni est gravius stultitiæ quam percŭti.—"To a foolish man, it is more bitter to be treated with contempt, than to receive a blow."

Contemni se impatienter ferunt princĭpes, quippe qui coli consuevērunt. TACIT.—"Princes, because they have been accustomed to receive homage, can ill brook being treated with contempt."

Contemnuntur ii qui nec sibi, nec altĕri prosunt, ut dicĭtur; in quibus nullus labor, nulla industria, nulla cura est. CIC.—"They are to be despised, who neither profit themselves nor others, as the saying is; in whom there is no exertion, no industry, no thought."

Contemporanea expositio est fortissima in lege. *Law Max.*—"A contemporary exposition prevails in law." A precedent drawn from the established practice of the time, when the law was promulgated, being made in accordance with the then prevailing notions and usages, ought to have the most force.

Contigĭmus portum, quo mihi cursus erat. OVID.—"I have reached the harbour, to which I steered my course."

Contĭnuò culpam ferro compesce, priusquam
Dira per incautum serpant contāgia vulgus. VIRG.
—"Instantly repress the mischief with the knife, before the dire contagion has infected the unthinking multitude." Even among civilized nations, we see life sacrificed for the common good.

Contra bonos mores.—"Contrary to good manners," or morals.

Contra malum mortis, non est medicāmen in hortis. *Med. Aphor.*—"Against the evil of death there is no remedy in gardens." A Leonine line.

Contra stimŭlum calcas. TER.—"You kick against the spur." So in *Acts* ix. 5, "It is hard for thee to kick against the pricks?" The meaning is, that you only injure yourself by resistance.

Contra verbōsos noli contendĕre verbis;
Sermo datur cunctis, animi sapientia paucis. CATO.
—"Strive not with words against the contentious; speech is given to all, wisdom to few."

Contumēliam si dices, audies. PLAUT.—"If you utter affronting speeches, you will have to hear them."

Convēniens vitæ mors fuit ista suæ. OVID.—"That was a death conformable to his life."

Conventio privatōrum non potest publico juri derogāre. COKE.—"An agreement between private persons cannot derogate from the rights of the public."

Convivæ certè tui dicant, Bibāmus, moriendum est. SEN.—"Your guests are for saying, no doubt, 'Let us drink, for die we must.'" See 1 *Cor.* xv. 32.

——*Convivatōris, uti ducis, ingĕnium res*
Adversæ nudāre solent, celāre secundæ. HOR.
—"Untoward circumstances usually bring out the talents of a host, as they do those of a general; while everything goes on well, they lie concealed."

Cor ne edito. Prov.—"Eat not your heart." A figurative expression, meaning, "Do not consume your life with cares."

Coram domĭno rege.—"Before our lord the king."

Coram nobis. Law Lat.—"Before us." Before the court. Before persons invested with due authority.

Coram non judĭce.—"Before a person who is not a judge." Before a tribunal which has no jurisdiction.

Cornix scorpium rapuit. Prov.—"The crow seized a scorpion," and was stung to death. Mischief recoils on its author. See *Neque enim*, &c.

Corōnat virtus cultōres suos.—"Virtue crowns her votaries."

Corpŏra lentè augescunt, citò extinguuntur. TACIT.—"All bodies are slow in growth, rapid in decay."

Corpŏra magnanĭmo satis est prostrāsse leōni:
Pugna suum finem, cum jacet hostis, habet. OVID.
—"It is sufficient for the noble-hearted lion to have brought the body to the ground: the contest is over when the enemy lies prostrate." The poets give the lion a better character than he really deserves.

Corpŏri tantum indulgeas quantum bonæ valetudini satis est. SEN.—"Indulge the body only so far as is necessary for good health." Be moderate in pleasures although harmless in themselves.

Corpŏris et fortūnæ bonōrum ut initium finis est. Omnia orta occĭdunt, et aucta senescunt. SALL.—"Of the blessings of health and fortune, as there is a beginning, so there is an end. Everything, as it is improved by art, hurries onward to decay, and increases only to become old."

Corpus adhuc Echo, non vox erat: et tamen usum
Garrŭla non ălium, quam nunc habet, oris habēbat;
Reddĕre de multis ut verba novissĭma posset. OVID.

—"Echo was then a body, not a mere voice; and yet the babbler had no other use of speech than she now has, to be able to repeat the last words out of many."

Corpus delicti. *Law phrase.*—"The body of the offence." The sum and substance of the crime.

Corpus omne sive arescit in pulvĕrem, sive in humōrem solvĭtur, vel in cinĕrem comprĭmitur, vel in nidōrem tenuātur, subducĭtur nobis; sed Deo elementōrum custōde reservātur. MINUCIUS FELIX.—"(When death happens) every body is reduced to dust, dissolved into fluid, converted to ashes, or wasted away by evaporation, and so withdrawn from our sight; but it is preserved in the hands of God, the guardian of the elements."

——*Corpus onustum*
Hesternis vitiis anĭmum quoque prægrăvat unà. HOR.

—"The body, oppressed by the debauch of yesterday, weighs down the mind as well."

Corpus quasi vas est aut alĭquod anĭmi receptācŭlum. CIC.—"The body is a vessel, as it were, or receptacle for the soul."

Corpus sine pectŏre.—"A body without a soul." A lump of flesh without spirit or animation. See *Sine pectore corpus.*

Corrumpunt bonos mores colloquia prava. *Prov.*—"Evil communications corrupt good manners." From the Greek.

Corrupti mores sunt depravātique admiratiōne divitiārum. CIC. —"Manners become corrupted and depraved through the hankering for riches."

Corruptio optĭmi pessĭma.—"The corruption of the best produces the worst." Nothing is so pernicious both in example and results as the rebound from very good to very bad. So our old proverb, "The sweetest wine makes the sharpest vinegar."

Corruptissimâ in republicâ plurĭmæ leges. TACIT.—"In the state which is the most corrupt, the laws are always the most numerous." Such a state of things necessitates a multiplicity of laws.

Cos ingeniōrum.—"A whetstone for the wits."

Cras credēmus, hodie nihil. Prov.—"To-morrow we will believe, not to-day." Let us wait and see what will happen to-morrow; for the present we will sleep upon it.

——*Credat Judæus Apella.* Hor.—"Let Apella the Jew believe it." An expression used in derision of the Jews, who were held in the greatest contempt among the Romans, every vice or weakness being imputed to them.

Crede mihi bene qui latuit, bene vixit, et intra
Fortūnam debet quisque manēre suam. Ovid.
—"Believe me, he who has the good fortune to escape notice, lives the happiest life, and every one is bound to live within his means."

Crede mihi, misĕros prudentia prima relinquit. Ovid.—"Believe me, prudence is the first thing to forsake the wretched."

Crede mihi, multos hăbeas cum dignus amicos,
Non fuit e multis quolibet ille minor. Ovid.
—"Believe me, although you deservedly have many friends, he out of those many was inferior to none."

Crede mihi, res est ingeniōsa dare. Ovid.—"Believe me, it is a noble thing to give."

Crede quod est quod vis; ac desĭne tuta verēri;
Deque fide certâ sit tibi certa fides. Ovid.
—"Believe that that is, which thou dost wish to be; cease to fear for what is secure, and have a certain assurance of undoubted constancy."

Crede quod habes, et habes.—"Believe that you have it, and you have it." This is not universally true—witness the unhappy termination of Alnaschar's reverie, whose story is told in the Spectator and the Arabian Nights.

Credēbant hoc grande nefas, et morte piandum,
Si juvĕnis vĕtŭlo non assurrexĕrat.—— Juv.
—"They used to hold it to be a heinous sin, and one that death alone could expiate, if a young man did not rise to pay honour to an elder."

——*Credĭte, postĕri!* Hor.—"Believe it, Posterity!"

Credo pudicitiam, Saturno rege, morātam
In terris.—— Juv.
—"In the reign of Saturn I believe that chastity did exist in the world." The reign of Saturn was the "golden

age" of the Romans. Juvenal is speaking of the almost universal corruption of the Roman females in his day.

Credŭla res amor est—— Ovid.—"Love is a credulous thing."

——*Credŭla vitam*
Spes fovet, ac mĕlius cras fore semper ait. Tibull.
—"Credulous hope cherishes life, and ever tells us that to-morrow will be better."

Crescentem sĕquĭtur cura pecūniam,
Majōrumque fames. Multa petentibus,
Desunt multa. Benè est cui Deus obtŭlit
Parcâ quod satis est manu. Hor.
—"Care attends accumulated wealth, and a thirst for still greater riches. They who require much are always in want of much. Happy is he to whom God has given a sufficiency with a sparing hand."

Crescit amor nummi quantùm ipsa pecūnia crescit:
Et minùs hanc optat, qui non habet—— Juv.
—"The love of money increases as fast as our wealth, and he who has none wishes for it the least."

Crescit indulgens sibi dirus hydrops. Hor.—"The fatal dropsy nursed by self-indulgence increases apace." This figure is here used in reference to the "greed for gain."

Crescit sub pondĕre virtus.—"Virtue grows under every weight;" shines forth with renewed lustre under every trial. The motto of the Earl of Denbigh.

Cressâ ne careat pulchra dies notâ. Hor.—"Let not a day so joyful be without its mark of Cretan chalk."

Cretâ an carbōne notandum. Hor.—"To be marked with chalk, or with charcoal." The Romans thus distinguished their lucky and unlucky days.

Cretâ notāre.—"To mark with chalk." To place a white line against the name of a person was to signify approval.

Cretizandum cum Crete. Prov.—"A man must be a Cretan with the Cretans." We must do at Rome as Rome does.

Crevĕrunt et opes, et opum furiōsa cupīdo:
Et cum possideant plurĭma, plura volunt. Ovid.
—"Both wealth has increased, and the maddening lust for wealth: and though men possess ever so much, they still wish for more."

Crimen læsæ majestātis. *Law Term.*—"The crime of lese-majesty," which involves the guilt of high-treason.

***Crimen** quod mihi dabĭtur, crimen non erat.* Cic.—"That which was imputed to me as a crime was no crime."

***Crimĭna** qui cernunt aliōrum, non sua cernunt,*
Hi săpiant aliis, desipiuntque sibi.
—"Those who see the faults of others, do not see their own; such men are wise towards others, and fools to themselves."

——***Crimĭne** ab uno*
Disce omnes—— Virg.
—"From one offence learn all."

***Crine** ruber, niger ore, brevis pede, lumĭne læsus:*
Rem magnam præstas, Zoïle, si bonus es. Mart.
—"With red hair, and tawny features, short of one foot, and blind of an eye—you do wonders, indeed, Zoilus, if you are a good man."

——***Crœsum,** quem vox justi facunda Solōnis*
Respĭcere ad longæ jussit spatia ultĭma vitæ. Juv.
—"Crœsus, whom the eloquent voice of the righteous Solon bade look upon the closing scene of a long life." See *Herodotus*, b. i c. 32.

***Crudēlem** medĭcum intempĕrans æger facit.* Syr.—"A disobedient patient makes an unfeeling physician." Because he is obliged to have recourse to harsher measures to effect a cure.

——***Crudēlis** ubique*
Luctus, ubique pavor, et plurĭma mortis imāgo. Virg.
—"Everywhere is cruel sorrow, terror on every side, and death in a thousand shapes."

Crux.—"A cross." Anything that frets or annoys us, a difficulty or stumblingblock is so called. Thus, *crux criticōrum*, "the cross of critics;" *crux medicōrum*, "the cross of physicians;" *crux mathematicōrum*, "the cross of mathematicians."

***Cucullus** non facit monăchum.* "The cowl does not make the monk." Trust not appearances.

Cui bono?—"For whose benefit?" *A maxim of* Cassius, *the judge, quoted by Cicero (Pro Milone).* It is generally used as signifying, "What is the good of it?"

——*Cui famulātur maxĭmus orbis*
Diva potens rerum, domĭtrixque pecūnia fati.
—"She to whom the great world is obedient, that goddess who rules mankind, money, the controller of fate."

Cui licet quod majus, non debet quod minus est non licēre. *Law Max.*—"He who has the greater right, ought not to be without the lesser one." Thus, in the transfer of property, a conveyance of the rights incident to it is always to be presumed.

Cui malo?—"To what evil?" What harm can result from it?

——*Cui mens divīnior atque os*
Magna sonatūrum des nōmĭnis hujus honōrem. HOR.
—"To him who is divinely inspired, and has a command of lofty language, you may grant the honour of this title." Said in allusion to the true poet.

Cui nihil satis, huic etiam nihil turpe.—"Nothing will be base to him for whom nothing is enough." The man is troubled with no scruples, who covets unlimited wealth.

Cui non convĕniat sua res, ut calceus olim,
Si pede major erit, subvertet; si minor, uret. HOR.
—"To him who is not satisfied with his fortune, it is as with a shoe; if it is too large for his foot it will upset him, if too small, it will pinch him."

Cui placet alterius, sua nīmīrum est odio sors. HOR.—"When a man is captivated with the lot of another, no wonder if he is discontented with his own."

Cui placet, oblivīscĭtur; cui dolet, memĭnit.—"He who is pleased at a thing, forgets it; he who is grieved at it, bears it in mind."

Cui prodest scelus, is fecit. SEN.—"He who profits by the villany, has perpetrated it." This is true in reference to the share of criminality which attaches to the "accomplice after the fact," but is not of universal application.

Cuicunque alĭquis quid concĕdit, concēdĕre vidētur et id, sine quo res ipsa esse non potest. *Law Max.*—"He who makes a grant to another, is held to have granted that as well, without which the thing so granted cannot be enjoyed." A house or land, for instance, cannot be sold without right of ingress to it, if in the vendor's power to grant it.

Cuilĭbet in arte suâ pĕrīto est credendum. COKE.—"Every man ought to have credit for skill in his own art."

Cuivis dolōri remĕdium est patientia. SYR.—"Patience is the remedy for every sorrow."

——*Cujus conātĭbus obstat*
Res angusta domi—— HOR.

—"Whose efforts are frustrated by the narrowness of his means." The fate of too many!

Cujus est solum, ejus est usque ad cœlum. *Law Max.*—"To him to whom the soil belongs, belongs everything over it, even to the sky." The building of no man, for instance, may project over the land of his neighbour.

Cujus summa est.—"Of which the sum and substance is." This is the long and short of it.

Cujus tu fidem in pecūniâ perspexĕris,
Verēre ei verba credĕre? TER.

—"Do you fear to trust a man with your secret, of whose honesty in pecuniary matters you have had experience?"

Cujus vita despĭcitur, restat ut ejus prædicātio contemnātur. ST. GREGORY.—"When a man's life is despised, it follows that his preaching must fall into contempt." The necessity of supporting precept by practice.

Cujus vultūris hoc erit cadaver? MART.—"To what vulture's share shall this carcass fall?"

Cujuslĭbet rei simulātor atque dissimulātor. SALL.—"A man who possessed the power on every occasion to seem to be what he was not, and to conceal what he really was." The character of Catiline, a finished hypocrite, as portrayed by Sallust.

Cujusvis hŏmĭnis est errāre, nullius nisi insipientis in errōre perseverāre. CIC.—"Every man is liable to err, but it is only the part of a fool to persevere in error."

Culpâ suâ damnum sentiens, non intellĭgĭtur damnum pati. *Law Max.*—"He who suffers a loss by his own fault, is not considered (by the law) a sufferer."

Culpam pœna premit comes. HOR.—"Punishment follows hard upon crime."

Cultaque Judæo septĭma sacra Syro. OVID.—"And the seventh day kept holy and observed by the Syrian Jew."

Cum domus ingenti sŭbĭto mea lapsa ruinâ
Concĭdit, in dŏmĭni prŏcubuitque caput. OVID.

—"When my house came suddenly down, and fell in ruins with a tremendous crash upon its master's head."

——*Cum corpŏre mentem*
Crescĕre sentīmus, parĭterque senescĕre.— LUCRET.
—"We feel that the mental powers increase with those of the body, and, in like manner, grow feeble with it."

Cum dubia et fragilis sit nobis vita tribūta,
In morte altĕrius spem tu tibi ponĕre noli. CATO.
—"Seeing that life has been given us precarious and full of uncertainty, fix not thy hopes on the death of another."

Cum duo inter se pugnantia repĕriuntur in testamento, ultĭmum ratum est. COKE.—"When two clauses are found in a will, repugnant to each other, the last holds good." But in deeds, the first holds good.

Cum duplicantur lătĕres venit Moses.—"When the tale of bricks is doubled, then comes Moses;"—to the rescue of the Israelites. A mediæval proverb, meaning that, "when things are at the worst they will mend."

Cum est concupīta pecūnia, nec ratio sanat cupidĭtātem, existit morbus anĭmi eique morbo nomen est avaritia. CIC.—"When money is coveted, and the desire is not cured by reason, there is a disease of the mind, and the name of that disease is 'avarice.'"

Cum fĕriunt unum, non unum fulmĭna terrent. OVID.—"When the lightning strikes but one, not one only does it alarm."

Cum fortūna manet, vultum servātis amīci;
Cum cedit, turpi vertĭtis ora fugâ. PETRON. ARB.
—"While prosperity lasts, you, my friends, give me your countenance; when it fails, you turn away your faces in disgraceful flight."

Cum fortūna perit, nullus amīcus erit.—"When fortune fails us, we shall have no friend left."

Cum fuĕris felix, quæ sunt adversa cavēto;
Non eădem cursu respondent ultĭma primis. CATO.
—"When you are enjoying prosperity, provide against adversity; the end of life will not be attended by the same train of fortunate circumstances as the beginning."

Cum furor haud dubius, cum sit manifesta phrenēsis,
Ut lŏcŭples mŏriāris, egentis vivĕre fato. JUV.

—"Since it is undoubted madness, manifest insanity, to live the life of a beggar that you may die rich."

Cum grano salis. *Prov.*—"With a grain of salt." With something which will help us to swallow it; with some latitude or allowance. Said of anything to which we are unable to give implicit credence.

Cum larvis luctāri. *Prov.*—"To wrestle with ghosts." To speak ill of the dead. See *De mortuis*, &c.

Cum licet fugĕre ne quære litem. *Prov.*—"When you can escape it, avoid a law-suit."

——*Cum lux altĕra venit,*
Jam cras hesternum consumpsĭmus; ecce aliud cras
Egĕrit hos annos.—— PERS.

—"When another day arrives, we have consumed the morrow of yesterday; behold, another morrow comes, and so wastes our years." A censure against procrastination, "the thief of time."

——*Cum magna malæ supĕrest audācia causæ,*
Credĭtur a multis fidūcia—— JUV.

—"When a bad cause is backed by great impudence, it is believed by many to be the boldness of innocence."

——*Cum magnis virtūtibus affers*
Grande supercilium.—— JUV.

—"With thy high virtues thou dost bring great superciliousness."

Cum mŏrĭtur dives concurrunt undĭque cives;
Paupĕris ad funus vix est e millibus unus.

—"When a rich man dies, the citizens flock together from every side; at a poor man's funeral there is hardly one out of thousands." Mediæval Leonine lines.

Cum multis aliis, quæ nunc perscribĕre longum est.—"With many other things which it would now be tedious to set forth in writing." A line often used in an ironical sense. To whom does it belong?

Cum plus sint potæ, plus potiuntur aquæ.—"The more water is drunk, the more is desired." See *Quo plus*, &c.

——*Cum prostrāta sopore*
Urget membra quies, et mens sine pondĕre ludit.
PETRON. ARBITER.

—"When repose steals over the limbs, extended in sleep, and the mind disports without restraint."

Cum pulchris tunĭcis sumet nova consilia et spes. HOR.—"Happy in his fine clothes, he will adopt new plans and cherish fresh hopes."

Cum surges abitūra domum, surgēmus et omnes. OVID.—"When you rise to go home, we will all rise too."

Cum tăbŭlis anĭmum censōris sumat honesti. HOR.—"Let him, with his papers, assume the spirit of an honest critic."

Cum tristĭbus sevērè, cum remissis jucundè, cum senĭbus grăvĭter, cum juventūte comĭter vīve. CIC.—"With those who are of a gloomy turn, be serious; with the idle, be cheerful; with the old, be grave; and with the young, be gay."

Cum volet illa dies, quæ nil nisi corpŏris hujus
Jus habet, incerti spatium mihi fīniat ævi. OVID.
—"Let that day, which has no power but over this body of mine, put an end to the term of my uncertain life, when it will."

Cuncta prius tentāta: sed immedicābĭle vulnus
Ense rĕcidendum, ne pars sincēra trahātur. OVID.
—"All methods have been already tried; but a wound that admits of no cure must be cut away, that the sounder parts may not be corrupted."

—*Cunctando restituit rem.* ENNIUS.—"He saved the state by delay." Said in praise of Fabius, who saved Rome by avoiding an engagement with Hannibal.

Cuncti adsint, mĕrĭtæque expectent præmia palmæ. VIRG.—"Let all attend, and await the reward of well-earned laurels."

Cunctis servatōrem liberatōremque acclamantĭbus.—"All hailing him as their saviour and deliverer."

Cupīdo dominandi cunctis affectĭbus flagrantior est. TACIT.—"The desire of rule is the most powerful of all the affections of the mind."

—*Cur ante tubam tremor occŭpat artus?* VIRG.—"Why does tremor seize the limbs before the trumpet sounds?" That is, before the signal for battle.

Cur in thĕātrum, Cato sevēre, venisti? MART.—"Why, Cato, with all thy gravity, didst thou come to the theatre?" On the occasion of the indecent celebration of the Floralia, when he only came that he might be seen to depart. See *An ideo*, &c. (App.)

——*Cur indecŏres in lĭmĭne primo*
Defĭcĭmus?—— VIRG.
—"Why faint we inglorious at the very outset?"

Cur me querēlis exanimas tuis? HOR.—"Why worry me to death with your complaints?"

Cur mŏriātur homo, cui salvia crescit in horto? Maxim of the School of Health at SALERNO.—"Why should the man die in whose garden sage grows?"

"He that would live for aye,
Must eat sage in May."

Sage is a good stomachic, and its medicinal qualities were highly valued in former times. It is said to have derived its name from the Latin *salvus*, "safe," or "healthy."

Cur mŏriātur homo qui sumit de cinamōmo? Maxim of the School of SALERNO.—"Why should the man die who takes cinnamon?"

Cur nescīre, pudens pravè, quam discĕre malo? HOR.—"Why do I prefer, through false modesty, to be ignorant rather than learn?"

Cur non, ut plenus vitæ conviva, recēdis?
Æquo anĭmoque capis secūram, stulte, quiētem. LUCRET.
—"Why not, fool, like a well-filled guest at life's banquet, withdraw, and, with contented mind, take a repose that is removed from every care?"

Cur opus affectas, ambitiōse, novum. OVID.—"Why, in your ambition, do you attempt a new task?"

Cura esse quod audis.—"Take care to be as good as you are esteemed to be."

Cura ut valeas.—"Take care of your health."

Cura pii Dis sunt—— OVID.—"The good are the care of the gods."

——*Curæ est sua cuique voluptas.* OVID.—"His own gratification is the object of each."

Curæ leves loquuntur, ingentes stupent. SEN.—"Light griefs find utterance, deeper ones are dumb."

Curas tolle graves, irasci crede profānum.—"Dispel anxious cares; consider it profane to be angry."

Curātio funĕris, conditio sepultūræ, pompæ exequiārum, magis sunt vivōrum solātia, quam subsidia mortuōrum. Words of the Emperor AUGUSTUS.—"The arrangements of the funeral, the place of burial, the procession and the ceremonial, are rather a consolation to the living, than of importance to the dead."

Cūria advisāre vult. *Law Latin.*—"The court wishes to advise thereon." The entry made when the court takes time to deliberate before giving judgment.

Cūria paupĕribus clausa est; dat census honōres. OVID.—"To the poor the senate-house is closed; wealth confers honours."

Currente călămo.—"With a running pen." The ancients sometimes wrote with a reed, whence this phrase. Equivalent to our English term, "off-hand."

Currus bovem trahit. *Prov.*—"The chariot is drawing the ox." "The cart is put before the horse." Said of anything done preposterously, or out of place.

Curtæ nescio quid semper abest rei. HOR.—"There is a something, I know not what, always found wanting in every man's too meagre fortunes."

Custos morum.—"The guardian of morality." A magistrate is so called.

Custos regni.—"The guardian of the realm." A person appointed to perform the sovereign's duties in his absence.

Custos rotulōrum.—"The master of the rolls." The principal justice of the peace in a county is also so called.

Cutem gerit lacerātam canis mordax. *Prov.*—"A snapping dog wears a torn skin."

"Those who in quarrels interpose,
Must often wipe a bloody nose." GAY.

Cutis vulpīna consuenda est cum cute leōnis. *Prov.*—"The fox's skin should be sewed to that of the lion." Where the strength of the lion fails, the cunning of the fox may prevail.

Cymīni sectōres. *Prov.*—"Splitters of cummin-seeds," or, as we say, "splitters of straws." An expression borrowed from Aristotle. Learned triflers, like many of the schoolmen of the middle ages.

D.

D. D. for *Dono dedit.*—"Has presented," or "has given."

D. D. D.—In presentation copies of books, these letters are inserted after the name of the giver, meaning either *donum dat, dicatque*, "presents (this book), and dedicates it;" or else, *dat, donat, dicatque*—"gives, presents, and dedicates (this book)."

D. M. for *Dis Manibus*.—"To the divine Manes," or "shades of the dead." The usual commencement of Roman sepulchral inscriptions.

D. O. M.—See *Deo optimo maximo*.

D. V.—See *Deo volente*.

Da juranti věniam.—"Pardon the oath." Forgive me for swearing.

Da locum mĕliōribus. Ter.—"Give way to your betters." The same maxim of modesty is inculcated by our Saviour, in Luke xiv. 8.

Da mihi mutuum testimōnium. Cic.—"Give me your testimony, and I 'll do as much for you." "Claw me, and I 'll claw thee."

Da modo lucra mihi, da facto gaudia lucro;
Et face ut emptōri verba dedisse juvet. Ovid.
—"Do but grant me profit, give me the delight that arises from making a bargain, and grant that it may prove to my advantage to have imposed upon my customers." The prayer of a fraudulent tradesman to Mercury.

Da, Pater, augustam menti conscendĕre sedem;
Da fontem lustrāre boni; da, luce repertā,
In te conspicuos ănĭmi defigĕre visus! Boeth.
—"Grant, Father, that my mind may climb to thy august abode; grant that it may survey the source of good; grant that, when it has gained the light, I may fix my full gaze on thee!"

Da popŭlo, da verba mihi; sine nescius errem. Ovid.—"Deceive the public, deceive me too; in my ignorance let me be mistaken."

Da, precor, ingĕnio præmia digna meo. Ovid.—"Grant, I pray, a reward worthy of my genius."

Da spatium tenuemque moram, male cuncta ministrat
Impĕtus.—— Stat.
—"Allow time and a short delay, haste and violence mar everything."

Da vĕniam lacrymis.—"Grant pardon to these tears."

——*Dabit Deus his quoque finem*. Virg.—"God will grant

an end to even these misfortunes." A phrase generally applied to public calamities, and the only real consolation that they will admit of.

——*Damna minus consuēta movent.* Juv.—"Misfortunes to which we are used affect us less severely." To the same effect is our vulgar adage—"Eels become accustomed to skinning."

Damnant quod non intellĭgunt. Cic.—"They condemn what they do not understand." They make up by positiveness of assertion for lack of real knowledge.

Damnōsa hærēdĭtas. Law Term.—"A losing property." A property, the possession of which entails loss on the owner.

Damnōsa quid non imminuit dies? Hor.—"What does not all-destructive time impair?"

——*Damnōsa senem juvat alea, ludit et hæres.* Juv.—"If the destructive dice have pleasures for the father, his son will be a gamester." So our proverb, "Bad hen, bad eggs." See *Mala gallina*, &c.

Damnum absque injūriâ. Law Term.—"Loss without injury." That kind of loss which all persons are liable to, who are exposed to the competition of others in the same business or profession as themselves. Loss, in fact, by *fair* competition.

Damnum appellandum est cum malâ famâ lucrum. Syr.—"That ought to be called a loss, which is gained by the sacrifice of character."

Dapes inemptæ. Hor. *and* Virg.—"Dainties unbought." The produce of the farm.

——*Dapibus suprēmi*
Grata testūdo Jovis. Hor.

—"The shell so loved at the feasts of supreme Jove." Mercury framed the *cithara*, (the origin of the modern guitar,) by stretching strings across the shell of a tortoise; his music was in high requisition at the table of Jupiter.

——*Dare jura marītis.* Hor.—"To lay down laws for husbands."

——*Dare pondus idōnea fumo.* Pers.—"Things suited to give weight to smoke." To impart value to that which is worthless.

Dat Deus immīti cornua curta bovi. *Prov.*—"God gives

short horns to the vicious ox." "God sends a curst cow short horns." *Much Ado About Nothing*, act ii. sc. 1.

——*Dat inānia verba,*
Dat sine mente sonum.—— VIRG.
—"He utters empty words, he utters sounds without meaning."

Dat vĕniam corvis, vexat censūra columbas. JUV.—"He grants pardon to the ravens, but visits with heavy censure the doves." A line often used to signify that the innocent man meets with injustice, while the guilty escape without censure.

——*Data tempŏre prosunt,*
Et data non apto tempŏre vina nocent. OVID.
—"Wine given at a proper time, is useful; given at an improper time, it is injurious."

Date obŏlum Belisārio.—"Give your mite to Belisarius." It is said that this great general, when blind and aged, was neglected by the emperor Justinian, and obliged to beg for charity. The tale is however treated as a fiction by Gibbon.

——*Datur ignis, tametsi ab inimīcis petas.* PLAUT.—"Fire is granted, even though you ask it of your enemies." It was considered unlucky to refuse fire to any one.

Davus sum, non Œdipus. TER.—"I am Davus, not Œdipus." I am a plain, simple man, not a conjuror. Œdipus was said to have solved the riddle of the Sphinx.

De aliĕno corio liberālis. *Prov.*—"Liberal of another man's leather."

De aliĕno largītor, et sui restrictus. CIC.—"A bestower of other men's property, but tenacious of his own." One who is liberal, but at the expense of others.

De ăsĭni umbrâ disceptāre. *Prov.*—"To dispute about an ass's shadow." To give one's attention to frivolous matters.

De bene esse. *Law Term.*—"As being well done for the present." A thing is done *de bene esse*, when it is done *conditionally*, and is to stand good till some time named, when the question of its being rightly or wrongly done will be determined. Depositions are often taken *de bene esse*, the question as to whether they shall be used for the benefit of the party so taking them, being reserved for consideration at a future time.

De calceo sollĭcĭtus, at pedem nihil curans. *Prov.*—"Anxious about the shoe, but careless about the foot." Said of those who are more thoughtful about outside appearances than the cultivation of the mind.

——*De duro est ultima ferro.*
———*Fugēre pudor, verumque, fidesque:*
In quorum subiēre locum fraudesque, doliquе,
Insidiæque, et vis, et amor scelerātus habendi. OVID.

—"The last age was of hard iron.—Modesty, and truth, and honour took to flight; in place of which succeeded fraud, deceit, treachery, violence, and the cursed hankering for acquisition." The condition of man after the fall, according to heathen tradition.

De facto.—"From the thing done." Because it is so. An usurper holds a throne *de facto*, not by right, but might.

De fumo disceptāre. *Prov.*—"To dispute about smoke." To wrangle about trifles. See *De asini*, &c.

De fumo in flammam. *Prov.*—"Out of the smoke into the flame." Quoted by Ammianus Marcellinus. Similar to our proverb, "Out of the frying-pan," &c.

De gustĭbus non est disputandum.—"There is no disputing about tastes." Like our saying, "What is one man's meat is another man's poison."

De hoc multi multa, omnes alĭquid, nemo satis.—"Of this matter many people have said many things, all something, no one enough."

De jure.—"From what is lawful," or "by law." Possession *de jure* is possession by right of law.

De lanā caprīnā.—"About goat's wool." About a worthless object.

De male quæsītis vix gaudet tertius hæres.—"A third heir seldom enjoys property dishonestly got." Hence the saying, "Badly got, badly gone." See *male parta*, &c.

De medietāte linguæ. *Law Term.*—"Of a moiety of languages." A jury empannelled to try a foreigner, when, at his request, one half of it is composed of foreigners, is a jury *de medietate linguæ*.

De mendīco male merētur, qui ei dat quod edat, aut quod bibat,
Nam et illud quod dat perdit, et illi prodūcit vitam ad miseriam. PLAUT.

—"He deserves ill of a beggar, who gives him to eat or

to drink; for he both loses that which he gives, and prolongs for the other a life of misery."

De minimis non curat lex. Legal Maxim.—"The law takes no notice of extreme trifles." The theft of a pin, for instance.

De missâ ad mensam.—"From mass to table," or, to preserve the jingle, "From mass to mess." A mediæval saying, implying that the only active employment of the monks was to eat and say their prayers.

De mortuis nil nisi bonum.—"Of the dead be nothing said but what is good." Silence, at least, is a duty where we cannot praise the dead.

De motu proprio.—"From his own impulse." "Of his own free will."

——*De multis grandis acervus erit.* OVID.—"Out of many things a large heap is made."

De nihilo nihil, in nihilum nil posse reverti. PERS.—"From nothing there is nothing made, and no existing thing can be reduced to nothing." The doctrine of the Epicureans as to the eternity of matter. See *Lucretius*, B. i. l. 160—265.

De non apparentibus, et non existentibus, eâdem est ratio COKE.—"The reasoning is the same as to things which do not appear, and those which do not exist."

De omnibus rebus, et quibusdam aliis.—"About everything, and something more besides." Said ironically of a voluminous book, or of a speech in which numerous topics are discussed. The saying is said to have derived its origin from the circumstance that Smalgruenius first wrote a work entitled *De omnibus rebus*, and then another, *De quibusdam aliis.* The same story has, however, been fathered on Thomas Aquinas.

——*De paupertāte tacentes*
Plus poscente ferent.—— HOR.
—"Those who are silent as to their poverty will obtain more than he who begs." So the lion rewarded the modest traveller, and rebuffed the importunate robber. See *Phædrus' Fables*, B. II. Fab. I.

De *pilo*, or *de filo, pendet. Prov.*—"It hangs by a hair," or "by a thread." The risk, or danger, is imminent. Originally said in reference to the sword which Dionysius of Syracuse caused to be suspended over the head of the courtier Damocles.

De quo libelli in celeberrimis locis proponuntur, huic ne perīre quidem tacĭtè concedĭtur. Cic.—"The man who is publicly arraigned is not allowed even to be ruined in quiet."

De vitâ homĭnis nulla cunctatio longa est. *Adapted from* Juvenal.—"When the life of a man is at stake, no delay can be too long." See *Audi, nulla, &c.*

Debētis velle quæ vĕlĭmus. Plaut.—"You ought to wish as we wish."

Dĕbĭle principium mĕlior fortūna sequētur.—"Better fortune will succeed a weak beginning."

Dĕbĭlem facĭto manu,
Dēbĭlem pede, coxâ,
Lūbrĭcos quate dentes,
Vita dum superest, bene est.

A portion of a fragment of Mæcenas, *as quoted by Seneca.*—"Make me weak in the hands, weak in the feet and hips, dash out my failing teeth. So long as life remains 'tis well." The words of a man who clings to life at any cost.

Debito justitiæ, or *E debito justitiæ.* *Law Phrase.*—"By debt of justice." By virtue of a claim justly established.

Deceptio visus.—"A deceiving of the sight." An illusion practised on the eye. "An ocular deception."

Decet affectus anĭmi neque se nimium erigĕre nec subjicĕre servilĭter. Cic.—"We ought neither to allow the affections of the mind to become too much elated, nor yet abjectly depressed."

Decet patriam nobis cariōrem esse quam nosmetipsos. Cic.—"Our country ought to be dearer to us than ourselves."

——*Decies repetīta placēbit.* Hor.—"Ten times repeated it will please." It will be encored again and again.

Decipĭmur specie recti.— Hor.—"We are deceived by an appearance of rectitude."

——*Decĭpit*
Frons prima multos; rara mens intellĭgit
Quod interiōre condĭdit cura angŭlo. Phædr.

—"First appearances deceive many; the penetration of but few enables them to discern that which has been carefully concealed in the inmost corners of the heart."

Decōrum ab honesto non potest separāri. Cic.—"Propriety cannot be separated from what is honourable."

Dedĕcet philosophum abjicĕre anĭmum. Cic.—"It is unbecoming in a philosopher to be dejected."

Dedĕcŏrant bene nata culpæ. Hor.—"Vices disgrace what is naturally good."

Dĕdĭmus potestātem. *Law Term.*—"We have given power." A writ, or commission, giving certain powers, for the purpose of speeding the business of the court.

Dediscit anĭmus sero quod dĭdĭcit diū. Sen.—"The mind is slow to unlearn what it has been long in learning." Impressions once made on the mind are not easily erased.

——*Dedit hanc contāgio labem,*
Et dabit in plures.—— Juv.
—"Contagion has caused this plague-spot, and will extend it to many more."

Defectio vīrium adolescentiæ vitiis efficĭtur sæpius quam senectūtis. Cic.—"Loss of strength is more frequently the fault of youth than of old age."

Defendit numĕrus junctæque umbōne phalanges. Juv.—"He is defended by their numbers, and the array of their serried shields."

Defluit saxis agitātus humor,
Concĭdunt venti, fugiuntque nubes,
Et minax, (nam sic voluĕre,) ponto
Unda recumbit. Hor.
—"The troubled surge falls down from the rocks, the winds cease, the clouds vanish, and the threatening waves, (for such is the will of the sons of Leda,) subside."

Deforme est de seipso prædicāre, falso præsertim. Cic.—"It is unseemly to talk of one's self, and more especially to state falsehoods."

Deformius nihil est ardeliōne sene. Mart.—"There is nothing more unseemly than an aged busybody."

Degĕnĕres anĭmos timor arguit.— Virg.—"Fear shows an ignoble mind."

Dei plena sunt omnia. Cic.—"All things are full of God." See *Sunt Jovis*, &c.

——*Delectando pariterque monendo.* Hor.—"Pleasing as well as instructing." Having an eye both to the useful and the ornamental. See *Omne tulit*, &c.

Delegāta potestas non potest delegāri. Coke.—"A power

that is delegated cannot again be delegated " That is, by the person to whom it is delegated.

Delenda est Carthāgo.—" Carthage must be destroyed." A phrase with which Cato the Elder used to end all his speeches, to stimulate the people to the destruction of Carthage, which from its wealth and commerce he looked upon as the most dangerous enemy of Rome.

Deleo omnes dehinc ex animo muliĕres. TER.—" From henceforth I blot out all women from my mind."

Deliberando sæpe perit occāsio. SYR.—" The opportunity is often lost by deliberating." This may occur where we have to perform a duty in a given time.

Deliberandum est diu quod statuendum est semel. SYR.—" Time must be taken for deliberation, where we have to determine once for all."

Deliberāre utĭlia, mora est tutissĭma. SYR.—" To deliberate about useful things is the safest of all delay."

Delibĕrat Roma, perit Saguntum. Prov.—" Rome deliberates, Saguntum perishes." The Saguntines, the brave allies of Rome, perished while the Romans were deliberating how to save them. Too much deliberation is nearly as dangerous as too little. See *Dum deliberamus,* &c.

Deliciæ illĕpĭdæ atque inelegantes. CATULL.—" Gross and vulgar pleasures."

Delīramenta doctrīnæ.—" The ravings of the learned." Such, for instance, as the question which was seriously argued among the schoolmen, how many angels could dance on the point of a needle.

——*Delīrant reges, plectuntur Achīvi.* HOR.—" The kings play the madman, the Achæans (the people) are punished for it." When kings fight, it is at the expense of the blood and treasure of their subjects.

Delphīnum natāre doces. Prov.—" You are teaching a dolphin how to swim." "You are teaching your grandam to suck eggs."

Delphīnum sylvis appingit, fluctĭbus aprum. HOR.—" He paints a dolphin in the woods, a boar in the waves." A description of the incongruities of a wretched painter.

——*Demētrî, teque Tigellî,*
Discipulārum inter jubeo plorāre cathĕdras. HOR.

—"You, Demetrius, and you, Tigellius, I bid lament among the forms of your female pupils." Addressed to frivolous authors.

Demitto aurĭcŭlas ut inīquæ mentis asellus. Hor.—"Like an ass of stubborn disposition, I drop my ears."

Denīque non omnes eādem mirantur amantque. Hor.—"All men, in fact, do not admire and love the same things." No two men probably have the same tastes, any more than exactly similar bodies and features.

Deo dante nil nocet invidia, et non dante, nil profĭcit labor. —"With the favour of God, envy cannot injure us; without that favour, all our labours are of no avail."

Deo favente.—"With God's favour."

Deo juvante.—"With God's help."

Deo optĭmo maxĭmo.—"To God, all good and all great." The usual beginning of epitaphs in Roman Catholic countries, denoted by the initials, D. O. M.

Deo volente.—"God willing." Often denoted by the initials, D. V.

Deōrum cibus est. *Prov.*—"'Tis food fit for the gods."

Deprendi mĭsĕrum est.— Hor.—"To be detected is a shocking thing."

Derelictio commūnis utilitātis contra natūram est. Cic.— "The abandonment of the common good is contrary to nature."

Derīdet, sed non derīdeor.—"He laughs, but I am not laughed at." Said by a wise man, who will not take an affront.

Derivatīva potestas non potest esse major primitīvâ. *Law Maxim.*—"A power that is derived cannot be greater than that from which it is derived."

Descriptas servāre vices, ŏpĕrumque colōres,
Cur ego, si nequeo ignōrōque, poëta salūtor? Hor.

—"If I am incapable of, and ignorant how to observe the distinctions described, and the complexions of works of genius, why am I saluted with the name of 'Poet'?"

Desiderantem quod satis est, neque
Tumultuōsum sollicitat mare,
* * *
Non verberātæ grandĭne vīneæ,
Fundusve mendax.—— Hor.

—"him who desires but a competence, neither the tempestuous sea renders anxious, nor yet vineyards pelted with hail, nor disappointments in his farm."

Designătio unius est exclusio altĕrius. COKE.—"The mention of one condition implies the exclusion of another."

——*Desĭnant*
Maledicĕre, facta ne noscant sua. TER.
—"Let them cease to speak ill of others, lest they should happen to hear of their own doings."

Desĭne fata Deum flecti sperāre precando. VIRG.—"Cease to hope that the decrees of the gods can be changed through your prayers."

Desĭnit in piscem mulier formōsa supernè. HOR.—"A woman beautiful above, ends in the tail of a fish." A description of bad taste and incongruity of style.

Destitūtus ventis remos adhĭbe.—"When the wind fails, ply your oars."

Desunt cætĕra.—"The rest is wanting." Words often placed at the end of an imperfect narrative.

Desunt inŏpiæ multa, avaritiæ omnia. *Prov.*—"Poverty is in want of much, avarice of everything." With the one, a wish to gain money is natural, with the other, a disease.

Det ille vĕniam facĭlè, cui vĕniâ est opus. SEN.—"He who needs pardon, should readily grant pardon."

Detĕriōres omnes sumus licentiâ. TER.—"We are all of us the worse for too much licence." There are *spoilt children* even among men.

Detestando illo crĭmĭne, scĕlĕra omnia complexa sunt. CIC.—"In that one detestable crime all wickedness is comprised."

Detrahĕre alĭquid altĕri, et homĭnem homĭnis incommŏdo suum augēre commŏdum, magis est contra natūram quam mors, quam paupertas, quam dolor, quam cætĕra quæ possunt aut corpŏri accidĕre, aut rebus externis. CIC.—"To deprive another of anything, and for one man to increase his own advantage by the distress of another, is more repugnant to nature, than death, or poverty, or grief, or any other contingencies that can possibly befall our bodies, or affect our external circumstances."

Detur aliquando otium quiesque fessis. SEN.—"Rest and repose should sometimes be granted to the weary." The bow must be sometimes unstrung.

Detur pulchriōri.—"Let it be given to the most beautiful." The inscription on the golden apple, by adjudging which to the goddess Venus, Paris offended Juno and Minerva, and ultimately caused the Trojan war.

——*Deum namque ire per omnes*
Terrasque, tractusque maris, cœlumque profundum. VIRG.
—"For God, they say, pervades all lands, the tracts of sea, and the heaven profound." In these lines Virgil gives a broad outline of the Pantheistic philosophy.

Deus det.—"May God grant." In the middle ages, grace at meat was so called, from the commencing words.

Deus est mortāli juvāre mortālem, et hæc ad æternam gloriam via. PLINY *the Elder.*—"For man to assist man is to be a god; this is the path that leads to everlasting glory."

Deus est summum bonum.—"God is the supreme good."

——*Deus hæc fortasse benignā*
Redūcet in sedem vice.— HOR.
—"God will, perhaps, by some propitious change, restore these matters to their former state."

Deus id vult.—"It is the will of God." The cry of the Crusaders at the siege of Jerusalem.

Deus misereātur nobis.—"God be merciful unto us." The beginning of the 67th Psalm.

——*Deus nobis hæc ōtia fecit.* VIRG.—"God has granted unto us this repose."

Deus omnĭbus quod sat est suppĕdĭtat.—"God supplies enough to all." Because God alone is properly the judge of what is enough.

Dextras dare.—"To give the right hands to each other." An assurance of mutual friendship, or at least of security, because two right hands, when clasped, cannot conceal any weapon.

Dextro tempŏre. HOR.—"At a propitious time." At a lucky moment.

Dī bene fecērunt, inŏpis me quodque pusilli
Finxĕrunt anĭmi, raro et perpauca loquentis. HOR.
—"The gods have dealt kindly with me, since they have framed me of an humble and meek disposition, speaking but seldom and briefly."

Dī bene vertant, tene crumēnam. PLAUT.—"May the gods send luck—take the purse."

——*Dî immortāles, obsĕcro, aurum quid valet.* PLAUT.—"Immortal gods, I do beseech you, how powerful is gold!"

Dî laneos pedes habent. *Prov.*—"The gods have feet made of wool." The judgments of Providence evertake us silently, and when we least expect them.

Dî mĕlius, quam nos moneāmus tālia quenquam. OVID.—"May the gods forbid that I should advise any one to follow such a course."

Dî nobis labōribus omnia vendunt. *Prov.*—"The gods sell us everything for our labours."

——*Dî nos quasi pilas hŏmĭnes habent.* PLAUT.—"The gods treat us men like balls."

Dî, quĭbus impĕrium est animārum, umbræque silentes,
Et Chaos, et Phlĕgĕthon, loca nocte tacentia late;
Sit mihi fas audīta loqui! sit nūmĭne vestro
Pandĕre res altâ terrâ et calīgĭne mersas. VIRG.

—"Ye gods, to whom belongs the empire of the ghosts, and ye silent shades, and Chaos, and Phlegethon, places where silence reigns around in night! permit me to utter the secrets I have heard; may I by your divine will disclose things buried deep in the earth and darkness."

——*Dî talem terris avertĭte pestem.* VIRG.—"Ye gods, avert from the earth such a scourge."

Dî tibi dent annos! a te nam cætĕra sumes;
Sint modo virtūti tempŏra longa tuæ. OVID.

—"May the gods grant thee length of years! All other blessings from thyself thou wilt derive, let only time be granted for thy virtues."

Dî tibi sint facĭles; et opis nullīus egentem
Fortūnam præstent, dissĭmĭlemque meæ. OVID.

—"May the gods be propitious to thee; may they also grant thee a fate that needs the aid of no one, and quite unlike to mine."

Dic mihi, cras istud, Posthŭme, quando vĕniet? MART.—"Tell, me, Posthumus, when will this to-morrow arrive?" Said to a procrastinating friend.

Dic mihi, si fias tu leo, qualis eris? MART.—"Tell me, if you were a lion, what sort of one would you be?" No man should speak too positively as to how he would conduct himself under a total change of circumstances and position.

Dicam insigne, recens adhuc
Indictum ore ălio. HOR.
—"I shall record a remarkable event, which is new as yet, and untold by the lips of another."

Dicēbam, Medicāre tuos desiste capillos:
Tingĕre quam possis, jam tibi nulla coma est. OVID.
—"I used to say—Do leave off doctoring your hair; and now you have no hair left for you to dye."

——*Dicenda, tacenda locūtus.* HOR.—"Speaking of things to be mentioned and to be kept silence upon."

——*Dicenda tacendaque calles?* PERS.—"Dost thou understand when to speak, and when to hold thy tongue?"

Dicĕre quæ puduit, scribĕre jussit amor. OVID.—"What I was ashamed to say, love has commanded me to write."

Dicētur mĕrĭtâ nox quoque næniâ. HOR.—"The night too shall be celebrated in an appropriate lay."

Dicĭte Iō Pæan, et Iō bis dicĭte Pæan;
Decĭdit in casses præda petīta meos. OVID.
—"Sing Io Pæan, and Io Pæan twice sing, the prey that was sought has fallen into our toils." Ovid says this, having taught the men the arts of successful courtship. *Art of Love*, B. ii.

Dicĭtis, omnis in imbecīllitāte est et gratia et carĭtas. CIC.—"You affirm that all kindness and benevolence is founded in weakness."

Dicĭtur certe vulgāri quodam proverbio; Qui me amat, amat et canem meum. ST. BERNARD.—"At all events there is a certain common proverb which says, Love me, love my dog."

——*Dicta tibi est lex.* HOR.—"The law has been laid down for you."

Dicto celĕrius hostis abscĭdit caput,
Victorque rĕdiit—— PHÆD.
—"Sooner than you could say it, he whipped off the head of the enemy, and returned victorious."

Dictum de dicto.—"A report founded on hearsay."

Dictum sapienti sat est. PLAUT. and TER.—"A word to the wise is enough." A hint is enough for a sensible man.

Dictus eram cuidam subĭto vĕnisse puellæ;
Turbĭda perversas induit illa comas. OVID.
—"I was unexpectedly announced as having paid a visit

to a certain lady; in her confusion she put on her wig the wrong side before."

Diem perdĭdi!—"I have lost a day!" The exclamation of the Emperor Titus, on finding at night that he had done nothing worthy of recollection during the day.

Dies adĭmit ægritudĭnem. Prov.—"Time removes afflictions."

Dies datus. Law Term.—"A day given." The day appointed for appearing.

Dies dolōrem minuit.—"Time alleviates grief."

Dies Domin ĭcus non est jurid ĭcus. COKE.—"Sunday is not a day in law."

Dies faustus.—"A lucky day."

Dies infaustus.—"An unlucky day."

Dies iræ, dies illa,
Sæclum solvet in favillâ
Teste David cum Sibyllâ.

"The day of wrath, that dreadful day,
The world in ashes all shall lay—
This David and the Sibyl say."

These are the commencing lines of the Sequence used by the Romish Church in the Office of the Dead. The authorship of this hymn, which is of considerable beauty, does not seem to be positively known. It has been attributed to Thomas de Celano, a Minorite friar of the fourteenth century, but, more generally, to Frangipani, Cardinal Malabrancia.

——*Dies, ni fallor, adest, quem semper acerbum,*
Semper honorātum, sic Di voluistis, habēbo. VIRG.
—"The day, if I mistake not, is at hand, which I shall always account a day of sorrow, always a day to be honoured, such, ye gods, has been your will."

Dies non (the word *juridicus* being understood).—"No legal day." A day on which the courts are closed, and no law proceedings are going on, which is therefore called "no day." Such days were by the Romans called "nefasti." Sunday is a *dies non* in law. See *Dies Dominicus*, &c.

Dies si in obligatiōnĭbus non pōnĭtur, præsente die debētur. Law Maxim.—"If a day for payment is not stated in a bond, the money is due on the day on which it is executed."

Dies solemnes.—"Holidays."

Difficĭle custodĭtur quod plures amant.—"That is preserved with difficulty which many covet."

Difficĭle est, făteor, sed tendit in ardua virtus. OVID.—"It is difficult, I confess; but true courage seeks obstacles."

Difficĭle est longum sŭbĭto depōnĕre amōrem. CATULL.—"It is difficult to relinquish on a sudden a long cherished love."

Difficĭle est mutāre ănĭmum, et si quid est pĕnĭtus insĭtum mōribus, id sŭbĭto evellĕre. CIC.—"It is difficult to alter the disposition, and, if there is anything deeply implanted in our nature, suddenly to root it out."

Difficĭle est plurĭmum virtūtem reverēri, qui semper secundâ fortūnâ sit usus. AD HERENN.—"It is difficult for him to have a very high respect for virtue, who has enjoyed uninterrupted prosperity." It is doubted if the four Books on Rhetoric, dedicated to Herennius, are the composition of Cicero.

Difficĭle est satĭram non scrībĕre—— JUV.—"It is hard to avoid writing satire." This was especially true in reference to the corrupt age in which Juvenal lived.

Difficĭle est temperāre felicitāti, quâ te non putes diu usūrum. TACIT.—"It is difficult to enjoy with moderation the happiness, which we suppose we shall not long enjoy."

Difficĭlem oportet aurem habēre ad crĭmina. SYR.—"One should be slow in giving ear to accusations."

Difficĭlia quæ pulchra. Prov.—"The best things are worst to come by."

Difficĭlis, facĭlis, jucundus, acerbus es idem ;
Nec tecum possum vīvĕre, nec sine te. MART.
—"Crabbed but kind, pleasant and sour together, I can neither live with you nor yet without you."

Difficĭlis, quĕrŭlus, laudātor tempŏris acti. HOR.—"Peevish, complaining, the praiser of by-gone times." A natural and not unamiable feature, if not carried to an extreme.

——*Difficulter contĭnētur spirĭtus,*
Integritātis qui sincēræ conscius,
A noxiōrum prĕmĭtur insolentiis. PHÆD.
—"The mind is with difficulty restrained, which, conscious of unsullied integrity, is exposed to the insults of spiteful men."

Difficulter rĕciduntur vitia quæ nobiscum crevērunt.—"Vices which have grown with our growth are with difficulty lopped away."

——*Diffugiunt, cadis*
Cum fæce siccātis, amīci
Ferre jugum pārĭter dolōsi. HOR.

—"Friends too faithless to bear equally the yoke of adversity, when the casks are emptied to the very dregs, fly off in all directions."

Dignior est vestro nulla puella choro. TIBULL.—"No maiden, (Muses,) is more worthy of your choir."

Dignum laude virum Musa vetat mori. HOR.—"The Muse forbids the man who is worthy of praise to die."

Dignum patellâ operculum.—"A cover worthy of the pot." What better could be expected of one coming of such a stock?

——*Dignum sapiente, bonoque est.* HOR.—"'Tis worthy a wise man, and a good."

Diis alĭter visum—— VIRG.—"It has seemed otherwise to the gods."

——*Diis proxĭmus ille est*
Quem ratio, non ira movet, qui facta rependens
Consĭlio punīre potest—— CLAUD.

—"He is nearest to the gods, whom reason, not passion, influences; and who, weighing the circumstances, can inflict punishment with discretion."

Dilatiōnes in lege sunt odiōsæ. *Law Maxim.*—"Delays in the law are odious."

Dīligĕre parentes prima natūræ lex est. VAL. MAX.—"To love one's parents is the first law of nature."

Dīlĭgĭmus omnia vera, id est fidēlia, simplicia, constantia; vana, falsa, fallentia ōdĭmus. CIC.—"We (naturally) love all qualities that are genuine, that is, that are faithful, frank, and constant; such as are vain, fickle, and deceitful, we abhor."

Dīlĭgĭtur nemo, nisi cui Fortūna secunda est,
Quæ, simul intŏnuit, proxĭma quæque fugat. OVID.

—"No one is beloved, but the man to whom Fortune is favourable; soon as she thunders, she chases away all that are near."

Dimĭdium facti, qui cœpit, habet—— HOR.—"He who has

made a beginning, has half done." This is sometimes quoted "*bene capit.*" So our old proverb, "Well begun is half done."

Dimĭdium plus toto. *Prov.*—"The half is more than the whole." Meaning that the half which we have with safety, is better than the whole when only to be obtained with danger. *A translation from* Hesiod.

Diruit, ædificat, mutat quadrāta rotundis. Hor.—"He pulls down, he builds up again, he changes square for round." Descriptive of a restless love of change.

Disce aut discēde.—"Learn or depart." A punning motto sometimes put up in school-rooms.

Disce docendus adhuc, quæ censet amicŭlus, ut si
Cæcus iter monstrāre velit; tamen aspĭce si quid
Et nos quod cures proprium fecisse loquāmur. Hor.

—"Hear what are the sentiments of your humble friend, who himself still requires teaching just as much as a blind man who undertakes to show the way; however, see if even I can advance anything which you may think it worth your while to adopt as your own."

Disce, puer, virtūtem ex me, verumque labōrem,
Fortūnam ex aliis—— Virg.

—"Learn, my son, valour and real exertion from me, good fortune from others." The words of Æneas to Iulus, when the former was about to engage Turnus in single combat.

Discĭpŭlus est priōris postĕrior dies. Syr.—"The day that follows is the scholar of that which has gone before."

Discit enim cĭtiùs, mĕmĭnitque libentiùs illud
Quod quis deridet quam quod probat et venerātur. Hor.

—"Each learns more readily, and retains more willingly, that which causes laughter than that which merits his approbation and respect." The poet here censures that love of scandal which prevails unfortunately among all grades and classes.

Discĭte justitiam monĭti et non temnĕre divos. Virg.—"Learn justice from my advice, and not to despise the gods." The words of one who spoke from bitter experience, and when repentance was too late.

Discrĕpant facta cum dictis. Cic.—"The facts differ from the statement."

——*Disjecti membra poëtæ.* HOR.—"The limbs of the dismembered poet."

Disjĭce compositam pacem, sere crīmĭna belli. VIRG.—"Cast aside this patched-up peace, sow the evils of war." The address of Juno to the Fury Alecto, when prompting her to "let slip the dogs of war."

Dissĭmile est, pecūniæ debĭtis et grātiæ. CIC.—"There is a difference between the owing of money and of gratitude."

Dissolve frigus, ligna super foco
Largè repōnens, atque benignius
Deprōme quadrīmum Sabīnâ,
O Thaliarche, merum diōtâ. HOR.

—"Dispel the cold, by heaping logs in plenty on the hearth, and bountifully pour, O Thaliarchus, the wine of four years old from the Sabine jar."

Distat opus nostrum; sed fontĭbus exit ab īsdem;
Artis et ingĕnuæ cultor uterque sumus. OVID.

—"Our pursuits are different; but they arise from the same source, and each of us is the cultivator of a liberal art."

Distrăhit ănĭmum librōrum multitūdo. SEN.—"A multitude of books distracts the mind." A hint to *dilettanti* students.

Districtus ensis cui semper impiâ
Cervīce pendet, non Sicŭlæ dapes
Dulcem elaborābunt sapōrem,
Non ăvium cithăræque cantus
Somnum rĕdūcent. HOR.

—"Sicilian dainties will not force a delicious relish for the man over whose impious neck ever hangs the naked sword; the songs of birds and of the lyre will not restore his sleep."

Distringas. *Law Phrase.*—"You may distrain." A writ issued to the sheriff, commanding him to distrain.

Diversum vĭtio vĭtium prope majus—— HOR.—"To this vice there is an opposite vice, almost the greater of the two."

Dives agris, dives pŏsĭtis in fœnŏre nummis. HOR.—"Rich in lands, rich in money placed out at interest."

——*Dives amīcus*
Sæpe decem vitiis instructior, odit et horret. HOR.

—"Your rich friend who has many a time been initiated into ten times as many vices as you have, hates and abhors vous (for yours)." He sees the mote in your eye, and takes no thought of the beam in his own.

Dives aut ĭnĭquus est, aut ĭnĭqui hæres. Prov.—"A rich man is either a knave, or the heir of a knave." As illiberal as the English adage:

"It is a saying, common more than civil,
The son is blest, whose sire is at the devil."

Dives eram dudum, fecĕrunt me tria nudum,
Alea, vina, Venus, per quæ sum factus egēnus.
—"I was rich of late; three things have made me poor, gaming, wine, and women; through these have I been brought to want." Leonine rhymes of the middle ages.

——*Dives qui fieri vult,*
Et citò vult fieri—— JUV.
—"The man who is anxious to become rich, is anxious to become so with all speed."

Dīvĭde et impĕra.—"Divide and rule." Not a Christian precept, but one which has been often acted upon by successful politicians.

——*Divīsum sic breve fiet opus.* MART.—"Thus divided, the work will become short." All difficulties are to be surmounted by method.

Divĭtiæ grandes hŏmĭni sunt, vīvĕre parcè
Æquo ănĭmo—— LUCR.
—"It is great wealth to a man, to live frugally, with a contented mind."

Divĭtiæ virum făciunt.—"Money makes the man." It is fortunate that this is not universally the case, and that people are *sometimes* estimated for other qualities. See *Et genus et proavos, &c.*

Divitiārum acquisitio magni labōris, possessio magni timōris, amissio magni dolōris.—"The gaining of wealth is a work of great labour; the possession, a source of great apprehension; the loss, a cause of great grief."

Divitiārum et formæ gloria fluxa atque frăgĭlis; virtus clara æternaque habētur. SALL.—"The glory of wealth and of beauty is fleeting and unsubstantial; virtue is brilliant and everlasting."

Dixĕrit e multis ălĭquis, Quid virus in angues
Adjĭcis? et rabĭdæ tradis ovīle lupæ? OVID.
—"One of the multitude may say, Why add venom to the

serpent? And why deliver the sheepfold to the ravening wolf?"

Dixĕro quid si forte jocōsius, hoc mihi juris
Cum vĕniâ dabis—— Hor.
—"If perchance I shall speak a little jocosely, you will kindly allow me that privilege."

——*Dŏcĭles imitandis*
Turpĭbus et pravis omnes sumus—— Juv.
—"We are all apt scholars in learning that which is base and depraved."

Docti non solum vivi atque præsentes studiōsos dicendi erudiunt, atque docent; sed hoc etiam post mortem monimentis literārum assequuntur. Cic.—"Learned men not only teach and instruct others desirous to learn during their life, and while they are still with us, but, even after death, they do the same by the records of literature which they leave behind them."

Docti ratiōnem artis intellĭgunt, indocti voluptātem. Quint. —"Learned men understand the principles of art, the unlearned have a perception of the pleasure only."

Doctrīna est ingĕnii naturāle quoddam pābŭlum. Cic.—"Learning is as it were the natural food of the mind."

Doctrīna sed vim promŏvet insĭtam,
Rectique cultus pectŏra rōbŏrant:
Utcunque dĕfēcĕre mores,
Dēdĕcŏrant bene nata culpæ. Hor.
—"But learning improves the innate force, and good discipline confirms the mind; whenever morals are deficient, vices disgrace what is naturally good."

Dolendi modus, timendi non autem. Pliny *the Younger.*—"To grief there is a limit, not so to fear."

Doli non doli sunt, nisi astu colas. Plaut.—"Fraud ceases to be a fraud, if not artfully planned." The *intention* with which an action is done gives it its real weight and importance.

Dōlium volvĭtur. Prov.—"A cask is soon set a rolling." A weak man is easily turned from his purpose.

Dolor decrescit, ubi quo crescat non habet. Syr.—"Grief decreases, when it has nothing to make it increase."

Dolōrem aut extimescĕre vĕnientem, aut non ferre præsentem, turpe est. Cic.—"To be terrified at an approaching evil, or not to be able to bear up against it when present, is disgraceful."

——*Dolus an virtus, quis in hoste requirat?* VIRG.—"Who inquires in an enemy whether it was stratagem or valour?"

Dolus versātur in generālibus. *Law Max.*—"Fraud employs generalities."

Domi manēre convĕnit felicĭbus.—"Those who are happy at home ought to remain there."

Domi mansit, lanam fecit.—"She stayed at home and spun her wool." An epitaph upon an exemplary wife.

Domi puer ea sola discĕre potest quæ ipsi præcipientur: in scholâ etiam quæ āliis. QUINT.—"A boy can only learn at home those things which are taught him individually; at school, he can learn by what is taught to others."

Dŏmĭne, exaudi.—"Lord, listen to my prayer."

Domĭnium a possessiōne cœpisse dicĭtur. *Law Maxim.*—"Right is said to have had its beginning in possession." Length of possession is sufficient to give a legal title.

Dominus vobiscum.—"The Lord be with you."

Dŏmĭtæ natūræ.—"Of a tame nature." See *Feræ naturæ*.

Domus amīca domus optĭma.—"The house of a friend is the best of houses."

Domus procĕrum.—"The house of peers." Often written *Dom. proc.*

Domus sua est unicuique tutissĭmum refugium. COKE.—"Every man's house is his safest refuge." "Every man's house is his castle."

Dona præsentis cape lætus horæ, et
Linque sevēra. HOR.
—"With cheerfulness enjoy the blessings of the present hour, and banish sad thoughts."

Donātio mortis causâ. *Law Term.*—"A gift made in apprehension of death." A death-bed disposition of property, when a person delivers his personal goods to another to keep, in case of his decease.

Donec eras simplex, ănĭmum cum corpŏre amāvi;
Nunc mentis vitio læsa figūra tua est. OVID.
—"So long as you were disinterested I loved both your mind and your person; now, to me, your appearance is affected by this blemish on your disposition."

Donec eris felix multos numerābis amīcos;
Tempŏra si fuĕrint nūbĭla, solus eris. OVID.
—"So long as you are prosperous you will reckon many friends; if the times become cloudy, you will be alone."

——*Donum exitiāle Minervæ.* VIRG.—"The fatal gift of Minerva." The wooden horse, by means of which the Greeks gained possession of Troy.

Dormiunt aliquando leges, nunquam moriuntur. COKE.—"The law sometimes sleeps, it never dies." It is not so much the law that sleeps, as those who ought to put it in force; often from a sense of the impolicy of asserting their legal rights to the very letter.

——*Dos est magna parentum*
Virtus—— HOR.
—"The virtue of one's parents is a great dowry."

Duābus anchŏris nītĭtur.—"She is held by two anchors." So our saying, "He has two strings to his bow."

Dubiam salūtem qui dat afflictis, negat. SEN.—"He who gives to the afflicted a dubious support, denies it." Such support is deprived of its grace, if not of its efficacy.

Duc me, Parens, celsique domināto poli,
Quocunque plăcuit; nulla parendi mora est;
Adsum impĭger. SEN.
—"Conduct me, Parent of all, and ruler over the lofty heavens, wherever it pleases thee; in obeying thee I make no delay; I am ever ready at thy command."

Duces tēcum. *Law Term.*—"Bring with you." A writ which commands a person to appear in court on a certain day, and bring with him certain writings or evidences.

——*Ducĭmus autem*
Hos quoque felīces, qui, ferre incommŏda vitæ,
Nec jactāre jugum, vitâ didicēre magistrâ. JUV.
—"We consider those men happy, who, from their experience in life, have learned to bear its inconveniences without struggling against the yoke."

——*Ducis ingĕnium, res*
Adversæ nudāre solent, celāre secundæ. HOR.
—"Disasters are wont to reveal the abilities of a general, good fortune to conceal them." Hence the most consummate abilities of a general are shown in a masterly retreat.

Ducunt *volentem fata, nolentem trahunt.* — "Fate leads the willing, and the unwilling drags." From the Greek of Cleanthes, in Seneca, Epistle 107.

Dulce *domum.*—"Sweet home." A Latin song is thus called, which is sung at Winchester College, on the evening preceding the Whitsun holidays.

Dulce est *desĭpĕre in loco.* Hor.—"It is pleasant to play the fool on the proper occasion." As there is "a time for everything," there is a time for merriment and relaxation.

Dulce est *mĭsĕris sŏcios hăbuisse dolŏris.*—"It is a comfort for the wretched to have companions in their sorrow."

Dulce *et decōrum est pro patriā mori.* Hor.—"It is sweet and glorious to die for one's country."

Dulces *moriens reminiscĭtur Argos.* Virg.—"And, as he dies, his thoughts revert to his dear Argos."

Dulcĭbus est *verbis alliciendus amor.*—"Love must be allured with kind words."

Dulcior *est fructus post multa perĭcŭla ductus.*—"The fruit is sweetest that is gained after many perils." A Leonine proverb quoted by Rabelais, "Stolen fruit is the sweetest."

——*Dulcique ănĭmos novitāte tenēbo.* Ovid.—"And I will enthral your mind with the charms of novelty."

Dulcis *amor patriæ, dulce vidĕre suos.*—"Sweet is the love of one's country, sweet to behold one's kindred."

Dulcis *inexpertis cultūra potentis amīci;*
Expertus mĕtuit—— Hor.

—"Worship of the great is pleasant to those who are inexperienced in the world, but he who has gained experience dreads dependence."

Dum *Aurōra fulget, monĭti adolescentes, flores collĭgĭte.*—"Take my advice, my young friends, and gather flowers while the morning shines." Employ the hours of sunshine, for "when the night cometh, no man can work."

Dum *bene dives ager; dum rami pondĕre nutant,*
Affĕrat in calătho rustĭca dona puer. Ovid.

—"While the country is bountifully rich, while the branches are bending beneath their load, let the boy bring your country presents in his basket."

Dum *caput infestat, labor omnia membra molestat.*—"While the head aches, weariness oppresses all the limbs."

Dum curæ ambĭguæ, dum spes incerta futūri. Virg.—"While I am immersed in doubtful care, with uncertain hopes of the future."

Dum deliberāmus quando incipiendum, incipĕre jam serum fit. Quint.—"While we are deliberating when to begin, it becomes too late to begin." See *Deliberat*, &c.

Dum fata fugĭmus, fata stulti incurrĭmus. Buchanan.—"While we fly from our fate, like fools we rush on to it."

Dum fata sinunt vīvĭte læti. Sen.—"So long as the Fates permit, live in cheerfulness."

Dum flammas Jovis et sŏnĭtus imitātur Olympi. Virg.—"While he imitates the flames of Jove, and the lightnings of Olympus."

Dum in dubio est ănĭmus, paulo momento huc illuc impellĭtur. Ter.—"While the mind is in suspense, it is swayed by a slight impulse one way or the other."

Dum lego, assentior. Cic.—"Whilst I read, I assent." The exclamation of Cicero, while reading Plato's reasoning on the immortality of the soul.

Dum licet, in rebus jucundis vive beātus,
Vive memor quàm sis ævi brevis. Hor.
—"While you have the power, live contented with happy circumstances, live mindful how short is life." See *Dum vivimus*, &c.

——*Dum loquor, hora fugit.* Ovid.—"While I am speaking, time flies."

Dum ne ob malefacta pĕream, parvi æstĭmo. Plaut.—"So I do not die for my misdeeds, I care but little."

Dum potuit sŏlĭtâ gĕmĭtum virtūte repressit. Ovid.—"So long as he is able, he suppresses his groans with his wonted fortitude." Said of Hercules when he has put on the fatal garment sent him by his wife.

——*Dum rĕcĭtas incĭpit esse tuus.* Mart.—"As you recite it, it begins to be your own." See *Mutato nomine*, &c.

Dum se bene gessĕrit.—"So long as he conducts himself well." "During good behaviour." The tenure upon which some official situations are held.

Dum singŭli pugnant, universi vincuntur. Tacit.—"While each is fighting separately, the whole are conquered." The Britons, being divided among themselves by the jealousies of their petty nations, and having no centre of action, were more easily conquered by the Romans than if they had acted in concert.

Dum spiro, spero.—"While I breathe I hope."

Dum tacent, clamant. Cic.—"While silent, they cry aloud." Their silence is expressive of their smothered discontent.

Dum vires annique sinunt, tolerāte labōres:
Jam vĕniet tăcito curva senecta pede. Ovid.
—"While strength and years permit, endure labour; soon will bowed old age come on with silent foot."

Dum vitant stulti vĭtia, in contrāria currunt. Hor.—"While fools are for avoiding one fault, they run into the opposite one."

Dum vīvĭmus, vivāmus. *From an ancient inscription in* Gruter, p. 609.—"While we live, let us live." Let us enjoy life, for existence without enjoyment is not living. This was the maxim of the Epicureans. See *Dum licet, &c.*

Dum vivit, hŏmĭnem nōvĕris; ubi mortuus est, quiescas. Plaut.—"While he is alive, you may know a person; when he is dead, keep yourself quiet."

Dummŏdo morāta recte vĕniat, dotāta est satis. Plaut.—"So long as a woman comes with good principles, she is sufficiently portioned."

Dummŏdo sit dives, barbărus ipse placet. Ovid.—"If he be only rich, a very barbarian is pleasing."

Duōbus modis, id est aut fraude aut vi, fit injūria—fraus quasi vulpĕcŭlæ, vis leōnis vidētur—utrumque ab hŏmĭne alienissimum est. Cic.—"Injury is done by two methods, either by deceit or by violence; deceit appears to be the attribute of the fox, violence of the lion; both of them most foreign to man."

Duos qui sequĭtur lepŏres neutrum capit. *Prov.*—"He who follows two hares catches neither." So our saying, "Between two stools," &c.

Duplex omnĭno est jocandi genus: unum illiberāle, pĕtŭlans, flagitiōsum, obscœnum; altĕrum, elĕgans, urbānum, ingeniōsum, facētum. Cic.—"There are two sorts of pleasantry; the one ungentlemanly, wanton, flagitious, obscene; the other elegant, courteous, ingenious, and facetious."

——*Dura*
Exerce impĕria, et ramos compesce fluentes. Virg.

—"Exert a rigorous sway, and check the straggling boughs."

Durante beneplăcĭto.—"During our good pleasure." The tenure by which most official situations are held in this country.

Durante vitâ.—"During life."

Durāte, et vosmet rebus servāte secundis. VIRG.—"Persevere, and reserve yourselves for better times."

Durum et durum non făciunt murum.—"Hard and hard do not make a wall." A mediæval proverb. As bricks require a soft substance to unite them, so proud men will never agree without the mediation of a mild and equable disposition.

Durum! Sed lĕvius fit patientiâ
Quicquid corrĭgĕre est nefas. HOR.

—"'Tis hard! But that which it is not allowed us to amend, is rendered more light by patience."

Durum telum necessĭtas. *Prov.*—"Necessity is a sharp weapon."

Dux fœmĭna facti. VIRG.—"A woman the leader in the deed." Said in reference to the valour and enterprise of Queen Dido.

E.

E contra.—"On the other hand."

E dĕbĭto justitiæ. See *Debito justitiæ.*

E flammâ cibum pĕtĕre. TER.—"To seek one's food in the very flames." Only the most abject and wretched would pick from out of the flames of the funeral pile the articles of food, which, in conformity with the Roman usage, were thrown there.

E multis paleis, paulum fructus collēgi. *Prov.*—"From much straw I have gathered but little fruit." "Much straw, but little grain." With much labour I have obtained but little profit.

E se finxit velut arāneus.—"He spun from himself like a spider." He depended solely on his own resources.

E tardigrădis ăsĭnis equus non prŏdiit. *Prov.*—"The horse does not spring from the slow-paced ass." Worthy children cannot be expected to spring from degenerate parents.

E tĕnui casâ sæpe vir magnus erit. Prov.—"From an humble cottage a hero often springs."

E terræ cavernis ferrum elĭcimus, rem ad colendos agros necessārium. Cic.—"We draw forth iron from the depths of the earth, a thing necessary for cultivating the fields."

Ea ănĭmi elātio quæ cernĭtur in perĭcŭlis, si justĭtiâ vacat, pugnatque pro suis commŏdis, in vitio est. Cic.—"That elevation of mind which is to be seen in moments of peril, if it is uncontrolled by justice, and strives only for its own advantages, becomes a crime."

Ea fama vagātur.—"That report is in circulation." There is a report to that effect.

Ea quŏniam nēmĭni obtrūdi potest,
Itur ad me—— Ter.
—"Because she cannot be pushed off on any one else, they come to me."

——*Ea sola voluptas*
Solāmenque mali—— Virg.
—"That was his only delight, and the solace of his misfortune."

Ea sub ŏcŭlis pŏsĭta neglĭgĭmus; proximŏrum incuriōsi, longinqua sectāmur. Pliny *the Younger*.—"Those things which are placed under our eyes, we overlook; indifferent as to what is near us, we long for that which is distant." The traveller abroad overlooks the beauties of his own country.

"'Tis distance lends enchantment to the view."

Ecce homo.—"Behold the man." The title given to pictures of our Saviour, wearing the crown of thorns and the purple robe—when Pilate said, "Behold the man," *John* xix. 5.

Ecce ĭtĕrum Crispīnus!—— Juv.—"Behold! Crispinus once again!" A notorious debauchee and favourite of the emperor Domitian, whom Juvenal has occasion more than once to make the object of his satire.

Ecquem esse dices in mari piscem meum? Plaut.—"Of which fish in the sea can you say, 'That is mine?'"

Edĕpol næ hic dies pervorsus et advorsus mihi obtĭgit. Plaut.

—"Upon my word, this day certainly has turned out both perverse and adverse for me."

Edĕre non pŏtĕris vocem, lupus est tibi visus. *Prov.*—"You cannot utter a word, you have surely seen a wolf." It was said that the wolf, by some secret power, deprived of their voice those who beheld it. See *Lupus in fabulâ.*

Edĕre oportet ut vivas, non vīvĕre ut edas. Ad Herenn.—"You ought to eat to live, not live to eat."

Edvardum occīdĕre nolīte timĕre bonum est.—The ambiguous message penned by Adam Orleton, bishop of Hereford, and sent by Queen Isabella to the gaolers of her husband, Edward II. Being written without punctuation, the words might be read two ways; with a comma after *timere*, they would mean, "Edward to kill fear not, the deed is good;" but, with it after *nolite*, the meaning would be, "Edward kill not, to fear the deed is good."

Effŏdiuntur opes irrītamenta malōrum. Ovid.—"Riches, the incentives of evil, are dug out of the earth."

Effŭgit mortem quisquis contemsĕrit, tĭmidissĭmum quemque consĕquĭtur. Curt.—"He who despises death, escapes it; while the most cowardly it overtakes."

Effutīre leves indigna tragœdia versus,
Ut festis matrōna movĕri jussa diĕbus. Hor.

—"Tragedy disdains to babble forth trivial verses, like a matron challenged to dance on festive days."

Ego apros occīdo, sed alter ūtĭtur pulpamento.—"I kill the boars, while another enjoys the flesh." "I beat the bush, another catches the hare." A proverb used by the emperor Diocletian. See *Sic vos, &c.*

Ego consuetūdĭnem sermōnis vocābo consensum eruditōrum; sicut vivendi consensum bonōrum. Quint.—"I shall consider the style of speaking adopted by men of education, as the model of correct language; as I do the example of good men the model of our conduct through life."

Ego ero post principia. Ter.—"I will be behind the first rank." I will get out of harm's way.

Ego et rex meus.—"I and my king." An expression attributed to Cardinal Wolsey. Though apparently egotistical and haughty, correct Latin would not admit of any other form.

——*Ego hæc mecum mussĭto,*
Bona mea inhiant; certātim dona mittunt et munĕra.
PLAUT.

—"I mutter this to myself—'They are gaping after my property, while, vying with each other, they are thus sending me gifts and presents.'"

Ego ita compĕrio omnia regna, civitātes, natiōnes, usque eo prospĕrum impĕrium hăbuisse, dum apud eos vera consĭlia valuĕrunt. SALL.—"I find that all kingdoms, states, and nations have enjoyed prosperity, so long as good counsels have had influence in their affairs."

——*Ego nec studium sine divĭte vena,*
Nec rude quid prosit vĭdeo ingĕnium.— HOR.

—"For my part, I can neither conceive what study can do without a rich natural vein, nor what rude genius can avail of itself."

Ego—quod te laudas, vehementer probo,
Namque hoc ab ălio nunquam continget tibi. PHÆD.

—"I greatly approve of your bestowing praise on yourself, for it will never be your lot to receive it from another." The answer of Æsop to a wretched author, who praised himself.

Ego, si bonam famam mihi servasso, sat ero dives. PLAUT.—"If I keep a good character for myself, I shall be quite rich enough."

——*Ego si risi, quod ineptus*
Pastillos Rufillus olet, Gargōnius hircum,
Lĭvĭdus et mordax vĭdeor tibi?— HOR.

—"If I laugh at the silly Rufillus, because he smells of perfumes, or at Gargonius, because he stinks like a he-goat, am I to be thought envious and carping?"

Ego spem pretio non emo. TER.—"I will not purchase hope with gold." I will not throw away what is of value upon empty hopes.

——*Egrĕgii mortālem, altique silentī.* HOR.—"A being of extraordinary silence and reserve."

Eheu! fugāces, Posthŭme, Posthŭme,
Labuntur anni; nec piĕtas moram
Rugis et instanti senectæ
Affĕret, indŏmĭtæque morti. HOR.

—"Alas! Posthumus, Posthumus, our years pass away,

nor can piety stay wrinkles, and approaching old age, and unconquerable death."

Eheu! quam brĕvĭbus pĕreunt ingentia causis! CLAUD.—"Alas! by what trifling causes are great states overthrown!" or, as Pope says, "What mighty contests spring from trivial things!"

Eheu! quam pingui macer est mihi taurus in arvo,
Idem amor exitium pĕcŏri est, pĕcŏrisque magistro. VIRG.
—"Alas! how lean is my bull amid the rich pastures! love is equally the destruction of the cattle, and of the cattle's master."

——*Eheu!*
Quam tĕmĕrè in nosmet legem sancīmus inīquam!
Nam vĭtiis nemo sine nascĭtur; optĭmus ille est,
Qui mĭnĭmis urgētur.—— HOR.
—"Alas! how rashly do we sanction severe rules against ourselves, for no man is born without faults; he is the best who is subject to the fewest."

Eja, age, rumpe moras, quo te spectābimus usque?
Dum quid sis dŭbĭtas, jam potes esse nihil. MART.
—"Come then, away with this delay, how long are we to be looking at you? While you are in doubt what to be, presently it will be out of your power to be anything at all."

Elāti ănĭmi comprimendi sunt.—"Minds which are too much elated must be humbled."

Elĕgit. Law Term.—"He has chosen." A writ of execution that lies for one who has recovered a debt, to levy from a moiety of the defendant's lands: while holding which moiety the creditor is tenant by *elegit*.

Elephantem ex muscâ facis. Prov.—"You are making an elephant of a fly."

Elephantus non capit murem. Prov.—"The elephant does not catch mice." Some annoyances are beneath our notice. See *Aquila non*, &c.

Elĭge eum cujus tibi plăcuit et vita et ōrātio. SEN.—"Make choice of him whose mode of living and whose conversation are pleasing to you."

Elĭgĭto tempus, captātum sæpe, rogandi. OVID.—"Choose your time for asking, after having often watched for it."

Elocūtio est idoneōrum verbōrum et sententiārum ad rem in-

ventam accommodātio. Cic.—"Elocution is an apt accommodation of the words and sentiments to the subject under discussion."

Eloquentia non modo eos ornat, penes quos est, sed etiam universam rempublĭcam. Cic.—"Eloquence is not only an ornament to those who possess it, but even to the whole community."

Emax fœmĭna. Ovid.—"A woman who is always buying." A lover of bargains.

Emĕre malo quam rogāre.—"Better to have to buy than to beg." Because in the former case there is no obligation.

——*Emĭtur solâ virtūte potestas.* Claud.—"(True) power is purchased by virtue alone."

Empta dolōre docet expĕrientia. *Prov.*—"Experience bought by pain teaches us a lesson."

Emunctæ naris homo.—"A man of sharp nose." One of quick perception.

En! hic declārat, quales sitis jūdĭces! Phæd.—"Look! This shows what sort of judges you are."

Eo crassior aër est, quo terris prŏpior. Cic.—"The air is the more dense, the nearer it is to the earth."

Eo instanti.—"At that instant."

Eo magis præfulgēbat quod non vidēbātur. Tacit.—"He shone with all the greater lustre, because he was not seen." Said of a great man whose statue was insidiously removed from public view.

Eōdem collyrio medēri omnĭbus. *Prov.*—"To heal all with the same ointment." To use the same argument, or adopt the same course, with persons of all ages and classes.

Eōdem modo quo quid constituĭtur eōdem modo dissolvĭtur. Coke.—"In the same manner in which an agreement is made, it is dissolved." If made by deed, it must be dissolved by deed.

——*Epicuri de grege porcum.* Hor.—"One of the swinish herd of Epicurus."

Eques ipso mĕlior Bellerophonte. Hor.—"A better horseman than Bellerophon himself." Bellerophon was master of the winged horse Pegasus.

——*Equo frænāto est auris in ore.* Hor.—"The ear of a bridled horse is in his mouth." He is guided by the bit, not by words.

Equĭtis quoque jam migrāvit ab aure voluptas
Omnis, ad incertos ŏcŭlos, et gaudia vana. HOR.
—"In these days, our knights have transferred all pleasure from the hearing to the eyes that may deceive, and frivolous amusements." The poet rebukes the Roman *equites* for their love of the shows of the Circus and the amphitheatre.

Equus Seiānus.—"The horse of Seius." Cneius Seius, a Roman citizen, possessed a horse of singular size and beauty, and supposed to be sprung from those of Diomedes, king of Thrace. Seius was put to death by Antony, and the horse was bought for a large price by Cornelius Dolabella. He in his turn was conquered by Cassius, and fell in battle; upon which the horse came into the hands of Cassius. He slaying himself on being defeated by Antony, the horse came into Antony's possession; who was afterwards defeated by Augustus, and put himself to death. The possession of this horse was considered so disastrous to its owner, that "The horse of Seius" became a proverbial expression for a thing that was supposed to bring ill luck.

Erant in officio, sed tamen qui mallent imperantium mandāta interpretāri, quam exsĕqui. TACIT.—"They attended to their duties, but still as preferring rather to cavil at the commands of their rulers, than to obey them." Quoted by Lord Bacon in his Essays.

Erant quibus appetentior famæ vĭderētur, quando sapientĭbus cupīdo gloriæ novissĭma exuĭtur. TACIT.—"There were some to whom he seemed too greedy of fame, at a time when the desire of glory, that last of all desires, is by the wise laid aside." Milton was probably indebted to this passage for his line on ambition,
"That last infirmity of noble minds."

Ergo haud diffĭcĭle est perĭtūram arcessĕre summam,
Lancĭbus oppŏsĭtis, vel matris imāgĭne fractā. JUV.
—"Therefore there is no scruple in borrowing a sum, soon to be squandered, by pawning their plate, or the battered likeness of their mother."

——*Erĭpe te moræ.* HOR.—"Away with all delay."

——*Erĭpe turpi*
Colla jugo. Liber, liber sum, dic age.— HOR.

—"Rescue your neck from this vile yoke; come, say, I am free, I am free."

Erĭpĭte isti gladium, qui sui est impos anĭmi. PLAUT.—"Take away the sword from him who is not in possession of his senses."

Erĭpit interdum, modo dat medicīna salūtem. OVID.—"Medicine sometimes takes away health, sometimes bestows it."

Erĭpuit cœlo fulmen, sceptrumque tyrannis.—"He snatched the lightning from heaven, and the sceptre from tyrants." This line, an adaptation of one from Manilius, was inscribed by the French minister Turgot on a medal struck in honour of Benjamin Franklin. The allusion is to his discovery that lightning is produced by electricity, and to the support which he gave to his country in the assertion of its independence of the British crown. See *Solvitque animis, &c.*

Errāmus si ullam terrārum partem immūnem a perīcŭlo credĭmus. SEN.—"We are mistaken if we believe that there is any part of the world free from danger."

Errantem in viam redŭcĭto.—"Bring back him who has strayed, into the right way." The duty of the pastor of the flock.

——*Errat, et illinc*
Huc venit, hinc illuc, et quoslĭbet occŭpat artus
Spīrĭtus; eque feris humāna in corpŏra transit,
Inque feras noster.—— OVID.

—"The soul wanders about and comes from that spot to this, from this to that, and takes possession of any limbs it may; it both passes from the beasts into human bodies, and from us into the beasts." The Pythagorean doctrine of the transmigration of the soul.

Esse bonum făcĭle est, ubi quod vetet esse remōtum est. OVID.—"It is easy to be good, when that which would forbid it is afar off." It is easy to be virtuous when we are not exposed to temptation.

Esse quam vidēri malim.—"I would rather *be*, than *seem* to be."

Esse quoque in Fatis reminiscĭtur affŏre tempus
Quo mare, quo tellus, correptaque rēgia cœli
Ardeat; et mundi moles operōsa labōret. OVID.

—"He remembers too that it was in the decrees of fate,

that a time should come when the sea, the earth, and the palace of heaven, seized by the flames, should be burnt; and the laboriously-wrought fabric of the universe should be in danger of perishing." So we read in Scripture, "But the day of the Lord will come as a thief in the night; in which the heavens shall pass away with a great noise, and the elements shall melt with fervent heat, the earth also, and the works that are therein, shall be burnt up." 2 *Pet.* iii.

Esse solent magno damna minōra bono. OVID.—"Trivial losses are often of great benefit."

Est amīcus socius mensæ, et non permanēbit in die necessitātis. —"Some friend is a companion at the table, and will not continue in the day of thy affliction."—*Ecclus.* vi. 10. This, however, is only said of the class of *so-called* friends.

——*Est anĭmus lucis contemptor!* VIRG.—"My soul is a contemner of the light!"

——*Est anĭmus tibi*
Rerumque prudens, et secundis
Tempŏrĭbus dubiisque rectus. HOR.
—"You have a mind endowed with prudence in the affairs of life, and upright, as well in prosperity as in adversity."

Est avidĭtas dives, et pauper pudor. PHÆD.—"Covetousness is rich, while modesty starves."

——*Est bonus ut mĕlior vir*
Non ălius quisquam.— HOR.
—"He is so good a man, that no one can be better."

Est brevitāte opus, ut currat sententia.— HOR.—"There is need of conciseness that the sentence may run agreeably."

Est demum vera felīcitas, felīcitāte dignum vidēri. PLINY *the Younger.*—"The truest happiness, in fine, consists in the consciousness that you are deserving of happiness."

Est egentissĭmus in suâ re.—"He is much straitened in circumstances."

Est etiam misĕris piĕtas, et in hoste probātur. OVID.—"Towards the wretched there is a duty, and even in an enemy it is praised."

Est etiam, ubi profecto damnum præstet făcĕre, quam lucrum. PLAUT.—"There are occasions when it is undoubtedly better to make loss than gain."

——*Est hic,*
Est ubi vis, animus si te non deficit æquus. HOR.
—"[Happiness] is to be found here, it is everywhere, if you possess a well-regulated mind."

Est in aquâ dulci non invidiōsa voluptās. OVID.—"In pure water there is a pleasure begrudged by none."

Est ipsi res angusta domi.—"His means are but very limited."

Est mihi, sitque, precor, nostris diuturnior annis,
Filia; quâ felix sospite semper ero. OVID.
—"I have a daughter, and long, I pray, may she survive my years; so long as she is in comfort I shall ever be happy."

Est miserōrum, ut malevolentes sint atque invideant bonis. PLAUT.—"'Tis the nature of the wretched to be ill-disposed, and to envy the fortunate."

Est modus in rebus; sunt certi dēnique fines,
Quos ultra citrāque nequit consistĕre rectum. HOR.
—"There is a medium in all things; there are, in fact, certain bounds, on either side of which rectitude cannot exist." The evils which have been produced by fanaticism, prompted by motives really good, are almost equal to those which have sprung from confirmed vice. The poet wisely commends the *golden mean.*

——*Est multi fābŭla plena joci.* OVID.—"It is a short story, but full of fun."

Est natūra hŏmĭnum novitātis ăvĭda. PLINY *the Elder.*—"Man is by nature fond of novelty."

Estne Dei sedes nisi terra, et pontus, et aër,
Et cœlum, et virtus? Supĕros quid quærĭmus ultra?
Jūpĭter est, quodcunque vides, quocunque movēris. LUCAN.
—"Has God any other seat than the earth, and the sea and the air, and the heavens, and virtue? Beyond these why do we seek God? Whatever you see, he is in it wherever you move, he is there." The doctrine of Pantheism.

Est nĭtĭdus, vitroque magis perlucĭdus omni
Fons.—— OVID.
—"The fountain is limpid and clearer than any glass."

Est ŏpĕræ prĕtium duplĭcis pernoscĕre juris
Natūram —— HOR.

—"'Tis worth your while to know the nature of these two kinds of sauce." A good motto for a disciple of Kitchener or Soyer.

Est pater ille quem nuptiæ demonstrant. *Law Max.*—"He is the father whom the marriage-rites point out as such." Each man must be content to father his wife's children, unless he can show a satisfactory reason to the contrary.

Est profectò Deus, qui quæ nos gĕrĭmus auditque et videt. PLAUT.—"There is undoubtedly a God who both hears and sees the things which we do."

Est proprium stultitiæ aliōrum cernĕre vĭtia, oblivisci suōrum. CIC.—"It is the province of folly to discover the faults of others, and forget its own."

——*Est quædam flere voluptas;*
Explētur lăchrymis, egĕrĭturque dolor. OVID.
—"There is, in weeping, a certain luxury; grief is soothed and alleviated by tears."

——*Est quiddam gestus edendi.* OVID.—"One's mode of eating is of some importance."

Est quoddam prodīre tenus, si non datur ultra. HOR.—"'Tis something to have advanced thus far, even though it be not granted to go farther." Failure in a laudable attempt is far from being a thing to be ashamed of.

Est quoque cunctārum nŏvĭtas carissĭma rerum. OVID.—"Novelty is, of all things, the most sought after."

Est rosa flos Vĕnĕris; quo dulcia furta latērent,
Harpŏcrăti matris dona dicāvit Amor.
Inde rosam mensis hospes suspendit amīcis,
Convīvæ ut sub eâ dicta tăcenda sciant.
—"The rose is the flower of Venus; in order that his sweet thefts might be concealed, Love dedicated this gift of his mother to Harpocrates. Hence it is that the host hangs it up over his friendly board, that the guests may know how to keep silence upon what is said beneath it." Harpocrates was the god of silence. Hence our expression, "It was said under the rose."

Est tempus quando nihil, est tempus quando ălĭquid, nullum tamen est tempus in quo dicenda sunt omnia.—"There is a time when nothing may be said, a time when some things may be said, but no time when all things may be said."

Est via sublīmis, cœlo manifesta serēno,
Lactea nomen habet, candōre notăbilis ipso. OVID.
—"There is a way on high, easily seen in a clear sky, and which, remarkable for its very whiteness, receives the name of the Milky Way."

Esto perpĕtua.—"Be thou everlasting." The last words of Father Paul Sarpi, spoken in reference to his country, Venice.

Esto quod es; quod sunt ălii, sine quemlĭbet esse:
Quod non es, nolis; quod potes esse, velis.
—"Be what you really are; let any other person be what others are. Do not wish to be that which you are not, and wish to be that which you can be."

Esto quod esse vidĕris.—"Be what you seem to be." Motto of Lord Sondes.

Esto, ut nunc multi, dives tibi, pauper amīcis. JUV.—"Be, as many are now-a-days, rich to yourself, poor to your friends."

Esurienti ne occurras.—"Do not encounter a starving man." An enemy reduced to desperation is likely to prove formidable.

Et cætĕra.—"And the rest." Denoted by—&c.

——*Et credis cĭnĕres curāre sepultos?* VIRG.—"And do you suppose that the ashes of the dead care for what passes on earth?"

Et dicam, Mea sunt; injĭciamque manus. OVID.—"And I will say, 'They are mine,' and will lay hands on them."

Et dubitāmus adhuc virtūtem extendĕre factis? VIRG.—"And do we hesitate to extend our glory by our deeds?"

Et errat longè meâ quidem sententiâ,
Qui impĕrium credit grăvius esse aut stabĭlius
Vī quod fit, quam illud, quod amicĭtiâ adjungĭtur. TER.
—"He is very much mistaken, in my opinion, at all events, who thinks that an authority is more firm, or more lasting, which is established by force, than that which is founded on affection."

Et făcĕre et pati fortia Romānum est. LIVY.—"To act bravely and to suffer bravely is the part of a Roman."

Et fert suspensos, corde micante, gradus. OVID.—"And with palpitating heart he advances on tiptoe."

Et genus et formam regīna pecūnia donat HOR.—"Money,

that queen, bestows both birth and beauty." Money becomes the substitute for high lineage and good looks.

Et genus et proăvos, et quæ non fēcĭmus ipsi,
Vix ea nostra voco.—— Ovid.
—"High lineage and ancestors, and such advantages as we have not made ourselves, all these I scarcely call our own."

Et genus et virtus, nisi cum re, vīlior algâ est. Hor.—"Virtue and high birth, unless accompanied by wealth, are deemed more worthless than sea-weed." That is, by the unthinking part of the community.

Et lăteat vĭtium proxĭmĭtāte boni. Ovid.—"And let each fault lie concealed under the name of the good quality to which it is the nearest akin." See *Et mala*, &c.

Et latro, et cautus præcingĭtur ense viātor;
Ille sed insĭdias, hic sibi portat opem. Ovid.
—"Both the cut-throat and the wary traveller is girded with the sword; but the one carries it for the purposes of crime, the other as a means of defence."

Et magis adducto pomum decerpĕre ramo,
Quam de cœlātâ sūmĕre lance juvat. Ovid.
—"It is more gratifying too, to pull down a branch and pluck an apple, than to take one from a graven dish."

Et mala sunt vīcīna bonis; errōre sub illo
Pro vĭtio virtus crīmĭna sæpe dedit. Ovid.
—"There are bad qualities too near akin to good ones: by confounding the one for the other, a virtue has often borne the blame for a vice." See *Et lateat*, &c.

Et male tornatos incūdi reddĕre versus. Hor.—"And to return ill-polished verses to the anvil."

Et mea cymba semel vastâ percussa procellâ
Illum, quo læsa est, horret adīre locum. Ovid.
—"My bark too, once struck by the overwhelming storm, dreads to approach the spot on which it has been shattered."

Et meæ, (si quid loquar audiendum,)
Vocis accēdet bona pars. Hor.
—"Then, if I can offer anything worth hearing, my voice shall readily join in the general acclamation."

Et mihi, Prōpŏsitum perfĭce, dixit, opus. Ovid.—"And said to me, Complete the work that you design."

Et mihi res, non me rebus, submittĕre conor. Hor.—"I endeavour to conquer circumstances, not to submit to them."

Et mĭnĭmæ vires frangĕre quassa valent. Ovid.—"A very little violence is able to break a thing once cracked." If we give way to dejection, we shall be unable to struggle against the caprice of fortune.

Et monēre, et monēri, proprium est veræ amicitiæ. Cic.—"To advise, and be advised, is the duty of true friendship."

Et moveant primos publĭca verba sonos. Ovid.—"And let the topics of the day lead to the first words."

Et nati natōrum, et qui nascentur ab illis. Virg.—"The children of our children, and those who shall be born of them." Our latest posterity.

Et neque jam color est misto candōre rubōri;
Nec vigor, et vires, et quæ modo visa placēbant;
Nec corpus rĕmănet—— Ovid.
—"And now, no longer is his complexion of white mixed with red; neither his vigour nor his strength, nor the points which charmed when seen so lately, nor even his body, now remains."

Et nova fictaque nuper habēbunt verba fidem, si
Græco fonte cadunt parcè detorta.—— Hor.
—"And new and lately invented terms will have authority, if they are derived from Greek sources, with but little deviation."

Et nulli cessūra fides, sine crīmĭne mores,
Nūdăque simplicitas, purpureusque pudor. Ovid.
—"A fidelity that will yield to none, manners above reproach, ingenuousness without guile, and blushing modesty."

Et nunc omnis ager, nunc omnis partŭrit arbos;
Nunc frondent sylvæ, nunc formosissĭmus annus. Virg.
—"And now every field, now every tree, is budding forth; now the woods look green; now most beauteous is the year." A description of Spring.

Et peccāre nefas, aut prĕtium est mori. Hor.—"It is forbidden to sin, or the reward is death." The sin to which the poet alludes, is that of adultery, as punished by the Scythians. So in Scripture, "The wages of sin is death" *Rom.* vi. 23.

——*Et Phœbo digna locūti,*
Quique sui mĕmŏres ălios fecēre merendo ;
Omnĭbus his nĭveâ cinguntur tempŏra vittâ. VIRG.
—"Those who have uttered things worthy of Phœbus, and those who have made others mindful of them by their merits, all these have their temples bound with the snow-white fillet." In his description of the rewards of Elysium, the poet classes his brethren, the disciples of Phœbus, with the benefactors of mankind.

Et pudet, et mĕtuo, semperque eădemque prĕcāri,
Ne subeant ănĭmo tædia justa tuo. OVID.
—"I am both ashamed and I dread to be always making the same entreaties, lest a justifiable disgust should take possession of your feelings."

——*Et quæ sibi quisque timēbat,*
Unĭus in misĕri exĭtium conversa tulēre. VIRG.
—"And what each man dreaded for himself, they bore lightly, when centred in the destruction of one wretched creature." A picture of the readiness with which man makes a scapegoat of his fellow-man.

Et quando ubĕrior vĭtiŏrum cōpia? Quando
Major avārĭtiæ pătuit sinus? Alea quando
Hos ănĭmos?—— JUV.
—"And when was vice ever in greater force? When was there ever a greater scope for avarice? When did the dice more thoroughly enthral the minds of men?"

Et qui ăliis nocent, ut in ălios liberāles sint, in eâdem sunt injustitiâ, ut si in suam rem aliēna convertant. CIC.—"And those who injure one party to benefit another, are quite as unjust, as if they converted the property of others to their own benefit."

——*Et qui nolunt occīdĕre quenquam*
Posse volunt.—— JUV.
—"Even those who have no wish to slay another, are wishful to have the power." In allusion to the ambitious thirst for power.

Et quiescenti agendum est, et agenti quiescendum est. SEN.—"He who is indolent should labour, and he who labours should take repose."

Et rident stŏlĭdi verba Latīna.— OVID.—"And the fools laugh at Latin words."

Et sanguis et spīrĭtus pecūnia mortālibus. *Prov.*—"Money is both blood and life to men."

Et sĕquentia.—"And what follows." Generally written in short, *et seq.*

Et si non ălĭquâ nocuisses, mortuus esses. VIRG.—"And if you could not have hurt him some way or other, you would have died (of spite)."

Et sic de simĭlĭbus.—"And so of the like."

Et tĕnuit nostras numerōsus Horātius aures. OVID.—"Horace too, with his varied numbers, charmed my ears."

Et vĕniam pro laude peto; laudātus abunde,
Non fastīditus si tibi, lector, ero. OVID.
—"Pardon too, in place of praise, do I crave; abundantly, reader, shall I be praised, if I do not cause thee disgust."

Et vitam impendĕre vero.—"And in the cause of truth to lay down life."

Etĕnim omnes artes quæ ad humanitātem pertĭnent, habent quoddam commūne vincŭlum, et quasi cognatiōne quâdam inter se continentur. CIC.—"All the arts appertaining to civilized life, are united by a kind of common bond, and are connected, as it were, by a certain relationship."

Etiam capillus unus habet umbram suam. SYR.—"Even a single hair has its shadow." The most trivial thing has its utility and importance.

Etiam cĕlerĭtas in desidĕrio, mora est. SYR.—"In desire, even swiftness itself is delay."

Etiam fera animālia, si clausa tĕneas, virtūtis obliviscuntur.—"Savage animals even, if you keep them in confinement, forget their ferocious disposition."

Etiam fortes viros subĭtis terrēri. TACIT.—"The minds of resolute men even may be alarmed by sudden events." And on the other hand, weak men are then found resolute.

Etiam in secundissĭmis rebus maxĭme est utendum consĭlio amīcōrum. CIC.—"Even in our greatest prosperity, we ought by all means to take the advice of our friends."

Etiam innocentes cogit mentīri dolor. SYR.—"Pain makes even the innocent liars."

Etiam oblivisci quod scis, interdum expĕdit. SYR.—"It is sometimes as well to forget what you know."

——*Etiam Parnassia laurus*
Parva sub ingenti matris se subjĭcit umbrâ. VIRG.

—"Even the Parnassian laurel shelters itself beneath the dense shade of its mother." Said of the suckers which shoot up from the root.

Etiam sanāto vulnĕre cicātrix manet. SYR.—"Even when the wound is healed the scar remains." Injuries are more often forgiven than forgotten.

Etiam si Cato dicat. Prov.—"Even if Cato were to say so" —I would not believe it: Cato being a man of the most scrupulous integrity.

——*Etiam stultis acuit ingĕnium fames.* PHÆD.—"Hunger sharpens even the wits of fools."

Etsi pervīvo usque ad summam ætātem, tamen
Breve spatium est perferundi quæ mĭnĭtas mihi. PLAUT.
—"Though I should live even to an extreme age, still, short is the time for enduring what you threaten me with."

——*Euge poetæ.* PERS.—"Well done, ye poets!"

Eum ausculta, cui quătuor sunt aures. Prov.—"Listen to him who has four ears." Attend to persons who show themselves more ready to hear than to speak.

Eventus stultōrum magister est. LIV.—"Experience is the master of fools." Fools are only to be taught by experience.

Eversis omnĭbus rebus, quum consĭlio profĭci nihil possit, una rătio vidētur; quidquid evĕnĕrit, ferre moderāte. CIC.—"When we are utterly ruined, and when no counsel can profit us, there seems to be one way open to us; whatever may happen, to bear it with moderation."

Evolāre rus ex urbe tanquam ex vincŭlis. CIC.—"To fly from the town into the country, as though from chains."

Ex abundanti cautēlā.—"From excess of precaution."

Ex abūsu non argŭitur ad usum. Law Max.—"We must not argue, from the *abuse* of a thing, against the *use* of it."

Ex abūsu non argumentum ad desuetūdinem. Law Max.—"The abuse of a thing is no argument for its discontinuance."

Ex æquo et bono judicāre.—"To judge in fairness and equity."

Ex arēnâ funĭculum nectis. Prov.—"You are for making a rope of sand." You are attempting an impossibility.

Ex aurĭbus cognoscĭtur ăsĭnus. Prov.—"An ass is known by his ears."

Ex căthĕdrâ.—"From the chair," or "pulpit." Coming from high authority, and therefore to be relied on.

Ex concesso.—"From what has been conceded." An argument *ex concesso*, or from what the opponent has admitted.

Ex contractu.—"From contract."

Ex curiâ.—"Out of court."

Ex dēbĭto justĭtiæ.—"From what is due to justice."

Ex delicto.—"From the crime."

Ex desuetūdĭne amittuntur privilĕgia. Law Max.—"Rights are forfeited by non-user."

Ex diuturnitāte tempŏris omnia præsumuntur esse solemnĭter acta. Law Max.—"From length of time everything is presumed to have been solemnly done."

Ex eōdem ore călĭdum et frīgĭdum efflāre.—"To blow hot and cold with the same mouth." This adage is founded on the Fable of the Satyr and the Traveller.

Ex factis non ex dictis amīci pensandi. LIV.—"Friends are to be estimated from their deeds, not their words."

Ex facto jus ŏrĭtur. Law Max.—"The law arises from the fact." Until the nature of the crime is known, the law cannot be put in force.

Ex hăbĭtu hŏmĭnes mĕtientes. CIC.—"Estimators of men from their outward appearances."

——*Ex humĭli magna ad fastigia rerum*
Extollit, quŏties vŏluit fortūna jocāri. JUV.
—"As oft as fortune is in sportive mood, she raises men from an humble station to the highest pinnacle of power."

Ex inimīco cōgĭta posse fiĕri amīcum. SEN.—"Think that you may possibly make of an enemy a friend." Avoid extremes in enmities. See *Amicum*, &c.

Ex magnâ cœnâ stŏmăcho fit maxĭma pœna,
Ut sis nocte levis, sit tibi cœna brevis.
—"From a heavy supper great uneasiness to the stomach is produced; that you may enjoy a good night's rest, let your supper be moderate." A Leonine or rhyming couplet, not improbably issued by the School of Health at Salerno.

Ex malis mōrĭbus bonæ leges natæ sunt. COKE.—"From bad manners good laws have sprung."

Ex mero motu.—"From a mere motion;" of one's own free will.

Ex necessitāte rei.—"From the urgency of the case."

Ex nihilo nihil fit.—"From nothing nothing is made." Nothing can come of nothing.

Ex officio.—"By virtue of his office."

Ex ōtio plus negōtii quam ex negōtio habēmus. *Old Scholiast.* —"From our leisure we get more to do, than from our business." Especially when it gives us the opportunity of falling into mischief.

Ex parte. *Law Term.*—"On one part." Evidence given on one side only is called *ex parte*.

Ex pede Hercŭlem. *Prov.*—"You may judge of Hercules from his foot." Pythagoras ascertained the length of the foot of Hercules by taking the length of the Olympic stadium or course, which was six hundred feet, originally measured by the foot of the hero. He thence came to the conclusion that his height was six feet seven inches. From this circumstance was formed the proverb, meaning that we may judge of the whole from the part.

Ex post facto. *Law Term.*—"Done after another thing." A law enacted purposely to take cognizance of an offence already committed, is, so far as that individual offence is concerned, an *ex post facto* law.

Ex quovis ligno non fit Mercurius. *Prov.*—"A Mercury is not to be made out of every log." Mercury being a graceful god, it was not out of every piece of wood that his statue could be made.

Ex tempŏre.—"Off-hand." On the spur of the moment, or, without preparation.

Ex umbrâ in solem. *Prov.*—"Out of the shade into the sunshine." You have rendered clear what was obscure before.

Ex ungue leōnem. *Prov.*—"You can tell the lion by his claw." The master's hand may be known in the specimen.

Ex uno disce omnes.—"From one learn all." From one example you may judge of all. What has been said of one may be said of the rest. See *Crimine ab uno*, &c.

Ex uno specta omnia. *Prov.*—"From one circumstance judge of all."

Ex vitâ discēdo, tanquam ex hospĭtio, non tanquam ex domo. Cic.—"I depart from life as from an inn, not as from my home." I die without regret, just as one quits an inn, where he has been a sojourner for a time only.

Ex vĭtio altĕrius săpiens emendat suum. Syr.—"From the faults of another a wise man corrects his own."

Ex vĭtŭlo bos fit.—"The calf becomes an ox." Small things enlarge to great.

Ex vultĭbus hŏmĭnum mores collĭgĕre.—"To judge of men's manners from their countenance."

Exceptio probat rĕgŭlam. *Law Max.*—"The exception prove the rule." The fact of there being an exception proves the existence of a rule.

Excepto quod non simul esses, cætĕra lætus.—"Except that you were not with me, I was in other respects happy."

Excessit ex ephēbis.—"He is out of his minority." He is of age, and has come to years of discretion.

——*Exclŭdat jurgĭa finis.* Hor.—"Let this settlement terminate all disputes."

Excusātio non petĭta fit accusātio manifesta. *Law Max.*—"An excuse that is uncalled for is a convincing proof of guilt."

Exeat.—"Let him depart." The leave given for temporary absence from college is so called.

——*Exeat aulâ*
Qui vult esse pius—— Lucret.
—"Let him withdraw from court, who wishes to remain uncorrupted."

Exēgi monumentum ære perennius. Hor.—"I have completed a monument more durable than brass." The prophecy of a poet, who formed a just estimate of his works.

Exempli gratia.—"For example." For instance. Usually written *e. g.*

Exemplo plus quam ratiōne vīvĭmus.—"We live more by example than by reason." On this is based the tyranny of fashion.

Exemplo quodcunque malo committĭtur ipsi
Displĭcet auctōri ; prima est hæc ultio, quod, se
Jūdĭce, nemo nocens absolvĭtur—— Juv.
—"Every deed that will furnish a precedent for crime, must be condemned by the author himself. This is his first punishment, that, being his own judge, no guilty man is acquitted."

——*Exempta juvat spinis e plūrĭbus una.* Hor.—"A single

thorn extracted out of many, is a point gained." As the passage stands in the original, the poet puts the question, "Of what use is it to have one thorn plucked out when you are smarting from many?"

Exercent illi sŏciæ commercia linguæ:
Per gestum res est significanda mihi. OVID.
—"They enjoy the intercourse of a common language: by me everything has to be signified by gestures."

Exercitātio optĭmus est magister. *Prov.*—"Practice is the best master."

Exercitātio potest omnia. *Prov.*—"Continued practice can accomplish everything." "Practice makes perfect."

Exeunt omnes.—"All depart." A stage direction.

——*Exi,*
Intŏnat horrendum. JUV.
—"Begone! she thunders out with awful voice."

Exĭgit et a stătuis farīnas. *Prov.*—"He exacts meal from a statue even." He can make something out of everything, and can "get blood out of a stone."

Exĭgĭte ut mores tĕnĕros ceu pollĭce ducat,
Ut si quis cerâ vultum facit—— JUV.
—"Require him, with his thumb, as it were, to press into shape their unformed morals, just as one forms a face from wax." Said with reference to the importance of good training in tender years. The poet alludes to the Roman mode of taking portraits in wax.

Exĭgua est virtus, præstāre silentia rebus;
At contra, gravis est culpa, tacenda loqui. OVID.
—"'Tis a small merit to hold silence upon a matter; on the other hand, it is a serious fault to speak of things on which we ought to be silent."

Exĭgui nŭmĕro, sed bello vīvĭda virtus. VIRG.—"Few in number, but valiant in spirit."

Exiguum est ad legem bonum esse. SEN.—"It is but a slight matter to be good to the letter of the law only."

Exīlis domus est, ubi non et multa supersunt,
Et dŏmĭnum fallunt, et prosunt fūrĭbus—— HOR.
—"It is a poor house indeed, in which there are not many superfluities, which escape the master's notice, and fall a prey to thieves."

——*Exĭtio est ăvĭdis mare nautis.* HOR.—"The sea is the

destruction of avaricious sailors." Few will think this an apposite maxim at the present day.

Exĭtus in dubio est: audēbĭmus ultĭma, dixit;
Vidērit, audentes forsne Deusne juvet. OVID.
—"'The result is doubtful, we will dare the utmost,' said he, 'Be it chance or be it a Providence that aids the bold, let him see to it.'"

Experientia docet. *Prov.*—"Experience teaches." Or, as our proverb has it, "Experience makes fools wise."

Expĕrimentum crucis.—"Trial by the cross." Alluding, probably, to a mode of eliciting truth by torture.

——*Experto crede.* VIRG.—"Believe one who speaks from experience."

Experto crede Roberto.—"Believe Robert, who speaks from experience." A proverb commonly used in the middle ages; but its origin does not appear to be known. Burton uses it in the Introduction to his Anatomy of Melancholy.

——*Expertus mĕtuit*—— HOR.—"He who has experienced it, dreads it."

Expĕtuntur divĭtiæ ad perficiendas voluptātes. CIC.—"Riches are sought to minister to our pleasures."

Explōrant adversa viros: perque aspĕra duro
Nītĭtur ad laudem virtus interrĭta clivo. SIL. ITAL.
—"Adversity proves men; and virtue, undaunted, struggles through difficulties, and up the steep height, to gain the reward of fame."

Expressa nocent, non expressa non nocent. *Law Max.*—"What is expressed may be injurious, what is not expressed is not so." Said in reference to written contracts.

Expressio unīus est exclūsio altĕrīus. *Law Max.*—"The naming of one man implies the exclusion of another."

——*Extinctus amābĭtur idem.* HOR.—"The same man will be beloved when dead." Men, in general, meet with more justice from their fellow-men, when dead, than when alive.

Extra lutum pedes habes. *Prov.*—"You have got your feet out of the mud." You are well out of that difficulty.

Extra telōrum jactum.—"Beyond bow-shot." Out of harm's way. See *Ego post*, &c.

Extrēma gaudii luctus occŭpat. *Prov.*—"Grief borders on the extremes of gladness." "If you laugh to-day, you may cry to-morrow," is an old saying.

Extrēma manus nondum opĕrĭbus ejus impŏsĭta est.—"The finishing hand has not yet been put to his work."

Extrēmis dĭgĭtis attingĕre.—"To touch with the finger ends." To handle a matter lightly.

Extrēmis malis extrēma remĕdia. *Prov.*—"Extreme evils require extreme remedies." "Desperate maladies require desperate remedies."

Exuĕrint sylvestrem ănĭmum, cultuque frequenti,
In quascunque voces artes, haud tarda sequentur. VIRG.
—"They lay aside their rustic nature, and by repeated instruction will advance apace in any arts into which you may initiate them."

Exul, inops erres, aliēnaque līmĭna lustres ;
Exiguumque petas ore tremente cibum. OVID.
—"An exile, and in need, mayst thou wander, and mayst thou survey the thresholds of others, and beg with tremulous lips a morsel of food."

F.

F. C. See *Fieri curavit.*

Fabas indulcet fames. *Prov.*—"Hunger sweetens beans." "Hunger is the best sauce."

Faber compĕdes quas fecit ipse
Gestet—— AUSON.
—"Let the blacksmith wear the fetters which he himself has forged." See *Tute hoc*, &c.

Faber quisque fortūnæ suæ. SALL.—"Every man is the architect of his own fortune."

Fabricando fabri fimus. *Prov.*—"By working we become workmen." "Practice makes perfect."

Fābŭla, nec sentis, totâ jactāris in urbe. OVID.—"You are the talk, and yet you do not perceive it, of the whole city."

Fac simile.—"Do the like." Read as one word, it means an exact imitation or copy of anything.

Fac totum.—"Do everything." Hence our word *factotum*, meaning a "handy man."

Facētiārum apud præpotentes in longum memŏria est. TACIT.—"Men in power do not readily forget a joke."

Faciam ut hujus loci semper memĭnĕris. TER.—"I will make you always remember this place."

——*Facies non omnĭbus una,*
Nec diversa tamen, qualis decet esse sorōrum. OVID.
—"The features are not the same in all, nor yet very different; they are such as those of sisters ought to be." A description of "a family likeness."

Facies *tua compŭtat annos.*—"Your face reckons your years;" or, "Your face tells your age."

Făcĭle *est impĕrium in bonis.* PLAUT.—"The sway is easy over the good."

Făcĭle *est inventis addĕre. Prov.*—"It is easy to improve what has been already invented."

Făcĭlè *imprŏbi malĭtiâ suâ aspergunt probos.*—"Wicked men with their malice easily asperse the characters of the good."

Făcĭlè *invĕnies et pejōrem, et pejus morātam,*
Meliōrem neque tu repĕries, neque sol videt. PLAUT.
—"You may easily find a worse woman, and one of worse manners; a better one you will not find, nor does the sun behold such."

Făcĭlè *omnes cum valēmus recta consĭlia*
Ægrōtis damus. Tu, si hic sis, ălĭter senties. TER.
—"When we are in health, we are all able to give good advice to the sick. You, if you were in my place, would think otherwise."

Făcĭlè *princeps.*—"The acknowledged chief." The one who stands first, beyond a doubt.

——*Făcĭlis descensus Averni,*
Sed rĕvocāre gradum, supĕrasque evādĕre ad aurās,
Hic labor, hoc opus est—— VIRG.
—"Easy the descent to hell; but to retrace your steps, and to regain the upper world, that is the difficulty, that the labour." The poet alludes to the descent of Æneas to the Infernal regions; but the figure may be applied to the readiness with which we may fall into evil courses, and the difficulty of retracing our steps.

Făcĭlius *crescit quam inchoātur dignĭtas.* SYR.—"Increase of dignity is more easily gained than the first step."

Făcĭlius *sit Nili caput invenīre. Prov.*—"It would be easier to discover the sources of the Nile."

——*Făcĭnus audax incĭpit,*
Qui cum opulento pauper hŏmĭne cœpit rem habēre aut negōtium. PLAUT.

—"A poor man who commences to have business or dealings with an opulent one, commences upon a rash undertaking."

——*Făcĭnus majōris abollæ.* JUV.—"The crime of a more dignified garb." A crime committed by a philosopher of more dignified character. The *abolla* was the cloak worn by philosophers.

——*Făcĭnus quos inquĭnat æquat.* LUCAN.—"Those whom guilt defiles, it places on a level." The highest and the lowest are equally degraded by guilt; but, if anything, the former is the most culpable.

Facit gratum fortūna, quam nemo videt. SYR.—"The good fortune which no one sees, makes a man grateful for it." Because he is not the object of envy.

Făcĭto alĭquid ŏpĕris, ut semper te diabŏlus invĕniat occupātum. ST. JEROME.—"Be busy about something; so that the devil may always find you occupied."

Făciunt næ intelligendo, ut nihil intellĭgant? TER.—"By being thus knowing, do they not show that they know nothing at all?"

Facta canam; sed erunt qui me finxisse loquantur. OVID.—"I shall sing of facts; but there will be some to say that I have invented fictions."

——*Factis ignoscĭte nostris,*
Si scelus ingĕnio scitis abesse meo. OVID.
—"Forgive my deeds, inasmuch as ye know that impiety was far from my intention."

——*Facto pius et scelerātus eōdem.* OVID.—"A father, affectionate and unnatural in the self-same act." Said of Agenor, when he dismissed his son Cadmus to roam over the world in search of his daughter Europa.

——*Factum ăbiit; monumenta manent.* OVID.—"The occurrence has passed away; the memorial of it still remains." The motto of the London Numismatic Society.

Factum est illud; fĭĕri infectum non potest. PLAUT.—"The thing is done, it cannot be undone."

Fæx pŏpŭli.—"The dregs of the people." The scum of the population.

Fallăcia alia aliam trudit. TER.—"One deception makes way for another." One lie is supported by another.

——*Fallentis sēmĭta vitæ.* HOR.—"The path of a life that passes unnoticed."

Fallit enim vĭtium, spĕcie virtūtis et umbrâ,
Cum sit triste habĭtu, vultuque et veste sevērum. JUV.
—"For vice deceives us, under the form and guise of virtue, when serious in manner and reserved in countenance and dress." A rebuke of sanctified hypocrisy.

Fallĭtur egrĕgio quisquis sub princĭpe credit
Servĭtium. Nunquam libertas grātior extat
Quam sub rege pio—— CLAUD.
—"He is mistaken who considers it slavery to be ruled by a virtuous prince. Never has liberty more charms, than under a pious king."

Fallor? An arma sonant? Non fallĭmur, arma sonābant;
Mars venit, et vĕniens bellĭca signa dabat. OVID.
—"Am I mistaken? Or is that the clash of arms? I am not mistaken, it was the clash of arms: Mars approaches; and, as he comes, he sounds the note of war."

Falsa grammatĭca non vĭtiat concessionem. COKE.—"Bad grammar does not vitiate a grant." See *Mala Grammatica, &c.*

——*Falso damnāti crimĭne mortis.* VIRG.—"On a false charge condemned to die."

Falsus honor juvat, et mendax infāmia terret,
Quem nisi mendōsum et mendācem?—— HOR.
—"Whom, but the vicious and the liar, does misplaced praise delight, or lying slanders alarm?"

Fama, malum quo non ălind velōcius ullum,
Mobilitāte viget, viresque acquirit eundo. VIRG.
—"Rumour, than which no pest is more swift, increases by motion, and gains strength as she goes."

Famâ nihil est celĕrius. LIVY.—"Nothing travels more swiftly than scandal."

Famæ damna majōra sunt, quam quæ æstimāri possint. LIVY.
—"The loss of reputation is greater than can be possibly conceived."

Famæ laboranti non facĭlè succurrĭtur. *Prov.*—"It is not easy to repair a character when falling." It is not easy to recover a lost character.

——*Famam extendĕre factis.* VIRG.—"To extend our fame by our deeds." The motto of Linnæus.

Fames est optĭmus coquus. *Prov.*—"Hunger is the best cook."

Fames et mora bilem in nasum conciunt. *Prov.*—"Hunger

and delay summon the bile to the nostrils," i. e. "excite our wrath."

Fames optĭmum condimentum. Prov.—"Hunger is the best sauce."

Fames, pestis, et bellum, pŏpŭli sunt pernĭcies.—"Famine, pestilence, and war, are the scourges of mankind."

Familiāre est homĭnĭbus omnia sibi ignoscĕre.—"It is usual with man to forgive all his own faults." A man is an indulgent censor to himself.

Farrāgo libelli. Juv.—"The medley of my book." The "something of everything" there to be found.

——*Fas est et ab hoste docēri.* Ovid.—"It is right to be taught by an enemy even." We may profit from the oversights of our adversaries, by learning to avoid them.

Fastidientis est stŏmăchi multa degustāre. Sen.—"To taste of many dishes is a sign of a delicate stomach."

Fastus inest pulchris, sequĭturque superbia formam;
Irrīsum vultu despĭcit illa suo. Ovid.

—"Cold disdain is innate in the fair, and haughtiness accompanies beauty. By her looks she despises and she scorns him."

Fata obstant.—"The Fates are opposed." It is not his destiny.

Fata volentem ducunt, nolentem trahunt.—"The Fates lead him who is willing, and drag him who is unwilling." A maxim of the believers in predestination, that it is as well to be resigned to our fate.

Fatētur făcĭnus is qui judĭcium fugit. Law Max.—"He who flies from trial confesses his guilt." At all events, his conduct is *primâ facie* evidence against him.

Fatigātis humus cubīle est. Curt.—"To the weary the earth is a bed."

——*Fatis accēde Deisque,*
Et cole fēlīces, mĭsĕros fuge. Sīdĕra cœlo
Ut distant, flamma mari, sic ŭtĭle recto. Lucan.

—"Welcome the Fates and the Gods, caress the fortunate, and shun the wretched. As much as the stars are distant in the heavens, as much as flame differs from the sea, so much does the expedient differ from the right."

Favēte linguis. Ovid.—"Favour by your tongues," or, "Be propitious in your language." This was an usual injunction with the Romans at their sacrifices, as a word of ill-omen spoken during their celebration was considered to have an evil influence.

Fecundi călĭces quem non fecēre disertum? Hor.—"Whom have not flowing cups made eloquent?"

——*Felīces errōre suo.* Lucan.—"Happy in their error." "Where ignorance is bliss, 'tis folly to be wise." Gray.

Felīces ter et amplĭus
Quos irrupta tenet cōpŭla, nec, malis
Divulsus quærimōniis,
Suprēmâ cĭtius solvet amor die. Hor.

—"Thrice happy they, and more, whom an indissoluble union binds together, and whom love, unimpaired by evil complainings, does not separate before the last day." Applicable to the delights of connubial happiness.

Felīcĭtas multos habet amīcos. Prov.—"Prosperity has many friends." Fair-weather followers, and sun-shine friends.

Felīcitas nutrix est iracundiæ. Prov.—"Prosperity is the nurse of anger." Men who have been successful are apt to forget themselves.

Felīciter is sapit, qui perīcŭlo aliēno sapit.—"He is happy in his wisdom, who is wise at the expense of another." From the interpolated Scene in the *Mercator* of Plautus, supposed to have been written by Hermolaüs Barbarus.

Felix est cui quantulumcunque tempŏris contĭgit, bene collocātum est. Sen.—"Happy is he who has well employed his time, however short it may have been."

Felix quem făciunt aliēna perīcŭla cautum.—"Happy is he whom the perils of others put on his guard."

Felix quem făciunt aliōrum cornua cautum. Owen [*Epigr.*].—"Happy the man whom the horns of others make wary."

Felix qui nihil debet. Prov.—"Happy is he who owes nothing."

Felix qui pŏtuit rerum cognoscĕre causas. Virg.—"Happy is he who can trace the causes of things." A compliment to the philosopher, who centres his pleasure in that which is for the benefit or instruction of mankind.

——*Felix quicunque dolōre*
Altĕrius disces posse carēre tuo. Tibull.

—"Happy you, who can, by the pain of another, learn to avoid it yourself."

Felo de se. Law Latin.—"A felon of himself." One who, being, in legal estimation, of sound mind, slays himself. One who commits felony by suicide.

Feræ natūræ.—"Of a wild nature." This term is applied to animals of a savage nature, in contradistinction to those, which are under the control of man, and are called *domitæ naturæ*, "of a tame nature."

Feras, non culpes, quod mutāri non potest. Syr.—"You must endure, not blame, that which cannot be altered." "What cannot be cured must be endured."

Feras quod lædit, ut id quod prodest perfĕras. Syr.—"You must bear that which hurts, that you may gain that which profits."

Fere libenter hŏmĭnes id quod volunt credunt. Cæs.—"Men generally are willing to believe what they wish to be true." Like our saying, "The wish is father to the thought."

Ferre pulcherrĭmè secundam fortūnam et æquè adversam. Cic.—"To bear with equal gracefulness good fortune or bad."

Ferrĕus assĭduo consūmĭtur annŭlus usu. Ovid.—"By continued use a ring of iron is consumed."

Fertĭlior seges est aliēnis semper in agris,
Vicīnumque pecus grandius uber habet. Ovid.
—"The crop is ever more fruitful in our neighbour's fields, and his cows have more distended udders than our own." It is the nature of man to repine at his own lot, and to envy that of another.

Ferto, ferēris.—"Bear, and you shall be borne with." Learn to "give and take."

Fervens difficili bile tumet jecur. Hor.—"My inflamed liver swells with bile, difficult to be repressed."

Fervet avaritiâ mĭsĕroque cupīdĭne pectus? Hor.—"Does your heart burn with avarice, and the direful greed for gain?"

Fervet olla, vivit amicitia. Prov.—"While the pot boils, friendship endures."

Festīna lentè.—"Hasten slowly." Be on your guard against impetuosity. A favourite saying of the emperors Augustus and Titus. It forms the punning motto of the Onslow family.

Festināre nocet, nocet et cunctātio sæpe;
Tempŏre quæque suo qui facit, ille sapit.
—"It is bad to be in a hurry, and delay is often as bad; he is wise who does everything at its proper time."

——*Festīnat decurrĕre velox*
Floscŭlus, angustæ, misĕræque brevissĭma vitæ
Portio; dum bĭbĭmus, dum serta, unguenta, puellas
Poscĭmus, obrēpit non intellecta senectus. Juv.
—"The short-lived flower, the limited span of our fleeting and wretched existence, hastens to decay; whilst we are drinking, calling for garlands, perfumes, and women, old age steals upon us unperceived." We learn from Ovid that wine and women, unguents and garlands, all played their part in the feasts of the sensualists of Rome.

Festinātio tarda est. *Prov.*—"Haste is slow." Real despatch is insured by prudence and caution: for a thing is done "*sat cito si sat benè*," "quick enough if well enough."

——*Festo die si quid prodĕgĕris*
Profesto egēre liceat, nisi pepercĕris. Plaut.
—"If you are guilty of any extravagance on a feast day, you may be wanting on a common day, unless you are frugal."

Fiat.—"Let it be done." "So be it." An order or assent given by one in authority.

Fiat expĕrimentum in corpŏre vili.—"Let the experiment be made on a worthless body."

Fiat justĭtia, ruat cœlum.—"Let justice be done, though heaven should fall." Said of a decision formed at all hazards.

Fiat lux.—"Let there be light." *Gen.* i. 3.

Fiat mixtūra secundum artem.—"Let the mixture be made according to the rules of art." Often placed at the end of medical prescriptions.

Ficos divĭdĕre. *Prov.*—"To split figs." Said of persons who would, as we say, "flay a flint."

Ficta voluptātis causâ sit proxĭma veris. Hor.—"Let whatever is devised for the sake of entertainment have as much resemblance as possible to truth."

Fictis mĕmĭnĕrit nos jocāri fābŭlis. Phædr.—"Let it be remembered that we are amusing you with tales of fiction."

Ficum cupit. Prov.—"He wants some figs." "He is paying me so much attention to suit his own purposes." The Athenian fashionables were in the habit of visiting the cottages of the peasants, on the approach of the fig season, and treating them with great courtesy, that they might obtain the choicest of the fruit when it came to maturity.

Ficus ficus, ligōnem ligōnem vocat. Prov.—"He calls a fig a fig, a spade a spade." He is a plain, straightforward man, one who speaks his mind.

Fide abrogātâ, omnis humāna sociĕtas tollĭtur. LIV.—"Good faith abolished, all human society is destroyed."

Fidēlius rident tuguria. Prov.—"The laughter of the cottage is the most hearty." Because the laughers are free from care.

Fidem qui perdit perdĕre ultra nil potest. SYR.—"He who loses his good faith has nothing else to lose." Integrity and honour are the most valuable inheritance.

Fidem qui perdit, quo se servat in rĕlĭquum? SYR.—"He who has lost his credit, with what shall he sustain himself in future?"

Fides servanda est. PLAUT.—"Faith must be kept."

Fides sit penes auctōrem.—"Let due faith be given to the author." A phrase used by a writer when quoting from a doubtful authority.

Fiĕri curāvit.—"Caused this to be done." Often represented in monumental inscriptions by the initial letters F. C.

Fiĕri făcias. Law Lat.—"Cause it to be done." A writ by which the sheriff is commanded to levy the debt, or damages, on the defendant's goods. Sometimes called, for brevity, a *fi fa.*

Fĭgŭlus figulo invĭdet, faber fabro. Prov.—"The potter envies the potter, the blacksmith the blacksmith." So we say, "Two of a trade never agree."

Filii non plus possessiōnum quam morbōrum hærēdes sumus.—"As sons we are heirs, no less to diseases than to possessions."

Filius nullius.—"The son of no man." A bastard is so called, for he has no legal rights as a son, in respect to the inheritance of property.

Filum aquæ.—"The thread of the stream." An imaginary

line in the middle of a river, which is supposed to be the boundary of the lordships or manors on either side.

***Finge datos currus; quid agas?*——** OVID.—"Suppose the chariot were given to you; what would you do?" The question put by Apollo, when Phaëton asks him for the loan of the chariot of the Sun. The same question may be asked of one who aspires to an office which he is unfit to fill.

Fingĕbat trĕmŭlâ rustĭca liba manu. OVID.—"She made her rustic cakes with trembling hand."

Fingit equum tĕnĕrâ dŏcĭlem cervīce magister
Ire viam quam monstrat eques—— HOR.
—"The trainer teaches the docile horse to turn, with tractable neck, whichever way the rider directs it."

Finis corōnat opus. *Prov.*—"The end crowns the work." A work cannot be appreciated until it is completed. The words are also capable of meaning the same as our saying, "The end sanctifies the means."

Fistŭla dulce canit vŏlŭcres dum dēcĭpit auceps;
Impia sub dulci melle venēna latent. OVID.
—"The pipe sounds sweetly, while the fowler is decoying the birds; beneath the sweet honey deadly poisons lie concealed."

Fit cito per multas præda petīta manus. OVID.—"The prey that is sought by many hands speedily accumulates."

Fit erranti medicīna confessio. CIC.—"Confession is as medicine to him who has erred." "Confess your faults one to another," says the apostle, *James* v. 16.

Fit fabricando faber. *Prov.*—"To become a blacksmith you must work at the forge."

Fit in domināttu servĭtus, in servitūte dominātus. CIC.—"He who should be the master, sometimes becomes the servant, he who should be the servant, the master.

Fit sonus; inclāmat cŏmĭtes, et lūmĭna poscit. OVID.—"An uproar is the consequence; she summons her attendants, and calls for lights."

Flagrante bello.—"While the war was raging."

Flagranti delicto.—"In the commission of the offence." "In the very act."

Flamma fumo est proxĭma. PLAUT.—"Flame is near akin to smoke." So our proverb, "Where there's smoke there's fire." No rumour is without some foundation.

Flamma per incensas citius sedētur aristas. PROPERT.—"Sooner might the flames be extinguished among the standing corn as it burns."

Flare simul et sorbēre haud făcĭle est. PLAUT.—"It is not easy to drink and whistle at the same moment." We must not try to do two things at once.

Flēbĭle ludĭbrium.—"A deplorable mockery." Such, for instance, as a woman of seventy marrying a boy of fourteen. [See an instance in the *Gentleman's Magazine*, vol. i. p. 177.]

Flebit, et insignis totâ cantābitur urbe. HOR.—"He shall lament it, and his name shall be sung the whole city through." The poet threatens his foes with this punishment.

Flectĕre si nĕqueo sŭpĕros, Acheronta movēbo. VIRG.—"If I cannot influence the gods of heaven, I will stir up Acheron itself." I will avail myself of every possible resource to accomplish my purpose. Words which are only likely to proceed from the mouth of a vindictive and unscrupulous opponent.

Flet victus, victor intĕriit.—"The conquered mourns, the conqueror is undone." A not uncommon result, both in war and law. This saying took its rise from the battle of Chæronea, which caused the destruction of both the Theban and the Athenian power.

Florĭfĕris ut apes in saltĭbus omnia libant. LUCRET.—"As bees sip of every juice in the flowery meads." Every one who makes selections *tries* to do this, the man of taste alone succeeds.

Flūmĭna jam lactis, jam flumĭna nectăris ibant. OVID.—"Now rivers of milk, rivers of nectar, were flowing." A description of the happy state of man in the Golden Age.

——*Flūmĭna libant*
Summa leves—— VIRG.
—"They lightly skim the surface of the rivers."

Fluvius cum mari certas. *Prov.*—"You, a river, are contending with the ocean." Said to a person of small means trying to imitate the affluent.

Fœdius hoc ălĭquid quandoque audēbis—— JUV.—"Ere long you will dare to commit some crime more base than this."

Fœdum inceptu, fœdum exĭtu. LIVY.—"A bad beginning leads to a bad ending."

Fœnum habet in cornu, longe fuge, dummŏdo risum
Excŭtiat sibi, non hic cuiquam parcit amīco. HOR.
—"He has hay upon his horn, fly afar from him, for so long as he can excite a laugh, he spares no friend." The ancients used to fasten a wisp of hay to the horns of a vicious bull. The poet speaks of an unscrupulous man, ready to say anything of another, to gratify his own vanity.

Fons omnium viventium.—"The fountain of all living things." The Deity.

Fontes ipsi sĭtiunt. *Prov.*—"Even the fountains are athirst." Said ironically of wealthy men who are covetous.

Forma bonum frăgĭle est—— OVID.—"Beauty is a frail advantage."

Formâ paupĕris. *Law Term.*—"In form of a poor man." See *In forma*, &c.

Forma viros neglecta decet—— OVID.—"A neglect of personal appearance becomes men."

Formam quidem ipsam, Marce fili, et tanquam făciem honesti vides; quæ si ŏcŭlis cernerĕtur, mirābĭles amōres excitāret săpientiæ. CIC.—"You see, my son Marcus, the very figure and features, as it were, of virtue; and, if it could only be beheld by our eyes, it would excite a marvellous love for wisdom."

Format enim natūra prius nos intus ad omnem
Fortunārum hăbĭtum; juvat, aut impellit ad iram,
Aut ad humum mærōre gravi dedūcit et angit;
Post effert ănimi motus interprĕte linguâ. HOR.
—"For nature forms us first within to every modification of circumstances; she delights us, impels us to anger, or depresses us to the earth, and afflicts us with heavy sorrow; and then expresses these emotions of the mind by the tongue, its interpreter."

Formīdābĭlior cervōrum exercĭtus, duce leōne, quam leōnum cervo. *Prov.*—"An army of stags would be more formidable under the command of a lion, than one of lions under the command of a stag." Everything depends upon generalship.

Formōsa făcies muta commendātio est. SYR.—"A handsome face is a silent recommendation."

——*Formōsos sæpe invĕni pessĭmos,*
Et turpi facie multos cognōvi optĭmos. PHÆD.
—"I have often found the good-looking to be very knaves, and I have known many with ugly features most worthy men."

——*Forsan et hæc olim mĕmĭnisse juvābit;*
Durāte, et vosmet rebus servāte secundis. VIRG.
—"Perhaps it may one day be a pleasure to remember these sufferings; bear up against them, and reserve yourselves for more prosperous fortunes."

——*Forsan mĭsĕros meliōra sequentur.* VIRG.—"Perhaps better fortunes await us wretched men."

Forsĭtan hic ălĭquis dicat, Quæ publĭca tangunt
Carpĕre concessum est; hoc via juris habet. OVID.
—"Perhaps some one here may say, 'What encroaches on the highway it is allowable to take; this right the road confers.'"

Fortem facit vicīna libertas senem. SEN.—"The prospect of liberty makes even an old man brave."

Fortem posee ănĭmum—— JUV.—"Pray for strong resolve." The motto of Lord Say and Sele.

Fortem posce ănĭmum, mortis terrōre carentem,
Qui spatium vitæ extrēmum inter mūnĕra ponat,
Natūræ—— JUV.
—"Pray for strong resolve, void of the fear of death, that reckons the closing hour of life among the boons of nature."

Fortes creantur fortĭbus et bonis;
Est in juvencis, est in equis patrum
Virtus, nec imbellem ferōces
Progĕnĕrant ăquĭlæ columbam. HOR.
—"The brave are generated by the brave and good: there is in steers and in horses the virtue of their sires, nor does the warlike eagle beget the peaceful dove."

Fortes fortūna adjŭvat. TER.—"Fortune favours the bold." These words were quoted by the elder Pliny shortly before he perished, in the eruption of Mount Vesuvius, a victim to his thirst for knowledge.

Fortior et potentior est disposĭtio legis quam hŏmĭnis. Law Max.—"The control of the law is stronger and more powerful than that of man."

K

Fortis cadĕre, cedĕre non potest.—"The brave may fall, but will never yield." A play upon the resemblance of the words *cadere* and *cedere*.

Fortis et constantis ănĭmi est, non perturbāri in rebus aspĕris. Cic.—"It is the proof of a brave and resolute spirit, not to be daunted in adversity."

——*Fortissĭmus ille est*
Qui promptus metuenda pati, si cŏmĭnus instent. Lucan.
—"He is the bravest, who is prepared to encounter danger on the instant."

Fortĭter ferendo vincĭtur malum quod evitāri non potest. Prov.—"By bravely enduring it, an evil which cannot be avoided is overcome."

Fortitūdo in labōribus perĭcŭlisque cernĭtur: temperantia in prætermittendis voluptātibus: prudentia in delectu bonōrum et malōrum: justitia in suo cuique tribuendo. Cic.—"Fortitude is to be seen in the endurance of toils and dangers; temperance, in a self-denial of luxuries; prudence, in a choice between good and evil; justice, in rendering to every one his due."

Fortius e multis mater desiderat unum;
Quam quæ flens clamat, Tu mihi solus eras. Ovid.
—"With greater fortitude does a mother bewail one out of many, than she who, weeping, exclaims, 'Thou wast my only one.'"

Fortūna favet fatuis.—"Fortune favours fools."

Fortūna humāna fingit artatque ut lubet. Plaut.—"Fortune moulds and fashions human affairs just as she pleases."

Fortūna magna magna dŏmĭno est servĭtus. Syr.—"A great fortune is a great slavery to its owner." He who has immense wealth, is troubled with cares unknown to others.

Fortūna multis dat nĭmium, nulli satis. Mart.—"Fortune gives to many too much, to none enough."

Fortūna nĭmium quem fovet, stultum facit. Syr.—"Fortune makes a fool of the man whom she favours too much."

Fortūna non mutat genus. Hor.—"Fortune does not change our nature." "What's bred in the bone won't out of the flesh."

Fortūna obesse nulli contenta est semel. Syr.—"Fortune is not content to do a man but one ill turn." "Misfortunes never come single."

Fortūna opes auferre, non ănĭmum potest. SEN.—"Fortune may deprive us of wealth, but not of courage."

"I care not, Fortune, what you me deny;
Of fancy, reason, virtue nought can me bereave."
THOMSON.

Fortūna parvis momentis magnas rerum commutatiōnes effĭcit.—"Fortune, in a short moment, effects vast changes in worldly affairs." The fate of a kingdom often depends upon the act of a moment.

Fortūna sævo læta negōtio, et
Ludum insolentem lūdĕre pertĭnax,
Transmūtat incertos honōres,
Nunc mihi, nunc alii benigna. HOR.

—"Fortune, delighting in her cruel pursuit, and persisting in playing her insolent game, shifts her uncertain honours, indulgent now to me, now to another."

Fortūna vitrea est, tum cum splendet frangĭtur. SYR.—"Fortune is like glass—while she shines she breaks." She has its splendour with its brittleness.

——*Fortūnæ cætĕra mando.* OVID.—"I confide the rest to fortune." I have taken all measures to ensure success, the rest remains in the hand of God.

Fortūnæ fīlius. HOR.—"A son of fortune." A favourite child of fortune; one of a number that are very often spoiled.

Fortūnæ majōris honos, erectus et acer. CLAUD.—"An honour to his elevated station, upright and brave."

——*Fortūnæ verba dĕdique meæ.* OVID.—"And I have deceived my destiny."

Fortūnam reverenter habe, quicunque repentè
Dives ab exīli progrĕdiēre loco. AUSON.

—"Behave with all respect to fortune, you who have suddenly risen to wealth from narrow circumstances."

Fortunāto omne solum patria est.—"To him who is fortunate every land is his country."

Fortunātus et ille deos qui novit agrestes. VIRG.—"Happy the man who makes acquaintance with the rural gods." Such a man knows the health and pleasures of a country life.

——*Frăgĭli quærens illīdĕre dentem*
Offendet sŏlĭdo—— HOR.

—"Trying to fix her tooth in some tender part, Envy will

strike it against the solid." In allusion to the Fable of the Serpent and the File.

Frangas, non flectes.—"You may break, you shall not bend, me." Motto of the Duke of Sutherland and Earl Granville.

Frange, miser, călămos, vigilātaque prælia dele,
Qui facis in parvâ sublimia carmina cellâ,
Ut dignus vĕnias hĕdĕris, et imāgĭne macrâ. Juv.
—"Break your pens, poor wretch! Blot out your battles that have kept you watching, you that write sublime poetry in your narrow room, that you may come forth worthy of an ivy crown and a meagre statue."

Fraudāre eos qui sciunt et consentiunt nemo vidētur. Law Max.—"It is not deemed that a fraud is committed upon those who are aware of the act and consent to it."

Fraus est celāre fraudem. Law Max.—"It is a fraud to conceal fraud." By doing so a person becomes in the eye of the law an accomplice.

Frigĭdam aquam effundĕre.—"To throw cold water on a matter." To discourage an undertaking, by damping the enthusiasm of the projector. To poo-pooh a thing as impracticable or unprofitable.

Frigŏra mitescunt Zĕphyris; ver prōtĕrit æstas
Interitūra, simul
Pōmifer autumnus fruges effūdĕrit; et mox
Bruma recurrit iners. Hor.
—"The colds are mitigated by the Zephyrs; the summer follows close upon the spring; shortly to die itself, as soon as the fruit-bearing autumn shall have poured forth her fruits; and then anon sluggish winter returns again."

Frons, ŏcŭli, vultus persæpe mentiuntur: orātio vero sæpissime. Cic.—"The forehead, eyes, and features often deceive; still oftener the speech." It is a maxim of Machiavellian policy that "the use of speech is to conceal the thoughts."

Fronti nulla fides —— Juv.—"There is no trusting the features." Judge not from outward appearances.

Fructu non foliis arbŏrem æstĭma. Phaed.—"Judge of a tree from its fruit, not from its leaves."

Fruges consumĕre nati. Hor.—"Born only to consume the fruits of the earth." Alluding to persons who pass their lives in eating and drinking, but are comparatively useless to society.

Frustra fit per plura, quod fieri potest per paucióra.—"It is useless to do by many, that which may be done by a few." The chances are that they will be in each other's way. "Too many cooks spoil the broth."

Frustra Hercŭli. Prov.—"It is in vain you speak against Hercules." Applied to those who speak ill of persons really above reproach.

Frustra labōrat qui omnĭbus placēre studet. Prov.—"He labours in vain who tries to please everybody." The Fable of the Old Man and the Ass teaches the same lesson.

——*Frustra retinācula tendens*
Fertur equis aurīga, neque audit currus habēnas. VIRG.
—"In vain as he pulls the reins, is the charioteer borne along by the steeds; they no longer heed his control."

——*Frustra vitium vitāvĕris illud,*
Si te alio pravus detorsĕris—— HOR.
—"In vain do you avoid one vice, if in your depravity you plunge into another."

Fucum facĕre.—"To give a false colour to a thing."

Fugam fecit. Law Term.—"He has taken to flight." Said of a person who has fled from trial.

——*Fuge magna; licet sub paupĕre tecto*
Reges et regum vitâ præcurrĕre amīcos. HOR.
—"Avoid an elevated station; under a poor roof one may surpass even kings and the friends of kings in what is really life."

Fugĕre est triumphus.—"Flight is a triumph." Said in the case of flight from temptation.

Fugiendo in mĕdia sæpe ruĭtur fata. LIVY.—"By precipitate flight we often rush into the very midst of destruction."

"Beware of desperate steps. The darkest day
(Live till to-morrow) will have pass'd away."
COWPER.

Fugit hora.—"Time flies." Lost moments can never be recovered.

——*Fugit imprŏbus, ac me*
Sub cultro linquit—— HOR.
—"The rogue runs away, and leaves me under the knife."

He deserts me in my danger, and leaves me to be sacrificed.

——*Fugit irrĕpărābĭle tempus.* VIRG.—"Time flies, never to be regained."

——*Fuit Ilium*—— VIRG.—"Ilium was." So said in reference to the former greatness of Ilium, or Troy, and the complete destruction which had befallen it. Commonly said of a thing long past. The expression may be appropriately applied to a man who is "a wreck of his former self."

Fuit ista quondam in hâc republicâ virtus, ut viri fortes acerĭōribus suppliciis, civem perniciōsum, quam hostem acerbissĭmum coercērent. CIC.—"Virtue once prevailed so far in this republic, that our stern rulers would subject a vicious citizen to a more severe punishment than even the most inveterate enemy."

——*Fulgente trahit constrictos gloria curru,*
Non minus ignōtos generōsis—— HOR.
—"Glory drags along chained to her glittering car, the humble no less than those of noble birth."

Fumos vendĕre. MART.—"To sell smoke." To barter for money that which is worth nothing. A favourite of the emperor Alexander Severus was in the habit of selling his pretended interest at court, as "smoke." The emperor, on hearing of it, had him smoked to death, and proclamation made to the effect that "the seller of smoke was punished by smoke."

Fumum et opes, strepĭtumque Romæ—— JUV.—"The smoke, the show, the rattle of the town."

Functus officio.—"Having discharged his duties." Said of one who no longer holds his former office.

Fundamentum est justitiæ fides. CIC.—"The foundation of justice is good faith."

Funem abrumpĕre nimium tendendo. *Prov.*—"To break the cord by stretching it too tight." In allusion to the mind, which becomes enfeebled if kept intensely applied too long.

Funĕra plango, fulgŭra frango, Sabbăta pango,
Excĭto lentos, dissĭpo ventos, paco cruentos.
—"I bewail deaths, I disperse lightnings, I announce the Sabbath, I arouse the slow, I dispel the winds, I appease the blood-thirsty." A mediæval inscription on a bell.

—— *Fungar ināni*
Munĕre—— VIRG.
—"I will discharge an unavailing duty."

——*Fungar vice cotis, acūtum*
Reddĕre quæ ferrum valet, exsors ipsa secandi. HOR.
—"I will act the part of a whetstone, which can give an edge to iron, while incapable of cutting itself." Literary critics, like whetstones, often give to others an edge.

Fungīno genere est, capĭte se totum tegit. PLAUT.—"He is of the mushroom kind—he covers all his body with his head." Said of a man having a *petasus*, or broad-brimmed hat.

Fungino gĕnĕre est, sŭbĭto crevit de nihilo.—"He is of the mushroom genus, he has suddenly sprung up from nothing."

Funicŭlis ligātum vel puer verberāret. Prov.—"A man bound with cords even a child can beat."

Furāri lĭtŏris arēnas. Prov.—"To steal the sands of the sea-shore." Said of those who prize things of no value to any one else.

Furiōsus absentis loco est. COKE.—"A madman is looked upon as absent." Because of the absence of reason.

Furiōsus furōre suo punītur. Law Max.—"A madman is punished by his own madness." The affliction of madness is quite sufficient, without the sufferer being made responsible for his acts. The sentence may also be made to mean that a furious man causes suffering and repentance to himself by giving way to passion.

——*Furor arma ministrat.* VIRG.—"Their rage supplies them with arms." Said of the desperation manifested in a popular insurrection, or in a captured city, when each uses as a weapon whatever comes to hand. Thus Abimelech and Pyrrhus were slain by missiles thrown by women, on the capture of a city.

——*Furor est post omnia perdĕre naulum.* JUV.—"It is sheer madness, when everything else is gone, to lose one's passage-money too." It is unwise to cut off every hope.

Furor fit læsâ sæpius patientiâ. Prov.—"Patience, when trespassed on too often, is converted into rage."

Furor loquendi, or *scribendi.* See *Cacoethes*, &c.

Futūra expectans presentĭbus angor.—"While awaiting the

future I am tormented by the present." The situation of a man in present difficulties, but with good prospects.

G.

——*Galeātum serò duelli*
Pœnitet—— JUV.
—"Having put on your helmet, it is late to repent of becoming a warrior." Good advice to a soldier before he takes the fatal shilling. See *Gladiator*, &c.

Gallus in suo sterquilīnio plurĭmum potest. SEN.—"Every cock is master of his own dunghill."

——*Garrit aniles*
Ex re fabellas—— HOR.
—"He relates old women's tales very much to the purpose."

Gaude, Maria Virgo.—"Rejoice, Virgin Mary." The beginning of an anthem chaunted by the monks of the Romish Church at nightfall; from which that particular period of time obtained the name of the *Godemarre.*

——*Gaudent prænōmine molles*
Aurĭcŭlæ—— HOR.
—"Delicate ears are tickled with a title."

Gaudet equis, canĭbusque, et aprĭci grāmĭne campi. HOR.
—"He delights in horses, and dogs, and the grass of the sunny plain."

——*Gaudetque viam fecisse ruīnâ.* LUCAN.—"He rejoices at having made his way by ruin." Said by Lucan of Julius Cæsar, against whom he manifests a most bitter prejudice.

Gĕnius loci.—"The Genius" or "presiding spirit, of the place."

——*Genus humānum multo fuit illud in arvis*
Dūrius—— LUCRET.
—"The human race was then far more hardy in the fields."

——*Genus immortāle manet, multosque per annos*
Stat fortūna domûs, et avi numerantur avōrum. VIRG.
—"The race continues immortal; throughout many years, the fortunes of the house still flourish, and grandsires of grandsires are to be numbered." A picture of a thriving community.

——*Genus irritābĭle vatum.* Hor.—"The sensitive race of poets." Who are peculiarly tenacious of their literary fame.

Gladiātor in arēnā consilium capit. *Prov.*—"The gladiator, having entered the lists, is taking advice." Said of a man taking counsel at a moment at which it is probably too late to use it. See *Galeatum, &c.*

Gloria est consentiens laus bonōrum, incorrupta vox bene judicantium de excellenti virtūte. Cic.—"Glory is the unanimous praise of the good, the unbought voice of those who can well discriminate as to surpassing virtue."

Gloria Patri.—"Glory be to the Father."

Gloria virtūtem tanquam umbra sequĭtur. Cic.—"Glory follows virtue, as though it were its shadow."

Gloriæ et famæ jactūra facienda est, publĭcæ utilitātis causâ. Cic.—"A sacrifice must be made of glory and fame for the public advantage."

Gnatum parĭter uti his dĕcuit, aut etiam amplius,
Quod illa ætas magis ad hæc utenda idōnea est. Ter.
—"Your son ought to have enjoyed these good things equally with you, or even more so, because his age is better suited for such enjoyments."

Græcia capta ferum victōrem cepit, et artes
Intŭlit agresti Latio—— Hor.
—"Greece, subdued, captivated her uncivilized conqueror, and imported her arts into unpolished Latium."

Græcōrum ănĭmi servitūte ac misĕriâ fracti sunt. Livy.—"The minds of the Greeks are broken down by slavery and wretchedness." The historian speaks of the time when Greece had succumbed to the Roman arms.

Græcŭlus esuriens ad cœlum jussĕris ibit. Juv.—"The hungry wretch of a Greek would attempt heaven even, were you to bid him." So the English line, "Bid him go to hell, to hell he goes." Said of the wretched sycophants who, in its degenerate days, left Greece, the country of their birth, to fawn on the great men of Rome.

Grammatĭci certant, et adhuc sub jūdĭce lis est. Hor.—"The grammarians disagree, and the matter in dispute is still undetermined."

Gram. loquitur; Dia. vera docet; Rhe. verba colōrat;
Mu. canit; Ar. numĕrat; Geo. pondĕrat; As. docet astra.

—"Grammar speaks correctly; Dialectics (Logic) teach us truth; Rhetoric gives colouring to our speech; Music sings; Arithmetic reckons; Geometry measures; Astronomy teaches us the stars." Two Latin hexameters, composed to assist the memory in conveying to it some correct information.

Grata supervĕniet quæ non sperābĭtur hora. HOR.—"The hour of happiness will be the more welcome, the less it is expected." Unexpected blessings are doubly acceptable.

Gratia ab officio quod mora tardat abest. OVID.—"Thanks are lost for a service tardily performed."

Gratia gratiam parit. *Prov.*—"Kindness produces kindness."

Gratia, Musa tibi. Nam tu solātia præbes;
Tu curæ rĕquies, tu medicīna mali. OVID.

—"Thanks to thee, my Muse. For it is thou that dost afford me solace; thou art a rest from care, a solace for my woes."

Gratia placendi.—"The delight of pleasing." The happiness we ought to feel in making others happy.

Gratia pro rebus mĕrito debĕtur inemtis. OVID.—"Thanks are justly due for things obtained without purchase."

Gratiæ expectātivæ.—"Anticipated benefits." Advantages in perspective.

Gratior et pulchro vĕniens in corpŏre virtus. VIRG.—"Even virtue appears more lovely, when it inhabits a beautiful form."

Gratis anhēlans, multa agendo nihil agens. PHÆD.—"Out of breath about nothing, with much ado doing nothing." The poet's picture of the busy-bodies of Rome.

Gratis assĕrĭtur.—"It is asserted, but not proved."

Gratis dictum.—"Said to no purpose." Irrelevant to the present question.

—— *Gratis pœnĭtet esse probum.* OVID.—"A man is sorry to be honest for nothing."

Gratŭlor quod eum quem necesse erat diligĕre, qualiscunque esset, talem habēmus, ut libenter quoque dilīgāmus. CIC.—"I rejoice that he, whom, whatever his character might have been, I was bound to love, should prove himself such, that I can feel a pleasure in bestowing my affections on him." A compliment paid by a son or a subject, who finds the object of his duteous respect equally that of his admiration.

Gratum est quod patriæ civem pŏpŭloque dedisti,
Si facis ut pătriæ sit idōneus, ūtĭlis agris ;
Utĭlis et bellōrum et pacis rebus agendis. JUV.
—"It deserves our gratitude that you have presented a citizen to your country and people, if you take care that he prove useful to the state, and of service to her lands; useful in transacting the affairs both of war and peace."

Gratum hŏmĭnem semper bĕneficium delectat; ingrātum semel. SEN.—"A benefit received is always delightful to a grateful man; to an ungrateful man, only at the time,"—that is, at the moment when it is bestowed.

Grave nihil est hŏmĭni quod fert necessĭtas.—"Nothing is really heavy to a man, which necessity brings upon him."

Grave paupertas malum est, et intolerābĭle, quæ magnum domat populum.—"The poverty which weighs down a great people is a grievous and intolerable evil."

Grave pondus illum, magna nobilĭtas premit. SEN.—"A grievous burden, his exalted rank weighs heavy on him."

Grave senectus est homĭnĭbus pondus.—"Old age is a heavy burden to man."

——*Grave virus*
Munditiæ pepulēre—— HOR.
—"Refinement expelled this offensive style." Horace alludes to the coarse and rugged lines of the early Roman authors, which became improved by their communication with the Greeks.

Graviōra quædam sunt remedia perĭcŭlĭs. SYR.—"Some remedies are worse than the disease." This can be only said with reference to so-called remedies administered by quacks.

Gravis ira regum semper. SEN.—"The anger of kings is always heavy." Because they have the means of showing their displeasure.

Gravissimum est imperium consuetūdĭnis. SYR.—"The empire of custom is most mighty." The tyranny of fashion is a penalty inflicted on us in conjunction with the blessings of civilization. See *Usus tyrannus est.*

——*Grex totus in agris*
Unius scabie cadit, et porrigine porci. JUV.
—"The entire flock dies in the fields of the disease introduced by one, and the swine of the measles."

Grex venālium. SUETON.—"A venal throng." An assembly whose votes are put up for sale.

Gustātus est sensus ex omnĭbus maxĭme voluptarius. CIC.—"The sense of taste is the most exquisite of all."
Edere oportet ut vivas, &c.

Gutta cavat lapĭdem, consūmĭtur annŭlus usu,
Et tĕrĭtur pressā vomer aduncus humo. OVID.
—"The drop hollows out the stone, the ring is worn by use, and the curved ploughshare is rubbed away by the pressure of the earth."

Gutta cavat lapĭdem non vi sed sæpe cadendo. *Prov.*—"Dripping water hollows the stone not by force, but by continually falling."

Gutta fortūnæ præ dolio sapientiæ. *Prov.*—"A drop of fortune is worth a cask of wisdom."

H.

Habeas corpus. *Law Term.*—"You are to bring up the body." The English subject's writ of right. Where a person has been imprisoned, having offered sufficient bail, which has been refused though the case is a bailable one, the judges of the court of Chancery or the Queen's Bench may award this writ, for the discharge of the prisoner, on receiving bail.

Habeas corpus ad prosequendum. *Law Term.*—"You are to bring up the body for the purpose of prosecuting." A writ for the removal of a person for trial in the proper county.

Habeas corpus ad respondendum. *Law Term.*—"You are to bring up the body to make answer." A writ to remove a prisoner from the jurisdiction of a lower court to that of a higher one.

Habeas corpus ad satisfaciendum. *Law Term.*—"You are to bring up the body to satisfy." A writ against a person in a lower court, where judgment has been pronounced against him, to remove him to a superior court, that he may be charged with process of execution.

Habēmus confitentem reum. Cic.—"We have his own confession of his guilt."

Habēmus luxuriam atque avaritiam, publicè egestātem, privātim opulentiam. Sall.—"We have luxury and avarice, public want, private opulence." Cato's description of Rome in the latter days of the republic.

Habent insĭdias hŏmĭnis blandĭtiæ mali. Phæd.—"The fair words of a wicked man are fraught with treachery."

Habeo senectūti magnam gratiam, quæ mihi sermōnis aviditātem auxit, potiōnis et cibi sustŭlit. Cic.—"I owe many thanks to old age, which has increased my eagerness for conversation, and has diminished my hunger and thirst."

Habēre derelictui rem suam. Aul. Gell.—"To abandon one's affairs to ruin."

Habēre facias possessiōnem. *Law Term.*—"You are to put in possession." A writ commanding the sheriff to give seisin of land recovered in ejectment.

Habet alĭquid ex inīquo omne magnum exemplum, quod contra singŭlos, utilitāte publĭcâ rependĭtur. Tacit.—"Every great example [of punishment] has in it some injustice, but, though it affects individuals, it is balanced by the promotion of the public good."

Habet et musca splenem. *Prov.*—"A fly even has its anger.' A warning that no enemy is to be despised, however weak and insignificant. See *Inest et*, &c.

Habet iracundia hoc mali, non vult regi. Sen.—"Anger has this evil, that it will not be governed."

Habet natūra, ut aliōrum omnium rerum, sic vivendi modum; senectus autem peractio ætātis est tanquam fabŭlæ, cujus defatigatiōnem fugĕre debēmus, præsertim adjunctâ satietāte. Cic.—"As in all other things, so in living, nature has prescribed to us a mean; but old age, like the last act of a play, is the closing of the scene, in which we ought to avoid too much fatigue, especially if we indulge to satiety."

Habet salem.—"He has wit." He is a wag.

Habet suum venēnum blanda orātio. Syr.—"A soft speech has its poison."

Habĭtus corpŏris quiescenti quam defuncto similior. Pliny

the Younger.—"The appearance of the body was more that of a person asleep than dead." His description of the appearance of the body of his uncle, the Elder Pliny, after his death.

Hâc jacet in tumbâ rosa mundi non rosa munda.—"In this tomb lies a rose of the world, but no chaste rose." A punning epitaph placed by the monks on the tomb of fair Rosamond, in reference to her name and lax morals.

Hâc sunt in fossâ Bedæ venerābilis ossa.—"In this grave lie the bones of venerable Bede." Inscription on the tomb of Beda in Durham cathedral.

Hactĕnus invĭdiæ respondĭmus—— OVID.—"Thus far do I give an answer to envy."

——*Hæ nugæ sēria ducent*
In mala, dērisum semel, exceptumque sinistrè. HOR.
—"These trifles will lead to mischiefs of serious consequence, when once made an object of ridicule, and used in a sinister manner."

*Hæ tĭbi erunt artes, pacisque impon*ĕ*re morem,*
Parcĕre subjectis et debellāre superbos. VIRG.
—"These shall be thy arts, to prescribe the conditions of peace, to spare the conquered, and to subdue the proud." The destinies of Rome.

Hæc amat obscūrum; volet hæc sub luce vidēri,
Judĭcis argūtum quæ non formĭdat acūmen;
Hæc placuit semel; hæc decies repetīta placēbit. HOR.
—"The one courts the shade; another, who is not afraid of the critic's caustic acumen, chooses to be seen in the light; the one has pleased once, the other will give pleasure if ten times repeated."

——*Hæc à te non multum ablūdit imago.* HOR.—"This picture bears no slight resemblance to you."

——*Hæc brevis est nostrōrum summa malōrum.* OVID.—"This is the short sum of our evils."

——*Hæc ego mecum*
Compressis agĭto labris; ubi quid datur otî,
Illūdo chartis—— HOR.
—"These things I revolve by myself in silence. When I have any leisure I amuse myself with my papers."

Hæc facit, ut vivat vinctus quoque compĕde fossor;
Libĕraque a ferro crura futūra putet. OVID.

—"Hope it is that makes even the miner, bound with the fetter, to live on, and to trust that his legs will be liberated from the iron."

——*Hæc perinde sunt, ut illīus ănĭmus, qui ea possĭdet,*
Qui uti scit, ei bona, illi qui non utĭtur recte, mala. TER.

—"These blessings are just according to the disposition of him who possesses them. To him who knows how to use them, they are blessings; to him who does not use them aright, they are evils."

Hæc prima lex in amicĭtiâ sanciātur, ut neque rogēmus res turpes, nec faciāmus rogāti. CIC.—"This is the first law to be established in friendship, that we neither ask of others that which is dishonourable, nor ourselves do it when asked."

Hæc, pro ămicĭtiâ nostrâ, non occultāvi. SUET.—"These things, in consideration of our friendship, I have not concealed from you." Said by Tiberius to his unworthy favourite, Sejanus.

Hæc scripsi non otii abundantiâ, sed amōris erga te. CIC.—"I have written this, not from having an abundance of leisure, but of love for you."

Hæc studia adolescentiam alunt, senectūtem oblectant, secundas res ornant, adversis solātium ac perfugium præbent, delectant domi, non impĕdiunt foris, pernoctant nobiscum, peregrinantur, rusticantur. CIC.—"These studies are as food to us in our youth, they are the solace of our old age, the ornament of our prosperity, the comfort and refuge of our adversity; they amuse us at home, they are no encumbrance abroad, they pass the night with us, accompany us on our travels, and share our rural retirement." So true it is, that books are the best, the most truthful, and the most constant of friends.

Hæc sunt jucundi causa cibusque mali. OVID.—"These things are at once the cause and the nutriment of the delightful malady."

Hæc sunt quæ nostrâ lĭceat te voce monēri.
Vade age—— VIRG.

—"These are all the points on which I am allowed to offer you advice. Begone then."

Hæc vivendi ratio mihi non convĕnit. CIC.—"This mode of living does not suit me."

Hærēdem Deus facit, non homo. COKE.—"It is God that makes the heir, not man." Because no man is the heir of another who is alive. See *Nemo est hæres*, &c.

Hærēdis fletus sub persōnâ risus est. SYR.—"The tears of an heir are laughter beneath a mask." It is to be hoped that this saying has more wit than truth in it.

Hærēdum appellātione vĕniunt hærēdes hærēdum in infinītum. COKE.—"Under the appellation of heirs come the heirs of heirs for everlasting."

Hæres hærēdem, &c. See *Perpetuus nulli*, &c.

Hæres jure repræsentatiōnis.—"An heir by right of representation." Thus, a grandson inherits from his grandfather, as representing his father.

Hæres legitĭmus est quem nuptiæ demonstrant. *Law Max.*—"He is the legitimate heir, whom the marriage ceremony points out as such." To be an heir, a person *must* be *born*, though he may not have been *procreated*, in wedlock.

——*Hæret latĕri lethālis arundo.* VIRG.—"The fatal shaft remains fixed in her side." Words emblematical of the deep-seated wounds of love, envy, or remorse.

Halcyŏnii dies.—"Halcyon days." The kingfisher, or halcyon, was supposed to sit upon her nest, as it floated, for seven days in the winter, upon the sea; during which time that element was always calm; hence the expression, "Halcyon days," expressive of a time of happiness or peace.

Hanc cupit, hanc optat; solâ suspīrat in illâ;
Signaque dat nutu, sollicitatque notis. OVID.
—"Her he desires, for her he longs, for her alone he sighs; he makes signs to her by nods, and courts her by gestures."

——*Hanc veniam petimusque damusque vicissim.* HOR.—"We expect this privilege, and we give it in return."

——*Has pœnas garrula lingua dedit.* OVID.—"This punishment has a prating tongue incurred."

Has vaticinatiōnes eventus comprobāvit. CIC.—"The event has verified these predictions."

——*Haud æquum facit,*
Qui quod didĭcit, id dediscit. PLAUT.
—"He does not do right who unlearns what he has learnt."

Haud facĭle emergunt quorum virtūtibus obstat
Res angusta domi—— JUV.

—"Those persons do not easily rise, whose talents are impeded by limited means."

——*Haud ignāra ac non incauta futūri.* Hor.—"Neither ignorant, nor regardless, of the future." Said of the ant.

Haud ignāra mali mĭsĕris succurrĕre disco. Virg.—"Not unacquainted with misfortune, I have learned to succour the wretched." The words of Dido, whom misfortunes had made more kind than wise, to the shipwrecked Æneas.

——*Haud passĭbus æquis.* Virg.—"Not with equal steps." These words are sometimes applied to a person who has been distanced by another in the race of life.

Hectŏra quis nosset, si felix Troja fuisset?
Publĭca virtūti per mala facta via est. Ovid.
—"Who would have known of Hector, if Troy had been fortunate? A path is opened to virtue through the midst of misfortunes."

Hei mihi! hei mihi! Istæc illum perdĭdit assentatio. Plaut.—"Ah me! ah me! this over-indulgence has proved his ruin."

Hei mihi! non magnas quod habent mea carmĭna vires,
Nostraque sunt mĕrĭtis ora minōra tuis! Ovid.
—"Ah me! that these my verses have so little weight, and that my praises are so inferior to your deserts."

Hei mihi, quod nostri toties pulsāta sepulcri
Janua, sed nullo tempŏre aperta fuit. Ovid.
—"Ah! wretched me! that the door of my tomb should so oft have been knocked at, but never opened!"

——*Heu! Fortūna, quis est crudēlior in nos*
Te Deus? Ut semper gaudes illūdĕre rebus
Humānis—— Hor.
—"Alas! O Fortune, what god is more cruel to us than thou? How much thou dost always delight in making sport of the fortunes of men!"

Heu mĕlior quanto sors tua sorte meâ! Ovid.—"Alas! how much better is your fate than mine!"

Heu piĕtas! Heu prisca fides!— Virg.—"Alas! for piety—Alas! for our ancient faith!"

Heu! quam diffĭcĭle est crimen non prodĕre vultu! Ovid.—"Alas! how difficult it is not to betray guilt by our looks!"

Heu! Quam diffĭcĭlis gloriæ custōdia est! Syr.—"Alas!

how difficult is the guardianship of glory!" Because more is expected of him who has once distinguished himself, than of the crowd of his fellow-men.

Heu! Quam misĕrum est ab eo lædi, de quo non ausis queri. SYR.—"Alas! how grievous is it to be injured by one against whom you dare make no complaint."

Heu! Quanto minus est cum rĕlĭquis versāri, quam tui meminisse!—"Alas! how little the pleasure of conversing with those who are left, compared with that of remembering thee." SHENSTONE'S epitaph on Miss Dolman.

"To live with them is far less sweet
Than to remember thee." MOORE.

Heu quantum fati parva tabella vehit! OVID.—"Ah! what a weight of destiny does one slight plank carry!" In allusion to a ship.

Heu! totum triduum. TER.—"Alas! a whole three days." The language of an impatient lover.

Hi motus animārum, atque hæc certāmĭna tanta
Pulvĕris exĭgui jactu compressa quiescent. VIRG.
—"These commotions of their minds, and these mighty frays, checked by the throwing of a little dust, will cease." Said of the battles of the bees. These lines have been applied to the Carnival of the Roman Church, and the season of repose which follows immediately after the ceremony of sprinkling the ashes on Ash Wednesday.

Hi narrāta ferunt aliò; mensūraque ficti
Crescit; et audītis ălĭquid novus adjĭcit auctor. OVID.
—"These carry elsewhere what has been told them; the sum of the falsehood is ever on the increase, and each fresh narrator adds something to what he has heard."

Hiātus maxĭmè deflendus.—"A deficiency very much to be deplored." Words used to mark a blank in a work, which has been rendered defective by accident or time. It is sometimes used in an ironical sense, in reference to speakers or other persons who make great promises, which they fail to perform.

Hibernĭcis ipsis Hibernior.—"More Irish than the Irish themselves." A specimen of modern dog Latin, quoted against those who are guilty of bulls or other absurdities.

Hic coquus scitè ac mundĭter condit cibos. PLAUT.—"This cook seasons his dishes well, and serves them up neatly."

Hic dies vere mihi festus atras
Exĭmet curas.—— Hor.
—"This day, to me a real festival, shall expel gloomy cares." Said originally in reference to the day on which Augustus returned to Rome from Spain.

Hic est aut nusquam quod quærĭmus. Hor.—"What we seek is either here or nowhere."

Hic est mucro defensiōnis meæ. Cic.—"This is my weapon of defence." This is the point of my argument.

Hic et ubīque.—"Here and everywhere." Words sometimes used in reference to the omnipresence of the Deity.

Hic finis fandi.—"Here ends the discourse." Let our conversation end here.

Hic funis nihil attraxit. *Prov.*—"This line has taken no fish." This plan has not answered.

Hic gĕlidi fontes, hic mollia prata, Lycōri,
Hic nemus, hic toto tecum consūmĕrer ævo. Virg.
—"Here are cooling springs, here grassy meads; here, Lycoris, the grove; here with thee could I pass my whole life."

Hic locus est, partes ubi se via findit in ambas. Virg.—"This is the spot where the road divides into two parts."

Hic manus, ob patriam pugnando vulnĕra passi,—
Quique pii vates, et Phœbo digna locūti:
Inventas aut qui vitam excoluĕre per artes,
Quique sui mĕmŏres ălios fecĕre merendo. Virg.
—"Here is a band of those who have sustained wounds in fighting for their country; pious poets, who sang in strains worthy of Apollo; those who improved life by the invention of arts, and who, by their deserts, have made others mindful of them."

——*Hic murus ahĕneus esto,*
Nil conscīre sibi, nullâ pallescĕre culpâ. Hor.
—"Let this be as a brazen wall of defence, to be conscious of no guilt, to turn pale at no accusation." An admirable picture of the advantages of a good conscience.

——*Hic nigræ succus lolīgĭnis, hæc est*
Ærūgo mera.—— Hor.
—"This is the invention of black envy, this is sheer cankered malice."

Hic patet ingĕniis campus, certusque merenti
Stat favor: ornātur propriis industria donis. CLAUD.
—"Here lies a field open for talent, and certain favour awaits the deserving; industry is graced with her appropriate reward."

Hic pŏtĕrit cavēre recte, jura qui et leges tenet. PLAUT.—"He will be able to take all due precautions, who understands the laws and ordinances."

Hic rogo, non furor est ne moriāre mori? MART.—"I ask, is it not downright madness to kill yourself, that you may not die?"

"How! leap into the pit our life to save?
To save our life leap all into the grave?" COWPER.

Hic secūra quies, et nescia fallĕre vita,
Dives opum variārum; hic latis ōtia fundis,
Spēluncæ, vivique lacus; hic frīgĭda Tempe,
Mūgītusque boum, mollesque sub arbŏre somni. VIRG.
—"Here is quiet free from care, and life ignorant of guile, rich in varied opulence; here are peaceful retreats in ample fields, grottoes and refreshing lakes; here are cool valleys, and the lowing kine, and soft slumbers beneath the tree." The first *hic* is here substituted for *at*.

Hic sĕgĕtes, illuc vĕniunt fēlīcius uvæ:
Arbŏrei fœtus ălibi, atque injussa virescunt
Grāmĭna—— VIRG.
—"Here grain, there grapes more abundantly grow; nurseries of trees elsewhere, and grass spontaneously spring up."

Hic situs est Phaëton currus aurīga paterni;
Quem si non tĕnuit, magnis tamen excĭdit ausis. OVID.
—"Here Phaëton lies buried, the driver of his father's car; which if he did not manage, still he miscarried in a great attempt." The epitaph on the rash son of Apollo.

Hic transĭtus effĭcit magnum vitæ compendium.—"This change effects a great saving of our time."

Hic ubi nunc urbs est, tum locus urbis erat. OVID.—"Here, where now the city stands, was then the city's site."

Hic ver assiduum, atque aliēnis mensĭbus æstas. VIRG.—"Here is everlasting spring, and summer in months that are not her own."

——*Hic vivĭmus ambĭtiōsâ*
Paupertāte omnes.—— JUV.
—"Here we all live in an ostentatious poverty." The poorest man in a company is very often found to have the best coat.

Hĭlărisque tamen cum pondĕre virtus. STATIUS.—"Virtue may be gay, but with dignity." "Be merry and wise."

Hinc illæ lachrymæ— HOR.—"Hence those tears." The cause of his grief is now seen.

Hinc omne principium, huc refer exĭtum. HOR.—"To this refer every undertaking, to this the issue thereof." To the decrees of Providence.

Hinc sŭbĭtæ mortes atque intestāta senectus. JUV.—"Hence arise sudden deaths, and an intestate old age." Debauchery and excesses cut short the lives of their votaries, and by a sudden death deprive them of the opportunity of making their will.

——*Hinc tibi copia*
Manābit ad plenum benigno
Ruris honōrum opulenta cornu. HOR.
—"Here plenty, rich in rural honours, shall flow for you, with her generous horn full to the very brim." In allusion to the *Cornucopia.*

Hinc totam infēlix vulgātur fama per urbem. VIRG.—"Hence the unhappy report was spread throughout the whole city."

Hinc usūra vorax, avĭdumque in tempŏre fœnus,
Et concussa fides, et multis utĭle bellum. LUCAN.
—"Hence devouring usury, and interest accumulating by lapse of time—hence shaken credit, and warfare profitable to the many."

Hinc venti docĭles rĕsŏno se carcĕre solvunt,
Et cantum acceptâ pro libertāte rependunt.
—"Hence the obedient winds are loosed from their durance as they sound, and give melody in return for the liberty they have received." Words very applicable to the Æolian harp.

Hirundĭnem sub eōdem tecto ne habeas. *Prov.*—"Do not have a swallow under the same roof." Do not make friends of those who will leave you when the spring and fair weather are past.

Hirundĭnes æstīvo tempŏre præsto sunt: frigŏre pulsæ recēdunt. Ita falsi amīci. AD HERENN.—"The swallows in summer are among us; in cold weather they are driven away. So it is with false friends." Such friends may justly be called *fair-weather* friends.

His lăchrymis vitam damus, et miserescĭmus ultro. VIRG.—"To these tears we concede his life, and willingly show mercy."

His lĕgĭbus solūtis respublĭca stare non potest. CIC.—"These laws once repealed, the republic cannot last."

His nunc præmium est, qui recta prava faciunt. TER.—"In these days they are rewarded who make right appear wrong."

His saltem accumŭlem donis, et fungar ināni
Munĕre.—— VIRG.

—"These offerings at least I would bestow upon him, and discharge this unavailing duty." A quotation often used with reference to distinguished men when deceased.

Hoc age.—"Do this," or "attend to this."

Hoc decet uxōres; dos est uxōria lites. OVID.—"This befits wives only; strife is the dowry of a wife."

Hoc erat in more majōrum. "This was the custom of our forefathers."

Hoc erat in votis; modus agri non ita magnus;
Hortus ubi, et tecto vicīnus jugis aquæ fons,
Et paulum silvæ super his foret.—— HOR.

—"This was ever the extent of my wishes; a portion of ground not over large, in which is a garden, and a fountain with its continual stream close to my house, and a little woodland beside."

Hoc est quod palles? cur quis non prandeat, hoc est? PERS.—"Is it for this you grow pale? Is it for this that one should go without his dinner?"

——*Hoc est*
Vivĕre bis, vitâ posse priōre frui. MART.

—"It is to live twice over, to be able to enjoy the retrospect of our past life."

——*Hoc fonte derivāta clades,*
In pătriam, pŏpŭlumque fluxit. HOR.

—"Derived from this source, perdition has overwhelmed the nation and the people." The poet says that the misfortunes of the Romans in their wars with the Parthians originated in the depravity then universally prevalent.

Hoc maxĭmè officii est, ut quisquis maxĭmè opus indigeat, ita ei potissimum opitulāri. Cic.—"It is more especially our duty, to aid him in preference who stands most in need of our assistance."

Hoc opus, hoc studium, parvi properēmus et ampli,
Si patriæ vŏlŭmus, si nobis vivĕre cari. Hor.
—"Let us, both small and great, push forward in this work, in this pursuit; if to our country, if to ourselves, we would be dear."

Hoc pretium ob stultitiam fero. Ter.—"This is the reward I gain for my folly."

Hoc quoque, quam volui, plus est. Cane, Musa, receptus. Ovid.—"Even this is more than I wished to say. My Muse, sound a retreat."

Hoc scio pro certo, quod si cum stercŏre certo,
Vinco seu vincor, semper ego maculor.
—"This I know for certain, that when I contend with filth, whether I vanquish or am vanquished, I am always soiled." Leonine rhymes.

——*Hoc scito, nĭmio celĕrius*
Venīre quod molestum est, quam id quod cupĭdè petas.
Plaut.
—"Know this, that that which is disagreeable comes much more speedily than that which you eagerly desire."

Hoc tibi sit argumentum, semper in promptu situm,
Ne quid expectes amīcos facĕre, quod per te queas.
—"Let this be your rule of life, always to be acted upon, expect not your friends to do anything that you can do yourself."

——*Hoc tolerābĭle si non*
Et furĕre incipias. Juv.
—"This might be endurable, if you did not begin to rave."

Hoc volo, sic jubeo, &c. See *Sic volo,* &c.

Hŏdie mihi, cras tibi. Prov.—"To-day for myself, to-morrow for you." Inscribed over the elder Wyatt's epitaph at Ditchley.

Hŏdie nihil, cras credo. Varro.—"To-morrow I will trust, not to-day." See *Cras credimus,* &c.

Hŏdie vivendum amissâ præteritōrum curâ.—"Let us live to

day, dismissing all care for the past." Epicurean advice, given by a boon companion.

Hŏmĭne impĕrīto nunquam quidquam injustius,
Qui, nisi quod ipse facit, nil rectum putat. TER.
—"There is nothing more unreasonable than a man who wants experience, one who thinks nothing right except what he himself has done."

Hŏmĭnem non odi sed ejus vitia.—"I hate not the man, but his vices."

——*Hŏmĭnem pāgĭna nostra sapit.* MART.—"Our pages understand human nature." We write from experience.

Hŏmĭnes ad deos nullâ re propius accēdunt quam salūtem homĭnĭbus dando. CIC.—"In nothing do men more nearly approach the gods, than in giving health to men."

Hŏmĭnes amplius ŏcŭlis quam aurĭbus credunt: longum iter est per præcepta, breve et effĭcax per exempla. SEN.—"Men believe their eyes rather than their ears—the road by precept is long, by example short and sure."

Hŏmĭnes nihil agendo discunt malè agĕre. CATO.—"By having nothing to do, men learn to do evil."

"For Satan always mischief finds
For idle hands to do." WATTS.

Hŏmĭnes proniōres sunt ad voluptātem, quam ad virtūtem. CIC.—"Men are more prone to pleasure than to virtue."

Hŏmĭnes qui gestant, quique auscultant crĭmĭna,
Si meo arbitrātu lĭceat, omnes pendeant,
Gestōres linguis, auditōres aurĭbus. PLAUT.
—"Those men who carry about, and those who listen to, accusations, should all be hanged, if I could have my way, the carriers by their tongues, the hearers by their ears."

Hŏmĭnes quo plura habent, eo ampliōra cupiunt. JUST.—"The more men have, the more they want."

Hŏmĭnis est errāre, insipientis perseverāre.—"It is the nature of man to err, of a fool to persevere in error."

Hŏmĭnis frugi et temperantis functus officio. TER.—"One who has acted the part of a virtuous and temperate man."

——*Hŏmĭnum sententia fallax.* OVID.—"The opinions of men are fallible."

Homo ad res perspĭcacior Lynceo vel Argo, et oculeus totus. APUL.—"A man more clear-sighted than Lynceus or Argus, and eyes all over."

Homo constat ex duābus partĭbus, corpŏre et ănĭmâ, quorum una est corpŏrea, altĕra ab omni matĕriæ concrētiōne sejuncta. Cic.—"Man is composed of two parts, body and soul, of which the one is corporeal, the other severed from all combination with matter."

Homo delīrus, qui verbōrum minūtiis rerum frangit pondĕra. A. Gell.—"A foolish man, who fritters away the weight of his subject by fine-spun trifling on words."

Homo extra est corpus suum cum irascĭtur. Syr.—"A man when he is angry is beside himself."

Homo fervĭdus et dīligens ad omnia parātur. A Kempis *de Imit. Christi.*—"The man who is earnest and diligent is prepared for all things."

Homo hŏmĭni aut deus aut lupus. *Prov.*—"Man is to man either a god or a wolf."

Homo hŏmĭni deus, si officium sciat. Cæcil.—"Man to man is a god, if he knows how to do his duty."

Homo hŏmĭni lupus. Plaut.—"Man to man is a wolf." One man's loss is, too often, another man's gain.

"Man's inhumanity to man makes countless thousands mourn." Burns.

Homo in Hispāniam natūra natūram vitium visum.—"A woman about to sail to Spain to see the nature of vines." A Latin puzzle; the sentence, at first, seeming to have neither grammar nor meaning.

Homo justus nil cuipiam dĕtrăhit. Cic.—"A just man speaks ill of no one."

Homo multa habet instrumenta ad adipiscendam sapientiam. Cic.—"Man possesses numerous means of acquiring wisdom."

Homo multārum literārum.—"A man of many letters." A man of extensive learning.

Homo multi consilii et optĭmi.—"A man always ready to give his advice, and that the best."

Homo qui erranti comĭter monstrat viam,
Quasi lumen de suo lūmĭne accendit, facit;
Nihilōmĭnus ipsi luceat, cum illi accendĕrit.
—"He who kindly shows the way to one who has gone astray, acts as though he had lighted another's lamp by his own; although it has given light to the other, it still

lights him on his way." So Shakspeare says, "The quality of mercy is twice blessed."

Homo qui in hŏmĭne calamitōso est misericors, mĕmĭnit sui. Prov.—"A man who is merciful to the afflicted, remembers what is due to himself." He remembers his duty as a man.

Homo sine religiōne, sicut equus sine fræno. Prov.—"A man without religion is like a horse without a bridle."

Homo solus aut deus aut dæmon. Prov.—"A man to live alone must be either a god or a dæmon."

Homo sum; humāni nihil à me aliēnum puto. TER.—"I am a man, and nothing that concerns a man do I deem a matter of indifference to me." St. Augustin tells us that on hearing these words of the poet, the theatre resounded with applause.

Homo tŏties mŏrĭtur, quŏties amittit suos. SYR.—"A man dies as many times as he loses his relatives."

Homo trium literārum. PLAUT.—"A man of three letters" —FUR, "a thief."

Homo unius libri.—"A man of one book." To fix one's mind intently on one book, and master it, is the only way to become truly learned, at least, according to Thomas Aquinas, as quoted by Jeremy Taylor.

Homuncŭli quanti sunt! cum recogito. PLAUT.—"What poor creatures are men! when I reflect upon it."

Honesta mors turpi vitâ potior. TACIT.—"An honourable death is better than an ignominious life." The maxim of a martyr.

Honesta paupertas prior quam opes malæ. Prov.—"Poverty with honesty is better than ill-acquired wealth."

Honesta quædam scĕlĕra successus facit. SEN.—"Success makes some crimes honourable." Thus rebellion and conspiracy, though based on fraud and ingratitude, are dignified, if successful, with the name of "revolution."

Honestum non est semper quod licet. Law Max.—"That is not always honourable which is lawful." If every one scrupulously insisted on his legal rights, the world would be a scene of tenfold litigation. We must "give and take."

Honestum quod vere dīcĭmus, etiamsi a nullo laudātur, laudăbĭle est suâ natūrâ CIC.—"That which we truly call virtuous, even though it be praised by no one, is praiseworthy in its own nature."

Honestus rumor altĕrum patrimōnium est. SYR.—"A good name is a second inheritance."

Honor est præmium virtūtis. CIC.—"Honour is the reward of virtue."

Honōra mĕdĭcum propter necessitātem. *Prov.*—"Make much of a physician through necessity."

Honōres mutant mores.—"Honours change manners."

Honos alit artes. CIC.—"Honours nurture the arts." See *Quis enim*, &c.

Horæ cedunt, et dies, et menses, et anni, nec prætĕrĭtum tempus unquam revertĭtur. CIC.—"Hours and days, and months and years, pass away, and no time that is once past ever returns."

——*Horæ*
Momento cita mors venit, aut victōria læta. HOR.—"In a moment of time comes sudden death, or joyous victory." The contingencies of a soldier's life.

Horrea formīcæ tendunt ad inānia nunquam;
Nullus ad amissas ibit amīcus opes. OVID.
—"Ants never bend their course to an empty granary; no friend will visit departed wealth." Said in reference to fair-weather or sun-shine friends.

Horresco rĕfĕrens. VIRG.—"I shudder as I tell it."

Horrĭdus miles esse debet, non cœlātus auro argentoque, sed ferro et anĭmis fretus. Virtus est mīlĭtis decus. LIVY.—"The soldier should inspire terror, and not be adorned with gold and silver, but rely upon his courage and his sword. Valour is the soldier's virtue."

Horror ubīque ănĭmos, simul ipsa silentia terrent. VIRG.—"Horror seizes their minds, and the very silence is dreadful."

Hortus siccus.—Literally, "a dry garden." A collection of dried plants for the purpose of classification. Applied figuratively to a recital of dry and uninteresting details.

Hos ego versĭcŭlos feci, tulit alter honōres;
Sic vos non vobis fertis arātra boves;
Sic vos non vobis mellĭfĭcātis apes;
Sic vos non vobis vellĕra fertis oves;
Sic vos non vobis nidĭfĭcātis aves. VIRG.

—"I wrote these lines; another has borne away the honour—Thus do ye, oxen, for others bear the yoke; thus do ye, bees, for others make honey; thus do ye, sheep, wear fleeces for others; thus do ye, birds, for others build nests."—On the occasion of some shows at Rome, the weather was remarkable for tempestuous nights, with fine days. Virgil, then a young man, and unknown, wrote these lines, and fixed them in a conspicuous place:

"*Nocte pluit totâ, redeunt spectăcula mane,*
Divīsum impĕrium cum Jove Cæsar habet."

"It rains all night, the games return with day,
Cæsar with Jove thus holds divided sway."

The author being inquired for, a poet of the name of Bathyllus claimed the distich, and was rewarded accordingly. Virgil, indignant at this, wrote under the verses the line "*Hos ego, &c.,*" and the words, "*Sic vos non vobis,*' four times. He alone proving able to complete the lines, of which these words were the beginning, the imposture of Bathyllus was detected, and he was dismissed with disgrace, while Virgil obtained the credit which was his due.

——*Hospes nullus tam in amīci hospitium devorti potest,*
Quin ubi trīduum contĭnuum fuĕrit, jam odiōsus siet,
Verum ubi trīduum continuos immorābitur,
Tametsi dŏmĭnus non invītus patītur, servi murmŭrant.
PLAUT.

—"No guest can be hospitably entertained by a friend, but what when he has been there three days together, he must become a bore; but when he prolongs his stay for ten successive days, even should the master willingly allow it, the servants grumble."

Hospĭtis antīqui solĭtas intrāvimus ædes. OVID.—"We entered the well-known abode of an old friend."

Hostis est uxor invĭta quæ ad virum nuptum datur. PLAUT. —"That wife is an enemy who is given to a man in marriage against her will."

——*Huc natas adjĭce septem,*
Et totĭdem jŭvĕnes, et mox gĕnĕrosque nurusque,
Quærĭte nunc, hăbeat quam nostra superbia causam. OVID.

—"Add to this my seven daughters, and as many sons, and ere long my sons-in-law and daughters-in-law; then inquire what reason I have for being proud." The vain-glorious words of the unfortunate Niobe.

——*Huc prŏpius me,*
Dum dŏceo insanīre omnes, vos ordĭne adīte. HOR.
—"Hither, all of you, come near me in order, while I convince you that you are mad."

Huic maxĭmè putāmus malo fuisse, nimiam opiniōnem ingĕnii atque virtūtis. CORN. NEPOS.—"This we think was his especial misfortune, that he entertained too high an opinion of his own genius and valour." The character of Themistocles.

Huic versātĭle ingĕnium sic părĭter ad omnia fuit, ut natum ad id unum dicĕres, quodcunque agĕret. LIVY.—"This man's genius was so versatile, so equally adapted to every pursuit, that in whatever he engaged, you would pronounce him to have been born for that very thing alone." The character of the elder Cato.

Hujus aquæ tactus depellit dæmŏnis actus.—"The contact of this water dispels the wiles of the devil." A mediæval line describing the alleged virtues of holy water.

Humāni nihil aliēnum. TER.—"Nothing that concerns a man is indifferent to me." Motto of Earl Talbot.

Humanitāti qui se non accommŏdat,
Plerumque pœnas oppĕtit superbiæ. PHÆD.
—"He who does not conform to courtesy, mostly pays the penalty of his superciliousness."

Humānum amāre est, humānum autem ignoscĕre est. PLAUT.
—"It is natural to love, and it is natural also to be considerate."

Humānum est errāre.—"It is the nature of man to err." The result of his finite comprehension.

"To err is human, to forgive divine." POPE.

——*Humānum făcĭnus factum est.*
Actūtum fortūnæ solent mutārier. Varia vita est. PLAUT
—"The common course of things has happened. Fortunes are wont to change upon the instant. Life is chequered."

Humĭles labōrant ubi potentes dissĭdent. PHÆD.—"The humble are in danger, when the powerful disagree." See *Quicquid delirant*, &c.

Hunc comedendum et deridendum vobis propīno. TER.—"I

make him over to you to eat and drink him to the very dregs." The figure is taken from the custom of tasting of a cup of wine, and then handing it to another.

Hystĕron prŏtĕron.—"The last first." The Greek ὕστερον πρότερον, Latinized. A figure of speech in which the order of things is inverted, as in the lines of Virgil, *Georg.* b. iii. l. 60, and *Æn.* b. iii. l. 662. See also *Æn.* b. ii. l. 353, —*Moriāmur, et in media arma ruāmus.*—"Let us die, and rush upon their weapons."

I.

I. E., for *id est.*—"That is."

I. H. S.—An inscription sometimes attached to the figure of the cross. It may mean, *Jesus hominum Salvator,* "Jesus the Saviour of men," or *In hoc salus,* "In him is salvation." Or for the beginning of the Greek ΙΗΣΟΥΣ, "Jesus."

I. N. R. I., for *Jesus Nazarēnus Rex Judæōrum.*—"Jesus of Nazareth, King of the Jews." The inscription over the cross.

I. Q. for *idem quod.*—"The same as."

I, bone, quo virtus tua te vocat; i pede fausto,
Grandia latūrus meritōrum præmia.—— Hor.
—"Go, my brave fellow, whither your valour calls you, go with prosperous step, certain to receive the ample rewards of your merit." Words addressed to a soldier who had by his valour already won a purse of gold. To which he made answer, *Ibit eo quo,* &c., which see.

——*I demens! et sævas curre per Alpes,*
Ut puĕris plăceas, et dēclāmātio fias. Juv.
—"Go, madman! run over the rugged Alps, that thou mayst amuse children, and become the subject of a theme."

I nunc, et vĕtĕrum nobis exempla virōrum,
Qui forti casum mente tulēre refer. Ovid.
—"Come now, and recount to me the examples of men of ancient times, who have endured evils with fortitude."

I nunc, magnĭfĭcos, victor, molīre triumphos,
Cinge comam lauro, votaque redde Jovi. Ovid.
—"Go now, thou conqueror, acquire splendid triumphs, encircle thy brows with laurel, and pay thy vows to Jove."

——*Ibi omnis*
Effūsus labor.—— VIRG.
—"There all his labour is lost." Said of Orpheus, who lost Eurydice when bringing her back from the infernal regions.

Ibis, redībis, non morières in bello.—"Thou shalt go, thou shalt return, thou shalt not die in battle." This may be also read, by changing the punctuation, *Ibis, redibis non, morieris in bello.* "Thou shalt go, thou shalt not return, thou shalt die in battle." An ambiguous answer given by an oracle; which, as punctuation was not used in ancient times, might save the credit of the oracle either way.

Ibit eo quo vis, qui zonam perdĭdit.— HOR.—"He who has lost his girdle, will go wherever you please." Among the ancients, money, or the purse, was sometimes kept within the girdle. It is of the same meaning as our homely adage, "Hungry dogs eat dirty puddings." See *Græculus esuriens*, &c.

——*Id arbĭtror,*
Adprīmè in vitâ esse utĭle, ne quid nimis. TER.
—"This I consider in life to be especially advantageous; that one do nothing to excess." See *Sunt certi*, &c.

Id cinĕrem aut manes credis curāre sepultos? VIRG.—"Do you suppose that the ashes of the dead, or the shades of the buried, care for that?" The poet's less enlightened countrymen believed, however, that ghosts ate and drank at certain periods of the year, and especially at the time of the *Feralia*, which they celebrated in February. See Ovid's *Fasti*, b. ii. l. 566, *et seq.*

Id commūne malum, semel insanīvĭmus omnes. MANTUANUS, Ecl. i.—"It is a common ill, that we have all been mad once."

Id demum est hŏmĭni turpe, quod mĕruit pati. PHÆD.—"That only is really disgraceful to a man, which he has deserved to suffer."

Id ego jam nunc tibi renuncio tibi ut sis sciens. TER.—"I now warn you of it, that you may be on your guard."

Id est.—"That is." Commonly expressed by the initials *i. e.*

Id făcĕre laus est quod decet, non quod licet. SEN.—"To do what is becoming, not what the law allows, is true merit." There are many moral offences, which it is impossible to bring within the strict letter of the law, but which it is our duty to avoid equally with those which are criminal.

——*Id genus omne.* Hor.—"All that class." An expression which contemptuously alludes to the scum of the populace.

Id maxĭmè quemque decet, quod est cujusque suum maxĭmè. Cic.—"That thing best becomes us, which belongs to our station." See *Ne sutor*, &c.

Id mutāvit quia me immutātum videt. Ter.—"Because he sees me unchanged he has changed."

Id nobis maxĭmè nocet, quod non ad ratiōnis lumen sed ad similitūdinem aliōrum vivĭmus. Sen.—"This is especially detrimental to us, that we live, not according to the light of reason, but after the fashion set by others." We "follow the multitude to do evil."

Id vero est, quod ego mihi puto palmārium,
Me reperisse, quo modo adolescentŭlus
Meretrīcum ingenia et mores posset noscĕre:
Matūre ut cum cognōrit, perpetuo odĕrit. Ter.
—"That is a thing that I really consider my crowning merit, to have found out the way by which a young man may be enabled to learn the dispositions and manners of courtesans, so that by knowing them betimes he may detest them for ever after."

——*Idem quod.*—"The same as." Commonly expressed by the initials, *i. q.*

Idem velle et idem nolle ea demum firma amicitia est. Sall.—"To have the same tastes and the same dislikes—this in fact is the basis of lasting friendship."

Idōneus quidem meâ sententiâ, præsertim quum et ipse eum audivĕrit, ut scribat de mortuo; ex quo nulla suspicio est, amicitiæ causâ, eum esse mentītum. Cic.—"In my opinion he is qualified to write (of the deceased), especially as he had been accustomed to hear him speak; for which reason there can be no ground for suspicion, that he has, for motives of friendship, stated what is false."

Ignāvis semper fĕriæ sunt. *Prov.*—"With fools it is always holiday." Idle persons can always find an excuse for indolence.

Ignavissĭmus quisque, et, ut res docuit, in perîcŭlo non ausūrus, nimio verbis et linguâ ferox. TACIT.—"Every cowardly fellow, who, as experience tells us, will skulk in the hour of danger, is noisy and blustering with his words and language." The best pictures of a blustering coward are the two captains, Thraso, in the *Eunuchus* of Terence, and Pyrgopolinices, in the *Miles Gloriosus* of Plautus, both of whom are first-rate vapourers.

Ignāvum fucos pecus a præsēpibus arcent. VIRG.—"[The bees] drive from their hives the drones, a lazy race."

Igne quid utilius? si quis tamen urĕre tecta
Compărat, audāces instruit igne manus. OVID.
—"What is there more useful than fire? and yet, if any one prepares to burn a house, it is with fire that he arms his rash hands." Every blessing may be abused.

Ignem ne glădio fŏdĭto. *Prov.*—"Stir not the fire with a sword." Do not irritate an angry person,—or, as we say, "add fuel to flame."

Ignis fătuus.—"A deceiving light." The Will o' the wisp, or Jack-a-lantern. These words are sometimes used figuratively to denote a false light, tending to lead men astray.

Ignis sacer. PLINY *the Elder*.—"St. Anthony's fire," or Erisypelas. Columella calls by the same name an incurable and contagious disease among sheep.

Ignorāmus.—"We are ignorant." A term employed when a grand jury ignores an indictment. The word is jokingly applied to an ignorant man, a dolt.

Ignorantia facti excūsat. *Law Max.*—"Ignorance of the fact excuses." A contract being falsely read or explained to an ignorant man, and executed by him under the false impression produced thereby, is void.

Ignorantia juris quod quisque tenētur scire nemĭnem excūsat. *Law Max.*—"Ignorance of a law which every man is bound to know is no excuse."

Ignorantia non excūsat legem. *Law Max.*—"Ignorance is no plea against the law." To the same effect as the last.

Ignoratiōne rerum bonārum et malārum, maxĭmè hŏmĭnum vita vexātur. CIC.—"Through ignorance of what is good and what is bad, the life of man is greatly troubled."

Ignōrent pŏpŭli, si non in morte probāris,
An scires adversa pati.—— LUCAN.
—"The people would be ignorant, if you did not prove by your death that you were capable of supporting adversity." Words addressed to Pompey, whom the poet represents as a hero, while he makes Julius Cæsar little better than a demon.

Ignoscas aliis multa, nil tibi. AUSON.—"Pardon others for many an offence, yourself for none."

Ignoscent si quid peccāvĕro stultus amici,
Inque vicem illōrum patiar delicta libenter. HOR.
—"If I, in my foolishness, commit any offence, let my friends pardon it; I, in my turn, will willingly bear with their failings."

Ignoscĭto sæpe altĕri, nunquam tibi. SYR.—"Pardon others often, yourself never."

Ignōti nulla cupīdo. Prov.—"There can be no desire for that which is unknown." Our wants are very much increased by knowledge and example.

Ignōtis errāre locis, ignōta vidēre
Flūmĭna gaudēbat, studio minuente labōrem. OVID.
—"He loved to wander over unknown spots, and to see unknown rivers, his curiosity lessening the fatigue."

——*Ignōtum argenti pondus et auri.* VIRG.—"An untold weight of silver and gold."

Ignōtum per ignōtius. Prov.—"A thing not understood by a thing still less understood." An attempt at illustration which only adds to the previous obscurity.

Iis qui vendunt, emunt, condŭcunt, locant, justitia necessāria est. CIC.—"Justice is necessary for those who sell, who buy, who hire, and who let on contract."

Iliăcos intra muros peccātur et extra. HOR.—"Sin is committed as well within the walls of Troy as without." Both sides are to blame.

Illa dolet verè quæ sine teste dolet. MART.—"She grieves sincerely who grieves when alone."

Illa est agrĭcŏlæ messis inĭqua suo. OVID.—"That is a harvest which ill repays its husbandman."

Illa fidem dictis addĕre sola potest. OVID.—"It is that

[the intention] alone that is able to give weight to what we say."

Illa laus est, magno in gĕnĕre et in divitiis maxĭmis,
Libĕros homĭnem educāre, gĕnĕri monumentum et sibi.
PLAUT.

—"'Tis some merit for a man of noble family and of ample wealth to bring up children, memorials of his race and himself."

Illa placet tellus in quâ res parva beātum
Me facit, et tenues luxuriantur opes. MART.

—"That spot has its especial delights, in which small means render me happy, and moderate wealth insures abundance."

Illâ victōriâ viam ad pacem patefēcit.—"By that victory he opened a way to peace."

Illæso lūmĭne solem.—"[To look] at the sun with sight uninjured." Eagles are said to be able to do so. This is the motto of the Earl of Rosslyn.

Illam, quicquid agit, quoquo vestīgia flectit,
Compōnĭt furtim, subsequiturque decor. TIBULL.

—"In whatever she does, wherever she turns, grace steals into her movements, and attends her steps." So Milton:

"Grace was in all her steps, heaven in her eye,
In every gesture dignity and love." *Par. Lost*, viii.

Ille crucem scĕlĕris pretium tulit, hic diadēma. JUV.—"This man found the cross the reward of his crime; that one, a diadem." History shows us how some men have gained a throne by the same steps which led others to the gallows.

——*Ille etiam cæcos instāre tumultus*
Sæpe monet, fraudesque et operta tumescĕre bella. VIRG.

—"He often warns too that secret revolt is impending, and that treachery and pent-up warfare are ready to burst forth." The duty of a skilful statesman.

Ille fuit vitæ Mario modus, omnia passo
Quæ pejor fortūna potest, atque omnĭbus uso
Quæ mĕlior.—— LUCAN.

—"Such was the course of Marius' life, who suffered all that ill fortune could inflict, and enjoyed all that good fortune could bestow." Marius experienced, perhaps, more vicissitudes than any man we read of in history. See Plutarch's Life of him.

Ille igĭtur nunquam direxit brăchia contra
Torrentem; nec civis erat qui libĕra posset
Verba ănĭmi proferre, et vitam impendĕre vero. Juv.
—"He never exerted his arms to swim against the stream, nor was he a citizen who would freely deliver the sentiments of his mind, and lay down his life for the truth."

——*Ille potens sui*
Lætusque degit, cui licet in diem
Dixisse, Vixi: *cras vel atrâ*
Nube polum pater occupāto
Vel sole puro; non tamen irrĭtum
Quodcunque retrò est efficiet. Hor.
—"The man is master of himself, and lives happy, who has it in his power to say, 'I have *lived* to-day; to-morrow let the Omnipotent invest the heavens, either with black clouds, or with clear sunshine, still, he shall not efface what is past.'"

Ille sinistrorsum, hic dextrorsum, abit: unus utrique
Error, sed variis illūdit partĭbus.—— Hor.
—"One digresses to the right, the other to the left; they are both equally in error, but are influenced by different delusions."

Ille tĕnet palmam; palma petenda mihi est.—"He holds the palm; the palm must be sought by me."

Ille terrārum mihi præter omnes
Angŭlus ridet.—— Hor.
—"That little spot of earth has charms for me before all others." The charms of home.

Ille vir, haud magnâ cum re, sed plenus fidei.—"He is a man, not of ample means, but full of good faith."

Illi inter sese magnâ vi brăchia tollunt. Virg.—"The workmen lift their arms in turns with mighty force." Said of the Cyclopes, working at the forges of Etna. This line, when scanned, is expressive of the sound of alternate strokes on the anvil:

Illin | ter se | se mag | nâ vi | brachia | tollunt—

by the figure *Onomatopœa.* See a similar instance in *Quadrupedante putrem,* &c.

Illi mors gravis incŭbat,
Qui, notus nimis omnĭbus,
Ignōtus mŏrĭtur sibi. Sen.

—"Death falls heavily upon him, who, too well known to all others, dies unknown to himself."

Illi robur et æs triplex
Circa pectus erat, qui frăgĭlem truci
Commīsit pĕlăgo ratem
Primus.—— Hor.

—"That man must have had oak and three-fold bronze around his breast, who first intrusted a frail bark to the raging seas."

Illiberāle est mentīri; ingĕnuum vērĭtas decet.—"It is a low thing to lie; truth alone bespeaks the man of high birth."

Illic appŏsĭto narrābis multa Lyæo. Ovid.—"There, with the wine on the table, you will tell many a story."

Illic et cantant quicquid didicēre theātris;
Et jactant faciles ad sua verba manus. Ovid.

—"There too they sing whatever snatches they have picked up at the theatres, and move their pliant arms in tune to their words."

Illōtis pĕdĭbus ingrĕdi. *Prov.*—"To enter with unwashed feet." In reference to the custom of the ancients of washing the feet before entering a sacred place, or sitting down at meals. Sometimes applied to those who talk irreverently of sacred subjects.

Illuc est sapĕre, qui ubicunque opus sit, anĭmum possis flectĕre. Ter.—"It is true wisdom to be enabled to govern the feelings whenever there is a necessity for it."

Illud amicitiæ sanctum ac venerābile nomen
Nunc tibi pro vili sub pĕdĭbusque jacet? Ovid.

—"Is the sacred and venerable name of friendship now held cheap by you, and trodden under foot?"

Illud maxĭmè rarum genus est eorum, qui aut excellenti ingĕnii magnitūdine, aut præclārâ eruditiōne atque doctrīnâ, aut utrâque re ornāti, spatium deliberandi habuĕrunt, quem potissĭmum vitæ cursum sequi vellent. Cic.—"The number is especially small of those, who, either by extraordinary genius, or by remarkable erudition and knowledge, or by being endowed with either, have enjoyed the opportunity of deciding what mode of life, in especial, they would wish to embrace."

Imberbis juvĕnis tandem custōde remōto
Gaudet equis canĭbusque, et aprīci grāmĭne campi,

Cēreus in vitium flecti, monitōribus asper,
Utilium tardus provīsor, prōdigus æris,
Sublīmis, cŭpĭdusque, et amāta relinquĕre pernix. Hor.
—"The beardless youth, his tutor at length dismissed devotes himself to horses and hounds, and the sward of the sunny Campus Martius; pliable as wax in receiving bad impressions, impatient of admonition, slow to see what is really for his good, profuse of money, high-spirited and full of eagerness, and prone to abandon the objects of his recent affection."

—— *Immensum gloria calcar habet.* Ovid.—"Glory affords an unbounded stimulus."

Immo, duas dabo, inquit ille adolescens, una si parum est,
Et si duarum pœnitēbit, inquit, addentur duæ. Plaut.
—"'Aye, I will give you two,' says this young man, 'if one is too little; and if you are not satisfied with two,' says he, 'two more shall be added.'"

Immŏrĭtur studiis, et amōre senescit habendi. Hor.—"He is dying from his very efforts, and in his eagerness to acquire wealth is becoming an old man."

Immortāle odium, et nunquam sanābĭle vulnus. Juv.—"An undying hatred, and a wound that can never be healed."

Immortālia ne speres monet annus, et almum
Quæ rapit hora diem—— Hor.
—"That we are not to expect permanence in things, the year, and the hour that is hurrying past this delightful day, admonish us."

Imperāre sibi maxĭmum impĕrium est. Sen.—"To command one's self, is to exercise the greatest command."

Impĕrat aut servit collecta pecūnia cuique. Hor.—"Money amassed either serves or rules us." It becomes either a slave or a tyrant, according to the way in which it is employed.

Impĕria dura tolle, quid virtus erit?—"Remove all harsh restraints, what will become of virtue?"

Impĕrium facĭlè iis artĭbus retinētur, quibus initio partum est. Sall.—"Empire is most easily retained by those arts by which it was originally acquired."

Impĕrium flagitio acquisītum nemo unquam bonis artĭbus exercuit. Tacit.—"No one ever employed sovereign power acquired by guilty measures, to promote good ends."

Impĕrium in impĕrio.—"One government existing within another." Said of a power assumed or set up in opposition to constituted authority.

Impetrāre oportet, quia æquum postŭlas. PLAUT.—"You ought to have your own way, as you only ask what is fair."

Implacābĭles plerumque læsæ muliĕres. *Prov.*—"Women when injured are generally implacable."

Implētus venter non vult studēre libenter.—"A belly well filled is not readily inclined to study." A mediæval line.

Impotentia excūsat legem. *Law Max.*—"Inability suspends the operation of the law." Natural infirmities disqualify a man from the performance of certain duties of a citizen; as in the case of lunatics, the blind, the dumb, &c.

Imprimātur.—"Let it be printed." The word generally used by the licenser of the press, in countries where the press is under the control of the government.

——*Imprŏbæ*
Crescunt divitiæ, tamen
Curtæ nescio quid sempĕr abest rei. HOR.
—"Iniquitous wealth increases, yet something or other is ever wanting to our still incomplete fortune."

Imprŏbe amor, quid non mortālia pectŏra cogis? VIRG.—"Oh, cruel love! to what dost thou not impel the human breast?"

Imprŏbè Neptunum accūsat, qui naufragium itĕrum facit. SYR.—"He who twice suffers shipwreck unfairly throws the blame on Neptune." Let experience teach you to avoid a danger which you have once escaped.

Imprŏbi hŏmĭnis est mendācio fallĕre. CIC.—"It is the act of a bad man to deceive by falsehood."

Imprŏbis aliēna virtus semper formidolōsa est. SALL.—"By wicked men the virtue of others is always dreaded." They are afraid that comparisons will be made to their disadvantage.

Impūnĭtas semper ad deteriōra invītat. COKE.—"Impunity always invites to still worse crimes."

In actu.—"In the very act."

In æquāli jure mĕlior est conditio possidentis. *Law Max.*—"Where the rights are equal the condition of him who is in possession is the best." Equivalent to "Possession is nine points of the law."

In aere piscāri; in mare venāri. *Prov.*—"To fish in the air; to hunt in the sea." Said of persons attempting things for which by nature or circumstances they are utterly unfitted.

In amōre hæc omnia insunt vitia; injūriæ,
Suspiciōnes, inimicitiæ, indūciæ,
Bellum, pax rursus.—— TER.
—"In love there are all these evils; wrongs, suspicions, enmities, reconcilements, war, and then peace again."

In Angliā non est interregnum. *Law Max.*—"In England there never is an interregnum." See *Rex nunquam*, &c.

In annūlo Dei figūram ne gestāto. *Prov.*—"Wear not the image of the Deity in a ring." Do not use the name of God on frivolous occasions.

In aquā scribis. *Prov.*—"You are writing on water." You are wasting your labour.

In arēnā ædificas. *Prov.*—"You are building on sand." You are raising a fabric which cannot stand.

In beāto omnia beāta. HOR.—"With him who is fortunate everything is fortunate."

In cadūcum parietem inclināre. *Prov.*—"To lean against a falling wall." To rely upon a false or a feeble friend.

In calamitōso risus etiam injūria est. SYR.—"Even to smile at the unfortunate is to do an injury."

In căpĭte.—"In chief." In the middle ages, those who held lands *immediately* of the king, and not of a mesne tenant, were called tenants *in capite*.

In capĭte orphani discit chirurgus.—"The surgeon practises on the orphan's head." A proverb of Arabian origin.

In causâ făcĭli, cuivis licet esse diserto. OVID.—"In an easy cause any man may be eloquent."

In cœlo nunquam spectātam impūnè comētam. CLAUD.—"A comet is never beheld in the sky without disastrous results." The appearance of a comet was supposed to be indicative of some calamity to mankind.

In cœlo quies.—"In heaven there is rest." A motto very commonly used on hatchments.

In cœlum jacŭlāris. *Prov.*—"You are aiming your dart against the heavens." Your anger cannot injure him against whom it is directed.

In commendam.—"As commended," or "intrusted." A

commendam implies a licence to hold a living jointly with some benefice of higher rank.

In contingentĭbus et lībĕris tota rătio facti stat in voluntāte facientis. *Law Max.*—"In contingencies and on occasions where we are free to act, the reason of our doing depends on the will of the doer."

In corpŏre.—"In a body."

In curiâ. *Law Term.*—"In court."

In dubiis benigniōra semper sunt præferenda. *Law Max.*—"In cases of doubt the side of mercy should always be preferred."

In eâdem re utĭlĭtas et turpitūdo esse non potest. CIC.—"In the same thing turpitude and advantage cannot coexist."

In eburnâ vagīnâ plumbeus glădius.—"A leaden sword in an ivory sheath." Said by Diogenes of a shallow, showy fop.

In equilibrio.—"In equilibrium."

In esse. *Law Term.*—"In actual being." That which exists.

In exornando se, multum tempŏris insūmunt mulĭĕres. TER.—"Females spend too much time in bedecking themselves."

In extenso.—"In full," or "at large." Without abridgment. Used in reference to written documents.

In flagranti delicto.—"In glaring delinquency." In the very commission of the act.

In flammam flammas, in mare fundis aquas. OVID.—"You heap flames upon flames, and pour water into the sea."

In flammam ne manum injĭcĭto. *Prov.*—"Thrust not your hand into the fire."

In fŏrĭbus scribat, occupātum se esse. PLAUT.—"Let him write upon the door that he is busy."

In formâ paupĕris. *Law Term.*—"In the form of a poor man." Where any person has just cause of suit, but is so poor that he is not worth five pounds when all his debts are paid, the court, on oath made to that effect, and a certificate from counsel that he has good ground of action, will admit him to sue *in formâ pauperis*, without paying any fees to counsel, attorney, or the court.

In foro conscientiæ. *Law Term.*—"At the tribunal of conscience." According to the test supplied by our own conscience.

In fugâ fœda mors est, in victōria gloriōsa. Cic.—"Death is shameful in flight, glorious in victory."

In furias ignemque ruunt; amor omnĭbus idem. Virg.—"They rush into fire and fury, love is the same in all."

In futūro.—"In future." At a future time.

In hoc signo vinces.—"By this sign shalt thou conquer." This motto was adopted by the emperor Constantine, after his assertion that he had beheld a cross in the heavens, the fancied precursor of victory. It is the motto of the Earl of Arran, and other persons of rank.

——*In horâ sæpe ducentos,*
Ut magnum, versus dictābat, stans pede in uno. Hor.
—"He would often, as a great feat, dictate two hundred lines in an hour, standing in the same position." A description of the fluency of Lucilius, a witty but inelegant poet.

In hunc scŏpŭlum cadāverōsi senes ut plurĭmum impingunt.—"Old men on the verge of the grave are mostly wrecked upon this rock"—that of avarice.

In illo viro, tantum robur corpŏris et ănĭmi fuit, ut quocunque loco natus esset, fortūnam sibi factūrus viderētur. Livy.—"In that man there was such great strength of body and mind, that in whatever station he had been born it seemed as though he was sure of making his fortune." Character of the elder Cato, as quoted by Lord Bacon.

In judĭcando crĭminōsa est celĕrĭtas. Syr.—"In giving judgment haste is criminal."

In limine.—"At the threshold." Preliminary.

In loco.—"In the place;" meaning, "in the proper place," "upon the spot." It may also mean, "instead of."

In loco parentis.—"In the place of a parent."

——*In lucro quæ datur hora mihi est.* Ovid.—"The hour which is granted me, is so much gained."

In magnis et vŏluisse sat est. Prop.—"In great undertakings to have even attempted is enough."

——*In malâ uxōre atque inimīco si quid sumas sumptus est;*
In bono hospĭte atque amīco, quæstus est, quod sumĭtur.
Plaut.
—"If you lay anything out on a bad wife or an enemy, that is an expense; but what is laid out on a deserving guest and a friend, is so much gained."

In malis sperāre bonum, nisi innŏcens, nemo potest.—"In adversity no one but the innocent can hope for happiness"

In manus.—A mediæval expression, meaning, "Into your hands I commend myself," *commendo me* being understood.

In mari aquam quærit. *Prov.*—"He is looking for water in the sea."

In mea vesānas habui dispendia vires,
Et valui pœnas fortis in ipse meas. OVID.
—"To my own undoing I had the strength of a madman; and for my own punishment did I stoutly exert it."

In mĕdias res. HOR.—"Into the very midst of a thing." Applicable to a person who without prelude plunges into the very midst of the matter in hand.

In mĕdio tutissĭmus ibis. OVID.—"You will go most safely in the middle." A middle course is the safest.

In melle sunt sitæ linguæ vestræ atque orātiōnes,
Corda felle sunt lita atque acēto. PLAUT.
—"Your tongues and your talk savour of honey; your hearts are steeped in gall and vinegar."

In memŏriam.—"In memory of."

In mercatūrâ faciendâ multæ fallāciæ et quasi præstĭgiæ exercentur.—"In commerce many deceptions, and, so to say, juggleries, are currently practised."

In monendo sapĭmus omnes, verum ubi
Peccāmus ipsi, non vidēmus propria.
—"We are all wise in giving advice, but when we ourselves commit faults, we see them not."

In nocte consĭlium. *Prov.*—"In the night is counsel." Act not precipitately, but take time for reflection, or, as we say, "sleep on it."

In nōmĭne Dŏmĭni incĭpit omne malum.—"In the Lord's name every evil begins." A mediæval proverb, implying that the most sacred pretences are often made an excuse for the infliction of the greatest injuries.

In nova fert ănĭmus mutātas dicĕre formas
Corpŏra.—— OVID.
—"My design leads me to speak of forms changed into new bodies."

In nubĭbus.—"In the clouds."

In nuce.—"In a nutshell."

In nullum avārus bonus est, in se pessĭmus. SYR.—"The

avaricious man is good to no one, but most hurtful to himself."

In nullum reipublĭcæ usum, ambitiōsâ loquēlâ inclāruit. TACIT.—"He distinguished himself by ambitious oratory, of no advantage to the state." A good description of the career of a demagogue.

In omnia paratus.—"Prepared for everything."

In omnĭbus ferè minōri ætāti succurrĭtur. *Law Max.*—"In nearly all respects a person under age is protected by the law." A minor can be sued only for money due for necessaries; for the law encourages no one to supply him with luxuries.

In omnĭbus quidem, maxĭmè tamen in jure, æquĭtas est. *Law Max.*—"In all things, but in law especially, equity is an ingredient." Equity tempers the asperity of the written law, and makes it pliable according to the requirements of the case.

In pace.—"In peace." The *in pace* was a monastic punishment in the middle ages. The offender was incarcerated or immured, the parting words addressed to him or her being *Vade in pace*, "Go in peace," which see.

In pace leōnes, in prælio cervi. *Prov.*—"Lions in peace, deer in war." The character of braggarts.

In partĭbus.—"In the parts (beyond sea)," *transmarinis* being understood. In the Roman Catholic Church, titular bishops are said to be bishops *in partibus.*

In perpĕtuam rei memŏriam.—"In everlasting remembrance of the event." A motto on a memorial of any great event.

In pertūsum ingĕrĭmus dicta dolium. PLAUT.—"We are casting our words into a leaky cask." We are throwing away our advice.

In pios usus.—"For pious uses."

In pleno.—"In full."

In pontificālibus.—"In pontificals," or priestly robes.

In portu navigāre. *Prov.*—"To sail into harbour." To overcome difficulties with final safety. See *Inveni portum*, &c.

In posse. *Law Term.*—"In possible being." A child unborn is *in posse.*

——*In prece totus eram.* OVID.—"I was wholly wrapt in prayer."

——*In principatu commutando sæpius*
Nil præter domĭni nomen mutant pauperes. PHÆD.
—"In a change of government, the poor mostly change nothing beyond the name of their master."

In prŏpriâ persōnâ.—"In proper person." Personal appearance, used in contradistinction to appearance by a representative.

In proverbium cessit, sapientiam vino obumbrāri. PLINY *the Elder.*—"It has passed into a proverb, that wisdom is overshadowed by wine."

In puris naturālĭbus.—"In a state of nature." Stark naked. An expression used in a jocular sense.

In quadrum redigĕre.—"To make a matter square." To reduce to order.

In re. Law Term.—"In the matter of."

In re malâ anĭmo si bono utāre, adjŭvat. PLAUT.—"In adversity, if you employ fortitude, it is of service."

In rebus dubiis plurĭmi est audācia. SYR.—"In matters of doubt, boldness is of the greatest value."

In rebus prospĕris superbiam magnŏpĕre, fastidium, arrogantiamque fugiāmus. CIC.—"In prosperity, let us especially avoid pride, disdain, and arrogance."

In referendâ gratiâ, debēmus imitāri agros fertĭles qui plus multo affĕrunt quam accepĕrunt. CIC.—"In making a return for kindness, we ought to imitate fertile lands, which give back much more than they have received."

In saltu uno duos apros capĕre. Prov.—"In one cover to take two boars." Similar to our proverb, "To kill two birds with one stone."

In se magna ruunt.—— LUCAN.—"Great interests clash with each other." Their very extent is apt to bring them into collision.

In secundis rebus nihil in quemquam superbè ac violenter consulĕre decet. LIVY.—"In prosperity it becomes us to act towards no one with pride and violence."

——*In seipso totus, teres, atque rotundus.* HOR.—"A man perfect in himself, polished, and round as a globe." A description of a man wholly occupied in mastering the inequalities of his own passions.

——*In servitūte expĕtunt multa inīqua;*
Habendum et ferendum hoc onus est cum labōre. PLAUT.

—"In servitude many hardships befall us; in pain this burden must be borne and endured."

In situ.—"In its site," or "position."

In solo Deo salus.—"Salvation in God alone." Motto of the Earl of Harewood.

In solo vivendi causa palato est. JUV.—"The pleasures of the palate are their only reason for living."

In studio rei amplificandæ apparebat, non avaritiæ prædam, sed instrumentum bonitati quæri. CIC.—"In his anxiety to increase his fortune, it was evident that it was not the gratification of avarice that was sought, but the means of doing good." A compliment paid by Cicero to the virtues of Rabirius Postumus.

In summâ inanitate versari.—"To be engaged in the very height of frivolity;" or, in a vain and silly pursuit.

In sylvam ligna ferre. *Prov.*—"To carry wood to the forest." As we say, "To carry coals to Newcastle."

In te, Domine, speravi.—"In thee, O Lord, have I put my trust." The first line of a Psalm, and the motto of the Earl of Strathmore.

——*In te omnis domus inclināta recumbit.* VIRG.—"In thee are centred all the hopes of thy house." The words of Amata to her son Turnus, when about to engage in combat with Æneas.

In tĕnui labor at tĕnuis non gloria.—— VIRG.—"It is labour bestowed on a trifling subject, but not trifling is the glory." Said by Virgil in reference to the Fourth Book of his Georgics, which treats of the production and habits of bees.

In terrōrem.—"In terror." By way of warning. Any power of enforcing the execution of a bond, or of inflicting punishment, or of revealing a secret, may be held *in terrorem* against another. The rod and fool's cap are exhibited *in terrorem.*

In toto.—"In the whole." Entirely.

In toto et pars continētur.—"In the whole the part is contained."

In transĭtu.—"On the passage." Goods are *in transitu* when on their passage from the owner to the consignee, so designated to free them from duties or excise in their passage through countries where they are not to remain.

In tuo regno es.—"You are in your own kingdom." You are omnipotent here, or you would not have insulted me thus.

In turbas et discordias pessĭmo cuique plūrĭma vis ; pax et quies bonis artĭbus indĭgent. TACIT.—"In times of turbulence and discord, whoever is the most abandoned has the greatest power; peace and good order stand in need of repose."

In unoquoque virōrum bonōrum habĭtat Deus. SEN.—"God dwells within every good man."

In utero.—"In the womb."

In utramvis dormīre aurem. *Prov.*—"To sleep on either ear." As we sleep most soundly when lying on the side, this proverb applies to a man who has made his fortune, and may take his ease.

In văcuo.—"In a vacuum."

In verbo.—"In a word."

In vino vēritas. *Prov.*—"In wine there is truth." Reserve is laid aside when a person is under the influence of wine. See *Quod in*, &c.

In vĭtium ducit culpæ fuga.—— HOR.—"In flying from one vice, we are led into another."

——*In vitium libertas excĭdit, et vim*
Dignam lege regi.—— HOR.
—"Freedom degenerated into excess and violence that required to be regulated by law."

——*In vultu signa dolentis erant.* OVID.—"On her features there were signs of grief."

Inānem inter magnātes versandi gloriam pertinacissĭmè sectāri.—"Inveterately to hanker after the glory of associating with the great."

Inānis torrens verbōrum. QUINT.—"An empty torrent of words."

——*Incedĭmus per ignes*
Supposĭtos cinĕri dolōso. HOR.
—"We are walking over fires that lie concealed beneath deceitful ashes." Our prospect of success appears encouraging, but we may encounter unforeseen disasters.

Incendit omnem fēmĭnæ zelus domum. *Prov.*—"A jealous woman sets a whole house in a flame."

Incenditque anĭmum famæ venientis amōre. VIRG.—"And fires his soul with the love of coming fame."

Incerta hæc si tu postŭles
Ratiōne certa facĕre, nihĭlo plus agas,
Quam si des opĕram ut cum ratiōne insānias. TER. —"If you expect to render these uncertain things certain by dint of reason, you will no more effect it than if you were to endeavour to be mad with reason."

Incerti sunt exĭtus belli. CIC.—"The results of war are uncertain."

Incertum est quo te loco mors expectet; itaque in omni loco illam expecta. SEN.—"It is uncertain in what place death awaits you; await it therefore in every place." "Live this day as if the last."

——*Incessu pătuit Dea.* VIRG.—"She stood revealed a goddess in her gait."

Incĭdit in Scyllam cupiens vitāre Charybdim. PHILIP GUALTIER DE LILLE, *a poet of the 13th century.*—"He falls into Scylla in endeavouring to escape Charybdis." These were two whirlpools on the coast of Sicily, of which Scylla was the most dangerous. They caused the destruction of a part of the fleet of Ulysses. It is sometimes quoted "*Qui vult vitare,* &c." See *Quo tendis,* &c.

Incipĕre multo est, quam impetrāre, facĭlius. PLAUT.—"It is much more easy to begin a thing than to complete it."

Incitamentum amōris musica.—"Music is an incitement to love."

Inclusio unius est exclusio alterius. *Law Max.*—"The inclusion of the one implies the exclusion of the other."

——*Incoctum generōso pectus honesto.* PERS.—"A breast imbued with generous honour."

Incūdi reddĕre. HOR.—"To return to the anvil." To reconsider a work, or return our performances to the anvil, to repair or repolish them.

Incultis aspĕrisque regiōnĭbus diūtius nives hærent, ast dŏmĭtā tellūre dilabuntur; simĭlĭter in pectŏrĭbus ira consīdit; feras quidem mentes obsĭdet, erudītas prælābĭtur. PETRON. ARBITER.—"In rugged and uncultivated regions the snow lies longer upon the ground, but on cultivated soil it soon disappears; in a similar manner anger affects our breasts; in those which are uncultivated it remains, but in those which are cultivated it quickly subsides."

Incurvat genu senectus. *Prov.*—"Old age bends the knee."

Inde datæ leges ne fortior omnia posset. *Law Max.*—"Laws

were given that the strongest might not have it all his own way."

Inde iræ.—"Hence this resentment."

Index expurgatōrius.—An "Index expurgatory," or "purifying index." A list of books denounced by the pope as improper to be read by members of the Romish Church. Since it was originally compiled this Index has been frequently modified according to circumstances.

Indictum sit.—"Let it be unsaid." Said by way of apology.

Indigna digna habenda sunt quæ hæres facit. PLAUT.—"Unworthy acts must be looked upon as worthy if done by your master." See *Ita servum*, &c.

Indigne vivit per quem non vivit alter.—"He by whom no one else lives, does not deserve to live."

Indignor quidquam reprehendi, non quia crasse Compŏsitum, illepĭdumve putētur, sed quia nuper. HOR. —"I am annoyed that a thing should be found fault with, not because it is a heavy composition, or inelegant, but because it is modern."

Indignum est in eâ civitāte, quæ lēgĭbus continētur, discēdi à lēgĭbus.—"In a state which is governed by laws, there ought to be no departure from them."

—— *Indŏcĭlis privāta loqui.*— LUCAN.—"Incapable of divulging secrets."

Indocti discant, et ament mĕmĭnisse perīti.—"Let the ignorant learn, and the learned take pleasure in remembering." A line by HENAULT, often attributed to Horace.

Industriæ nil impossĭbĭle.—"To industry there is nothing impossible." A Latinized saying of Periander of Corinth, one of the seven wise men of Greece.

Indūtus virtūte ab alto.—"Endued with virtue from on high."

Inĕrat Vitellio simplĭcĭtas ac liberālĭtas, quæ, nisi adsit modus, in exĭtium vertuntur. TACIT.—"There was in Vitellius a frankness and liberality, which, unless tempered with moderation, must lead to ruin." Virtues in excess, unless guided by prudence, are frequently productive of ultimate evil. See *Insani sapiens*, &c.

Inest et formīcæ sua bilis. *Prov.*—"Even the ant can feel anger." The humblest of beings in the animated world is influenced by passion, though it often lacks the means of showing it. See *Habet et*, &c.

Inest sua gratia parvis.—"Trifles have their own peculiar charms."

Infandum, regīna, jubes renovāre dolōrem. VIRG.—"You command me, O queen, to renew an unspeakable grief." Said by Æneas, with reference to the destruction of Troy, his native city, when requested by Dido to relate the history of its downfall.

Infantem nudum cùm te natūra creāvit,
Paupertātis onus patienter ferre memento. CATO.
—"As nature created you a naked infant, remember to bear with patience the burden of poverty."

Infēlix Dido, nulli bene juncta marīto;
Hoc pereunte fugis, hoc fugiente peris. AUSON.
—"Hapless Dido, wedded under no good auspices to either husband; the one dying thou didst fly, the other flying thou didst die." Sichæus is here alluded to as her first husband, Æneas as the second.

Infinīta est velōcĭtas tempŏris, quæ magis appāret respicientĭbus. SEN.—"The swiftness of time is infinite, as is still more evident when we look back on the past."

Infra dignitātem.—"Below his dignity." In cant parlance called *Infra dig.*

Infra tuam pellĭcŭlam te contĭne. Prov.—"Content yourself with your own skin." Live as becomes your circumstances. Said to the ass who was found wearing a lion's skin, and got cudgelled to death.

——*Ingĕminant curæ, rursusque resurgens*
Sævit amor, magnoque irārum fluctuat æstu. VIRG.
—"Her cares redouble, and love, again arising, rages in her breast, and swells with a vast tide of passion."

Ingĕnio făcies concĭliante placet. OVID.—"When the disposition charms, the features are pleasing."

——*Ingĕnio stat sine morte decus.* PROPERT.—"The honours of genius are immortal." See *Exegi monumentum*, &c., and *Jamque opus*, &c.

Ingeniōrum cos æmulātio. Prov.—"Emulation is the whetstone of genius."

Ingĕnium cui sit, cui mens divīnior, atque os
Magna sonātūrum, des nōmĭnis hujus honōrem. HOR.

—"To him who possesses genius, a soul of diviner cast, and greatness of expression, to him give the honour of the name of poet."

——*Ingĕnium ingens*
Inculto latet hoc sub corpŏre.— Hor.
—"A great intellect lies concealed beneath that uncouth exterior."

——*Ingĕnium mala sæpe movent.*— Ovid.—"Misfortunes often sharpen the genius."

——*Ingĕnium res*
Adversæ nudāre solent, celāre secundæ. Hor.
—"Adversity is wont to reveal genius, prosperity to conceal it."

Ingens telum necessĭtas. Sen.—"Necessity is a powerful weapon."

——*Ingentem fŏrĭbus domus alta superbis*
Mane salūtantum totis vomit ædĭbus undam. Virg.
—"The lofty palace, with its gorgeous portals, pours forth from every part whole torrents of courtiers, who have been paying their morning homage."

Ingentes ănĭmos angusto in corpŏre versant. Virg.—"In diminutive bodies they display mighty souls." Said by Virgil of the bees, but applicable to men, like Alexander the Great, and Buonaparte, small in person, but great in spirit.

Ingentes domĭnos, et claræ nōmĭna famæ,
Illustrique graves nobilitāte domos
Dēvīta, et longè cautus fuge; contrăhe vela,
Et te littŏrĭbus cymba propinqua vehat. Sen.
—"Shun mighty lords, and names illustrious in fame, and houses ennobled by exalted rank, and, ever on your guard, fly from them afar; take in your sails, and let your bark hug the shore as it bears you along."

——*Ingĕnuas didicisse fidēlĭter artes*
Emollit mores, nec sinit esse feros. Ovid.
—"To have thoroughly learned the liberal arts refines the manners, and permits them not to be unpolished."

Ingrāto hŏmĭne terra pejus nil creat.—"The earth produces nothing worse than an ungrateful man."

Ingrātum est bĕnĕfĭcium quod diu inter manus dantis hæsit; at bis gratum est, quod ultro affertur.—"The favour that has been long delayed in the hands of the giver loses its value; but that is doubly grateful, which is offered voluntarily." See *Bis dat*, &c., and *Inopi beneficium*, &c.

Ingrātum si dixĕris, omnia dicis. *Prov.*—"If you say he is ungrateful, you say everything." The ungrateful man is capable of any criminality.

Ingrātus est qui remōtis testĭbus agit gratiam. SEN.—"He is an ungrateful man who acknowledges his obligation when all witnesses are removed." A truly grateful man does not content himself with secret thanks for benefits conferred.

Ingrātus unus misĕris omnĭbus nocet. SYR.—"One ungrateful man does an injury to all who are in distress." Many wretched but deserving persons go unrelieved, in consequence of the ingratitude of others.

Ingrĕdĭturque solo, et caput inter nūbĭla condit. VIRG.—"She roves over the earth, while her head is hid among the clouds." A description of scandal.

Inimīci famam non ita ut nata est ferunt. PLAUT.—"Enemies carry about reports not in the form in which they have originated."

Inimicus et invĭdus vicinōrum ŏcŭlus. *Prov.*—"An enemy and an envious man is an eye over his neighbours."

Iniqua nunquam regna perpetua manent. SEN.—"Rule unjustly gained is never of long duration."

Iniquissĭmam pacem justissĭmo bello antĕfĕro. CIC.—"I prefer the most unjust peace to the most just war."

Iniquum est alĭquem rei sui esse jūdĭcem. COKE.—"It is unfair that any one should be judge in his own cause."

Initia magistrātuum nostrōrum meliōra et firma finis inclīnat. TAC.—"The commencement of our official duties is characterized by greater vigour and alacrity, but towards the end they flag." Too often the case in new undertakings.

Injūriâ injūriam cohibēre licet.—"We may escape an injury by the infliction of another." According to the law of nations, not of Christianity.

Injūriæ spretæ exolescunt, si irascāris agnĭtæ videntur. *Prov.*—"Injuries unnoticed lose their effect; if you are angry, they are seen to be acknowledged." You thereby afford a triumph to him who gave the affront.

Injuriam qui factūrus est jam facit. SEN.—"He who is

about to commit an injury, has committed it already." "Whoso hateth his brother, is a murderer: and ye know that no murderer hath eternal life abiding in him." 1 *John* iii. 15. See also *Matt.* v. 28.

Injuriārum remĕdium est oblivio. *Prov.*—"Oblivion is the best remedy for injuries."

——*Injusta ab justis impetrāri non decet;*
Justa autem ab injustis, pĕtĕre, insipientia 'st. PLAUT.
—"From the reasonable to ask what is unreasonable is not right; from the unreasonable to ask what is reasonable is sheer folly."

Innătat unda freto dulcis, lēviorque marīnâ est,
Quæ proprium mixto de sale pondus habet. OVID.
—"Fresh water swims on the surface of the deep, and is lighter than that of the sea, which derives its peculiar weight from the admixture of salt."

Innuendo.—"By making signs," or, "By nodding at." A covert hint or intimation is so called.

——*Inŏpem me copia fecit.* OVID.—"Plenty has made me poor." Narcissus says this, on finding that self-love has deprived him of a valuable treasure, the love of others. It may be applied to a writer, or speaker, whose expression is embarrassed by the copiousness of his thoughts.

Inŏpi bĕnĕficium bis dat, qui dat celĕrĭter. SYR.—"He confers a two-fold benefit on the needy man who confers it speedily." See *Bis dat*, &c., and *Ingratum est*, &c.

Inops, potentem dum vult imitāri, perit. PHÆD.—"The needy man, while affecting to imitate the powerful, comes to ruin." Witness the Fable of the Frog and the Ox.

Inquĭnat egrĕgios adjuncta superbia mores. CLAUD.—"If pride accompanies, it is a blemish to the best of manners."

Insāni săpiens nomen ferat, æquus inīqui,
Ultra quod satis est virtūtem si petat ipsam. HOR.
—"Let the wise man bear the name of fool, the just of unjust, if he pursues even virtue herself beyond the proper bounds." See *Inerat Vitellio*, &c.

Insanientis dum sapientiæ
Consultus erro.—— HOR.
—See *Parcus Deorum*, &c.

Insanīre parat certâ ratiōne modoque HOR.—"He is preparing to show his madness with a certain degree of reason and method." There is "method in his madness."

Insanīre putas solennia me, neque rides. HOR.—"You think me mad like everyone else, and you do not laugh."

Insānus mĕdio flumĭne quæris aquam.—"You madly search for water, in the middle of a stream." Said of one who searches for what is wrong where there is nothing good to be found.

Insānus omnis furĕre credit cætĕros. SYR.—"Every madman believes that all others are mad."

——*Insequĭtur cumŭlo præruptus aquæ mons.* VIRG.—"A steep mountain of waters follows with its towering height."

Insipientis est dicĕre, Non putārem. CIC.—"It is the part of a fool to say, 'I should not have thought so.'"

Insĭta homĭnĭbus natūra violentiæ resistĕre. TACIT.—"It is by nature implanted in man to resist oppression."

——*Insperāta accĭdunt magis sæpe quam quæ speres.* PLAUT.—"Things not hoped for happen more frequently than things which you do hope for."

Inspicĕre, tanquam in spĕcŭlum, in vitas omnium
Jubeo, atque ex ăliis sumĕre exemplum sibi. TER.
—"I advise you to look into the lives of men, as though into a mirror, and from others to take an example for yourself."

Intĕger vitæ scĕlĕrisque purus
Non eget Mauri jăcŭlis neque arcu. HOR.
—"The man whose life is unblemished, and unstained by crime, needs not the javelins nor bow of the Moor." Such a man may be wounded in body, but will remain unscathed in soul.

Intĕgra mens augustissĭma possessio. *Prov.*—"A mind unblemished is the noblest possession."

Intentio inservīre debet lĕgĭbus, non leges intentiōni. COKE.—"The intention ought to obey the laws, not the laws the intention." The laws ought not to be wrested from their original meaning, to suit the purposes of any one.

Inter alia.—"Among other things."

Inter amīcos omnium rerum commūnĭtas. CIC.—"Among friends all property is common."

Inter arma leges silent. CIC.—"In the midst of arms the laws are silent." Martial law then takes the place of civic sway.

Inter cuncta leges, et percontābĕre doctos,
Quâ ratiōne queas tradūcĕre lēnĭter ævum. HOR.
—"Under every circumstance you must read and consult the learned how you may be enabled to pass your life in quiet."

Inter delicias semper alĭquid sævi nos strangŭlat. *Prov.*—"Amid our enjoyments there is always some vexation to torment us." See *Medio de fonte*, &c.

Inter fīnĭtĭmos vetus atque antīqua simultas,
Immortāle odium et nunquam sanābĭle vulnus
Ardet adhuc——
Inde furor vulgo, quod nūmĭna vīcīnōrum
Odit uterque locus, cum solos credit habendos
Esse deos, quos ipse colit.—— JUV.
—"An ancient and inveterate enmity between neighbours, an everlasting hatred, and an ever-rankling wound, still galls them both. Hence has sprung universal rancour, because each community hates the worship of its neighbour, as it believes that those gods only which itself holds sacred ought to be esteemed as such."

Inter indoctos etiam cŏrȳdus sonat. *Prov.*—"To the unskilled the voice of the sparrow is music." A dunce even may impose on the illiterate. The *corydus* was a lark with an inferior note, found in the neighbourhood of Athens.

Inter malleum et incūdem. *Prov.*—"Between the hammer and the anvil." Said of a person between the horns of a dilemma.

Inter nos.—"Between ourselves." "Not to let it go any further."

Inter pŭĕros senex. *Prov.*—"An old man among boys." Said of a person who by his gravity of manners affects to be wiser than he really is.

Inter quadrupĕdes gloria prima lepus. MART.—"Of quadrupeds the chief glory is the hare." The Roman gourmands seemed to esteem this animal higher than we do; for we find Horace saying, *Fœcundi lepŏris sapiens sectābĭtur armos.*—"A man of taste will look out for the shoulders of a pregnant hare."

Inter spem curamque, timōres inter et iras,
Omnem crede diem tibi diluxisse suprēmum:
Grata supervĕniet quæ non sperābĭtur hora. HOR.

—"In the midst of hope and care, in the midst of fears and disquietudes, think every day that dawns upon you to be your last; the hour which shall not be expected will come upon you as a grateful boon."

——*Inter strepit anser olōres.* VIRG.—"A goose he gabbles among the swans."

——*Inter sylvas Acadēmi quærĕre verum.* HOR.—"Amid the woods of Academus to seek for truth." A spot near Athens where Plato lectured, and the philosophers met for discussion.

——*Inter utrumque tene.* OVID.—"Keep a mid course between the two extremes." See *In medio*, &c.

Inter vivos.—"Between" or "among the living."

Interdictum est ne bonus cum malĕfico usum ullīus rei consociētur. PHÆD.—"It is forbidden a good man to hold any intercourse with an evil-doer."

Interdum lăcrymæ pondĕra vocis habent. OVID.—"Sometimes tears have the weight of words."

Interdum stultus benè lŏquĭtur. *Prov.*—"Sometimes a fool speaks to the purpose." We may learn something of even a fool.

——*Interdum vitia prosunt homĭnĭbus,*
Sed tempŏre ipso tamen appăret vĕrĭtas. PHÆD.—"Vices are sometimes profitable to men, but still, in time, the truth transpires."

Interdum vulgus rectum videt, est ubi peccat. HOR.—"Sometimes the populace sees things aright; at other times it errs."

Intĕrea dulces pendent circum oscŭla nati;
Casta pudicitiam servat domus. VIRG.
"Meantime his sweet children hang about his lips, and his chaste abode is the dwelling of virtue." See *At jam*, &c., and the corresponding lines in *Gray's Elegy*, Stanza vi.

Intĕrea gustus elementa per omnia quærunt,
Nunquam ănĭmo prĕtiis obstantĭbus; intĕrius si
Attendas, magis illa juvant, quæ pluris emuntur. JUV.
—"Meantime they search for delicacies throughout all the elements, with minds regardless of expense; watch them narrowly, and you will see that those things please most which cost the highest price."

Intĕrĕrit multum Davusne loquātur an heros. HOR.—"It is

of considerable consequence whether (the servant) Davus is speaking, or a hero." The poet here warns dramatic writers to make their characters speak in language appropriate to their station in life.

Intĕrest reipublĭcæ ut quisque re suâ benè utātur.—"It is of importance to the state that every one should make a good use of his property."

Interpōne tuis interdum gaudia curis.—"Season your cares with joys sometimes."

Intolerābilius nihil est quam fœmĭna dives. JUV.—"Nothing is more unbearable than a woman with a full purse."

Intonuēre poli et crebris micat ignibus æther. VIRG.—"The heavens thunder and the sky flashes with vivid lightnings."

——*Intra*
Fortūnam debet quisque manēre suam. OVID.
—"Every one is bound to live within his means." See *Crede mihi*, &c.

——*Intus et in cute novi.* PERS.—"I know thee inside and out." See *Ad populum*, &c.

——*Intus et in jĕcŏre ægro*
Nascuntur dŏmĭni.—— PERS.
—"In our own breasts, and from a morbid liver, our masters spring up." Our passions, if they are not our servants, will become our masters.

Intūta quæ indĕcōra. TACIT.—"Those things which are unbecoming are unsafe."

Invendĭbĭli merci oportet ultro emptōrem abducĕre,
Proba merx făcĭle emptorem rĕpĕrit, tametsi in abstrūso sit. PLAUT.
—"To unsaleable wares it is necessary to try to entice the buyer; good wares easily meet with a purchaser, although they may be hid in a corner."

Invēni portum, Spes et Fortūna valēte;
Sat me lusistis, ludĭte nunc ălios.
"I've reach'd the harbour, Hope and Chance, adieu!
You've play'd with me, now play with others too."
Lines at the end of Le Sage's Gil Blas. Translated from the *Anthologia Græca.* See *Jam portum,* &c. Burton ascribes this version, with some variations, to Prudentius.

Invĕnies vestri præcōnia nōmĭnis illic;
Invĕnies ănĭmi pignŏra multa mei. OVID.

—"There wilt thou find the commendations of thy name: there wilt thou find full many a pledge of my esteem."

Inventas aut qui vitam excoluēre per artes,
Quique sui mĕmŏres alios fecēre merendo. VIRG.

—"Men who have improved life by their discoveries in art, and who have insured remembrance by their good deserts."

Invĭdiâ Sicŭli non invenēre tyranni
Tormentum majus.—— JUV.

—"Sicilian tyrants invented nothing that is a greater torment than envy." He alludes to the brazen bull of Perillus, made for the Sicilian tyrant Phalaris, in which his victims were roasted to death. This, as well as the cave of Dionysius of Syracuse, were productive of slight tortures compared with those produced by envy.

Invĭdiam ferre aut fortis aut felix potest. SYR.—"The brave or the fortunate are able to endure envy."

Invĭdiam placāre paras, virtūte relictâ? HOR.—"Do you think of appeasing envy by forsaking virtue?"

Invĭdus altĕrius macrescit rebus opīmis. HOR.—"The envious man grows lean on seeing the prosperity of another." A description of the cankering effects of envy.

Invĭdus, iracundus, iners, vinōsus, amātor,
Nemo adeo ferus est, ut non mitescĕre possit,
Si modo cultūræ patientem commŏdet aurem. HOR.

—"The envious, the choleric, the indolent, the slave to wine, to women—none is so savage that he cannot be tamed, if he will only lend a patient ear to discipline."

Invīsa nunquam impĕria retinentur diu. SEN.—"A sway that has incurred hatred is never held long."

Invīsa potentia, atque miseranda vita eōrum, qui se mĕtui quam amāri malunt. CORN. NEP.—"The power is detested, and the existence wretched, of those who would rather be feared than loved."

Invīso semel princĭpe seu bene, seu male, gesta premunt. TACIT.—"A ruler once detested, his deeds, whether good or bad, lead to his downfall." Somewhat similar to our proverb—"Give a dog a bad name and hang him."

Invītâ Minervâ. CIC. *and* HOR.—"Minerva being unwilling." Minerva being the goddess of wisdom, it was supposed that she was the bestower of that invaluable attribute.

If a work appeared to be destitute of wisdom, or genius, it was said to have been composed *invitâ Minervâ*, "against the will of Minerva."

Invĭtat culpam qui peccātum prætĕrit. Syr.—"He who passes a crime unpunished, encourages sin."

Invĭtum qui servat ĭdem facit occidenti. Hor.—"He who saves a man's life against his will does just the same as if he murdered him." His benevolence is as little estimated as if he were his most bitter enemy.

Involvĕre diem nimbi et nox humĭda cœlum
Abstŭlit.—— Virg.
—"Clouds enwrapped the day, and humid night withdrew the heavens from our view."

Ipsa hæret scŏpŭlis, et quantum vertĭce ad auras
Æthĕrias, tantum radĭce in Tartăra tendit. Virg.
—"[The tree] itself cleaves fast to the rocks, and as high as it shoots upwards into the æthereal regions, so deep does it descend with its roots to Tartarus below."

——*Ipsæ rursum concĕdĭte sylvæ.* Virg.—"And you, ye woods, once more farewell!"

Ipse dies agĭtat festos; fususque per herbam,
Ignis ubi in medio, et socii cratĕra corōnant,
Te lĭbans, Lenæe, vocat.—— Virg.
—"The swain himself keeps holiday; and stretched on the grass, where there is a fire in the middle, and where his companions crown the bowl, he invokes thee, Lenæus, as he makes the libation."

Ipse dixit.—"He himself said it." He said it on his *ipse dixit.* A mere saying or assertion without proof.

Ipse Jupiter, neque pluens omnĭbus placet, neque abstĭnens. *Prov.*—"Not even Jupiter himself can please all, whether he sends rain or whether he leaves off."

Ipse pavet; nec qua commissas flectat habĕnas,
Nec scit quà sit iter; nec si sciat impĕret illis. Ovid.
—"He becomes alarmed, nor knows which way to turn the reins intrusted to him, nor does he know the way; nor if he did know, could he control the steeds." Persons who undertake what they cannot accomplish are in the predicament of Phaëton, when he attempted to guide the horses of the Sun.

Ipse semet canit. *Prov.*—"He sings about himself." In our phrase, "He is his own trumpeter."

Ipsi lætitiâ voces ad sidĕra jactant
Intonsi montes; ipsæ jam carmĭna rupes,
Ipsa sonant arbusta.—— VIRG.

—"The unshorn mountains themselves send forth their voices to the stars; even the rocks utter their song, the very shrubs resound."

Ipsissĭma verba.—"The very identical words."

Ipso facto.—"In fact itself." "Absolutely," or "actually."

Ipso jure.—"By the law itself."

——*Ira furor brevis est.*— HOR.—"Anger is a short madness."

——*Ira quæ tĕgĭtur nocet;*
Professa perdunt odia vindictæ locum. SEN.

—"Resentment which is concealed is baneful; hatred avowed loses the opportunity of revenge." The object of the resentment is put upon his guard.

Iracundiam qui vincit, hostem supĕrat maxĭmum. SYR.—"He who overcomes his anger, subdues his greatest enemy."

Irārum tantos volvis sub pectŏre fluctus? VIRG.—"Do you harbour such torrents of anger in your breast?"

——*Iras et verba locant.*— MART.—"They let out for hire their anger and their words." A satirical view of the duties of a pleader.

Irātus cum ad se redit, sibi tum irascĭtur. SYR.—"An angry man, when he returns to himself, is angry with himself." He is overwhelmed with self-reproach.

Ire tamen restat, Numa quo devēnit et Ancus. HOR.—"It still remains for you to go where Ancus and Numa have gone before."

Irrĕpit in homĭnum mentes dissimulatio. CIC.—"Dissimulation creeps apace into the minds of men."

Irrĭgat ros herbam virentem, et calor solāris tĕpĕfăcit.—"The dew waters the growing grass, and the sun's heat warms it."

Irritābis crabrōnes. PLAUT.—"You will irritate the hornets." Or, as we say, You will bring a hornet's nest about your ears.

Is cadet ante senem qui sapit ante diem. *Prov.*—"He dies

before he is old, who is wise before his day." See *Cito maturum*, &c.

Is est honos hŏmĭni pudīco, meminisse officium suum. PLAUT. —"To be mindful of his duty is true honour to an upright man."

Is hăbĭtus animōrum fuit, ut pessĭmum făcĭnus audērent pauci, plures vellent, omnes păterentur. TACIT.—"Such was the state of feeling, that a few dared to perpetrate the worst of crimes, more wished to do so, all suffered it."

Is maxĭmè divĭtiis utĭtur, qui mĭnĭmè divĭtiis indĭget. SEN. —"He uses riches to the best purpose, who stands the least in need of riches."

Is mihi demum vivĕre et frui ănĭmâ vidētur, qui ălĭquo negōtio intentus, præclāri facĭnŏris aut artis bonæ famam quærit. SALL.—"That man in fine appears to me to live and to enjoy life, who, being engaged in any business, seeks the reputation attendant upon some illustrious deed, or upon the discovery of some useful art."

Is mihi vidētur amplissimus qui suâ virtūte in altiōrem locum pervĕnit. CIC.—"He is, in my opinion, the greatest man, who has by his own virtues raised himself to a higher station."

Is mĭnĭmo eget mortālis, qui mĭnĭmum cupit. SYR.—"He of all mortals is the least in want, who desires the least."

Is ordo vĭtio carēto, cætĕris spĕcĭmen esto.—"Let this order be free from vice, and an ensample to the others." This injunction was contained in the Twelve Tables at Rome, and was addressed to the Senatorial or Patrician order. The highest in rank should be most careful to set a good example.

Is săpiens qui se ad casus accommŏdet omnes;
Stultus in adversis ire natātor aquis.
—"He is the wise man who can accommodate himself to all contingencies; the fool struggles, like a swimmer, to go against the stream." This is not the motto of the *Justus et tenax propositi vir*, but it is the one usually adopted by the man who "wants to get on in the world."

——*Istam*
Oro, (si quis adhuc prĕcĭbus locus) exue mentem. VIRG.
—"I beseech you (if my entreaties can still have any effect) lay aside that intention."

Ista decens facies longis vitiābĭtur annis ;
Rugaque in antiquā fronte senīlis erit. OVID.
—"That beauteous face will be spoiled by length of years, and the wrinkle of age will be on thy antiquated brow."

Isthuc est sapĕre, non quod ante pedes modo est
Vidēre, sed etiam illa quæ futūra sunt
Prospicĕre.—— TER.
—"That is wisdom indeed, not to look at the present moment, but to look forward to what is to come."

Ita comparātam esse hŏmĭnum natūram omnium,
Aliēna ut mĕlius vĭdeant et dijudĭcent,
Quam sua !—— TER.
—"That the nature of men should be so constituted, that they can see and judge of other men's affairs better than their own!"

Ita dis est placĭtum, voluptātem ut mœror comes consequātur. PLAUT.—"It has so pleased the gods that Sorrow should attend as companion on Pleasure."

Ita fīnĭtĭma sunt falsa veris, ut in præcipĭtem locum non dēbeat se sapiens committĕre. CIC.—"Falsehood borders so closely upon truth, that a wise man should not trust himself too near the precipice." A rebuke against quibbling.

Ita lex scripta est.—"To such effect is the law written." The words of a man who argues tersely, and by the letter.

Ita me Dii ament! ubi sim nescio. TER.—"May the gods so love me, I know not where I am." I am bewildered, quite beside myself.

Ita nobilissĭma Græciæ cīvĭtas, quondam vero etiam doctissĭma sui civis unius acutissĭmi monumentum ignorāsset, nisi ab hŏmĭne Arpināte dĭdicisset. CIC.—"So the most noble city of Greece, once too the most distinguished for learning, would have remained in ignorance of the monument of her most talented citizen, had it not learned from a man of Arpinum" (now Abruzzo). Cicero speaks of the city of Syracuse; he himself having found there the tomb of Archimedes, covered with weeds, and abandoned to oblivion.

Ita oportŭit intrāre in gloriam suam.—"Thus ought he to enter upon his career of glory."

——*Ita servum par vidētur frugi se instituĕre ;*
Proinde heri ut sint, ipse item sit, vultum e vultu compăret ;
Tristis sit, si heri sint tristes ; hilăris sit si gaudeant
PLAUT.

—"Thus does it seem becoming for a trusty servant to conduct himself; just as his superiors are should he be too; by their countenances he should fashion his own countenance; if his superiors are grave, let him be grave; if they rejoice, let him be merry." See *Indigna digna*, &c.

——*Ita vertĕre sēria ludo.* Hor.—"Thus to turn serious matters into jest."

Ita vita est hŏmĭnum, quasi, cum ludas tessĕris;
Si illud quod maxĭme opus est jactu non cadit,
Illud quod cĕcĭdit forte id arte ut corrĭgas. Ter.
—"The life of man is just like playing with dice; if that which you most want to throw does not turn up, that which turns up by chance you must correct by skill."

Ita voluĕrunt, ita factum est.—"So they willed it, and so it has been done."

——*Iter factum corruptius imbre.* Hor.—"The way being rendered more disagreeable by the rain."

Iter pigrōrum quasi sepes spinārum. From *Proverbs* xv. 19.
—"The way of the slothful is as a hedge of thorns."

Itĕrum ille eam rem judicātam jūdĭcat
Majōreque mulctâ mulctat.—— Plaut.
—"He is trying a matter again that has been tried already, and is mulcting us again with a still heavier fine."

Ixīon quod versāri narrātur rotâ
Volūbĭlem fortūnam jactāri docet. Phæd.
—"The story of Ixion whirling round upon the wheel, teaches us how changeful a thing is fortune."

J.

——*Jacet ecce Tibullus,*
Vix manet e toto parva quod urna capit. Ovid.
—"See, here Tibullus lies; of one so great there hardly remains enough to fill a little urn."

Jacta est alea.—"The die is cast." The deed is done, and there is now no room for deliberation.

Jactitātio. *Law Term.*—"A boasting." Jactitation of marriage is a false boasting of a person that he, or she, is married to another, such not being the case. On a libel brought against the party guilty of jactitation, the ecclesiastical courts will impose silence on him or her

——*Jam desuetūdĭne longā*
Vix subeunt ipsi verba Latīna mihi. OVID.
—"From long disuse scarcely do Latin modes of expression recur to me." The complaint of Ovid, when in exile at Tomi in Pontus.

——*Jam istæc insipientia est,*
Sic viam in promptu gĕrĕre.—PLAUT.
—"Why, this is sheer folly, thus to keep your wrath always bottled up in readiness."

Jam nunc minăci murmŭre cornuum
Perstringis aures; jam lĭtui strepunt. HOR.
—"Even now you stun our ears with the threatening murmur of horns; now the clarions sound."

Jam pauca arātro jūgĕra rēgiæ
Moles relinquent.—— HOR.
—"Princely palaces will soon leave but few acres to the plough." The allusion is to the vast tracts of land enclosed by the rich for purposes of ornament, and no longer available for the public benefit.

Jam portum invĕni, Spes et Fortūna valēte!
Nil mihi vobiscum est, lūdite nunc alios.
—"I have now gained the harbour, Hope and Fortune, adieu! I have nothing to do with you, now go play with others." A translation by Sir Thomas More of an Epigram in the Greek Anthology. See *Inveni portum, &c.*

——*Jam protervā*
Fronte petit Lălăge marītum. HOR.
—"Already, with unblushing face, does Lalage seek a husband."

Jam redit et Virgo, rĕdeunt Sāturnia regna. VIRG.—"Now the Virgin returns, now the Saturnian age returns." The supposed reign of Astræa, the goddess of justice, in the Golden Age.

——*Jam sævus apertam*
In răbiem cœpit verti jocus, et per honestas
Ire minax impūne domos.—— HOR.
—"At length the bitter raillery began to be turned into open rage, and menaces with impunity to stalk through reputable houses."

Jam satis—ohe. AUSON.—"Hold—enough!"

——*Jam summa procul villārum culmĭna fumant.* VIRG.—"Now the high tops of the villages afar send forth their smoke."

Jamque opus exēgi, quod nec Jovis ira, nec ignis,
Nec pŏtĕrit ferrum, nec edax abŏlēre vetustas. OVID.
—"I have now completed a work which neither the anger of Jove, nor fire, nor the sword, nor consuming time, will be able to destroy." A prediction of the poet, which, thus far, has been verified, and deservedly so.

Jamque quiescēbant voces hŏmĭnumque canumque;
Lunaque nocturnos alta regēbat equos. OVID.
—"And now the voices of men and the baying of dogs were lulled, and the moon on high was guiding the steeds of night."

——*Jānua lethi*
Sed patet immāni, et vasto respectat hiātu. LUCRET.
—"But the gate of death yawns with its wide and vast entrance." "Broad is the way that leadeth to destruction." *Matt.* vii. 13.

Jānuis clausis.—"With closed doors;" that is, "in secrecy."

Jasper fert myrrham, thus Melchior, Balthazar aurum.
Hæc quicum secum portet tria nŏmĭna regum,
Solvĭtur a morbo, Dŏmĭni pietāte, cadūco.
—"Jasper brings myrrh, Melchior frankincense, and Balthazar gold. Whoever carries with him the names of these three kings will be exempt, by the goodness of God, from the falling sickness." A mediæval charm. These were said to be the names of the kings of the Magi, who were led by the star to the cradle of our Saviour in Bethlehem. They are usually called the Three Kings of Cologne.

Jejūnus raro stŏmăchus vulgāria temnit. HOR.—"A hungry stomach rarely despises plain food."

——*Jovis omnia plena.* VIRG.—"All things are full of Jove." The hand of Providence is visible everywhere.

——*Jubeo totas aperīre fenestras.* OVID.—"I bid you open all the windows."

Jubilāte Deo.—"O be joyful in the Lord." The beginning of the Hundreth Psalm.

——*Jucunda et idōnea dīcĕre vitæ.* HOR.—"To relate what

is agreeable and suited to our conduct in life." The useful as well as the amusing. See *Omne tulit, &c.*

Jucunda est memŏria prætĕritōrum malōrum. CIC.—"The recollection of past evils is pleasant."

Jucunda rerum vicissitūdo.—"A delightful change of circumstances."

Jucundi acti labōres. CIC.—"The remembrance of difficulties overcome is delightful."

Jucundum et carum stĕrĭlis facit uxor amicum. JUV.—"A barren wife makes a dear and interesting friend." To those, namely, who are looking for her husband's money after his decease.

Jucundum nihil est, nisi quod rĕfĭcit variĕtas. SYR.—"Nothing is pleasant that is not enlivened with variety."

Judex damnātur cum nocens absolvĭtur. SYR.—"The judge is condemned when the guilty is acquitted." That is, when the sentence is supposed to be dictated by corrupt motives, or to betray incapacity.

Judex non potest esse testis in prŏpriâ causâ. COKE.—"A judge cannot be a witness in his own cause."

Judex non solum quid possit, sed ĕtiam quid dĕceat pondĕrāre debet. CIC.—"A judge ought to weigh well not only what he may do, but also what he ought to do."

Judicandum est lĕgĭbus, non exemplis. *Law Max.*—"We must judge according to law, not by precedent."

Judĭce te mercēde caret, per seque petenda est
Externis virtus incomĭtāta bonis. OVID.

—"In thy judgment, virtue needs no reward, and is to be sought for her own sake, unaccompanied by external benefits."

Judĭces qui ex lege judicātis, lĕgĭbus obtemperāre dĕbētis. CIC.—"You judges who judge according to the law, ought to be obedient to the law."

Judĭcia Dei sunt ita recondĭta ut quis illa scrutāri nullātĕnus possit. CIC.—"The decrees of God are so impenetrable, that no one can possibly scrutinize them." The ways of Heaven are unsearchable. See *Job* v. 9; *Rom.* ii. 33.

Judĭcio acri perpendĕre. LUCRET.—"To weigh with keen discernment."

Jūdĭcis est innocentiæ subvĕnīre. CIC.—"It is the duty of the judge to succour innocence."

Jūdĭcis offĭcium est, ut res, ita tempŏra rerum Quærĕre.—— OVID.
—"It is the duty of a judge, to consider not only the facts, but the circumstances of the case."

Judĭcium Dei.—"The judgment of God." The name by which the *ordeal* by fire or water was called in the middle ages, because it was supposed that God would by his intervention manifest the guilt or innocence of the party tried.

Judĭcium pārium aut leges terræ.—"The judgment of our peers, or the laws of the land." By these only can an Englishman be condemned. Words from the *Magna Charta*, selected as his motto by that eminent judge, Lord Camden. The nobles are judged by the nobles, the commons by the commons, each by their peers.

Judĭcium subtīle videndis artĭbus.—— HOR.—"An acute discernment in understanding the arts."

Jugulāre mortuos. Prov.—"To stab the dead." To be guilty not only of needless cruelty, but also of cowardice.

Juncta juvant.—"United, they assist." Said of things trifling in themselves, but which, put together, acquire strength.

Jungĕre dextras. VIRG.—"To join right hands." Or, as we say, "to shake hands."

Jungĕre equos Titan vēlōcĭbus impĕrat Horis. OVID.—"Titan commands the swift-flying Hours to yoke the horses." The poet speaks of the *Hours*, which were personified under the names of *Eunomia*, *Dice*, *Irene*, *Carpo*, and *Thallo*, as harnessing the horses of the sun.

Jupĭter est quodcunque vides, quocunque movĕris. LUCAN.—"Where'er you turn your eyes, where'er you move, 'tis God you see." The doctrine of Pantheism.

Jupĭter in multos tĕmerārĭa fulmĭna torquet,
Qui pœnam culpâ non meruēre pati. OVID.
—"Jupiter hurls his lightnings at random against many who have not deserved punishment for any commensurate fault."

Jupĭter tonans.—"The thunderer Jove." "The *Jupiter tonans* of debate," i. e. a "great gun" in argument.

Jura negat sibi nata, nihil non arrŏgat armis. HOR.—"He denies that laws were framed against him; he arrogates everything to himself by force of arms." The acts of a tyrant or usurper.

Juratōres sunt jūdĭces facti. Law Max.—"The jurors are the judges of the facts."

Jurāvi linguā, mentem injurātam gero. Cic.—"I have sworn with my tongue, but I have a mind unsworn." I feel no constraint to perform my oath. The words of a man from whom an oath has been extorted by unlawful means and under duress, or the mental reservation of a subtle casuist.

Jure divino.—"By Divine law," meaning, "by the will of Heaven," irrespective of the will of the people. The sovereigns of the line of the Stuarts were the last monarchs of Great Britain who claimed to govern by this title.

Jure humāno.—"By human law." By laws made and upheld by men. The present emperor of France professes to reign *jure humano*, "by the will of the people."

Jure repræsentatiōnis. Law Term.—"By right of representation." As representing another party.

Jurgia præcĭpue vino stimulāta cavēto. Ovid.—"Especially avoid quarrels excited by wine."

Jus alĭquod făciunt affīnia vincŭla nobis. Ovid.—"The links of connexion form a certain tie between us."

Jus civīle.—"The civil law," i. e. the Roman law, which, to a certain extent, is still used in our ecclesiastical courts.

Jus civīle neque inflecti grātiā, neque perfringi potentiā, neque adulterāri pecūniā debet. Cic.—"The law of the land ought neither to be warped by favour, nor broken through by power, nor corrupted by money."

Jus divīnum.—"Divine right."

Jus gentium.—"The law of nations." Laws formed on strict principles of universal justice, and acknowledged by all nations of the civilized world as the basis of their international relations.

Jus postlimĭnii.—"The law of recovery." A Roman law which restored certain rights and privileges to one who had lost them was thus called.

Jus primogenitūræ.—"The right of eldership."

Jus proprietātis.—"The right of property."

Jus rēgium.—"Royal right."

Jus sanguĭnis, quod in legitĭmis successiōnibus spectātur, ipso nativitātis tempŏre quæsītum est. *Law Max.*—"The right of consanguinity, which is regarded in successions by law, is established at the very moment of our birth."

Jus summum sæpe summa malitia est. TER.—"Extreme law is often extreme wrong." See *Summum jus*, &c.

Justæ causæ făcĭlis est defensio. CIC.—"It is easy to defend a just cause."

——*Justissĭmus unus*
——*Et servantissĭmus æqui.* VIRG.

—"Most just and most observant of what is right." The character of Ripheus.

Justitia erga Deum relĭgio dĭcĭtur; erga parentes piĕtas.—CIC.—"Fulfilment of our duty towards God is called religion; towards our parents, piety."

Justitia est obtemperātio scriptis lĕgĭbus. CIC.—"Justice is obedience to the written law."

Justitia nihil expĕtit præmii. CIC.—"Justice seeks no reward."

Justitia non novit patrem nec matrem, solum veritātem spectat. *Law Max.*—"Justice knows neither father nor mother; it looks at truth alone."

Justitiâ tanta vis est, ut ne illi quidem, qui malĕfĭcio et scĕlĕre pascuntur, possint sine ullâ particŭlâ justitiæ vīvĕre. CIC. —"There is so vast a power in justice, that those even who live by crime and wickedness, cannot live without some small portion of justice among them." Hence the proverb which says that "There is honour among thieves."

Justitiæ partes sunt, non violāre hŏmĭnes, verecundiæ non offendĕre. CIC.—"It is the duty of justice to do injury to no man; of propriety, to offend none."

Justum bellum quibus necessārium, et pia arma quibus nulla nisi in armis relinquĭtur spes. LIVY.—"War is just to those to whom it is necessary; and an appeal to arms is a sacred duty with those who have no hope left except in arms."

Justum et tenācem propŏsĭti virum,
Non cīvium ardor prava jubentium,
Non vultus instantis tyranni
Mente quatit sŏlĭdâ. HOR.

—"Not the rage of the people pressing to hurtful measures, not the aspect of the threatening tyrant, can shake from his settled purpose the man who is just and determined in his resolution."

Juvenile vitium regĕre non posse impĕtum. SEN.—"It is the failing of youth, not to be able to restrain its own impetuosity."

Juxta flŭvium pŭteum fodit. *Prov.*—"He is digging a well close by a river." Said of a person adding to a supply which is already more than sufficient.

K.

Kyrie eleeison.—"Lord, have mercy upon us." Two Latinized Greek words in common use in the responses of the Romish Church.

L.

LL. D. for "*Legum Doctor*," "Doctor of Laws."

L. S. for "*Locus sigilli*," which see.

Labĭtur et labĕtur in omne volŭbilis ævum. HOR.—See *Rusticus expectat*, &c.

Labĭtur occulte, fallitque volŭbilis ætas. OVID.—"Age glides stealthily on, and beguiles us as it flies."

——*Labor omnia vincit*
Imprŏbus.—— VIRG.
—"Incessant labour conquers everything."

——*Labŏrum*
Dulce levămen.—— HOR.
—"The sweet soother of my cares." The words addressed by the poet to his lyre, the solace of his leisure hours.

——*Lăchrymæque decōræ,*
Grătior et pulchro vĕniens in corpŏre virtus. VIRG.
—"His graceful tears, and a merit that still more commends itself in a beauteous person."

——*Lactŭca innătat acri*
Post vinum stŏmăcho.—— HOR.
—"Lettuce after wine floats on an acrid stomach." Words to be borne in mind by the *bon vivant.*

Lætus in præsens ănĭmus, quod ultra est
Odĕrit curāre, et amāra lento
Tempĕret risu. Nihil est ab omni
Parte beātum. HOR.

—"The mind that is cheerful at the present hour, will be indifferent about anything beyond it, and meet the bitters of life with a complacent smile. Nothing is blessed on every side."

Lætus sorte tuâ vives sapienter.—"If you are wise you will live contented with your lot."

Lăpĭdes lŏquĭtur, căveant lectōres ne cĕrĕbrum iis excŭtiat.—"He speaks stones; let his readers take care that he does not knock their brains out." See *Plautus, Aulul.* II. i. 29.

Lapis philosophōrum.—"The philosopher's stone." A supposed mineral, sought by the alchemists of the middle ages, the property of which was to transmute the base metals into gold.

Lapis qui volvĭtur algam non gĕnĕrat. Prov.—"A rolling stone finds no sea-weed." Or as we say, "A rolling stone gathers no moss." The figure, in the Latin, refers to the stone on the sea-shore, upon which, as it rolls to and fro, the sea-weed does not collect.

Lapsus calămi.—"A slip of the pen."

Lapsus linguæ.—"A slip of the tongue."

Lascīvi sŏbŏles gregis. HOR.—"The descendants of a wanton race."

Lateat scintillŭla forsan.—"Some small spark may lie perchance concealed." These words (in reference to the vital spark) have been adopted as the motto of the Humane Society for the recovery of persons apparently drowned.

Lătĕrem lavas. Prov.—"You are washing a brick." This was originally said of unburnt bricks, which the more they were scoured, the more muddy they became. "You are making bad worse."

——*Latet anguis in herbâ.* VIRG.—"A snake lies hidden in the grass." Individuals, like armies, suffer most from perils that lie in ambush.

Lātius regnes, ăvĭdum domando
Spīrĭtum, quam si Lĭbyam remōtis
Gādĭbus jungas, et ŭterque Pœnus
Serviat uni. HOR.

—"You may possess a more extensive dominion by controlling a craving disposition, than if you could unite Libya to the distant Gades, and the natives of either Carthage were subject to you alone."

Latrant me, lăteo ac tăceo.—"They bark at me, but I lie hid, and hold my tongue."

Latrante uno, latrat statim et alter canis. Prov.—"When one dog barks, another at once barks too."

Latrantem curatne alta Diāna canem? Prov.—"Does Diana on high care for the dog that bays her?"

Laudări a laudāto viro. CIC.—"To be praised by a man who deserves praise."

Laudat vēnāles qui vult extrūdĕre merces. HOR.—"He praises the wares he has to sell who wishes to push them off upon others."

——*Laudāto ingentia rura,*
Exiguum cŏlĭto. VIRG.

—"Commend large estates, but cultivate a small one." You will both avoid giving offence to others, and will insure your own happiness and peace of mind.

——*Laudātor tempŏris acti.* HOR.—"A praiser of times past." An old man, who, like Nestor in the Iliad, is always praising the men and manners of former times. A weakness both amiable and natural. See *Ætas parentum*, &c.

——*Laudātur ab his, culpātur ab illis.* HOR.—"He is praised by these, censured by those."

Laudĭbus arguitur vini vinōsus.—— HOR.—"The drunkard is convicted by his praises of wine."

Laudis amōre tumes? sunt certa piācŭla quæ te
Ter purè lecto, pŏtĕrunt recreāre, libello. HOR.

—"Do you swell with the love of praise? There are [in philosophy] certain purgations which can restore you, a certain treatise being thrice perused with purity of mind."

Laudo Deum verum, plebem voco, congrĕgo clerum,
Defunctos ploro, pestem fugo, festa decoro.

—"I praise the true God, I summon the people, I assemble the clergy, I mourn the dead, I put to flight the plague, I celebrate festivals." Inscription on a church bell. See *Funera*, &c.

Laudo, malum cum amīci tuum ducis malum. PLAUT.—"I

commend you for considering the affliction of your friend your own affliction."

Laureum băcŭlum gesto. Prov.—"I carry a sprig of laurel." I am proof against all dangers. The laurel was thought by the ancients to be an antidote against poison, and to afford security against lightning.

Laus Deo.—"Praise be to God."

Laus in proprio ore sordescit. Prov.—"A man's own praise of himself is unseemly." "Self-praise is no recommendation."

Lebĕrĭde cæcior. Prov.—"Blinder than a serpent's slough." Which has holes only instead of eyes.

Lege totum si vis scire totum.—"Read the whole if you wish to know the whole." It is not easy to judge of a book on one connected subject, by reading a bit here and there.

Legem brevem esse oportet quo făcĭlius ab impĕrītis tĕneātur. SEN.—"A law ought to be short that it may be the more easily understood by the unlearned."

Leges a victōrĭbus dicuntur, accipiuntur a victis. CURT.—"Conditions are made by the conquerors, accepted by the conquered."

Leges ad cīvium salutem, civitātumque incolumitātem condĭtæ sunt. CIC.—"Laws were made for the safety of citizens, and the security of states."

——*Leges mori serviunt.* PLAUT.—"The laws are subservient to usage."

Leges sunt inventæ quæ cum omnĭbus semper unâ atque eâdem voce lŏquerentur. CIC.—"Laws are so made that they may always speak with one and the same voice to all." Good laws are no respecters of persons.

Legis constructio non facit injuriam. Law Max.—"The construction of the law does injury to no man." For instance, it will not suppose a man to grant away that which rightfully belongs to another.

——*Legĭtĭmâ fraudātur lĭtĕra voce;*
Blæsaque fit jusso lingua coacta sono. OVID.
—"The letters are deprived of their full sound, and the lisping tongue is contracted with an affected pronunciation."

Legum ministri magistrātus, legum interprĕtes judĭces; legum dĕnĭque idcirco omnes servi sumus, ut lĭbĕri esse possĭmus. CIC.—"The magistrates are the ministers of the law, the judges the interpreters of the laws; we all, in fine, are the servants of the law, that we may be free."

Lēnior et mĕlior fis, accēdente senectâ? Hor.—"Do you become milder and better, as old age approaches?"

Lēnĭter ex mĕrĭto quidquid patiāre ferendum est,
Quæ venit indignè pœna dolenda venit. Ovid.
—"Whatever you suffer deservedly should be borne with patience; the penalty that comes upon us undeservedly comes as a ground for complaint." The poet thus consoles himself, upon his banishment to Thrace without having deserved it.

Lentiscum mandĕre. *Prov.*—"To chew mastich." Said of people over-nice about their personal appearance. Gum mastich is a whitener of the teeth, and a preserver of the gums.

Leōnem larvâ terres. *Prov.*—"You are for frightening a lion with a mask."

Leonīna societas. *Prov.*—"A lion's society." A partnership where one individual engrosses the whole power and authority. See the Fable of the Lion in Partnership, in *Phædrus*, b. i. f. 1.

Leonīni versus.—"Leonine verses." These consist of Latin hexameters, or hexameters and pentameters, in rhyme. There are various kinds; but the most common is that in which the cæsura in the fifth syllable rhymes with the end of the line, thus:

En rex Edvardus debacchans ut leopardus.
("Lo! king Edward, raging like a leopard.")

Other metres are however used in the Leonine hymns of the Roman Catholic Church. The name is said to have been derived from Leoninus, a monk of the twelfth century. He may very possibly have revived the use of these rhymes; but we find them composed as far back as the third century.

Leōnum ora a magistris impūnè tractantur. Sen.—"The mouths of lions are handled with impunity by their keepers." That which is dangerous to one man may be done in safety by another.

Lĕpĭdi mores turpem ornātum făcĭlè factis comprŏbant. Plaut.—"Good morals have no difficulty in setting off a lowly garb."

Lĕpŏris vitam vivit. *Prov.*—"He lives the life of a hare." He is always full of fears and anxiety.

Lepos et festīvĭtas ōrātiōnis. Cic.—"The pleasantry and playfulness of his conversation."

——*Leve fit quod benè fertur onus.* Ovid.—"The load becomes light which is borne with cheerfulness."

Leves hŏmĭnes futūri sunt imprŏvĭdi. Tacit.—"Light-minded men are careless of the future."

Lĕvia perpessi sumus, si flenda pătĭmur. Sen.—"We have had to suffer but trifles if our sufferings are merely such as we should weep for." Real misfortunes require something more than tears as their remedy.

Leviōra sunt injūria, quæ repentīno ălĭquo motu accĭdunt, quam ea quæ meditāte præparāta inferuntur. Cic.—"The injuries which befall us unexpectedly are less severe than those which we are deliberately anticipating."

Levis est dolor qui capĕre consĭlium potest. Sen.—"That grief is but light which can take counsel."

Lĕvius solet timēre qui prŏpĭus timet. Sen.—"A man's fears are diminished when the danger is near at hand." Dangers appears less formidable when looked in the face.

Lex appĕtit perfectum. *Law Max.*—"The law aims at perfection."

Lex cĭtĭus tolerāre vult privātum damnum quam publĭcum malum. Coke.—"The law will sooner tolerate a private loss than a public evil."

Lex est, quæ in Græcōrum convīviis obtinētur, aut bibat aut ăbeat. Et rectè. Aut enim fruātur ălĭquis, părĭter cum ăliis, voluptāte potandi; ut ne sobrius in violentiam vinolentōrum incĭdat ante discēdat. Cic.—"At the banquets of the Greeks a custom prevails, that every man shall either drink or begone: and with good reason: for every man should enjoy, equally with the rest, the pleasure of drinking; lest he, being sober, should witness any violence of conduct, before he departs, on the part of those who are overtaken with wine."

Lex nĕmĭnem cogit ad impossibĭlia. *Law Max.*—"The law compels no man to do impossibilities." If a man under a penalty in a bond undertakes to do a physical impossibility, the law will not allow the penalty to be recovered.

Lex nĕmĭni operātur inīquum; nĕmini facit injuriam. *Law Max.*—"The law works injustice to no man, does injury to none."

Lex non scripta.—"The unwritten law." The common law of England, which originated in custom prior to the time of Richard I., and has never been committed to writing. The eldest son inherits realty to the exclusion of the younger children under the *Lex non scripta.*

Lex prospĭcit non respĭcit. *Law Max.*—"The law is prospective, not retrospective."

Lex scripta.—"The written" or "statute law."

Lex taliōnis.—"The law of retaliation," or "of requital." "An eye for an eye, a tooth for a tooth." This is the law of revenge, not of justice, and not unlike what the Americans call "Lynch Law."

Lex terræ.—"The law of the land." A term used in contradistinction to the "civil law."

Lex universa est quæ jubet nasci et mori. SYR.—"There is one universal law which commands that we shall be born and shall die."

Lĭbĕra te metu mortis. SEN.—"Deliver thyself from the fear of death." By doing your best to insure the reward of a good life.

Lībĕri parentes alant, aut vinciantur.—"Let children support their parents, or be imprisoned." A Roman law.

Lībĕrius quam ut imperantium mĕmĭnissent. TACIT.—"Too freely to remember their own rulers."

Libertas est potestas faciendi id quod jure licet. *Law Max.*—"Liberty is the power of doing that which the law permits." The proper estimate of real liberty.

Libertas, quæ sera, tamen respexit inertem. VIRG.—"Liberty which, though late, looked back upon me in my helpless state."

——*Libertas ultĭma mundi*
Quo stĕtĕrit fĕrienda loco.—— LUCAN.

—"In the spot where liberty has made her last stand must she be smitten." A sentiment attributed by Lucan to Julius Cæsar.

Libidinōsa et intempĕrans adolescentia effœtum corpus tradit senectūti. CIC.—"A youth of sensuality and intemperance transmits to old age a worn-out body."

Libĭdo effrenāta effrenātam appetentiam effĭcit. Prov.—"Unbridled gratification produces unbridled desire." See *Sic quibus*, &c.

Lĭbra justa justĭtiam servat.—"A just balance preserves justice."

——*Lĭceat concēdĕre veris.* Hor.—"It is only right to yield to truth."

Licĕt superbus ambŭles pecuniâ,
Fortūna non mutat genus. Hor.
—"Although you may strut about, proud of your money, fortune does not change birth." Words addressed to a conceited *parvenu.*

——*Lĭcuit, semperque licēbit*
Parcĕre persōnis, dīcĕre de vitiis.
—"It ever has been lawful, and ever will be, to spare the person, but to censure the vice."

Lignum vitæ.—"The wood of life." Boxwood, or the wood of the *guaiacum officinale*, is popularly so called.

——*Limæ labor et mora.* Hor.—"The labour and tediousness of the file." The wearisome labour of correcting and giving the last polish to a work.

Lingua mali loquax malæ mentis est indicium. Syr.—"An evil tongue is the proof of an evil mind." Because "Out of the abundance of the heart the mouth speaketh." *Luke* vi. 4, 5.

——*Lingua mali pars pessĭma servi.* Juv.—"The tongue is the worst part of a bad servant." If a servant is unprincipled, the opportunities which he has for slander render his power for evil ten-fold greater.

——*Linguâ mĕlior, sed frĭgĭda bello*
Dextĕra.—— Virg.
—"Excelling in speech, but of a right hand slow to war." The description given of Drances.

Lingua, sile; non est ultra narrābĭle quicquam. Ovid.—"My tongue, be silent; not another word must be said."

——*Linguæ centum sunt, oraque centum,*
Ferrea vox.—— Virg.
—"It has a hundred tongues, a hundred mouths, a voice of iron." The attributes of rumour.

——*Linguæ prorsus non nego*
Habēre atque agĕre maxĭmas me gratias·
Verum ocŭlis ut privēris opto perfĭdis. Phæd.

—"I do not deny that to your tongue I owe most sincere thanks, and I return them; but I wish you may be deprived of your perfidious eyes." Said to one who, though he may hold his tongue, still acts the traitor by his significant looks.

Linguam alicŭjus fŭtĭlem ac ventōsam retundĕre. LIVY.—"To silence the babbling empty tongue of a person."

Linguam compescĕre, virtus non mĭnĭma est.—"To restrain the tongue is not the least of virtues."

Linquenda tellus, et domus, et placens
Uxor, neque harum, quas colis, arbŏrum,
Te, præter invīsas cupressos,
Ulla brevem dŏmĭnum sequĕtur. HOR.

—"Your estate, your house, and your pleasing wife must be left, nor shall any of these trees which you are tending follow you, their owner for a brief space, except the hated cypresses." The cypress was planted near the graves of the dead.

Lis litem gĕnĕrat. *Prov.*—"Strife begets strife."

Litem parit lis, noxa item noxam parit. *Prov.*—"Dispute begets dispute, and injury begets injury."

Lĭtĕra canīna.—"The canine letter." The letter R is so called, as it seems to be pronounced by a dog when he snarls, "Grr, Grrr," as Rabelais says.

Lĭtĕra scripta manet.—"The written letter remains." Words may escape our memory, but that which is written remains established as proof of the intention of the writer. Probably a portion of a mediæval pentameter.

Litĕræ Bellĕrophontis. *Prov.*—"Letters of Bellerophon." Prœtus, king of Argos, suspecting that Bellerophon had attempted to corrupt the chastity of his wife, sent him to the king of Syria with a sealed letter directing him to put the bearer to death. Hence letters which are dangerous to the bearer are called *Literæ Bellerophontis.*

Lĭtĕræ humaniōres.—"Polite literature," or "arts," in University parlance.

Littus ama, altum alii teneant.—— VIRG.—"Hug the shore, let others stand out into the deep." Figuratively applied, these words warn us not to launch out into hazardous enterprises, but to consult the dictates of prudence.

Lĭvĭdi limis ocŭlis semper aspiciunt aliōrum commŏda. CIC.—

"Envious men always view with jealousy the prosperity of others."

Loc. cit. for *Loco citāto.*—"In the place quoted."

Locum tenens.—"Holding his place," meaning, a person acting for, or holding the office of, another. A substitute or deputy, or, more strictly speaking, a *lieutenant.*

——*Locus est et plurĭbus umbris.* Hor.—"There is room enough for more to introduce their friends." The "*umbra,*" or "shadow," was a guest's friend, allowed by the Roman custom to accompany him at banquets and entertainments.

Locus in quo.—"The place in which." Meaning, the place or position which was previously occupied.

Locus sigilli.—"The place for the seal"—which is pointed out in copies of deeds or sealed documents by the letters L. S.

Locus standi.—"A place for standing." A position assumed in argument.

——*Longa est injūria, longæ*
Ambāges.—— Virg.

—"Lengthened is the story of my wrongs, tedious the detail."

Longa mora est, quantum noxæ sit ubīque repertum
Enumerāre: minor fuit ipsa infāmia vero. Ovid.

—"It were an endless task to enumerate how great an amount of guilt everywhere prevailed; even the report itself was below the truth." The words of Jupiter when he found it necessary to destroy mankind by the deluge.

—— *Longa via est, nec tempŏra longa supersunt,*
Dixit; et hospĭtĭbus jānŭa nostra patet. Ovid.

—"'Long is the road,' said he, 'and little of the day remains; my door too is ever open to the stranger.'"

Longè aberrat scopo.—"He is wide of the mark." "He has wandered far from his sphere."

Longè absit.—"Far be it from me." Or as we say, "God forbid."

——*Longè mea discrĕpat istis*
Et vox et ratio.—— Hor.

—"Both my language and my sentiments differ widely from theirs."

Longum iter est per præcepta, breve et effĭcax per exempla.

Sen.—"The road by precept is long; by example, short and effectual."

Loquendum ut vulgus, sentiendum ut docti. Coke.—"We should speak with the populace, think with the learned."

Lotis manĭbus.—"With clean hands."

Lubrĭca nascentes implent conchylia lunæ. Hor.—"The increasing moon plumps up the slippery oyster." A dictum to be remembered by the epicure.

Lūbrĭca statio et proxĭma præcĭpĭtio.—"A slippery spot, and on the edge of a precipice."

Lubrĭci sunt fortūnæ gressus.—"The footsteps of fortune are slippery."

Lubrĭcum linguæ non facile in pœnam est trahendum. *Law Max.*—"A slip of the tongue ought not to be punished without due consideration."

Lucem redde tuæ, dux bone, patriæ;
Instar veris enim vultus ubi tuus
Affulsit pŏpŭlo, grātior et dies,
Et soles mĕlius nitent Hor.

—"Restore, O excellent prince, light to thy country; for, like the spring, wherever thy countenance has shone, the day passes more agreeably for the people, and the sun has a superior lustre." An eulogium, addressed by the poet to the emperor Augustus, during his absence from Rome.

——*Lucet, eāmus*
Quo ducit gula.—— Hor.

—"It is day, let us go whither appetite leads us."

Lucĭdus ordo. Hor.—"Perspicuous arrangement." Method.

——*Lucri bonus est odor ex re*
Quālĭbet.—— Juv.

—"The smell of gain is good, come from what it may." Vespasian made this reply to his son Titus, when he expostulated with him upon his imposing a tax upon urine.

——*Lucrum amāre nullum amatōrem decet.* Plaut.—"No lover ought to be in love with pelf."

Lucrum malum æquāle dispendio. *Prov.*—"An evil gain is equal to a loss." "What is ill-gotten rarely thrives."

Luctantem Icăriis fluctĭbus Afrĭcum
Mercātor metuens, otium et oppĭdi
Laudat rura sui: mox refĭcit rates
Quassas, indŏcĭlis paupĕriem pati. Hor.

—"The merchant, dreading the south-west wind contending with the Icarian waves, commends the tranquillity and the rural retirement of the country-town; but soon, incapable of being taught to endure poverty, he refits his shattered bark."

Luctantes ventos tempestātesque sonōras
Impĕrio premit.—— VIRG.
—"He represses by his control the struggling winds, and the resounding tempests." Said in allusion to the sway of Æolus, the god of the winds.

Lucus à non lucendo.—That is, *Lucus*, "a grove," is derived, by antiphrasis, from *non lucere*, "not to admit light," because, as the grammarians said, it does not allow the light of the sun to shine through it. This derivation is found in Servius on Æneid I., Charisius, and Diomedes. Quintilian (i. 6) also notices it, but merely to ask whether such derivations from contraries can possibly be received by reasonable people; some critics having also imagined that *ludus*, "a school," was so called *à non ludendo*, because no play was allowed in it, and that Pluto was called *Ditis*, "rich," because he was *minime dives*, "not at all rich." Vossius condemns the derivation of *lucus* from *luceo* as a mere fancy of the grammarians, and alludes to another given by Isidore, xiv. 8, *à collucendo crebris luminibus religionis causâ*, "from the number of lamps or torches that were often lighted in the sacred groves," *lucus* being properly a grove consecrated to some deity, though often used in a general sense. But Vossius prefers on the whole to derive it from λόχος, "an ambush." Others would have it for *lugus* from λύγη, "darkness." The real etymology is quite uncertain. Servius, who favours the derivation from *luceo*, adduces, in support of it, another imagination of the grammarians, *bellum*, "war," *à nullâ re bellâ*, because it has nothing pleasing in it; and Varro, de L. L., book v., rather inclines to think that *cœlum*, "heaven," may be derived *à celando*, from "to conceal," *quia apertum est*, "because it is open." *Lucus à non lucendo* has become proverbial in ridicule of absurd or far-fetched etymologies. See *Non sequitur*, and *Obscurum per obscurius*.

Lūdĕre cum sacris.—"To play with holy things." To jest on sacred subjects.

Ludit in humānis Dīvīna potentia rebus;
Et certam præsens vix habet hora fidem. Ovid.
—"The Divine power finds sport in the affairs of men, and the present moment hardly carries positive assurance."

——*Ludus ănĭmo debet ălĭquando dari,*
Ad cŏgitandum mĕlior ut rĕdeat tibi. Phæd.
—"Recreation ought sometimes to be given to the mind, that it may return to you better fitted for thought."

Lūgēte Vĕnĕres Cupīdĭnesque. Catull.—"Mourn, ye Venuses and Cupids." These words, used by the poet in commemorating the death of Lesbia's favourite sparrow, are sometimes employed ironically.

Lumen soli mutuum das. Prov.—"You are lending light to the sun." Said of persons who affect to explain what is perfectly clear and intelligible, or, as Young says of commentators, "Hold their farthing candle to the sun."

Lupus in fābŭlā. Prov.—"The wolf in the fable." Alluding to the accidental arrival of the person who happens at that moment to be the subject of conversation. Like the wolf of ancient fable, which was said to have that power, his appearance deprives the speakers of their voice, or, in other words, puts a stop to their conversation. See *Edere non poteris*, &c.

Lupus pilum mutat, non mentem. Prov.—"The wolf changes his hair, but not his nature." See *Naturam expellas*, &c.

Lusisti satis, edisti satis, atque bibisti.
Tempus abīre tibi est.—— Hor.
—"Thou hast trifled enough, hast eaten and drunk enough, 'tis time for thee to depart." Words addressed to an aged sensualist, on the verge of the grave.

Lusit amābĭlĭter, donec jam sævus apertam
In răbiem verti cœpit jocus.—— Hor.
—"This raillery sported on pleasantly enough, till at length, becoming bitter, it began to turn into virulence."

Lusus natūræ.—"A freak of nature." A deformed or unnatural production is so called.

Lutum nisi tundātur, non fit urcĕus. Prov.—"Unless the clay be well pounded, no pitcher can be made." Nothing of value can be produced without industry.

Luxum pŏpŭli expiāre solent bella.—"The luxury of a people is usually expiated by war." Luxury and dissipation produce disorder, the fruitful parent of turbulence and war.

Luxuriæ desunt multa, avaritiæ omnia. SYR.—"Luxury is in want of many things; avarice, of everything."

Luxŭriant ănĭmi rebus plerumque secundis;
Nec făcĭle est æquâ commŏda mente pati. OVID.
—"The feelings often run riot amid prosperity; and to bear good fortune with evenness of mind is no easy task."

M.

M. D. "*Medicīnæ Doctor.*"—"Doctor in Medicine."

M. S. See *Manu scriptum.*

Macte virtūte. VIRG.—"Be strong in virtue." These words are sometimes used ironically.

Macte virtūte diligentiâque esto. LIVY.—"Be strong in virtue and diligence."

——*Măcŭlæ quas aut incūria fudit,*
Aut humāna parum cavit natūra.—— HOR.
—"The blemishes which carelessness has produced, or against which human nature is not sufficiently on its guard."

——*Mădĭdis Notus ēvŏlat alis.* OVID.—"The south-west wind flies forth with dripping wings."

——*Magālia quondam.* VIRG.—"Once cottages." The same may be said, as to the ground on which they stand, of some of the most gorgeous palaces of the present day.

Magis gaudet quam qui senectam exŭit. *Prov.*—"He is more delighted than one who has put off old age," *i. e.* has become young again.

——*Magis illa juvant quæ pluris emuntur.* JUV.—"Those things please most which cost most."

Magis magni clērĭci non sunt magis săpientes. *Prov.*—"The greatest scholars are not the wisest men;" in a worldly point of view. A mediæval proverb.

Magis mutus quam piscis. *Prov.*—"More dumb than a fish."

Magister ălius casus. PLINY *the Elder.*—"Chance is a second master."

Magister ărtis ingĕnĭque largītor
Venter.—— PERS.

—"Hunger, the teacher of the arts, and the bestower of invention."

Magistrătus indĭcat virum.—"Office proves the man." Motto of the Earl of Lonsdale.

Magna Charta. — "The Great Charter." The Charter which was obtained from King John by the barons of England, in the year 1215, and which has ever since been regarded as the great bulwark of the liberties of Great Britain.

Magna cīvĭtas, magna sōlĭtudo. *Prov.*—"A great city, a great desert." A Latin adage taken from a Greek comic poet, who said of the city of Megalopolis in Arcadia, Ἐρημία μεγάλη 'στὶν ἡ Μεγάλη πόλις. "The great city, (or Megalopolis,) is a great wilderness."

Magna est admiratio copiōsè săpienterque dicentis. Cic. —"Great is our admiration of one who expresses himself with fluency and wisdom."

Magna est vĕrĭtas et prævalēbit.—"Truth is powerful, and she will prevail." An adaptation of the words in *I. Esdras*, iv. 41.

Magna est vis consuetūdĭnis: hæc ferre labōrem, contemnĕre vulnus et dolōrem docet. Cic.—"Great is the power of habit: this teaches us to bear fatigue, and to despise wounds and pain."

Magna fuit quondam căpĭtis reverentia cani,
Inque suo prĕtio ruga senīlis erat. Ovid.

—"In days of yore great was the respect paid to the hoary head, and honoured were the wrinkles of age."

——*Magnâ mĕdius cŏmĭtante catervâ.* Virg.—"In the midst of a vast crowd which attended him."

Magna movet stŏmăcho fastīdia, si puer unctis
Tractāvit călĭcem mănĭbus.—— Hor.

—"The stomach is sensible of great loathing, if the servant touches your cup with his greasy hands."

Magna quidem sacris quæ dat præcepta libellis
Victrix Fortūnæ Săpientia. Ducĭmus autem
Hos quoque fēlices, qui ferre incommŏda vitæ,
Nec jactāre jugum vitâ dĭdĭcēre magistrâ. Juv.

—"Noble indeed are the precepts which Philosophy, that triumphs over Fortune, lays down in her sacred pages. Yet we deem those happy too, who, with daily life for their preceptress, have learnt to endure with patience the evils of life, and not to struggle against the yoke."

Magna servĭtus est magna fortūna. SEN.—"A great fortune is a great servitude;"—in consequence of the many and imperative duties which it entails.

Magna vis est conscientiæ in utramque partem, ut neque tĭmeant qui nihil commisĕrunt, et pœnam ante ŏcŭlos versāri putent qui peccārunt." CIC.—"The power of conscience is great in both ways; those have nothing to fear who have committed no crime; and those who have sinned always have punishment before their eyes."

Magna vis est, magnum nomen, unum et idem sentientis senātûs. CIC.—"Great is the power, great the name, of a senate which is unanimous in its opinions."

Magnæ fēlīcitātes multum calīgĭnis mentĭbus hūmānis objĭciunt. SEN.—"Great prosperity involves the human mind in extreme darkness." Men who are suddenly prosperous are apt to lose sight of their duties and obligations.

Magnæ fortūnæ comes adest adulātio.—"Adulation is the attendant on great wealth."

Magnas inter opes inops. HOR.—"Poor in the midst of great wealth." A description of a miser, who knows not the proper use of money, and dares not spend it.

Magne pater divûm, sævos punīre tyrannos
Haud ălĭā rătiōne velis——
Virtūtem vĭdeant, intābescantque videndo. PERS.
—"Great father of the gods, be pleased to punish cruel tyrants in no other way than that they may behold virtue, and pine in despair as they behold her." The pangs of remorse are the severest punishment.

Magni ănĭmi est injūrias despĭcĕre. SEN.—"It is the duty of a great mind to despise injuries."

Magni est ingĕnii revocāre mentem à sensĭbus, et cōgitatiōnem à consuetūdĭne abdūcĕre. CIC.—"It requires great intellect to release the mind from the thraldom of the senses, and to wean the thoughts from confirmed habits."

——*Magni nōmĭnis umbra.* LUCAN.—"The shadow of a great name." These words are sometimes applied to the degenerate son or descendant of an illustrious father or ancestor. The son of Cicero, for instance, was only the shadow of his father's great name. See *Stat magni*, &c.

Magni refert quibuscum vixĕris. Prov.—"It is of great consequence with whom you live." People are generally estimated according to the character of their associates.

——*Magnis tamen excĭdit ausis.* Ovid.—"He fell, however, in a great attempt." See *Hic situs est*, &c.

Magno conātu magnas nugas. Ter.—"Great efforts on great trifles."

Magno cum perīcŭlo custoditur, quod multis placet. Syr.—"That is kept with great danger, which is coveted by many."

——*Magno de flūmĭne mallem*
Quam ex hoc fontĭcŭlo tantundem sūmĕre.—— Hor.
—"I had rather draw my glass of water from a great river than the same quantity from this little spring." Said ironically in reproof of those who lay by large stores and never use them.

——*Magnōrum haud unquam indignus avōrum.* Virg.—"Never proving unworthy of his illustrious ancestors."

Magnos hŏmĭnes virtūte metĭmur, non fortūnâ. Corn. Nep.—"We estimate great men by their virtue, not by their success." Philosophers may do this, but the public does not.

Magnum bonum.—"A great good." A species of plum is so called.

Magnum est argumentum in utrōque fuisse moderātum.—"It is greatly in a man's favour, to have shown himself moderate, when placed in either situation."

——*Magnum hoc ego duco,*
Quod plăcui tibi, qui turpi secernis honestum,
Non patre præclāro, sed vitâ et pectŏre puro. Hor.
—"I esteem it a great blessing that I pleased you, who distinguish probity from baseness, not by the illustriousness of a father, but by the purity of the heart and feelings."

——*Magnum hoc vĭtium vino est,*
Pedes captat primum; luctātor dolōsus est. Plaut.
—"This is the great fault in wine; it first trips up the feet: it is a cunning wrestler."

Magnum paupĕries opprŏbrium jubet
Quidvis aut făcĕre aut pati. Hor.
"Poverty, a great reproach, impels us to do or to suffer anything."

Magnum vectīgal est parsimōnia. CIC.—"Economy is a great revenue." On the principle of Franklin's favourite saying—"A penny saved is a penny earned."

Magnus Alexander corpŏre parvus erat. *Prov.*—"The great Alexander was small in stature."

Major e longinquo reverentia. TAC.—"Respect is greater at a distance." Similar to our proverb, "Familiarity breeds contempt." The French have a saying, that "No man is a hero to his valet."

——*Major famæ sitis est quam*
Virtūtis; quis enim virtūtem amplectĭtur ipsam,
Præmia si tollas? JUV.

—"The thirst for fame is greater than for virtue; for, take away the reward, and who would embrace virtue?" Strictly speaking, there is selfishness, though of a laudable character, in the motives of the best of men; they, at least, look for the reward of a good conscience.

Major hærēdĭtas venit unicuique nostrûm à jure et lēgĭbus, quàm à parentĭbus. CIC.—"We each of us receive a more valuable inheritance in our civil and legal rights, than any we derive from our fathers."

Major privāto visus, dum privātus fuit, et omnium consensu capax impĕrii, nisi imperâsset. TACIT.—"He appeared greater than a private individual, so long as he remained a private individual, and, by the consent of all, would have been deemed fit to rule had he never ruled." Said of the Emperor Galba.

——*Major rerum mihi nascĭtur ordo.* VIRG.—"A more extended range of things presents itself to me." My views become enlarged.

Majōresque cadunt altis de montĭbus umbræ. VIRG.—"And the shadows lengthen as they fall from the lofty mountains"—upon the approach of evening.

——*Mala causa silenda est.* OVID.—"It is best to be silent in a bad cause."

Mala conscientia etiam sōlitūdĭne anxia atque sollĭcĭta est.—"An evil conscience is anxious and solicitous, even in solitude."

Mala fides.—"Bad faith."

Mala gallīna, malum ovum. *Prov.*—"Bad hen, bad egg." So *Matt.* vii. 16, "Do men gather grapes of thorns, or figs of thistles?"

Mala grammătĭca non vĭtiat chartam. COKE.—"Bad grammar does not vitiate a deed." A deed is construed according to the manifest intention of the writer.

Mala mali malo mala contŭlit omnia mundo;
Causa mali tanti fœmĭna sola fuit.
—"The jaw-bone of a bad man with the aid of an apple brought all evil into the world; woman alone was the cause of all this evil." A play on the Latin words, *māla,* "a jaw-bone," *mălus,* "bad," *mălum,* "evil," and *malum,* "an apple."

Mala mens, malus ănĭmus. TER.—"Bad heart, bad disposition."

Mala ultro adsunt. PROV.—"Misfortunes come unsought."

——*Malè cuncta ministrat*
Impĕtus.—— STAT.
—"Violence conducts everything badly." When we are influenced by passion, we do everything amiss. See *Da spatium,* &c.

Malè imperando summum impĕrium amittĭtur. SYR.—"By bad government the supreme rule is lost."

Malè narrando fābŭla depravātur.—"A story is spoiled by being badly told."

Malè partum malè dispĕrit. PLAUT.—"Property ill got, ill spent." "Lightly come, lightly go." See *De malè quæsitis,* &c.

Malè secum agit æger, mĕdĭcum qui hærēdem facit. SYR.—"The sick man does injustice to himself who makes his physician his heir."

——*Malè si mandāta loquāris,*
Aut dormītābo aut rīdĕbo.—— HOR.
—"If you pronounce the parts assigned you badly, I shall either fall asleep or laugh." Addressed to an actor in tragedy.

——*Malè verum exămĭnat omnis*
Corruptus judex.—— HOR.
—"Every corrupt judge imperfectly examines into the truth." He shuts his eyes to such parts of the matter as do not suit his purpose. The poet is speaking of the intemperate man as ill qualified to judge of temperance.

Malè vivunt qui se semper victūros putānt. SYR.—"They live ill, who think they will live for ever." Because they are always deferring repentance and amendment.

Malĕdĭcus à malĕfĭco non distat nisi occăsiōne. QUINTILL.—"An evil-speaker differs from an evil-doer in nothing but want of opportunity." A person who stabs our good name will not hesitate to stab the body if it suits his purpose, and he can insure impunity.

Malĕfacĕre qui vult, nusquam non causam invĕniet. SYR.—"He who wishes to do evil will never be at a loss for a reason." See Æsop's Fable of the Wolf and the Lamb.

Malesuāda fames. VIRG. — "Hunger that persuades to evil."

Mali princĭpii malus finis. TER.—"Bad beginnings have bad endings."

Malim inquiētam lĭbertātem quàm quiētum servĭtium.—"I would prefer liberty with unquiet to slavery with quiet." The sentiments of a lover of freedom at any price.

Malis ăvĭbus.—"With bad birds," *i. e.* "with a bad omen."

Malĭtia est versūta et fallax rătio nocendi. CIC.—"Malice is a subtle and deceitful engine of mischief."

Malo accepto stultus sapit. *Prov.*—"After suffering an evil the fool becomes wise." "Experience is the mistress of fools."

Malo bĕnĕfăcĕre tantumdem est perĭcŭlum
Quantum bono mălĕfăcĕre.—— PLAUT.
—"To do good to the bad is a danger just as great as to do bad to the good."

Malo cum Platōne errāre, quam cum ălìis rectè sentīre. CIC.—"I had rather be wrong with Plato, than think aright with the others."

Malo indisertam prudentiam, quàm loquācem stultĭtiam. CIC.—"I prefer ineloquent prudence to fluent folly."

Malo malo malo malo.
—"*Malo*, I would rather be
Malo, in an apple tree,
Malo, than a wicked man
Malo, in adversity."
A play upon the different meanings of apparently the same word.

Malo mihi malè quàm mollĭter esse. SEN.—"I prefer being unfortunate to being effeminate."

Malo nodo malus quærendus cuneus. *Prov.*—"For a hard knot a hard tool must be sought."

Malo si quid bĕnĕfăcias, id bĕnĕfĭcium intĕrit,
Bono si quid mălĕfăcias, ætătem expĕtit. Plaut. —"If you do any good to the bad, the benefit is lost at once if you do any bad to the good, it lasts for a length of time."

Malōrum facinŏrum ministri quasi exprobrantes aspiciuntur. Tacit.—"The accomplices in evil actions are generally looked upon as our censors." There is no dependence upon them beyond the present moment.

Malōrum immensa vorāgo et gurges. Cic.—"A boundless abyss and gulf of evils."

Malum bene condĭtum ne movĕris. *Prov.*—"Do not disturb an evil that has been fairly buried." "Let well alone"—or, as we say, "Do not rip up old sores."

Malum consĭlium consultōri pessĭmum. Ver. Flaccus.—"Bad advice is most fatal to the adviser." Its ill effects are apt to recoil upon himself. See *Nec enim*, &c.

Malum est consĭlium quod mutări non potest. Syr.—"That is bad counsel, which cannot be changed." See *Vestigia nulla*, &c.

Malum in se.—"An evil in itself." That which is universally acknowledged to be bad among civilized men, and is stigmatized as such by the laws of nature.

Malum nascens făcĭlè opprĭmĭtur; inveterătum fit robustius. Cic.—"An evil habit in the beginning is easily subdued, but when it becomes inveterate, it gains strength."

Malum prohĭbĭtum.—"An evil from prohibition." That which is conventionally an evil, from being so defined by law; such, for instance, as smuggling.

Malum vas non frangĭtur. *Prov.*—"A worthless vessel does not get broken." "Nought comes to no harm."

Malus bonum ubi se sĭmŭlat, tunc est pessĭmus. Syr.—"A bad man is worst of all, when he pretends to be a good one." Because we are not on our guard against him.

Malus clandestīnus est amor, damnum est merum. Plaut.—"Clandestine courtship is bad; it is downright ruin."

Malus est enim custos diuturnitătis metus, contràque benevolentia fidēlis vel ad perpetuitătem. Cic.—"Fear is a bad preserver of that which is intended to endure; on the other hand, considerateness will insure fidelity for ever." A contrast of the comparative results of despotic sway and free government.

Malus malum vult, ut sit sui sĭmĭlis.—"A bad man wishes another to be bad, that there may be one like himself."

Malus usus abolendus est. *Law Max.*—"An evil custom ought to be abolished." In states this should be done with a sense that every usage is not necessarily bad because it is old.

Mandāmus. *Law Term.*—"We command." A writ or command issuing from the Queen's Bench, commanding certain things to be done, which it lies within its power to enforce.

Mandāre suspendium ălĭcui. Apul.—"To bid a man go and be hanged."

Mandrabūli more res succēdit. *Prov.*—"The business goes on as as it did with Mandrabulus:" i. e. worse and worse. Mandrabulus was a man who found a treasure, on which he presented to Juno a golden ram, meaning to make a similar offering each year: but repenting of his liberality, the next year he offered one of silver, and the following, one of bronze. Hence this phrase, very similar to our saying, "Out of the frying-pan into the fire."

Manēbant vestīgia morientis libertātis. Tacit. — "Traces still remained of expiring liberty." The spirit of freedom was not utterly crushed.

——*Manet altâ mente repôstum,*
Judicium Parĭdis spretæque injuria formæ. Virg.
—"There remains deeply seated in her mind the judgment of Paris, and the injustice done to her slighted beauty." In allusion to the vengeance of Juno.

Mănĭbus pĕdĭbusque.—"With hands and feet." With all one's energies; "With tooth and nail."

Manliāna impĕria. *Prov.*—"A Manlian order." In reference to Titus Manlius, who ordered his son to be scourged and beheaded for fighting contrary to orders.

Mantua me gĕnuit, Calăbri rapuēre, tenet nunc
Parthenŏpe. Cĕcĭni pascua, rura, duces.
—"Mantua bore me, Calabria witnessed my death, Parthenope [or Naples] now receives me. I sang of pastures, fields, and heroes." The epitaph of Virgil, written by himself, Donatus says, though without much appearance of probability.

Mantua, væ! mĭsĕræ nĭmium vĭcīna Cremōnæ. Virg.—

"Mantua, alas! how much too near to the unfortunate Cremona!" These words are said to have been most aptly quoted by Dean Swift, on seeing a valuable Cremona violin swept from a table to the floor by a lady's mantua or gown.

Manu forti.—"With a strong hand."

Manu scriptum.—"Written by the hand." Hence our word manuscript—sometimes written MS. and in the plural MSS.

Manum de tăbŭlâ!—"Hands off the picture!" Meaning that by touching and retouching you may at last injure a work. Said originally by Apelles to Protogenes, when still labouring to add to the beauties of a picture already beautiful.

Manum non vertĕrim, dĭgĭtum non porrexĕrim.—"I would not turn my hand, or hold out my finger for it."

Manus manum fricat, et manus manum lavat. *Prov.*—"Hand rubs hand, and hand washes hand." Nature teaches us that we were made to assist each other.

Marĕ apertum.—"A sea open,"—to commerce.

Mare clausum.—"A sea shut up,"—against the commerce of the world at large.

Mare quidem commūne certo est omnĭbus. PLAUT.—"Surely the sea is common to all."

Margarīta e stercŏre. *Prov.*—"A pearl from a dunghill."

Marmŏreo Lĭcĭnus tŭmŭlo jacet, at Cato parvo,
Pompeius nullo. Quis putet esse deos?
Saxa premunt Lĭcĭnum, levat altum Fama Catōnem,
Pompeium tĭtŭli. Crēdĭmus esse deos.

—"Licinus lies in a marble tomb, Cato in an humble one, Pompey in none. Who can think that the gods exist? Heavy lies the stone on Licinus; Fame raises Cato on high; his glories, Pompey. We believe that the gods do exist." The first two lines are an epigram from the Latin Anthology in reference to the magnificent tomb of one Licinus, the slave and steward of Julius Cæsar. The two lines in answer, which are equally good, are of more recent origin.

Mars grăvior sub pace latet.—— CLAUD.—"A more serious warfare lies concealed beneath a show of peace."

——*Martem accendĕre cantu.* VIRG.—"To kindle the warfare by his note." Said of a trumpeter, and the effects of martial music.

Mater ait natæ, dic natæ, Fīlia, natam
Ut mŏneat natæ, plangĕre fīliŏlam.

"The mother to her daughter spake,
Daughter, said she, arise,
Thy daughter to her daughter take,
Whose daughter's daughter cries."

A distich, according to Zuinglius, on a lady of the family of the Dalburgs, who saw her descendants to the sixth generation.

Mater artium necessĭtas. *Prov.*—"Necessity is the mother of arts." Or, as we say, "Necessity is the mother of invention."

Mater familias.—"The mother of a family."

Mātĕriem, qua sis ingĕniōsus, habes. OVID.—"You have a subject on which to prove your ingenuity."

Matĕriem superābat opus.—— OVID.—"The workmanship surpassed the material." The mechanical skill displayed rendered the material more than doubly valuable.

Matūre fias senex, si diu velis esse senex. *Prov.*—"You must become an old man soon, if you would be an old man long." "Old young and old long." You must leave off the irregularities of youth early, if you wish to attain old age. Quoted by Cicero, *De Senectute.*

Māvĕlim mihi inimīcos invidēre quam me inimīcis meis :
Nam invidēre alii bene esse, tibi male esse, mĭsĕria est.
PLAUT.

—"I had rather that my enemies should envy me than I my enemies; for to feel envy because it goes well with another, and badly with yourself, is wretchedness."

Maxĭma debētur puĕris reverentia.—— JUV.—"The greatest respect is due to youth." Everything said and done in the presence of youth should be weighed more carefully even than our conduct in the company of old age. It has its effect for good or for bad.

Maxĭme illĕcĕbra est peccandi impunitātis spes. CIC.—"The greatest allurement to guilt, is the hope of escaping with impunity." It is the certainty of punishment that deters from the commission of crime.

Maxĭma pœna mihi est ipsum offendisse—— OVID.—"It is my greatest punishment to have offended him."

Maxĭma quæque domus servis est plena superbis. JUV.—"Every great house is full of insolent servants."

Maximas virtūtes jacēre omnes necesse est, voluptāte dominante. CIC.—"Where a love of pleasure reigns paramount, the greatest of virtues must necessarily lie inactive."

Maxĭmus in mĭnĭmis.—"Very great in very little things." The character of a laborious trifler.

——*Me antehac*
Supremum habuisti cŏmĭtem consiliis tuis. PLAUT.
—"Till now you have had me as the most intimate sharer in your counsels."

Me duce, damnōsas, hŏmĭnes, compescĭte curas. OVID.—"With me for your guide, ye men, dispel your anxious cares."

Me justum esse gratis oportet. SEN.—"It is my duty to be just without reward."

Me lĭceat casus miserēri insontis amīci? VIRG.—"May it be allowed me to pity the misfortunes of my guiltless friend?"

Me, me, adsum qui feci, in me convertĭte ferrum. VIRG.—"On me! on me! here am I who did the deed, oh turn your sword on me." See *Mea fraus*, &c.

Me mĭsĕrum! paucas mŏnui quod prosit in horas. OVID.—"Wretched me! I have been giving advice to be of use for a few hours only."

——*Me non orācŭla certum,*
Sed mors certa facit.——
—These words are part of a speech of Cato in Lucan, ix. 582. Cato says,

Sortilegis egeant dubii, semperque futuris
Casibus ancipites, *me non oracula certum,*
Sed mors certa facit; pavido fortique cadendum est.

—"Let those who are doubtful, and always perplexed about future events, seek the aid of diviners; *as for me, it is not oracles that render me decided, but death, which is itself decided;* for the coward and the hero must perish alike."

Me non solum piget stultitiæ meæ, sed etiam pudet. CIC.—"I am not only grieved at, but even ashamed of, my folly."

——*Me Parnassi deserta per ardua dulcis*

Raptat amor; juvat ire jugis, qua nulla priōrum
Castălian molli divertĭtur orbĭta clivo. VIRG.
—"The sweet love [of the Muses] transports me along the lonely heights of Parnassus; I delight to range those mountain-tops, where no path, trodden by the ancients, winds down to Castalia with gentle descent."

——*Me pascant olīvæ,*
Me cichorēa, levesque malvæ.
Frui parātis, et vălĭdo mihi,
Latöe dones, et, precor, intĕgrâ
Cum mente, nec turpem senectam
Dĕgĕre, nec cithărâ carentem. HOR.
—"May olives support me, succory too and soft mallows. O son of Latona, grant me to enjoy what I have, and to possess my health, with an unimpaired understanding, I beseech thee; and not to pass a wretched old age, or deprived of my lyre."

Mea culpa, Deus.—"My fault, O God." A mediæval expression, like our "God forgive me," used by a person when sensible of having done or said anything profane.

——*Mea fraus omnis: nihil iste nec ausus,*
Nec pŏtuit, cœlum hoc, et conscia sīdĕra testor. VIRG.
—"Mine is all the offence, he neither dared, nor could do, aught. This I call heaven and the conscious stars to witness." (See *Me, me, adsum,* &c.) The words of Nisus, when attempting to save Euryalus, in the 9th Æneid. A celebrated statesman, having quoted the passage, "*Me, me, adsum,*" &c., was reminded by his opponent, that he had omitted the "*Mea fraus omnis,*" which was much more applicable to him.

Meārum rerum me novisse æquum est ordĭnem. PLAUT.—"It is right that I should know the state of my own circumstances."

——*Mecum făcĭlè rĕdeo in grātiam.* PHÆD.—"I am easily reconciled to myself."

——*Mĕdia inter prœlia semper*
Stellārum, cœlique plagis, sŭpĕrisque vacāvi. LUCAN.
—"Ever, amid battles, have I found time to contemplate the stars, and the tracts of heaven, and the realms above."

Mĕdĭci, causâ morbi inventâ, curatiōnem inventam putant. CIC.

—"Physicians think that, the cause of the disease being discovered, they have also discovered its cure."

Mĕdĭci graviōres morbos aspĕris remĕdiis curant. Curt.—"Physicians cure severe diseases with sharp remedies."

Mĕdĭcus dedit qui tempŏris morbo moram,
Is plus rĕmĕdii quam cutis sector dedit.
—"The physician who gives to the disease time for cure, finds a better remedy than he who cuts the skin." A gradual cure is more desirable than recourse to violent remedies.

——*Mĕdio de fonte lepōrum*
Surgit amāri ălĭquid quod in ipsis flōrĭbus angat. Lucret.
—"From the midst of the very fountain of delight something bitter arises, to vex us even amid the flowers themselves."

"Full from the fount of joy's delicious springs
Some bitter o'er the flowers its bubbling venom flings."
Childe Harold, c. i. § 82.

——*Mĕdio tutissĭmus ibis.* Ovid.—"You will go most safely in the middle." By avoiding extremes you will insure comparative security.

——*Mediŏcrĭbus esse poētis*
Non Di, non hŏmĭnes, non concessēre columnæ. Hor.
—"Mediocrity in poets not gods, nor men, nor booksellers will permit."

Mĕdiŏcrĭtas est inter nĭmĭum et parum.—"Mediocrity is the mean between too much and too little."

Mel in ore, verba lactis,
Fel in corde, fraus in factis.
—"Honey in his mouth, words of milk, gall in his heart, fraud in his deeds." A Leonine couplet of the middle ages, descriptive of a hypocrite.

Mĕlior est condĭtio possidentis. *Law Max.*—"The condition of him who is in possession is the most advantageous." "Possession is nine points of the law," where the rights are equal.

Mĕlior est condĭtio possidentis, ubi neuter jus habet. *Law Max.*—"Where neither has a right, the condition of him who is in possession is the best."

Mĕlior tūtiorque est certa pax, quam sperāta victōria. Liv.
—"Certain peace is better and safer than expected victory."

Mĕliōra sunt ea quæ natūrâ, quam quæ arte perfecta sunt. Cic.—"Those things which are perfect by nature are better than those which are made perfect by art."

Mĕlius est cavēre semper, quàm pati semel. *Prov.*—"It is better to be always on one's guard, than once to suffer." On the other hand, Julius Cæsar used to hold that it was better to suffer once, than to be kept continually on the rack of apprehension.—*Mĕlius est pati semel, quàm cavēre semper.*

Mĕlius est modo purgāre peccāta, et vĭtia resecāre, quam in futūrum purganda reservāre. Th. a Kempis.—"It is better now to cleanse ourselves of our sins, and to lop off our vices, than to reserve them, to be cleansed at some future time."

Mĕlius est peccāta cavēre, quam mortem fŭgĕre. Si hŏdie non es parātus, quōmŏdo cras eris? Cras est dies incertus: et qui scis si crastĭnum habēbis? Th. a Kempis.—"It is better to avoid sin, than to fly from death. If to-day you are not prepared, how will you be to-morrow? To-morrow is an uncertain day, and how do you know whether you will have a to-morrow?"

——*Mĕlius non tangĕre, clamo.* Hor.—"I give notice, 'tis best not to touch me." The words of a man who is on his guard against every attack.

Mĕlius, pejus, prosit, obsit, nil vident nisi quod libuerit. Ter.—"Better or worse, for their advantage or disadvantage, they see nothing but what they please."

Mellītum venēnum, blanda orātio. *Prov.*—"A flattering speech is honied poison." It tends to disarm the person to whom it is addressed.

Membra refōrmīdant mollem quoque saucia tactum;
Vanaque sollicitis incŭtit umbra metum. Ovid.
—"The wounded limb shudders at even a gentle touch: and to the timid the unsubstantial shadow creates alarm."

Memento mori.—"Remember you must die." Anything which reminds us of our end is called a *memento mori.* At their banquets the Egyptians were in the habit of introducing a mummy or a skeleton, and addressing words to this effect to their guests.

Memento semper finis, et quia perdĭtum non redit tempus.

TH. A KEMPIS.—"Always be in remembrance of your end, and that time lost never returns."

——*Mĕmĭnĕrunt omnia amantes.* OVID.—"Lovers remember everything."

Memorābĭlior prima pars vitæ quam postrĕma fuit. LIVY.—"The first part of his life was more distinguished than the latter." Said of Scipio Africanus the Younger.

Mĕmŏrem immĕmorem facit, qui monet quod memor mĕmĭnit. PLAUT.—"He who is continually reminding a man who has a good memory, makes him forget."

Memŏria est per quam mens rĕpĕtit illa quæ fuĕrunt. CIC.—"The memory is that by which the mind recalls the things that have been."

Memŏriâ in æternâ.—"In eternal remembrance."

Memŏria technĭca.—"An artificial memory." Words or signs adapted for aiding the memory.

Mendācem mĕmŏrem esse oportet. QUINT.—"A liar should have a good memory."

Mendāci hŏmĭni, ne verum quidem dicenti crēdĕre solēmus. CIC.—"We are accustomed to give no credit to a liar, even when he tells the truth." Illustrated by the Fable of the Shepherd Boy and the Wolf.

——*Mendīci, mimi, balatrōnes.* HOR.—"Beggars, buffoons, and scoundrels." "Tag, rag, and bobtail."

Mendīco ne parentes quidem amīci sunt. *Prov.*—"To a beggar not even his own parents are friendly." Poverty has the effect of blighting the natural affections.

Mene fugis? per ego has lăchrymas dextramque tuam, te
Per connūbia nostra, per inceptos Hymenæos,
Si bene quid de te mĕrui, fuit aut tibi quicquam
Dulce meum, miserĕre domûs lābentis, et istam
Oro, siquis adhuc prĕcĭbus locus, exue mentem. VIRG.

—"Dost thou fly from me? I conjure thee, by these tears, by thy own right hand, by our marriage rites, by our new-made wedding tie, if ever I have deserved well of thee, or if aught of my charms were sweet unto thee, pity my falling house, and if there is still any room for my prayers, lay aside, I beseech thee, this thy intention." Dido thus appeals to Æneas, when he is about to abandon her, and fly from Carthage.

Mene salis plăcĭdi vultum fluctusque quiētos
Ignorāre jubes? Mene huic confīdĕre monstro? VIRG.
—"Dost thou command me not to understand the countenance of the placid ocean and the waves? Am I to put any faith in this monster?"

—*Mens ăgĭtat molem*—— VIRG.—"A mind informs the mass."

Mens bona regnum possĭdet. Prov.—"A good mind possesses a kingdom." "My mind to me a kingdom is." The motto of the Emperor Nerva.

Mens conscia recti.—"A mind conscious of rectitude." See *Conscia mens recti*, &c.

Mens cujusque is est quisque.—"The mind of the man is the man himself."

Mens immōta manet, lăchrymæ volvuntur inānes. VIRG.—"His mind remains unmoved. Tears are shed of no avail."

——*Mens interrĭta lethi.* OVID.—"A mind unawed by death." The feelings of a good man in his last moments.

Mens invicta manet.—"The mind remains unsubdued." This is especially proved in the case of those who have died martyrs for their faith.

Mens peccat, non corpus, et unde consĭlium abfŭit culpa abest. LIV.—"The mind sins, not the body, and where reason is wanting there is no criminality." Hence it is that lunatics are not subject to the penal laws.

Mens sine pondĕre ludit.—"The mind is playful when free from pressure."

Mensque pati durum sustĭnet ægra nihil. OVID.—"A mind diseased can bear nothing that is harsh." Its susceptibility is increased by suffering.

—— *Mensūraque juris*
Vis erat.—— LUCAN.
—"And might was the measure of right." This takes place in the lawless days of anarchy.

——*Mentis gratissĭmus error.* HOR.—"A most delightful reverie of the mind." See *Pol me*, &c.

Mentis pĕnĕtrālia. CLAUD.—"The inmost recesses of the mind." The secret thoughts of the heart.

——*Meo sum pauper in ære.* HOR.—"I am poor, but at my own expense." Though I am poor, I am out of debt.

Merces virtūtis laus est. *Prov.*—"Praise is the reward of virtue."

Merx ultrōnea putet. *Prov.* — "Proffered wares stink." Quoted by St. Jerome, and meaning that proffered services are despised. In either case we are apt to suspect the sincerity of the person making the offer.

Messe tenus prŏpriâ vive.—— Pers.—"Live within your own harvest." Live within your means.

Messis erant primis vĭrĭdes mortālĭbus herbæ,
Quas tellus nullo sollicitante dabat. Ovid.
—"Green grass, which the earth yielded, unsolicited by man, was, to the first mortals, in place of harvest."

Mētīri se quemque suo mŏdŭlo ac pede verum est. Hor.—"It is just that every man should estimate himself by his own measure and standard." Stretch your arm no further than your sleeve will reach.

Meum and *tuum.*—"Mine and thine." The "law of *meum* and *tuum*," means "the law of property;" in contradistinction to what is called at the present day *communism* or *socialism.*

Meum est propŏsĭtum in tabernâ mori ;
Vinum sit appŏsĭtum mŏrientis ori.
—"In a house of carousal, well primed will I die,
With the cup to my lips, while expiring I lie."

The commencement of the so-called drinking-song of Walter Mapes. It consists of some stanzas selected from his *Goliæ Confessio.*

Meus mihi, suus cuique est carus. Plaut.—"Mine is dear to me, and dear is his own to every man."

——*Micat inter omnes.* Hor.—"It shines above all." These words have been used as a punning inscription under the picture of a favourite cat. "My cat above all others."

——*Mīgrāvit ab aure voluptas*
Omnis.—— Hor.
—"All pleasure has fled from the ear." Said in reference to those who preferred pantomimic exhibitions on the stage to the dialogue of the legitimate drama.

Mihi forsan, tibi quod nĕgāvit,
Porrĭget hora.—— Hor.

—"Time may, perhaps, extend to me that which it has denied to thee."

Mihi *istic nec sĕrĭtur nec mĕtĭtur.* PLAUT. — "There is neither sowing nor reaping for me in this matter."

——*Mihi res, non me rebus, subjungĕre conor.* HOR. —"I endeavour to make events submit to me, and not to submit myself to them."

——*Mihi tarda fluunt ingrātaque tempŏra*—— HOR.—"The time flies slowly and heavily to me."

Mīlĭtat *omnis amans.*—— OVID.—"Every lover is a soldier." The lover requires vigilance, wariness, resolution, and fortitude. Ovid wrote his "Art of Love" to instruct in this kind of warfare.

Mīlĭtiæ *spĕcies amor est.* OVID.—"Love is a kind of warfare."

——*Mille ănĭmos excĭpe mille modis.* OVID.—"Treat a thousand dispositions a thousand different ways."

Mille *hŏmĭnum spĕcies et rerum discŏlor usus;*
Velle suum cuique est, nec voto vīvĭtur uno. PERS.
—"There are a thousand kinds of men, and different hues in the colour of things; each one follows his own inclination, nor do they all agree in their desires." It is one of the most admirable dispensations of Providence, that the tastes of men are suited to the infinite variety of circumstances. See *Quot homines*, &c.

Mille *modi Vĕnĕris.*—— OVID. "A thousand-fold are the ways of love."

Mille *trahens vărios adverso sole colōres.* VIRG.—"Drawing a thousand colours from the opposite sun." Said of the rainbow.

Millia *frumenti tua trīvĕrit ārea centum,*
Non tuus hoc căpiet venter plus ac meus.—— HOR.
—"Though your threshing-floor should yield a hundred thousand bushels of corn, your belly will none the more hold more than mine."

Minātur *innocentĭbus qui parcit nocentĭbus.* COKE.—"He threatens the innocent who spares the guilty."

Minor *est quàm servus, dŏmĭnus qui servos timet.*—"A master who fears his servants is lower than a servant." He should take care therefore not to put himself in their power.

——*Minuentur atræ*
Carmĭne curæ. Hor.
—"Black cares will be soothed by verse."

——*Minuit præsentia famam.* Claud.—"Our own presence diminishes the exaggeration of report." See *Majore longinquo*, &c., and *Vindictam*, &c.

Minus afficit sensus fătigătio quam cōgitătio. Quint.—"Bodily fatigue affects the mind less than deep thought."

——*Minus aptus acūtis*
Nārĭbus horum hŏmĭnum.—— Hor.
—"Not proof against the sharp-witted sneers of these men."

Minus in parvos fortūna furit,
Lĕviusque ferit leviōra Deus. Sen.
—"Fortune rages less against the humble, and God strikes more lightly the lowly." See the Fable of the Oak and the Thistle.

——*Minūti*
Semper et infirmi est ănĭmi exĭguique voluptas
Ultio.—— Juv.
—"Revenge is always the pleasure of a narrow, diseased, and little mind." Any person capable of thinking twice must see that no practical utility can result from the gratification of revenge.

Minūtiæ.—"Trifles." Meaning the most minute and trifling circumstances connected with any matter.

Minūtŭla plŭvia imbrem parit. *Prov.*—"Many little drops make a shower." "Many littles make a mickle."

Mira cano; sol occŭbuit, nox nulla secūta est.—"Wonders I sing; the sun has set, no night has ensued." See *Sol occubuit*, &c.

Mira quædam in cognoscendo suāvĭtas et delectātio.—"There is a certain wonderful gratification and delight in gaining knowledge."

Mirābĭle dictu. Virg.—"Wonderful to be told."

Mirāmur ex intervallo fallentia. *Prov.*—"We admire at a distance things which are deceptive." Both morally and physically the sight is often deceived by objects beheld from a distance. "'Tis distance lends enchantment to the view." See *Major e*, &c., and *Minuit præsentia*, &c.

Mirantur tăcĭti, et dŭbio pro fulmĭne pendent. Statius.—

"In silence they are amazed, and stand in expectation of the thunderbolt, doubtful where it shall fall."

Miris modis Dî ludos făciunt homĭnĭbus ;
Mirisque exemplis somnia in somnis danunt. PLAUT. —"In wondrous ways do the gods make sport of men ; and in wondrous fashions do they send dreams in sleep."

Misce stultitiam consĭliis brevem. HOR.—"Mingle a little gaiety with your grave pursuits." "Be merry and wise."

——*Mĭsĕra est magni custōdia censûs.* JUV.—"The charge of a great estate is a misery." If the duties of the owner are properly attended to they will entail labour, if neglected he must make up his mind to be robbed.

Mĭsĕra est servĭtus ubi jus est aut vagum aut incognĭtum. *Law Max.*—"Servitude is a wretched state where the law is either undefined or unknown."

Mĭsĕra mors săpienti non potest accĭdĕre. CIC.—"A wretched death cannot fall to the lot of a wise man." To him death, in whatever shape, will be welcome.

Mĭsĕram pacem vel bello benè mutāri. TACIT.—"A peace that is productive of wretchedness, may be profitably exchanged for war." The one is a certain evil, from the other good *may* result.

——*Mĭsĕri, quibus*
Intentāta nites.—— HOR.
—"Wretched are they to whom you, untried, seem fair!" They will be sadly duped on finding your beauty accompanied by deceit and ingratitude.

Mĭsĕricordia Dŏmĭni inter pontem et fontem. ST. AUGUSTIN. —"Between bridge and stream the Lord's mercy may be found." True repentance, though at the last moment, will find favour in the sight of God.

——*Mĭsĕris succurrĕre disco.* VIRG.—"I have learned to succour the wretched." See *Haud ignara,* &c.

Miserrĭma est fortūna quæ inimīco caret. SYR. — "Most wretched is the fortune of him who has not an enemy." Meaning that to be envied by none, a man must be low down in the world indeed.

——*Miserrĭma isthæc misĕria est servo bono,*
Apud herum qui vera lŏquĭtur, si id vi verum vincĭtur.
PLAUT

—"It is the greatest of misfortunes to a good servant, who is telling the truth to his master, if that same truth is overpowered by violence."

Miserrĭmum est timēre cum speres nihil. SEN.—"It is a most wretched thing to be in dread, when you have nothing to hope for."

——*Mĭsĕrum est aliēnâ vīvĕre quadrâ.* JUV.—"Wretched is it to live at the expense of another."

——*Mĭsĕrum est aliōrum incumbĕre famæ,*
Ne collapsa ruant subductis tecta columnis. JUV.
—"It is wretched to be dependent on another's fame; the chance is, that the props by which you are supported will be withdrawn, and the roof come tumbling down in one common ruin."

——*Mĭsĕrum est opus,*
Igĭtur demum fŏdĕre pŭteum, ubi sitis fauces tenet. PLAUT.
—"It is a shocking thing to have to dig a well at the last moment, just when thirst has seized your throat." The disadvantage of having deferred till the last moment a matter of vital importance.

Mĭsĕrum istuc verbum et pessĭmum est,
Hăbuisse, et nihil habēre.—— PLAUT.
—"A shocking expression that, and a most grievous one, 'I had, and I have not.'"

Mitte ambos nudos ad ignōtos, et vidēbis.—"Send them both naked among strangers, and then you will see." The old rule (attributed by Bacon, in his Apophthegms, to "one of the philosophers,") for knowing a fool from a wise man. See the Fable of Simonides preserved from Shipwreck, in Phædrus.

——*Mitte hanc de pectŏre curam.* VIRG.—"Dismiss these anxieties from your breast."

Mitte superba pati fastīdia, spemque cadūcam
Despĭce; vive tibi, nam mŏriēre tibi. SEN.
—"Cease to endure a patron's proud insolence, and despise all transitory hopes; live for yourself, for for yourself you will die."

Mittĭmus. Law Term.—"We send." A writ for the removal of records from one court to another, also a precept in writing, under which a person accused of a crime is committed to prison by a justice of the peace.

Mŏbĭlis et văria est fermè natūra malōrum. JUV.—"The nature of evils is generally variable and changing."

Mōbilitāte viget, viresque acquīrit eundo. VIRG.—"It lives by moving, and gains strength as it goes." Said with reference to the activity of Rumour, which gains strength as it travels.

——*Mōbĭlium turba Quirītium.* HOR.—"A crowd of fickle citizens." The mob, so called from their *mobilitas,* or fickleness.

Moderāri ănĭmo et orātiōni, cum sis irātus, non mĕdiŏcris ingĕnii est. CIC.—"To keep the mastery over your indignation and language, when you are angry, is no mean effort of the mind."

Moderāta durant. SEN.—"Things enjoyed in moderation last long." Whereas excess entails speedy exhaustion.

Modestè tamen et circumspecto judĭcio de tantis viris pronunciandum est, ne, quod plerisque accĭdit, damnent quæ non intellĭgunt. QUINTILL.—"We should, however, pronounce our opinions with reserve and cautious judgment, concerning such eminent men, lest, as is the case with many, we should be condemning what we do not understand."

Modestia famæ neque summis mortālĭbus spernenda est. TACIT. —"Fame is not to be despised by even the most eminent of men, if sought with modesty." A high reputation is a legitimate object of ambition so long as it is sought by fair means.

——*Modo me Thebis, modo ponit Athēnis.* HOR.—"He now places me at Thebes, now at Athens." Said of a dramatic writer, whose art and talent enable him to carry his audience along with him whenever he changes the scene.

Modus omnĭbus in rebus optĭmum est hăbĭtu. PLAUT.—"A medium is best to be observed in all things." See *Est modus,* &c.

Modus ŏperandi.—"The mode of operation." The way in which a thing is done.

Molesta et importūna salutantium frequentia.—"A troublesome and annoying crowd of persons paying their court."

Molle meum lĕvĭbus cor est violābĭle telis. OVID.—"My tender heart is vulnerable by his light arrows." In allusion to the darts of Cupid.

——*Mollia tempŏra fandi.* HOR.—"The favourable moment

for speaking." There is a season for everything, and among them, for asking a favour.

Mollis educātio nervos omnes et mentis et corpŏris frangit. Quint.—"An effeminate education weakens all the powers both of mind and body."

Mollis in obsĕquium făcilisque rogantĭbus esses. Ovid.—"You should be kindly obsequious and yielding to any entreaties."

——*Mollissĭma corda*
Hūmāno gĕnĕri dare se nātūra fatētur,
Quæ lăchrymas dedit.—— Juv.
—"Nature confesses that she has bestowed on man a most susceptible heart, in that she has granted tears."

Mollĭter austēro stŭdio fallente labōrem. Hor.—"While your eagerness in the pursuit beguiles fatigue."

——*Mollĭter ossa cubent.* Ovid.—"Softly may his bones repose."

——*Momento mare vertĭtur:*
Eōdem die ubi lūsĕrunt, nāvĭgia sorbentur.
—"In a moment the sea is changed, and on the same day on which they have gaily sported along, ships are swallowed up." Human life and the lot of the sailor are equally subject to vicissitudes.

——*Mŏnĭti, meliōra sequāmur.* Virg.—"Advised, let us follow better counsels."

Mons cum monte non miscēbĭtur. Prov.—"Mountain will not mingle with mountain." Haughty persons will rarely agree.

Mons partŭrĭbat, gĕmĭtus immānes ciens,
Eratque in terris maxĭma expectatio,
At ille murem pĕpĕrit.—— Phæd.
—"A mountain was in labour, sending forth dreadful groans, and there was in the districts the highest expectation. But after all, it brought forth a mouse." See *Parturiunt montes,* &c.

Monstra evĕnĕrunt mihi!
Introiit in ædes ater aliēnus canis!
Anguis per implŭvium dĕcĭdit de tĕgŭlis!
Gallīna cĕcĭnit!—— Ter.
—"Prodigies have befallen us! A strange black dog came into the house! a snake came down from the tiles

through the sky-light! a hen crowed!" All these were bad omens with the ancients.

Monstrum horrendum, informe, ingens, cui lumen ademptum. VIRG.—"A monster horrible, misshapen, huge, and deprived of his eye." The description given by Virgil of the Cyclops Polyphemus, after his one eye had been put out by Ulysses with a red-hot spit.

——*Monstrum nullâ virtūte redemptum*
A vĭtiis.—— JUV.
—"A monster whose vices are not redeemed by a single virtue."

Mora omnis ŏdio est, sed facit săpientiam. SYR.—"All delay is distasteful, but it produces wisdom."

Morbi perniciōres sunt ănĭmi quam corpŏris. CIC.—"The diseases of the mind are more hurtful than those of the body."

More majōrum.—"After the manner of our ancestors."

More suo.—"After his usual manner."

Mores detĕriōres increbrescunt, nec qui amīci, qui infidēles sint, pernoscas. PLAUT.—"Bad manners gain apace, nor can you distinguish who are your friends, and who are false to you."

Mores dispăres dispăria stŭdia sequuntur. CIC.—"Persons of different manners follow different pursuits." "Every man to his taste." See *Non omnia*, &c.

——*Mores multōrum vidit.*—— HOR.—"He saw the manners of many men." Said of Ulysses.

Mori est felīcis, antĕquam mortem invŏcet. SYR.—"He who dies before he calls for death is a happy man."

——*Moriāmur, et in mĕdia arma ruāmus.* VIRG.—"Let us die, and rush into the thick of the fight." See *Hysteron proteron.*

Mōrĭbus antīquis stat Roma.—"Rome stands by her ancient manners." The stability of the Roman republic was based on the simplicity of the manners of its citizens, and their resistance to all innovations.

Mōrĭbus et formâ conciliandus amor. OVID.—"Pleasing manners and good looks conciliate love."

Mors et fugācem persĕquĭtur virum,
Nec parcit imbellis juventæ
Poplĭtĭbus, tĭmĭdoque tergo. HOR.

—"Death pursues the man as he flies, nor spares the trembling knees of the unwarlike youth, or his timid back." The impartial advance of death, who strikes down all before him, the coward equally with the brave.

Mors et vita in mănĭbus linguæ. *Prov.*—"Life and death are in the hands of the tongue."

Mors jānua vitæ.—"Death is the gate of life," *i. e.* of everlasting life.

Mors omnĭbus commūnis.—"Death is the common lot of all."

——*Mors sola fatĕtur*
Quantŭla sint hŏmĭnum corpuscŭla.—— Juv.

—"Death alone discloses how insignificant are the puny bodies of us men." Death, the universal leveller, shows the emptiness of human pride and ambition, and the feebleness of man.

——*Mors ultĭma lĭnea rerum est.* Hor.—"Death is the closing limit of human affairs."

Mortālia acta nunquam Deos fallunt.—"The deeds of man never deceive the gods."

——*Mortālia facta perĭbunt;*
Nedum sermōnum stat honos et grātia vivax,
Multa renascentur quæ jam cĕcidēre, cadentque
Quæ nunc sunt in honōre vocābŭla, si volet usus,
Quem penes arbĭtrium est, et jus, et norma loquendi. Hor.

—"Mortal works must perish; much less can the honour and elegance of language be long-lived. Many words shall revive which have now fallen into disuse, and many shall fall into disuse which are now esteemed, if it is the will of custom, in whose power is the decision, and the right to form the standard of correct speaking."

Mortālis nemo est, quem non attingat dolor morbusque.—"There is no mortal being whom grief and disease cannot reach."

Mortalitāte relictā vivit immortalitāte indūtus.—"Mortality left behind, he lives clothed in immortality."

Mortem Parca affert, opes rursus ac facultātes aufert.—"Fate brings death, and deprives us of wealth and riches."

Mortua manus. *Law Term.*—"Mortmain." Lands which were transferred to ecclesiastical corporations, and thereby became inalienable and not liable to secular services, were said to be, so far as the community at large was concerned, placed *in mortuâ manu*, "in a dead man's hand." There is, however, some doubt as to the origin of the term.

Mortuis nōn conviciandum. *Prov.*—"We must not speak ill of the dead." See *De mortuis*, &c.

Mortuo leōni et lĕpŏres insultant. *Prov.*—"Even hares insult a dead lion." It is only a poor-spirited creature that will insult departed greatness. See the Fable of the Aged Lion and the Ass, in Phædrus, B. i. F. 21.

Mortuum flagellas. *Prov.*—"You are beating a dead man." Said to one who reproves a man incorrigibly wicked.

Mortuus per somnum vacābis curis. "Having dreamed that you are dead you will be free from care." This was a current opinion of the ancient Greeks, and still prevails with some superstitious persons.

——*Mos est oblivisci hŏmĭnĭbus, neque novisse, cujus nihĭli sit făciunda gratia.* PLAUT.—"It is the fashion for persons to forget and not to know him whose favour is esteemed as worth nothing."

Mos pro lege. *Law Max.*—"Usage for law." Long established usage is the basis of our common law.

Motus in fine velōcior.—"Motion, towards its conclusion, is more swift." The law of falling bodies.

——*Movet cornīcŭla risum*
Furtīvis nūdāta colōrĭbus.—— HOR.
—"The crow, deprived of its stolen colours, excites our laughter." A picture of the detected hypocrite or braggart.

Mūgītus lăbyrinthi. *Prov.*—"The roaring of the labyrinth." A phrase used at Rome, to signify any common topic or hackneyed subject; this being a favourite theme with wretched poets.

Mulgēre hircum. *Prov.*—"To milk a he-goat." To attempt an impossibility.

——*Mŭlier cŭpĭdo quod dicit amanti,*
In vento et răpĭdâ scrībĕre oportet aquâ. CATULL.
—"What a woman says to an anxious lover, ought to be written on the winds and the water as it swiftly flows." In allusion to the fickleness of the fair sex; but more particularly the fair sex of ancient Rome.

Mŭlier profecto nata est ex ipsâ morâ. PLAUT.—"Woman is surely born of tardiness itself."

Mŭlier quæ sola cŏgĭtat malè cŏgĭtat. *Prov.*—"A woman who meditates alone, meditates to evil purpose."

Mŭlier tum bene olet ubi nihil olet. PLAUT.—"A woman smells sweetly, when she smells of nothing at all."

Multa cadunt inter călĭcem suprēmaque labra. LABER.—"Many things fall between the cup and the edge of the lips." To the same purpose as our favourite proverb,

"There is many a slip
'Twixt the cup and the lip."

Multa dies, văriusque labor mutābĭlis ævi,
Rĕtŭlit in mĕlius; multos alterna revisens
Lusit, et in sŏlĭdo rursus fortūna locāvit. VIRG.

—"The lapse of time, and the varying revolutions of changing years, have improved many things, and capricious fortune, after many changes, has placed them once again on a solid basis." In allusion to the changing destinies of states, and the transitions from anarchy to peace and order.

Multa diūque tuli: vĭtiis pătientia victa est. OVID.—"Much and long time have I suffered; by your faults is my patience overcome."

Multa docet fames. *Prov.*—"Hunger teaches many things." To the same effect as "Necessity is the mother of invention."

——*Multa et præclāra minantis.* HOR.—"Threatening things many and great." Of great and wondrous promise.

Multa ferunt anni vĕnientes commŏda secum;
Multa recēdentes ădĭmunt.—— HOR.

—"Our years as they advance bring with them many advantages; as they recede they take many away." Our early years are gilded by the pleasures of hope and anticipation: our declining ones are embittered either by satiety or disappointment.

Multa gemens. VIRG.—"Deeply lamenting." Said of one who relates a sorrowful tale.

Multa me dŏcuit usus, magister egrĕgius. PLIN. *the Younger.*—"Necessity, that excellent master, hath taught me many things."

Multa novit vulpes, sed felis unum magnum. *Prov.*—"A fox knows many things, but a cat one great thing." Said by the cat, who could climb the tree and so escape the hounds, while the bragging fox could only run for it. See *Ars varia*, &c.

——*Multa petentĭbus*
Desunt multa.—— Hor.
—"Those who desire much are in want of much." The number of our wants (not our *necessities*) is in proportion to the extent of our desires.

Multa præter spem scio multis bona ēvĕnisse. Plaut.—"I know that many a lucky thing has happened to many a one beyond his hopes."

Multa quidem scripsi; sed quæ vitiōsa putāvi,
Emendātūris ignĭbus ipse dĕdi. Ovid.
—"Much did I write; but what I considered faulty I myself committed to the all-correcting flames."

Multa rogant utenda dari; data reddĕre nolunt. Ovid.—"They ask for many a sum to be lent them; but when it is lent they are loth to repay."

Multa senem circumvĕniunt incommŏda.—"Many inconveniences surround the aged man."

——*Multa vidēmus*
Quæ miser et frugi non fecit Apĭcius.—— Juv.
—"We see many things which even Apicius (mean and stingy compared with him) never was guilty of."

Multa viri nequicquam inter se vulnĕra jactant,
Multa cavo lătĕri ingĕmĭnant, et pectŏre vastos
Dant sŏnĭtus; erratque aures et tempŏra circum
Crebra manus · duro crĕpĭtant sub vulnĕre malæ. Virg.
—"The men deal many blows to one another with erring aim, and many redouble on their hollow sides; from their breasts the thumps resound, and round their ears and temples thick blows at random fly; their jaws crack beneath the heavy hits."

Multæ manus onus lĕvius făciunt. *Prov.*—"Many hands make a burden light."

Multæ terricŏlis linguæ, cœlestĭbus una.—"The inhabitants of earth have many tongues, those of heaven but one." A much quoted line, written by the late Rev. H. Carey of the British Museum.

Multārum palmārum causidĭcus.—"A pleader who has gained many victories."

Multas amicitias silentium dĭrĕmit. *Prov.*—"Silence severs many friendships." It requires considerable energy and warmth of feeling long to maintain a correspondence with friends at a distance. See *Non sunt amici*, &c.

Multi adorantur in arâ qui cremantur in igne. St. Augustin. —"Many are worshipped at altars, who are burning in flames." Not every man that has been canonized is really a saint.

——*Multi*
Committunt eădem diverso crīmĭna fato. Juv.
—"Many men commit the same crimes, with very different fates." See *Ille crucem*, &c.

Multi more isto atque exemplo vivunt, quos cum censeas
Esse ămīcos, rĕpĕriuntur falso falsimōniis. Plaut.
—"Many live after this manner and method; when you think them to be your friends, they are found to be false with their deceitfulness."

Multi multa, nemo omnia novit. Coke.—"Many people know many things, no one everything."

(*Multi*) *nil rectum nisi quod plăcuit sibi ducunt.* Hor.—"Many esteem nothing right, but what pleases themselves."

——*Multi si pauca rogābunt,*
Postmodo de stipŭlâ grandis acervus erit. Ovid.
—"If many ask for but a little, very soon will a heap be formed from the gleanings." "Many littles make a mickle."

Multi te ōdĕrint si teipsum ames.—"Many will hate you if you love yourself." Selfishness and self-love beget hatred and contempt.

Multi tristantur post delĭcias, convīvia, dies festos.—"Many persons feel dejected after pleasures, banquets, and holidays."

Multis commoditātĭbus et elegantiis, suas ædes commŏdiōres aptiōresque fecit. Cic.—"By many appliances and elegancies, he has rendered his house more commodious and convenient."

——*Multis ille bonis flĕbĭlis occĭdit*
Nulli flĕbĭlior quam tibi—— Hor.
—"He died lamented by many good men, by none more lamented than by thee."

Multis minatur, qui uni facit injūriam. Syr.—"He who injures one, threatens many."

Multis parâsse dīvĭtias non finis misĕriārum fuit, sed mūtātio; non est in rebus vĭtium sed in ănĭmo. SEN.—"To have become possessed of riches, is, to many, not the end of their miseries, but a change in them; the fault is, not in the riches, but in the disposition."

Multis terrĭbĭlis cavēto multos. AUSON.—"If you are terrible to many, then beware of many." The number of your enemies is proportionably increased.

Multitūdĭnem decem făciunt. COKE.—"Ten make a multitude."

Multo mĕlius ex sermōne quam lineamentis, de mōrĭbus hŏmĭnum judicāre.—"It is much better to judge of men's characters from their words than their features."

Multò plures satiĕtas quam fames perdĭdit viros.—"Surfeit has killed many more men than hunger."

Multōrum annōrum opus.—"The labour of many years."

Multōrum mănĭbus grande levātur opus.—"By the hands of many a great work is made easy." See *Multæ manus*, &c

Multos castra juvant, et lĭtuo tubæ
Permistus sŏnĭtus, bellaque mātrĭbus
Detestāta.—— HOR.

—"The camp, and the sound of the trumpet mingled with that of the clarion, and war, detested by mothers, have delights for many."

Multos ingrātos invĕnĭmus, plures făcĭmus. *Prov.*—"We find many men ungrateful; we make still more." By throwing the opportunity of showing themselves ungrateful in the way of undeserving persons.

——*Multos in summa perĭcŭla misit*
Ventūri timor ipse mali.—— LUCAN.

—"The very fear of approaching evil has driven many into peril." See *Incidit in Scyllam*, &c.

Multos qui conflictāri adversis videantur, beātos; ac plerosque, quanquam magnas per opes, miserrĭmos; si illi gravem fortūnam constanter tŏlĕrent, hi prospĕrâ inconsulte utantur. TACIT.—"Many who appear to be struggling against adversity, are happy; and more, although possessed of great wealth, are most wretched. The former support their adverse fortune with firmness, the latter inconsiderately abuse their prosperity."

Multos timēre debet quem multi timent. SYR.—"He of

whom many are afraid has reason to be afraid of many." See *Multis terribilis*, &c.

——*Multum ablūdit imāgo.* HOR.—"The picture is most ludicrously unlike."

Multum demissus homo. HOR.—"An extremely reserved man."

Multum habet jucunditātis soli cælique mutātio. PLINY *the Younger.*—"Change of soil and climate is productive of considerable pleasure."

Multum ille periclitātur, qui in negotiatiōnem marĭtĭmam pecūniam impendit suam.—"He runs many risks who expends his money on maritime speculations."

Multum in parvo.—"Much in little." Much in a little compass. A compendium.

Multùm sapit qui non diù desĭpit. *Prov.*—"He is very wise who does not long persist in folly." This is said, taking into consideration the limited extent of the human powers of discernment.

Multum te opinio fallit. CIC.—"Your opinion is extremely fallacious."

Mundæque parvo sub lare pauperum
Cœnæ, sine aulæis et ostro,
Sollicĭtam explicuēre frontem. HOR.

—"A cleanly meal in the little cottage of the poor has smoothed an anxious brow, without hangings and purple."

Munditiæ, et ornātus, et cultus, hæc fœminārum insignia sunt, his gaudent et gloriantur. LIVY.—"Neatness, ornament, and dress, are distinctions peculiar to women; in these they delight and glory."

——*Munditiis căpĭmur.* OVID.—"We are captivated by neatness."

Mundus scena, vita transĭtus, venisti, vidisti, abiisti.—"This world is a stage, and life your walk across; you have come, you have seen, you are gone."

Mundus universus exercet histriōnem. PETRON. ARB.—"All men practise the player's art." So Shakspeare—

"All the world 's a stage,
And all the men and women merely players."
As You Like It.

Mūnĕra accĭpit frequens, remittit nunquam. PLAUT.—"He

often receives presents, but never makes them in return."

Mūnĕrum ănĭmus optĭmus est. *Prov.*—"Goodwill is the best of gifts." The goodwill of the giver constitutes the real value of the gift.

——*Munus Apollĭne dignum.* HOR.—"A present worthy of Apollo." A compliment to a meritorious poem.

Munus ornāre verbis. TER.—"To enhance the value of a present by one's words." To double the value of a gift by the grace with which it is presented.

Muri coctiles. OVID.—"Walls of brick;" and *not* "cock-tailed mice," a translation facetiously suggested in the "Art of Pluck."

Mus in pice.—"A mouse in pitch." A man who is always immersed in useless researches: Swift's dirty philosopher of Lagado in "Gulliver's Travels," for instance.

Mus non uni fidet antro. PLAUT.—"The mouse does not trust to one hole only."

——*Musæo contingĕre cuncta lepōre.* LUCRET.—"To touch upon everything with a lively wit."

Mustēlam habes. *Prov.*—"You have a weasel (in your house)." To meet a weasel was considered an omen of misfortune.

Mutātis mutandis.—"Changing what should be changed." A warrant made out against B will do for E, *mutatis mutandis*, *i. e.* changing one name for the other.

——*Mutāto nōmĭne, de te*
Fābŭla narrātur.—— HOR.
—"Change but the name, the story 's told of you." Such was the gist of Nathan's parable to David.

Mutiāna cautio.—"The quirks" or "cozenage of Mutius." In allusion to Mutius Scævola, the great Roman lawyer.

Mutum est pictūra poēma.—"A picture is a poem without words." See *Si poēma*, &c., and *Ut pictura poēsis*, &c.

N.

N. B. See *Nota bene.*

Næ amīcum castigāre ob mĕrĭtam noxiam
Immūne est facĭnus.—— PLAUT.

—"To reprove one's friend for a fault that deserves it, is decidedly a thankless task."

Nævia sex cyăthis, septem Justīna bibātur. MART.—"Let Nævia be toasted with six cups, Justina with seven."

Nam bonum consilium surripĭtur sæpissĭme,
Si minus cum curâ aut cate locus loquendi lectus est. PLAUT.
—"For a well-devised plan is very often filched away, if the place for deliberating has not been chosen with care or caution."

Nam curiōsus nemo est, quin idem sit malĕvŏlus. PLAUT.—"For no person is a busy-body, but he is ill-natured as well."

Nam de mille fabæ mŏdiis dum surrĭpis unum,
Damnum est, non făcĭnus, mihi pacto lĕnius isto. HOR.
—"For when from a thousand bushels of beans you steal a single one, the loss to me is trifling, but none the less is the crime on your part." Although the law does not take cognizance of extreme trifles, still, morally speaking, if there is the *animus furandi*, "the intention to steal," the guilt is the same.

Nam ego illum pĕriisse duco, cui quidem pĕriit pudor. PLAUT. "For I consider that man to be lost who is lost to shame."

Nam et majōrum institūta tuĕri, sacris cerimōniisque rĕtinendis, săpientis est.—"For it is the part of a wise man to defend the institutions of his forefathers, and uphold the sacred rites and ceremonies."

Nam et stultè făcĕre et stultè fābŭlārier,
Utrumque in ætāte haud bonum est. PLAUT.
—"For to act unwisely and to talk unwisely, are neither of them profitable at times."

Nam mora dat vires, tĕnĕras mora percŏquit uvas;
Et vălĭdas sĕgĕtes, quod fuit herba, facit. OVID.
—"For time supplies strength; time thoroughly ripens the tender grapes; and it makes that into standing corn which was before only blades of grass."

Nam non est verisĭmĭle hŏmĭnem paupĕrem
Pauxillum parvi făcĕre, quin nummum petat. PLAUT.
—"For it is not very likely that a poor man would despise ever such a trifle, and not be glad of a piece of money."

Nam nunc mores nihil făciunt quod licet, nisi quod lubet.

Plaut.—"For now-a-days it is the fashion to reckon of no value what is proper, but only what is agreeable."

Nam pro jucundis aptissĭma quæque dabunt Dî;
Cārior est illis homo quam sibi.—— Juv.
—"For the gods will bestow what is most suitable, rather than what is agreeable; man is more dear to them than he is to himself."

Nam qui injuste impĕtum in quempiam facit, aut irâ, aut ălĭquâ perturbātiōne incitātus, is quasi manus afferre vidētur sŏcio. Cic.—"For when a man, in the heat of anger, or agitated by some other cause, makes an attack upon another unjustly, it would seem as though he had laid hands upon an ally." Because man is a social animal.

Nam sapiens quidem pol ipsius fingit
Fortūnam sibi.—— Plaut.
—"The prudent man really frames his own fortunes for himself."

Nam scelus intra se tăcĭtum qui cōgĭtat ullum
Facti crimen habet.—— Juv.
—"For he who secretly meditates a crime within himself, has all the guilt of the deed." The *animus*, and not the act, constitutes the crime; although the laws of man can only take cognizance of the *animus* when manifested by the act.

Nam vĭtiis nemo sine nascĭtur; optĭmus ille est,
Qui mĭnĭmis urgētur.—— Hor.
—"For no man is born without faults; he is the best who is beset by the fewest."

——*Namque inscĭtia est*
Adversum stĭmŭlum calces. Ter.
—"For it is mere folly to kick against the spur." So in *Acts* ix. 5, the Lord says to Saul, "It is hard for thee to kick against the pricks;" i. e. to resist a superior power which has you under its control.

Narrātur et prisci Catōnis
Sæpe mero căluisse virtus. Hor.
—"It is said that the virtues even of old Cato were often warmed by wine." Said in allusion to the rigid Cato, the Censor.

Nascentes mŏrĭmur, finisque ab orĭgĭne pendet. Manil.—

"We are born to die, and our end is the necessary consequence of our birth."

Nascĭmur poëtæ, fimus orātōres. CIC.—"We are born poets, we become orators." Poetical genius is a gift, but oratory may be acquired by education and perseverance. Witness the instance of Cicero, who in vain tried to become a poet, and of Demosthenes, who by perseverance became the greatest of orators. See *Poëta nascitur*, &c.

Natio comœda est. JUV. — "The nation is a company of players."

Natis in usum lætitiæ scyphis
Pugnāre Thracum est; tollĭte barbărum
Morem.—— HOR.
—"To quarrel over your cups, which were made to promote good fellowship, is like the Thracians: away with a habit so barbarous." The battles of the Centaurs and Lapithæ, the near neighbours of the Thracians, commenced in a drunken brawl.

——*Natos ad flūmina primum*
Defĕrĭmus, sævoque gelu durāmus et undis. VIRG.
—"Our infants, as soon as born, we convey to the rivers, and harden them in the freezing ice and waves."

——*Natūra beātis*
Omnĭbus esse dedit, si quis cognōvĕrit uti. CLAUD.
—"Nature has given unto all to be happy, if each did but know how to make a proper use of her gifts." The same objects and opportunities may be blessings or curses to us, according as they are used.

Natūra dedit usūram vitæ tanquam pecūniæ nullâ præstitūtâ die. CIC.—"Nature has bestowed life on us, at interest, like money, no day being fixed for its recall."

Natūrâ ipsâ valēre, et mentis vīrĭbus excitāri, et quasi quodam divīno spīrĭtu afflāri. CIC.—"To be endowed with strength by nature, to be impelled by the powers of the mind, and to be inspired by a certain divine spirit as it were." A recital of the endowments of true genius.

Natūra naturans—natūra naturāta.—"Nature formative—nature formed." The two ultimate principles of the Dualistic Philosophy are technically so called.

Natūra non dat virtūtem; nascĭmur quidem ad hoc, sed sine

hoc. Cic.—"Nature does not bestow virtue; we are born indeed to it, but without it."

Natūra! quam te cŏlĭmus invīti quoque. Sen.—"O nature! how much do we worship thee, however unwilling!"

Natūra tenacissĭmi sumus eorum quæ puĕri percipĭmus, ut sapor, quo nova vasa imbuuntur, durat. Sen.—"We are naturally most tenacious of those impressions which we receive in childhood, just as a flavour remains in those vessels with which they were imbued when new."

Naturālem quamdam voluptātem habent lusus jocusque; at eorum frequens usus omne ănĭmis pondus, omnemque vim ērĭpit. Sen.—"There is a certain delight in pleasantry and jesting; but a too frequent use of them deprives the mind of all weight and vigour."

Natūram expellas furcâ, tamen usque recurret. Hor.—"Though you should check Nature by force, she will still resume her sway."

Naufrăgium rerum est mŭlier malefīda marīto.—"A faithless wife is the shipwreck of her husband's fortunes." These words were quoted by William the Conqueror to his wife Matilda, on finding that she encouraged his son Robert in his rebellious designs.

Nauseanti stŏmăcho effluunt omnia.—"Everything is thrown off from a sick stomach."

——*Nāvĭbus atque*
Quadrīgis pĕtĭmus bene vīvĕre.—— Hor.
—"With the help of ships and chariots we endeavour to make ourselves happy." By moving from place to place.

Ne ad aures quidem scalpendas otium est. *Prov.*—"He has not time even to scratch his ears."

Ne Æsōpum quidem trivit. *Prov.*—"He has not so much as thumbed Æsop." Said of a person extremely illiterate; the Fables of Æsop being among the ancients an elementary school book.

——*Ne cede malis, sed contra audentior ito.* Virg.—"Yield not to misfortunes, but meet them with still greater firmness." The first three words are the motto of the Earl of Albemarle.

Ne cuivis dextram injĕcĕris. *Prov.*—"Don't give your right hand to every one." Use discrimination in the selection of your friends.

Ne depugnes in aliēno negōtio. *Prov.*—"Fight not in another person's concerns."

Ne exeat regno. *Law Term.*—"Let him not leave the kingdom." A writ issued by the courts of Equity to prevent a person from leaving the kingdom without the royal licence.

Ne glădium tollas, mŭlier. *Prov.*—"Woman, do not wield the sword." Persons should not wield "edged tools," which they know not how to use.

Ne Hercŭles quidem contra duos. AUL. GEL.—"Not Hercules even could struggle against two."

Ne intellĭgis, dŏmĭne? "Don't you understand, good sir?" See *Love's Labour's Lost*, Act V. sc. 1.

Ne Jupĭter quidem omnĭbus placet. *Prov.*—"Not Jupiter himself can please everybody."

Ne mente quidem recte ŭti possŭmus, multo cibo et potiōne complēti. CIC.—"We cannot use the mind aright when filled with much food and drink."

Ne mihi contingant quæ volo, sed quæ sunt utĭlia.—"Let those things happen to me, not which I most wish, but which are most for my good."

Ne neglĭgas amĭcĭtiæ consuetūdĭnem, aut viŏles jura ejusdem.—"You must not omit the usages of friendship, or violate the rights thereof."

——*Ne non procumbat honestè,*
Extrēma hæc ĕtiam cura cadentis erat. OVID.
—"That she might fall in no unseemly manner—this was her care even as she died." Said of Lucretia when about to stab herself.

Ne plus ultra.—"No farther." "This is my *ne plus ultra*"—much the same as This is my *ultimatum*, (or, as the newspapers have it at the present day, my *ultimatissimum*,)—"beyond this I will not go."

Ne præsentem aquam effundas, priusquam ălium sis adeptus. *Prov.*—"Do not throw away the water you have, until you have got more." Do not throw away a present advantage for a problematical one.

Ne prius antĭdŏtum quam venēnum. *Prov.*—"Don't take the antidote before the poison." Do not exculpate yourself before you are accused.

Ne, puĕri, ne tanta ănĭmis assuescĭte bella;
Neu patriæ vălĭdas in viscĕra vertĭte vīres. VIRG

—"Do not, my sons, accustom your minds to such cruel wars, nor turn your mighty strength against the vitals of your country."

Ne pŭĕro glădium. *Prov.*—"Do not give a child a sword." Let every person act in his proper sphere of life.

Ne, pulvis et cinis, superbe te geras,
Omnipotentis ne fulmĭna feras.
—"Dust and ashes, be not elate with pride, lest the lightnings of the Omnipotent should reach thee." The commenting lines of a Sequence used by the Romish Church.

Ne qua meis esto dictis mora—— VIRG.—"Let there be no delay in the execution of my injunctions."

Ne quid abjectè, ne quid tĭmĭdè făcias. CIC.—"Do nothing meanly, nothing timidly."

Ne quid detrimenti respublĭca căpiat.—"That the republic shall receive no detriment." The injunction given at ancient Rome to the Dictator, when invested with the supreme authority.

Ne quid falsi dīcĕre audĕat, ne quid veri non audĕat. CIC.—"Let him not dare to say anything that is false, nor let him fear to say what is true." Advice given to an historian.

Ne quid nimis. TER.—"Not too much of anything." Do nothing to excess. See *Id arbitror*, &c.

Ne scŭtĭcâ dignum horrĭbĭli sectĕre flagello. HOR.—"Do not punish with an unmerciful scourge that which is only deserving of the whip." The censure of the satirist, as well as of every one that reproves, should be proportionate to the fault.

Ne sibi deesset in his angustiis. CIC.—"Lest, in circumstances of such great difficulty, he should be found wanting to himself."

Ne sus Minervam. *Prov.*—"A pig must not talk to Minerva." Ignorant persons must not censure those wiser than themselves.

Ne sutor ultra crĕpĭdam.—"Let not the shoemaker go beyond his last." Words addressed by Apelles to a shoemaker, who pointed out errors in a slipper painted in one of his pictures; but when he was proceeding to criticise other parts of the painting, he was met by the artist with this rebuke.

——*Ne te longis ambāgĭbus ultra*
Quàm satis est morer.—— Hor.
—"That I may not, by a long circumlocution, delay you longer than is necessary."

Ne tentes, aut perfĭce. Prov.—"Attempt not, or achieve."

Ne verba pro farīnâ. Prov.—"Don't give me words for meal." Similar to our expression, "Sweet words butter no parsneps."

——*Nec bellua tētrior ulla est,*
*Quam servi răbies in lib*ĕ*ra terga furentis.* Claud.
—"No monster is there more baneful, than the fury of a slave wreaking his vengeance on the backs of freemen."

Nec caput nec pedes. Cic.—"Neither head nor feet;" or, as we say, "Neither head nor tail."

Nec cibus ipse juvat morsu fraudātus acēti. Mart.—"Not food itself is palatable when deprived of the relish given by vinegar."

Nec citò crēdĭdĕris; quantùm citò crēdĕre lædat,
Exemplum vobis, non leve, Procris erit. Ovid.
—"Be not too ready to believe; the fate of Procris will be no slight example to you how disastrous it is to believe things readily." See *Ovid's Met.* b. vii. l. 394, *et seq.*

Nec cui de te plusquam tibi credas. Prov.—"Give no man more credit than yourself about yourself." Do not acquiesce in either praises or censures pronounced on you, which you know to be undeserved.

Nec deus intersit, nisi dignus vindĭce nodus. Hor.—"Nor let a god interfere, unless there be a difficulty worthy of a god's assistance." Advice to dramatic writers, not to introduce personages too exalted, except on occasions of the highest importance.

Nec domo dŏmĭnus, sed dŏmĭno domus honestanda est. Cic.—"The master ought not to be honoured by the house, but the house by the master."

Nec făcĭle invĕnias multis in millĭbus unum;
Virtūtem prĕtium qui putet esse sui. Ovid.
—"Among many thousands you would not easily find one who believes that virtue is its own reward."

Nec fuge collŏquium; nec sit tibi jānua clausa. Ovid.—"Fly not from conversation; and let not your door be shut."

——*Nec imbellem ferōces*
Progĕnĕrant ăquĭlæ columbam. HOR.
—"Nor do ferocious eagles beget the unwarlike dove."

Nec levis, ingĕnuas pectus coluisse per artes,
Cura sit; et linguas edĭdicisse duas. OVID.
—"And be it no light care to cultivate the mind with the liberal arts, and to learn thoroughly the two languages." The Latin and the Greek.

——*Nec longum tempus, et ingens*
Exiit ad cœlum ramis felīcĭbus arbos,
Mirātur que novas frondes, et non sua poma. VIRG.
—"In no long time a huge tree shoots up to heaven with verdant boughs, and admires its new leaves, and fruits not its own." Said of the results of grafting trees.

Nec loquor hæc, quia sit major prūdentia nobis;
Sed sim, quam mĕdĭco, notior ipse mihi. OVID.
—"And I say this, not because I have any greater foresight, but because I am better known to myself than to a physician."

Nec lusisse pudet, sed non incīdĕre ludum. HOR.—"It is no disgrace to have been gay, but it is, not to have renounced those gaieties." The shame does not lie in having joined in gaieties, but in not having quitted them at a proper season. A man must not be *always* "sowing his wild oats."

Nec magis sine illo nos esse fēlīces, quam ille sine nobis pŏtuit. PLINY's *Panegyric on Trajan.*—"No more could we live happily without him, than he could without us."

Nec me pudet, ut istos, fatēri nescīre quod nesciam. CIC.—"Nor am I ashamed, like those men, to acknowledge that I do not know the things which I do not know."

——*Nec meus audet*
Rem tentāre pudor, quam vires ferre recūsent. VIRG.
—"Nor does my modesty presume to attempt a thing which my powers are unable to accomplish."

Nec meus hic sermo est, sed quæ præcĕpit Ofellus. HOR.—"Nor is this my language, but a precept which Ofellus has given."

——*Nec mihi dīcĕre promptum,*
Nec făcĕre est isti.—— OVID.
—"Neither does my talent lie in talking, nor his in act-

ing." The words of Ajax when pleading against Ulysses for the arms of Achilles.

Nec mĭnĭmum refert, intacta rosāria primus,
An serâ carpas pæne relicta manu. OVID.
—"Nor does it make a slight difference only, whether you cull from rosebeds before untouched, or whether, with a late hand, when there are hardly any roses left."

Nec minor est virtus, quam quærĕre, parta tuēri:
Casus inest illic; hic erit artis opus. OVID.
—"'Tis no less merit to keep what you have got, than to gain it. In the one there is some chance; the other will be a work of art."

Nec mirum, quod divīna natūra dedit agros, ars humāna ædificāvit urbes. VARRO.—"Nor is it wonderful, as divine nature has given us the country, and human art has built the cities." Similar to the line of Cowper,
"God made the country, and man made the town."

Nec mora, nec rĕquies.—— VIRG.—"Neither rest nor cessation." No intermission is allowed.

Nec morti esse locum.—— VIRG.—"Nor is there scope for death." Virgil says, that after their dissolution on earth, all things return to God, and that death has no further power over them.

——*Necnon et apes exāmĭna condunt*
Cortĭcĭbusque cavis vitiōsæque ilĭcis alveo. VIRG.
—"Bees also conceal their swarms in the hollow bark and in the trunk of a decayed holm oak."

Nec nos obnīti contra, nec tendĕre tantum
Suffĭcĭmus; sŭpĕrat quŏniam Fortūna, sequāmur,
Quoque vocat vertāmus iter.—— VIRG.
—"We are neither able to make head against (the storm), nor even to withstand it; since Fortune overpowers us, let us follow her, and turn our course whither she invites us." The words of Æneas to his followers.

——*Nec plăcĭdam membris dat cura quiētem.* VIRG.—"Nor does care allow placid quiet to the wearied limbs."

Nec plūrĭbus impar.—"No unequal match for many." The motto assumed by Louis XIV. when he formed his project for the subjugation for Europe.

Nec plŭteum cædit, nec demorsos sapit ungues. PERS.—"It neither thumps away at the desk, nor savours of nails gnawed to the quick" Said of poor spiritless poetry.

Nec, quæ prætĕriit, ĭtĕrum revocābĭtur unda;
Nec, quæ prætĕriit hora redīre potest. OVID.
—"Neither shall the wave, which has passed by, ever be recalled; nor can the hour which has passed ever return."

Nec quare et unde—quid hăbeat tantum rogant.—"People ask not *how* and *whence*, but only *what* a man possesses."

Nec quicquam ad nostras pervĕnit acerbius aures. OVID.—"Nothing more distressing has come to my ears."

Nec satis est pulchra esse poĕmata, dulcia sunto. HOR.—"It is not enough that poems be beautiful; let them be pleasing also."

Nec scire fas est omnia. HOR.—"Nor is it allowed us to know all things."

Nec semper fĕriet quodcunque minābĭtur arcus. HOR.—"Nor will the arrow always hit the object aimed at."

Nec servum mĕliōrem ullum, nec detĕriōrem dŏmĭnum fuisse. SUETON.—"There never was a better servant or a worse master." Said of the emperor Caligula.

Nec, si me sŭbĭto vĭdeas, agnoscĕre possis. OVID.—"Nor could you recognise me, if you were to see me on a sudden."

Nec si non obstātur proptĕrea ĕtiam permittĭtur. CIC.—"Though an act is not prohibited, it does not therefore follow that it is permitted." Moral duties go beyond the mere letter of the law.

Nec sibi cœnārum quivis tĕmĕrè arrŏget artem,
Non prius exactâ tĕnui ratiōne sapōrum. HOR.
—"Let no man rashly arrogate to himself a knowledge of the art of catering, if he has not previously acquired an intimate knowledge of the delicate distinctions of flavours."

Nec sibi, sed toti gĕnĭtum se crēdĕre mundo. LUCAN.—"To believe that he was born not for himself alone, but for the whole world." The principle acted upon by the benefactors of mankind.

Nec sum ădeo informis, nuper me in littŏre vidi. VIRG.—"Nor am I so very ugly, I lately viewed myself on the shore." Self-commendation.

Nec tamen ignōrat, quid distent æra lupīnis. HOR.—"Nor

is he ignorant of the vast difference between money and lupines." He can distinguish between the worthy and the worthless. Lupines were used as counters among the Romans, and to represent money on the stage.

Nec tamen in dando mensūram dēsĕrit; immo,
Singŭla descrībit certo modĕrāmĭne finis.

—"Nor yet in giving does he go beyond all bounds; nay, rather, to each he assigns a portion fixed and definite."

Nec tamen indignum est, quod vobis cura placendi,
Cum comptos hăbeant sæcŭla nostra viros. OVID.

—"And yet it is not unbecoming for you to have a care to please, since our age produces men of taste." Advice to the ladies.

Nec tibi quid lĭceat, sed quid fecisse decēbit
Occurrat; mentemque domet respectus honesti. CLAUD.

—"And let it not be the subject of your thoughts what you may do, but what you ought to do; let a regard for what is honourable ever govern your mind."

Nec vagus in laxâ pes tibi pelle natet. OVID.—"And do not let your foot wallop about in your shoe down at heel."

Nec Vĕnĕris phărĕtris macer est, aut lampăde fervet:
Inde faces ardent, vĕniunt a dote sagittæ. JUV.

—"It is not from Venus' quiver that he grows thin, or with her torch that he burns; it is from this that his fires are fed, from her dowry the arrows come." Said of a fortune-hunter.

Nec verbum verbo curābis reddĕre fidus
Interpres.—— HOR.

—"Nor, even if a faithful translator, should you make it your care to render the original word for word." The meaning of the original might be lost thereby.

Nec vīdisse semel satis est, juvat usque morāri,
Et conferre gradum, et vĕniendi discĕre causas. VIRG.

—"Nor is it enough to have merely seen him; they are delighted to prolong the interview, and to approach him, and to learn the cause of his coming." The ghosts of the departed Trojans thronging around Æneas, when he visits the infernal regions.

Nec vixit malè qui natus mŏriensque fefellit. HOR.—"Nor has he lived to no purpose, who, from his birth to his death, has lived in retirement."

Nec vos, turba fere censu fraudāta, magistri
Spernĭte: discĭpŭlos attrăhit illa novos. OVID.
—"Neither do you, schoolmasters, a set too often cheated of your pay, despise her; 'tis she that brings you new pupils." Minerva, the goddess of wisdom, is alluded to.

——*Nec vultu destrŭe dicta tuo.* OVID.—"And do not undo your sayings with your looks."

Necesse est cum insanientĭbus fŭrĕre, nisi solus relinquĕris. PETRON. ARB.—"It is necessary to be mad with the insane, if you would not be left alone." It is as well to appear to conform to the prejudices of the day.

Necesse est eum qui velit peccāre ăliquando primum delinquĕre. CIC.—"It is a matter of course that he who would sin must first fail in his duty." See *Nemo repente*, &c.

Necesse est făcĕre sumptum, qui quærit lucrum. PLAUT.—"It is necessary for him who looks for gain, to incur some expense." "Nothing venture, nothing win."

Necesse est in immensum exeat cupĭdĭtas quæ naturālem modum transĭliit. SEN.—"Avarice, when it has once passed the proper limits, of necessity knows no bounds."

Necesse est ut multos tĭmeat, quem multi timent. SYR.—"He whom many fear, must of necessity fear many." The condition of the tyrant. See *Multos timere*, &c., and *Multis terribilis*, &c.

Necessĭtas est lex tempŏris et loci. *Law Max.*—"Necessity is the law of time and place."

Necessĭtas non habet legem. *Law Max.*—"Necessity knows no law." In a sinking ship, for instance, the laws of life and property are but little regarded.

Necessitūdĭnis et libertātis infinīta est æstimātio. *Law Max.*—"Necessity and liberty should receive the very greatest consideration."

Nefas nocēre vel malo fratri puta. SEN.—"Consider it a crime to do an injury to a bad brother even." Similar to the Scripture precept, by which we are commanded to return good for evil.

Negat quis? Nego. Ait? Aio. Postrēmo impetrāvi ĕgŏmet mihi omnia assentāri. CIC.—"Does any one deny a thing? Then I deny it. Does he affirm? Then I affirm. In fine, I have prevailed upon myself to agree to everything."

——*Neglecta solent incendia sūmĕre vires.* HOR.—" Fire neglected is wont to gain strength."

Neglĭgĕre quid de se quisque sentiat, non solum arrogantis est, sed omnino dissolūti. CIC.—" To be careless of what any one may think of him, is not only the conduct of an arrogant man, but of one utterly abandoned."

Negōtiis par.—" Equal to business." Able to manage affairs.

Nem. con. Abbreviation of *nēmĭne contradicente.*—" No one contradicting " any question proposed.

Nem. diss. Abbreviation of *nēmĭne dissentiente.*—" No one disagreeing " with a proposition made.

Nēmĭnem id ăgĕre, ut ex alterius prædētur inscitiâ. CIC.—" No man should so act as to take advantage of another man's ignorance."

Nēmĭnem tibi adjungas amīcum prinsquam explorāvĕris quōmŏdo priōrĭbus amīcis sit usus.—" Make no man your friend before you have ascertained how he has behaved towards his former friends."

Nēmĭni dixĕris, quæ nolis efferri. *Prov.*—" Tell no one that which you do not wish repeated again."

Nēmĭni fidas, nisi cum quo prius mĕdium salis absumpsĕris. *Prov.*—" Trust no man till you have eaten a bushel of salt with him."

Nemo allēgans suam turpitūdĭnem audiendus est. *Law Max.*—" No man bearing testimony of his own baseness ought to be heard."

Nemo an bonus, an dives omnes quærĭmus. *Prov.*—" No one asks whether a man is good; we all ask whether he is rich."

Nemo benè impĕrat nisi qui paruĕrit impĕrio. *Prov.*—" No man is fully able to command, unless he has first learned to obey."

Nemo dat quod non habet. *Law Max.*—" No man gives that which he does not possess."

Nemo debet bis punīri pro uno delicto. COKE.—" No man ought to be punished twice for one offence."

Nemo dextĕrius fortūnâ sit usus.—" No man has more judiciously employed his good fortune."

Nemo doctus mutātiōnem consĭlii inconstantiam dixit esse. CIC.—" No well-instructed man has called a change of opinion inconstancy." Acknowledgment of error is a duty, upon the observance of which our improvement depends.

Nemo errat uni sibi, sed dementiam spargit in proxĭmos. SEN —"No man commits error for himself alone, but scatters his folly among all around him." Error is doubly injurious; first in itself, and then by example.

Nemo est ab omni parte beātus.—"No man is happy in every respect." See *Nihil est*, &c.

Nemo est hæres viventis. *Law Max.*—"No man is the heir of one who is alive." He is only an "heir apparent." See *Hæredem Deus*, &c.

——*Nemo in sese tentat descendĕre? Nemo!* PERS.—"Does no one attempt to explore himself? No one!" Instead of looking into the faults of others, we should examine our own hearts.

Nemo ire quenquam publĭcâ prohĭbet viâ. PLAUT.—"No one forbids another to go along the highway." No one is likely to interfere with you so long as you keep the beaten path.

Nemo ita pauper vivit, quam pauper natus est. SYR.—"No man ever lived so poor as he was born."

Nemo lædĭtur nisi à seipso. *Prov.*—"No man is hurt but by himself."

Nemo malus felix, mĭnĭmè corruptor.—— JUV.—"No wicked man can be happy, least of all one who corrupts others."

Nemo me impūnè lacessit.—"No one provokes me with impunity." The motto of the Order of the Thistle, a plant which is protected by its prickles.

Nemo mīlĭtans Deo implicĕtur secularĭbus negōtiis. COKE.—"No one in the service of God should be involved in secular affairs."

Nemo mortālium omnĭbus horis sapit. PLINY *the Elder.*—"No man is wise at all times."

Nemo plus juris in ălium transferre potest quam ipse habet. *Law Max.*—"No man can transfer to another a right or title greater than he himself possesses."

Nemo potest nudo vestimenta detrahĕre. *Prov.*—"No man can strip a naked man of his garment." Like our saying, "You cannot get blood out of a stone."

Nemo prudens punit quia peccātum est, sed ne peccĕtur. SEN. —"No man of prudence punishes because a fault has been committed, but that it may not be committed." If this were not the object of punishment, it would degenerate into revenge.

Nemo puniātur pro ălieno delicto. *Law Max.*—"Let no man be punished for the fault of another."

Nemo qui suæ confīdit, altĕrius virtūti invĭdet. Cic.—"No man who confides in his own virtue, envies that of another."

Nemo repentè fuit turpissĭmus—— Juv.—"No man ever became extremely wicked all at once." Men sink into the depths of vice step by step.

Nemo sic impar sibi.—"No man was ever so unequal to himself." See *Nil fuit,* &c.

Nemo solus satis sapit. Plaut.—"No man is sufficiently wise of himself."

Nemo suâ sorte contentus.—"No one is contented with his own lot."

Nemo tam divos hăbuit faventes,
Crastĭnum ut possit sibi pollicēri. Sen.
—"No man was ever so favoured by the gods as to be able to promise himself a morrow."

Nemo tenētur ad impossĭbile. *Law Max.*—"No one is bound to do that which is impossible."

Nemo tenētur seipsum accusāre. *Law Max.*—"No one is bound to accuse himself."

Nemo vir magnus, sine ălĭquo afflātu divīno, unquam fuit. Cic. —"No man was ever great without some portion of Divine inspiration."

Neptūnum, procul a terrâ, spectāre furentem.—"From the land to view the ocean raging afar."

Nequam hŏmĭnis ego parvipendo grātiam. Plaut.—"I set little value on the esteem of a worthless man."

Nequam illud verbum est, Bene vult, nisi qui bene facit. Plaut. —"That expression, 'he wishes well,' is worthless unless a person *does well* besides."

Nequāquam satis in re unâ consūmĕre curam. Hor.—"It is by no means enough to devote our care exclusively to one object."

Neque cæcum ducem, neque amentem consultōrem.—"[Select] neither a blind guide nor a silly adviser." A sentiment from Aristophanes.

Neque cuiquam tam clarum ingĕnium est, ut possit emergĕre nisi illi matĕria, occāsio, fautor etiam commendātorque contingat. Pliny *the Younger*.—"No man possesses a genius so commanding, as to be able to rise in the world, unless these means are afforded him:—opportunity, and a friend to promote his advancement."

Neque culpa neque lauda teipsum.—"Neither blame nor praise yourself." Avoid egotism, and pretend not to be either better or worse than you are.

——*Neque enim conclūdĕre versum*
Dixĕris esse satis: neque, si quis scribat, uti nos,
Sermōni prŏpiōra, putes hunc esse poētam. Hor.
—"For you must not deem it enough to tag a verse; nor if any person, like me, writes in a style more nearly resembling conversation, must you esteem him to be a poet."

——*Neque enim lex æquior ulla,*
Quam necis artĭfices arte perīre suâ. Ovid.
—"For there is no law more just than that the contrivers of death should perish by their own contrivances."

Neque enim quies gentium sine armis, neque arma sine stipendiis, neque stipendia sine tribūtis. Tacit.—"The repose of nations cannot be insured without arms, arms without pay, nor pay without taxes." An armed peace is the best guarantee against war.

Neque extra necessitātes belli præcipuum ŏdium gero.—"Beyond that necessitated by war, I feel no particular resentment."

Neque fēmĭna, amissâ pudicitiâ, ălia abnuĕrit. Tacit.—"When a woman has once lost her chastity, she will deny nothing." She will most probably be induced by circumstances to submit to any degradation.

Neque mala vel bona quæ vulgus putet. Tacit.—"Things are not to be pronounced either good or bad on public opinion."

Neque mel, neque apes. Prov.—"No bees, no honey." "Every rose has its thorns."

Neque opiniōne sed natūra constitūtum est jus. Cic.—"Not in opinion but in nature is law founded."

Neque semper arcum
Tendit Apollo. Hor.
—"Nor is Apollo always bending his bow."

——*Nĕqueo monstrāre, et sentio tantum.* Juv.—"I cannot describe it, I only feel it."

Nequicquam Deus abscīdit
Prudens ocĕăno dissociăbĭli
Terras, si tamen impĭæ
Non tangenda rates transĭliunt vada. Hor.
—"In vain has God in his wisdom divided the countries of the earth by the separating ocean, if nevertheless profane barks bound over the forbidden waters."

Nequicquam exornāta est bene, si morāta est male,
Pulchrum ornātum turpes mores pejus cœno collĭnunt.
Plaut.
—"It is in vain that a woman is well dressed, if she is ill conducted; misconduct soils a fine dress worse than dirt."

Nequicquam pŏpŭlo bĭbŭlas donāvĕris aures;
Respue quod non es.—— Pers.
—"You cannot possibly give the people ears that will drink in everything: aim not at that for which you are not made." You cannot long impose even on the credulity of the public.

Nequicquam sapit qui sibi non sapit. *Prov.*—"He is wise to no purpose who is not wise for himself."

Nequissĭmi hŏmĭnis est prōdĕre amīcum.—"It is the part of the most abandoned of men to betray his friend."

Nequĭtiam vīnōsa tuam convīvĭa narrant. Ovid.—"Your drunken banquets bespeak your debauchery."

Nervi belli pecūnia infīnīta. Cic.—"Endless money is the very sinews of war." Both Bacon and Machiavelli question the truth of this saying.

Nervis ălĭēnis mŏbĭle lignum.—"A wooden puppet moved by strings in the hands of others." Said with reference to those who allow themselves to be made the tools of others.

Nervis omnĭbus. *Prov.*—"Straining every nerve."

Nescia mens hŏmĭnum fati sortisque futūræ,
Et servāre modum rebus sublāta secundis! Virg.
—"How blind is the mind of men to fate and future events, how unwilling to practise moderation, when elated with prosperity!"

Nescio quâ natāle solum dulcēdĭne cunctos
Ducit, et immĕmŏres non sinit esse sui. Ovid.

—"The land of our birth allures us by an unaccountable attraction, and permits us not to be forgetful of it."

Nescio quâ præter sŏlĭtum dulcēdĭne læti. VIRG.—"By some inconceivable charm animated beyond their wont."

Nescio quis tĕnĕros ŏcŭlus mihi fascĭnat agnos. VIRG.—"I know not what evil eye has bewitched my tender lambs." Said in reference to the notion among the ancients, that evil resulted from the glance of the envious eye.

Nescio quōmŏdo inhæret in mentĭbus quasi sæculōrum augŭrium futūrōrum; idque in maxĭmis ingĕniis, altissĭmisque ănĭmis, et existit maxĭme et appāret facillĭme. CIC.—"There is, I know not how, inherent in the minds of men, a certain presage as it were of a future state; and this chiefly exists and appears the most manifest, in those of the greatest genius and of the most exalted mind."

Nescīre quid antĕa quam natus sis accĭdĕrit, id est semper esse puĕrum; quid enim est ætas hŏmĭnis, nisi memŏria rerum nostrārum cum supĕriōrum ætāte contexĕrit? CIC.—"To be unacquainted with what has taken place before you were born, is to be always a child; for what is human life, unless memory is able to compare the events of our own times with those of by-gone ages?"

Nescis quid serus vesper vehat. *Prov.*—"You know not what night-fall may bring."

Nescis tu quam metĭcŭlōsa res sit ire ad jūdĭcem. PLAUT.—"You little know what a ticklish thing it is to go to law."

Nescit plebs jejūna timēre. *Prov.*—"A starving populace knows no fear."

——*Nescit vox missa reverti.* HOR.—"The word which has been once uttered, can never be recalled." Hence the mischief that may result from an unguarded expression or the disclosure of a secret.

——*Neu fluĭtem dŭbiæ spe pendŭlus horæ.* HOR.—"That I may not fluctuate in the hope dependent on each uncertain hour." The blessings of a competency.

Neutĭquam offĭcium lībĕri esse hŏmĭnis puto,
Cum is nihil promĕreat, postulāre id grātiæ appōni sibi. TER.
—"I do not think it the part of a man of a liberal mind to ask that a thing should be granted him when he has done nothing to deserve it."

——*Ni*

Posces ante diem librum cum lūmĭne, si non
Intendes ănĭmum stŭdiis et rebus honestis,
Invĭdiâ vel amōre vigil torquēbĕre. Hor.

—"Unless before day you call for your book with a light, unless you occupy your mind with study and becoming pursuits, you will, when waking, be tortured by envy or by love." By idleness the passions are let loose, and mischief is a probable result.

——*Ni vis boni*
In ipsâ inesset formâ, hæc formam extinguĕrent. Ter.

—"Had there not been great force of beauty in her very form, these things must have extinguished it." Her neglected dress and disheveled hair.

Nihil a Deo vacat : opus suum ipse implet. Sen.—"Nothing is void of God: He himself fills all his works." The doctrine of Pantheism.

Nihil ad versum.—"Not corresponding to the words," meaning, "not to the purpose." This adage is supposed to have had reference to the representations by gesticulation of the sense of the part recited. Hence, when the actor failed to represent the sense conveyed by the line, the prompter used this expression.

Nihil agendo hŏmĭnes malè ăgĕre discunt.—"By doing nothing, men learn to do ill."

Nihil agit qui diffidentem verbis solātur suis ;
Is est amīcus qui in re dŭbiâ re juvat, ubi re est opus.
Plaut.

—"He does nothing who consoles a desponding man with words; he is a true friend, who, under doubtful circumstances, aids in deed when deeds are necessary."

Nihil ăliud necessārium, ut sis miser, quam ut te mĭsĕrum credas.—"Nothing is wanting to make you wretched but to fancy yourself so."

Nihil altum, nihil magnĭfĭcum ac divīnum suscĭpĕre possunt, qui suas omnes cōgitātiōnes abjēcērunt in rem tam hŭmĭlem atque abjectam. Cic.—"They can attempt nothing elevated, nothing noble and divine, who have expended all their thoughts upon a thing so low and abject."

Nihil credam et omnia cavēbo.—"I will trust to nothing, and be on my guard against everything."

Nihil differt utrum ægrum in ligneo lecto an in aureo collŏces: quocumque illum transtŭlĕris, morbum suum secum transfert. SEN.—"It matters not whether you place the sick man on a wooden bed, or on one of gold; wherever you lay him, he carries his disease along with him."

Nihil diffĭcĭle est Natūræ, ubi ad finem
Sui prŏpĕrat—— Momento fit cinis, diu silva. SEN.
—"Nothing is difficult to Nature, when she is pursuing her end. A wood is long in making, ashes are made in an instant." Said in reference to the final destruction of the earth by fire. See *Esse quoque*, &c.

Nihil doli subesse credens. CORN. NEP.—"Suspecting no deceit."

Nihil ērĭpit fortūna nisi quod et dedit. SYR.—"Fortune takes nothing away but what she has given."

Nihil est ab omni
Parte beatum. HOR.
—"There is nothing that is blessed in every respect." There is a dark side to every picture.

Nihil est ălud magnum, quam multa minūta. *Prov.*—"That which is great is nothing but many littles." "Many littles make a mickle."

Nihil est aptius ad delectatiōnem lectōris, quam tempŏrum varietātes, fortūnæque vicissitūdĭnes. CIC.—"Nothing is better suited for the entertainment of a reader, than the varying features of times, and the vicissitudes of fortune." It is the varieties and contrasts of history that make "truth stranger than fiction."

——*Nihil est furācius illo:*
Non fuit Autŏlyci tam pĭceāta manus. MART.
—"There is nothing in the world more pilfering than he; not even the hand of Autolycus was so gluey (filching) as his."

Nihil est in vitâ magnŏpĕre expetendum nisi laus et honestas. CIC.—"There is nothing in life so earnestly to be sought as character and probity."

Nihil est mĭsĕrius, quam ănĭmus hŏmĭnis conscius. PLAUT.—"There is nothing more wretched than the mind of a man with a guilty conscience."

——*Nihil est*
Quin male narrando possit depravārier. TER.—"There is no story but what may be made worse by being badly told."

——*Nihil est quod crēdĕre de se*
Non possit.—— JUV.
—"There is nothing that he cannot believe about himself."

Nihil est quod non expugnet pertĭnax ŏpĕra, et intenta ac dīlĭgens cura. SEN.—"There is nothing which persevering industry may not overcome, with continued and diligent care."

Nihil est sānitāti multo vino nocentius.—"There is nothing more prejudicial to health than much wine."

Nihil est tam ūtĭle quod in transĭtu prosit. SEN.—"Nothing is so useful that it can be profitable from only a hasty perusal." No lasting benefit can be derived from careless or hasty studies.

Nihil est tam vŏlūcre quam măledictum, nihil făcĭlius emittĭtur, nihil cĭtius excĭpĭtur, nihil lātius dissipātur. CIC.—"Nothing is so swift in flight as slander, nothing more easily propagated, nothing more readily received, nothing more widely disseminated."

Nihil eum commendat præter simulātam versūtamque tristĭtiam. CIC.—"He has nothing to recommend him, except an assumed and deceitful seriousness."

——*Nihil hic nisi carmĭna desunt.* VIRG.—"Nothing is wanting here but a song."

Nihil hŏmĭni amīco est opportūno amīcius. PLAUT.—"There is nothing more desirable to a man than a friend in need."

Nihil honestum esse potest, quod justĭtiâ vacat. CIC.—"Nothing can be honest which is destitute of justice."

Nihil largiundo glōriam adeptus est. SALL.—"He acquired glory by no bribery." He rose by his own merits.

Nihil legĕbat quod non excerpĕret. PLINY *the Younger.*—"He read no work from which he did not cull something." Said of his uncle the Elder Pliny, author of the *Historia Naturalis.*

Nihil Lysiæ subtīlĭtāte cedit, nihil argūtiis et acūmĭne Hyperĭdi. CIC.—"He yields not a jot to Lysias in subtlety, nor to Hyperides in acumen and sharpness of repartee." Lysias was a celebrated orator of Syracuse, Hyperides of Athens.

Nihil magis consentāneum est quam ut iisdem modis res dissolvātur quibus constituĭtur. *Law Max.*—"Nothing is more consistent with reason than that everything should be undone by the same means by which it was done." A deed under seal, for instance, can only be varied by a deed under seal.

Nihil potest rex nisi quod de jure potest. Law Max.—"The king can do nothing but what he is allowed to do by law." In a country, namely, which is governed on constitutional principles.

Nihil prĕtio parco, amīco dum opĭtŭlor.—"I spare no expense so long as I can serve my friend."

Nihil prodest imprŏbam mercem ĕmĕre. Prov.—"There is no advantage in buying bad wares."

Nihil scire est vita jucundissĭma. Prov.—"To know nothing at all is the happiest life." So our old English proverb, "Children and fools have merry lives."

Nihil scriptum mirăcŭli causâ. TACIT.—"There is nothing written here to excite wonder." Said of a plain unvarnished narrative.

Nihil semper floret; ætas succĕdit ætati.—"Nothing flourishes for ever; age succeeds age."

Nihil simul inventum est et perfectum. COKE.—"Nothing is invented and brought to perfection at the same moment."

Nihil sub sole novi.—"There is no new thing under the sun." *Eccl.* i. 9.

Nihil tam absurdum dici potest ut non dicātur à philŏsŏpho. CIC.—"There is nothing so absurd but what it may have been said by some philosopher."

Nihil tam diffĭcĭle est, quin quærendo investigāri possit. TER.—"There is nothing so difficult, but what it may be found out by research."

Nihil tam firmum est, cui perīcŭlum non sit ĕtiam ab invălĭdo. QUINT. CURT.—"There is nothing so secure, but what there may be danger from even the weakest." A mouse may put the finishing stroke to the ruin of a castle-wall.

Nihil tam firmum est, quod non expugnāri pecūniâ possit. CIC.—"Nothing is so well fortified that it cannot be taken by money."

Nihil turpius est quam gravis ætāte senex, qui nullum ălius habet argumentum, quo se probet diu vixisse, præter ætātem. SEN.—"There is nothing more despicable than an old man, who has no other proof to give of his having lived long than his age."

Nihil unquam peccāvit, nisi quod mortua est.—"She only did amiss in this, that she died." An epitaph on a virtuous wife, given by Camerarius as having been found near the Jews' Quarter at Rome.

Nihil unquam sic impar sibi. See *Nil fuit*, &c.

——*Nihil vidētur mundius.* Ter.—"Nothing seems more neat."

Nihĭli cŏcio est. Plaut.—"Trusting is good for nought."

Nil actum credens, dum quid superesset agendum. Lucan.—"Considering nothing done, whilst aught remained to be done." Said of Julius Cæsar. The principle adopted by a man of energy and talent.

Nil ădeo fortūna gravis miserābĭle fecit,
Ut mĭnuant nullâ gaūdia pace malum. Ovid.
—"Misfortune has made no lot so wretched, but what a respite of the evil is productive of some delight."

Nil admirāri prope est res una, Numĭci,
Solăque, quæ possit făcĕre et servāre beātum. Hor.
—"Never to lose one's self-possession is almost the one and only thing, Numicius, which can make and keep a man happy."

Nil agit exemplum litem quod lite resolvit. Hor.—"That illustration is of no use which extricates us from one difficulty by involving us in another."

Nil conscīre sibi, nullâ pallescĕre culpâ. Hor.—See *Hic murus*, &c.

——*Nil consuetūdĭne majus.* Ovid.—"There is nothing more powerful than custom."

——*Nil cupientium*
Nudus castra peto. Hor.
—"Naked I commit myself to the camp of those who desire nothing."

Nil debet. *Law Term.*—"He owes nothing." The common plea in defending an action for debt.

Nil despĕrandum.—"Nothing is to be despaired of."

Nil despĕrandum Teucro duce, et auspĭce Teucro. Hor.—"We must despair of nothing, Teucer being our leader, and we under his command."

Nil dicit. *Law Term.*—"He says nothing." When the defendant fails to put in his answer to the plaintiff's declaration, judgment is given against him, because he does not say anything why it should not be

Nil dictu fœdum visūque hæc līmĭna tangat,
Intra quæ puer est.—— Juv.
—"Let nothing unfit to be said or seen, enter those thresholds where youth inhabits." See *Maxima debetur*, &c.

Nil dictum quod non dictum prius. Prov.—"Nothing can be said which has not been said before." See *Nihil sub*, &c.

Nil ego contŭlĕrim jucundo sanus amīco. Hor.—"There is nothing which, in my senses, I should prefer to an agreeable friend."

Nil erit ultĕrius quod nostris mōrĭbus addat
Postĕrĭtas; eădem cŭpient făcientque minōres:
Omne in præcĭpĭti vĭtium stetit.—— Juv.
—"There will be nothing left for posterity to add to our manners; those who come after us will act as we do, and have the same desires: every vice has reached its culminating point." The complaint of the moralist in every age against the luxury and vice of his time.

Nil feret ad Manes dīvĭtis umbra suos. Ovid.—"The ghost of the rich man will carry nothing to the shades below."

——*Nil fuit unquam*
Sic impar sibi.—— Hor.
—"Never was there anything so unlike itself." The extreme of inconsistency.

Nil habet infēlix paupertas dūrius in se,
Quam quod rīdĭcŭlos hŏmĭnes facit.—— Juv.
—"Unhappy poverty has nothing in it more galling, than that it exposes men to laughter."

Nil hăbuit in tĕnementis. Law Term.—"He had no such tenement." The plea denying the title of the plaintiff in an action of debt by a lessor against a lessee without deed.

Nil hŏmĭni certum est. Fiĕri quis posse putāret? Ovid.—"There is nothing assured to mortals. Who could have thought that this would come to pass?"

Nil intra est ŏlĕam, nil extra est in nuce duri. Hor.—"[If such is not the case] then there is no kernel in the olive, no shell outside the nut." A person who will maintain that, will swear that black is white.

——*Nil me offĭcit unquam,*
Dītior hic, aut est quia doctior; est locus uni
Cuique suus.—— Hor.

—"It nothing affects me that this man is more wealthy or more learned than I am; every man has his own station."

Nil mihi das vivus, dicis post fata datūrum;
Si non insānis, scis, Maro, quid cŭpiam. MART.
—"You give me nothing during your life, you say you will leave me something after your death; if you are not a fool, Maro, you know what I wish for." The thoughts of the man who is waiting to slip "into dead men's shoes."

Nil mihi vobiscum est; hæc meus ardor erit. OVID.—"I have nought to do with you; she shall be my flame."

Nil mortālibus arduum est. HOR.—"Nothing is too arduous for mortals." With patience and perseverance there is no difficulty in that which is not in itself impossible.

——*Nil obstat. Coïs tibi pene vidēre est*
Ut nudam, ne crure malo, ne sit pede turpi:
Mētiri possis ŏcŭlo latus.—— HOR.
—"There is nothing in your way; through the thin gauze dress you may discern her almost as well as if she were naked; you may see that she has neither a bad leg nor an ugly foot; you may survey her form from top to toe with your eye."

Nil opus est dĭgĭtis, per quos arcāna loquāris. OVID.—"There is no need there of using the fingers to talk over your secrets."

Nil ŏritūrum ăliās, nil ortum tale fatentes. HOR.—"Confessing that none had arisen before, or would arise, like unto thee." A compliment to his patron, Augustus.

Nil peccent ŏcŭli, si ŏcŭlis ănĭmus impĕret. SYR.—"The eyes cannot sin if the understanding governs the sight." Cicero too says that it is necessary to exercise chastity of sight. See also *Matt.* v. 28.

Nil prodest quod non lædĕre possit idem. OVID.—"There is nothing advantageous, which may not also be injurious." These evils may be caused by carelessness, precipitation, or want of moderation.

Nil prŏprium ducas quod mutāri potest. SYR.—"Reckon nothing your own, that can be changed." All worldly possessions are of doubtful tenure; but virtue, philosophy, and an enlightened mind, we may call our own.

——*Nil sciri si quis putat, id quoque nescit*
An sciri possit, qui se nil scire fatĕtur. LUCRET.

—"If a person thinks that nothing can be known, it necessarily follows that he does not know whether or not nothing can be known, from his very confession that he knows nothing." An answer to the scepticism of the disciples of Pyrrho, who maintained that "all that we know is, that nothing can be known."

Nil simĭlius insāno quam ēbrĭus. *Prov.*—"Nothing more strongly resembles a madman than a man who is drunk."

——*Nil sine magno*
Vita labōre dedit mortālĭbus. HOR.
—"Life has bestowed nothing on man without great labour."

——*Nil sine te me*
Prosunt honōres.—— HOR.
—"My honours are nothing worth without thy aid." An address by the poet to his Muse, entreating her to continue her inspiration.

Nil spernat auris, nec tamen credat statim. PHÆD.—"Let the ear despise nothing, nor yet let it accord implicit belief at once."

Nil tam diffĭcĭle est, quin quærendo investigāri possit. TER.—"There is nothing so difficult but what it may be found out by seeking."

Nil tam diffĭcĭle est quod non solertia vincat. *Prov.*—"There is nothing so difficult that skill will not overcome it."

Nil tĕmĕre novandum. *Law Maxim.*—"Innovations should not be rashly made."

Nil tĕmĕre uxōri de servis crede querenti;
Sæpe ĕtĕnim mŭlier quem conjux dīlĭgit, odit. CATO.
—"Do not rashly give credit to a wife complaining of servants; for very often the wife hates the person whom the husband most regards."

Nil vŏlĭtum quin præcognĭtum.—"Nothing can be wished for without our having had some thought of it beforehand." See *Consentire non*, &c.

Nĭmia cura dētĕrit magis quam emendat. *Prov.*—"Too much care injures rather than improves." A good thing may be spoiled by overdoing it. "Too many cooks spoil the broth."

Nĭmia est misĕria pulchrum esse hŏmĭnem nimis. PLAUT.—"It is a very great plague to be too handsome a man." The words of Pyrgopolinices, a braggart and a fop.

——*Nĭmia est voluptas, si diu abfuĕris a domo*
Domum si redĭĕris, si tibi nulla est ægritūdo ănĭmo obviam. PLAUT.
—"It is a great pleasure, if you have been long absent, when you return home to have no anxieties to grate your feelings."

Nĭmia famĭliārĭtas parit contemptum. *Prov.*—"Too much familiarity breeds contempt."

——*Nĭmia illæc licentia*
Profecto evādet in ălĭquod magnum malum. TER.
—"This extreme licentiousness will assuredly end in some great disaster."

Nĭmia subtīlĭtas in jure reprobātur. *Law Max.*—"Excessive refinements in the law are to be reproved."

Nĭmio id quod pudet făcĭlius fertur, quam illud quod piget. PLAUT.—"That which we are ashamed of is more easily endured than that which we are vexed at."

Nĭmio præstat impendiōsum te quàm ingrātum dicĭer;
Illum laudābunt boni, hunc ĕtiam ipsi culpābunt mali. PLAUT.
—"It is much better to be called over-liberal, than ungrateful; the first, good men will applaud; the latter, even bad men will condemn."

Nimīrum insānus paucis vĭdeātur, eo quod
Maxĭma pars hŏmĭnum morbo jactātur eōdem. HOR.
—"He, for instance, appears to be mad to but a few, because the greater part of them are infected with the same disease."

Nimis arcta premunt ŏlĭdæ convīvia capræ. HOR.—"Rank and sweaty odours annoy us at overcrowded entertainments." A good suggestion for those who think that they cannot overcrowd a room.

——*Nimis uncis*
Nārĭbus indulges.—— PERS.
—"You indulge your upturned nostrils too much." The nostrils, as Pliny says, were considered the exponents of sarcasm and ridicule.

Nĭmium altercando verĭtas amittĭtur. *Prov.*—"In too eager disputation, the truth is lost sight of."

Nĭmium diffĭcĭle est rĕpĕrīri, ita ut nomen ducit,
Cui tuam cum rem crēdĭdĕris sine omni curâ dormias. PLAUT.

—"It is an extremely difficult thing for a friend to be found to act up to his title, and to whom when you have intrusted your interests you may sleep without care."

——*Nĭmium ne crede colōri.* Virg.—"Trust not too much to your good looks." Said by the poet to a conceited youth, but applicable to outward appearances in general.

Nĭmium risūs prĕtium est, si prŏbitātis impendio constat. Quint.—"A laugh costs too much, if it is bought at the expense of propriety."

Nĭmius in veritāte, et similitūdĭnis quàm pulchritūdĭnis amantior. Quint.—"Too scrupulous as to the truth, and more desirous of exactness than beauty." There are disagreeable traits in nature, which an artist need not go out of his way to copy. Some of the Dutch painters have been guilty of this.

Nisi caste, saltem caute. *Prov.*—"If not chastely, at least cautiously." A Jesuitical hint that at all events we should study appearances.

——*Nisi dextro tempŏre Flacci*
Verba per attentam non ibunt Cæsăris aurem. Hor.
—"Unless at an appropriate time, the words of Flaccus will not reach the attentive ear of Cæsar."

Nisi Dŏmĭnus, frustra.—"Unless the Lord is with us, our efforts are vain." From *Psalm* cxxvii. 1. The motto of the city of Edinburgh, where it has been ludicrously translated, "You can do nothing here unless you are a lord!"

Nisi prius. *Law Term.*—"Unless before." A writ by which the sheriff is commanded to bring a jury to Westminster Hall on a certain day, unless the justices shall previously come into his county.

Nisi ūtĭle est quod făcĭmus, stulta est gloria. Phæd.—"Unless what we do is useful, vain is our glory." This line is said to have been found copied on a marble stone, as part of a funeral inscription, at Alba Julia, or Weissemberg, in Transylvania.

Nītĭmur in vĕtĭtum semper, cŭpĭmusque negāta. Ovid.—"We are ever striving for what is forbidden, and are coveting what is denied us."

Nitor in adversum, nec me, qui cætĕra vincit
Impĕtus, et rapĭdo contrārius ēvĕhor orbi. Ovid.
—"Against this I have to contend; that force which over-

comes all other things, does not overcome me; and I am borne in a contrary direction to the swiftly moving world."

Nobĭlĭtas sola est atque ūnĭca virtus. JUV.—"Virtue is the sole and only nobility."

Nobis cum semel occĭdit brevis lux,
Nox est perpĕtua una dormienda. CATULL.
—"As soon as our brief day has closed, we shall have to sleep in everlasting night." The words of one who did not believe in the immortality of the soul.

Nobis non licet esse tam disertis,
Qui Musas cŏlĭmus sevĕriōres. MART.
—"We, who cultivate the severer Muses, are not allowed to be so discursive."

——*Nocet empta dolōre voluptas.* HOR.—"Pleasure purchased by pain is injurious." Because pleasure of this kind arises from immoderate indulgence.

——*Noctemque diemque fatīgat.* VIRG.—"He labours both night and day."

Noctis erat mĕdium; quid non amor imprŏbus audet? OVID.
—"'Twas midnight; what does not unscrupulous passion dare?"

Nocturnâ versāte manu, versāte diurnâ. HOR.—"Ponder these matters by night, ponder them by day."

Nŏcumentum, dŏcumentum. *Prov.*—"Harming's warning." "Forewarned, forearmed."

Nodum in scirpo quærĕre. *Prov.*—"To look for a knot in a bulrush." To be too fastidious.

Nolens volens.—"Whether he will or no." "Will he, nill he."

Noli affectāre quod tibi non est datum,
Delūsa ne spes ad querēlam recĭdat. PHÆD.
—"Covet not that which has not been granted you, lest your baffled hopes sink down to useless repinings."

Noli equi dentes inspĭcĕre donāti. *Prov.*—"Look not a gift-horse in the mouth." Quoted by St. Jerome.

Noli me tangĕre.—"Touch me not." A plant of the genus *impatiens.* On being touched when ripe, it discharges its seeds from the capsule with considerable force. The term is also applied to an ulcer or cancer; and sometimes an object of extreme costliness is called a "Touch me not." See also *John* xx 17.

——*Noli pugnāre duōbus.* CATULL.—"Don't fight against two." "Two to one is odds."

Nolle prŏsĕqui. *Law Term.*—"To be unwilling to prosecute." An acknowledgment by the plaintiff that he will not proceed any further with his suit.

Nolo episcopāri.—"I have no wish to be a bishop." A phrase which, with a semblance of modesty, was used as a matter of form by those who were elevated to a bishopric. Hence it is used to imply an affectation of indifference about a thing which a person has the greatest ambition to obtain.

Nomen amicĭtia est, nomen ināne fides. OVID.—"Friendship is but a name, constancy an empty title."

Nōmĭna honesta prætenduntur vĭtiis. TAC.—"Honourable names are given as a screen to vices."

Nōmĭne pœnæ. *Law Term.*—"Under name of a penalty." A penalty agreed to be incurred on non-payment of rent by a given day.

Non adeo cĕcĭdi, quamvis dejectus, ut infra
Te quoque sim; infĕrius quo nihil esse potest. OVID.
—"Although prostrate, I have not fallen so low that I am beneath even thee, than whom nothing can be lower."

Non ætāte verum ingĕnio adipiscĭtur săpientia. PLAUT.—"Not by years but by disposition is wisdom acquired."

Non ălĭter quam qui adverso vix flūmĭne lembum
Rēmĭgiis sŭbĭgit: si brăchia forte remīsit,
Atque illum in præceps prono rapit alveus amni. VIRG.
—"Not otherwise than is he who rows his skiff with much ado against the tide; if by chance he slackens his arms, the tide hurries him headlong down the stream."

Non amo te, Săbĭdi, nec possum dīcĕre quare;
Hoc tantum possum dicĕre, non amo te. MART.
—"I do not love thee, Sabidius, nor can I say why; this only I can say, I do not love thee." A description of an unaccountable aversion. This epigram has been thus translated by the facetious Tom Brown;

"I do not love thee, Doctor Fell:
The reason why I cannot tell;
But this alone I know full well,
I do not love thee, Doctor Fell."

T·

Dr Fell being the dean of Christ Church, who had threatened him with expulsion.

Non amplĭter sed mundĭter convīvium; plus salis quam sumptûs. CORN. NEP.—"An entertainment not profuse but elegant; more of true relish than expense."

Non assumpsit. *Law Term.*—"He did not undertake." The general issue in an action of *assumpsit*, where the defendant denies that he undertook to do the thing stated. See *Assumpsit.*

Non aurīga piger.—"No lazy charioteer." Said of a director or managing man who will not "let the grass grow under his feet" in carrying out an undertaking.

Non bene conducti vendunt perjūria testes. OVID.—"Witnesses hired dishonestly make sale of their perjuries."

Non bene convĕniunt, nec in unâ sede morantur
Majestas et amor.—— OVID.
—"Majesty and love do not well agree, nor do they dwell in the same place."

Non bene junctārum discordia sēmĭna rerum. OVID.—"The discordant atoms of things not harmonizing." A description of the state of Chaos.

Non bene pro toto libertas vendĭtur auro;
Hoc cœleste bonum prætĕrit orbis opes.
—"Liberty is not well sold for all the gold; this heavenly blessing surpasses the wealth of the world."

Non bonus somnus est de prandio. Apage. PLAUT.—"Sleep is not good after a morning meal—out upon it!"

Non caret is, qui non desīdĕrat.—"He is not in want who has no desires."

Non compos mentis.—"Not master of his mind." In an unsound state of mind.

Non constat. *Law Term.*—"It does not appear." It is not shown by evidence before the court.

Non cuicunque datum est habēre nasum.—— MART.—"It is not every one to whom it has been given to have a nose:" meaning a keen wit, and power of satire.

Non cuivis hŏmĭni contingit adīre Corinthum. HOR.—"It is not the lot of every man to visit Corinth." It is not the lot of all men to enjoy the same opportunities of travel or improvement. Corinth was the head quarters of luxury and refinement, and it was only the more wealthy who could afford to pay a visit to it.

Non de ponte cadit, qui cum săpientiā vadit.—"He falls not from the bridge who walks with prudence." A mediæval Leonine proverb.

Non decet superbum esse hŏmĭnem servum. PLAUT.—"It is not proper for a servant to give himself airs."

Non decĭpĭtur qui scit se dĕcĭpi. COKE.—"He is not deceived who knows that he is being deceived."

Non dĕĕrat voluntas, sed facultas.—"Not the will, but the means, were wanting."

——*Non dĕfĭcit alter.* VIRG.—"Another is not wanting." We sustain no loss but what can easily be replaced; or the loss of one will be the gain of another.

Non Dindymēne, non ădytis quatit
Mentem sacerdōtum incŏla Pythius,
Non Liber æque; non acūta
Sic gĕmĭnant Cŏrybantes æra,
Tristes ut iræ.—— HOR.

—"Nor Cybele, nor Pythian Apollo, the dweller in the shrines, so convulses the breasts of his priests, nor so does Bacchus; nor do the Corybantes so loudly redouble their blows on the shrill cymbals, as direful anger (inflames the mind)."

Non domus et fundus, non æris acervus et auri
Ægrōto dŏmĭni deduxit corpŏre febres,
Non ănĭmo curas.—— HOR.

—"Neither house nor land, nor heaps of brass and gold, can remove the fever from their sick possessor, nor banish cares from his mind."

Non eădem est ætas, non mens.—— HOR.—"My age, my tastes are now no longer the same."

Non eădem rătio est, sentīre et dēmĕre morbos:
Sensus inest cunctis; tollĭtur arte malum. OVID.

—"The art of perceiving diseases and of removing them is not the same. Perception exists in all; by skill alone disease is removed."

——*Non ebur neque aureum*
Meā rĕnīdet in domo lacūnar. HOR.

—"No ivory or golden ceiling shines resplendent in my house."

——*Non ego avārum*
Cum te veto fiĕri, vappam jŭbeo ac nebŭlōnem. Hor.
—"When I forbid you to be a miser, I do not bid you become a prodigal and a spendthrift."

Non ego illam mihi dotem esse puto, quæ dos dīcĭtur,
Sed pudicĭtiam, et pudōrem, et sedātam cupīdĭnem. Plaut.
—"That which is called a dowry, I do not deem my dowry, but chastity, modesty, and subdued desires."

Non ego mendōsos ausim defendĕre mores,
Falsăque pro vĭtiis arma tenēre meis. Ovid.
—"I would not presume to defend my faulty morals, and to wield deceitful arms in behalf of my frailties."

Non ego mordāci destrinxi carmĭne quenquam;
Nec meus ullius crīmĭna versus habet. Ovid.
—"I have pulled no one to pieces in spiteful verse; nor does my poetry contain a charge against any man."

Non ego omnīno lucrum omne esse ūtĭle hŏmĭni existimo. Plaut.—"I do not quite believe that every kind of gain is serviceable to mankind."

——*Non ego paucis*
Offendar măcŭlis, quas aut incūria fudit,
Aut humāna parum cavit natūra.—— Hor.
—"I will not take offence at a few blemishes which either carelessness has caused, or against which human nature has failed to be on its guard."

Non ego ventōsæ venor suffrāgia plebis. Hor.—"I do not hunt after the suffrages of the unsteady multitude." I do not solicit their votes.

Non enim gazæ neque consulāris
Summŏvet lictor mĭsĕros tumultus
Mentis et curas lăqueāta circum
Tecta volantes. Hor.
—"For neither regal treasure, nor the consul's lictor, can remove the direful tumults of the mind, nor the cares that hover about the carved ceilings."

Non enim potest quæstus consistĕre, si eum sumptus supĕrat. Plaut.—"There cannot any profit remain, if the expenditure exceeds it."

Non enim tam auctoritātis in disputando, quam rătiōnis momenta quærenda sunt. Cic.—"In discussing a question, more reliance ought to be placed on the influence of reason than on the weight of authority."

Non ĕquĭdem invĭdeo, miror magis.—— Virg.—"For my part, I feel no envy, I am surprised rather."

Non ĕquĭdem stŭdeo, bullātis ut mihi nugis
Pāgĭna turgescat, dare pondus idōnea fumo. Pers.
—"I do not study that my page may be swelled out with bubbly trifles, suited only to give weight to smoke."

Non ĕquĭdem vellem; sed me mea fata trahēbant,
Inque meas pœnas ingĕniōsus eram. Ovid.
—"I wish indeed that I had not; but my destiny drew me on, and I exercised my ingenuity to my own undoing."

Non esse cŭpĭdum pecūnia est: non esse emācem vectīgal est. Cic.—"Not to be covetous is money: not to be fond of buying, a revenue."

Non est. See *Non est inventus.*

Non est ad astra mollis à terris via. Sen.—"Not easy is the passage from the earth to the stars." It is only by great efforts that immortality is to be attained.

Non est arctius vincŭlum inter hŏmĭnes quam jusjurandum. Law Max.—"There is no stronger bond among men than an oath."

Non est beātus, qui se non putat; quid enim refert qualis status tuus sit, si tibi vidētur malus? Sen.—"No man is happy who does not think himself so; for what does it signify how exalted your position may be, if it appears to you undesirable?"

Non est bonum lūdĕre cum Diis. Prov.—"It is not good to trifle with the gods." It is impossible to deceive an all-wise Providence.

Non est de sacco tanta fărīna tuo.—"All that meal is not out of your own sack." Said to a man who is palming off the work of another as his own. A mediæval proverb.

Non est ejusdem et multa et opportūna dīcĕre. Prov.—"It is not easy for the same person to talk much and to the purpose."

Non est factum. Law Term.—"It was not done." The general issue in an action on bond or other deed, whereby the defendant denies that to be his deed on which he is impleaded.

Non est in mĕdĭco semper rĕlevētur ut æger :
Interdum doctâ plus valet arte malum. OVID.
—"It is not always in the physician's power that the invalid should recover; sometimes the disease is more powerful than the resources of art."

Non est inventus. *Law Term.*—"He has not been found." The return made by the sheriff when a person whom he has been ordered to produce cannot be found by him. When a man disappears or is not forthcoming, he is jocosely said to be *non est inventus*, or *non est.*

——*Non est jocus esse malignum.* HOR.—"There is no joking in being spiteful." Genuine humour is compatible only with good nature.

Non est magnus pūmĭlio licet in monte constĭtĕrit: Colossus magnitūdĭnem suam servābit, etiam si stĕtĕrit in pŭteo. SEN.—"A dwarf is no bigger, though he stand on the summit of a mountain: a Colossus will preserve its magnitude, though it should stand in a well." You cannot improve a fool whatever advantages you give him, while the man of genius will attain eminence in the greatest obscurity

Non est meum contra auctōrĭtātem senātûs dicĕre. CIC.—"It is not for me to speak against the authority of the senate."

Non est mihi cornea fibra. *Prov.*—"My nerves are not made of horn." I am not unmoved by a tale of misery and woe.

Non est rĕmĕdium adversus sycophantæ morsum. *Prov.*—"There is no remedy against the bite of a flatterer."

Non est vīvĕre, sed valĕre, vita. MART.—"Not existence, but health, is life."

Non exercĭtus, neque thesauri, præsĭdia regni sunt, verum amīci. SALL.—"Neither armies, nor treasures, are the safeguards of a state, but friends."

Non făcias malum ut inde vĕniat bonum. COKE.—"You must not do evil that good may come of it."

Non fas est scire omnia.—"We are not allowed to know everything."

Non formōsus erat, sed erat facundus Ulysses. OVID.—"Ulysses was not handsome, but then he was eloquent."

Non fumum ex fulgōre, sed ex fumo dare lucem. HOR.—"Not to produce smoke from light, but light from smoke."

In this, says Horace, consists the difference between a bad and a good poet. The first begins with a florid and inflated prelude, and ends in smoke; the latter, beginning with reserve, attains the height of poetic grandeur.

Non habet commercium cum virtūte voluptas. Cic.—"Pleasure has no fellowship with virtue." Said in reference to that kind of pleasure which delights in excess.

Non habet in nobis jam nova plaga locum. Ovid.—"A fresh wound can now no longer find room in me."

Non hæc in fœdĕra.—— Virg.—"Not into such alliances as these."

Non hoc de nĭhĭlo est.—"This does not come of nothing." There is some foundation for this story—there is something in it.

Non hoc ista sibi tempus spectācŭla poscit. Virg.—"The present moment does not require such an exhibition as this."

——*Non hŏmĭnis culpa, sed ista loci.* Ovid.—"It is not the fault of the man, but of the place."

Non horam tecum esse potes, non ōtia rectè
Pōnĕre, teque ipsum vitas fŭgĭtīvus et erro,
Jam vino quærens, jam somno fallĕre curam;
Frustrà, nam comes atra premit sĕquĭturque fŭgācem. Hor.

—"You cannot endure an hour by yourself, nor apply your leisure advantageously; a fugitive and vagabond, you endeavour to escape from yourself, now endeavouring with wine, now with sleep, to cheat care—but all in vain: for the gloomy companion presses on you, and pursues you as you fly." A fine description of the torture endured by the wicked man, under the stings of self-reproach.

Non id quod magnum est pulchrum est, sed id quod pulchrum magnum.—"Not that which is great is praiseworthy, but that which is praiseworthy is great."

Non id videndum, conjŭgum ut bonis bona,
At ut ingĕnium congrŭat et mores mōrĭbus;
Prōbĭtas, pudorque virgĭni dos optĭma est. Ter.

—"It is not requisite that the possessions of the married couple should be equal in amount; but that, in disposition and manners, they should be alike. Chastity and modesty are the best dower a young woman can have."

Non ignāra mali mĭsĕris succurrĕre disco. VIRG.—"Not unversed in suffering, I learn to succour the wretched." The words of Dido to Æneas. See *Haud ignara*, &c.

——*Non illa colo călăthisve Minervæ*
Fœmĭneas assuēta manus.—— VIRG.
—"Not to the distaff or the work-baskets of Minerva had she accustomed her womanly hands." Though originally said of Camilla, the female warrior, these words are applicable to an indolent and ignorant woman.

Non ille pro caris amīcis
Aut patriā tĭmĭdus pĕrīre. HOR.
—"He fears not to die for his beloved friends or for his country." The sentiment of a hero and a patriot.

——*Non in caro nidōre voluptas*
Summa, sed in teipso est, tu pulmentāria quære
Sudando.—— HOR.
—"The chief pleasure [in eating] does not lie in the rich flavour, but in yourself. Do you seek dainties by sweating." The benefit of exercise and the value of a good appetite.

Non intellĭgĭtur quando obrēpit senectus. CIC.—"We do not perceive it, while old age creeps on apace."

Non intellĭgunt hŏmĭnes quam magnum vectīgal sit parsimōnia. CIC.—"Men do not understand how great a revenue is economy." In accordance with Franklin's saying, that "a penny saved is a penny earned."

Non invisa feres pŭĕris munuscŭla parvis. HOR.—"You will be the bearer of no unwelcome presents to the children."

Non ita est, neque cuique mortālium injūriæ suæ parvæ videntur. SALL.—"It is not so, nor do his own injuries appear light to any man."

Non letum timeo; genus est miserābĭle leti;
Dēmĭte naufrăgium; mors mihi minus erit. OVID.
—"I fear not death; it is the dreadful kind of death; take away the shipwreck, and death will be a gain to me."

Non licet hŏmĭnem esse sæpe ita ut vult, si res non sinit. TER.—"A man often cannot be what he would, if circumstances do not permit it."

Non licet in bello bis peccāre. *Prov.*—"In war, it is not permitted twice to err."

Non liquet.—"It is not clear." Words used in the Roman law, when the judge gave the verdict *ignoramus*, similar to that of the Scotch at the present day, "not proven." It is called "Ampliation," or a "verdict of ignoramus," and neither acquits nor convicts the party accused.

Non lugenda est mors quam consĕquĭtur immortălĭtas. Cic.—"That death is not to be mourned which is followed by immortality."

Non magni pendis quia contĭgit.- - Hor.—"You do not value it greatly, because it came by accident."

Non me pudet fatēri nescīre quod nesciam. Cic.—"I am not ashamed to confess myself ignorant of that which I do not know."

Non mĕtuis dubio Fortūnæ stantis in orbe
Numen, et exōsæ verba superba Deæ? Ovid.
—"Dost thou not fear the Divine power of Fortune, as she stands on the unsteady wheel, and of the goddess who abhors all boastful words?"

Non mihi mille placent; non sum desultor amōris. Ovid.—"A thousand girls have no charms for me; I am no rover in love."

Non mihi sapit qui sermōne, sed qui factis sapit. Greg. Agrigent.—"I esteem a man wise, not according to his words, but according to his deeds."

Non mihi si linguæ centum sint, oraque centum,
Ferrea vox, omnes possim comprendere. Virg.
—"Not though a hundred tongues were mine, a hundred mouths, and iron voice, could I include them all."

Non missūra cutem, nisi plena cruōris hirūdo. Hor.—"A leech that will not leave the skin until sated with blood."

Non nobis, Dŏmĭne.—"Not unto us, O Lord." The beginning of the 115th Psalm. Some verses of this Psalm, beginning as above, have been used for ages as a grace after dinner, and are still chaunted at public festivals.

Non nobis solum nati sumus. Cic.—"We are born not for ourselves alone."

"Not for thyself alone,
Did Nature form thee." Armstrong.

Non nostrum inter vos tantas compōnĕre lites. Virg.—"It is not for me to settle for you such serious disputes."

Non nunc ăgĭtur de vectīgălĭbus, non de sociōrum injūriis; libertas et ănĭma nostra in dubio est. Cic.—"The question is not now as to our revenues, not as to the injuries sustained by our allies; our liberties and our lives are at stake."

Non obstante veredicto. Law Term.—"The verdict notwithstanding."

Non ŏcŭli tăcuēre tui.—— OVID.—"Your eyes were not silent."

Non omnem mŏlĭtor quæ fluit unda videt.—"The miller does not see everything which is carried past by the stream." A mediæval proverb.

Non omne quod nitet aurum est. Prov.—"All is not gold that glitters."

Non omnes arbusta juvant hŭmĭlesque myrīcæ. VIRG.—"The shrubs and the humble tamarisks have not their charms for all."

——*Non omnes eădem mirantur amantque.* HOR.—"All men do not admire and love the same objects." Tastes differ. So our proverb, "So many men so many minds." See *De gustibus*, &c., and *Quot homines*, &c.

Non omnia eădem æque omnĭbus suāvia esse scito. PLAUT.—"Know that all things are not equally sweet to all men."

——*Non omnia possŭmus omnes.* VIRG.—"We cannot any of us do everything." Each one is suited for his own sphere, and that alone.

Non omnis error stultitia est dicendus.—"Every error must not be called foolishness." A mistake need not be the result of systematic folly or weakness.

Non omnis fert omnia tellus.—"Not every land bears everything."

Non omnis mŏriar; multăque pars mei
Vitābit Lĭbĭtīnam.—— HOR.

—"I shall not wholly die; and a great part of me shall escape Libitina." Libitina was the goddess who was supposed to preside over funerals.—Horace here anticipates undying fame.

Non opus admisso subdĕre calcar equo.—"There is no need to spur a horse at full speed." "We must not ride a willing horse too hard." A mediæval adaptation from Ovid

Non opus est magnis plăcĭdo lectōre poētis;
Quamlibet invītum difficilemque tenent. OVID.

—"Great poets have no need of an indulgent reader; they captivate one however unwilling and difficult to please."

Non placet quem scurræ laudant, mănĭpŭlāres mussitant. PLAUT.—"I like not the man whom the town-gossips praise aloud, but of whom his neighbours are silent."

Non posse benè geri rempublĭcam multōrum impĕriis. CORN. NEP.—"Under the command of many, the affairs of the commonwealth cannot be well conducted." "No man can serve two masters." See *St. Matt.* vi. 24.

Non possidentem multa vocāvĕris
Rectè beātum. Rectius occŭpat
Nomen beāti, qui Deōrum
Mūnĕrĭbus săpienter uti,
Duramque callet paupĕriem pati. HOR.
—"You cannot properly call a man happy because he possesses much. He more justly claims the title of happy, who understands how to make a wise use of the gifts of the gods, and how to endure the privations of poverty."

——*Non possum ferre, Quĭrītes,*
Græcam urbem.—— JUV.
—"I cannot endure, O Romans! a Grecian city."

Non potest sevĕrus esse in judicando, qui ălios in se sevĕros esse jūdĭces non vult. CIC.—"He cannot be impartial in judging others, who does not wish others to be strict judges of himself."

Non prōgrĕdi est rĕgrĕdi. *Prov.*—"Not to go on is to go back." Nothing in this world is stationary, and that which does not advance retrogrades.

——*Non prōnŭba Juno,*
Non Hymĕnæus adest, non illi Grātia lecto;
Eumĕnĭdes strāvĕre torum.—— OVID.
—"No Juno, guardian of the marriage rites, no Hymenæus, no one of the Graces, attended those nuptials. The Furies strewed the marriage bed."

Non propter vitam făciunt patrimōnia quidam,
Sed vitio cæci propter patrimōnia vivunt. JUV.
—"Some persons do not acquire estates for the enjoyment of life, but, blind in error, live only for their estates."

Non pŭdendo, sed non făciendo id quod non decet, impudentiæ effŭgĕre nomen debēmus. CIC.—"Not by being ashamed of doing, but by avoiding to do, what is unbecoming, we ought to shun the imputation of effrontery."

Non purgat peccāta qui negat. Prov.—"He who denies his offences does not atone for them."

Non quam diu, sed quam benè vixĕris refert. Sen.—"Not how long, but how well, you have lived, is the question."

Non qui solētur, non qui labentia tardè
Tempŏra narrando fallat, amicus adest. Ovid.
—"There is no friend nigh to console me, no one to beguile my moments with his converse, as they slowly creep along."

Non quia tu dignus, sed quia mitis ego. Ovid.—"Not that you were worthy, but because I was indulgent."

Non quisquam fruĭtur veris odōribus,
Hyblæos latĕbris nec spŏliat favos,
Si frontem căveat, si tĭmeat rubos.
Ornat spina rosas, mella tegunt apes.
—"No one will enjoy the sweet-smelling flowers of spring, nor spoil the Hyblæan honeycombs in their concealment, if he dreads his face being stung, or fears the brambles. The rose is provided with its thorn, the honey protected by the bees."

Non quivis suāvia comĕdit edūlia. Prov.—"Not every one eats nice dainties." See *Non cuivis*, &c.

Non quo sed quŏmŏdo.—"Not by whom, but how." Motto of Lord Howard de Walden.

Non refert quam multos sed quam bonos libros hăbeas ac legas. Sen.—"It matters not how many, but how good, are the books you possess and read."

Non satis fēlĭcĭter solēre procēdĕre quæ ŏcŭlis agas aliēnis. Livy.—"That business does not usually go on well, which you transact with the eyes of other persons."

Non scholæ, sed vitæ discĭmus. Sen.—"We learn not at school, but in life." Our education is only *commenced* at school.

Non scribit, cujus carmĭna nemo legit. Mart.—"That man is not a writer, whose verses no one reads."

Non semper ea sunt quæ videntur; dĕcĭpit
Frons prima multos.—— Phæd.
—"Things are not always what they seem to be; first appearances deceive many."

Non semper erit æstas.—"It will not always be summer." A translation from Hesiod.

Non semper erunt Saturnālia. *Prov.*—"It will not always be holiday time."

Non semper idem flōrĭbus est honos
Vernis; neque uno luna rubens nitet
Vultu.—— HOR.
—"The same glorious colour does not always remain in the flowers of spring, nor does the ruddy moon shine with the same aspect."

Non sĕquĭtur.—"It does not follow." It is not a necessary inference. The phrase is sometimes used as a substantive.

Non si malè nunc et olim sic erit. HOR.—"Though matters may be bad to-day, they may be better to-morrow." "It is a long lane that has no turning." "Heaviness may endure for a night, but joy cometh in the morning." *Psalm* xxx. 5.

Non sibi sed toti genĭtūm se crēdĕre mundo. LUCAN.—"To believe himself born not for himself, but for the whole world."

Non soles respĭcere te, cum dicas injustè altĕri? PLAUT.—
—"Are you not accustomed to look at yourself when you abuse another?"

Non solum scientia quæ est remōta à justĭtiâ, callĭdĭtas pŏtiùs quàm săpientia est appellanda; verum ĕtiam ănĭmus parātus ad perĭcŭlum, si suâ cupĭdĭtāte, non utĭlitāte commūni impellĭtur, audācia pŏtiùs nomen habet quàm fortitūdĭnis. CIC.—"Not only may that knowledge which is not governed by justice be called cunning rather than wisdom; but that courage also which is ready to encounter every danger, when impelled by avarice and not the common good, may be called audacity, rather than fortitude."

Non solum natūra sed ĕtiam lēgĭbus popŭlōrum constitūtum est, ut non lĭceat sui commŏdi causâ nocēre altĕri. CIC.—"It is ordained not only by nature, but also by the law of nations, that it shall not be allowable for a person to injure another for his own benefit."

Non sum informātus. *Law Latin.*—"I am not informed thereon."

Non sum qualis eram.—— HOR.—"I am not what I once was." The words of one who feels the effects of old age.

Non sum quod fuĕram.—— OVID.—"I am not what I once was."

Non sum uni angŭlo natus: patria mea totus hic est mundus. SEN.—"I was not born for one corner: all the world is my country." I am a citizen of the world.

Non sunt amici qui degunt procul. *Prov.*—"They are not your friends who live at a distance." See *Multas amicitias*, &c.

Non sunt jūdĭciis omnia danda meis. OVID.—"Every point is not to be yielded to my recommendations."

Non tali auxĭlio, nec defensōrĭbus istis,
Tempus eget.—— VIRG.
—"We do not, at this time, want such aid as that, nor such defenders."

Non tam ovum ovo sĭmĭle. *Prov.*—"More like than one egg is to another."

——*Non tam portas intrāre patentes,*
Quam frēgisse juvat; nec tam patiente colōno
Arva premi, quam si ferro pōpulentur et igni.
Concessâ pudet ire viâ.—— LUCAN.
—"It does not give him so much delight to enter by open gates, as to have forced them; nor so much that the fields be ploughed by the patient husbandman, as laid waste by fire and sword. He is reluctant to enter by a path conceded." One of this poet's usual misrepresentations of Julius Cæsar.

——*Non tamen intus*
Digna geri promes in scenam: multăque tolles
Ex ŏcŭlis, quæ mox narret făcundia præsens. HOR.
—"You must not, however, bring upon the stage things fit only to be acted behind the scenes; and you must take away from view many actions which an eloquent reciter may afterwards in person relate." Murders for instance.

——*Non tamen irrĭtum*
Quodcunque retro est, effĭcĭet; neque
Diffinget, infectumque reddet,
Quod fŭgiens semel hora vexit. HOR.
—"Not Heaven will render ineffectual what is past, or annihilate and undo what the fleeting hour has once carried away with it."

Non tĕmĕrārium est, ubi dives blandè appellat paupĕrem PLAUT.—"It is not for nothing, when a rich man accosts a poor one courteously."

Non tĕmĕre est, quod corvus cantat mihi nunc ab lævâ manu. PLAUT.—"It was not for nothing that the raven was just now croaking on my left hand." So in Gay's Fables:

"That raven on yon left-hand oak
(Curse on his ill-betiding croak!)
Bodes me no good."——

Non tu corpus eras sine pectŏre. Dî tibi formam,
Dî tibi divĭtias dĕdĕrant, artemque fruendi. HOR.

—"You are not a body without a soul. The gods have given you a beauteous form, the gods have given you wealth and the faculty of enjoying it." An elegant compliment paid by Horace to his friend the poet Tibullus.

Non tu scis, cum ex alto pŭteo sursum ad summum ascendĕris,
Maxĭmum perīcŭlum inde esse, a summo ne rursum cadas? PLAUT.

—"Do you not know that when you have ascended from a deep well to the top, there is the greatest danger lest you should fall back again from the top?"

——*Non umbras nocte volantes,*
Non tĭmeo strictas in mea fata manus. OVID.

—"I fear not ghosts that flit by night, or hands armed for my destruction."

Non unquam tăcuisse nocet, nocet esse locūtum.—"It never hurts us to have kept silence, it hurts us to have spoken."

Non usĭtātâ, nec tĕnui ferar
Pennâ.—— HOR.

—"I shall soar on no common, no feeble, wing."

Non ut diu vīvāmus curandum est, sed ut satis. SEN.—"It should be our care to live not long, but well enough." Life ought to be distinguished not so much by a number of years as by good actions.

——*Non ut plăcĭdis coëant immītia, non ut*
Serpentes ăvĭbus geminentur, tĭgrĭbus agni. HOR.

—"Not to such a degree that the tame should unite with the savage; nor that serpents should be coupled with birds, lambs with tigers." A sample of inconsistency.

Non uti libet, sed uti licet, sic vīvĭmus. Prov.—"We must live not as we like but as we can." We must "make a virtue of necessity." See *Ut quimus*, &c.

Non uxor salvum te vult, non fīlius: omnes
Vicīni ōdĕrunt, noti, puĕri, atque puellæ. HOR.

—"Neither thy wife nor thy son wishes well to thee; all thy neighbours hate thee, thy acquaintances, even the very boys and girls." Addressed to a miser, hated by all.

Non vis esse iracundus? ne sis curiōsus. Qui inquīrit, quid in se dictum sit, se ipse inquiĕtat. SEN.—"Do you wish not to be angry? be not inquisitive. He who inquires what has been said of him, torments himself."

Non zelus sed chărĭtas.—"Not your good wishes, but your charity." A mediæval expression.

——*Nonumque premātur in annum.* HOR.—"And let it be kept back up to the ninth year." A recommendation to dramatic writers to expend the greatest care upon their productions.

——*Noris quam ĕlĕgans formārum spectātor fiem.* TER.—"You shall see how nice a judge of beauty I am."

——*Nos decĕbat*
Lūgēre ubi esset ălĭquis in lucem ēdĭtus,
Humānæ vitæ văria rĕpŭtantes mala,
At qui labōres morte finisset graves,
Omnes amīcos laude et lætĭtiā exĕqui. CIC.

—"We ought to grieve when a being is born into the world, thinking of the various evils of human life; but when, by death, a man has closed his toilsome labours, all his friends should be affected with feelings of congratulation and joy." A quotation from Euripides.

Nos frăgĭli vastum ligno sulcāvĭmus æquor. OVID.—"We have ploughed the vast ocean in a frail bark."

——*Nos hæc nōvĭmus esse nihil.* MART.—"We know that these things are nothing at all." Mere trifles.

——*Nos in vĭtium crēdŭla turba sumus.* OVID.—"We are a multitude prone to vice, ever ready to be led astray."

Nos patriæ fines et dulcia linquĭmus arva. VIRG.—"We quit the limits of our native land, we bid our pleasant plains farewell."

Nos pŏpŭlo damus. SEN.—"We go with the crowd." We do as the world does.

Nos quoque, quæ fĕrĭmus, tŭlĭmus pătientius ante;
Et mala sunt longo multiplicāta die. OVID.

—"I too at first endured my sufferings with patience; and by length of time my evils have been multiplied."

——*Nos te,*
Nos făcĭmus, Fortūna, deam.—— JUV.
—"It is we, Fortune, it is we that make thee a goddess." See *Nullum numen habes*, &c.

Nosce tempus. Prov.—"Know your opportunity." "Make hay while the sun shines."

Noscenda est mensūra sui spectandaque rebus
In summis mĭnĭmisque.—— JUV.
—"One should know one's own measure, and keep it in view, in the greatest and in the most trifling matters."

Noscĭtur ex sŏciis. Prov.—"He is known from his companions." An estimate of his character is to be formed from the company he keeps. "Birds of a feather," &c.

Nosse hæc omnia salus est adolescentŭlis. TER.—"To know all these things is salvation for youth."

Nostra sine auxĭlio fŭgiunt bona; carpĭte florem. OVID.—"Our advantages fly irretrievably; then gather flowers while ye may."

——*Nostri farrāgo libelli.* HOR.—"The medley of my book."

Nota bene.—"Mark well!" note well. Often signified by N.B., calling the reader's attention in especial to what follows.

——*Nota mala res optŭma est.* PLAUT.—"A bad thing is best known."

Notæ Tirōniānæ.—"Tironian notes." Short-hand writing was so called in the earlier part of the middle ages, from Tullius Tiro, the freedman of Cicero, who was supposed to have invented it.

——*Notandi sunt tĭbi mores.* HOR.—"You must study the manners of men."

Notĭtiam primosque gradus vicīnia fĕcit;
Tempŏre crevit amor.—— OVID.
—"Proximity caused their first acquaintance, and their first advances in love; with time their affection increased."

Novăcŭla in cotem. Prov.—"The razor against the whetstone." Sharp as he is, he has met his match. See *Fragili quærens*, &c.

Novi ego hoc sæcŭlum, mōrĭbus quibus siet. PLAUT.—"I know this age, what its manners are."

——*Novi ingĕnium muliĕrum,*
Nolunt ubi velis, ubi nolis cŭpiunt ultro. TER.
—"I know the disposition of women; when you will they won't, when you won't they will."

Novos amīcos dum paras, vĕtĕres cole.—"While you cultivate new friendships, preserve your old ones." For remember, that it takes time to make friends.

——*Novum intervĕnit vĭtium et călămĭtas,*
Ut neque spectāri neque cognosci potuĕrit:
Ita pŏpŭlus stŭdio stŭpĭdus in funambŭlo
Anĭmum occupārat.—— TER.
—"An universal disaster and calamity interrupted [my play], so that it could not be witnessed throughout or estimated: so much had the populace, carried away with silly admiration, devoted their attention to some rope-dancing."

Novus homo.—"A new man." A man of yesterday; a mushroom, an upstart.

——*Nox atra cavâ circumvŏlat umbrâ.* VIRG.—"Black night envelopes them with her surrounding shade."

Nox erat; et bĭfŏres intrābat luna fenestras. OVID.—"It was night, and the moon entered at the windows with their double shutters."

Noxiæ pœna par esto. CIC.—"Let the punishment be equal to the offence."

Nuces relinquĕre.—"To leave the nuts." To lay aside childish amusements.

Nudum pactum. *Law Term.*—"A naked agreement." A bare promise, made in words only, and not confirmed by a written contract.

Nugæ canōræ. HOR.—"Melodious trifles." Agreeable nonsense.

——*Nugis addĕre pondus.* HOR.—"To add weight to trifles."

——*Nulla aconīta bibuntur*
Fictĭlĭbus.—— JUV.
—"No wolf'sbane is drunk out of earthen vessels." The peasant is in no danger of poison when eating from his humble dish—because there is no inducement to put an end to his life.

Nulla ætas ad perdiscendum est. ST. AMBROSE.—"There is no age past learning."

Nulla bona. *Law Phrase.*—"No goods," or "no assets."

Nulla capitălior pestis quam voluptas corpŏris hŏmĭnĭbus a natūrâ data. Cic.—"No pest more deadly has by nature been allotted to men than sensual indulgences."

Nulla dies ăbeat, quin līnea ducta supersit. *Prov.*—"Let no day pass by, without a line being drawn and left in remembrance of it." No day should be allowed to pass without leaving some memorial of itself.

Nulla discordia major quam quæ a religiōne fit.—"No animosities are more bitter than those which arise from religion." See *Odium theologicum.*

——*Nulla est sincēra voluptas;*
Sollĭcĭtique ălĭquid lætis intervĕnit.—— Ovid.

—"No pleasure is without alloy; some anxiety always interferes with our joys." See *Medio de,* &c.

Nulla falsa doctrīna est, quæ non permisceat ălĭquid vēritātis.—"There is no doctrine so false as not to be mingled with some truth."

Nulla ferè causa est, in quâ non fœmĭna litem
Mŏvĕrit.—— Juv.

—"There is hardly any dispute, in which a woman did not cause the breach."

Nulla ferent talem sæcla futūra virum.—"No future ages will produce such a man."

Nulla fides regni sŏciis, omnisque potestas
Impătiens consortis erit.—— Lucan.

—"There is no faith between the sharers in rule, and all power will be impatient of a sharer." See *Summa sedes,* &c.

Nulla herba aut vis mortis tela frangit.—"No herb or might can break the darts of death."

Nulla potentia supra leges esse debet. Cic.—"There ought to be no power above the laws."

Nulla quidem sano grăvior mentisque potenti
Pœna est, quam tanto displĭcuisse viro. Ovid.

—"There is no punishment more severe to a man of principle and good sense, than to have displeased so distinguished a person."

Nullâ re făcĭlius concilĭātur benevolentia multitūdĭnis, quam abstinentiâ et continentiâ. Cic.—"By nothing is the good will of the multitude more easily conciliated, than by abstinence and moderation."

Nulla recordanti lux est ingrāta gravisque,
Nulla fuit cujus non mĕmĭnisse velit.
Ampliat ætātis spătium sibi vir bonus, hoc est
Vīvĕre bis, vitâ posse priōre frui. MART.

—"No day can be cause of grief and bitter reflection to a good man, none is there which he is unwilling to remember: he prolongs the period of existence, and may be said to live twice, in that he can enjoy the days that are past."

——*Nullâ reparābĭlis arte,*
Læsa pudīcĭtia est. OVID.

—"Chastity, once tarnished, can be restored by no art."

Nulla res tantum ad discendum prōfĭcit quantum scriptio. CIC. —"Nothing has so greatly assisted learning, as the art of writing."

Nulla salus bello.—— VIRG.—"There is no safety in war."

Nulla scăbies scăbiōsior superstitiōne.—"No itch more infectious than superstition."

Nulla tam bona est fortūna, de quâ nil possis queri. SYR.— "There is no fortune so good, but you may find something to complain of."

Nulla unquam de morte hŏmĭnis cunctātio longa est. JUV.— "When a man's life is at stake, no deliberation can be too long."

Nulla venēnāto litĕra mixta joco est. OVID.—"Not a letter of my writings is sullied by a malevolent joke."

Nulla vitæ pars vacāre offĭcio potest. CIC.—"No period of life is exempt from its duties."

Nullæ sunt occultiōres insĭdiæ quam eæ quæ latent in simulātiōne offĭcii, aut in ălĭquo necessitūdĭnis nōmĭne. CIC.— "There are no acts of treachery more deeply concealed than those which lie veiled beneath a semblance of kindness, or under some plea of necessity."

Nullam habent personārum rătiōnem. CIC.—"They are no respecters of persons."

Nullăque mortāles præter sua littŏra norant. OVID.—"And mortals knew no shores beyond their own." A description of the ignorance of mankind in the earlier ages of the world.

Nulli est hŏmĭni perpĕtuum bonum. PLAUT.—"No man enjoys blessings to last for ever."

Nulli jactantiùs mœrent, quam qui maxĭmè lætantur. TAC.—"None mourn with such loud sorrow as those who are in reality the most delighted."

Nulli negābĭmus, nulli differēmus justĭtiam.—"To no man will we deny, to no man will we delay, the administration of justice." This assurance is given in Magna Charta, the charter of our liberties.

Nulli secundus.—"Second to none."

Nulli suis peccātis impĕdiuntur quo minus altĕrius peccāta demonstrāre possint.—"None are prevented by their own faults from pointing out the faults of another."

——*Nulli tăcuisse nocet, nocet esse locūtum.*—"To be silent hurts no one; to be talkative does the mischief."

Nulli tam feri affectus ut non disciplīnâ perdomentur.—"No propensities are so unbridled that they may not be subdued by discipline."

——*Nullis amor est medicābĭlis herbis.* OVID.—"Love is to be cured by no drugs."

——*Nullis fraus tuta latĕbris.* CAMERARIUS.—"In no concealment is fraud safe."

Nullĭus addictus jurāre in verba magistri,
Quo me cunque rapit tempestas, dēfĕror hospes. HOR.
—"Not pledged to swear by the words of any master, I am borne as a guest wherever the weather drives me." Horace here owns himself an eclectic philosopher, and not an adherent of any one sect.

Nullum à labōre me reclīnat ōtium. HOR.—"No intermission affords me repose from my labours."

Nullum anarchiâ majus est malum.—"There is no greater evil than anarchy."

Nullum ego sum numen, quid me immortālĭbus æquas?—"I am no divinity; why do you put me on a level with the gods?"

Nullum est malum majus, quam non posse ferre malum.—"There is no greater misfortune than not to be able to endure misfortune."

Nullum est nunc dictum, quod sit non dictum prius. TER.—

"There is nothing said now, that has not been said before."

Nullum impĕrium tutum nisi benevolentiâ munītum. CORN. NEP.—"No empire is secure unless it is supported by the good will [of the people]."

Nullum infortūnium solum.—"No misfortune comes singly." Misfortunes never come alone. "It never rains but it pours." A mediæval proverb.

Nullum inīquum in jure præsumendum est. Law Max.—"No injustice is to be presumed in the law." It is not to be presumed that the law will sanction anything that is unjust.

Nullum magnum ingĕnium sine mixtūrâ dementiæ. SEN.—"There is no great genius without a tincture of madness." It is a common saying, that every man is mad upon some point. Dryden says,

> "Great wits are sure to madness near allied,
> And thin partitions do their bounds divide."

This was originally a saying of Aristotle.

Nullum magnum malum quod extrēmum est. CORN. NEP.—"No evil is great if it is the last we have to bear." Death being the last.

Nullum numen abest si sit prudentia.—"No protecting deity is wanting, if there is prudence." An adaptation of the following line of Juvenal.

Nullum numen habes, si sit prudentia: nos te,
Nos făcĭmus, Fortūna, deam, cœlōque locāmus. JUV.
—"Had we but foresight, thou wouldst have no divinity. It is we, Fortune, it is we that make thee a goddess, and place thee in the heavens."

Nullum sĭmĭle quatuor pĕdĭbus currit. Prov. quoted by Lord COKE.—"No simile runs on all fours;" or, as Coke says, "No simile holds in everything." There are no two things alike in every respect.

——*Nullum sine nōmĭne saxum.* LUCAN.—"Not a stone is without a name." Every spot in such a city as Troy had been distinguished by some memorable event.

Nullum tempus occurrit regi. COKE.—"No time precludes the king." No lapse of time bars the rights of the crown.

Nullus argento color est,—
———nisi temperāto
Splendeat usu. **HOR.**
—"Money has no splendour of its own, unless it shines by temperate use."

Nullus commŏdum căpĕre potest de injūriâ suâ prŏpriâ. Law Max.—"No person may take advantage of his own wrong." The law will not allow a man to derive advantage from an act in which he has wrongfully taken part.

Nullus dolor est quem non longinquĭtas tempŏris mĭnuat ac molliat. CIC.—"There is no suffering which length of time will not diminish and soften."

Nullus est liber tam malus, ut non ălĭquâ parte prosit.—"There is no book so bad, as not to be useful in some way or other." A saying of the Elder Pliny, quoted by his nephew, Pliny the Younger.

Nullus illi nasus est.—"He has no nose." He is dull and void of sagacity.

Nullus perniciōsior hostis est, quam familiāris inimīcus.—"No foe is more pernicious than an enemy in the disguise of a friend."

Nullus tantus quæstus, quam quod habes parcĕre. Prov.—"There is no gain so sure as that which results from economizing what you have." "A penny saved is a penny gained." See *Non intelligunt homines, &c.*

Nullus unquam amātor adeo est callĭdè
Facundus, quæ in rem sint suam, loqui possit. PLAUT.
—"No lover is ever so skilled in eloquence, as to be able to give utterance to that which is for his own interest."

Num vobis tinniēbant aures? PLAUT.—"Did not your ears tingle?" A sign that somebody is talking of you.

——Numĕrisque fertur
Lege solūtis. HOR.
—"And he is borne along in numbers unfettered by laws." He treats with utter contempt all poetic rules. This quotation was happily applied by Burke when the mob carried Wilkes on their shoulders.

Nŭmĕrus certus pro incerto pōnĭtur.—"A certain number is used for an uncertain one." That is to say, when we speak *in round numbers*, as we call them.

Nunc ănĭmis opus, Ænēa, nunc pectŏre firmo. VIRG.—"Now, Æneas, you have need of courage, and a resolute heart."

Nunc dimittis.—"[Lord,] now lettest thou [thy servant] depart [in peace.]" The beginning of the song of Simeon in the Temple. *Luke* i. 29

Nunc ĕtiam somni pingues, nunc frīgĭdus humor;
Et liquĭdum tenui guttŭre cantat avis. OVID.

—"Now the slumbers are sound, now the moisture of the morn is refreshing; the birds too are sweetly warbling with their little throats."

Nunc mare, nunc sylvæ
Threĭcio Aquilōne sonant; răpiāmus, amīci,
Occăsiōnem de die.—— HOR.

—"Now the sea, now the woods resound with the Thracian north-east wind; let us, my friends, seize the opportunity offered by this auspicious day."

——*Nunc omnis ager, nunc omnis partŭrit arbos,*
Nunc frondent sylvæ, nunc formosissĭmus annus. VIRG.

—"Now every field is green, every tree puts forth its shoots, now are the woods in leaf, and the season is most beauteous."

Nunc pătĭmur longæ pacis mala; sævior armis
Luxŭria incŭbuit, victumque ulciscĭtur orbem. JUV.

—"Now do we suffer the evils of prolonged peace; luxury more ruthless than the sword broods over us, and avenges a conquered world." A picture of Rome in its decline.

Nunc pro tunc. *Law Term.*—"Now for then."

——*Nunc retrorsùm*
Vela dare, atque ĭterāre cursus
Cogor relictos.—— HOR.

—"I am now obliged to tack about, and to regain the track I had deserted."

Nunc scio quid sit Amor: duris in cautĭbus illum
Ismărus, aut Rhŏdŏpe, aut extrēmi Gărămantes,
Nec gĕnĕris nostri puĕrum, nec sanguĭnis, edunt. VIRG.

—"Now I know what Love is: Ismarus, or Rhodope, or the remotest Garamantes produced him on rugged cliffs, a child not of our race or blood."

Nunc si nos audis, atque es divīnus, Apollo,
Dic mihi, qui nummos non habet unde petat?

—"Now if you listen to us, and are a god, Apollo, tell me whence he who has got no money is to get it?"

Nunc tuum ferrum in igni est. Prov.—" Now your iron is in the fire." "Strike while the iron is hot."

Nunquam ad lĭquĭdum fama perdūcĭtur.—" Rumour never can be brought to state things with clearness."

Nunquam ălĭud natūra, aliud săpientia dicit. Juv.—" Nature never says one thing, wisdom another."

Nunquam erit aliēnis gravis, qui suis se concinnat levem. Plaut. —" He will never be despised by others, who makes himself respected by his own relations."

Nunquam est fidēlis cum potente socĭĕtas. Phæd.—" An alliance with the powerful is never sure."

Nunquam ĭgĭtur satis laudāri dignè pŏtĕrit philŏsŏphia, cui qui pāreat, omne tempus ætātis sine molestiâ possit dēgĕre. Cic. —" Philosophy therefore can never be sufficiently praised; for he who is obedient to her laws may pass through every stage of life without discontent."

Nunquam in vitâ mihi fuit mĕlius. Plaut.—" Never in my life was I better,"—in better circumstances.

Nunquam ita quisquam benè subductâ ratiōne ad vitam fuit,
Quin res, ætas, usus, semper ălĭquid apportet novi,
Alĭquid mŏneat; ut illa, quæ te scire credas, nescĭas,
Et quæ tibi putâris prima, in expĕriundo nunc rĕpudĭes.
Ter.

—" Never was there any person of such well-trained habits of life, but experience, age, and custom were always bringing him something new, or suggesting something; so much so, that what you believe you know, you don't know, and what you have fancied of first importance to you, on making trial you reject."

——*Nunquam libertas grātior extat*
Quam sub rĕge pio.—— Claud.

—" Liberty is never more inviting than under a pious king." Good government and a rational degree of liberty are then united.

Nunquam minus solus quam cum solus. Cic. — " Never less alone than when alone." The words of a philosopher, who estimated the pleasures of self-communion and reflection.

Nunquam nimis curāre possunt suum parentem filiæ. Plaut.

—"Daughters can never take too much care of their father."

Nunquam nimis dīcĭtur, quod nunquam satis discĭtur SEN.—"That is never too often repeated, which is never sufficiently learned."

Nunquam potest non esse virtūti locus. SEN.—"Room can never be wanting for virtue."

Nunquam sunt grati qui nŏcuēre sales.—"Witticisms are never agreeable which are productive of injury."

Nunquam vidi inīquius concertatiōnem compărātam. TER.—"I never saw a more unequal contest."

Nunquid vitæ mimum commŏde perēgisset?—"Whether he had not well played his part in the comedy of life?" The question put to his friends by Augustus Cæsar on his death-bed.

Nusquam nec ŏpĕra sine emolumento, nec emolumentum ferme sine ŏpĕrâ, impensa est. LIVY.—"There is nowhere labour without profit, and seldom profit without labour."

Nusquam tuta fides.—— VIRG.—"Confidence is nowhere safely placed." Such is the case in times of civil commotion.

Nutrit pax Cĕrĕrem, pacis amīca Ceres. OVID.—"Peace nourishes Ceres, Ceres is the friend of peace."

Nutu Dei, non cæco casu, rĕgĭmur et nos et nostra.—"By the will of God, not by blind chance, are we and all things belonging to us governed."

O.

O, O, O.—Certain prayers or anthems in the Roman Catholic church were called the O, O, O's, as they severally begin with *O sapientia*, *O radix*, *O Adonaï*, &c.: they are sung in the evening for nine days before Christmas day.

O beāta sānĭtas, te præsente amœnum
Ver floret gratiis; absque te nemo beātus.
—"Oh blessed health! when thou art present the joyous spring blossoms in all its gracefulness: without thee no one is happy."

——*O cæca nocentum*
Consilia, O semper timidum scelus! STATIUS.
—"Oh how blind are the counsels of the guilty! Oh how cowardly at all times is wickedness!"

O Corydon, Corydon, secrētum dīvĭtis ullum
Esse putas? Servi ut tăceant.—— JUV.
—"Oh Corydon, Corydon, do you suppose that anything a rich man does can be secret? even if the servants hold their tongues."

O curas hŏmĭnum! O quantum est in rebus ināne! PERS.—"Oh! the cares of men! Oh! how much vanity there is in human affairs!" "Vanity of vanities; all is vanity." *Eccles.* i. 2.

O curvæ in terris ănĭmæ, et cœlestium inānes!—"Oh! groveling souls on earth, how devoid of all that is heavenly!"

O facĭles dare summa Deos, eădemque tuēri
Difficĭles.—— LUCAN.
—"How ready are the gods to bestow on us prosperity, how averse to insure our tenure of it!"

O fortūna, viris invĭda fortĭbus,
Quam non æqua bonis præmia dīvĭdis! SEN.
—"Oh fortune, envious of able men, what an unequal share of thy prizes dost thou award to the good!"

O fortunātam, natam, me consŭle, Romam!—"Oh happy Rome, when I was consul, born." The only line that has come down to us of Cicero's unfortunate attempts at poetry. The jingle between the second and third words is the great deformity, though the line is otherwise meagre enough. Juvenal, to whom we are indebted for the preservation of it, says that Cicero "might have scorned the sword of Antony, if all he uttered had been like this."

O fortunāti nimium, sua si bona norint,
Agrĭcŏlæ, quibus ipsa, procul discordĭbus armis,
Fundit humo facĭlem victum justissĭma tellus. VIRG.
—"Oh! husbandmen more than happy, if they did but know their own advantages; for whom, far from discordant arms, the grateful earth pours forth from her bosom a ready abundance." The first line is often applied to that rather large class of people who "don't know when they are well off."

O! hebetūdo et durĭtia cordis humāni, quæ solum præsentia meditātur et futūra non magis prævĭdet. A Kempis, *De Im. Christi.*—"Oh! the dulness and the hardness of the heart of man, which contemplates only the present, and not rather the things of futurity."

O! imitatōres! servum pecus!—— Hor.—"Oh! ye imitators, a servile herd!" In allusion to the low position occupied by the plagiary and copyist.

O major tandem, parcas, insāne, minōri. Hor.—"Oh! thou who art still more mad, spare me, I pray, who am not sc mad." A phrase used ironically in paper warfare.

O mihi prætĕrĭtos rĕfĕrat si Jūpĭter annos! Virg.—"Oh! that Jupiter would but give me back the years that are past!"

O mihi tam longæ mănеat pars ultĭma vitæ,
Spīrĭtus et quantum sat erit tua dicĕre facta! Virg.
—"Oh! may my last stage of life continue so long, and may so much breath be granted me as shall suffice to sing thy deeds!"

O misĕras hŏmĭnum mentes, O pectŏra cæca! Lucret.—"Oh! how wretched are the minds of men, oh! how blind are their understandings!" Applicable to popular delusions.

——*O mūnĕra nondum*
Intellecta Deûm.—— Lucan.
—"Oh gifts from the gods, not yet understood."

O nimium făcĭles! O toto pectŏre captæ! Ovid.—"Oh people too credulous! Oh people utterly gone mad!"

——*O nimium nimiumque oblīte tuōrum.* Ovid.—"Oh, far too far, forgetful of your kin!"

O passi graviŏra!—— Virg.—"Oh ye who have suffered greater dangers than these."

O præclārum diem cum ad illud divīnum animōrum concĭlium cœtumque proficiscar. Cic.—"Oh happy day, when I shall hasten to join that holy council and assemblage of spirits!" A proof how highly this great philosopher appreciated the doctrine of the immortality of the soul.

O quanta spĕcies cĕrebrum non habet! Phædr.—"Oh that such beauty should have no brains." See the Fable of the Fox and the Mask.

O rus, quando te aspiciam? quandŏque licēbit

Nunc vĕtĕrum libris, nunc somno et inertĭbus horis
Dūcĕre sollĭcitæ jucunda oblīvia vitæ? HOR.
—"Oh rural retreat, when shall I behold thee? and when shall it be in my power to enjoy the pleasing forgetfulness of an anxious life, one while with the books of the ancients, another while in sleep and leisure?"

O! si sic omnia!—"Oh! had he acted thus in all things!" or, "Oh! that all were thus!"

O suavis ănĭma! qualem te dicam bonam
Antĕhac fuisse, tales cum sint relĭquiæ! PHÆDR.
—"Oh the delicious fragrance! how good I should say were your former contents, when the remains of them are such!"

O tempŏra! O mores! CIC.—"Oh times! Oh manners!" The exclamation of Cicero when inveighing against the impunity of wicked men.

O vita, mĭsĕro longa, felīci brevis! SYR.—"Oh life, how long to the wretched, how short to the happy!"

O vitæ philosophia dux! O virtūtis indagātrix, expultrixque vitiōrum! quid non modo nos, sed omnīno vita hŏmĭnum sine te esse pŏtuisset. Tu urbes pĕpĕristi; tu dissipātos hŏmĭnes in societātem vitæ convocasti. CIC.—"Oh! Philosophy, guide of life. Oh! searcher out of virtues and expeller of vices! what could we have done without thee? And not only we, but every age of man? It is thou that didst form cities; thou that didst call together solitary men to the enjoyment of the social intercourse of life."

Obĭter cantāre. PETRON. ARBITER.—"To sing by the way."

Obĭter dictum.—"A thing said incidentally," or "by the way." Parenthetically.

Oblātam occasiōnem tene. CIC.—"Seize the opportunity when it offers." Seize "the golden moments as they fly." "Take time by the forelock."

Obruat illud malè partum, malè retentum, malè gestum, impĕrium. CIC.—"May that sovereignty fall which has been evilly acquired, which is evilly retained, and which is evilly administered."

Obscūris vera involvens.—— VIRG.—"Involving the truth in obscurity." The subterfuge of the person who has the worst of an argument.

Obscūrum facĕre per obscūrius.—"To make that darker

which was dark enough before." To render, in an attempt to illustrate, obscurity doubly obscure. See *Lucus a non*, &c., and *Non sequitur*.

Obsĕcro, tuum est? vetus credĭdĕram.—"Pray, is it yours? I really had thought it old." The proper answer to a plagiary.

Obsĕquium amīcos, vērĭtas odium parit. TER.—"Obsequiousness begets friends, truth hatred." Words uttered in a complaining spirit.

——*Observantior æqui*
Fit pŏpŭlus, nec ferre vetat cum vīdĕrit ipsum
Auctōrem parēre sibi.—— CLAUD.
—"The people becomes more observant of justice, and refuses not to support the laws, when it sees the author of them obeying his own enactments."

Obstŭpui, stĕtĕruntque comæ, et vox faucĭbus hæsit. VIRG.—"I was amazed, my hair stood erect, and my voice cleaved to my throat." A picture of horror and alarm.

Obstŭpui, tăcĭtus sustinuique pedem. OVID.—"I stood amazed, and in silence I made a pause."

Occāsio facit furem. *Prov.*—"Opportunity makes the thief."

Occasiōnem cognosce.—"Know your opportunity."

Occāsio primâ sui parte comōsa, posteriōri parte calva, quam si occupāris, tĕneas; elapsam semel, non ipse Jūpĭter possit reprehendĕre.—"Opportunity has hair in front, behind she is bald; if you seize her by the forelock, you may hold her; but, if she once escapes, not Jupiter himself can catch her again." See also *Rem tibi*, &c., and Phædrus, Fab. B. v. F. viii., from which the latter part of the quotation is taken.

Occĭdit mĭsĕros crambe repetīta.—— JUV.—"The same stale cabbage, everlastingly hashed up, wears out their wretched lives." Said in reference to the drudgery of a teacher's life.

Occĭdit una domus: sed non domus una perire
Digna fuit.—— OVID.
—"Thus did one house fall: but not one house alone deserved to perish."

Occultāre morbum funestum.—"To conceal disease is fatal." See *Principiis obsta*, &c.

Occŭpet extrēmum scăbies!—— HOR.—"May the itch seize

the hindmost." Like our proverb, "The devil take the hindmost."

Ocŭli tanquam speculatōres altissĭmum locum obtĭnent. CIC. —"The eyes, like sentinels, occupy the highest place [in the body]."

Ocŭlis magis habenda fides quam aurĭbus. *Prov.*—"It is better to trust our eyes than our ears." Ocular demonstration is better than hearsay.

——*Ocŭlos, paulum tellūre morātos,*
Sustŭlit ad procĕres; expectātoque resolvit
Ora sono; nec abest facundis grātia dictis. OVID.

—"Fixing his eyes for a short time on the ground, he raised them towards the chiefs, and opened his lips in accents not unlooked for; nor was persuasiveness wanting to his eloquent words." Descriptive of the manner of Ulysses, when pleading before the Grecian chiefs for the arms of Achilles.

Ocŭlus dexter mihi salit. *Prov.*—"My right eye twitches." I shall see the person whom I have long wished to see.

Ocŭlus dŏmĭni sagĭnat equum. *Prov.*—"The master's eye makes the horse fat." This is illustrated in Phædrus' Fable of the Stag and the Oxen, B. ii. F. viii.

Odĕrint modo mĕtuant.—"Let them hate, so long as they fear me." The sentiments of a tyrant. These words were often in the mouth of the Emperor Tiberius, who, in his turn, lived in perpetual fear of his subjects.

Odĕro si potĕro, si non, invītus amābo. OVID.—"I will hate if I can; if not, I will love against my will." Heinsius doubts however if this line was written by Ovid.

Odĕrunt hilărem tristes, tristemque jocōsi,
Sedātum cĕlĕres, agĭlem gnavumque remissi. HOR.

—"The melancholy hate those who are cheerful; the gay, the melancholy; the bustling hate the sedate; the indolent, the brisk and active." These opposite classes of people have few or no sympathies in common.

Odĕrunt peccāre boni virtūtis amōre,
Odĕrunt peccāre mali formīdĭne pœnæ.

—"The good hate to sin from love of virtue; the bad hate to sin from fear of punishment." The first line is from Horace, the second from an unknown source.

Odi ego aurum! multa multis sæpè suasit perpĕram. PLAUT. —"Gold I detest; many a one has it persuaded to many an evil course."

Odi mĕmŏrem compotōrem.—"I hate a boon companion with a good memory." See *Aut bibeat*, &c.

Odi, nec possum cupiens non esse quod odi. OVID.—"I hate this state; nor, though I wish it, can I be otherwise than what I hate to be."

Odi profānum vulgus et arceo. HOR.—"I hate the profane vulgar, and I spurn them."

Odi puĕrŭlos præcōci ingĕnio. CIC. *and* APUL.—"I hate your bits of boys of precocious talent."

Odia in longum jăciens, quæ recondĕret, auctăque promĕret. TACIT.—"Treasuring hatred, to be long stored up, and brought forward with an increase of virulence." This, as Junius remarks, is a description of the worst of characters.

Odia qui nĭmium timet, regnāre nescit. SEN.—"He who too much fears hatred, is unfit to reign."

Odimus accĭpitrem quia semper vivit in armis. OVID.—"We hate the hawk because he always lives in a state of warfare." This line was held to apply not inaptly to the first emperor Napoleon.

Odiōsa est orātio, cum rem agas, longinquum loqui. PLAUT. —"It is a tiresome way of speaking, when you should despatch the business, to be beating about the bush."

Odium effugĕre est triumphāre.—"To escape hatred is to gain a triumph."

Odium theologĭcum.—"Theological hatred." A hatred of the bitterest kind, engendered by differences on theological points. See *Nulla discordia*, &c.

——*Odōra canum vis.* VIRG.—"The sharp scent of the hounds."

Offĭcit adulātio vĕritāti. TAC.—"Flattery is hurtful to truth."

——*Ohe!*
Jam satis est.—— HOR.

—"Hold, there is now enough." An expression used to signify satiety.

Oleo tranquillior. *Prov.*—"More smooth than oil." Oil poured on water in agitation renders the surface smooth and placid.

Olet lucernam. *Prov.*—"It smells of the lamp." Said of any mental production that bears the marks of midnight study. The phrase was especially applied to the orations of Demosthenes.

——*Oleum adde camīno.* Hor.—"Add oil to the fire." To add fuel to flame, or as we say, "To let the fat in the fire."

Oleum et opĕram perdĕre. *Prov.*—"To lose one's oil and pains." This may allude either to the oil of the midnight lamp, or that with which the candidates at the public games anointed themselves.

——*Olim meminisse juvābit.* Virg.—"It will one day be pleasing to remember these sufferings." See *Forsan et*, &c.

Ollæ amicitia.—"Platter-friendship." Cupboard love. See *Fervet olla*, &c.

Omĭna sunt ălĭquid. Ovid.—"There is something in omens."

Omne actum ab agentis intentiōne judicandum. *Law Max.*—"Every act is to be judged of by the intention of the agent." In all legal inquiries the main object is to ascertain the *animus* or intention of the agent.

Omne anĭmal seipsum dīlĭgit. Cic.—"Every animal loves itself."

Omne anĭmi vitium tanto conspectius in se
Crimen habet, quanto major qui peccat habĕtur. Juv.
—"Every fault of the mind becomes the more conspicuous and more culpable, the higher the rank of the person who is guilty."

Omne capax movet urna nomen. Hor.—"The capacious urn [of death] sends forth every name in turn." Comparing death to a lottery, each name is drawn from his urn in its turn. See *Omnes eodem*, &c.

Omne corpus mutābĭle est; ita effĭcĭtur ut omne corpus mortāle sit. Cic.—"Every body is subject to change; hence it is that every body is mortal."

Omne Epigramma sit instar apis, acūleus illi,
Sint sua mella, sit et corpŏris exigui. Mart.
"Three things must Epigrams, like bees, have all,
A sting, and honey, and a body small."

Omne ignōtum pro magnĭfico est. Tac.—"Everything unknown is taken for magnificent." We are apt to magnify things that are mysterious in themselves or only seen from a distance. It is sometimes quoted "*pro mirifĭco,*" "as marvellous."

——*Omne in præcipĭti vitium stetit.* JUV.—"Every vice has reached its climax."

Omne malum nascens făcĭle opprĭmĭtur: inveterātum fit plerumque robustius. CIC.—"Every evil at its birth is easily rooted out; when grown old, it mostly becomes stronger." See *Principiis obsta*, &c.

Omne nimium vertĭtur in vitium. Prov.—"Every excess becomes a vice."

Omne solum forti patria est. OVID.—"To the resolute man every soil is his country." A stout heart will support us even in exile.

Omne supervăcuum pleno de pectŏre manat. HOR.—"Every thing superfluous overflows from a full bosom." A hint to poets not to overload their poems with unnecessary descriptions, or rambling digressions.

Omne tulit punctum qui miscuit ŭtĭle dulci,
Lectōrem delectando păriterque monendo. HOR.
—"He has carried every point who has blended the useful with the agreeable, amusing his reader while he instructs him."

Omne vafer vitium ridenti Flaccus amīco
Tangit, et admissus circum præcordia ludit,
Callĭdus excusso popŭlum suspendĕre naso. PERS.
—"The subtle Flaccus touches every failing of his smiling friend, and once admitted sports around his heart; well-skilled in sneering at the public with upturned nose." Said with reference to the satire of Horace.

——*Omne vovĕmus*
Hoc tibi; ne tanto căreat mihi nōmĭne charta. TIBULL.
—"All this I dedicate to thee; that this my book may not be deprived of a name so great as thine."

Omnem crede diem tibi diluxisse suprĕmum. HOR.—"Believe that each day that shines is your last." In the words of the Morning Hymn, "Live this day as if the last."

Omnem movēre lăpĭdem. Prov.—"To leave no stone unturned."

——*Omnem, quæ nunc obducta tuenti*
Mortāles hĕbĕtat visus tibi, et hūmĭda circum
Calīgat, nubem eripiam.—— VIRG.

—"I will dissipate every cloud which now, intercepting the view, bedims your mortal sight and spreads a humid veil of mist around you."

Omnes amicitias familiārităt esque afflixit. SUETON.—"He has violated all the ties of friendship and of intimacy."

Omnes amīcos habēre operōsum est; satis est inimīcos non habēre. SEN.—"It is an arduous task to make all men your friends; it is enough to have no enemies."

Omnes attrăhens ut magnes lapis. *Prov.*—"Attracting all to himself, like a loadstone." Said of a person of a conciliatory and winning disposition.

Omnes autem et habentur et dicuntur tyranni, qui potestāte sunt perpĕtuâ, in eâ civitāte quæ libertāte usa est. CORN. NEPOS.—"All men are considered and called tyrants who possess themselves of perpetual power in a state which has before enjoyed liberty."

Omnes bonos bonasque accurāre addĕcet
Suspiciōnem et culpam ut ab se segrĕgent. PLAUT.
—"It becomes all good men and good women to be careful and keep suspicion and guilt away from themselves."

Omnes compŏsui. HOR.—"I have buried them all." My relations are all gone to their repose.

——*Omnes, cum secundæ res sunt maxĭme, tum maxĭme*
Meditāri secum oportet, quo pacto advorsam ærumnam ferant.
TER.
—"When their fortunes are the most prosperous it is then most especially the duty of all men to reflect within themselves how they are to endure adversity." Cicero quotes this passage in the Third Book of his Tusculan Questions, and the maxim here inculcated was a favourite one with the Stoic philosophers.

Omnes eōdem cōgĭmur; omnium
Versātur urnâ, sērius, ocius,
Sors exitūra.—— HOR.
—"We are all impelled onward alike; the urn of death is shaken for all, and sooner or later the lot must come forth." See *Omne capax*, &c.

Omnes hŏmĭnes, qui de rebus dubiis consultant, ab odio, amicitiâ, irâ, atque misericordiâ vacuos esse decet. SALL.—"It is proper that all men, who consult on doubtful matters, should be unbiassed by hatred, friendship, anger, and pity."

Omnes in malōrum mari navigāmus.—"We are all embarked on a sea of woes."

Omnes insanīre. Hor.—"That all men are mad." The doctrine of Licinius Damasippus, the Stoic philosopher, satirized by Horace: b. i. Sat. 3.

Omnes omnium carităes patria una complectĭtur. Cic.—"Our country comprehends all the affections of life."

Omnes pari sorte nascĭmur, solâ virtūte distinguĭmur.—"All men are equal by birth, we become distinguished by merit alone."

Omnes quibus res sunt minus secundæ, magis sunt nescio quōmŏdo
Suspiciōsi; ad contumēliam omnia accipiunt magis;
Propter suam impotentiam se credunt neglĭgi. Ter.
—"All who are in distressed circumstances are suspicious, to I know not what degree; they take everything too readily as an affront, and fancy themselves neglected on account of their helpless condition."

——*Omnes sapientes decet conferre et fabulāri.* Plaut.—"It behoves all prudent persons to confer and discourse together."

Omnes sibi mĕlius esse malunt quam altĕri. Ter.—"All would rather it went well with themselves than with another."

——*Omnes una manet nox,*
Et calcanda semel via lethi. Hor.
—"The same night awaits us all, and the road of death must once be travelled by us."

Omnes ut tecum mĕrĭtis pro tālĭbus annos
Exĭgat, et pulchrâ făciat te prole parentem. Virg.
—"That with thee, for such thy merits, she may pass all her years, and make thee sire of a beauteous offspring."

Omni ætāti mors est commūnis. Cic.—"Death is common to every age."

Omni exceptiōne major.—"A man beyond all exception."

Omni malo pūnĭco inest granum putre. Prov.—"Every pomegranate has its rotten pip." So our proverb, "Every rose has its thorns."

Omni personārum delectu et discrīmĭne remōto. Cic.—"All respect or partiality for persons being laid aside."

Omnia bene, sine pœnâ, tempus est ludendi,
Absque morâ venit hora libros deponendi.

"All things go well, the hour for play,
No fear of rod, so books away."

A favourite rhyme with school-boys.

Omnia bonos viros decent. *Prov.*—"All things are becoming to good men." A favourable construction is put upon all they do.

Omnia Castor emit, sic fiet ut omnia vendat. MARTIAL.—"Castor is buying everything, it will so happen that he will have to sell everything." The probable fate of a greedy buyer.

Omnia conando dŏcĭlis solertia vincit. MANIL.—"By endeavour, a pliant and industrious disposition surmounts every difficulty."

Omnia cum amīco delībĕra, sed de te ipso prius. SEN.—"Consult your friend on everything, but first of all about yourself."

Omnia ejusdem farīnæ. *Prov.*—"All things are of the same grain." There is no mark of distinction in the eyes of Providence.

Omnia fanda nefanda, malo permista furōre,
Justifĭcam nobis mentem avertēre deorum. CATULL.
—"The confusion of all right and wrong, in this accursed war, has turned from us the gracious favour of the gods."

Omnia fert ætas, anĭmum quoque.—— VIRG.—"Age bears away all things, the mental powers even."

Omnia fert ætas secum, aufert omnia secum;
Omnia tempus habent, omnia tempus habet.
—"Age brings all things with it, and carries all things away. All things have time, time has all things."

——*Omnia Græcè!*
Cum sit turpe magis nostris nescīre Latīnè. JUV.
—"All things must be Greek! when it is more disgraceful for us Romans to be ignorant of Latin." A sarcasm on those who study foreign languages, without being masters of their own.

Omnia idem pulvis. *Prov.*—"All things are dust alike," or "of the same mould."

Omnia inconsulti impĕtus cœpta, initiis valĭda, spatio languescunt. TACITUS.—"The undertakings of inconsiderate impulse are full of vigour at the outset, but soon wither."

Omnia jam fient, fiĕri quæ posse negābam :
Et nihil est de quo non sit habenda fides. OVID.
—"All things shall now come to pass which I used to say could not come to pass; and there is nothing which is not deserving of belief."

Omnia mala exempla bonis princĭpiis orta sunt.—"All bad precedents have had their rise in good beginnings."

Omnia mea mecum porto.—"I carry all my property about me." The words of Simonides at the time of his shipwreck, in allusion to his mental acquirements; also of Bias, one of the Seven Wise Men.

Omnia munda mundis.—"To the pure all things are pure."

Omnia mutantur, nihil intĕrit.—— OVID.—"All things are ever changing, nothing comes to an end." The doctrine of Pythagoras.

Omnia mutantur, nos et mutāmur in illis. BORBONIUS.—"All things are subject to change, and we change with them." This hackneyed line is generally quoted as "*Tempora mutantur,*" &c.

Omnia non părĭter rerum sunt omnĭbus apta. PROPERT.—"All things are not equally fit for all men."

Omnia orta occĭdent. SALL.—"All created things shall perish."

Omnia patefacienda, ut nihil quod vendĭtor norit emptor ignōret. CIC.—"Everything should be disclosed, that the buyer may be ignorant of nothing which the seller knows." The proper way of dealing; and then the maxim *Caveat emptor* applies.

Omnia perdĭdĭmus. Tantummŏdo vita relicta est. OVID.—"We have lost everything. Life alone is left."

Omnia perversas possunt corrumpĕre mentes. OVID.—"All things can lead astray perverted minds."

Omnia pontus erant, deĕrant quoque littŏra ponto;
Nat lupus inter oves, fulvos vehit unda leōnes. OVID.
—"It was all ocean, and to that ocean shores were wanting—the wolf swims among the sheep, the wave carries along the tawny lions." Ovid's description of the Deluge.

Omnia præcĕpi, atque ănĭmo mecum ante perĕgi. VIRG.—"I have anticipated all things, and have acted them over already in my mind."

Omnia præsumuntur legĭtĭmè facta donec probĕtur in contrārium. COKE.—"All things are presumed to be lawfully done, until it is proved to the contrary."

Omnia priùs verbis experīri, quam armis, sapientem decet. TER. —"It becomes a wise man to try everything that can be done by words, before he has recourse to arms."

Omnia profectò, cum se à cœlestĭbus rebus rĕfĕret ad humānas, excelsiùs magnificentiùsque et dicet et sentiet. CIC.—"When a man turns his attention from heavenly things to human affairs, he will assuredly be able to speak and to think on all subjects on a more sublime and a more elevated scale."

Omnia quæ nunc vetustissima creduntur nova fuēre; et quod hodie exemplis tuēmur inter exempla erit. TACIT.—"All things which are now believed to be of the greatest antiquity were once new; and what we now defend by example will one day be quoted as an example."

Omnia quæ sensu volvuntur vota diurno
Pectŏre sōpīto reddit amīca quies. CLAUD.
—"Kindly repose restores to the slumbering breast all the thoughts that are revolved in our mind during the day."

Omnia risus, omnia pulvis, et omnia nil sunt.—"All things are ridiculous, all things are as dust, and all things are as nothing."

——*Omnia Romæ*
Cum prĕtio.—— JUV.
—"All things at Rome are coupled with high price."

Omnia si perdas, famam servāre memento;
Quâ semel amissâ postea nullus eris.
—"Though you should lose everything else, remember to preserve your good name, which once lost, you will be undone."

Omnia subjecisti sub pĕdĭbus, oves et boves.—"Beneath our feet Thou hast placed everything, both sheep and oxen." Motto of the Butchers' Company.

Omnia sunt hŏmĭnum tenui pendentia filo;
Et sŭbĭto casu, quæ valuēre, ruunt. OVID.
—"All things belonging to man are hanging from a slender thread; and that which was firm before falls headlong with a sudden descent."

Omnia tuta timens.—— VIRG.—"Fearful of everything, even where there is safety." The state of a mind which has been harassed by dangers and anxieties.

Omnia venālia Romæ. Prov.—"All things are to be bought at Rome." Said of Rome in the days of her corruption.

Omnia vincit amor, nos et cedāmus amōri. VIRG.—"Love conquers all things, let us too yield to love." "Love rules the court, the camp, the grove."

Omnĭbus bonis expĕdit rempublĭcam esse salvam. CIC.—"It is the interest of every good man that his country shall be safe."

Omnĭbus hoc vitium est cantōrĭbus, inter amīcos
Ut nunquam indūcant ănĭmum cantāre rogāti,
Injussi nunquam desistant.—— HOR.
—"This is a fault common to all singers, that among their friends when asked to sing they never will bring their minds to comply, but when not requested they will never leave off." See *Novi ingenium*, &c.

——*Omnĭbus hostes*
Reddĭte nos pŏpŭlis, civīle avertĭte bellum. LUCAN.
—"Make us the enemies of every nation, avert from us civil war." Any bloodshed is preferable to that of citizens by the hands of citizens.

Omnĭbus in terris, quæ sunt à Gādĭbus usque
Aurōram et Gangem, pauci dignoscĕre possunt
Vera bona, atque illis multùm diversa, remōtâ
Errōris nĕbŭlâ.—— JUV.
—"In all the lands which lie from Gades even to the land of the morn and the Ganges, few are able to remove the clouds of prejudice, and to discern those things which are really for their good, and those which are directly the contrary."

Omnĭbus invĭdeas, Zōĭle, nemo tibi. MART.—"You envy everyone, Zoilus, no one envies you." Said to a sarcastic but contemptible writer.

Omnĭbus modis, qui paupĕres sunt hŏmĭnes, mĭsĕri vivunt;
Præsertim quibus nec quæstus est, nec dĭdĭcēre artem ullam. PLAUT.
—"Those who are poor live wretchedly in every way; especially those who have no calling and have learned no pursuit."

Omnĭbus nobis ut res dant sese, ita magni atque humĭles sumus. TER.—"Just as matters befall us, so are we all elated or depressed."

Omnis ars imitātio est natūræ. SEN.—"All art is an imitation of nature."

Omnis commŏdĭtas sua fert incommŏda secum.—"Every convenience has its own inconveniences."

Omnis doctrīnæ ac scientiæ thesaurus altissĭmus.—"A most copious repository of every kind of learning and science."

Omnis dolor aut est vehĕmens, aut levis; si levis, facĭlè fertur, si vehĕmens, certè brevis futūrus est. CIC.—"All pain is either severe or moderate; if moderate it will be easily endured; if severe it will at least be short-lived."

——*Omnis enim res,*
Virtus, fama, decus, divīna humānăque, pulchris
Divitiis parent.—— HOR.

—"For all things divine and human, virtue, fame, and honour, obey the influence of alluring wealth." Said in reference to the venality of Rome.

Omnis fama a domestĭcis emānat. *Prov.*—"All fame emanates from our servants." They are the first to teach the world how to estimate us, according to the character which we receive from them. But in spite of this it is a saying that "No man is a hero to his valet."

Omnis pœna corporālis, quamvis mĭnĭma, major est omni pœnâ pecuniāriâ, quamvis maxĭmâ. *Law Max.*—"The very slightest corporal punishment falls more heavily than the most weighty pecuniary penalty." Because there is a disgrace attached to the one which does not result from the other.

Omnium consensu capax impĕrii, nisi imperâsset. TACIT—"By the consent of all, fit to govern had he never ruled." Said of the Emperor Galba, who did not answer the expectations which had been previously formed of him.

Omnium horārum homo. QUINTILL.—"A man ready at all hours."

Omnium pestium pestilentissĭma est superstitio.—"Of all pests the greatest pest is superstition."

Omnium quæ dixĕrat fĕcĕratque, arte quâdam ostentātor. TACIT.—"One who set off everything that he said and did with a certain skill." Said of Licinius Mucianus, the consul.

Omnium rerum ex quibus ălĭquid acquīrĭtur, nihil est agricultūrâ mĕlius, nihil ubĕrius, nihil hŏmĭne lībĕro dignius. CIC. —"Of all the pursuits by which anything is acquired, there is nothing preferable to agriculture, nothing more productive, nothing more worthy the attention of a man of liberal education."

——*Omnium rerum, heus! vicissitūdo.* TER.—"Hark you! there are changes in all things."

Omnium rerum principia parva sunt. CIC.—"The beginnings of all things are small."

Omnium rerum quarum usus est potest esse abūsus, virtūte solâ exceptâ. *Law Max.*—"Of all things of which there is a use there may be an abuse, virtue alone excepted."

Omnium rerum vicissitūdo est. TER.—"Everything is liable to change."

Onus probandi.—"The burden of proving." A responsibility which by our law lies on the person making the charge.

Onus segni impōne asello.—"Lay the burden on the slow-paced ass."

Opem ferre in tempŏre.—"To bring aid in time." To show oneself a friend in need.

Opĕræ prĕtium est.—"'Tis worth your while." It is worth attending to.

——*Opĕre in longo fas est obrēpĕre somnum.* HOR.—"In a long work we must expect sleep to steal upon us." We must naturally expect mistakes in a work of any magnitude. See *Quandoque bonus*, &c.

Operōsè nihil agunt. SEN.—"They take great pains in doing nothing." They make much ado about nothing.

Opes invīsæ mĕrĭto sunt forti viro,
Quia dives arca veram laudem intercĭpit. PHÆD.
—"Riches are deservedly despised by a man of worth, because a well-stored chest intercepts genuine praise."

Opiniōnum commenta delet dies, natūræ judicia confirmat. CIC. —"Time effaces speculative opinions, but confirms the judgments of nature." Speculative opinions are but short-lived, while theories founded upon nature are immutably upheld.

——*Opīnor,*

Hæc res et jungit, junctos et servat, amicos.
At nos virtūtes ipsas invertĭmus, atque
Sincērum cŭpĭmus vas incrustāre.—— Hor.
—"This method, in my opinion, both unites friends, and keeps them so united. But we invert the very virtues themselves, and are desirous of soiling the untainted vessel." Horace alludes to the practice of not making allowance for the failings of our friends.

Oportet testūdĭnis carnes aut ĕdĕre aut non ĕdĕre. Prov.—"You must either eat the flesh of turtle, or not eat it." Either do a thing well or don't do it at all. "There is no mincing the matter." The flesh of the turtle eaten sparingly was said to be hard of digestion, but, if taken plentifully, to be extremely wholesome.

Opprobrium medicōrum.—"The disgrace of the physicians." Any incurable disorder.

Optandum est ut ii qui præsunt reipublĭcæ legum simĭles sint, quæ ad puniendum non iracundiâ, sed æquitāte ducuntur. Cic.—"It were to be wished that they who are set over the republic should be like the laws, which, in inflicting punishment, are influenced not by anger but by justice."

Optat ephippia bos, piger optat arāre caballus. Hor.—"The ox wishes for the horse's trappings, the lazy nag wishes to plough." Few are content with the station in which Providence has placed them.

Optĭma quæque dies mĭsĕris mortālĭbus ævi
Prima fugit; subeunt morbi tristisque senectus,
Et labor; et duræ rapit inclĕmentia mortis. Virg.
—"Each best day of life flies fast away for wretched mortals; diseases succeed, and morose old age, and pain; and the inclemency of inexorable death tears us away."

Optĭmi consiliārii mortui. Prov.—"The best counsellors are the dead."

Optĭmum cibi condimentum fames, sitis potus.—"The best seasoning for food is hunger, for drink, thirst." An aphorism of Socrates quoted by Cicero.

Optĭmum custōdem ovium quem dicam esse lupum!—"What a pretty shepherd a wolf would make!"

Optĭmum ĕlĭge, suave et facĭle illud făciet consuetūdo.—"Choose what is best; habit will soon render it agreeable and easy." A saying of Pythagoras, translated from Plutarch by Lord Bacon.

Optĭmum est aliēnā frui insāniā. CATO.—"It is the best plan to profit by the folly of others."

Optĭmum est non nasci. *Prov.*—"Better not to be born." We should then escape "the thousand ills that flesh is heir to."

Optĭmum obsonium labor. *Prov.*—"Labour is the best food," or as we say, "Hunger is the best sauce."

Optĭmus ille fuit vindex, lædentia pectus
Vincŭla qui rŭpit, dēdoluitque semel. OVID.
—"He is the best asserter of his liberties who bursts the chain that galls his breast, and at the same moment ceases to grieve."

——*Opum furiāta cupīdo.* OVID.—"An ungovernable passion for wealth."

Opus opĭficem probat. *Prov.*—"The work proves the workman."

Orandum est ut sit mens sana in corpŏre sano. JUV.—"We should pray for a healthy mind in a healthy body."

Orāte pro ănĭmā.—"Pray for the soul of." The ordinary commencement of mediæval epitaphs.

Orationis summa virtus est perspicuitas. QUINT.—"The greatest excellency of oratory is perspicuity."

Orātor imprŏbus leges subvertit.—"An evil-minded orator subverts the laws." He uses the arts of persuasion to a bad purpose, by prevailing on others to disregard the laws.

Orci habet găleam. *Prov.*—"He has the helmet of Pluto." Said of persons who incite others to crime without appearing themselves to be accomplices. The helmet of Pluto was said to render the wearer invisible.

——*Ordĭne gentis*
Mores, et studia, et popŭlos, et prælia dicam. VIRG.
—"I will in their proper order relate the manners and pursuits, the tribes and the battles of the race."

Ore tenus. *Law Term.*—"From the mouth." By word of mouth. His testimony was *ore tenus*, "by parole," in contradistinction to written evidence.

Ornamentum figurārum ad elegantiam verbōrum adjungĕre. CIC.—"To unite figurative embellishment with elegance of language."

Os dignum æterno nĭtĭdum quod fulgeat auro,

Si mallet laudāre Deum ; cui sordĭda monstra
Prætŭlit, et liquĭdam temerāvit crīmĭne vocem. PRUD.
—"Features so beauteous that they had been worthy to shine in everlasting gold, if he had chosen rather to praise our God; to whom he preferred foul monsters, and defiled his fluent language with obscenity."

Os hebes est, pŏsĭtæque movent fastĭdia mensæ ;
Et queror, invīsi cum venit hora cibi. OVID.
—"My appetite is blunted, food set before me creates loathing; and I complain when the hour comes for my hated repast."

Os hŏmĭni sublīme dedit cœlumque tuēri. OVID.—"To man [God] gave a countenance to look on high and to behold the heavens."

Oscitante uno deinde oscĭtat et alter.—"When one yawns, another yawns too." A saying of the middle ages, the truth of which most persons know by experience.

——*Ostrōque insignis et auro*
Stat sŏnĭpes, ac fræna ferox spumantia mandit. VIRG.
—"Splendidly caparisoned in purple and gold, her courser stands, and impatient champs the froth-covered bit." A description of Dido's steed.

Otia corpus alunt, ănĭmus quoque pascĭtur illis ;
Immŏdĭcus contrà carpit utrumque labor. OVID.
—"Relaxation strengthens the body and invigorates the mind; while immoderate fatigue exhausts both."

Otia secūris invidiōsa nocent.—"Idleness, so much envied, injures those who are self-confident."

Otia si tollas, periēre Cupīdĭnis arcus,
Contemptæque jacent et sine luce faces. OVID.
—"Take away the temptations of idleness, and Cupid's bow is useless: his torches lie neglected and without their light." The mind that is immersed in business has no time to think of love. See *Quæritis Ægisthus*, &c.

Otiōsa sedūlĭtas.—"Idle industry." Laborious trifling.

Otiōsis nullus adsistit Deus. Prov.—"No deity assists the idle." "Help yourself, and God will help you."

Otiōsus ănĭmus nescit quid volet.—"The unemployed mind knows not what it wants."

Otium cum dignitāte.—"Leisure with dignity." Applied to a man who is living in the retirement earned by his worth.

Otium divos rogat in patenti
Prensus Ægæo, simul atra nubes
Condĭdit lunam, neque certa fulgent
Sīdĕra nautis. HOR.
—"He that is overtaken in the wide Ægean, when black clouds have obscured the moon and not a star shines with its steady light for mariners, supplicates the gods for repose."

Otium multa mala adolescentes docet.—"Idleness teaches the young many vices."

Otium naufrăgium castitātis.—"Idleness is the shipwreck of chastity." See *Quæritis Ægisthus*, &c.

Otium omnia vitia parit.—"Idleness produces every vice." "Idleness is the mother of all evil."

Otium sine dignitāte.—"Leisure without dignity." A vulgar arrogant man in retirement.

Otium sine litĕris mors est, et hŏmĭnis vivi sepultūra. SEN. —"Leisure without literary resources is death, and the entombment of a man alive."

Otium umbrātĭle.—"Ease in retirement," or, "in the shade."

Ovem lupo committĕre. *Prov.*—"To intrust the sheep to the wolf." To leave unprotected persons to the mercy of the rapacious.

P.

P. D. for ***Post Diluvium.***—"After the flood."

P. M. for ***Post Meridiem.***—"After mid-day"—"afternoon."

P. S. for ***Post Scriptum.***—"After-written"—a postscript.

Pābŭlum Acherontis. PLAUT.—"Food for Acheron." An old man at the very verge of the grave. Acheron was a river, according to Grecian mythology, in the infernal regions.

Pace tanti viri.—"With the leave of so great a man." Sometimes said ironically.

Pacem hŏmĭnĭbus habe, bellum cum vitiis.—"Be at peace with men, at war with vices."

Pacta conventa.—"Conditions agreed upon." A diplomatic phrase used to describe terms that have been agreed on between two powers.

Palam mutīre plebeio piācŭlum est.—"It is a dangerous thing for a man of humble birth to mutter in public." Quoted by Phædrus from the Telephus of Ennius.

Palindromicus, or *Sotadicus versus.*—See *Roma tibi*, &c.

Palinōdiam cănĕre.—"To make one's recantation." "To eat one's words." The poet Stesichorus, having in an ode censured Helen, was deprived of his sight by the gods; upon which, in another ode which he called his *Palinodia*, he made his recantation by extolling her as highly as he had censured her before; whereupon he regained his sight.

Pallĭda mors æquo pulsat pede paupĕrum tabernas,
Regumque turres. O beāte Sexti,
Vitæ summa brevis spem nos vetat inchoāre longam. HOR.

—"Pale death with impartial foot knocks at the cottages of the poor, and the palaces of kings. O happy Sextius! the short sum total of life forbids us to form remote expectations."

Pallor in ore sedet; măcies in corpŏre toto:
Nusquam recta ăcies: livent rubīgĭne dentes:
Pectŏra felle virent: lingua est suffūsa venēno:
Risus abest.—— OVID.

—"Paleness rests upon her countenance, and leanness in all her body; she never looks direct on you; her teeth are black with rust; her breast is green with gall; her tongue is dripping with venom; smiles there are none." A beautiful description of Envy.

Palmam qui mĕruit ferat.—"Let him who has deserved the palm bear it." The motto assigned to Nelson. It is derived from Dr. Jortin's *Lusus Poetici.*

Par bene comparātum.—"A pair well matched."

Par negŏtiis neque supra. TACIT.—"Equal to, but not above, his business." Said of a person whose talents fit him exactly for his situation.

Par nōbĭle fratrum. HOR.—"A noble pair of brothers." Used ironically, to denote two associates well suited to each other.

Par pari rĕfĕro.—"I return like for like." I give "tit for tat,"—"a rowland for an oliver."

Parasītĭcam cœnam quærit.—"He seeks the meal of a parasite." In the character of a sponger.

Parce, puer, stĭmŭlis, et fortius ūtĕre loris. OVID.—"Boy, spare the whip, and firmly grasp the reins."

Parcendum est ănĭmo miserābĭle vulnus habenti. OVID.—"We must make allowance for the mind that bears the wound of sorrow."

Parcĕre persōnis, dicĕre de vitiis. MART.—"To spare persons, to speak of vices." Advice to a satirist.

Parcĕre subjectis, et debellāre superbos. VIRG.—"To spare the conquered, and to pull down the haughty." This maxim was adopted by France in the time of the first Revolution.

Parcimōnia est scientia vitandi sumptus supervacuos, aut ars re familiāri moderātè utendi. SEN.—"Frugality is the science of avoiding superfluous expenses, or the art of using our means with moderation."

——*Parcit*
Cognātis măcŭlis sĭmĭlis fera.—— JUV.
—"The beast of like kind will spare those of kindred spots."

Parcĭte paucōrum diffundĕre crimen in omnes. OVID.—"Forbear to lay the culpability of the few upon the many."

Parcus Deōrum cultor, et infrĕquens,
Insanientis dum sapientiæ
Consultus erro; nunc retrorsum
Vela dare, atque iterāre cursus
Cogor relictos.—— HOR.
—"A thrifty and irregular worshipper of the gods, while I professed the errors of a senseless philosophy, I am now obliged to set sail back again, and to renew the course that I had deserted." The confession made by Horace on abandoning the tenets of the Epicureans.

Pares cum păribus (ut est in vĕtĕri proverbio) facillĭme congregantur. CIC.—"To use the old proverb, 'Like most readily associates with like.'" "Birds of a feather," &c.

Pari passu.—"With equal steps." Neck and neck.

Pari ratiōne.—"By similar reasoning." For a like cause.

Părĭbus sententiis reus absolvĭtur. COKE.—"Where the opinions are equally divided the accused is acquitted."

Părĭtur pax bello. CORN. NEP.—"Peace is the result of war." Peace is also insured by showing that we are prepared for war.

Pars adaperta fuit, pars altĕra clausa fenestræ:
Quale ferè sylvæ lumen habēre solent. Ovid.
—"A part of the window was thrown open; the other part shut; the light was just such as the woods are wont to have."

Pars bĕnĕfĭcii est quod pĕtĭtur si bellè neges. Syr.—"To refuse graciously, is half to grant a favour."

Pars bĕnĕficii est quod pĕtĭtur si citò neges. Syr.—"To refuse quickly, is half to grant a favour."

Pars hŏmĭnum vitiis gaudet constanter, et urget
Propŏsĭtum; pars multa natat, modo recta capessens,
Interdum pravis obnoxia.—— Hor.
—"A portion of mankind constantly glory in their vices, and pursue their purpose; a great portion fluctuate, sometimes practising what is right, sometimes giving way to what is wrong."

——*Pars mĭnĭma est ipsa puella sui.* Ovid.—"The girl herself is the least valuable part of herself." Her portion is better worth having than herself.

Pars mĭnĭma sui.—"The smallest remains of himself," or "itself." "The wreck of his former self."

Pars pede, pars ĕtiam cĕlĕri decurrĭte cymbâ. Ovid.—"Some of you go on foot, some run down the stream in the rapid skiff." An appropriate address to the spectators of a boat-race.

Pars sanitătis velle sanāri fuit. Sen.—"It is a part of the cure to wish to be cured."

Pars tui mĕlior immortālis est. Sen.—"Your better part is immortal."

Parthis mendăcior. Hor.—"More lying than the Parthians." The Parthians were looked upon by the Romans as peculiarly faithless, and in that respect occupied the same place in their estimation that the Carthaginians had formerly done.

Partĭbus locāre.—"To let land, going halves in the crop," instead of rent.

Partĭceps crĭmĭnis.—"A partaker in the crime." An accessory either before or after the fact.

Partŭriunt montes, nascĕtur rĭdĭcŭlus mus. Hor.—"The mountains are in labour, a silly mouse will be produced." An application of the fable of the Mountain in Labour, to an author whose pompous pretences end in little or nothing.

Parva leves capiunt ănĭmos.—— Ovid.—"Trifles captivate weak minds." "Little things please little minds."

——*Parvis compōnĕre magna.*—— Virg.—"To compare great things with small."

Parvŭla, pūmĭlio, χαριτων μια, tota, merum sal. Lucr.—"A little, tiny, pretty, witty, charming, darling she."

Parvŭla scintilla sæpe magnum suscitāvit incendium.—"A tiny spark has often kindled a great conflagration."

Parvum addas parvo, magnus acervus erit.—"Add little to little, and there will be a large heap." See *De multis*, &c., and *Multi si*, &c.

Parvum, non parvæ amicitiæ, pignus.—"A little pledge of no little friendship." A motto for a gift to a friend.

Parvum parva decent.—— Hor.—"Small things best suit the small."

Pascitur in vivis livor, post fata quiescit;
Tunc suus, ex mĕrito, quemque tuĕtur honos. Ovid.
—"Envy feeds upon the living, after death it is at rest; then a man's deserved honours protect him." The world seldom does justice to living merit.

Passĭbus ambiguis Fortūna volūbĭlis errat,
Et manet in nullo certa tenaxque loco. Ovid.
—"Fleeting fortune wanders with doubting steps, remaining in no one place for certain and to be relied upon."

Pater familias.—"The father of a family."

——*Pater ipse colendi*
Haud făcĭlem esse viam vŏluit, primusque per artem
Movit agros, curis acuens mortālia corda. Virg.
—"The Father himself did not ordain the ways of tillage to be easy; he first, by art, aroused the soil, whetting the skill of mortals by care."

Pater noster.—"Our Father." The Lord's Prayer, from its commencing words, is so called.

Pater patriæ.—"The father of his country."

Pati necesse est multa mortālem mala. Nævius.—"Man must of necessity suffer many evils." "Man is born to trouble as sparks fly upwards." *Job* v. 7.

——*Pati*
Nos oportet quod ille făciat cujus potestas plus potest. Plaut.

—"It befits us to submit to what he does whose power is the stronger."

Patientia læsa fit furor.—"Patience abused becomes fury." Patience must not be trespassed upon too far.

Patientia—quæ pars magna justitiæ ĕst. PLINY *the Younger.* —"Patience, which is a great part of justice."

——*Patĭtur pœnas peccandi sola voluntas.* JUV.—"The bare wish to sin incurs the penalty." See *Scelus intra,* &c.

Patriâ quis exul
Se quoque fugit? HOR.
—"Who, though flying from his country, can fly from himself?"

Patriæ fumus igne aliēno luculentior. Prov.—"The smoke of our own country is brighter than the fire of another." Though ever so homely, home is home still. Ulysses felt this in his wanderings, when he longed to behold the smoke of his native land.

——*Patriæ pietātis imāgo.* VIRG.—"The image of filial affection."

——*Patriæque impendĕre vitam,*
Nec sibi, sed toti gĕnĭtum se crēdĕre mundo. LUCAN.
—"To devote his life to his country, and to think that he was born, not for himself alone, but for all mankind." Said of Cato of Utica. The principles of a benefactor of mankind.

Patrimōnium non comēsum sed devorātum. CIC.—"An inheritance, not merely eaten, but devoured."

Patris est filius. Prov.—"He is his father's son." "He is a chip of the old block."

Pauca abundè mediocrĭbus sufficiunt.—"A few things suffice abundantly for the moderate."

Pauca verba.—"Few words.

Pauci ex multis sunt amīci hŏmĭni qui certi sient. PLAUT. —"Out of many, there are but few friends on whom a man can depend."

Pauci vident morbum suum, omnes amant. Prov.—"Few see their own failings, all are in love with them."

Paucis cārior est fides quam pecūnia. SALL.—"To few is good faith more valuable than money." The author is speaking of the declining years of the Roman republic.

Paucis temĕrĭtas est bono, multis malo. PHÆD.—"Rashness brings luck to a few, misfortune to most."

Paulum sepultæ distat inertiæ
Celāta virtus.—— HOR.
—"Valour unsung is little better than cowardice in the grave." See *De non apparentibus*, &c.

Pauper enim non est cui rerum suppĕtit usus.
Si ventri bene, si lătĕri pĕdĭbusque tuis, nil
Divĭtiæ pŏtĕrunt rēgāles addĕre majus. HOR.
—"For that man is not poor who is in the enjoyment of the necessaries of life. If it is well with your stomach, your body, and your feet, regal wealth can add no more."

Pauper eris semper, si pauper es, Æmiliāne ;
Dantur opes nullis nunc nisi dīvĭtibus. MART.
—"You will always be poor, if you are poor now, Æmilianus; riches are given now-a-days to none but the wealthy."

Pauper sum, făteor, pătior ; quod Di dant fero. PLAUT.—"I am poor, I confess; I put up with it. What the gods send I endure."

Paupĕris est numerāre pecus. OVID.—"It is for a poor man to count his flock."

Paupertas fŭgĭtur, totōque arcessĭtur orbe. LUCAN.—"Poverty is shunned and persecuted throughout the world."

——*Pavor est utrīque molestus.* HOR.—"Fear is troublesome on either side."

Pavōre carent qui nihil commīsĕrunt ; at pœnam semper ob ŏcŭlos versāri putant qui peccārunt.—"Those are free from fear who have done no wrong; but those who have sinned have always the dread of punishment before their eyes."

Pax in bello.—"Peace in war." A war waged without vigour. Dr. Johnson remarks that "the king who makes war on his enemies tenderly, distresses his subjects most cruelly."

Pax potior bello.—"Peace is preferable to war."

Pax vobiscum.—"Peace be with you." Used in the ritual of the Roman Church.

——*Peccāre docentes*
Fallax histŏrias movet. HOR.
—"The deceiver quotes stories that afford precedents for sinning."

Peccāvi.—"I have sinned." To "make a man cry *peccavi*," to make him acknowledge his error.

——*Pectus præceptis format amīcis.* Hor.—"He influences the mind by the precepts of a friend."

Pecūniæ fugienda cupĭdĭtas: nihil est tam angusti ănĭmi tamque parvi quam amāre divitias. Cic.—"We should avoid the love of money: nothing so much shows a little and narrow mind as the love of riches."

Pecūniæ obēdiunt omnia. — "All things are obedient to money."

Pecūniam in loco neglĭgĕre interdum maxĭmum est lucrum. Ter.—"To despise money on proper occasions is sometimes the greatest gain."

Pecūniam perdidisti; fortasse illa te perdĕret manens.—"You have lost your money; perhaps, if you had kept it, it would have lost you."

——*Pĕdĭbus timor addĭdit alas.* Virg.—"Fear added wings to his feet."

——*Pendent ŏpĕra interrupta.*—— Virg.—"The progress of the works remains interrupted."

Pendente lite.—"The strife still pending." The trial not being concluded.

——*Pene gemelli*
Fraternis ănĭmis.—— Hor.
—"Almost twins in the strong resemblance of their dispositions."

—— *Pĕnĭtus toto divīsos orbe Britannos.* Virg.—"The Britons, a race almost severed from the rest of the world." The people of this island, as spoken of a few years after the invasion by Cæsar.

Pennas incīdĕre ălĭcui. *Prov.*—"To clip a person's wings;" or, as we say, "To bring him down a peg."

Per accĭdens.—"Through accident." A term used to denote an effect not following from the nature of the thing, but from some extrinsic circumstance. It is opposed to *per se*, "of itself"—thus, fire burns *per se*, heated iron *per accidens*.

Per annum.—"By the year." Yearly.

Per căpĭta. *Law Phrase.*—"By the head." In contradistinction to *Per stirpes*, which see.

Per centum.—"By the hundred."

Per contra.—"On the other side." By way of equivalent.

Per diem.—"By the day."

Per fas et nefas.—"By right or by wrong." He pursued his object *per fas et nefas*, i. e. he left no means untried, disregarding all consequences, and troubled by no scruples.

Per incūriam.—"Through carelessness."

——*Per multas ădĭtum sibi sæpe figūras*
Repĕrit.—— OVID.
—"He often gains admission under various disguises."

Per ōbĭtum.—"Through the death of"——

Per quod servitium amīsit. Law Term.—"By which he lost his, or her, services." Words used to describe the injury sustained by the plaintiff by reason of the seduction of his daughter.

Per risum multum possis cognoscĕre stultum.—"By much laughter you may distinguish a fool." A mediæval proverb.

Per saltum.—"By a leap." A man attains high rank *per saltum*, i. e. passing over the heads of others.

Per scĕlĕra semper scĕlĕrĭbus certum est iter. SEN.—"The sure way to wickedness is always through wickedness." One crime ever leads to another.

Per se.—"By itself," or, "For its own sake." "No man likes mustard *per se.*" *Johnson.* See *Per accidens.*

Per stirpes. Law Phrase.—"According to the original stock." See *Per capita.*

Per tantum terræ, tot aquas, vix crēdĕre possim
Indĭcium studii transiluisse mei. OVID.
—"Through such vast tracts of land, across so many seas, I could hardly have believed that any evidence of my pursuits could make its way."

Per testes.—"By witnesses."

Per varios casus, per tot discrīmĭna rerum. VIRG.—"Through various hazards, through so many changes in our fortunes." "Chances and changes."

——*Perăgit tranquilla potestas*
Quod violenta nequit, mandātăque fortius urget
Imperiōsa quies.—— CLAUD.
—"Power exercised with moderation can effect what by violence it could never have accomplished; and calmness enforces, with more energy, imperial mandates."

Peras impŏsuit Jupĭter nobis duas:

Propriis replĕtam vitiis post tergum dedit;
Aliēnis ante pectus suspendit gravem. PHÆD.
—"Jupiter has loaded us with a couple of wallets: the one, filled with our own vices, he has placed at our backs; the other, heavy with those of others, he has hung before." See *Aliena vitia*, &c.

Percunctāre à perītis. CIC.—"Make inquiries of persons who are skilled." Seek information from the learned.

Percunctatōrem fugĭto, nam garrŭlus idem est;
Nec rĕtĭnent pătŭlæ commissa fidēlĭter aures. HOR.
—"Avoid an inquisitive person, for he is a babbler; nor do ears which are always open faithfully retain what is intrusted to their keeping."

Perdĭdit arma, locum virtūtis dēsĕruit, qui
Semper in augendâ festīnat et obruitur re. HOR.
—"He has lost his arms, and deserted the cause of virtue, who is ever eager and engrossed in increasing his wealth."

Perdiffĭcĭle est, cum præstāre cætĕris concupiĕris, servāre æquitātem. CIC.—"It is very difficult to observe justice when you are striving to surpass others."

Perdis, et in damno gratia nulla tuo. OVID.—"You lose, and you get no thanks for your loss."

Perdĭtio tua ex te.—"Your ruin is owing to yourself."

Perdĭtur hæc inter mĭsĕro lux, non sine votis. HOR.—"With all this, the day is wasted to unhappy me, not without many regrets." The poet censures the trifles which consume the day in town.

Pĕreant amīci, dum unà inimīci intercĭdant. CIC.—"Let our friends perish, provided our enemies fall with them." This was both a Greek and a Roman proverb; quoted as the sentiment of a calculating ungenerous man.

Pĕreant illi qui ante nos nostra dixĕrunt. DONATUS.—"Perish they who have said our good things before us." The exclamation of a man who does not like to be forestalled in his good sayings. See *Nil dictum*, &c.

Pĕreunt et imputantur. MART.—"They perish, and are placed to our account." Said with reference to the hours. These words form an inscription on a clock at Exeter Cathedral, as also in the Temple, London.

Perfer; et invītos currĕre coge pedes. OVID.—"Persist, and compel your feet to hasten, however unwillingly."

Perfer et obdūra; dolor hic tibi prōdĕrit olim. OVID.—"Have patience and endure it; this grief will one day avail you."

Perfer et obdūra; multo graviōra tulisti. OVID.—"Have patience and endure it; you have endured much greater misfortunes than these."

Perfĭda, sed quamvis perfĭda, cara tamen. TIBULL.—"Perfidious, but, though thus perfidious, dear."

Perfĭde! sed duris gĕnuit te cautĭbus horrens
Caucăsus, Hyrcānæque admōrunt ubĕra tigres. VIRG.
—"Perfidious man! Caucasus hath borne thee among its flinty rocks, and Hyrcanian tigers have given thee suck." Dido's reproaches uttered against Æneas, when he resisted her attempts to dissuade him from leaving Carthage.

——*Pergis pugnantia secum*
Frontibus adversis compōnĕre.—— HOR.
—"You are trying to reconcile things which are opposite in their natures."

Pergo ad ălios; vĕnio ad ălios; deinde ad ălios;
Una res.—— PLAUT.
—"I go to others, I come to others, and then to others again, 'tis all one."

Perībo, si non fĕcĕro; si faxo, vapulāvĕro. PLAUT.—"I shall perish if I do it not—if I do it I shall get a drubbing." The horns of a dilemma.

Periculōsæ plenum opus ăleæ. HOR.—"A work full of dangerous hazard." As precarious as the faithless dice.

Periculōsior casus ab alto. *Prov.*—"A fall from on high is most dangerous." The higher the station the greater the fall.

Periculōsum est crēdĕre et non crēdĕre;
Ergo exploranda est verĭtas, multum prius
Quam stulta pravè jūdĭcet sententia. PHÆD.
—"It is dangerous alike to believe or to disbelieve; therefore we ought to examine strictly into the truth of a matter, rather than suffer an erroneous impression to pervert our judgment."

Perīcŭlum ex ăliis făcĭto, tibi quod ex usu siet. TER.—"Take warning from others of what may be to your own advantage."

Perière mores, jus, decus, piĕtas, fides,
Et, qui redīre nescit cum perit, pudor. SEN.
—"Morals, justice, honour, piety, good faith, have perished; that sense too of shame, which, once destroyed, can never be restored."

——*Periĕrunt tempŏra longi*
Servitii.—— JUV.
—"The fruits of a prolonged servitude are now lost."

Periissem nisi periissem.—"If I had not undergone it, I had been undone." A play on the meanings of the verb *pereo.*

Perit quod facis ingrāto. Prov.—"What you do for an ungrateful man is thrown away."

Peritūræ parcĭte chartæ.—"Spare the paper which is doomed to perish." An appeal to the kind feeling of the reader, by the author of a work of a light and ephemeral nature. Adapted from Juvenal.

——*Perjūria ridet amantum.* OVID.—"He laughs at the perjuries of lovers." Ovid says this of Jupiter, who calls to mind his own intrigues.

Perjūrii pœna divīna exĭtium, humāna dēdĕcus.—"Perdition is the punishment of perjury in heaven, on earth disgrace." This was one of the laws of the "*Twelve Tables,*" at Rome.

Permissu superiōrum.—"With the permission of the superior authorities."

Permitte divis cætĕra. HOR.—"Leave the rest to the gods." Do your duty, and leave the rest to Providence.

Permittes ipsis expendĕre numĭnĭbus quid
Convĕniat nobis, rebusque sit ūtĭle nostris:—
Cārĭor est illis homo quam sibi.—— JUV.
—"You will allow the deities themselves to determine what may be expedient for us, and suitable to our circumstances. Man is dearer to them than to himself."

Perpĕtuo risu pulmōnem agitāre solēbat. JUV.—"He used to shake his sides with an everlasting laugh."

——*Perpĕtuus nulli datur usus, et hæres*
Hærēdem altĕrius, velut unda supervĕnit undam. HOR.
—"Perpetual possession is allowed to none, and heir succeeds another's heir, as wave follows wave."

Perque dies plăcĭdos hiberno tempŏre septem
Incŭbat Halcyŏne pendentĭbus æquŏre nidis;

Tum via tuta maris, ventos custōdit et arcet
Æŏlus egressu.—— OVID.
—"And during seven calm days, in the winter season, does Halcyone brood upon her nest that floats on the sea; then the passage of the deep is safe, and Æolus shuts in and restrains the winds." The alcedo, halcyon, or king-fisher, was supposed by the ancients to incubate only seven days, and those in the depth of winter; during which period the mariner might sail in security. Hence the expression "Halcyon days," a term employed to denote a season of peace and happiness.

Persæpe ĕvĕnit ut utilitas cum honestāte certat. CIC.—"It often happens that self-interest has to struggle with honesty."

Persĕquĭtur scelus ille suum.—— OVID.—"He perseveres in his wicked design."

Persōnæ mutæ.—"Mute" or "dumb characters."

Pertūrbabantur Constantinŏpŏlitāni
Innumerabĭlibus solicitudĭnĭbus.
—"The Constantinopolitans were alarmed with cares innumerable." Cambridge, it is said, proposed the first line, and challenged Oxford to cap it, which it did with the second, at the same time pointing out the false quantity in *li*, which is properly long. The same story is told of Eton and Winchester, and Oxford is sometimes spoken of as the challenger. The syllable *no*, strictly speaking, ought to be short.

Pessĭmum genus inimicōrum laudantes. TACIT.—"Flatterers are the worst kind of enemies."

Pĕtĕre honōres per flagĭtia, more fit. PLAUT.—"To seek honours by base acts, is the habit of the age."

——*Petĭte hinc, juvĕnesque, senesque,*
Finem ănĭmo certum, mĭsĕrisque viătĭca canis. PERS.
—"From this source seek ye, young and old, a definite object for your mind, and a provision for your wretched gray hairs."

Petitio ad misericordiam.—"An appeal to compassion."

Petĭtio princĭpii.—"A begging of the question."

Pharmăca das ægrōto, aurum tibi porrĭgit æger;
Tu morbum curas illĭus, ille tuum. MART.
—"You give medicine to the sick man, the patient hands

you your fee; you cure his complaint, he yours." Lines aptly addressed to a poor physician.

Philosŏphia stemma non inspĭcit, Platŏnem non accĭpit nobĭlem philosŏphia, sed fecit. SEN.—"Philosophy does not regard pedigree, she did not find Plato noble, but she made him so."

Pia fraus.—"A pious fraud." Deceit practised, for instance, to save a life that is to be sacrificed illegally, is a *pia fraus*. See *Splendide mendax*.

——*Pictŏrĭbus atque poĕtis*
Quidlĭbet audendi semper fuit æqua potestas. HOR.
—"The power to dare everything always belonged equally to the painter and the poet." Boldness of invention is equally the characteristic of the pictorial and the poetical art.

Piĕtas fundamentum est omnium virtūtum. CIC.—"Piety is the foundation of all virtues."

Pietāte ac religiōne, atque hâc unâ sapientiâ, quod Deōrum immortālium numĭne omnia regi gubernārīque perspexĭmus, omnes gentes natiōnesque superāvĭmus. CIC.—"By piety and religion, and this, the only true wisdom, a conviction that all things are regulated and governed by the providence of the immortal gods, have we [Romans] subdued all races and nations."

Pietāte adversus Deum sublātâ, fides etiam et sociĕtas humāni gĕnĕris tollĭtur. CIC.—"Piety to God once removed, all faith and social intercourse among men is at an end."

——*Pietāte gravem, ac mĕrĭtis, si forte virum quem*
Conspexêre, silent, arrectisque aurĭbus astant. VIRG.
—"If they [the populace] perceive a man distinguished for piety and virtue, they are silent, and listen with attentive ear."

——*Piger scribendi ferre labōrem,*
Scribendi recte; nam, ut multum, nil moror.—— HOR.
—"Too lazy to endure the toil of writing well; for as to the quantity, that is not worth speaking of." Said of Lucilius, but applicable to that class of careless writers who will not take the trouble of correcting their works.

Pignŏra jam nostri nulla pudōris habes. OVID.—"Now hast thou no pledges of our disgrace."

Pingĕre cum glădio. *Prov.*—"To paint with a sword over

one's head." To do that which requires thought and retirement in the midst of confusion and danger.

Pinguis item quæ sit tellus, hoc dēnĭque pacto
Discĭmus; haud unquam manĭbus jactāta fatiscit,
Sed picis in morem ad dĭgĭtos lentescit habendo. VIRG.
—"We may learn what soil is rich in this manner; it never crumbles when pressed in the hand, but adheres to the fingers like pitch on being handled." Pliny disputes this.

Pinguis venter non gignit sensum tenuem. *Prov.*—"A fat paunch does not produce fine sense." Translated by St. Jerome from the Greek.

Pirāta est hostis humāni gĕnĕris. COKE.—"A pirate is an enemy to all mankind."

Piscātor ictus săpiet. *Prov.*—"The fisherman when stung will be wiser." When wounded by the spines on the fishes in his net, he will learn to handle them with caution.

Piscem natāre doces. *Prov.*—"You are teaching a fish how to swim." You are wasting your time and labour.

Plăceat hŏmĭni quidquid Deo plăcuit. SEN.—"That which is pleasing to God should be pleasing to man." The duty of resignation.

Placet ille meus mihi mendīcus; suus rex regīnæ placet. PLAUT.—"This beggar of mine is pleasing to me; her own king pleases the queen."

Planta genĕti.—"A plant of broom." From this plant, which formed their crest, the Plantagenet family derived its name.

Plausĭbus ex ipsis pŏpŭli, lætōque furōre,
Ingĕnium quodvis incăluisse potest. OVID.
—"At the applauses of the public, and at its transports of joy, every genius may grow warm."

——*Plausu frĕmĭtūque virûm studiisque faventûm*
——*Pulsāti colles clamōre resultant.* VIRG.
—"The shaken hills reëcho with the plaudits, the cries of men, and the cheers of partisans." A description of a boat-race or any other friendly trial of strength.

——*Plausus tunc arte carēbat.* OVID.—"In those days applause was devoid of guile." There was no canvassing for applause.

Plebs venit, ac vĭrĭdes passim disjecta per herbas
Potat, et accumbit cum pare quisque suâ. OVID.

—"The multitude repair thither and carouse, scattered in all quarters upon the green grass; each with his sweetheart is reclining there."

Plena fuit vobis omni concordia vitâ,
Et stetit ad finem longa tenaxque fides. OVID.
—"Throughout life there was a firm attachment between you, and your prolonged and lasting friendship endured to the end."

Plene administrāvit. *Law Phrase.*—"He administered in full."

Plenus inconsideratissĭmæ ac dementissĭmæ temeritātis. CIC. —"Full of the most inconsiderate and most precipitate rashness."

Plenus rimārum sum. TER.—"I am full of outlets." "I am leaky." You must not confide anything to me.

Plerumque gratæ divĭtĭbus vices. HOR.—"Change is generally pleasant to the rich." *Ennui* very often gives a taste for rambling. See *Romæ Tibur*, &c.

——*Plerumque modestus*
Occŭpat obscūri spĕciem, taciturnus acerbi. HOR.
—"The modest man has often the look of the designing one, the silent of the sullen."

Plerumque stulti risum dum captant levem,
Gravi distringunt alios contumēliâ,
Et sibi nocīvum concĭtant perīcŭlum. PHÆD.
—"Fools often, while trying to raise a silly laugh, provoke others by gross affronts, and cause serious danger to themselves."

Plorātur lăcrymis amissa pecūnia veris. JUV.—"The loss of money is lamented with unaffected tears." A loss which, through the pocket, strikes home to the feelings.

Plōravēre suis non respondēre favōrem
Sperātum mĕrĭtis.—— HOR.
—"They lamented that the encouragement they had hoped for was not commensurate with their merits."

Pluma haud intĕrest. PLAUT.—"It matters not one feather."

Plura făciunt hŏmĭnes è consuetūdĭne, quam è ratiōne.—"Men do more things from custom than from reason."

Plura locutūri sŭbĭto sedūcĭmur imbre. OVID.—"About to say more we are separated by a sudden shower."

Plura mala contingunt quam accĭdunt.—"More evils befall

us, than happen to us by accident." i. e. We bring many evils upon ourselves.

Plura sunt quæ nos terrent, quam quæ premunt; et sæpius opiniōne quam re laborāmus. SEN.—"There are more things to alarm than to afflict us, and we suffer much oftener from apprehension than in reality." We are apt to be "more frightened than hurt."

Plures adōrant solem orientem quam occidentem. *Prov.*—"More adore the rising sun than the setting one."

Plures crāpŭla quam glădius. *Prov.*—"Gluttony [kills] more than the sword."

Plūrĭbus intentus minor est ad singŭla sensus.—"The senses, when intent on many objects, can pay the less attention to each individually." So our proverb which warns us not to have "too many irons in the fire."

——*Plūrĭma mortis imāgo.* VIRG.—"Death in full many a form." Hogarth makes this the motto for his "Consultation of Physicians."

——*Plūrima sunt quæ*
Non audent hŏmĭnes pertūsâ dicĕre lænâ. JUV.
—"There are a great many things which men with a tattered garment dare not say."

Plūrĭmum făcĕre, et mĭnĭmum ipso de se loqui. TACIT.—"To do the most, and say the least of himself." The character of a man of energy, no talker but a doer.

Pluris est oculātus testis unus quam aurīti decem. PLAUT.—"One eye-witness is better than ten from hearsay."

Plus aloës quam mellis habet.—"He has in him more aloes than honey." Said of a sarcastic writer.

Plus apud nos vera ratio văleat quam vulgi opīnio. CIC.—"Genuine reason should prevail with us more than public opinion."

Plus dolet quam necesse est, qui ante dolet quam necesse est. SEN.—"He grieves more than is necessary who grieves before it is necessary." It only adds to our miseries to meet troubles half way.

——*Plus est quam vita salusque,*
Quod perit: in totum mundi prosternĭmur ævum. LUCAN.
—"What we lose is more than life and safety; we are laid prostrate even to the latest ages of the world." Prophetically said with reference to the consequences of the battle

of Pharsalia, fought between Cæsar and Pompey, and applicable to any man who forfeits his good name.

——*Plus et enim fati valet hora benigni,*
Quam si nos Vĕnĕris commendet epistŏla Marti. JUV.
—"For one hour of benignant fate is of more avail than a letter of recommendation from Venus herself to Mars." See *Gutta fortunæ*, &c.

Plus exempla quam peccāta nocent. *Prov.*—"The example does more injury than the offence itself."

Plus impĕtûs, majōrem constantiam, penes mĭsĕros. TACIT.—"There is greater energy, and more perseverance, among the wretched." Having less to lose and more to gain they are reckless of consequences.

Plus in amicitiâ valet similitūdo morum quam affinĭtas. CORN. NEP.—"Similarity of manners unites us more strongly in friendship than relationship."

Plus in posse quam in actu.—"More in the possible than in the actual."

——*Plus lædunt, quam juvet una, duæ.* OVID.—"Two can do more harm than one can do good." Said with reference to the enmity of Juno and Pallas against Troy, which was favoured by Venus.

Plus oportet scīre servum quam loqui. PLAUT.—"A servant should know more than he tells."

Plus rătio quam vis cæcæ valēre solet. GALLUS.—"Reason is generally able to effect more than blind force."

Plus salis quam sumptûs. CORN. NEPOS.—"More good taste than expense." A description of a philosophical entertainment.

——*Plus scire satius est, quam loqui,*
Servum hŏmĭnem; ea sapientia est. PLAUT.
—"It is best for a man in servitude to know more than he says: that is true wisdom." See *Plus oportet*, &c.

Plus sonat quam valet. SEN.—"It is more noise than strength, with him." "Great cry and little wool."

Plus vident ŏcŭli quam ŏcŭlus. *Prov.*—"The eyes see more than the eye." Two eyes see better than one.

Plusve minusve.—"More or less."

——*Pœnas garrŭlus ipse dabit.* OVID.—"That blabbing person shall be punished."

Poēta nascĭtur non fit.—"The poet is born a poet, not made so." See *Nascimur poetæ*, &c.

——*Poētĭca surgit*
Tempestas.—— Juv.
—"A storm of poetry is gathering."

Pol me occidistis, amīci,
Non servâstis, ait; cui sic extorta voluptas,
Et demptus per vim mentis gratissĭmus error. Hor.
—"By Pollux, my friends, you have undone, not saved, me; my delight has been torn from me, and a most pleasing delusion of the mind taken by force."

——*Pol meo ănĭmo omnes sapientes*
Suum officium æquum est colĕre, et făcĕre. Plaut.
—"I' faith, in my opinion, it is proper for all prudent persons to observe and to do their duty."

Pŏlypi mentem obtīne. *Prov.*—"Follow the plan of the polypus." Accommodate yourself to the changes of circumstances, and the dispositions of those around you. The polypus was supposed to be able to assume the colour of the rocks to which it adhered, and thus to be able to escape notice.

Poma, ova, atque nuces, si det tibi sordĭda, gustes. A mediæval proverb.—"An apple, an egg, and a nut, you may eat after a slut."

Pompa mortis magis terret quam mors ipsa.—"The array of the death-bed has more terrors than death itself." Quoted by Lord Bacon as from Seneca.

Ponāmus nimios gĕmĭtus; flagrantior æquo
Non debet dolor esse viri, nec vulnĕre major. Juv.
—"Let us dismiss excessive sorrow; a man's grief ought not to be immoderate, nor disproportioned to the wound."

Ponderanda sunt testimōnia, non numĕranda.—"Testimonies are to be weighed, not counted." It is to be considered not how many they are, but from whom they come. The golden rule of criticism.

Pone metum, văleo.—— Ovid.—"Lay aside your fears, I am well."

Pone seram, cŏhĭbe; sed quis custōdiet ipsos
Custōdes? cauta est, et ab illis incĭpit uxor. Juv.
—"Use bolts and restraint; but who is to watch the

watchers themselves? your wife is cunning, and will begin by seducing them." A woman who is inclined to evil, will find modes of evading every restraint.

Pons asinŏrum.—"The asses' bridge." The Fifth Proposition of the 1st book of Euclid is so called; partly from the figure of the diagram, and partly because it presents the first great difficulty to the beginner.

——*Populāres*
Vincentem strĕpĭtus. HOR.
—"Overcoming the clamour of the mob."

——*Popŭlumque falsis dēdŏcet uti*
Vōcĭbus.—— HOR.
—"And he teaches the people how to discredit false rumours."

——*Pŏpŭlus me sībĭlat; at mihi plaudo*
Ipse domi, simul ac nummos contemplor in arcâ. HOR.
—"The people hiss me; but I console myself at home as soon as I gaze upon the money in my chest." The consolation of a miser.

Pŏpŭlus vult dēcĭpi; decipiātur.—"The people wish to be deceived; then let them be deceived." This adage is found in the works of De Thou, but it is probably older than his time. Cardinal Caraffa said of the Parisians, *Quandoquidem populus decipi vult, decipiatur,* "Since these people *will* be deceived, let them be deceived."

Porrecto jŭgŭlo, histŏrias, captīvus ut, audit. HOR.—"With outstretched neck, like some slave, he listens to his tales." Said of a dependant listening to the long stories of his patron.

Portātur lĕvĭter quod portat quisque libenter.—"What a man bears willingly is lightly borne."

Poscentes vărio multum diversa palāto. HOR.—"Requiring with varying taste things widely different from each other." The words of an author on finding how difficult it was to please the various tastes of his readers.

Posse comitātûs. *Law Lat.*—"The power of the county." A levy which the sheriff is authorized to summon, when opposition is made to the king's writ, or the execution of justice.

Possessio fratris. *Law Term.*—"The possession of the brother." The name given to the right which a sister has to succeed her full brother as heir of what was her father's real estate, in preference to her younger half-brother.

Possunt quia posse videntur. VIRG.—"They are able because they seem to be so." The result of confidence in our own powers. "Where there 's a will there 's a way."

Post acclamātiōnem bellĭcam jăcŭla volant.—"After the shout of war the arrows fly."

Post amicitiam credendum est, ante amicitiam judicandum. SEN.—"After forming a friendship you should place implicit confidence; before it is formed you must exercise your own judgment." True friendship is endangered by mistrust; it ought not therefore to be lightly formed.

Post bellum auxilium. *Prov.*—"Aid after the war." Useless assistance. Succour when the danger is over.

—— *Post cinĕres glōria sera venit.* MART.—"Glory comes too late, when we are reduced to ashes."

Post diluvium. See *P. D.*

Post ĕpŭlas stabis vel passus mille meābis.—"After eating, either stand, or walk a mile." A maxim of the School of Health at Salerno.

—— *Post ĕquĭtem sedet atra cura.* HOR.—"Behind the horseman sits livid care." Said of a guilty man who attempts to fly from his own reflections.

Post factum nullum consĭlium.—"After the deed, counsel is in vain."

Post festum venisti. *Prov.*—"You have come after the feast." Like our proverb, "You have come a day after the fair." Said to indolent and unpunctual persons who are always too late.

Post folia cadunt arbŏres. PLAUT.—"After the leaves have fallen the tree has to fall." If an injury is too patiently submitted to, others will follow.

Post hoc, propter hoc.—"After this, therefore on account of this." An ironical expression implying that the propinquity of two events does not of necessity imply cause and effect.

Post malam sĕgĕtem serendum est. SEN.—"After a bad crop you should sow again." Instead of being discouraged by misfortune, we should take measures to repair our loss, and not give way to despondency. See *Tu ne cede, &c.*

Post mĕdiam noctem visus, cum somnia vera. HOR.—"A vision after midnight, when dreams are true." The ancients believed that visions beheld after midnight were always true.

Post meridiem.—" After mid-day." Generally written P. M.

Post mortem nulla voluptas.—" After death there are no pleasures." The maxim of the Epicureans, who taught that life ought to be enjoyed while it lasted.

Post nubĭla Phœbus. *Prov.*—" After cloudy weather comes the sun." Prosperity succeeds adversity.

Post prandium stabis, post cœnam ambulābis.—" After dinner take rest, after supper use exercise." A maxim of the School of Health at Salerno. So our common adage,

" After dinner sit a while,
After supper walk a mile."

Post tenĕbras lux.—" After darkness light." So, in the moral world, the clouds of ignorance are dispelled by the light of knowledge.

Post tot naufragia portum.—" After so many shipwrecks we reach harbour." Motto of the Earl of Sandwich.

Postea. *Law Term.*—" Afterwards." The name given to the return made by the judge, after verdict, of what has been done in the cause; endorsed on the record and beginning with the word *Postea*, &c., ' Afterwards,' on issue joined, &c. &c.

Postĕri dies testes sunt sapientissĭmi.—" Succeeding days are the wisest evidences." Actions cannot well be judged of till we have seen the results.

Posthabui tamen illōrum mea sĕria ludo. VIRG.—" After all, I deferred my serious business for their sport."

——*Postquam fregit subsellia versu,*
Esŭrit intactam Părĭdi nisi vendit Agăven. JUV.

—" But while the very benches are broken down by the ecstasies with which his verses are applauded, he may starve unless he sells his unpublished ' Agave ' to Paris."

Postulāta.—" Things required." In a disputation, there are certain self-evident propositions which form the basis of an argument. Hence they are termed "*postulates*," as their admission is absolutely necessary.

Potentes ne tentes æmulāri. PHÆD.—" Attempt not to rival your superiors."

Potentia cautis quam acrĭbus consiliis tūtius habētur. TACIT.

—"Power is more securely maintained by prudent than by harsh counsels."

Potentissĭmus est qui se habet in potestāte. SEN.—"He is the most powerful who can govern himself."

Potest exercitātio et temperantia etiam in senectūte conservāre ălĭquid pristĭni robŏris. CIC.—"Exercise and temperance may preserve some portion of our youthful strength, even in old age."

——*Pŏtuit fortasse minŏris*
Piscātor quam piscis emi.—— JUV.
—"The fisherman might perhaps be bought for less money than the fish." In the days of Juvenal, incredible sums were spent at Rome on the luxuries of the table.

——*Præceps in omnia Cæsar.* LUCAN.—"Cæsar, prompt in all his resolves."

Præcepto mŏnĭtus sæpe te considĕra. PHÆD.—"Warned by my lesson, often examine yourself."

Præcĭpitatque moras omnes, ŏpĕra omnia rumpit. VIRG.—"Headlong he resists all delay, breaks through every impediment." A description of the ardour with which Æneas hastens to meet Turnus.

Præcĭpua tamen ejus in commovendâ miserātiōne virtus, ut quidam in hac eum parte omnĭbus ejusdem ŏpĕris autōrĭbus præfĕrant. QUINT.—"His great excellence, however, was in moving compassion; so much so, that many give him the first place among the writers of that kind."

Præcĭpuum munus annālium reor, ne virtūtes sileantur, utque pravis dictis factisque, ex posteritāte et infāmiâ metus sit. TACIT.—"I hold it to be the especial office of history, that virtuous actions be not buried in oblivion, and that men feel a dread of being deemed infamous by posterity for their evil words and actions." The utility and advantage of history.

Præferre patriam lībĕris regem decet. SEN.—"It becomes a king to prefer his country even to his children." His duty to his subjects is paramount to every other consideration.

Præmŏnĭtus, præmūnītus. *Prov.*—"Forewarned, forearmed."

——*Præmonstro tibi*
Ut ita te aliōrum mĭsĕrescat, ne tui ălios mĭsĕreat. PLAUT.
—"I warn you beforehand, so to have compassion on

others that others may not have to pity you." A warning to those inclined to be extravagant or over-generous.

Præmunīre. *Law Term.*—The first word of a writ issued for the offence of contempt of the king and his government.

Præprŏpĕra consĭlia raro sunt prospĕra. COKE.—"Over-hasty counsels are rarely prosperous."

Præsentemque refert quælĭbet herba Deum.—"And every herb reveals a present God." The physical world gives abundant proof of the existence of a Providence.

Præsertim ut nunc sunt mores, ădeo res redit,
Si quisquis reddit, magna habenda est gratia. TER.
—"According to the present state of manners, things are come to such a pass, that if anybody pays a debt it must be considered as a great favour."

Præstant æterna cadūcis.—"Things eternal are better than those that fade." Formerly on a clock at Tetbury.

Præstat amicitia propinquitāti. CIC.—"Friendship is better than relationship." See *Plus in amicitiâ*, &c.

Præstat cautēla quam medēla. COKE.—"Precaution is better than cure."

Præstat habēre acerbos inimīcos, quam eos amīcos qui dulces videantur. CATO.—"It is better to have open enemies than pretended friends."

——*Præstat mihi lītĕra linguam;*
Et, si non lĭceat scrībĕre, mutus ero. OVID.
—"This letter gives me a tongue; and were I not allowed to write, I should be dumb."

Præstat otiōsum esse quam malè ăgĕre.—"It is better to be idle than to do evil." But unfortunately the one almost invariably leads to the other.

Præstat otiōsum esse quam nihil ăgĕre. PLINY, *Epist.*—"Better be idle than do that which is to no purpose."

Prævīsus ante, mollior ictus venit. *Prov.*—"Seen beforehand, the blow comes more lightly." "Forewarned is forearmed." See *Præmonitus*, &c.

Pravo favōre labi mortāles solent. PHÆD.—"Men are wont to err through prejudice."

——*Pravo vīvĕre naso,*
Spectandum nigris ŏcŭlis, nigrōque capillo. HOR.
—"To have a badly-shaped nose, but to be admired for

black eyes and black hair." The poet hints that good hair and eyes will only make an ugly nose the more conspicuous.

Preces armātæ. Auson.—" Armed prayers." Claims made with pretended submission, but which are intended to be supported by force if necessary: like those of the beggar on the bridge of Segovia, in Gil Blas.

Prima cāritas incĭpit a seipso. *Prov.*—" Charity begins with oneself." "Charity begins at home."

Prima et maxĭma peccantium est pœna peccâsse. Sen.—"The first and greatest punishment of sin is the having sinned." In allusion to the pangs inflicted on us by shame and conscience.

Primâ făcie.—" On the first face." On the first view, or at the first glance: according to a first impression.

Prima fuit rerum confūsa sine ordĭne moles:
Unăque erant făcies, sīdera, terra, fretum. Ovid.
—" At first there was a confused mass of things without arrangement: and the stars, the earth, and the ocean were of but one appearance."

——*Prīmâque e cæde fĕrārum*
Incaluisse putem maculātum sanguĭne ferrum. Ovid.
—" I can believe that the steel, since stained with blood, first grew warm from the slaughter of beasts."

——*Primo avulso non dĕfĭcit alter.* Virg.—" One being torn away, another is not wanting."

Primo intuĭtu.—" At the first glance." "At sight,"—to use a commercial expression.

Primum ex natūrâ hanc habēmus appetitiōnem ut conservēmus nosmet ipsos. Cic. — " Before everything, we have by nature the instinct to preserve ourselves." Self-preservation is the first law of nature.

Primum mŏbile.—" The primary motive power." An imaginary centre of gravitation, or central body, in the Ptolemaic Astronomy, which was supposed to set all the other heavenly bodies in motion.

Primus ego aspĭciam notum de littŏre pinum. Ovid.—" I shall be the first to behold the well-known bark from the shore."

Primus in orbe Deus est timor.—" The ruling deity in the world is fear."

Primus inter pares.—"The first among his equals." The one who, among those of equal rank, in courtesy takes the precedence: generally the senior, or the one whose turn it is in rotation.

Primus non sum nec imus.—"I am neither first nor last."

Primus sapientiæ gradus est falsa intellĭgĕre.—"The first step towards wisdom is to know what is false."

Princĭpes—plus exemplo quam peccāto nocent. CIC.—"Princes do more mischief by the example they set than by the crimes they commit."

Princĭpĭbus placuisse viris non ultĭma laus est. HOR.—"To have pleased great men deserves no slight degree of praise." Horace was a courtier, and he knew that it requires good management to do so.

Principiis obsta; sero mĕdĭcīna parātur,
Cum mala per longas convaluĕre moras. OVID.

—"Resist the first advances; a cure is attempted too late, when through long hesitation the malady has waxed strong." A precept equally good in medicine and in morals.

Princĭpis est virtus maxĭma nosse suos. MART.—"'Tis the especial virtue of a prince to know his own men."

Principium dimidium totius. *Prov.*—"The beginning is half of the whole." See *Dimidium facti*, &c.

Prisciāni caput frangĕre.—"To break Priscian's head." A mediæval expression, signifying, "To be guilty of a violation of the rules of Grammar." Priscian, who flourished in the fifth century, and Donatus, who lived in the fourth, were the standard Grammarians of the middle ages.

Priusquàm incipias consulto, et ubi consulŭeris maturè facto opus est. SALL.—"Before you begin, take counsel; but having maturely considered, use despatch."

Privātum commŏdum publĭco cedit. *Law Maxim.*—"Private advantage must give way to the public good." See *Publicum bonum*, &c.

Privātus illis census erat brevis,
Commūne magnum.—— HOR.

—"Their private property was small, the public revenue great." The state of the Roman republic in her early days: when luxury and corruption crept in, individuals became possessed of enormous wealth, while the public treasury was thinned.

Privilēgium est quasi privāta lex. *Law Definition.*—"**Privilege** is, as it were, *private law.*" In allusion to its derivation, *privâ lege*, from "private law."

Pro aris et focis.—"For our altars and our hearths." In defence of our religion and our country.

Pro bono publĭco.—"For the public good."

Pro confesso.—"As confessed."

Pro et con. (*Con.* abbrev. of *contra.*)—"For and against." The arguments *pro* and *con*, "on both sides of the question."

Pro formâ.—"For form's sake."

Pro hâc vice.—"For this turn."

Pro interesse suo. *Law Term.*—"As to his interest."

Pro pudōre, pro abstinentiâ, pro virtūte, audācia, largitio, avaritia vigebant. Sall.—"Instead of modesty, instead of temperance, instead of virtue, effrontery, corruption, and avarice flourished." The state of society in Rome in the days of Catiline.

Pro quibus ut mĕrĭtis refĕrātur gratia, jurat
Se fore mancipium, tempus in omne, tuum. Ovid.
—"For which kindnesses, that due thanks may be returned, he swears he will, for all future time, be your slave."

Pro ratâ.—"In proportion"—the word "*parte*" being understood.

Pro re natâ.—"For a special purpose." An assembly held *pro re natâ*, on a particular occasion, or an emergency. Used also by physicians in reference to medicines to be taken *pro re natâ*, as occasion or symptoms may require.

Pro re nitōrem, et gloriam pro cōpia.
Qui habent, memĭnĕrint sese unde oriundi sunt. Plaut.
—"Show for substance, pretence for abundance; those who have should remember what they sprung from."

Pro salūte ănĭmæ.—"For the safety of the soul."

Pro tanto.—"For so much." So far, to such an extent.

Pro tempŏre.—"For the time." Sometimes written *Pro tem.* A thing done *pro tempore*, is a temporary expedient.

Pro virtūte felix temĕrĭtas. Sen.—"Instead of valour, successful rashness." Said by the philosopher in speaking of Alexander the Great.

Proba merx făcĭle emptōrem reppĕrit. PLAUT. — "Good wares easily find a buyer."

——*Probamque*
Paupĕriem sine dote quæro. HOR.
—"I court virtuous poverty without a portion." I seek tranquillity and happiness, unalloyed by avarice.

Probatum est.—"It has been tried and proved."

——*Prŏbĭtas laudātur et alget.* JUV.—"Honesty is praised and freezes." Cold commendation is often all that is bestowed on honesty. See *Aude aliquid*, &c.

Probum patrem esse oportet, qui gnatum suum
Esse probiōrem, quam ipse fuĕrit, postŭlet. PLAUT.
—"It befits the father to be virtuous who wishes his son to be more virtuous than himself."

Procellæ quanto plus habent vīrium tanto minus tempŏris. SEN.—"Storms, the more violent they are, the sooner they are over." So it is usually with violent outbursts of anger.

Procul à Jove, procul à fulmĭne. Prov.—"Far from Jupiter, far from his thunderbolts." Those who do not feel the sunshine of court-favour are safe from the vexations and dangers of courtly intrigue. In allusion to the fate of Semele.

——*Procul, o procul este, profāni.* VIRG.—"Afar! hence, afar! ye profane." A warning to keep at a distance, sometimes used ironically.

——*Procul, o procul este, profani,*
Conclāmat vates, totoque absistĭte luco. VIRG.
—"'Afar! hence, afar! ye profane,' the priestess cries aloud, 'retire from all the sacred grove.'" This was the solemn preface to the Eleusinian Mysteries, pronounced by the officiating priest.

——*Procul omnis esto*
Clamor et ira. HOR.
—"Let all bickerings and tumults be afar removed."

Prodent auctōrem vires.—— OVID.—"His powers betray the author."

Prodesse cīvĭbus.—"To be of service to one's fellow-citizens." To be engaged in promoting the public good.

Prōdĭga non sentit pereuntem fœmĭna censum:
At velut exhaustâ redivīvus pullŭlet arcâ

Nummus, et e pleno semper tollātur acervo,
Non unquam rĕpŭtat, quanti sibi gaudia constent. Juv.
—"Woman in her prodigality perceives not that her fortune is coming to an end; and as if money, always reviving, would shoot up afresh from the exhausted chest, and she be able to take from a heap always full, she never reflects how great a sum her pleasures cost her."

Prodigiōsa loquor vĕtĕrum mendācia vatum;
Nec tulit hæc, nec fert, nec feret ulla dies. Ovid.
—"I speak of the marvellous fictions of the ancient poets; no time has produced, does produce, or will produce such wonders."

Prōdĭgus et stultus donat quæ spernit et odit;
Hæc seges ingrātos tulit, et feret omnĭbus annis. Hor.
—"The prodigal and fool gives away the things which he despises and hates: this crop (of fools) has ever produced, and at all times will produce, ungrateful men."

Proditiōnem amo, sed proditōrem non laudo.—"I like the treason, but I praise not the traitor." A proverb borrowed from Plutarch; and said to have been used by Richard the Third, on the betrayal of the Duke of Buckingham.

Prōdĭtor pro hoste habendus. Cic.—"A traitor must be looked upon as an enemy."

Prodĭtōres etiam iis quos anteponunt, invīsi sunt. Tac.—"Traitors are hated even by those whom they favour."

Profecto delīrāmus interdum senes. Plaut.—"In truth, we old men are sometimes out of our senses."

Profundæ impensæ abeunt in rem marĭtĭmam. Cic.—"A naval establishment is supported at an enormous expense."

Proh sŭpĕri! quantum mortālia pectŏra cæcæ
Noctis habent! Ovid.
—"Ye gods! what blind night envelopes the breasts of men!"

Prohibenda est ira in puniendo. Cic.—"Anger is to be avoided in inflicting punishment."

Prohibētur ne quis faciat in suo, quod nocēre potest in aliēno. *Law Max.*—"It is unlawful for any man to do, with his own property, that which may injure another's." See *Sic utere*, &c.

oinde tona elŏquio, sŏlĭtum tibi. VIRG. — "Wherefore thunder on in noisy eloquence, as thou art wont."

Prōjĭcit ampullas et sesquipedālia verba,
Si curat cor spectantis tetigisse querēlā. HOR.
—"He lays aside his bombastic expressions, and his words half a yard long, when it is his object to move the heart of his hearer by his plaints."

Promiscuam habēre et vulgārem clementiam non decet; et tam ignoscēre omnibus crudēlitas est quam nulli. SEN.—"It is not proper to indulge an indiscriminate and universal mercy; to forgive all is as cruel as to forgive nobody." Misplaced lenity is an offence against society.

Promissio boni viri fit obligātio.—"The promise of a good man is as good as his bond."

Promittas făcĭto: quid enim promittēre lædit?
Pollĭcĭtis dives quīlĭbet esse potest. OVID.
—"Take care and promise; for what harm is there in promising? Any person can be rich in promises."

Pronunciātio est vocis, et vultûs, et gestûs moderātio cum venustāte.—"Delivery is the graceful management of the voice, countenance, and gestures."

Prope ad summum, prope ad exĭtum.—"The nearer the summit, the nearer a fall." The danger attendant on all high stations. See *Procul a Jove.* &c.

——*Propĕrat cursu*
Vita citāto—— SEN
—"With quickened step life hastens on."

Propōne Deum ante ŏcŭlos. CIC.—"Have God before your eyes."

——*Propŏsiti nondum pudet, atque eadem est mens,*
Ut bona summa putes, aliēnā vīvēre quadrā. JUV.
—"You are not yet ashamed of your course of life, and your feeling is still the same, that you consider living at another man's table the chief good." Addressed to a spunger or hanger-on.

Propria domus omnium opĭma. Prov.—"One's own house is the best of all." "There is no place like home."

Propriæ tellūris herum natūra, neque illum,
Nec me, nec quemquam stătuit. Nos expŭlit ille:
Illum aut nequitiës, aut vafri inscĭtia juris,
Postrēmò expellet certe vivācior hæres. HOR.

—"Nature has constituted neither him, nor me, nor any one else, the absolute possessor of the soil. That man ejected me; either fraud or the quirks and absurdities of the law will eject him, or, last of all, some more long-lived heir will certainly take his place." See *Perpetuus nulli*, &c.

Proprio motu. — "Of his own motion." Spontaneously; uninfluenced by others.

Proprium est stultitiæ aliōrum vitia cernĕre, oblivisci suōrum. Cic.—"It is the nature of folly to see the faults of others, and to forget its own."

Proprium hoc esse prudentiæ conciliāre sibi ănĭmos hŏmĭnum et in suos usus adjungĕre. Cic.—"It is the part of prudence to conciliate the minds of one's fellow-men, and to turn them to one's own account."

Proprium humāni ingĕnii est odisse quem læsĕris. Tac.—"It is the nature of the human disposition to hate him whom you have injured." This arises from a consciousness that he has reason to dislike you, and that his forgiveness may not be sincere.

——*Propter vitam vivendi perdĕre causas.* Juv.—"For the sake of living to forfeit every inducement to live."

Prospectandum vĕtŭlo latrante. *Prov.*—"When the old dog barks it is time to look out."

Prospĕra lux ŏrĭtur, linguisque ănĭmisque favēte;
Nunc dicenda bono sunt bona verba die. Ovid.
—"A prosperous day is dawning, be ye propitious both in your words and thoughts; now on the auspicious day must auspicious language be used."

Prospĕrum et felix scelus virtus vocātur. Sen.—"Crime, when it is fortunate and successful, is called virtue." Revolution is the name given to successful treason and rebellion. Hence the English epigram,

"Treason does never prosper: what 's the reason?
That when it prospers, none dare call it treason."

Protectio trahit subjectiōnem, et subjectio protectiōnem. *Law Max.*—"Protection implies allegiance, and allegiance protection."

Prōtĭnus ad censum, de mōrĭbus ultĭma fiet
Quæstio.—— Juv.
—"The question first put will be as to his income; that about his morals will be the last of all."

Prōtĭnus appāret quæ arbŏres frugĭferæ futūræ. *Prov.*—"It it is soon seen which trees will yield fruit."

——*Prout cuique libīdo est,*
Siccat inæquāles călĭces convīva solūtus
Insānis legĭbus. Hor.
—"The guests, each according to his inclination, quaff from glasses of different sizes, unconstrained by absurd laws."

Prout res nobis fluit, ita et ănĭmus se habet.—"As things go with us, so are our spirits affected."

Proximōrum incuriōsi, longinqua sectāmur. Pliny, *Epist.*—"Regardless of things that are near to us, we pursue those which are at a distance."

Proxĭmus à tectis ignis defendĭtur ægrè. Ovid.—"One's house is saved with difficulty when one's neighbour's is on fire." To the same effect as the next.

——*Proxĭmus ardet*
Ucalĕgon.—— Virg.
—"Your neighbour Ucalegon is on fire." Meaning his house; words used as a warning that danger is at hand.

Proxĭmus hinc gradus est, bene dēspērāre salūtem,
Seque semel verâ scire perisse fide. Ovid.
—"The next step after this is entirely to despair of safety; and to feel thoroughly convinced, once for all, that we are ruined."

Proxĭmus sum ĕgŏmet mihi. Ter.—"I am nearest akin to myself." "I love my friends well, but myself better."

Prudens futūri tempŏris exĭtum
Caliginōsâ nocte premit Deus;
Ridetque, si mortālis ultra
Fas trĕpĭdat.—— Hor.
—"A wise Deity shrouds in obscure darkness the events of time to come; and smiles if a mortal is solicitous beyond the law of nature."

Prudens in flammam ne manum injĭcĭto. *Prov.*—"If you are wise thrust not your hand into the flame." Quoted by St. Jerome.

Prudens interrogātio quasi dimidium sapientiæ.—"A prudent question is, as it were, one half of wisdom." A maxim of Lord Bacon.

Prudentis est mutāre consilium; stultus sicut luna mutātur.

—"A wise man may change his opinion; but the fool changes as often as the moon."

Prudentis est nonnunquam silēre.—"It is the part of a prudent man to be sometimes silent." Where no probable good can result from babbling.

Publĭcum bonum privāto est præferendum. *Law Max.* —"The public good must be preferred to private advantage."

——*Pudet et hæc oppröbria nobis*
Et dici potuisse, et non potuisse refelli. Hor.
—"It is shameful both that such reproaches should be uttered against us, and that we should be unable to refute them."

Pudet me et misĕret qui harum mores cantābat mihi,
Monuisse frustra.—— Ter.
—"I am ashamed and grieved that he who used to lecture me about the manners of these women, advised me in vain."

Pudor demissus nunquam redit in gratiam. Syr.—"Shame, once banished, never returns into favour."

Pudor docēri non potest, nasci potest. Syr. — "Modesty cannot be taught, it may be born."

Pudōre et liberalitāte libĕros
Retinēre, satius esse credo, quam metu. Ter.
—"I think it better to restrain children through a sense of shame and by liberal treatment, than through fear."

Pugna suum finem, cum jacet hostis, habet. Ovid.—"The battle has come to an end when the enemy is fallen." It is ungenerous to exult over a vanquished foe.

——*Pulchra*
Edĕpol pecūnia dos est. Plaut.
—"I'faith, money is a prepossessing dowry."

Pulchritūdo mundi, ordo rerum cœlestium, conversio solis, lunæ, sidĕrumque omnium indicant satis aspectu ipso ea omnia non esse fortuīta. Cic.—"The beauteous aspect of the world, the order of the celestial bodies, the revolutions of the sun, the moon, and all the stars, indicate sufficiently, at a mere glance, that all this is not the work of chance."

Pulchrōrum autumnus pulcher.—"The autumn of the beautiful is beautiful."

Pulchrum est accusāri ab accusandis.—"It is honourable to be accused by those who deserve to be accused." The censure of the bad is praise.

Pulchrum est benefăcĕre reipublĭcæ, etiam benedīcĕre haud absurdum est. SALL.—"It is becoming to act well for the republic, to speak well of it even is not discreditable."

——*Pulchrum est dĭgĭto monstrāri et dicier, Hic est.* PERS. —See *At pulchrum*, &c.

Pulvis et umbra sumus, fruges consūmĕre nati.—"We are but dust and shadows, born to consume the fruits of the earth." See *Fruges consumere*, &c.

Punctum comparātiōnis.—"The standard of comparison." The fixed measure of value.

Pūnĭca fides.—"Punic faith." Among the Romans the bad faith of the Carthaginians was proverbial.

Punītis ingĕniis gliscit auctŏrĭtas. TACIT.—"When men of genius are punished, their influence is increased." A work well abused is pretty sure of a good sale, and persecuted sects flourish most.

Puras Deus non plenas adspicit manus. SYR.—"God looks to pure hands, not to full ones." The Deity values innocence, not wealth.

Purgamenta hujus mundi sunt tria, pestis, bellum, et frateria. —"There are three modes of purging this world of ours; the plague, war, and monastic seclusion."

Puris omnia pura.—"Unto the pure all things are pure." From *Titus* i. 15. Equivalent to the motto of the Garter, "Honi soit qui mal y pense," "Evil be to him who evil thinks thereof."

Purpŭrâ indūtus pauper, sui ipsīus immĕmor est.—"A beggar clothed in purple is unmindful of himself." See *Asperius nihil*, &c.

Purpŭreus latè qui splendeat unus et alter
Assŭĭtur pannus.—— HOR.

—"One or two verses of purple patch-work, to make a great show, are tagged on."

Pythăgŏras non sapientem se, sed studiōsum sapientiæ vocāri voluit. QUINT.—"Pythagoras wished to be called not wise, but a lover of wisdom." He wished to be called not a "sophist" but a "philosopher."

Q.

Q. V.—See *Quod vide.*

Quâ vincit victos prōtĕgit ille manu. OVID.—"With the same hand with which he conquers he shields the conquered."

——*Quâcumque potes, dote placēre, place.* OVID.—"By whatever talent you can please, please."

Quadrupedante putrem sonĭtu quatit ungŭla campum. VIRG. —"The hoof shakes with prancing din the crumbling plain." [This line exemplifies the poetical figure Onomatopœia, the sound echoing the meaning. The galloping of the horse is admirably expressed, if the line is read as it is scanned, thus:

Quadrupe-dante pu-trem soni-tu quatit-ungula-campum.]

See *Illi inter*, &c.

Quæ accessiōnum locum obtinent extinguuntur cùm principāles res peremptæ fuĕrint. *Law Max.*—"That which is only an accessory is rendered null when the principal is abolished."

Quæ caret ora cruōre nostro? HOR.—"What shores are without our blood?" In what country has not our blood been shed? The poet speaks exultingly in reference to the valour of the Romans, and the successes of their arms.

Quæ culpāre soles, ea tu ne fēcĕris ipse;
Turpe est doctōris cum culpa redarguit ipsum. CATO.
—"Do not that yourself which you are wont to censure in others. It is bad when the censure of the teacher recoils upon himself."

Quæ dubitatiōnis tollendæ causâ contractĭbus inferuntur, jus commūne non lædunt. *Law Max.*—"Glosses imported into a contract for the purpose of removing a doubt, are not adverse to a common-law right."

Quæ e longinquo magis placent. *Prov.*—"The further fetch'd, the more things please."

Quæ fuĕrant vitia mores sunt. SEN.—"What were vices once are now the fashion." Said in reference to the impunity with which vice is practised in a corrupt age.

Quæ fugiunt, cělěri carpĭte poma manu. OVID.—"With speedy hand, pluck the fruit that passes away."

—— *Quæ fuit durum pati*
Meminisse dulce est. SEN.
—"What was hard to suffer is pleasant to remember."

Quæ in terris gignuntur omnia, ad usum hŏmĭnum creantur. CIC.—"Everything that the earth produces is created for the use of man." See *Genesis* i. 28.

Quæ in testamento ita sunt scripta ut intellĭgi non possint perinde sunt ac si scripta non essent. *Law Max.*—"What has been so written in a will as to be unintelligible, is to be regarded as though it had not been written."

Quæ in vitâ usurpant hŏmĭnes, cōgĭtant, curant, vident; quæque agunt vigilantes, agitantque, ea cuique in somno accĭdunt. CIC.—"Those things which engross men in life, which they think upon, care for and observe, which employ and excite them during the day, present themselves also in sleep."

Quæ infra nos nihil ad nos. *Prov.*—"The things that are below us are nothing to us." We must look upwards.

Quæ lædunt ŏcŭlos festinas dĕmĕre: si quid
Est ănĭmum, differs curandi tempus in annum. HOR.
—"The things which offend your eyes you are in haste to remove: if anything affects your mind, you defer the cure of it for a year." More attention is given by us to the cure of physical than moral evils.

Quæ legi commūni dērŏgant stricte interpretantur. *Law Max.*—"That which is adverse to a right at common law is to be interpreted rigidly."

——*Quæ lucis mĭsĕris tam dira cupīdo?* VIRG.—"How is it that there should be with the wretched so strong a desire to live?"

——*Quæ nec reticēre loquenti,*
Nec prior ipsa loqui dĭdĭcit.—— OVID.
—"[Echo] who has neither learned to hold her tongue after another has spoken, nor to speak first herself."

——*Quæ nec Sarmentus iniquas*
Cæsaris ad mensas, nec vilis Galba tulisset. JUV.
—"Such things as neither Sarmentus, nor the worthless Galba, would have borne at the obscene table of Cæsar."

——*Quæ non prosunt singŭla, multa juvant.* OVID.—"Things which singly are of no avail, when united are of service."

Quæ non valeant singŭla juncta juvant. *Law Max.*—"Facts

of little consequence individually are weighty when united."

Quæ peccāmus jŭvĕnes ea luĭmus senes. *Prov.*—"We pay when old for the misdeeds of our youth." As Colton says, The excesses of youth are bills drawn by time, payable thirty years after date with interest.

Quæ rĕgio in terris nostri non plena labōris? VIRG.—"What region of the earth is not full of our works?" Said by Æneas of the Trojans. Great Britain might justly assume this as her motto.

Quæ sint, quæ fuĕrint, quæ mox ventūra trahantur. VIRG.—"What is, what has been, and what is to be."

Quæ sunt igitur epulārum, aut ludōrum, aut scortōrum voluptātes, cum his voluptātibus comparandæ? CIC.—"What then are the gratifications to be derived from feasts, from pageants, or from women, when compared with these delights?"—the pleasures of the intellect, namely.

Quæ supra nos nihil ad nos. *Prov.*—"Those things which are above us are nothing to us." This was sometimes said of astrologers, and with truth. See *Quæ infra.*

Quæ uncis sunt unguĭbus ne nutrĭas. *Prov.*—"Do not foster animals with hooked claws." Do not enter into friendship with persons of dangerous character.

Quæ venit ex tuto, minus est accepta voluptas. OVID.—"The pleasure that is enjoyed in safety is the least valued of all." "Stolen pleasures are the sweetest."

Quæ virtus et quanta, boni, sit vīvĕre parvo! HOR.—"How great, my friends, is the merit of living upon a little!"

Quæ volŭmus et crēdĭmus libenter, et quæ sentīmus ipsi relĭquos sentīre putāmus. CÆSAR.—"What we wish, we readily believe, and whatever we think, we imagine that others think as well." Hence our proverb, "The wish is father to the thought."

Quælibet concessio fortissĭmè contra donatōrem interpretanda est. *Law Max.*—"Every grant shall be interpreted most strongly against the giver."

——*Quæque ipse miserrĭma vidi,*
Et quorum pars magna fui.—— VIRG.
—"Scenes of wretchedness which I beheld myself, and in which I was a principal party." The words of Æneas when relating to Dido the destruction of Troy.

Quære peregrīnum, vicīnia rauca reclāmat. HOR.—"'Go seek some stranger (to tell it to),' the screaming neighbours bawl aloud."

——*Quærenda pecūnia primùm,*
Virtus post nummos.—— HOR.
—"Money must first be sought for; after riches virtue." The maxim of a worldly man.

Quærĕre ut absūmant, absumpta requīrĕre certant;
Atque ipsæ vitiis sunt alimenta vices. OVID.
—"They struggle to acquire, that they may lavish, and then to obtain again what they have lavished; and the very vicissitudes of life afford nourishment to their vices."

Quærit aquas in aquis, et poma fugăcia captat
Tantălus; hoc illi garrŭla lingua dedit. OVID.
—"In the midst of water, Tantalus is in want of water, and catches at the apples as they ever escape him: 'twas his babbling tongue caused this."

Quærit, et inventis miser abstīnet et timet uti. HOR.—"The miser is ever seeking gain, and yet abstains, and dreads to use what he has gained."

——*Quærit, pŏsĭto pignŏre, vincat uter.* OVID.—"The stake deposited, he asks which has won." The inquiry anxiously made by one who has bet upon a race.

Quærĭtis, Ægisthus quare sit factus adulter?
In promptu causa est; desidiōsus erat. OVID.
—"Do you inquire why Ægisthus became an adulterer? The cause is self-evident: he was an idler."

Quærĭtur, sitne æquum amīcos cognātis anteferre. CIC.—"It is a question whether it is just to prefer our friends to our relations."

Quæsītam merĭtis sume superbiam. HOR. — "Assume the honours which you have sought to gain by your deserts."

Quæstio fit de lĕgĭbus non de persōnis. *Law Term.*—"The question is, what is the law? not, who is the offender?" The law must be construed with equal impartiality, whether for rich or poor.

Quævis terra alit artĭficem. *Prov.*—"Every land will support the artisan." His assistance is so necessary, that he will find bread anywhere.

Quale per incertam lunam sub luce malignâ
Est iter in sylvis.—— VIRG.

—"As a path in the woods, seen by the deceiving light of the uncertain moon."

Quale sit id quod amas cĕlĕri circumspĭce mente;
Et tua læsūro subtrăhe colla jugo. OVID.
—"Examine quickly and circumspectly what sort of object it is with which you are in love; and withdraw your neck from a yoke that is sure to gall."

Quale solet sylvis, brumāli frigŏre, viscum
Fronde virēre novâ, quod non sua sēmĭnat arbos,
Et crŏceo fœtu tĕrĕtes circumdăre truncos. VIRG.
—"As the mistletoe is wont to flourish in the woods throughout the winter cold, with its verdant leaves, which spring from no trunk of its own, and to embrace with its yellow offspring the tapering stem."

Qualem commendes etiam atque etiam aspĭce, ne mox
Incutiant aliēna tibi peccāta pudōrem. HOR.
—"Examine again and again into the worth of a person you would recommend, lest the faults of others bring shame upon you."

Qualis ab incepto processĕrit et sibi constet. HOR.—"As he begins, so let him proceed, and be consistent with himself." Instruction offered to a tragic poet.

Qualis hera tales pedissĕquæ. CIC.—"Like mistress, like maids."

Qualis populĕâ mœrens Philomēla sub umbrâ
Flet noctem, ramŏque sedens miserăbĭle carmen
Intĕgrat, et mæstis latè loca questĭbus implet. VIRG.
—"As mourning Philomel, under a poplar shade, weeps the night through, and sitting upon a bough renews her plaintive song, and fills the places around with piteous complaints."

Qualis rex, talis grex. *Prov.*—"Like king, like people."

Qualis sit ănĭmus, ipse ănĭmus nescit. CIC.—"What the soul is, the soul itself knows not."

Quales sunt summi civitātis viri talis est civĭtas. CIC.—"The character of a community depends upon that of its rulers."

Qualis ubi audīto venantum murmŭre tigris,
Horrescit măcŭlis.—— STAT.
—"As when the tigress, on hearing the cry of the hunters, looks terrible with her spotted skin."

Qualis vita, finis ita. *Prov.*—"As a man's life has been, so will be his end." This proverb apparently leaves no room for repentance.

Quam ad probos propinquitāte proxĭme te adjunxĕris,
Tam optĭmum est. PLAUT.
—"The nearer you can unite yourself in alliance with the virtuous, the better."

——*Quam contĭnuis et quantis longa senectus*
Plena malis!—— JUV.
—"With what continuous and great evils is a prolonged old age replete!"

Quam diffĭcĭlis est virtūtis diuturna simulātio! CIC.—"How difficult it is to feign virtue for any length of time!"

Quam diu se bene gessĕrit.—"So long as he shall conduct himself properly." A term first used in the letters patent, under which the chief baron of the exchequer held his office: all the judges now hold their offices by a similar tenure. Down to the reign of George the Third, they only held them, "*Durante beneplacito,*" which see. See also *Dum se, &c.*

Quam inīque comparātum est, ii qui minus habent
Ut semper ălĭquid addant divitiōrĭbus! TER.
—"How unfairly it has been ordained that those who have the least should be always adding to the stores of the more wealthy!"

Quam male consuēvit, quam se parat ille cruōri
Impius humāno, vitŭli qui guttŭra cultro
Rumpit, et immōtas præbet mugītibus aures!
Aut qui vagītus simĭles puerīlibus hædum
Edentem jugulāre potest!—— OVID.
—"How greatly does he disgrace himself, how in his impiety does he prepare himself for shedding human blood, who cuts the throat of the calf with the knife, and turns a deaf ear to its lowings! or who can slay the kid as it sends forth cries like those of a child!"

Quam multa injusta ac prava fiunt mōrĭbus! TER.—"How many unjust and improper things are sanctioned by custom!"

Quam prope ad crimen sine crimĭne!—"How near to guilt, without being guilty!" Put interrogatively, this was a favourite query with the Jesuits, who refined very extensively upon the point.

Quam quisque novit artem in hâc se exercĕat. Cic.—"Let every man employ himself in the pursuit which he best understands." See *Ne sutor*, &c.

——*Quam sæpe fortè tĕmĕrè*
Eveniunt, quæ non audĕas optāre! Ter.
—"How often things happen by mere chance which you would not have dared hope for!"

Quam scipsum amans sine rivāli! Cic.—"How much in love with himself, and that without a rival!" A man entirely absorbed in self-love, and beloved by nobody else.

Quam tĕmĕrè in nosmet legem sancīmus inīquam! Hor.—"How rashly do we sanction a precedent to tell against ourselves!" Men in their rashness concur in adopting measures of which they themselves become the victims, and thus as it were "make a rod for their own back."

——*Quam veterrĭmus hŏmĭni optĭmus est amīcus.* Plaut.
—"The oldest friend is the best friend for a man."

Quamvis digressu vĕtĕris confūsus amīci
Laudo tamen.—— Juv.
—"However concerned for the loss of my old friend, I commend him"—for changing his residence.

Quamvis sublīmes debent humĭles metuĕre,
Vindicta dŏcĭli quia patet solertiæ. Phæd.
—"Men, however high in station, ought to be on their guard against the lowly; because to skill and address revenge lies near at hand."

Quando alĭquid prohibētur, prohibētur et omne per quod devĕnitur ad illud. *Law Max.*—"When a thing is forbidden (by law) everything is forbidden as well which tends to it." Whatever is prohibited by law to be done directly, cannot legally be effected by an indirect and circuitous contrivance.

Quando ea accĭdunt nobis quæ nullo consilio vitāre possŭmus, eventis aliōrum memŏriā repetendis, nihil novi accidisse nobis cōgitĕmus. Cic.—"When those things befall us which by no prudence we can avoid, we shall, by calling to memory what has happened to others, be able to reflect that nothing new has befallen ourselves."

Quando *jus domĭni regis et subdĭti concurrunt jus regis præferri debet. Law Max.*—"Where the title of the king and the title of a subject come into collision, the king's title shall be preferred."

Quando *plus fit quam fiĕri debet, videtur etiam illud fiĕri quod faciendum est. Law Max.*—"Where more is done than ought to be done, that portion for which there was authority shall hold good."

Quando *res non valet ut ago, valeat quantum valēre potest. Law Max.*—"When an instrument will not operate to the extent intended, it shall operate in law so far as it can."

Quando *ullum inveniēmus parem?*—"When shall we find his like again?"

——*Quandŏque bonus dormītat Homērus!* Hor.—"Even the worthy Homer is caught napping sometimes." The most distinguished of men will sometimes make mistakes.

Quandŏquĭdem *inter nos sanctissĭma divitiārum*
Majestas.—— Juv.
—"Seeing that the majesty of riches is, among us, held the most sacred."

——*Quanta est gula, quæ sibi totos*
Ponit apros, ănĭmal propter convīvia natum! Juv.
—"What a gullet he must have who sets before himself whole boars,—an animal born for feasting only!"

Quanta *pătĭmur!*—"How great the evils we endure!"

Quanta *sit admirabilĭtas cœlestium rerum atque terrestrium!* Cic.—"How admirable are the heavens and the earth!"

Quantæ *sunt tĕnĕbræ! væ mihi, væ mihi, væ!*—"The gloom how great! woe, woe is me! woe, woe!" A monkish Pentameter, inserted as a specimen of *wretchedness* in both senses.

Quanti *casus humāna rotant!*—"How many ups and downs there are in human affairs!"

Quanti *est æstimanda virtus quæ nec ērĭpi nec surrĭpi potest; et neque naufrăgio neque incendio amittĭtur.* Cic.—"How truly valuable is virtue, which cannot be taken from us either by force or fraud, and which is not to be lost by shipwreck or by fire!"

Quanti *est săpĕre!* Ter.—"How valuable is wisdom!"

Quanto *plura recentium seu vĕtĕrum revolvo, tanto ludibria* *rerum mortālium cunctis in negōtiis observantur.* TACIT.—"The more I revolve in my mind the transactions of the moderns or of the ancients, the more conspicuous appears the absurdity of human affairs in every point of view." A remark in accordance with the diplomatic saying, that it is "astonishing with how little wisdom the world is governed."

Quanto quisque sibi plura negāvĕrit,
A Dis plura feret.—— HOR.

—"The more a man denies himself, the more shall he receive from the gods."

Quanto sibi in prælio minus parcunt, tanto tutiōres sunt. SALL.—"The less careful they are of themselves in battle, the safer they are." They insure safety by trusting to their valour.

Quanto superiōres sumus, tanto nos gerāmus submissius. CIC.—"The higher our rank, the more humbly let us behave ourselves."

Quantum.—"How much." "His *quantum*," his proper allowance, his due proportion.

Quantum a rerum turpitūdine abes, tantum te a verbōrum libertāte sejungas. CIC.—"As much as you are incapable of a base action, so much should you be averse to loose language."

——*Quantum est in rebus ināne!* PERS.—"What emptiness there is in human affairs!" How frivolous are the doings and fancied interests of men! See *Eccles.* i. 2.

——*Quantum inter viburna cupressus.* VIRG.—"[Excelling] as much as the cypress does the shrubs."

Quantum mĕruit. *Law Term.*—"As much as he deserved." An action grounded on a promise, actual or implied, that the defendant should pay to the plaintiff for his services as much as he should reasonably deserve.

——*Quantum mutātus ab illo.* VIRG.—"How greatly changed from what he was!" Said of the ghost of Hector when it appeared to Æneas.

Quantum quisque feret, respiciendus erit. OVID.—"Each man must be regarded according to what he gives."

Quantum quisque suâ nummōrum servat in arcâ
Tantum habet et fidei.—— JUV.

—"The credit of every man is exactly in proportion to the

money he holds treasured up in his chest." In a corrupt state of things wealth alone commands respect.

Quantum relĭgio potuit suadēre malōrum! LUCRET.—"To such enormous wrongs could superstition persuade!" The poet is speaking of the sacrifice of Iphigenia by her father Agamemnon, when ordered by the priest of Diana to propitiate the goddess. The line is applicable to the mischiefs which have been wrought among mankind by fanaticism.

Quantum suffĭcit.—"As much as is sufficient." Sometimes written or pronounced *Quantum suff.*

Quantum vălеat.—"For as much as it is worth."

——*Quantum vertĭce ad auras*
Æthĕrias, tantum rādīce in Tartăra tendit. VIRG.

—"As far as it lifts its branches towards the sky, so far does it strike its roots to the depths below." Description of the oak and the beech.

Quare facit opium dormīre? Quia in eo est virtus dormitīva.—"Why does opium produce sleep? Because it has in it a sleepy quality." This question and answer were written by Molière, the French dramatist, in ridicule of that ignorance which affects to solve every difficulty by repeating the terms of the original question in words a little varied.

Quare impĕdit? Law Lat.—"Why does he disturb?" The name of a writ which lies for the patron of an advowson against one who has disturbed his right.

Quare obstruxit? Law Term.—"Why has he obstructed?" The name of a writ lying for him who has a right of passage through his neighbour's land, but has been obstructed therein.

Quare, si fieri potest, et verba omnia, et vox hujus alumnum urbis oleant; ut orātio Romāna plane videātur, non cīvitāte donāta. QUINTILL.—"If then it can be done, let all your words and your pronunciation lead to the impression that you are a native of this city; so that your speech may appear to be unquestionably Roman, and not that of an alien who has been presented with its freedom." A warning from high authority against the use of dialects and provincialisms.

Quare vitia sua nemo confitētur?

Quia etiam nunc in illis est. Somnum Narrāre vigilantis est. SEN.—"Why does no man confess his vices? Because he still persists in them. It is for the man who has awoke to tell his dreams."

Quartâ lunâ nati. Prov.—"Born in the fourth moon." Such persons were thought to be particularly unfortunate. Hercules was born in that month; whose labours, though beneficial to the world, were of little advantage to himself.

Quas dĕdĕris, solas semper habēbis opes. MART.—"Only the wealth which you give away will be yours for ever." He that giveth to the poor, lendeth to the Lord.

Quasi dicas.—"As though you were to say."

Quasi mures, semper ĕdĭmus aliēnum cibum. PLAUT.—"Like mice, we always eat the food of others." The mode of life pursued by a spunger or parasite.

Quatuor pĕdĭbus currit.—"It runs on all fours"—with it.

Queis păria esse ferè placuit peccāta, labōrant
Cùm ventum ad verum est; sensus moresque repugnant,
Atque ipsa utĭlĭtas, justi propè mater et æqui. HOR.

—"They who are pleased to rank all faults as nearly equal, find themselves in a difficulty when they come to the truth of the matter; sense and morality are opposed to them, and expediency itself, the mother almost of right and equity."

Quem casus transit aliquando invĕniet. SYR.—"Misfortune will one day find him whom it has till then passed by." "The pitcher that goes oft to the well comes home broken at last."

Quem damnōsa Venus, quem præceps ălea nudat. HOR.—"Him whom baneful lust, and the ruinous dice, have stripped bare."

Quem Deus vult perdĕre, prius dementat.—See *Quem Jupiter,* &c., and *Quos Deus,* &c.

Quem di dĭlĭgunt adolescens morĭtur. PLAUT.—"He whom the gods love dies young."

Quem ego ut mentiātur indūcĕre possum, eum făcĭlè exorāre pŏtĕro ut pējĕret. CIC.—"Him whom I can induce to tell a lie I can easily prevail upon to commit perjury."

Quem ferret, si parentem non ferret suum? TER.—"Whom should he bear with, if not with his own father?"

Quem Jupiter vult perdĕre dementat prius.—"Him whom Jupiter wishes to ruin, he first deprives of his senses" Barnes' translation of the Greek fragment—"Οταν δε δαίμων, &c. See *At dæmon*, &c.

Quem penes arbitrium est, et jus et norma loquendi. HOR.—"Whose province it is to regulate the propriety and rules of speech."

Quem pœnitet peccâsse penè est innŏcens. SEN.—"He who repents of having committed a fault is almost innocent."

Quem præstāre potest mulier galeāta pudōrem
Quæ fugit à sexu?—— JUV.
—"What modesty can the woman possess who, with a helmet on, flies her own sex?"

Quem res plus nimio delectavĕre secundæ,
Mutātæ quătient.—— HOR.
—"The man for whom prosperity has had unbounded charms will be most affected by reverses."

Quem sæpe transit, aliquanto invĕnit. SEN.—"That which is often overlooked is detected at last." See *Quem casus*, &c.

——*Quem semper acerbum,*
Semper honōrātum (sic, Dî, voluistis) habēbo. VIRG.
—"Though the day be for ever embittered, I will, (as ye gods have so decreed,) always hold it in honour and respect." In allusion to the day on which a person has lost a dear and esteemed friend.

Quem si puellārum insĕrĕres choro,
Mire sagāces fallĕret hospĭtes
Discrīmen obscūrum, solūtis
Crīnĭbus, ambĭguōque vultu. HOR.
—"If you were to place him in a throng of damsels, the undistinguishable difference occasioned by his flowing locks and doubtful features would wonderfully impose even on discerning strangers."

Quemcunque mĭsĕrum vĭdĕris, hŏmĭnem scias. SEN.—"Whenever you behold a fellow-creature in distress, remember that he is a man."

Quemcunque popŭlum tristis eventus premit,
Periclitātur magnitūdo princĭpum;
Minūta plebes făcĭli præsidio latet. PHÆD.
—"Whenever a people is reduced to extremity, the high

position of its chiefs is in danger: the humble easily find safety in obscurity."

Quemque suæ malæ cogitatiōnes conscientiæque ănĭmi terrent. Cic.—"His own galling reflections and the stings of conscience fill the mind (of the evil-doer) with alarm."

Qui altĕrum incūsat probri eum ipsum se intuēri oportet. Plaut.—"He who accuses another of dishonesty ought to look narrowly into himself." An accuser should always appear with *clean hands.*

Qui amat, tamen herclè si ēsŭrit, nullum ēsŭrit. Plaut.—"He that's in love, i'faith, even if he is hungry, isn't hungry at all." He is not sensible of hunger or other sufferings.

Qui amīcus est amat; qui amat non utĭque semper amīcus est. Itaque amicitia semper prodest; amor etiam aliquando nocet. Sen.—"He who is a friend must love (the object of his regard); but he who loves is not therefore a friend. Hence, friendship is always productive of good, while sometimes love is injurious even." He alludes to that *so-called* love which seeks its own gratification at any cost.

Qui e nuce nucleum esse vult, frangat nucem. Plaut.—"He who would eat the kernel must crack the shell." He who would attain perfection in any pursuit must submit to toil.

Qui aut tempus quid postŭlet non videt, aut plura lŏquĭtur, aut se ostentat, aut eōrum, quibuscum est, ratiōnem non habet, is ineptus esse dĭcĭtur. Cic.—"He who does not regard what the occasion demands, or talks too much, or swaggers, or does not pay becoming respect to the company, may be pronounced a fool."

Qui Bavium non odit, amat tua carmĭna, Mævi. Virg.—"He who does not hate Bavius must be pleased with thy lines, Mævius." The names of two wretched poets in Virgil's days.

Qui bellus homo, Cotta, pusillus homo est. Mart.—"He, Cotta, who is a pretty man is a trifling man."

Qui bene conjĭcĭet, hunc vatem perhĭbēto optĭmum.—"Consider him the best prophet who forms the best conjectures." Put the most confidence in him who draws the most rational conclusions.

Qui bene impĕrat, paruĕrit aliquando necesse est. CIC.—"He who governs well must, of necessity, have at some time obeyed."

Qui capit ille facit. *Prov.*—"He who takes it to himself has done the deed." "If the cap fits him, let him wear it."

Qui cibum è flammâ petit. PLAUT.—"A man who will snatch victuals from the flames [of a funeral pile]." The lowest of the low.

Qui cum triste ălĭquid stătuit, fit tristis et ipse;
Cuique fere pœnam sūmĕre pœna sua est. OVID.

—"One who, when he has come to a sad decision, himself is sad; and to whom it is almost a punishment to inflict punishment." This may be said of a merciful judge.

Qui Cŭrios sĭmŭlant, et Bacchanālia vivunt. JUV.—"Who pretend to be Curii and live like Bacchanals." Curius was a Roman noted for his extreme frugality and temperance.

Qui de contemnendâ gloriâ libros scribunt, nomen suum inscribunt.—"Those who publish books warning us to despise fame insert their own names in the title-page." Thus showing that very desire for fame which they affect to censure. See *Quid nostri*, &c.

Qui dedit bĕnĕficium tăceat; narret qui accĕpit. SEN.—"Let him who has bestowed a benefit be silent; let him who has received it tell of it."

Qui dedit hoc hŏdie, cras, si volet, aufĕret.—— HOR.—"He who has given to-day may, if he please, take away to-morrow." The public may in their caprice recall the honours they have lavished, as easily as they have bestowed them.

Qui deōrum consilia culpet, stultus inscītusque sit,
Quique eos vitŭpĕret.—— PLAUT.

—"He who would blame the ordinances of the gods must be as foolish and ignorant as he who censures them."

Qui dĭdĭcit patriæ quid dĕbeat, et quid amīcis,
Quo sit amōre parens, quo frater amandus, et hospes;
Quid sit conscripti, quid jūdĭcis officium, quæ
Partes in bellum missi ducis; ille profectò
Reddĕre persōnæ scit convenientia cuique. HOR.

—"He who has learned what he owes to his country, and what to his friends; with what affection a parent, a brother, and a guest are to be beloved; what is the duty of a senator, what of a judge; what the duties of a general sent forth to war;—he surely knows how to assign suitable attributes to every character."

Qui ex damnāto coïtu nascuntur inter libĕros non computantur. *Law Max.*—"The issue of illicit intercourse are not reckoned as children."

Qui facit per alium facit per se. COKE.—"He who does a thing by the agency of another does it himself." He is equally guilty and equally responsible for the consequences. This adage was probably derived from the Roman Law. See *Consentientes et*, &c.

Qui fert malis auxilium, post tempus dolet. PHÆD.—"He who helps the wicked repents it before long."

——*Qui finem quæris amōris,*
Cedit amor rebus; res age, tūtus eris. OVID.
—"You who seek to end your passion, love gives way to employment; attend to business, then you will be safe."

Qui fit, Mæcēnas, ut nemo, quam sibi sortem
Seu rătio dĕdĕrit, seu fors objēcĕrit, illā
Contentus vivat; laudet diversa sequentes? HOR.
—"How happens it, Mæcenas, that no one lives content with his lot, whether reason gave it him or chance threw it in his way; but is loud in his commendations of those who follow other pursuits?"

Qui fugit molam farīnam non invĕnit. *Prov.*—"He who flies from the mill does not get any meal." The lazy man cannot expect to eat the fruits of industry.

Qui genus humānum ingĕnio superāvit, et omnes
Præstinxit, stellas exortus uti aërius Sol. LUCRET.
—"Who in genius surpassed mankind, and outshone all, as the rising sun obscures the stars."

Qui genus jactat suum aliēna laudat. SEN.—"He who boasts of his descent boasts of that which he owes to others." See *Et genus*, &c.

Qui homo matūre quæsīvit pecūniam,
Nisi eam matūre parcit, matūre ēsŭrit. PLAUT.
—"He who has in good time acquired wealth, unless in good time he saves it, will in good time come to starvation." This maxim was often repeated by Louis XIII. of France, who was a great admirer of Plautus.

——*Qui in amōrem*
Præcipitāvit, pejus perit quam si saxo saliat. PLAUT.
—"He who plunges headlong into love, perishes more irremediably than if he leapt from a rock."

Qui in jus dominiumve alterius succedit jure ejus uti debet. *Law Max.*—"He who succeeds to the right or property of another ought to enjoy the privileges appertaining thereto."

Qui invĭdet minor est.—"He who envies admits his inferiority." Motto of Earl Cadogan.

Qui ipse haud amāvit, ægre amantis ingĕnium inspĭcit. PLAUT. —"He who has not been in love himself, with difficulty sees into the feelings of one who is in love."

Qui ipsus se contemnit, in eo est indŏles industriæ. PLAUT. —"He who thinks but poorly of himself, in him there is a tendency to well-doing."

Qui jacet in terrâ non habet unde cadat. *Prov.*—"He who lies on the ground cannot fall." When we are in the utmost misery, there can be no change but for the better.

Qui jure suo utĭtur, nēmĭni facit injūriam. *Law Max.*—"He who uses his own rights does wrong to no man."

Qui jussu judĭcis aliquod fēcĕrit non vidētur dolo malo fecisse, quia parēre necesse est. *Law Max.*—"He who does an act under the direction of judicial authority, is not held to have acted from any wrongful motive, because it was his duty to obey."

Qui malè agit, odit lucem. *Prov.*—"He who works evil hates the light." See *St. John* i. 20.

Qui mare et terras, variisque mundum
Tempĕrat horis :
Unde nil majus generātur ipso,
Nec viget quicquam sĭmĭle aut secundum. HOR.
—"[God] who rules the sea and the earth, and the whole world with the varying seasons : from whom proceeds nothing greater than himself; nor does there exist anything either like him or approaching to him."

Qui mare tĕneat, eum necesse est rerum potīri. CIC.—"The state which has the dominion of the ocean must of necessity be the master."

Qui mĕdĭce vivit mĭsĕre vivit. *Prov.*—"He who lives by prescription lives wretchedly."

Qui mentīri aut fallĕre insuēvit patrem,
Tanto magis is audēbit cætĕros. TER.
"He who has made it a practice to lie to or to deceive his father will the more readily venture to deceive others."

Qui mentītur fallit quantum in se est. AUL. GELL.—"He who tells a lie deceives so far as he can."

Qui mori dĭdĭcit, servīre dedĭdĭcit; supra omnem potentiam est, certè extra omnem. SEN.—"He who has learned how to die has learned how not to be a slave: he is above all power, at all events beyond it." Said in accordance with the philosophy of the Stoics, who deemed it meritorious to escape by a suicidal death the ills of this life. Cato of Utica thus escaped being made captive by Cæsar.

Qui——multōrum provĭdus urbes
Et mores homĭnum inspexit.—— HOR.
—"Who carefully viewed the cities, and examined the manners, of various nations." Said in commendation of Ulysses.

Qui ne tubĕrĭbus propriis offendat amicum,
Postŭlat, ignoscet verrūcis illīus.—— HOR.
—"He who wishes his friend not to take offence at his own protuberances, will excuse his friend's warts."

Qui nescit dissimulāre nescit vīvĕre.—"He who knows not how to dissemble knows not how to live." This was a favourite maxim with the emperor Frederic Barbarossa, Louis the Eleventh of France, and Philip the Second of Spain. Though dissimulation is an abominable vice, there are times when it is absolutely necessary to restrain our feelings and check our resentments.

Qui nihil potest sperāre, despĕret nihil.—"Let him who can hope for nothing despair of nothing."

——*Qui nil molĭtur ineptè.* HOR.—"A man who attempts nothing without success." Said in reference to the superior merits of Homer as a poet.

Qui nimis prŏpĕre, minus prospĕre. *Prov.*—"He who makes too much haste will have but little success." "The more haste, the worse speed."

Qui non est hŏdie, cras minus aptus erit. OVID.—"He who is not prepared to-day will be less so to-morrow."

Qui non prŏfĭcit, dĕfĭcit. *Prov.*—"He who does not advance loses ground."

Qui non labōrat non mandūcet.—"If any work not, neither should he eat." 2 *Thess.* iii. 10.

Qui non prohibet quod prohibēre potest assentīre vidētur. Law Max.—"He who does not prevent that which he can prevent, is held to assent."

Qui non vetat peccāre cum possit, jubet. SEN. — "He who does not prevent a crime when he can, encourages it."

Qui non vult fiĕri desidiōsus, amet. OVID.—"Let him who would not be an idler, fall in love." Implying that passion stirs up the energies, and promises success in the pursuit. The same author says, however, in another passage, that idleness is the parent of guilty passion. See *Quæritis Ægisthus*, &c.

Qui novit mollissĭma fandi tempŏra.—"Who well knows the most favourable moment to speak." Adapted from Virgil.

Qui nunc it per iter tenebricōsum,
Illuc unde negant redīre quenquam. CATULL.
—"Who now is travelling along the shaded path to the spot from which, they say, no one ever returns." The germ probably of the lines in *Hamlet*, "The undiscover'd country, from whose bourne no traveller returns."

——*Qui paupĕriem verĭtus, potiōre metallis*
Libertāte caret, dŏmĭnum vehet imprŏbus, atque
Serviet æternum, quia parvo nesciet uti. HOR.
—"He who, fearing poverty, forfeits his liberty more precious than golden ore, shall, avaricious wretch, submit to a master, and be a slave for ever, because he knew not how to use a little." Alluding to the Horse in the Fable.

Qui peccat ebrius, luat sobrius. Law Max.—"He who offends when drunk must pay for it when sober."

Qui pendet aliēnis promissis sæpe decĭpĭtur.—"He who depends on the promises of others is often deceived."

Qui per alium facit per seipsum făcĕre vidētur. Law Max.
—"He who does a thing by another is held to have done it himself." See *Qui facit*, &c.

Qui per virtūtem pĕrītat, non intĕrit. PLAUT.—"He who dies for virtue's sake, does not perish."

——*Qui prægrăvat artes*
Infra se pŏsĭtas, extinctus amābĭtur idem. HOR.

—"He who outweighs the energies of those beneath him, will still be loved when dead."

Qui prior est tempŏre potior est jure. COKE.—"He who is the first in time has the preferable right." As in the case of mortgagees; the first is to be paid before the second.

Qui pro quo.—"Who for whom." One thing instead of another. Something quite different. The nominative *qui*, and the ablative *quo*, here given, are the most distant cases.

Qui quæ vult dicit, quod non vult audiet. TER.—"He who says what he likes, will hear what he does not like."

Qui se committit hŏmĭni tutandum imprŏbo,
Auxilia dum requīrit, exĭtium invĕnit. PHÆD.
—"He who intrusts himself to the protection of a wicked man, while he seeks assistance, meets with destruction."

Qui se laudāri gaudet verbis subdŏlis,
Fere dat pœnas turpi pœnitentiâ. PHÆD.
—"He who is delighted at being flattered with artful words, generally pays the penalty by ignominious repentance."

Qui se ultro morti offĕrant, facilius repĕriuntur, quam qui dolōrem patienter ferant. CÆSAR.—"It is easier to find men who will volunteer to die than who will endure suffering with patience."

Qui seipsum laudat, cito derisōrem invĕniet. SYR.—"He who praises himself will soon find some one to laugh at him."

Qui semel aspexit quantum dimissa petītis
Præstant, matūrè redeat, rĕpĕtatque relicta. HOR.
—"Let him, as soon as he has discovered how much the life he has abandoned is preferable to that which he has chosen, immediately return, and resume that which he had relinquished."

Qui semel est læsus fallāci piscis ab hamo,
Omnĭbus unca cibis æra subesse putat. OVID.
—"The fish that has been once hurt by the deceitful hook thinks that the barbed metal lies concealed in every morsel."

Qui semel gustārit canis, à corio nunquam absterrētur. Prov.
—"The dog that has once tasted the flesh, is never to be frightened from the skin."

Qui semel scurra, nunquam paterfamilias. Cic.—"He who has once been a buffoon will never make a father of a family."

Qui sentit commŏdum, sentīre debet et onus. *Law Max.*—"He who derives the advantage ought also to sustain the burden." He who reaps the benefit must share in the expense.

Qui sibi amīcus est, scito hunc amīcum omnĭbus esse. Sen.—"Know that he who is a friend to himself is a friend to all." He who does his duty to himself must of necessity do his duty to all the world.

Qui sic jocātur, tractantem ut sĕria vincat ;
Seria quum făciet, dic rogo, quantus erit ?
"He who a tale so learnedly could tell,
That no true history ever pleased so well ;
How much in serious things would he excel ?"
An Epigram by Theodore Beza upon the works of Rabelais.

Qui sĭmŭlat verbis, nec corde est fidus amīcus ;
Tu quoque fac sĭmĭle, et sic ars delūdĭtur arte. Cato.
—"If any one tries to deceive you with his words, and is not, at heart, a sincere friend, do you act the same with him, and so art will be foiled by art."

Qui spe aluntur, pendent, non vivunt. *Prov.*—"Those who feed on hope, exist in suspense, they do not live."

Qui stădium currit, niti et contendĕre debet ut vincat. Cic.—"He who runs a race ought to strive and endeavour to win."

Qui stătuit ălĭquid parte inaudītâ altĕrâ,
Æquum licet statuĕrit, haud æquus fuerit. Sen.
—"He who comes to any decision while one side is unheard, even though his decision should be just, is not just himself."

Qui studet optātam cursu contingĕre metam,
Multa tulit fecitque puer, sudāvit et alsit,
Abstĭnuit Vĕnĕre et vino.—— Hor.
—"He who is eager to reach the wished-for goal, has done and suffered much in his youth ; he has sweated and shivered with cold, he has abstained from love and wine."

Qui suis rebus contentus est, huic maxĭmæ ac certissĭmæ sunt divĭtiæ.—"He who is contented with his own, possesses the greatest and most certain riches."

Qui tacet consentīre vidētur. *Law Maxim.*—"He who is silent is assumed to consent." "Silence gives consent."

Qui tam. *Law Lat.*—"Who so." The title given to an action in the nature of an information on a penal statute.

Qui terret plus ipse timet. CLAUD.—"He who causes terror to others feels still more dread himself." The despot, who rules by arbitrary sway, lives in a state of continual apprehension and alarm.

Qui tĭmĭdè rogat, docet negāre. SEN.—"He who asks timidly courts a denial." Requests made with a certain degree of confidence are the most likely to be successful.

Qui venit hic fluctus, fluctus superēmĭnet omnes;
Postĕrior nono est, undĕcĭmoque prior. OVID.
—"The wave that approaches overtops all the others, it follows the ninth, and comes before the eleventh." See *Vastius insurgens*, &c.

Qui vitat molam, vitat farīnam. *Prov.*—"He who shuns the mill, shuns the meal." With everything we must be content to take the attendant evils. See *Qui fugit*, &c.

Qui vult decipi, decipiātur. *Prov.*—"He who wishes to be deceived, let him be deceived."

——*Quibus res tĭmĭda aut turbĭda est;*
Pergunt turbāre usque, ut ne quod possit conquiescĕre.
PLAUT.
—"They whose affairs are in a critical or perplexed state proceed to render them more perplexed, so that nothing can be settled."

Quicquid agcs ĭgĭtur, magnâ spectābĕre scenâ. OVID.—"Whatever you do, therefore, you will be acting upon an extended stage."

Quicquid agunt hŏmĭnes nostri est farrāgo libelli.—Adapted from Juvenal. "Whatever men are engaged in makes the medley of my book."

Quicquid delīrant reges, plectuntur Achīvi. HOR.—See *Delirant reges*, &c.

Quicquid erit, superanda omnis fortūna ferendo est. VIRG.
—"Whatever may befall us, all (adverse) fortune can be surmounted by enduring it."

Quicquid est boni moris levitāte extinguĭtur. SEN.—"Whatever is good and virtuous is obscured by levity of conduct."

Quicquid est illud, quod sentit, quod sapit, quod vult, quod viget, cœleste et divīnum est, ob eamque rem æternum sit necesse est. Cic.—"Whatever that be, which thinks, which understands, which wills, which acts, it is something heavenly and divine, and, for that reason, must necessarily be eternal."

Quicquid excessit modum
Pendet instābili loco. Sen.
—"Whatever has exceeded its due bounds is always in a state of instability." See *Est modus in rebus*, &c.

Quicquid in altum fortūna tulit, ruitūra levat. Sen.—"Whatever fortune has raised aloft, she has raised only to let it fall." See *Prope ad*, &c.

Quicquid in eum officii contulĕris, id ita accĭpio, ut in me ipsum te putem contulisse. Cic.—"Whatever kindness you may confer upon him, I shall esteem it as though you conferred it upon myself."

Quicquid in linguam vēnĕrit offundĕre.—"To pour out whatever comes upon the tongue." To say whatever comes uppermost.

——*Quicquid multis peccātur, inultum est.* Lucan.—"Wherever a crime is shared by many, no punishment follows." Unless it is agreed that atonement shall be made by a scape-goat.

Quicquid plantātur solo solo cedit. *Law Max.*—"Whatever is affixed to the soil belongs thereto.

Quicquid præcĭpies esto brevis.—— Hor.—"Whatever you may enjoin, be brief."

Quicquid servātur, cŭpĭmus magis, ipsăque fūrem
Cura vocat: pauci, quod sinit alter, amant. Ovid.
—"Whatever is treasured up, we long for it the more, and the very care bestowed on it invites the thief; few care for that which another grants."

Quicquid sub terris est, in aprīcum profĕret ætas;
Defŏdiet condetque nitentia.—— Hor.
—"Whatever there is concealed beneath the ground, time will bring it to open sunshine; and will bury and consign to darkness things which are now conspicuous."

Quicquid vult habēre nemo potest.—"No man can have everything he wishes for."

Quicunque amīsit dignitātem pristĭnam,
Ignāvis est etiam jocus in casu gravi. PHÆD.
—"Whoever has fallen from his previous high estate, is in his heavy calamity the butt even of cowards."

Quicunque turpi fraude semel innŏtuit,
Etiamsi verum dicit, amittit fidem. PHÆD.
—"Whoever has once become notorious by base fraud, even if he speaks the truth, gains no belief."

Quicunque vult servāri.—"Whosoever will be saved." The beginning of the Athanasian Creed.

Quid ad farĭnas? Prov.—"How will this find you in flour?" What profit do you expect from this?

Quid ad Mercurium? Prov.—"What has this to do with Mercury?" He was the god of eloquence, and this question was put to one who wandered away from his subject.

——*Quid æternis minŏrem*
Consiliis ănĭmum fătīgas? HOR.
—"Why fatigue your mind, unequal to eternal projects?"

Quid afferre consĭlii potest, qui seipse eget consĭlio? CIC.
—"What counsel can he give to others, who has need of counsel himself?"

Quid brevi fortes jaculāmur ævo
Multa?—— HOR.
—"Why do we, whose life is so short, so resolutely aim at so many things?"

Quid datur à Divis felīci optātius horâ? CATULL.—"What can be granted us by the gods more desirable than a happy hour?" Meaning favourable opportunity, or lucky occasion, which was termed "*Felix hora.*"

Quid deceat, quid non; quo virtus, quo ferat error. HOR.—"What is becoming, what not; what is the tendency of excellence, what of error."

Quid dĕceat vos, non quantum lĭceat vobis, spectāre debētis.—"You ought to consider, not what is lawful for you to do, but what is becoming." There are acts not forbidden by law which it would not be justifiable to commit.

Quid de quoque viro, et cui dicas, sæpe cavēto. ——"Be ever on your guard what you say about another man, and to whom you say it." Properly *Quod de*, &c., which see.

Quid dem? quid non dem? rĕnuis tu quod jubet alter. Hor. —"What shall I give? what shall I not give? you refuse what another demands." The difficulties of authors who have to write for capricious readers.

Quid dignum tanto feret hic promissor hiātu? Hor.—"What will this promiser produce, worthy of all this gaping?"

Quid dignum tanto tibi ventre gulâque precābor? Mart.—"What shall I pray for as worthy of so vast a paunch and appetite as yours?"

Quid dŏmĭni făcient audent cum tālia fures? Virg.—"What will the masters be doing when the knaves dare do such things?"

Quid dulcius hŏmĭnum gĕnĕri à natūrâ datum est, quàm sui cuique lībĕri? Cic.—"What has been given by Nature more dear to man than his children?"

Quid ego ex hâc inopiâ nunc căpiam? Ter.—"What am I now to take from such a scarcity?" Where there is such a want of everything, who can take from the little there is?

——*Quid enim? Concurrĭtur—horæ*
Momento cito mors venit, aut victōria læta. Hor.
—"For why? They join battle, and in a moment of time there comes speedy death or joyous victory."

——*Quid enim ratiōne timēmus*
Aut cŭpĭmus?—— Juv.
—"For what is there that we either fear or wish for as reason would direct?"

——*Quid enim salvis infāmia nummis.* Juv.—"For what matters infamy so long as the money is safe?"

——*Quid est somnus, gĕlĭdæ nisi mortis imāgo?* Ovid.—"What is sleep but the image of cold death?"

Quid est tam inhumānum quam eloquentiam, a natūrâ ad salūtem hŏmĭnum et ad conservatiōnem datam, ad bonōrum pestem perniciemque convertĕre? Cic.—"What is so inhuman as to convert that eloquence, which by nature has been granted for the safety and preservation of man, into the annoyance and destruction of the good?"

Quid est turpius quàm senex vīvĕre incĭpiens? Sen.—"What is more shocking than to see an old man only just beginning to live?" What can be more dreadful than to see a man advanced in years, and yet a child in the practice of virtue?

Quid făcient pauci contra tot millia fortes? OVID —"What can a few brave men do against so many thousands?"

Quid făcies, făcies Vĕnĕris si vĕnĕris ante:
Ne pĕreas per eas; ne sĕdeas, sed eas.
—"What should you do if you come into Venus' presence? That you may not perish through it, sit not down—but begone." A punning distich, written by the Marquis De Bierve in the 17th century, on the words *facies, veneris, pereas,* and *sedeas.* Quoted in *Notes and Queries,* viii. 539.

Quid facis, infelix? Perdis bona vota.—— OVID.—"What are you doing, unhappy man? You are losing our good wishes."

——*Quid frustra simulacra fugăcia captas?*
Quod petis, est nusquam: quod amas avertĕre, perdes.
Ista repercussæ quam cernis imăginis umbra est,
Nil habet ista sui.—— OVID.
—"Why dost thou vainly catch at the flying image? What thou art seeking is nowhere: what thou lovest, turn but away and thou shalt lose; what thou seest, is but the shadow of a reflected form; it has nothing of its own." From the story of Narcissus.

Quid furor est, census corpŏre ferre suo! OVID.—"What madness it is, to be carrying a whole fortune on one's back!"

——*Quid habet pulchri constructus acervus?* HOR.—"What beauty is there in money piled up in heaps?"

Quid juvat immensum te argenti pondus et auri
Furtim defossâ tĭmĭdum depŏnĕre terrâ? HOR.
—"What pleasure can it afford you to bury stealthily and in fear immense sums of silver and gold under ground?"

——*Quid leges sine mŏrĭbus*
Vanæ proficiunt?—— HOR.
—"Of what avail are empty laws, without good morals?"

Quid magis est durum saxo, quid mollius undâ?
Dura tamen molli saxa cavantur aqua. OVID.
—"What is there harder than stone, what more yielding than water? Yet hard stones are hollowed by yielding water."

——*Quid, mea cum pugnat sententia secum?*
Quod pĕtiit spernit, rĕpĕtit quod nuper omīsit?
Æstuat, et vitæ disconvĕnit ordĭne toto? Hor.
—"What think you of me when my judgment is at variance with itself? When it despises what it just before desired, and desires what it lately rejected? When it is agitated by passion, and disturbs the whole tenor of life?"

Quid mentem traxisse polo, quid prŏfuit altum
Erexisse caput, pĕcŭdum si more pererrant? Claud.
—"What profits it to man to have derived a soul from heaven, what to lift his head with look erect, if, after the manner of brutes, he goes astray?"

Quid moror exemplis, quorum me turba fatīgat? Ovid.—"Why occupy myself with illustrations, the number of which exhausts me?"

Quid nisi victis dolor?—"What is there but misery for the conquered?"

Quid non ebriĕtas designat? Operta reclūdit;
Spes jubet esse ratas; in prælia trudit inertem;
Sollicitis ănĭmis onus exĭmit; addŏcet artes. Hor.
—"What does not drink achieve? it discloses secrets; commands our hopes to be ratified; urges the dastard to the fight; removes pressure from troubled minds; teaches the arts."

——*Quid non mortālia pectŏra cogis,*
Auri sacra fames?—— Virg.
—"To what crimes dost thou not impel the mortal breast, cursed greed for gold?"

——*Quid nos dura refugĭmus*
Ætas? Quid intactum nefasti
Lĭquĭmus? Hor.
—"What have we, an evil generation, deemed too bad? What have we, a wicked race, left inviolate?"

Quid nostri philosŏphi? Nonne in his libris ipsis, quos scribunt de contemnendâ gloriâ, sua nōmĭna inscrĭbunt? Cic.
—"What do our philosophers? Do they not, in those very books which they write on the contempt of glory, inscribe their own names?" See *Qui de*, &c.

Quid nunc?—"What now?" What news? A person who, like the Athenians in Saint Paul's time, is always on the hunt for news is satirically called a ***quidnunc.***

——*Quid oportet*
Nos făcĕre, à vulgo longè latèque remōtos? Hor.
—"What then must we do, when our sentiments differ so far and wide from those of the vulgar?"

Quid pro quo.—"One thing for another." "He expects a *quid pro quo*,"—he looks for something in return.

Quid prodest, Pontĭce, longo
Sanguĭne censēri, pictosque ostendĕre vultus
Majōrum?—— Juv.
—"What boots it, Ponticus, to be accounted of a long line, and to display the painted busts of our ancestors?"

Quid prosunt leges sine mōrĭbus?—See *Quid leges*, &c.

Quid quæque ferat rĕgio, et quid quæque recūset. Virg.—"What crop each soil produces, and what each soil refuses to bear." A subject for the chemical agriculturists.

Quid quisque vitet, nunquam hŏmĭni satis
Cautum est in horas.—— Hor.
—"Against that which each should avoid, no man takes sufficient precaution at all hours."

——*Quid rides? Mutāto nōmĭne de te*
Fābŭla narrātur.—— Hor.
—"Why do you laugh?" &c. See *Mutato nomine*, &c.

Quid Romæ făciam? mentīri nescio.—— Juv.—"What shall I do at Rome? I know not how to lie." He alludes to the corruption prevalent in Rome, where lying was the fashion.

Quid si cœlum ruat? Prov.—"What if the sky should fall?" Signifying the height of improbability.

Quid? si quis vultu torvo ferus, et pede nudo,
Exiguæque togæ sĭmŭlet textōre Catōnem;
Virtutemne repræsentet, moresque Catōnis? Hor.
—"What! If any savage, by a stern countenance and bare feet, and the texture of a scanty gown, were to ape Cato; would he represent the virtue and morals of Cato?"

Quid sit fŭtūrum cras fuge quærĕre, et
Quem sors diērum cunque dabit, lucro
Appōne.—— Hor.
—"Avoid inquiring what may happen to-morrow, and every day that fortune shall bestow on you, set down to your gain."

——*Quid sit pulchrum, quid turpe, quid ŭtĭle, quid non.* Hor. —"What is lovely, what base, what profitable, or what the contrary." Horace says that Homer excels in the investigation of all these points.

——*Quid tam dextro pede concĭpis, ut te*
Conātûs non pœniteat, votīque peracti? Juv.
—"What is there that you enter upon under such favourable auspices, as not to repent of your undertaking and the accomplishment of your wish?"

Quid tam rīdĭcŭlum quam appĕtĕre mortem, cum vitam tibi inquiētam fĕcĕris metu mortis? Sen.—"What is so ridiculous, as to seek death, when you have made your life miserable by the fear of death?" Addressed to those who would justify suicide.

Quid te exempta juvat spinis de plūrĭbus una? Hor.—"What does it avail you if one thorn is extracted out of many?" The removal of a single grievance is little felt if many are allowed to remain. See *Exempta juvat*, &c.

—— *Quid te ĭgĭtur rĕtŭlit*
Beneficum esse oratiōne, si ad rem auxilium emortuum est? Plaut.
—"What does it signify your being bounteous in talk, if all *real* aid is dead and gone?"

——*Quid terras ălio calentes*
Sole mutāmus?—— Hor.
—"Why do we change our own country for climates warmed by another sun?" Addressed to men of unsettled dispositions.

Quid tibi cum glădio? Dŭbiam rege, nāvĭta, pinum:
Non sunt hæc dĭgĭtis arma tenenda tuis. Ovid.
—"What hast thou to do with the sword? Steersman, guide the veering bark. These are not the implements that should be grasped by thy fingers." Lines which may be aptly addressed to one who vainly endeavours to distinguish himself both as a soldier and a statesman.

Quid tibi cum pĕlăgo? Terrâ contenta fuisses. Ovid.—"What have you to do with the sea? With the land you might have been content."

Quid tristes querimoniæ
Si non supplicio culpa recīdĭtur? Hor.

—"To what purpose are our woeful complaints, if sin is not checked with punishment?"

Quid turpius quam sapientis vitam ex insipientis sermōne pendĕre?—"What more unjust than to form an estimate of the life of a wise man from the words of a fool?"

Quid verum atque decens curo et rogo, et omnis in hoc sum. Hor.—"My care and study is what is genuine and proper and in this I am wholly engaged."

Quid vetat a magnis ad res exempla minōres
Sūmĕre?—— Ovid.
"What forbids me to apply illustrations from great matters to small ones?"

Quid vici prosunt aut horrea?——
——*Si metit Orcus*
Grandia cum parvis, non exorābĭlis auro. Hor.
—"Of what use are estates or granaries, if death, who cannot be bribed by gold, mows down equally the great with the small?"

Quid, victor, gaudes? Hæc te victōria perdet. Ovid.—"Why, victor, dost thou rejoice? This victory shall prove thy ruin."

——*Quid violentius aure tyranni?* Juv.—"What is more intemperate than the ear of a tyrant?" He, least of all, will brook advice or the honest truth.

——*Quid virtus, et quid sapientia possit,*
Utile proposuit nobis exemplar Ulyssem. Hor.
—"To show what virtue and what wisdom can do, [Homer] has propounded Ulysses as an instructive pattern."

Quid vŏveat dulci nutrĭcŭla majus alumno,
Quam săpĕre, et fari ut possit quæ sentiat, et cui
Gratia, fama, vălētūdo contingat abundè,
Et mundus victus, non deficiente crumēnâ? Hor.
—"What greater blessing could a tender nurse solicit for her beloved child, than that he might be wise, and able to express his sentiments, and that respect, reputation, and health might be his lot in abundance, and a respectable living with a never-failing purse?"

Quidam ex vultu conjectūram faciunt quantum quisque anĭmi habēre videātur. Cic.—"Some persons are able to judge from the countenance, how much intelligence each person is likely to have."

Quidque agat, ignārus stupet, et nec fræna remittit
Nec retinēre valet.—— OVID.
—"Ignorant what to do, he is stupefied; he neither lets go the reins, nor holds fast." Said of Phaëton.

Quidquid dicunt, laudo; id rursum si negant, laudo id quoque. TER.—"Whatever they say, I praise it; again, if they deny it, I praise that too." The rule of conduct of a time-serving flatterer. Such persons the Romans called *assentatores.*

Quidquid præter spem evēnit, id omne in lucro est deputandum. TER.—"Whatever has resulted beyond our expectations, must all be set down as clear gain."

Quiēta non movēre. Prov.—"Not to move things at rest." "To let well alone."

Quiētè et purè atque eleganter actæ ætātis, plăcĭda et lenis recordātio. CIC.—"Of a life passed in tranquillity, and in innocent and elegant pursuits, the remembrance is pleasing and delightful."

Quilibet potest renunciāre juri pro se introducto. Law Max. —"Any one may renounce the benefit of a stipulation introduced exclusively in his own favour."

Quique ălīis cavit, non cavet ipse sibi. OVID.—"And he that has defended others fails to defend himself."

Quique magis tĕgĭtur, tectus magis æstuat ignis. OVID.— "And the more the flame is covered, the more it spreads."

Quique sui memŏres ălios fecēre merendo. VIRG.—See *Inventas aut,* &c.

Quis custōdiet ipsos custōdes? JUV.—See *Pone seram,* &c.

Quis desidĕrio sit pudor aut modus
Tam cari căpĭtis?—— HOR.
—"What moderation or limit can there be to our regret at the loss of so dear a friend?"

Quis deus hanc, Musæ, quis nobis extŭdit artem? VIRG.— "What god, ye Muses, first revealed to us this art?"

——*Quis enim virtūtem amplectĭtur ipsam,*
Præmia si tollas?—— JUV.
—"For who would embrace virtue herself, if you take away the reward?" No man is utterly disinterested in the practice of the greatest virtue; he expects at least the reward of a good conscience. See *Si cum,* &c., and *Scire tuum,* &c.

Quis est enim, qui totum diem jacŭlans, non ălĭquando collĭneat? CIC.—"For who is there that will not, when shooting all day long, at last hit the mark?"

Quis expedĭvit psittăco suum χαῖρε? PERS.—"Who taught that parrot his 'how d'ye do?'" Who taught that fool to quote Greek?

Quis fallĕre possit amantem? VIRG.—"Who can deceive a man in love?" Who can escape a lover's jealous vigilance?

Quis fămŭlus amantior dŏmĭni quam canis? COLUM.—"What servant is more attached to his master than the dog?"

Quis fuit, horrendos primus qui prōtŭlit enses?
Quam ferus, et verè ferreus ille fuit! TIBUL.
—"Who was the man that first produced the dreadful sword? how savage, how truly iron-hearted was he!" The play upon the resemblance of the words *ferus* and *ferreus* cannot be expressed in English.

Quis furor, O cives, quæ tanta licentia ferri? LUCAN.—"What madness, O citizens! why this dreadful licence of the sword?" An appeal which may be made in a case of popular insurrection.

——*Quis inīquæ*
Tam patiens urbis, tam ferreus, ut tĕneat se? JUV.
—"Who can be so tolerant of the iniquities of the city, so steeled, as to contain himself?"

——*Quis neget arduis*
Pronos relābi posse rivos
Montĭbus, et Tĭbĕrim reverti? HOR.
—"Who can deny, that rivers may flow upwards to the mountains, and that the Tiber can be turned back?" Said in derision of an argument which cannot be supported upon natural grounds.

Quis nescit primam esse histŏriæ legem ne quid falsi dīcĕre audeat? CIC.—"Who knows not that it is the first law of history not to dare to say anything that is false?"

Quis non odit vărios, leves, fūtĭles? CIC.—"Who does not dislike the fickle, frivolous, and trifling?"

Quis novus hic nostris successit sēdĭbus hospes?
Quam sese ore ferens!—— VIRG.
—"What think you of this wondrous guest who has come to our abode? In mien how graceful he appears!"

Quis potest aut corpŏris firmitāti, aut fortūnæ stabilitāti confīdĕre? Cic.—"Who is there that can have confidence in the strength of his body, or the stability of his fortune?"

Quis scit an adjiciant hodiernæ crastīna summæ
Tempŏra Dī sŭpĕri?—— Hor.
—"Who knows whether the gods above will add a morrow to the existence of to-day?"

——*Quis talia fando*
Tempĕret a lăcrymis?—— Virg.
—"Who, in recounting such misfortunes, can refrain from tears?"

Quis tŭlĕrit Gracchos de seditiōne querentes? Juv.—"Who could endure the Gracchi complaining of sedition?" The Gracchi were tribunes of Rome, and demagogues concerned in every seditious movement of the people. The quotation has the same meaning as *Clodius accusat mœchos.*

Quisnam ĭgĭtur liber? Sapiens sibi qui imperiōsus;
Quem neque paupĕries, neque mors, neque vincŭla terrent;
Responsāre cupīdĭnĭbus, contemnĕre honōres
Fortis, et in seipso totus teres atque rotundus. Hor.
—"Who then is free? The wise man who has dominion over himself; whom neither poverty, nor death, nor chains affright; resolute in checking his appetites, and in contemning honours; perfect in himself, polished and round as a globe."

Quisque suos pătĭmur Manes.—— Virg.—"We each of us have to put up with his own destiny."

Quisquis amat ranam, ranam putat esse Diānam.—"If a man is in love with a frog, he will think his frog a very Diana." A mediæval saying.

Quo ănĭmo.—"With what mind," or intention. The criminality of an act greatly depends upon the animus with which it was committed.

Quo bene cœpisti, sic pede semper eas. Ovid.—"Mayest thou always proceed well in the path which thou hast commenced so well to tread."

——*Quo fata trahunt rĕtrăhuntque, sequāmur.* Virg.—"Wherever the fates lead us, let us follow." Let us submit to the decrees of Providence.

Quo jure. *Law Term.*—"By what right."

Quo jure, quâque injūriâ. TER.—"Whether right or whether wrong." "By hook or by crook."

Quo major gloria, eo propior invidiæ est. LIV. — "The greater the glory, the nearer it is to envy."

Quo me cunque rapit tempestas, dēfĕror hospes. HOR. — See *Nullius addictus*, &c.

Quo mihi fortūnas, si non concēdĭtur uti? HOR. — "Of what use is fortune to me, if I am not permitted to enjoy it?"

——*Quo more pyris vesci Călăber jubet hospes.* HOR.—"After the manner in which a Calabrian invites his guest to feed on pears." Pears so abounded in Calabria, that hogs were fed with them. Applicable to those who would force on you that which is of little value and for which you have no liking.

Quo nihil majus meliusve terris. HOR.—"Than which there is nothing greater or more august on earth."

Quo non ars pĕnĕtrat? Discunt lăcrymāre decenter. OVID. —"To what point does not art proceed? Some even study how to weep with grace."

Quo plus sunt potæ, plus sitiuntur aquæ. OVID.—"The more water we drink, the more we thirst."—The more we have, the more we want. A simile derived from the dropsy.

Quo quisque stultior, eo magis insolescit.—"The more foolish a man is, the more insolent he becomes."

Quo res cunque cadent, unum et commūne periclum,
Una salus ambōbus erit.—— VIRG.

—"However things may turn out, we shall share one common danger, enjoy the same security."

Quo rŭĭtis generōsa domus? male crēdĭtur hosti,
Simplex nobilĭtas, perfĭda tela cave. OVID.

—"Whither rush ye, high-born house? It is unsafe to trust a foe. Unsuspecting nobles, beware of the weapons of treachery."

Quo semel est imbūta recens servābit odōrem
Testa diu.—— HOR.

—"A cask will long preserve the flavour with which, when new, it was once impregnated." Early youth is especially susceptible of impressions for good or for bad.

Quo tamen adversis fluctĭbus ire paras? OVID.—"Whither

then do you prepare to go against the tide of circumstances?"

——*Quo tendis inertem,*
Rex perĭtūre, fugam? nescis heu, perdĭte! nescis
Quem fugias; hostes incurris, dum fugis hostem.
Incĭdis in Scyllam cŭpiĕns vitāre Charybdim.
PHILIP GUALTIER.

—"Whither, unfortunate king, dost thou direct thy unavailing flight? Thou knowest not, alas! doomed man, whom to fly; while thou fliest from one foe thou art running into the hands of another. Thou fallest into Scylla while endeavouring to escape Charybdis." See *Incidit in*, &c.

Quo tĕneam vultus mutantem Prōtea nodo? HOR.—"In what noose shall I hold this Proteus, who is always changing his countenance?" How confine to one point the man who is always shifting his ground of argument?

Quo tua non possunt offendi pectŏra facto;
Forsĭtan hoc ălio jūdĭce crimen erit. OVID.
—"Perhaps the commission of that by which your own feelings are not hurt, may be a fault in the opinion of another."

Quoad hoc.—"Thus far." "*Quoad hoc*, I agree with you."

Quocunque aspĭcias, nihil est nisi pontus et aer;
Nūbĭbus hic tŭmĭdus, fluctĭbus ille minax. OVID.
—"Whichever way you look, there is nothing but sea and air; the latter laden with clouds, the former threatening with billows."

Quocunque nōmĭne gaudet.—"In whatever name he rejoices." By whatever name he may be known.

——*Quocunque volent, ănĭmum audităris agunto.* HOR.—"Let them lead just as they please the passions of the audience." The great object of the poet and the orator.

Quod absurdum est.—"Which is absurd." See *Reductio ad absurdum.*

Quod ălĭbi diminūtum, exæquātur ălĭbi. Prov.—"That which is curtailed one way may be made up another." See *Non omnia*, &c.

Quod avertat Deus!—"Which may God forbid!" Or, more tersely, "God forbid!"

Quod caret alternâ rĕquie durābĭle non est. OVID.—"That which is without alternate repose is not durable."

Quod certamĭnĭbus ortum, ultra metam durat. VELL. PATER. —"What is begun in strife lasts beyond our calculations." Contention should if possible be avoided while there is still room for negotiation.

Quod cessat ex rĕdĭtu, frugalitāte supplеātur. PLINY *the Younger.*—"Let that which is wanting in our revenue be made up by frugality."

Quod cibus est ăliis, ăliis est atre venĕnum.—"What is food for some is black poison to others." Tastes differ. "What is one man's meat is another man's poison."

Quod cuique tempŏris ad vivendum datur, eo debet esse contentus. CIC.—"Each ought to be content with the period of existence allotted."

Quod de quoque viro, et cui dicas, sæpe cavēto.—"Be constantly on your guard to whom you speak and what you say."

Quod decet honestum est, et quod honestum est decet. CIC. —"Whatever is becoming is honourable, and whatever is honourable is becoming."

Quod defertur non aufertur.—"That which is deferred is not relinquished." "Omittance is no quittance." SHAKSP.

Quod erat demonstrandum.—"Which was to be proved." Abbreviated *Q. E. D.*, and generally appended to the Theorems of Euclid.

Quod erat faciendum.—"Which was to be done." Abbreviated *Q. E. F.*, and appended to the Problems of Euclid.

Quod est violentum non est durābĭle. *Prov.*—"That which is violent cannot last long."

Quod huic officium, quæ laus, quod decus erit tanti quod adipisci cum dolōre corpŏris velit, qui dolōrem summum malum sibi persuasĕrit? quam porro quis ignominiam, quam turpitūdĭnem non pertŭlĕrit, ut effugiat dolōrem, si id summum malum esse decrēvit? CIC.—"What office, what commendation, what honours, will be so highly valued by him who considers pain the greatest of evils, that he will earn them at the expense of bodily pain? And what ignominy, what baseness, will he not submit to, merely to avoid pain, if he is of opinion that it is the greatest of ills?"

Quod in corde sobrii, id in linguâ ebrii. *Prov.*—"What a man keeps in his breast when sober is at his tongue's end when drunk." See *In vino*, &c.

Quod latet ignōtum est, ignōti nulla cupīdo. OVID.—"That which lies hid is unknown; for what is unknown there is no desire." "What the eye sees not, the heart rues not."

Quod licet ingrātum est, quod non licet, ācrius urit.—OVID. —"What is accessible is but little esteemed, what is denied is eagerly desired."

Quod male fers, assuesce; feres bene. Multa vetustas
Lenit.—— OVID.

—"What you endure with impatience, accustom yourself to; and you will endure it with patience. Time makes many things endurable." See *Optimum elige*, &c.

Quod medicamenta morbis exhĭbent, hoc jura negotiis.—"Laws are of the same use in the affairs of men, as medicines in diseases."

——*Quod medicōrum est,*
Promittunt mĕdĭci, tractant fabrīlia fabri. HOR.

—"Physicians undertake what belongs to physicians, mechanics handle the tools of mechanics."

Quod munus reipublĭcæ afferre majus mĕliusve possŭmus, quam si docēmus atque erudīmus juventūtem? CIC.—"What greater benefit can we confer upon the state, or what more valuable, than if we teach and train up the young?"

Quod naturālis rătio inter omnes hŏmĭnes constĭtuit, vocātur jus gentium.—"That which natural reason has established among all men, is called the law of nations."

Quod nescias damnāre, summa est temĕrĭtas.—"It is extreme presumption to condemn what you do not understand."

Quod nimis mĭsĕri volunt, hoc făcĭle credunt.—"That which the wretched anxiously wish for, they are ready to believe."

Quod non opus est, asse carum est.—"What is not wanted is dear at a penny." A saying of Cato, quoted by Seneca.

Quod non potest, vult posse qui nimium potest. SEN.—"He who is able to do too much, wishes to do more than he is able." The thirst for power becomes the more insatiate the more it is gratified.

——*Quod nunc rătio est, impĕtus ante fuit.* Ovid.—"What is now an act of reason was an impulse before."

——*Quod optanti Divûm promittĕre nemo*
Audĕret, volvenda dies, en! attŭlit ultro. Virg.
—"That which not one of the gods would have ventured to promise to your supplications, behold! the revolving day has spontaneously bestowed." Said of some unlooked-for piece of good fortune.

Quod pĕtiit spernit, repĕtit quod nuper omīsit. Hor.—"What he formerly sought, he now despises, and seeks again that which he lately rejected." A description of the unsettled mind of a wayward and capricious man.

——*Quod petis hic est;*
Est Ulŭbris.—— Hor.
—"What you seek is here—it is at Ulubræ." Happiness may be enjoyed even in the meanest of places.

Quod petis, id sanè invīsum est ăcĭdumque duōbus. Hor.—"What you ask for is detestable and nauseous to two other persons." Said of an author, desirous, but unable, to please the tastes of three different readers.

Quod præstāre potes, ne bis promisĕris ulli;
Ne sis verbōsus, dum vis urbānus habēri. Cato.
—"Promise not twice to any man the service you may be able to render him; and be not loquacious, if you wish to be esteemed for your kindness."

Quod pŭdeat socium prudens celāre memento.—"What shames thy friend, be prudent and conceal."

Quod quisque vitet, nunquam hŏmĭni satis
Cautum est in horas.—— Hor.
—"Man is never sufficiently on his guard from hour to hour what to avoid."

Quod rătio nĕquiit, sæpe sanāvit mora. Sen.—"Time and patience have often cured what reason could not."

Quod satis est cui contingit, nihil amplius optet. Hor.—"He whose lot it is to have enough should wish for nothing more."

Quod scis, nihil prodest: quod nescis, multum obest. Cic.—"What you know profits you nothing, what you don't know is a great loss." An instance of Antithesis.

Quod sĕquĭtur, fŭgio; quod fugit, usque sequor. Ovid.—"What follows me, I fly; what flies me, I continue to pursue."

Quod si deficiant vires, audācia certe
Laus erit; in magnis, et voluisse sat est. PROPERT.
—"Even though the strength should fail, still boldness shall have its praise; in great undertakings it is enough to have attempted."

Quod si tantus amor menti, si tanta cupīdo est,
——Et insāno juvat indulgĕre labōri,
Accĭpe quæ peragenda prius.—— VIRG.
—"But if so great a passion, so ardent a love of enterprise, influences your mind, and you delight to undertake a task so desperate, hear what must first be done."

Quod sis esse velis, nihilque malis. MART.—"Wish to be what you are, and consider nothing preferable."

Quod sors feret, ferēmus æquo ănĭmo. TER.—"Whatever fortune may bring, let us bear it with equanimity."

Quod supra nos, nihil ad nos. *Prov.* —"That which is above us is nothing to us." Originally a saying of Socrates, intimating that we ought not to attempt to pry into mysteries beyond our comprehension. See *Quæ supra*, &c.

Quod tam grande sophos clamat tibi turba togāta,
Non tu, Pomponi, cœna discrta tua est. MART.
—"The reason why the gown-clad multitude receives you, Pomponius, with such loud plaudits is, not that you, but that your dinner, speaks with eloquence."

Quod tantis Romāna manus contexĕrit annis,
Prōdĭtor unus incrmi, angusto tempŏre vertit. CLAUD.
—"What the Roman hand constructed in so many years, a single traitor, unarmed, overthrew in one short moment." A censure against Rufinus.

Quod tibi fiĕri non vis, altĕri ne fēcĕris.—"Do not unto another what you would not have done unto yourself."

Quod verum, simplex, sincĕrumque est, id natūræ hŏmĭnis est aptissĭmum. CIC.—"That which is true, honest, and sincere, is most congenial to the nature of man."

Quod vide.—"Which see." Often written *q. v.*

Quod vīdĭmus testāmur.—"We testify that we have seen." 1 *John* iii. 11.

Quod vile est carum, quod carum est vile, putāto;
Sic tibi nec parcus, nec avārus habēbĕris ulli. CATO.

—"Consider that what is inferior is dear, and what is dear is inferior; so you will neither appear stingy to yourself, nor be considered avaricious by others."

Quod volunt hŏmĭnes, se bene velle putant.—"What men wish for, they think themselves right in wishing for."

Quod vos jus cogit, id voluntāte impĕtret. Ter.—"That which the law would compel you to do, let him obtain as of your own free will." Concede with a good grace that which the law will not allow you to withhold.

Quodcunque attĭgĕrit, si qua est studiōsa sinistri,
Ad vitium mores instruet inde suos. Ovid.

—"Whatever comes in a woman's way, if she is at all inclined to do wrong, she will strain to her vicious purposes."

Quodcunque ostendis mihi sic, incrēdulus odi. Hor.—"Whatever you show me in such a manner, I detest and disbelieve." Said with reference to the exhibition on the stage of shocking and disgusting objects.

Quodlĭbet.—"Whatever you please." A farrago or miscellany. This name is also given to a *pot-pourri*, or song, composed of scraps or verses of other songs, much after the fashion of the *Cento* of the later Roman poets.

Quōmŏdo hăbeas, illud refert; jurĕne an injuriâ. Plaut.—"The question is, In what way you get it, whether rightfully or wrongfully."

Quondam etiam victis redit in præcordia virtus. Virg.—"Sometimes valour will return even into the breasts of the conquered." When it is prompted by despair.

Quoniam diu vixisse denegātur, ălĭquid faciāmus quo possimus ostendĕre nos vixisse. Cic.—"As length of life is denied us, let us do something by which we may show that we have lived."

Quoniam id fiĕri quod vis non potest,
Velis id quod possit.—— Ter.

—"As that cannot be done which you desire, wish for something that can be done."

Quoniam quidem circumventus ab inimīcis præceps agor, incendium meum ruīnâ restinguam. Sall.—"Since, then, I am so beset by foes and hurried on to destruction, I will extinguish the flame in which I perish by their ruin."

From the speech of Catiline to the senate, when accused by them of conspiring against the state.

Quorum æmulāri exoptat negligentiam
Potius quam ipsōrum obscūram diligentiam. TER.
—"Whose carelessness (of style) he prefers to emulate, rather than the laboured abstruseness of the others."

Quorum ănĭmus meminisse horret luctuque refūgit. VIRG.—"At the remembrance of which my soul shudders, and has shrunk back with grief."

Quorum pars causas, et res, et nōmĭna quæret;
Pars rĕfĕret, quamvis nōvĕrit ipsa parum. OVID.
—"Some will be making inquiries as to the reasons, the circumstances, and the names; some again will be explaining, although they themselves know but little about it."

——*Quorum pars magna fui.* VIRG.—See *Quæque ipse*, &c.

Quos Deus vult perdĕre dementat priùs.—"Those whom God has a mind to ruin he first deprives of their senses." Aptly applied to persons whose obstinacy, or pride, leads them into errors portentous of their fall. See *At Dæmon*, &c., and *Quem Jupiter*, &c.

Quos ego—— VIRG.—"Whom I——" will chastise. A good illustration of the figure Aposiopesis.

——*Quos ille timōrum*
Maxĭmus haud urget lethi metus: inde ruendi
In ferrum mens prona viris, ănĭmæque capāces
Mortis.—— LUCAN.
—"The dread of death, that greatest of fears, does not influence them: hence they are inspired to rush upon the sword, and are ever ready for death."

——*Quos nunc perscrībĕre longum est.*—"Whom it would be tedious just now to enumerate." See *Cum multis*, &c.

——*Quot căpĭtum vivunt, tŏtĭdem studiōrum*
Millia.—— HOR.
—"As is the number of men who exist, so is the diversity of their pursuits."

Quot hŏmĭnes, tot sententiæ. TER.—"So many men, so many minds." See the preceding, and *Denique non*, &c.

Quot servi, tot hostes. SEN.—"As many servants, so many enemies." Every servant you keep has an opportunity of becoming your enemy.

——*Quotīdie*
Prīdie caveat, ne făciat quod pĭgeat postrīdie. PLAUT.
—"Let each man take care not to do to-day what he may regret to-morrow."

——*Quoties flenti Thesēius heros*
Siste modum, dixit, neque enim fortūna querenda
Sola tua est; sĭmĭles aliōrum respĭce casus,
Mitius ista feres.—— OVID.
—"How often did the hero, the son of Theseus say to her as she wept, 'Restrain thy grief; for thy lot is not the only one to be lamented; consider the like calamities of others, thou wilt then bear thine own better.'"

Quotiescumque gradum făcies, toties tibi tuārum virtūtum vĕniat in mentem. CIC.—"As often as you make a step so often let your merits occur to your mind." The words addressed by his mother to Spurius Carvilius, who had been rendered lame by a wound received in battle.

Quousque tandem abutĕre patientiâ nostrâ? CIC.—"How long, pray, will you abuse our patience?" The beginning of Cicero's first Philippic against Catiline.

Quum labor extudĕrit fastidia, siccus, inānis,
Sperne cibum vilem; nisi Hymettia mella Falerno
Ne bĭbĕris dilūta.—— HOR.
—"When exercise has worked off squeamishness, dry and hungry as you are, then despise plain food; and don't drink anything but Hymettian honey qualified with Falernian wine." Said ironically, of course.

Quum sunt partium jura obscūra, reo potius favendum est quam actōri. *Law Max.*—"When the rights of the parties are doubtful, favour must be shown to the defendant rather than the complainant."

R.

R. I. P., for *Requiescat in pace.*—"May he rest in peace." These initials frequently terminate the epitaph of persons of the Roman Catholic persuasion.

Radit usque ad cutem. *Prov.*—"He shaves close to the skin." Applied to a person who is rigorously exacting.

——*Rami felīcia poma ferentes.* OVID.—"Branches bearing beauteous fruit."

——*Răpĭdus montāno flūmĭne torrens*
Sternit agros, sternit sata læta, boumque labōres,
Præcipitesque trahit sylvas.—— VIRG.

—"The raging torrent of the mountain-stream sweeps over the fields, levels the smiling crops and the labours of the oxen, and carries headlong the trees of the forest."

Rara avis in terris, nigroque simillĭma cygno. OVID.—"A bird rarely seen on earth, and very like a black swan." A thing so utterly unknown in those times, that it was supposed not to exist. The first four words are often used ironically.

——*Rara est ădeo concordia formæ*
Atque pudicitiæ.—— JUV.

—"So rare is the union of beauty and virtue." Beauty is greatly exposed to the arts of temptation, which in the corrupt age of Juvenal were exercised with almost universal success.

Rara fides pietasque viris qui castra sequuntur. LUCAN.—"Faith and piety are rarely found among the men who follow the camp." This is a severe, and it is to be hoped undeserved, censure against the military profession.

Rara quidem virtus, quam non fortūna gubernat. OVID.—"Rare indeed is that virtue which fortune does not govern."

Rarâ tempŏrum felicitāte, ubi sentīre quæ velis, et quæ sentias dīcĕre licet. TACIT.—"Such was the uncommon happiness of the times, that you might think what you would and speak what you thought." A description of the freedom and happiness enjoyed by the Roman empire in the reigns of Nerva and Trajan.

——*Rari nantes in gurgĭte vasto.* VIRG.—"A few swimming here and there in the vasty deep." A description of sailors endeavouring to escape from shipwreck; but sometimes applied to literary works, in which a few happy thoughts may be found here and there amid an ocean of nonsense. See *Apparent rari*, &c.

Rari quippe boni; nŭmĕro vix sunt totĭdem quot
Thebārum portæ, vel dīvĭtis ostia Nili. JUV.

—"Few indeed are the good; their number is scarce so

many as the gates of Thebes, or the mouths of fertilizing Nile." The gates of Thebes in Egypt were one hundred in number, those of Thebes in Bœotia seven.

Raro antecedentem scelestum
Desĕruit pede pœna claudo. Hor.
—"Justice has rarely, with halting foot, failed to overtake the evil-doer in his flight."

Rarus enim ferme sensus commūnis in illâ
Fortūnâ.—— Juv.
—"Common sense is seldom found with great fortune." Men when suddenly elevated are apt to lose their senses.

Rarus sermo illis, et magna libīdo tacendi. Juv.—"They speak but seldom, and show a great love of silence." Said with reference to men who affect a silent and solemn deportment, as indicative of wisdom and solid sense: copyists of Lord Burleigh's expressive nods.

Rătio et auctŏrĭtas, duo clarissĭma mundi lumĭna. Coke.—"Reason and authority, the two brightest lights of the world."

Rătio et consilium propriæ ducis artes. Tacit.—"Thought and deliberation are the proper qualifications of a general."

Rătio et orătio conciliant inter se hŏmĭnes. Neque ullâ re longius absūmus a natūrâ ferārum. Cic.—"Reason and speech unite men to each other. Nor is there anything in which we differ more entirely from the brute creation."

Ratio justifica.—"The reason which justifies."

Rătio quasi quædam lux lumenque vitæ. Cic.—"Reason is, as it were, the guide and light of life."

Ratio suasoria.—"The reason which persuades."

Rătionābĭle tempus.—"A reasonable time."

Re infectâ.—"The business being unfinished." His object being unaccomplished.

——*Re ipsâ rĕppĕri,*
Facilitāte nihil esse hŏmĭni melius neque clementiâ. Ter.
—"I have found by experience that there is nothing better for a man than an easy temper and complacency."

Re opĭtulandum non verbis. Prov.—"We must assist in deeds, not in words."

Re secundâ fortis, dubiâ fugax. Phæd.—"In prosperity courageous, in danger timid."

Rebus angustis animōsus atque
Fortis appāre; sapienter idem
Contrăhes vento nimĭum secundo
Turgĭda vela. HOR.

—"In adversity, appear full of resolution and undaunted; in like manner prudently reef your sails, when too much distended by a prosperous gale."

Rebus in angustis făcĭle est contemnĕre mortem;
Fortĭter ille facit qui miser esse potest. MART.

—"In adversity it is easy to show contempt for death; he acts with fortitude, who can endure being wretched." Suicide is cowardice:

"The coward dares to die, the brave live on."

Rebus secundis etiam egregios duces insolescĕre. TACIT.—"In the moments of prosperity, even the best of generals are apt to be too much elated."

Rebus sic stantĭbus.—"Such being the state of things."

——*Recenti mens trĕpĭdat metu.* HOR.—"My mind is still agitated with terror."

——*Recepto*
Dulce mihi furĕre est amīco. HOR.

—"It is delightful to launch out on receiving my friend once more."

Recipiunt fœminæ sustentācula a nobis.—"Women receive support from us." Motto of the Patten-makers' Company.

Recta actio non erit, nisi recta fuit voluntas, ab hâc enim est actio. Rursus, voluntas non erit recta, nisi hăbĭtus ănĭmi rectus fuerit, ab hoc enim est voluntas. SEN.—"An action will not be right unless the intention is right, for from it springs the action. Again, the intention cannot be right unless the state of the mind is right, for from it proceeds the intention."

Rectius vives, Lĭcĭni, neque altum
Semper urgendo, neque, dum procellas
Cautus horrescis, nimium premendo
Littus inīquum. HOR.

—"You will live more prudently, Licinius, by neither always keeping out at sea, nor, while you are cautiously in dread of storms, by hugging too much the hazardous shore." A lesson to avoid extremes.

Rectus in curiâ. *Law Phrase.*—"Upright in the court." The state of a man who comes into a court of justice with clean hands.

Recusātio jūdĭcis.—"Exception taken to the judge."

Reddas amīcis tempŏra, uxōri vaces,
Anĭmum relaxes, otium des corpŏri. PHÆD.
—"Give time to your friends, your leisure to your wife, relax your mind, and refresh your body." Lines addressed to a man immersed in business.

Redde vicem mĕrĭtis; grato licet esse.—— OVID.—"Make some return for my kindness; you may now be grateful."

Reddĕre persōnæ scit convenientia cuique. HOR.—"He knows how to assign to each person a suitable part." He knows what best suits each character. Said of a dramatic writer.

Reddĕre qui voces jam scit puer, et pede certo
Signat humum, gestit părĭbus collūdĕre, et iram
Collĭgit ac ponit tĕmĕrè, et mutātur in horas. HOR.
—"The child who just knows how to talk and to walk, delights to play with his equals, is easily provoked and appeased, and changes with every hour."

Reddĭte depŏsĭtum; piĕtas sua fœdĕra servet;
Fraus absit; văcuas cædis habēte manus. OVID.
—"Restore the pledge intrusted; let affection observe her duties; be there no fraud; keep your hands free from bloodshed."

——*Rĕdeat mĭsĕris, ăbeat fortūna superbis.* HOR.—"May fortune revisit the wretched, and forsake the proud!"

Redīre ad nuces.—"To return to the nuts." To become a child again.

——*Redit agrĭcŏlis labor actus in orbem,*
Atque in se sua per vestīgia volvĭtur annus. VIRG.
—"The farmer's toil returns in a circle, and the year revolves in its former footsteps."

Redŏlet lucernam.—"It smells of the lamp." See *Olet lucernam.*

Reductio ad absurdum.—"A reduction to an absurdity." A phrase used in logical or mathematical reasoning, when the adversary is *reduced* to submission by proving the *absurdity* of his position.

Refricāre cicatrīcem.—"To open a wound afresh." "To rip up an old sore." To revert to a former grievance.

——*Rege incŏlŭmi, mens omnĭbus una est;*
Amisso, rupēre fidem, constructaque mella
Diripuēre ipsæ, et crates solvēre favōrum. VIRG.

—"While the king is safe one mind animates all; when he is dead they dissolve their union, and themselves tear to pieces the fabric of their honey, and demolish the structure of their combs." From this circumstance, Virgil expresses his opinion that bees are endowed with something more than instinct. The presiding bee was, by the ancients, erroneously called the "king."

Reges dicuntur multis urgēre culullis,
Et torquēre mero, quem perspexisse labōrent,
An sit amicitiâ dignus.—— HOR.

—"Certain kings are said to ply with many a cup, and to test with wine, the man whom they are anxious to prove, whether he be worthy of their friendship."

Rēgia, crede mihi, res est, succurrĕre lapsis. OVID.—"'Tis a kingly act, believe me, to succour the distressed."

Rēgĭbus boni quam mali suspectiōres sunt, semperque his aliēna virtus formidolōsa est. SALL.—"Good men are more suspected by kings than bad ones; and distinguished virtues in other men are always to them a ground of apprehension." When a man has no rivals in station, he is apt to become suspicious of those who are his successful rivals in the practice of virtue.

Rēgĭbus hic mos est; ubi equos mercantur opertos
Inspiciunt; ne si facies, ut sæpe, decōra
Molli fulta pede est, emptōrem indūcat hiantem,
Quod pulchræ clunes, breve quod caput, ardua cervix. HOR.

—"This is the custom with men of fortune when they purchase horses, they inspect them covered; that if, as often happens, a fine forehand is supported by a tender hoof, it may not deceive the buyer, eager for the bargain, because the buttocks are handsome, the head small, and the neck stately."

Regis ad exemplar totus compōnĭtur orbis.—"The whole community is regulated by the example of the king." See *Componitur orbis*, &c.

Rēgium donum.—"The royal gift." A sum of money granted

yearly by the Crown to the Presbyterian clergy of Ireland is so called.

Rēgius morbus.—"The royal disease." In the classical authors this means the jaundice, but when used by mediæval writers, it signifies the malady now known as the "king's evil."

Regnāre nolo, liber ut non sim mihi. PHÆD.—"I would not be a king to lose my liberty."

Regŭla ex jure, non jus ex regŭlâ sūmĭtur. Law Max.—"The practice is taken from the law, not the law from the practice."

Regum æquābat opes ănĭmis; serâque revertens
Nocte domum, dăpĭbus mensas onerābat inemptis. VIRG.
—"He equalled the wealth of kings in contentment of mind; and at night returning home, would load his board with unbought dainties." A description of the happy life of the old man Corycius.

Regum fēlīcitas multis miscētur malis.—"The happiness of kings is alloyed by many evils."

Rei mandātæ omnes sapientes primum prævorti decet. PLAUT.—"It behoves all wise men to give their first attention to the business intrusted to them."

Reipublĭcæ forma laudāri facilius quam evenīre, et si evenit, haud diuturna esse potest. TACIT.—"It is more easy to praise a republican form of government than to establish it; and when it is established it cannot be of long duration." So far as Europe is concerned, the historian seems to be right.

Relāta rĕfĕro.—"I tell the tale as it was told to me." I do not vouch for its truth.

Relegāre bona religiōnĭbus. Law Phrase.—"To bequeath one's property for pious purposes."

——*Relictâ non bene parmŭlâ.* HOR.—"Ingloriously leaving my shield behind." Horace confesses that he did this at the battle of Philippi, when he saved himself by flight See *Tanquam Argivum, &c.*

Religentem esse oportet, religiōsum nefas. AUL. GELL. *from an ancient poem.*—"A man should be religious, not superstitious." A play upon the resemblance of the two words.

Rem acu tĕtĭgit.—"He has touched the matter with a needle." "He has hit the right nail on the head."

——*Rem, făcias rem;*
Si possis recte, si non, quocunque modo rem. Hor.
—"Wealth, acquire wealth; by honest means if you can, if not, by any means gain wealth." "Get money, my son, get money, honestly if you can, but get money."

Rem tibi quam nosces aptam, dimittĕre noli;
Fronte capillātâ, post est occăsio calva. Cato.
—"Lose not the thing that thou knowest to be suitable for thee; Opportunity has locks before, but behind is bald." See *Occasio prima*, &c.

——*Rem tu strenuus auge.* Hor.—"Exert every endeavour to increase your property."

Remis velisque. *Prov.*—"With oars and sails." Using every possible endeavour. "With tooth and nail."

Rĕnŏvet pristīna bella.—"Let him fight his battles over again."

——*Reparābĭlis adsŏnat echo.* Pers.—"Repeating echo resounds."

Repente dives nemo factus est bonus. Syr.—"No good man ever became rich all of a sudden." Fortunes rapidly made are often owing to advantage being taken of others.

Rĕpĕrit Deus nocentem. *Prov.*—"God finds out the guilty man." Our sins "come home to us at last."

Rĕquiem æternam dona eis, Dŏmĭne.—"Grant them eternal rest, O Lord." The beginning of the *Requiem*, or chaunt for the dead, of the Romish Church.

Requiescat in pace.—"May he rest in peace." A common inscription on tomb-stones. It is sometimes used ironically in reference to the departed greatness of persons dismissed from office. See *R. I. P.*

Rerum ipsārum cognĭtio vera, e rebus ipsis est. Jul. Scalig.—"The true knowledge of things must be derived from the things themselves." Mastery of a subject can only be acquired by attentive study and examination.

Res amīcos invĕnit. Plaut.—"Money finds friends."

——*Res angusta domi.* Juv.—"Narrowed circumstances at home;" limited means. "The *res angusta domi* obliges him to live in retirement." An euphemism for poverty.

Res est blanda canor; discant cantāre puellæ. Ovid.—"Music is an insinuating thing: let the fair learn to sing."

Res est sacra miser.—— OVID.—"A man in distress is a sacred object." Respect is due to the sufferings of the wretched.

Res est solliciti plena timōris amor. OVID.—"Love is full of anxious fears."

Res humānæ instābĭles sunt, et nihil habent firmitātis. CIC. —"Human affairs are unstable, and have in them nothing lasting."

Res in cardĭne est. *Prov.*—"The business is on the hinge." It is now in suspense, but will soon be terminated one way or the other.

Res judicāta.—"A thing adjudged." A matter decided.

Res rustĭca sic est, si unam rem sero fēcĕris omnia ŏpĕra sero făcies. CATO.—"The nature of husbandry is such, that if you do one thing too late, you will do everything too late."

Res sunt humānæ flēbĭle lūdĭbrium.—"Human affairs are a mournful jest."

Res ubi magna nitet.—— HOR.—"Where an ample fortune shines." Where splendid circumstances are evident.

Res unīus ætātis.—"A thing of only one age." A phrase employed in the law to denote a legal provision, which cannot extend to the circumstances of more than one generation.

Respĭce finem.—"Look to the end." "Respect your end." *Comedy of Errors*, act iv. sc. 4.

Respĭcĕre exemplar vitæ morumque jubēbo
Doctum imitātōrem, et veras hinc dūcĕre voces. HOR.
—"I would direct the learned imitator to study closely nature and manners, and thence to draw his expressions to the life."

Respondeat supĕrior. *Law Max.*—"The principal must answer." The master must answer for the acts of his servant when acting as such.

Respŭe quod non es.—— PERS.—"Reject what you are not." Assume not a character to which you have no just claim.

Restat iter cælo: cælo tentābĭmus ire;
Da vĕniam cœpto, Jūpĭter alte, meo. OVID.
—"There remains a path through the heavens; through the heavens we will attempt to go Great Jupiter, grant

pardon to my design." The words of Dædalus, when about to make his escape on wings from the Cretan Labyrinth.

Rete non tendĭtur accĭpĭtri neque milvio. TER.—"The net is not spread for the hawk or the kite."

Reverendo admŏdum.—"To the very reverend."

——*Revocāte ănĭmos, mœstumque timōrem*
Mittĭte.—— VIRG.
—"Resume your courage, and cast off this desponding fear."

Rex datur propter regnum, non regnum propter regem. Potentia non est nisi ad bonum. *Law Max.*—"A king is given for the sake of the kingdom, not the kingdom for the sake of the king. Power is only given for the public good."

Rex est major singŭlis, minor universis. BRACTON.—"The king is greater than any individual, but less than the whole community."

Rex est qui mĕtuit nihil;
Rex est qui cupit nihil. SEN.
—"He is a king who fears nothing; he is a king who desires nothing."

Rex nunquam mŏrĭtur. *Law Max.*—"The king never dies." The office is supposed to be filled by his successor at the instant of his decease.

——*Ridentem dīcĕre verum*
Quid vetat?—— HOR.
—"What forbids a man to convey the truth laughingly?" Why may not truth be conveyed under the form of pleasantry?

Ride si sapis. MART.—"Laugh if you are wise." Enjoy the ridicule which is directed against the follies of the age. "It is good to be merry and wise."

Ridēre in stŏmăcho. CIC.—"To laugh inwardly." "To laugh in one's sleeve," as we say.

Ridet argento domus. HOR.—"The house smiles with silver." Almost every article is of plate.

Ridētur chordâ qui semper oberrat eâdem. HOR.—"He is laughed at who is for ever blundering on the same string." A man who is always harping on one subject or talking about himself becomes ridiculous.

——*Ridicŭlum acri*
Fortius ac melius magnas plerumque secat res. HOR. —"Ridicule often settles an affair of importance better and more effectually than severity."

Ridiculus æque nullus est, quam quando ēsŭrit. PLAUT.—"A man is never so droll as when he is hungry." That is, of course, when he expects to satisfy his hunger by his buffoonery.

Risu dissolvit īlia. PETRON. ARBITER.—"He bursts his sides with laughing."

Risu inepto res ineptior nulla est. MART.—"Nothing is more silly than silly laughter."

——*Risum tenеātis, amīci?* HOR.—"Can you refrain from laughter, my friends?"

Risus abundat in ore stultōrum.—"Laughter abounds in the mouths of fools."

Rivālem patienter habe.—— OVID.—"With patience bear a rival (in love)."

Rixātur de lanâ caprīnâ.—"He would quarrel about a goat's hair." A captious, litigious person. See *Alter rixatur*, &c.

Roma, tibi sŭbito mōtĭbus ibit amor. SIDON. APOLLINARIS.—"Rome, upon thee suddenly love with its commotions shall come." Inserted as a specimen of the Palindrome or Sotadic verse, a trifling composition, which reads the same from left to right, and from right to left. This line has also been attributed to Aldhelm. See another instance, *Sacrum pingue*, &c.

Romæ Tibur amem, ventōsus, Tibŭre Romam. HOR.—"At Rome I Tibur love, wind-like, at Tibur Rome." The picture of a man who does not know his own mind, but is always in an unsettled state.

Rore vixit more cicādæ. *Prov.*—"He lived upon dew, like a grasshopper." Said ironically of luxurious persons, who pretend to be very abstemious.

——*Rudis indigestăque mōles.* OVID.—"A rude and undigested mass." A description of Chaos; but often quoted as meaning a mass of confusion.

Rumor est sermo quidam sine ullo certo auctōre dispersus, cui malignĭtas initium dedit, incrementum credulĭtas. QUINT. —"Rumour is, as it were, a report spread without any certain author, begotten by malignity, and nourished by credulity."

Rumpĭtur innumĕris arbos uberrĭma pomis,
Et sŭbĭto nimiæ præcipitantur opes.
—"The most fruitful tree is weighed down by fruit innumerable, and wealth too abundant is suddenly brought to the ground."

Rura mihi et rĭgui plăceant in vallĭbus amnes.
Flūmĭna amem sylvasque inglōrius.—— VIRG.
—"Let fields and streams, purling through the valleys, be my delight. Inglorious, may I court the rivers and the woods."

——*Rursum si reventum in gratiam est,*
Bis tanto amīci sunt inter se quam prius. PLAUT.
—"When they become reconciled, they are twice as loving as they were before."

Rus in urbe. MART.—"Country in town." A residence situate in town or its vicinity, possessing many of the advantages of the country. A Cit's "box."

—*Rustĭcus expectat dum dēfluat amnis; at ille*
Lābĭtur et labĕtur in omne volūbĭlis ævum. HOR.
—"The peasant waits until the river shall cease to flow: but still it glides on, and will glide on for all time to come." It is vain to expect a change in the laws of nature.

S.

S. P. for *Sine prole.*—"Without issue."

S. P. Q. R.—*Senātus Pŏpŭlusque Romānus.*—"The Roman Senate and people." These initials were placed upon the Roman standards and public buildings.

Sacrum pinque dabo, non macrum sacrĭficābo.—"I will give a fat sacrifice, I will not make a lean offering." The line, read thus, is an Hexameter, and refers to Abel's sacrifice. Read backwards it is a Pentameter, and reads thus, "I will make a lean offering, I will not give a fat sacrifice,"—in reference to that of Cain. It is of the Palindrome genus, and was probably composed by a poet of the middle ages. See *Roma, tibi*, &c.

2 D 2

Sæpe bibi succos, quamvis invītus, amāros
Æger; et oranti mensa negāta mihi. OVID.
—"Often when ill have I, though reluctantly, had to drink bitter potions; and, though I begged for it, food was refused me."

Sæpe ego, ne bĭbĕrem, vŏlui dormīre vidēri;
Dum vĭdeor, somno lūmĭna victa dedi. OVID.
—"Often, that I might not drink, I have wished to appear asleep; while I have seemed to be so, I have surrendered my overpowered eyes to slumber."

Sæpe est sub pallio sordĭdo sapientia. CIC.—"Wisdom is often found under a mean cloak."

Sæpe etiam est ŏlĭtor valde opportūna locūtus. *Prov.*—"Even a costermonger very often speaks to the purpose."

——*Sæpe exiguus mus*
Sub terris pŏsuitque domos et horrea fecit. VIRG.
—"The little mouse often constructs its abode and its granary under ground."

——*Sæpe illi dixĕrat Almo,*
Nata, tene linguam; nec tamen illa tenet. OVID.
—"Often had Almo said to her, 'Daughter, do hold your tongue;' but still she held it not."

Sæpe in conjugiis fit noxia, cum nĭmia est dos. AUSON.—"Mischief is often the result in marriage, when the dowry is too large."

Sæpe in magistrum scĕlĕra redierunt sua. SEN.—"His own faults often recoil upon the author's head."

——*Sæpe ingĕnia calamitāte intercĭdunt.* PHÆD.—"Genius is often wasted through misfortune."

Sæpe intĕreunt aliis meditantes necem.—"Men often perish when meditating the destruction of others." The wicked often fall into the pit which they dig for others.

Sæpe premente Deo, fert Deus alter opem.—"Often when we are hard pressed by one deity, another comes to our aid." When we think we are overwhelmed with misfortunes, unexpected relief often comes to our rescue.

Sæpe rogāre soles qualis sim, Prisce, futūrus,
Si fiam lŏcŭples, simque repente potens.
Quemquam posse putas mores narrāre futūros?
Dic mihi, si fias tu leo, qualis eris? MART.
—"Priscus, you are wont often to ask me how I would

live, if I should become rich and be a great man all at once. Do you think that any one can foretell what his conduct will be? Tell me, if you were to become a lion, what sort of one would you be?"

Sæpe solet sĭmĭlis fīlius esse patri;
Et sĕquĭtur lĕvĭter fīlia matris iter.
—"The son is usually wont to be like the sire; and lightly does the daughter follow in her mother's footsteps."

Sæpe sonant moti glăcie pendente capilli;
Et nitet inducto candĭda barba gelu. OVID.
—"Full oft do the hairs rattle with the pendent icicles, as they move, and the white beard sparkles with the frost that has gathered upon it."

Sæpe stylum vertas itĕrum quæ digna legi sint
Scriptūrus.—— HOR.
—"You must often correct your language if you mean to write anything worthy of being read a second time."

Sæpe sub attrītâ lătĭtat săpientia veste.—"Often does wisdom lie concealed beneath a thread-bare garment."

Sæpe summa ingĕnia in occulto latent. PLAUT.—"The greatest talents often lie concealed." "Full many a gem of purest ray serene," &c. See *Gray's Elegy.*

Sæpe tacens vocem verbăque vultus habet. OVID.—"The silent features have often both words and expression of their own."

Sæpe viâ oblīquâ præstat quam tendĕre rectâ.—"The circuitous road is often better than the direct one." The same as our English proverb, "The longest way about is often the shortest way home."

Sæpius ventis agitātur ingens
Pinus, et celsæ grăviōre casu
Dĕcĭdunt turres, fĕriuntque summos
Fulgŭra montes. HOR.
—"The lofty pine is oftenest shaken by the winds, high towers fall to the earth with a heavier crash, and lightnings strike the summits of the mountains." The advantages of a middle station.

Sæva jussa, continuas accusātiōnes, fallāces amicĭtias, pernĭciem innocentium. TACIT.—"Cruel commands, continual denunciations, deceitful friendships, and the destruction of the innocent." A description of the state of Rome in the days of Tacitus.

Sævi inter se convĕniunt ursi.—— Juv.—"Even savage bears agree among themselves." The wild beasts agree with others of their own species; man alone is perpetually at war with his fellow-men.

Sævit amor ferri, et scelerāta insānia belli. Virg.—"The love of arms rages, and the frenzied wickedness of war."

——*Sævitque ănĭmis ignōbĭle vulgus;*
Jamque faces et saxa volant; furor arma ministrat. Virg.—"The rude rabble are enraged; and now fire-brands and stones are seen to fly; rage supplies arms." A description of a popular tumult.

Sal Attĭcum.—"Attic salt." The poignancy of wit and brilliancy of style peculiar to the Athenian writers was so called by the Romans.

Saltābat mĕlius quam necesse est probæ. Sall.—"She danced better than became a modest woman." Among the Romans it was only loose women that were expected to excel in this art.

——*Saltat Milōnius, ut semel icto*
Accessit fervor căpĭti, numĕrusque lucernis. Hor.
—"Milonius begins to dance as soon as his head is heated with wine, and the lights begin to multiply."

Salus popŭli suprēma est lex.—"The well-being of the people is the first great law." Said to have been derived from the Laws of the Twelve Tables at Rome. Aristotle has a similar maxim.

Salus ubi multi consiliārii. Coke.—"In the multitude of counsellors there is safety." See *Proverbs* xi. 14, and xxiv. 6.

Salūti consulĕre et incolumitāti suæ. Cic.—"To study his health and his welfare." The legitimate object of a man's life, so long as he is observant of his duty to others.

Salvâ dignitāte.—"Without compromising his dignity."

Salve, magna parens.—— Virg.—"All hail! thou great parent!"

Salve Pæōniæ largĭtor nōbĭlis undæ,
Salve Dardănii gloria magna soli:
Publĭca morbōrum rĕquĭes, commūne medentum
Auxilium, præsens numen, inempta Salus. Claud.

—"Hail! thou noble bestower of the Pæonian wave; hail! thou great glory of the Dardanian soil; thou universal relief from maladies, thou common aid of the healing craft, propitious deity—Health! unbought by gold."

Salvo jure.—"Saving the right." A grant is made *salvo jure regis*, "saving the right of the king," his rights and prerogatives being preserved from encroachment.

Salvo pudōre.—"Modesty saved." Without a violation of modesty. With proper regard to decency.

Salvum fac regem.—"God save the king!" *Salvam fac reginam.*—"God save the queen!"

Sanctio justa, jubens honesta, et prohĭbens contrāria. BRACTON. —"A just decree, enforcing what is honest, and forbidding the contrary." A characteristic of a good law.

Sanctius his animal, mentisque capācius altæ,
Dĕerat adhuc et quod domināri in cætĕra possit:
Natus homo est.—— OVID.

—"But an animated being, more holy than these, more fitted to receive higher faculties, and one to rule over the rest, was still wanting. Then man was formed." Ovid's account of the creation of man.

Sanctum sanctōrum.—"The holy of holies." In the Ecclesiastical Law the chancel of a church is so called. Commonly applied to a study or private room.

——*Sanctus habēri*
Justĭtiæque tenax, factis dictisque merēris?
Agnosco prŏcĕrem.—— JUV.

—"If you deserve to be accounted a man of blameless integrity and staunch in your love of justice, both in word and deed, then I recognise the real nobleman."

——*Săpĕre aude.* HOR.—"Dare to be wise." Adhere to the dictates of wisdom, in spite of fear or temptation. Motto of the Earl of Macclesfield.

Săpĕre isthac ætāte oportet, qui sunt căpĭte candĭdo. PLAUT. —"They who have grey heads are old enough to be wise."

——*Săpias, vina liques, et spatio brevi*
Spem longam rĕsĕces.—— HOR.

—"Be wise, rack off your wines, and abridge your hopes in proportion to the shortness of your life."

Săpiens domirābitur astris.—"The wise man will govern the stars."

Săpiens nihil facit invītus, nihil dolens, nihil coactus. CIC. —"A wise man does nothing against his will, nothing repiningly, or under compulsion."

Săpiens quidem pol ipse fingit fortūnam sibi. PLAUT.—"The wise man surely carves out his own destiny."

——*Sapientem pascĕre barbam.* HOR.—"To nourish a wise beard." To affect wisdom, by wearing the beard of a philosopher.

Sapienter vitam instituĕre. TER.—"Wisely to regulate the conduct of one's life."

——*Sapientia prima*
Stultitiâ caruisse.—— HOR.
—"The first step towards wisdom is to be exempt from folly."

Sapientissimum esse dicunt eum cui, quod opus sit, ipsi vĕniat in mentem. CIC.—"He is reckoned the wisest to whom that which is required at once suggests itself." The definition of a wise man, as being one possessed of a store of wisdom, so well arranged in his memory that he can make it useful upon any emergency.

Sapientissĭmus inter sapientes. CIC.—"The wisest of the wise." Said of the philosopher Thales.

Săpientum octāvus. HOR.—"An eighth wise man." One added to the number of the Seven Wise Men of Greece. Applied ironically to a person who affects to be remarkably wise, or, as we say, "a second Solomon."

Sardonius risus.—"A Sardonic grin." A certain herb which grew in Sardinia by the extreme acridity of its taste was said to distort the features of those who ate of it.

Sat cito, si sat bene. Prov.—"Quick enough, if well enough." Attributed by St. Jerome to Cato; but at present the words *Si sat bene* are alone to be found in his works.

Sat cito, si sat tuto.—"Quick enough, if safe enough." This motto was a favourite maxim with the great Lord Eldon, who was struck with it in his school days, and made it his future rule of life. See Twiss's Life of Lord Eldon, vol. i. p. 49.

Sat pulchra, si sat bona. Prov.—"Fair enough, if good enough." "Handsome is who handsome does."

Satis eloquentiæ, sapientiæ parum. SALL.—"Eloquence enough, but little wisdom."

Satis quod suffĭcit—"What suffices is enough." "Enough is as good as a feast." See *Love's Labour's Lost*, Act v. Sc. 1.

Satis superque.—"Enough, and more than enough." An expression used by Pliny, and not uncommon in other authors.

Satis superque me benignĭtas tua
Ditāvit.—— Hor.
—"Your bounty has enriched me enough, and more than enough." Said by the poet of his patron Mæcenas.

Satius est inĭtiis medēri quam fini.—"It is better to cure at the beginning than at the end." See *Principiis obsta*, &c.

Satius est prodesse etiam malis propter bonos, quam bonis deesse propter malos.—"It is better even to profit the bad for the sake of the good, than to injure the good for the bad." Hence the legal maxim, that it is better that ten guilty men should escape, than that one innocent man should suffer.

Satius est recurrĕre, quam currĕre male. Prov.—"It is better to run back than to run the wrong way." When we are in a wrong course it is best to retrace our steps at once.

Saucius ejūrat pugnam gladiātor, et idem
Immĕmor antīqui vulnĕris arma capit. Ovid.
—"The wounded gladiator forswears all fighting, and yet forgetful of his former wound he takes up arms."

Saxum volūtum non obdūcĭtur musco. Prov.—"A rolling stone gathers no moss."

Scabiem et contāgia lucri. Hor.—"The contagious itch for gain." The passion with which a miser collects his heaps of gold.

Scandălum magnātum. Law Lat.—"An offence against nobles." A reflection against a peer, or the body of peers. A statute to punish this offence has remained on our statute-book since the time of Richard II.

Scelĕre velandum est scelus. Sen.—"One crime has to be concealed by another."

——*Scelus est jugulāre Falernum,*
Et dare Campāno toxĭca sæva mero. Mart.
—"It is a crime to kill Falernian wine (by mixing), and to give (to your guests) deleterious poison in pure Campanian."

——*Scelus intra se tăcĭtum qui cōgĭtat ullum*
Facti crimen habet.—— JUV.
—"He who silently meditates the perpetration of a crime, incurs the guilt of the deed." It is the intention that constitutes the crime.

——*Scena sine arte fuit.* OVID.—"The stage was devoid of art."

Scientia popīnæ. SEN.—"The knowledge of cook-shop-keeping." The art of cookery.

Scientiæ non visæ ut thesauri abscondĭti nulla est utĭlĭtas.—"Knowledge not seen, like hidden treasure, is utterly useless." See *De non apparentibus*, &c., *Paulum*, &c., and *Scire tuum*, &c.

Scilicet a spĕcŭli sumuntur imāgĭne fastus. OVID.—"Pride, forsooth, is caught from the reflection in the mirror."

Scilicet expectes, ut tradet mater honestos
Atque ălios mores, quam quos habet?—— JUV.
—"Can you expect, forsooth, that the mother will inculcate virtuous principles, or other than she possesses herself?"

Scilicet ingĕniis ălĭqua est concordia junctis,
Et servat stŭdii fœdĕra quisque sui. OVID.
—"In truth there is a certain alliance between kindred minds, and each one cherishes the ties of his own pursuit." This feeling makes good the proverb, "Birds of a feather," &c.

Scilicet ut fulvum spectātur in ignĭbus aurum,
Tempŏre sic duro est inspicienda fides. OVID.
—"As the yellow gold is assayed in the fire, so is the faith (of friendship) to be tested in moments of adversity."

Scindentur vestes, gemmæ frangentur et aurum;
Carmĭna quam tribuent, fama perennis erit. OVID.
—"Garments will rend, gems and gold will spoil; the fame which poesy confers is everlasting."

Scindĭtur incertum stŭdia in contrāria vulgus. VIRG.—"The wavering multitude is divided into opposite opinions."

Scio, coactus tuâ voluntāte es. TER.—"I know, you are led by your own will." You plead necessity when you are governed solely by your own inclination.

Scio quid văleant hŭmĕri et quid ferre recūsent.—"I know what shoulders can bear, and what they will refuse to bear." Adapted from Horace, *Ars Poet.* 39, 40.

Scire facias. Law Term.—"You are to let know." The name given to a judicial writ, usually issued to call on a person to show cause to the court why execution of a judgment passed should not issue.

Scire potestātes herbārum usumque medendi. VIRG.—"To know the virtues of herbs, and their use in healing."

Scire tuum nihil est, nisi te scire hoc sciat alter. PERS.—"Your knowledge is nothing, unless others know that you possess it." See *Quis enim*, &c.

Scire ubi ălĭquid invĕnīre possis, ea demum maxĭma pars ērudītiōnis est.—"To know where you can find a thing, is in fact the greatest part of learning."

Scire volunt omnes, mercēdem solvĕre nemo. JUV.—"All would like to know, but few choose to pay the price." Most would like to possess knowledge, but few like to incur the expense and trouble of learning.

Scire volunt secrēta domûs, atque inde timēri. JUV.—"They wish to know the family secrets, and thence to be feared." Said in reference to persons at Rome, who got introduced into families as slaves, and having gained possession of the family secrets, extorted money under threat of denunciation.

Scis ĕtĕnim justum gĕmĭnâ suspendĕre lance
Ancĭpĭtis libræ.—— PERS.

—"For you know well how to weigh the justice of the case in the double scale of the poised balance."

Scit gĕnius, natāle comes qui tempĕret astrum. HOR.—"The genius, our companion from our birth, who regulates the planet of our nativity, knows best"—how to account for our various dispositions and propensities.

Scit uti foro.—"He knows how to take advantage of the market." How to make his bargains, when to buy and when to sell.

——*Scŏpŭlis surdior Icări*
Voces audit.—— HOR.

—"He receives his injunctions more deaf than the Icarian rocks."

Scribendi rectē, săpĕre est et principium et fons. HOR.—"Wisdom is the guiding principle and main source of all good writing."

Scribentem juvat ipse favor, mĭnuitque labōrem ;
Cumque suo crescens pectŏre fervet opus. OVID.

—"Enthusiasm itself aids the writer and diminishes his toil; and, as the work grows, it warms with his feelings."

Scrībĭmus, et scriptos absūmĭmus igne libellos;
Exĭtus est studii parva favilla mei. OVID.
—"I write, and I burn my books when written: a few ashes are the result of all my labours."

Scrībĭmus indocti doctīque.—— HOR.—"Unlearned and learned, we all of us write." Descriptive of the *Cacoēthes scribendi.*

Scripta ferunt annos; scriptis Agamemnŏna nosti,
Et quisquis contra, vel simul arma tulit. OVID.
—"Writings survive the lapse of years; through writings you know of Agamemnon, and who bore arms against or who with him."

Scriptōrum chorus omnis amat nemus et fugit urbes;
Ritè cliens Bacchi somno gaudentis et umbrâ. HOR.
—"The whole band of poets loves the groves and shuns cities; genuine votaries of Bacchus, delighting in repose and the shade."

——*Secrēta hæc murmŭra vulgi.* JUV.—"These sullen murmurings of the populace."

Secrēte amīcos admŏne, lauda palam. SYR.—"Advise your friends in private, praise them openly."

Secundæ cōgitatiōnes meliōres.—"Second thoughts are best."

Secundas fortūnas decent superbiæ. PLAUT.—"High airs befit prosperous fortunes."

Secundo amne deflŭit.—"He floats with the stream."

Secundum artem.—"According to the rules of art."

Secundum gĕnĕra.—"According to classes."

Secundum usum.—"According to usage," or "to the use of."

——*Secūra quies, et nescia fallĕre vita.* VIRG.—"Repose unfraught with care, a life that knows no guile."

Sed de hoc tu vidēbis. De me possum dicĕre ĭdem quod Plautīnus pater in Trinummo, 'mihi quidem ætas acta ferme est.'
—"But as for that matter, it is your concern. For my own part, I may say with the father in the Trinummus of Plautus, 'my life is nearly at an end.'" The words of Cicero in his Second Epistle to Brutus.

Sed exsequāmur cœptum propŏsĭti ordĭnem. PHÆD.—"But let us pursue our purpose in the order we proposed."

Sed fugit intĕrea, fugit irreparābĭle tempus. VIRG.—"But meanwhile time flies, never to be regained." "Time and tide wait for no man."

Sed justitiæ primum munus est, ut ne cui quis noceat nisi lacessītus injūriâ. CIC.—"But it is the first rule of justice, that you offend no one, unless provoked thereto by an act of injustice." Unless you are acting in defence of your legal rights.

Sed nil dulcius est, bene quam munīta tenēre
Edĭta doctrīnâ săpientum templa serēnâ;
Despĭcĕre unde queas ălios, passimque vidēre
Errāre, atque viam palanteis quærĕre vitæ. LUCR.
—"But nothing is there more delightful than to occupy the elevated temples of the wise, well fortified by tranquil learning; whence you may be able to look down upon others, and see them straying in every direction, and wandering in search of the path of life."

Sed nisi peccassem, quid tu concēdĕre posses?
Mātĕriam vĕniæ sors tibi nostra dedit. OVID.
—"Had I not sinned, what had there been for thee to pardon? My fate has given thee the opportunity for mercy."

——***Sed non ego crēdŭlus illis.*** VIRG.—"But I do not believe them." I do not give credit to all their flattery.

Sed notat hunc omnis domus et vicīnia tota,
Introrsum turpem, speciōsum pelle dĕcōrâ. HOR.
—"But all his family and the entire neighbourhood look upon him as inwardly base, though of a specious, showy exterior." Description of a hypocrite.

Sed plures nĭmiâ congesta pecūnia curâ
Strangŭlat.—— JUV.
—"But money heaped up with overwhelming care torments many."

Sed præsta te eum, qui mihi, a tĕnĕris (ut Græci dicunt) unguicŭlis, es cognĭtus. CIC.—"But prove yourself to be the same person that I have known you to be, 'from your tenderest finger-nails,' as the Greeks say." See *A teneris unguiculis.*

——***Sed quæ præclāra et prospĕra tanti,***
Ut rebus lætis par sit mensūra malōrum? JUV.
—"But what brilliant or prosperous fortune is of suffi-

cient worth that your measure of evils should equal your success?"

Sed satis est orāre Jovem, quæ donat et aufert;
Det vitam, det opes, æquum mî ănĭmum ipse parābo. Hor.
—"But it is sufficient to pray to Jove for those things which he gives and takes away at pleasure; let him grant life, let him grant wealth; I myself will provide a well-regulated mind."

——*Sed summa sequar fastigia rerum.* Virg.—"But I will trace the principal heads of events." I will relate the most prominent parts of the subject.

Sed tăciti fecēre tamen convīcia vultus. Ovid.—"But still her silent features censured me."

——*Sed te decor iste, quod optas*
Esse vetat, votōque tuo tua forma repugnat. Ovid.
—"But that very beauty forbids thee to be what thou wishest, and the charms of thy person are an impediment to thy desires."

——*Sed tu*
Ingĕnio verbis concĭpe plura meis. Ovid.
—"But do you conceive in imagination more than is expressed in my words."

Segnem ac dĕsĭdem, et Circo et theātris corruptum mīlĭtem. Tacit.—"A soldiery slothful and indolent, debauched by the Circus and the theatres." Enervated by the dissipations of the metropolis.

Segnius hŏmĭnes bona quam mala sentiunt.—"Men have a slower perception of benefits than of injuries."

Segnius irrĭtant ănĭmos demissa per aurem,
Quam quæ sunt ocŭlis subjecta fidēlibus. Hor.
—"Facts of which we have information merely through the ear, make less impression upon the mind than those which have been presented to the more trustworthy eye."

Semel abbas semper abbas.—"Once an abbot, always an abbot." A mediæval expression.

Semel in anno licet insanīre.—"We may play the fool once a year."

Semel insanīvĭmus omnes. Mant.—"We have all been mad at some time." Few men do not feel, that at some moments of their lives they have been uninfluenced by reason. See *Id commune*, &c.

Semel malus, semper præsūmĭtur esse malus. Law Max.—"A man once bad is always to be presumed bad." The presumptions will be *against* a man of known bad character.

——*Sēmĭta certè*
Tranquillæ per virtūtem patet ūnĭca vitæ. Juv.
—"The only sure path to a tranquil life is through virtue."

Semper avārus eget; certum voto pete finem. Hor.—"The avaricious man is ever in want; prescribe a fixed limit to your desires."

——*Semper bonus homo tiro est.* Mart.—"A beginner is always a good man." To the same effect as our proverb, "A new broom sweeps clean."

Semper causæ eventōrum magis mŏvent, quam ipsa eventa.—"The causes which produce great events are always regarded with more interest than the events themselves."

Semper habet lites alternăque jurgia lectus,
In quo nupta jacet; mĭnĭmum dormītur in illo. Juv.
—"The bed in which a wife lies has always its disputes and wranglings; there is little chance of sleep there." A rather too sweeping censure, in reference to what are called *Curtain lectures.*

Semper honos, nomenque tuum, laudesque manēbunt. Virg.—"Thy honour, thy renown, and thy praises shall be everlasting."

Semper idem.—"Always the same"—applied to the masculine gender. *Semper eadem,* to the feminine.

Semper inops, quicunque cupit.—— Claud.—"He is always poor who is for ever wishing for more." See *Semper avarus, &c.*

——*Semper nŏcuit differre parātis.* Lucan.—"It has ever been prejudicial for those who are prepared to admit of delay."

Semper parātus.—"Always ready."

——*Semper tibi pendeat hamus;*
Quo mĭnĭme credas gurgĭte, piscis erit. Ovid.
—"Let your hook be always ready; in waters where you least think it there will be a fish."

Senectus non impĕdit quōmĭnus literārum studia teneāmus usque ad ultĭmum tempus senectūtis. Cic.—"Old age does not hinder us from continuing our studies, even to the latest period of our existence."

Senem juventus pigra mendicum creat. *Prov.*—"Youth passed in idleness produces an old age of beggary."

Senīlis stultitia, quæ delirātio appellāri solet, senum levium est, non omnium. Cic.—"That foolishness, which in old men is termed *dotage*, is not common to all who are old. but to those who are of a frivolous disposition."

Seniōres priōres.—"The older ones first." "Little boys last," as they say at school.

Seniōrĭbus gravis est inveterāti moris mutātio. Quintus Curt.—"A change of confirmed habits is severely felt by aged persons."

——*Sensim labefacta cadēbat*
Religio.—— Claudian.
—"By degrees religion was undermined and fell."

——*Sensit pœnamque peti, vēniamque timēri;*
Vive, licet nolis, et nostro mūnĕre, dixit,
Cerne diem.—— Lucan.
—"He perceived that punishment was courted, and pardon dreaded. 'Live on,' said he, 'although thou art unwilling, and, by my bounty, behold the light of day.'"

——*Sententia prima*
Hujus erit: post hanc ætāte atque arte minōres
Censēbunt: tanquam famæ discrimen agātur,
Aut ănĭmæ: tanta est quærendi cura decōris. Juv.
—"Her opinion will be asked first. Then those who are her inferiors in years and skill will give their votes, as though their mistress's good name or life were at stake. So great is the anxiety for gaining beauty." A consultation of lady's-maids upon their mistress's toilet.

Sentio te sedem hŏmĭnum ac domum contemplāri; quæ si tibi parva (ut est) ita vidētur, hæc cœlestia semper spectāto; illa humāna contemnĭto. Cic.—"I perceive that you contemplate the seat and the habitation of man; now, if it appears as little to you as it really is, you should fix your eyes steadily upon heavenly objects, and despise those of this world."

Septem convīvium, novem convīcium.—"Seven's a banquet,

nine's a brawl." A favourite dinner maxim of the ancients.

Septem horas dormisse sat est juvĕnique, senique.—"Seven hours of sleep is enough for old or young." A mediæval aphorism probably.

Septennis quum sit, nondum ēdĭdit dentes. Prov.—"Though he is seven years of age, he has not yet cut his teeth." Said ironically of men who devote themselves to frivolous or childish pursuits.

——*Sepulchri*
Mitte supervăcuos honōres. Hor.
—"Dispense with the superfluous honours of the tomb." Abstain from all vain parade and show.

Sequentem fugit, fŭgientem sĕquĭtur.—"It flies from him who pursues it, it pursues him who flies." Said of glory. See *Quod sequitur*, &c.

Sequestrāri făcias. Law Lat.—"Cause to be sequestrated." An order for sequestration.

Sĕquĭtur superbos ultor a tergo Deus. Sen.—"An avenging God follows close at the back of the proud."

Sĕquĭtur ver hyĕmem. Prov.—"Spring follows winter." Bad fortune will not last for ever.

——*Sĕquĭturque patrem non passĭbus æquis.* Virg.—"And he follows his father, not with equal steps." These words may be applied to a son who fails to equal the talent displayed by his father.

Sera in fundo parsimonia. Sen.—"Economy is too late at the bottom of the purse." "Too late when all is spent."

Sera nunquam est ad bonos mores via. Sen.—"The way to good manners is never too late."

Sĕria cum possim, quod delectantia malim
Scrībĕre, tu causa es, lector.—— Mart.
—"That I prefer to write of lighter subjects, when I am able to treat of serious ones, thou, reader, art the cause." Address of an author whose only object is to consult the taste of his readers.

Seriătim.—"In order." According to rank or priority.

Series implexa causārum. Sen.—"The complicated chain of causes." Fate.

Serit arbŏres quæ in altĕra sæcŭla prosint. An adaptation from Statius.—"He plants trees for the benefit of a future age."

Sĕrius aut cĭtiùs sedem prŏperāmus ad unam.—— OVID.—"Sooner or later we all hasten to one place." All are born to die.

Sermo datur cunctis, ănĭmi săpientia paucis.—"Language is given to all, wisdom to few."

Sermōne huic obsōnas. PLAUT.—"By your talking you drown his voice."

——*Sero clypĕum post vulnĕra sumo.* OVID.—"Wounded, too late I take my shield."

Sero recūsat ferre quod sŭbiit jugum. SEN.—"Too late he refuses to bear the yoke to which he has submitted."

Serò respĭcĭtur tellus, ubi fune solūto,
Currit in immensum panda carīna salum. OVID.
—"Too late we look back upon the land when the moorings are loosed, and the curved keel runs out into the boundless deep."

Sero săpiunt Phryges. Prov.—"The Trojans become wise too late." When their city was on the point of being taken, they began to think of restoring Helen.

Sero vĕnientĭbus ossa.—"The bones for those who come late." The share left for those who come late to dinner.

Serpens ni edat serpentem, draco non fiet. Prov.—"A serpent, unless he devours a serpent, will not become a dragon." This adage implies that kings only become great by the destruction of neighbouring potentates.

——*Serpens, sitis, ardor, arēnæ*
Dulcia virtūti.—— LUCAN.
—"Serpents, thirst, heat, sands, are all sweet to heroic valour." The speech of Cato to his troops when about to cross the deserts of Libya.

Serum est cavendi tempus in mĕdiis malis. SEN.—"It is too late to be on our guard when we are in the midst of misfortunes."

Serus in cœlum rĕdeas, diuque
Lætus intersis popŭlo.—— HOR.
—"May it be long before you return to heaven, and may you long live happily among your people!" A flattering compliment addressed to Augustus; and since paid to other potentates.

Servāre cives, major est virtus patriæ patri. SEN.—"To preserve his fellow-citizens is the greatest of virtues in the father of his country."

Servāre leges patrias pulchrum ac bonum.—"To observe the laws of our country is honourable and good."

Servātâ semper lege et ratiōne loquendi. JUV.—"Always observing the rules and principles of grammar."

——*Servētur ad imum*
Qualis ab incepto processĕrit, et sibi constet. HOR.
—"Let [the character] be maintained to the very last, just as it begins, and so be consistent with itself."

Servientes servitūte ego servos introduxi mihi,
Non qui mihi impĕrārent.—— PLAUT.
—"I have brought servants into my house to serve, not to command, me."

Serviet æternum, quia parvo nesciet uti. HOR.—"He will be always a slave, because he knows not how to enjoy a little." A slave to his own boundless and ungratified desires.

Seu cālĭdus sanguis seu rerum inscītia vexat. HOR.—"Whether it is the heat of your blood, or your ignorance of the world, that influences you."

Seu quis Olympiăcæ mirātus præmia palmæ
Pascit equos, seu quis fortes ad arātra juvencos;
Corpŏra præcĭpuè matrum legat.—— VIRG.
—"Whether any one, aspiring to the praises of the Olympic palm, breeds horses, or sturdy bullocks for the plough, let him choose, with especial care, the dams for their shape." The qualities of the *sire* are most regarded at the present day.

Seu recreāre volet tenuātum corpus; ubīve
Accēdent anni, et tractāri mollius ætas
Imbecilla volet.—— HOR.
—"Or if he shall desire to refresh his emaciated body; or if, when years approach, his feeble old age shall require to be treated more tenderly." Words quoted by Lord Monboddo, shortly before his death.

Sex horas somno, tŏtĭdem des lĕgĭbus æquis;
Quātuor orābis, des ĕpŭlisque duas.
Quod sŭpĕrest ultra, sacris largīre Camœnis. COKE.
—"Give six hours to sleep, as many to the study of just

laws. Pray four hours, and give two to refreshment. All that remains, bestow upon the sacred Muses."

Sexu fœmĭna, ingĕnio vir.—"In sex a woman, in genius a man." Epitaph of Maria Theresa of Austria.

Si ad honestātem nati sumus, ea aut sola expetenda est, aut certe omni pondĕre grăvior est habenda quam relĭqua omnia. Cic.—"If we are born for the practice of virtue, it ought either to be our only object, or at least deemed of far more weighty importance than anything else."

Si ad natūram vivas, nunquam eris pauper; si ad opiniōnem, nunquam dives. Sen.—"If you live according to what nature requires, you will never be poor; if according to the notions of men, you never will be rich."

——*Si ad paupertātem admigrant infāmiæ,*
Grăvior paupertas fit, fides sublestior. Plaut.
—"If disgrace is added to poverty, poverty will be more unendurable, character more frail."

Si antiquitātem spectes, est vetustissĭma; si dignitātem, est honoratissĭma; si jurisdictionem, est capacissĭma. Coke.—"If you consider its antiquity, it is most ancient; if its dignity, it is most honourable; if its jurisdiction, it is most extensive." A description by Coke of the English House of Commons.

Si benè commemĭni, causæ sunt quinque bibendi;
Hospĭtis adventus, præsens sitis, atque futūra,
Aut vini bŏnĭtas, aut quælĭbet altĕra causa.
—"If I remember right, there are five excuses for drinking: the visit of a friend, thirst existing, thirst to come, the goodness of the wine, or any other excuse you please." These lines have been translated by Dean Aldrich, a good scholar and musician, and a lover of his pipe and good-fellowship. Attributed by Menage (i. 172) to Père Sirmond.

Si cădĕre necesse est, occurrendum discrīmĭni. Tacit.—"If we must fall, let us boldly face the danger." Misfortune ought to be met with energy.

Si caput dolet omnia membra languent. *Aphorism.*—"If the head aches, all the members of the body are languid." In the body politic, incompetence in the ruler entails disorder among those below him.

Si claudo cohăbĭtes, subclaudicāre disces.—"If you live with him who is lame, you will learn to limp." The result of evil associations. A mediæval proverb.

Si cui vis aptè nūbĕre, nube pari. OVID.—"If you wish to marry suitably, marry your equal." The poet alludes to equality of years; he might, with equal justice, have alluded to equality of condition.

Si cum hâc exceptiōne detur săpientia, ut illam inclūsam tĕneam, nec enunciem, rejĭciam. SEN.—"If wisdom were offered me on condition that I should keep it bottled up, I would not accept it." See *Quis enim*, &c., and *Scire tuum*, &c.

Si Deus nobiscum, quis contra nos?—"If God is with us, who shall be against us?"

Si dicentis erunt fortūnis absŏna dicta,
Romāni tollent ĕquĭtes pĕdĭtesque cachinnum. HOR.
—"If the words of the speaker are at variance with his fortunes, both Roman knights and plebeians will laugh at your expense."

——*Si dixĕris, Æstuo, sudat.* JUV.—"If you say 'I am warm,' he sweats." Applied to one of those truckling hangers-on who are always of the same opinion with their patrons. See *Græculus esuriens*, &c.

——*Si dum vivas*
Tibi bene facias, jam, pol, id quidem esse haud perlonginquum,
Neque si hoc hŏdie amīsĕris, post in morte id eventūrum esse unquam. PLAUT.
—"If while you live you enjoy yourself, why, really, that is for no very long time: so too, if you lose the present day, it can never return to you after you are dead."

Si est ănĭmus æquus tibi, satis habes, qui bene vitam colas. PLAUT.—"If you have a well-regulated mind, you are possessed of abundance, in leading a good life."

Si ex re sit popŭli Romāni, feri.—"If it be for the good of the Roman people, strike the blow." The dying words of the Emperor Galba, as given by Tacitus and Suetonius, and quoted by Lord Bacon.

Si foret in terris, rīdĕret Democrĭtus.—— HOR.—"If Democritus were on earth, he would laugh." Democritus laughed at the follies of mankind: hence he was called, "The laughing philosopher."

Si foret in terris, rideret Heraclitus.—"If Heraclitus were on earth, even he would laugh." This philosopher was continually weeping for the follies of mankind. A proverb, adapted from the preceding line.

Si fortūna juvat, cavēto tolli;
Si fortūna tonat, cavēto mergi. Auson.
—"If fortune favours you, be not elated; if fortune thunders, do not sink." In all circumstances preserve equanimity.

Si fractus illābātur orbis,
Impăvĭdum fĕrient ruīnæ. Hor.
—"If the world's wreck should fall about him, the ruins would crush him unconcerned." Said of the man conscious of his integrity.

Si fuit errandum, causas habet error honestas. Ovid.—"If I was to err, my error has a fair excuse."

Si genus humānum, et mortālia temnĭtis arma;
At sperāte Deos mĕmŏres fandi atque nefandi. Virg.
—"If you despise the human race and mortal arms, still expect that the gods will be mindful of right and wrong."

Si in hoc erro quod ănĭmos hŏmĭnum immortāles esse credam, libenter erro; nec mihi hunc errōrem quo delector dum vivo extorquēri volo. Cic.—"If in this I err, that I believe the souls of men to be immortal, I err willingly; nor do I wish this error, in which I take a delight, to be wrested from me whilst I live."

Si incŏlæ bene sunt morāti, pulchre munītum arbĭtror. Plaut.—"If the inhabitants of a city have good morals, I consider it well fortified."

Si jūdĭcas, cognosce; si regnas, jube. Sen.—"If you are a judge, investigate; if you are a ruler, command." The difference between judicial and ministerial duties. In the one you must be governed by evidence; in the other, by your own perception of right and wrong.

Si juxta claudum habĭtes, subclaudicāre disces. *Prov.*—"If you live near a lame man, you will learn to limp." See *Claudicantis*, &c., and *Si claudo*, &c.

Si laus hŏmĭnem allĭcĕre ad rectè faciendum non potest, ne metus quidem à fœdissĭmis factis potest avocāre. Cic.—"If the love of praise cannot induce a man to act honestly, the fear of punishment can never restrain him from the basest of actions."

***Si** leonīna pellis non satis est, assuenda vulpīna. Prov.*—"If the lion's skin will not do, we must sew on that of the fox." What cannot be effected by force may be compassed by craft.

***Si** me mendācii captas, non potes me căpĕre.*—"If you are trying to catch me in a lie, you cannot catch me."

***Si** meliōres sunt quos ducit amor, plures sunt quos corrĭgit timor.* COKE.—"If those are the best whom love induces, they are the most whom fear holds in check."

***Si** mihi pergit quæ vult dīcĕre, ea quæ non vult audiet.* TER. —"If he persists in saying whatever he likes against me, he shall hear what he will not like himself."

***Si** (Mimnermus uti censet), sine amōre jocisque*
Nil est jucundum, vivas in amōre jocisque. HOR.
—"If (as Mimnermus thinks) there is no pleasure without love and mirth, live amid love and mirth."

***Si** monumentum requiris, circumspĭce.*—"If you seek my monument, look around." Epitaph of Sir Christopher Wren, the architect who designed St. Paul's Cathedral in London, the greatest memorial of his fame.

——*Si mutābĭle pectus*
Est tibi, consĭliis, non currĭbus, ŭtĕre nostris. OVID.
—"If you have a mind capable of change, use my advice and not my chariot." The advice of Apollo to Phaethon.

***Si** natūra negat, facit indignātio versum.* JUV.—"Though Nature denied the power, indignation would give birth to verses."

***Si** nihil infesti durus vidisset Ulysses;*
Pēnĕlŏpe felix, sed sine laude, foret. OVID.
—"If the hardy Ulysses had seen no adversity, Penelope would have been happy, but unknown to fame." Virtue is only proved by misfortune.

***Si** non errâsset, fĕcĕrat ille minus.* MART.—"If he had not committed an error, he would have done less." Said of a person who, having been negligent in his duty, exerts all his energy to retrieve his character.

***Si** non esse domi, quos des, causābĕre nummos;*
Lītĕra poscētur.—— **OVID.**

—"If you say that you have no money at home to pay with, a bill will be asked for."

——*Si non*
Intendes ănĭmum stŭdiis et rebus honestis,
Invidiâ vel amōre vigil torquēbĕre.—— Hor.

—"If you do not apply your mind to study and laudable pursuits, you will be tormented and kept awake by envy or by love."

Si non pertæsum thălămi, tædæque fuisset;
Huic uni forsan pŏtui succumbĕre culpæ. Virg.

—"Had I not been tired of the marriage-bed and nuptial endearments, to this one frailty I might perhaps give way" —Of marrying in her widowhood.

Si nŭmĕres anno soles et nūbĭla toto,
Invĕnies nĭtĭdum sæpius esse diem. Ovid.

—"If you count the fine days and the cloudy ones throughout the year, you will find that the bright days are the most in number."

——*Si parva licet compōnĕre magnis.* Virg.—"If I may be allowed to compare small things with great."

Si poēma loquens pictūra est, pictūra tăcĭtum poēma debet esse. Ad Herenn.—"If a poem is a speaking picture, a picture ought to be a silent poem." See *Mutum est*, &c.

Si possis suāvĭter, si non quocunque modo.—"Gently if you can, if not, by any means."

Si præsens bene collocāvĕris, de futūro tibi dŭbium non erit.—"If you make a good use of the present time, you need not be apprehensive as to the future."

Si qua fidem tanto est ŏpĕri latūra vetustas. Virg.—"If posterity will give any credit to so great an exploit."

Si qua, metu dempto, casta est, ea dēnĭque casta est. Ovid.—"If any woman preserves her chastity when fear of detection is removed, she, indeed, is chaste." Ovid had only experience of the more worthless part of the sex, and believed, with Pope, that every "woman is at heart a rake."

Si quid amīcum erga bene feci, aut consului fidēlĭter,
Non vĭdeor mĕruisse laudem; culpâ cāruisse arbĭtror.
Plaut.

—"If I have in any way acted well towards my friend, or have faithfully consulted his advantage; I deem myself not deserving of praise; I consider only that I am free from blame."

***Si** quid fēcĕris honestum cum labōre, labor abit, honestum manet. Si quid fēcĕris turpe cum voluptāte, voluptas abit, turpitūdo manet.*—"If you have done anything honourable by dint of labour, the labour is past, the honour survives. If you have done anything base for pleasure's sake, the pleasure is past, the baseness survives."

***Si** quid ingĕnui sanguĭnis habes, non pluris eum facies quam lutum.* PETRON. ARBITER.—"If you have any free-born blood in you, you will esteem him no more than you would a lump of clay."

——*Si quid novisti rectius istis*
Candĭdus imperti; si non, his utĕre mecum. HOR.
—"If you know anything better than these maxims, candidly impart it; if not, with me adopt these."

***Si** quis.*—"If any one." A notification by a candidate for orders, inquiring if any impediment is alleged against him, is so called.

***Si** quis clērĭcus, aut mŏnăchus, verba joculatōria risum moventia serat, anathĕmăta esto.*—"If any clerk or monk shall use a jocular expression exciting laughter, let him be excommunicated." An ordinance of the 2nd Council of Carthage.

***Si** quis dat mannos, ne quære in dentibus annos.*—"You must not look a gift horse in the mouth." A mediæval Leonine proverb.

***Si** quis Deus mihi largiātur ut hāc ætāte repuerascam et in cunis vāgiam, valde recūsem.* CIC.—"If any god were to grant that at this age I should become a child again and cry in the cradle, I should decidedly refuse."

***Si** quis mutuum cui dĕdĕrit, fit pro proprio perdĭtum.* PLAUT.
—"If one lends money to another, it is lost so far as being one's own."

***Si**, quŏties hŏmĭnes peccant, sua fulmĭna mittat*
Jupiter, exĭguo tempŏre inermis erit. OVID.
—"If, as oft as mortals sin, Jove were to hurl his lightnings, in a little time he would be without weapons."

***Si** res ita sit, vāleat lætĭtia!*—"If this is the fact, then farewell happiness!"

Si Romæ fuĕris, Romāno vivĭto more;
Si fuĕris ălĭbi, vivĭto sicut ibi. St. Ambrose.
—"If you are at Rome, live after the Roman fashion; if you are in any other place, live as they do there."

Si săpias, săpias; hăbeas quod Di dabunt boni. Plaut.—"If you are wise, be wise. Take the good the gods provide you."

——*Si sapis,*
Neque præterquam quas ipse amor molestias
Habet, addas, et illas, quas habet, rectè feras. Ter.
—"If you are wise, you will not add to the troubles which love brings, but will bear with patience those which belong to it."

Si sitis, nihil intĕrest utrum aqua sit an vinum: nec refert utrum sit aureum pōcŭlum an vitreum. Sen.—"If you are thirsty, it matters not whether it be water or wine; nor does it signify whether the cup be of gold or of glass."

Si sol splendescat Mariā purificante,
Major erit glăcies post festum quam fuit ante.
—"If the sun shines on the Purification of St. Mary, the frost will be greater after the feast than it was before." A mediæval proverb; similar to

"If Candlemas day be fair and bright,
Winter will have another flight."

——*Si stĭmŭlos pugnis cædis, mănĭbus plus dolet.* Plaut.
—"If you thump a goad with your fists, your hands suffer the most." An evil is aggravated by foolish opposition.

Si tamen, e nobis ălĭquid, nisi nomen et umbra,
Restat, in Elysiā valle Tibullus erit. Ovid.
—"If however aught of us but the name and shade remains, Tibullus will exist in the Elysian vales."

Si te fēcĕrit secūriōrem. *Law Term.*—"If he gives you security." If he holds you harmless.

Si te nulla movet tantārum gloria rerum. Virg.—"If you are unmoved by the glory of exploits so mighty."

——*Si te proverbia tangunt,*
Mense malas Maio nūbĕre vulgus ait. Ovid.
—"If proverbs have any weight with you, the common people say that 'bad prove the wives that are married in

May.'" Because the Lemuria, or rites of the dead, were celebrated in that month.

***Si** tempus in studia confĕras, omne vitæ fastīdium effŭgĕris; nec noctem fiĕri optābis tædio lucis, nec tibi gravis eris, nec aliis supervăcuus.* SEN.—"If you devote your time to study, you will avoid all the irksomeness of life; you will neither long for the night, being tired of the day; nor will you be a burden to yourself, or make your society insupportable to others."

Si tibi deficiant mĕdĭci, mĕdĭci tibi fiant
Hæc tria; mens hĭlăris, rĕquies, moderāta diæta.
Maxim of the School of Health at Salerno.
—"If you stand in need of physicians, let these three things be your physicians; a cheerful mind, relaxation from business, and a moderate diet."

Si turpia sunt quæ facis, quid refert nēmĭnem scire, cum tu scias? O te mĭsĕrum, si contemnis hunc testem. SEN.—"If what you do is criminal, what matters it that no one else knows, when you know it yourself? O miserable man, if you despise this testimony." The condemning power of a bad conscience.

Si vales, bene est; ego quidem valeo.—"If you are well, 'tis good; as for me, I am well."

Si vir es, i.—— OVID.—"If you are a man, go."

Si vis incŏlŭmem, si vis te reddĕre sanum,
Curas tolle graves, irasci crede profānum.
—"If you wish to be safe in person and in health, shun weighty cares, and deem it profane to be angry." Mediæval lines.

——*Si vis me flere, dolendum est*
Primum ipsi tibi.—— HOR.
—"If you wish me to sympathize, you must first show grief yourself." Advice given to the actor or writer of tragedy.

Si vis pacem, para bellum.—"If you wish for peace, be prepared for war." An armed peace is the best security against war.

Si vos valetis, bene est, ego quidem valeo.—"If you are well, 'tis good; I myself am well." Sometimes abbreviated thus, *Si Vos V. B. E. E. Q. V.*

Si vulnus tibi, monstrātâ rādīce vel herbâ,

Non fiĕret lĕvius, fŭgĕres rădīce vel herbâ
Proficiente nihil curārier.—— HOR.
—"If you had a wound which was not relieved by the application of a plant or root prescribed for it, you would reject the plant or root that had not effected a cure."

Sibi quisque peccat. *Prov.*—"Every one who sins sins against himself." Our sins fall *on our own heads*, whatever may be our object in sinning.

——*Sibi quivis*
Speret idem: sudet multum, frustrāque labōret
Ausus idem.—— HOR.
—"Anybody might hope to do the same thing, but would sweat much and labour in vain, in attempting it." The result of a vain attempt to imitate a great author.

Sibi uni fortūnam debet.—"He owes his fortune to himself alone."

Sic ăgĭtur censūra, et sic exempla parantur;
Cum vindex, ălios quod monet, ipse facit. OVID.
—"Thus is a censorship discharged, and thus is an example given; when the assertor of morality himself practises that which he enjoins on others."

Sic ait, et dicto cĭtius tŭmĭda æquora placat. VIRG.—"He so says, and quicker than speech he lulls the swelling seas."

Sic ănĭmum tempusque traho; meque ipse redūco
A contemplātu, summŏveōque, mali. OVID.
—"Thus do I occupy my mind and my hours; and thus do I take myself away and withdraw myself from the contemplation of my woes."

Sic cŏgitandum est tanquam ălĭquis in pectus intĭmum inspĭcĕre possit. SEN.—"You ought so to regulate your thoughts, as if any one could look into the inmost recesses of your breast."

Sic cum infĕriōre vivas, quemadmŏdum tecum supĕriōrem velis vīvĕre. SEN.—"So live with your inferior, as you would wish a superior to live with you."

——*Sic cum manus impia sævit,*
Sanguĭne Cæsareo Romānum extinguĕre nomen;
Attŏnĭtum tantæ sŭbĭto terrōre ruīnæ
Hūmānum genus est, totusque perhorruit orbis. OVID.
—"Thus, when an impious band of traitors madly raged

to extinguish the Roman name in the blood of Cæsar, the human race was astounded with sudden terror at ruin so universal, and the whole earth shook with horror." In allusion to the prodigies which were said to have happened at the time of the murder of Julius Cæsar.

Sic delatōres, genus hŏmĭnum publĭco exitio repertum, et pœnis nunquam satis coercĭtum, per præmia eliciebantur. TACIT. —"Thus were informers, a description of men introduced for the public destruction, and never sufficiently restrained by penalties, invited to action by rewards." The historian is speaking of the informers, who swarmed and flourished in imperial Rome.

Sic ego nec sine te nec tecum vīvĕre possum;
Et vĭdeor voti nescius esse mei. OVID.
—"Thus I can neither live without you nor yet with you; and I seem not to know my own wishes."

——*Sic itur ad astra.* VIRG.—"Thus do we reach the stars." By the path of virtue.

Sic noctem pătĕrâ, sic duram carmĭne, donec
Injĭciat rădios in mea vina dies. PROPERT.
—"Thus will I pass the night with the goblet and the song, until the day shall shed its rays upon my wine."

——*Sic omnia fatis*
In pejus ruĕre et retro sublapsa referri. VIRG.
—"Thus, by the Fates' decree, all things change quickly for the worse and retrograde." A destiny fixed and immutable was held by the ancients to rule all things.

Sic passim.—"So in various places."

Sic præsentĭbus utāris voluptātĭbus ut futūris non noceas. SEN. —"So enjoy present pleasures as not to alloy those which are to come." Beware of being cloyed by satiety.

Sic quibus intumuit suffusâ venter ab undâ;
Quo plus sunt potæ, plus sitiuntur aquæ. OVID.
—"So, with those troubled with dropsy, the more water they drink, the more they thirst."

——*Sic quisque pavendo*
Dat vires famæ, nullōque auctōre malōrum
Quæ finxēre timet.—— LUCAN.
—"Thus each person by his fears gives strength to rumour; and without any real ground for apprehending evil fears what he has conjured up."

Sic transit gloria mundi. —"Thus passes away the glory of this world." Beginning of a Sequence of the Romish Church, and said to have been formerly used at the inauguration of the popes of Rome.

Sic ŭtĕre tuo ut aliēno ne lædas. COKE.—"So use your own, as not to injure the property of another." So use your own property, as not to cause a nuisance or injury to others.

Sic visum Vĕnĕrī; cui placet impăres
Formas, atque ănĭmos sub juga ahĕnea
Sævo mittĕre cum joco. HOR.
—"Such is the will of Venus; who delights, in cruel sport, to subject to her brazen yoke persons and tempers ill suited to each other."

Sic vita erat; făcĭlĕ omnes perferre ac pati;
Cum quibus erat cunque unà, his sese dedĕre;
Eōrum obsĕqui studiis; adversus nĕmĭni,
Nunquam præpōnens se ăliis.—— TER.
—"Such was his life; readily to bear and comply with all; with whomsoever he was in company, to them to resign himself; to devote himself to their pursuits; at variance with no one, and never preferring himself to others."

Sic vive cum homĭnĭbus tanquam Deus vĭdeat, et videt. SEN. —"So live with men, as if God might see, and does see you."

Sic volo, sic jubeo, sit pro ratiōne voluntas. JUV.—"So I will it, so I command it, let my pleasure stand for my reason." In the original, the line begins, *Hoc volo,* &c.

Sic vos non vobis. See *Hos ego*, &c.

Sicut ante.—"As before."

——*Sicut meus est mos,*
Nescio quid mĕdĭtans nugārum, totus in illis. HOR.
—"Meditating on some trifle or other, as is my habit, and totally intent upon it."

Sicut Notus pulvĕrem, sic luxuries imprŏbos gyrat.—"As the south wind carries along the dust, so does sensuality the wicked." A mediæval passage.

——*Sicut*
Parvŭla (nam exemplo est) magni formīca labōris
Ore trahit quodcunque potest, atque addit acervo
Quem struit; haud ignāra, ac non incauta futūri. HOR.

—"Thus the little ant (for she is an example) with vast toil carries in her mouth all she can, and adds to the heap which she piles up, by no means ignorant or regardless of the future."

Sĭcŭti aurum ignis, ita etiam amīcos tempus jūdĭcat.—"As fire tries gold, so does time try friends."

Silent leges inter arma. Cic.—See *Inter arma*, &c.

——*Silvis, ubi passim*
Palantes error certo de trămĭte pellit,
Ille sinistrorsum, hic dextrorsum, abit.—— Hor.

—"As in the woods, where a mistake leads people to wander from the proper path; one deviates to the right, another to the left."

Sĭmia, quam sĭmĭlis, turpissĭma bestia, nobis!—"The ape, that most vile beast, how like it is to ourselves!"

Sĭmia sĭmia est, etiamsi aurea gestet insignia. *Prov.*—"An ape is an ape still, though it wear jewels of gold."

——*Sĭmĭle gaudet sĭmĭli.* *Prov.*—"Like loves like." See *Pares cum*, &c.

——*Sĭmĭles aliōrum respĭce casus,*
Mitius ista feres.—— Ovid.—See *Quoties flenti*, &c.

Sĭmĭles habent labia lactūcas. *Prov.*—"Like lips like lettuce." Every class has its own tastes and predilections. Said by Crassus, on seeing an ass eat thistles; the only occasion on which he was known to laugh.

Simĭlia simĭlĭbus curantur.—"Like things are cured by like." The basis of Homœopathy.

Simplex munditiis. Hor.—"Simple in neat attire." "Neat but not gaudy."

——*Simul ac durăvĕrit ætas*
Membra ănĭmumque tuum, nabis sine cortĭce.—— Hor.

—"As soon as age shall have strengthened your limbs and your mind, you will swim without cork."

——*Simul et jucunda et idōnea dīcĕre vitæ.* Hor.—"To tell at the same time what is pleasant and what is suited to life." To blend amusement with instruction.

Simulātio amōris pejor odio est. Pliny *the Younger.*—"Pretended love is worse than hatred."

Sincĕrum est nisi vas, quodcunque infundis acescit. Hor.—"Unless the vessel is clean, whatever you pour into it turns sour." If the youthful mind is not properly prepared, the lessons of instruction will be turned to bad purpose. We see daily instances in the perverted use made of the arts of reading and writing.

Sine Cĕrĕre et Baccho friget Venus.—"Without Ceres and Bacchus, Venus will starve." Without the support of wine and food, love would soon perish.

Sine curâ.—"Without care." A *sinecure* is a place or appointment of which the only duty is that of receiving the salary.

Sine die.—"Without a day." An assembly is adjourned *sine die* when no time is named for its reässembling for the consideration of the business for which it originally met.

Sine fuco et fallăciâ homo. Cic.—"A man without guile and deceit."

Sine invidiâ.—"Without envy." Not invidiously.

Sine me, văcuum tempus ne quod dem mihi
Labōris.—— Ter.
—"Allow me to grant myself no leisure, no respite from labour."

Sine me vocāri pessĭmum, ut dives vocer. *Prov.*—"Call me all that's bad, so you call me rich." The maxim of one who makes money his chief object.

——*Sine mīlĭtis usu*
Mollia sĕcūræ peragĕbant ōtia mentes. Ovid.
—"Without occasion for soldiers, the minds of men, free from care, enjoyed an easy tranquillity." The happy state of man in the Golden Age.

Sine odio.—"Without hatred."

Sine pectŏre corpus.—"A body without a heart."

Sine pennis volāre haud făcĭle est. Plaut.—"It is not easy to fly without wings." Said of those who attempt to do what is beyond their natural capacity.

Sine probâ causâ.—"Without approved cause."

Sine prole.—"Without offspring." Sometimes abbreviated, *S. P.*

Sine quâ non.—"Without which, not." Anything indispensable, and without which another cannot exist.

Sine quereiâ mortalitātis jura pendāmus. Sen.—"Let us abide by the laws of mortality without complaining."

Sine virtūte argūtum civem mihi hăbeam pro præficâ,
Quæ alios collaudat, eapse se vero non potest. PLAUT.
—"Without valour an eloquent citizen is like a hired mourner, who praises other people for that which he cannot do himself." The *præficæ*, or hired mourners, were females.

Sine virtūte esse amicitia nullo pacto potest; quæ autem inter bonos amicitia dīcĭtur, hæc inter malos factio est. SALL.—"There can be no true friendship without virtue; for that bond which, among good men, is called friendship, among wicked men becomes faction."

Singŭla de nobis anni prædantur euntes. HOR.—"Each passing year deprives us of something."

Singŭla quæque locum teneant sortīta decenter. HOR.—"Let each keep the place assigned it by its respective properties." The character of Tragedy is not to be blended with that of Comedy.

Singŭla quid rĕfĕram? nil non mortāle tenēmus,
Pectŏris exceptis ingĕniique bonis. OVID.
—"Why should I enter into details? we have nothing that is not perishable, except the blessings of the heart and of the intellect."

Sint Mæcenātes, non dĕrunt, Flacce, Marōnes;
Virgiliumque tibi vel tua rura dabunt. MART.
—"Let there be Mæcenases, Flaccus, and Maros will not be wanting; and even your own fields will give you a Virgil." In allusion to the patronage given by Mæcenas to Virgil.

Sint sales sine vilitāte.—"Let your jests be without vulgarity."

Sit bona librōrum et provīsæ frugis in annum
Cōpia.—— HOR.
—"Let me have a good supply of books, and a store of provisions for the year." The great necessaries with Horace for the true enjoyment of life.

Sit brevis aut nullus tibi somnus meridiānus. *Maxim of the School of Salerno.*—"At midday take either a short nap or none at all."

Sit mihi fas audīta loqui; sit nūmĭne vestro
Pandĕre res altâ terra et calīgĭne mersas. VIRG.
—"Be it permitted me to utter what I have heard; may

I by your divine will disclose things buried in the depths of the earth and in darkness."

——*Sit mihi mensa tripes et*
Concha salis puri, et toga, quæ defendĕre frigus,
Quamvis crassa queat.—— HOR.

—"Let me have but a three-legged table, a shell full of pure salt, and a garment, which, though coarse, may keep off the cold."

Sit mihi quod nunc est, ĕtiam minus; ut mihi vivam
Quod sŭpĕrest ævi, si quod sŭperesse volunt Dī. HOR.

—"May my fortune be as it is now, or even less; so I enjoy myself for the remainder of my days, if the gods will that any do remain."

Sit modus lasso maris, et viārum,
Militiæque. HOR.

—"Let there be an end to my fatigues by sea, by land, and in warfare."

Sit piger ad pœnas princeps, ad præmia velox. OVID.—"A prince should be slow to inflict punishment, prompt to reward."

Sit procul omne nefas; ut amēris, amābĭlis esto. OVID.—"Afar be all criminal designs; that you may be loved, be worthy to be loved."

Sit tibi crēdĭbĭlis sermo, consuētăque verba. OVID.—"Let your language be intelligible, and your words such as are commonly used."

Sit tibi terra levis.—"May the earth lie light upon thee." Often found in Roman Epitaphs, as also in the abbreviated form, *S. T. T. L.* These words are wittily parodied in the well-known Epitaph on Sir John Vanbrugh, the architect:

"Lie heavy on him, earth, for he
Laid many a heavy load on thee."

Sit tua cura sequi, me duce tutus eris. OVID.—"Be it your care to follow, with me your guide you will be safe."

Sit venia verbis.—"May pardon be granted to my words."

Sive pium vis hoc, sive hoc muliēbre vocāri;
Confĭteor mĭsĕro molle cor esse mihi. OVID.

—"Whether you call it affectionate, or whether womanish, I confess that the heart of poor me is but tender."

Societātis vincŭlum est ratio et orātio. CIC.—"Reason and speech are the bond of human society."

Socius atque comes, tum honōris, tum etiam calamitātis. Cic. —"The companion and sharer as well of my honours as of my misfortunes."

Socius fidēlis anchŏra tuta est.—"A faithful companion is a sure anchor."

Socrates, cui nulla pars săpientiæ obscūra fuit, non erŭbuit tunc, cum interpŏsĭtâ arundĭne crūrĭbus suis, cum parvŭlis filiŏlis ludens, ab Alcibiăde risus est. Valer. Max.— "Socrates, to whom no branch of wisdom was unknown, was not ashamed, when, being found astride a stick, playing with some little children, he was laughed at by Alcibiades."

Socrates quidem cum rogārētur cujātem se ipse dicĕret, mundānum inquit; totius enim mundi se incŏlam et civem arbitrabātur. Cic.—"Socrates, when asked of what country he called himself, answered, of the world; for he considered himself an inhabitant and citizen of the whole world."

——*Sol crescentes dēcēdens duplĭcat umbras.* Virg.—"The setting sun doubles the lengthening shadows."

Sol occŭbuit; nox nulla secūta est.—"The sun has set; no night has ensued." A piece of flattery addressed to a son, and equally complimentary to his father. Burton applies it to Charles I., as the successor of James. Camden says it is ascribed to Giraldus, and refers to the succession of Richard on the death of Henry II. See *Mīra cano*, &c.

Solāmen mĭsĕris sŏcios habuisse dolōris.—"It is some comfort to the wretched to have partners in their woes."

——*Solēbāmus consūmĕre longa loquendo*
Tempŏra, sermōnem deficiente die. Ovid.
—"We were in the habit of spending much of our time in conversation; and the day sufficed not for our discourse."

Solem e mundo tollunt qui amicĭtiam e vitâ tollunt.—"They deprive the world of the sun who deprive life of friendship."

——*Solem quis dīcĕre falsum*
Audeat?—— Virg.
—"Who dares call the sun a deceiver?" Virgil says this when about to mention the prognostics afforded by the sun for fair or foul weather.

Solent mendāces luĕre pœnas malĕfici. Phæd. — "Liars generally pay the penalty of their guilt."

Solet a despectis par referri gratia. Phæd.—"Repayment in kind is generally made by those who are despised."

Soli lumen mutuāri; cœlo stellas; ranæ aquam. ***Prov.***—"To lend light to the sun, stars to the heavens, and water to the frogs."

Sŏlitūdĭnem faciunt, pacem appellant. TACIT.—"They make a desert and call it peace." The conduct pursued by some *civilized* nations in exterminating what they call ***barbarians.***

Sollicitant ălii remis freta cæca, ruuntque
In ferrum: pĕnĕtrant aulas, et līmĭna regum. VIRG.
—"Some harass unknown seas with oars; some rush into arms; some work their way into courts and the palaces of kings." Virgil contrasts the quiet of a country life with the conditions of the sailor, the soldier, and the courtier. See *O fortunati nimium*, &c.

Solo cedit, quicquid solo plantātur. *Law Max.*—"Whatever is planted in the soil goes with the soil."

Solum patriæ omnĭbus est carum, dulce, atque jucundum. CIC.—"His native soil is sweet, dear, and delightful to every one."

Solve senescentem matūre sanus equum, ne
Peccet ad extrēmum ridendus.—— HOR.
—"Wisely in time dismiss the aged courser, lest, an object of derision, he stumble at last."

Solvit ad diem. *Law Term.*—"He paid to the day." A plea to an action of debt.

Solvĭte tantis ănĭmum monstris,
Solvĭte, Sŭpĕri.—— SEN.
—"Save, ye gods of heaven, from such chimæras, save the mind!"

——*Solvitque ănĭmis mirācŭla rerum,*
Erĭpuitque Jovi fulmen, vīresque tonanti. MANIL.
—"He both freed our minds from dread of things above, and snatched the lightnings from Jove, and from the thunderer his might." See *Eripuit cœlo*, &c.

Solvuntur tabŭlæ.—"The bills are dismissed."

Somne quies rerum, placidissĭme, somne, Deōrum,
Pax ănĭmi, quem cura fugit, qui corda diurnis
Fessa ministeriis mulces, repărasque labōri. OVID.
—"Sleep, thou repose of all things; sleep, thou gentlest of the deities; thou peace of the mind, from whom care flies; who dost soothe the hearts of men wearied with the toils of the day, and dost recruit them for labour."

Somnia me terrent veros imitantia casus;
Et vigĭlant sensus in mea damna mei. OVID.
—"Visions alarm me, that portray my real misfortunes; and my senses are ever awake to my sorrows."

Somnia, terrōres măgĭcos, mīrăcŭla, sagas,
Nocturnos Lĕmūres, portentăque Thessăla, rides? HOR.
—"Can you laugh at dreams, magic terrors, wonders, witches, goblins of the night, and Thessalian prodigies?"

——*Somnus agrestium*
Lenis virōrum non hŭmĭles domos
Fastīdit, umbrōsamque ripam. HOR.
—"Light slumbers do not disdain the humble dwelling of the peasant, or the shady bank."

Sorex suo perit indĭcio. Prov.—"The mouse perishes, by being his own informer." His hole being seen is the cause of his destruction.

——*Sors et virtus miscentur in unum.* VIRG.—"Chance and valour are blended together." It is equally doubtful which may prevail.

Sortes Virgiliānæ.—"The Virgilian Chances." A species of divination practised by the ancients, by opening the works of Virgil, and remarking the lines beneath the fingers the instant the leaves were opened. Spartianus tells us that it was much practised by the Emperor Adrian. When the works of Homer were used, it was called, "*Sortes Homericæ.*" The ancient Christians used a similar kind of divination with the Holy Scriptures, or the Psalter, which was called "*Sortes Sanctorum,*" and was repeatedly condemned by the councils of the Church. King Charles the First is said to have tried the "*Sortes Virgilianæ,*" in the Bodleian Library at Oxford, when on a visit there in company with Lord Falkland, and to have opened at the prophetic lines in the 4th Book of the Æneid, l. 615, beginning,

At bello audăcis popŭli vexātus et armis.

"Harassed in warfare by the arms of a valiant people—" This is Dr. Wellwood's account, but Aubrey relates the same story of the poet Cowley and Charles, Prince of Wales, at Paris, in 1648.

Sospes eas, semperque parens; mihi fīlia rapta est.
Heu! mĕlior quanto sors tua sorte meâ! OVID.

—"Unharmed mayest thou be, and a parent mayest thou ever remain. From me my daughter has been removed. Alas! how much happier is thy lot than mine!"

——*Spargĕre voces*
In vulgum ambĭguas.—— VIRG.
—"To scatter doubtful rumours among the mob."

——*Spatio brevi*
Spem longam rĕsĕces. Dum lŏquĭmur, fŭgĕrit invĭda
Ætas. Carpe diem, quam mĭnĭme crēdŭla postero. HOR.
—"Abridge your hopes in proportion to the shortness of your life. While we are conversing, envious time has been flying. Seize the present day, trusting as little as possible in the morrow."

Spectas et tu spectābĕris.—"You see and you shall be seen." You here see the characters of others, and if necessary you shall see your own held up to view.

Spectātum vĕniunt, vĕniunt spectentur ut ipsæ. OVID.—"They come to see, they come too to be seen." Said by Ovid with reference to the motives with which the Roman females flocked to the Circus and the Theatres.

Spectātum admissi, risum teneātis, amīci? HOR.—"Being admitted to see [the picture], can you, my friends, refrain from laughter?"

Spem bonam certamque domum reporto.—"I bring home a good and assured hope." I announce hopes not likely to be disappointed.

Spem prĕtio non emo. TER.—"I do not buy hopes with money." I do not give gold for mere expectations.

Sperat infestis, mĕtuit secundis
Altĕram sortem bene præparātum
Pectus.—— HOR.
—"The heart that is well prepared, hopes in adversity, and fears a change of fortune in prosperity."

Sperāte, et vosmet rebus servāte secundis. VIRG.—"Hope on, and reserve yourself for prosperous times."

Sperāte mĭsĕri, cavēte felīces.—"Live in hope, you who are wretched; you who are in prosperity, beware."

——*Sperāvĭmus ista*
Dum fortūna fuit.—— VIRG.
—"We once had such hopes, while fortune favoured us."

Sperēmus quæ volŭmus, sed quæ accĭdĕrit ferāmus. CIC.—

"Let us hope for what we will; but let us endure what befalls us."

Sperne voluptātes, nocet empta dolōre voluptas. HOR.—"Despise pleasures; pleasure purchased by pain is injurious."

Spes bona dat vires, ănĭmum quoque spes bona firmat;
Vivĕre spe vidi qui mŏrĭtūrus erat.
—"Good hope gives strength, good hope also confirms the resolution; even him who was on the point of death, I have seen kept alive by hope."

Spes est vigilantis somnium. COKE.—"Hope is the dream of a man awake." An adaptation from Quintilian.

Spes facit, ut vĭdeat cum terras undĭque nullas,
Naufrăgus in mĕdiis brăchia jactet aquis. OVID.
—"Hope it is that makes the shipwrecked mariner strike out in the midst of the waves, even when he beholds no land on any side."

Spes gregis. VIRG.—"The hope of the flock." Sometimes applied to one particular child, the hope of the family. "The flower of the flock." It is also used ironically.

——*Spes incerta futūri.* VIRG.—"Hopes of the future full of uncertainty."

Spes sibi quisque. VIRG.—"Let every man's hope be in himself." Let every man trust to his own resources.

Spes tenet in tempus, semel est si crēdĭta, longum;
Illa quidem fallax, sed tamen apta Dea est. OVID.
—"Hope, if once indulged, endures for a long time; although a deceitful goddess, she is nevertheless a convenient one."

——*Spirat adhuc amor,*
Vivuntque commissi calōres
Æŏliæ fĭdĭbus puellæ. HOR.
—"Still breathes his love, and still lives the glowing warmth, imparted to the lyre by the Æolian fair." Said in allusion to Anacreon and Sappho.

——*Spirat trăgĭcum satis, et felĭcĭter audet.* HOR.—"He breathes a spirit tragic enough, and is happy in his attempt."

Splendĭde mendax. HOR.—"Nobly false." Untrue for a noble object. Sometimes used ironically in reference to an egregious liar. See *Pia fraus.*

Sponde, noxa præsto est. Prov.—"Be surety, and harm is at hand." From the Greek.

——*Spretæque injūria formæ.* VIRG.—"And the affront offered to her slighted beauty." In allusion to the resentment of Juno at the judgment of Paris.

Sta, viātor, herōem calcas.—"Pause, traveller; thou treadest on a hero's dust!" The epitaph inscribed by the great Condé over the remains of his antagonist, the brave Merci.

Stabat Mater dolorōsa.—"There stood the Mother, bathed in tears." The beginning of the Prose, or Sequence, of the Mass for the Dead in the Roman Church.

Standum est contra res adversas.—"We must stand up against adversity."

Stans pede in uno. HOR.—"Standing on one leg." Applied to a work, this phrase means that it bears no marks of extraordinary exertion.

Stare decīsis, et non movēre quiēta. Law Max.—"To abide by decisions made, and not to stir up points set at rest."

Stare putes, adeo procēdunt tempŏra tarde. OVID.—"The time proceeds so slowly, you would think that it was standing still."

Stare super vias antīquas.—"To stand upon old ways." To be attached to old habits or customs, and to resist novelties or innovations.

Stat fortūna domus, &c. VIRG.—See *Genus immortale*, &c.

——*Stat magni nōmĭnis umbra.* LUCAN.—"He stands, the shadow of a mighty name." The poet says this in reference to the titles gained by Pompey in his younger days; but it is sometimes quoted as though meaning that the lustre of a person's former greatness is impaired by his late conduct, and he is no more than the faint image of what he was. See *Magni nominis*, &c.

Stat nōmĭnis umbra.—An adaptation of the above, used by 'Junius' as the motto of his pseudonymous Letters.

Stat pro ratiōne voluntas.—"My pleasure stands as my reason." See *Hoc volo*, &c., and *Sic volo*, &c.

Stat sua cuique dies; breve et irrĕparābĭle tempus

Omnĭbus est vitæ; sed famam extendĕre factis,
Hoc virtūtis opus.—— VIRG.
—"For every one his day is fixed; a short and unalterable term of life is given to all; but by deeds to extend our fame, this is virtue's task."

Statim daret, ne differendo viderētur negāre. CORN. NEP.—"He would give at once, lest, by deferring, he should seem to deny." Said of Themistocles. See *Bis dat*, &c.

Status quo, *Status in quo*, *Statu quo*, or *In statu quo.*—"The state in which, [it was]."

Status quo ante bellum.—"The state in which the belligerent nations stood before war commenced." A term used in diplomatic communications. The opposite term is the *Uti possidetis*, which see.

Stemmăta quid făciunt? Quid prodest, Pontĭce, longo
Sanguĭne censēri?—— JUV.
—"What do pedigrees avail? Of what use, Ponticus, is it to be descended from a long line of ancestors?"

Stercus et ūrīna medicōrum ferŭla prima.—"To regulate the natural evacuations is the first rule of physicians."

——*Stĕrĭlisque diu palus, aptăque remis*
Vīcīnas urbes alit, et grave sentit arātrum. HOR.
—"And the swamp, long sterile, and plied by the oar, now maintains the neighbouring cities, and feels the heavy plough."

Sternĭtur, exănĭmisque tremens procumbit humi bos. VIRG.—"The ox is felled, and, quivering, lies expiring on the ground." Porson is said to have exclaimed, on letting Bos's Ellipses fall upon some volumes of Hume's History of England, "*Procumbit Humi Bos!*"

Stet processus. *Law Lat.*—"Let process be stayed."

——*Stillicĭdi casus lapĭdem cavat.*—— LUCR.—"The falling drop hollows out the stone."

——*Stĭmŭlos dedit æmŭla virtus.* LUCAN.—"Valorous rivalry spurred him on."

——*Stŏlĭdam præbet tibi vellĕre barbam.* PERS.—"He holds out his silly beard for thee to pluck."

Stomachātur omnia. CIC.—"He frets about everything." He takes everything to heart.

Strata jacent passim sua quæque sub arbŏre poma. VIRG.—

"The fruits lie scattered here and there beneath their trees."

Strātum super strātum.—"Layer upon layer," or "stratum upon stratum," as geologists would say.

Strēnua nos exercet inertia; nāvībus atque
Quadrīgis pĕtĭmus bene vīvĕre.—— Hor.
—"A useless activity urges us on; by ships and by chariots we seek to live happily."

Studēre suis commŏdis. Cic.—"To study one's own convenience."

——*Studiis florentem ignōbĭlis oti.* Virg.—"Indulging in the pursuits of inglorious ease." Said by the poet of himself, when writing the Georgics.

Studio culinæ tenētur. Cic.—"He is possessed by thoughts of the kitchen." "His heart is in the kitchen." He thinks of nothing but eating. See *Animus est in*, &c.

——*Studio minuente labōrem.* Ovid.—"His zeal diminishing his toil."

——*Studium famæ mihi crescit amōre.* Ovid.—"My zeal increases with my eagerness for fame."

——*Stulta est clementia, cum tot ubīque*
Vātĭbus occurras, peritūræ parcĕre chartæ. Juv.
—"It were misplaced forbearance, when you meet so many poets everywhere, to spare paper that is sure to be wasted." The words of an indignant critic.

Stulte, quid o frustra votis puerīlĭbus optas,
Quæ non ulla tulit, fertque feretque dies? Ovid.
—"O fool! why, with thy childish aspirations, dost thou vainly wish for that, which no time, past, present, or to come, will realize?"

——*Stultĭtia est, cui bene esse licet, eum prævorti*
Lītĭbus.—— Plaut.
—"It is sheer folly for a man who can enjoy himself, to turn to brawling in preference."

Stultĭtia est ei te esse tristem, cujus potestas plus potest. Plaut.—"It is sheer folly to be morose towards him whose rule is the stronger."

——*Stultĭtia est, făcĭnus magnum tĭmĭdo cordi crēdĕre, nam omnes*
Res perinde sunt ut agas.—— Plaut.

—"It is sheer folly to intrust a bold design to a timorous heart, for all things are just as you make them."

Stultĭtia est venātum dūcĕre invītos canes. Plaut.—"It is folly to take out unwilling dogs to hunt."

Stultĭtiam dissimulāre non potes nisi tăcĭturnitāte.—"There is no way to conceal folly but by silence."

Stultĭtiam patiuntur opes.—— Hor. — "Riches license folly." Follies are often passed over in the rich.

Stultĭtiam simulāre loco, săpientia summa est.—"To affect folly is, on some occasions, consummate wisdom." The foolishness, for instance, affected by Brutus in the house of Tarquinius.

Stultōrum calămi carbōnes, mœnia chartæ. *Prov.*—"Coals are the fool's pen, the walls his paper." So the English proverb, "A white wall is a fool's paper."

Stultōrum incūrāta malus pudor ulcĕra celat. Hor.—"It is the false shame of fools that makes them conceal their uncured wounds." This maxim may be applied both to wounds of the mind and of the body.

Stultum consĭlium non modo effectu caret
Sed ad pernĭciem quoque mortāles avŏcat. Phæd.
—"An ill-judged project is not only profitless, but lures mortals to their destruction as well."

Stultum est dicere, Non putarem.—"It is foolish to say, 'I could not have thought it.'" See *Nil admirari, &c.*

Stultum est in luctu capillum sibi evellĕre, quasi calvitio mœror levētur. Cic.—"It is folly to tear one's hair in sorrow, just as though grief could be assuaged by baldness."

Stultum est timēre quod vitāri non potest. Syr.—"It is foolish to fear that which cannot be avoided."

Stultus es, qui facta infecta făcĕre verbis postŭlas. Plaut.—"You are a fool to expect by words to make undone what has been done."

Stultus es, rem actam agis. Plaut.—"You are a simpleton, you are doing what has been done already."

Stultus labor est ineptiārum. Mart.—"The labour is foolishly thrown away that is bestowed on trifles."

Stultus nisi quod ipse facit, nil rectum putat.—"The fool thinks nothing well done but what he does himself." Self-sufficiency is a sign of a weak mind.

Stultus, qui, patre occīso, libĕros relinquat. *Prov.*—"He is a fool who kills the father and leaves the children." Things must never be done by halves.

Stultus semper incĭpit vīvĕre. *Prov.*—"The fool is always beginning to live." He is always putting off settled habits and amendment till to-morrow.

Stylus virum arguit.—"The style proclaims the man."

Sua comparāre commŏda ex incommŏdis altĕrius. TER.—"To build up his own fortunes on the misfortunes of another."

Suâ confessiōne hunc jŭgŭlo. CIC.—"I convict him by his own confession." His own testimony condemns him. See *Suo sibi*, &c.

——*Sua cuique deus fit dira cupīdo.* VIRG.—"Each one's ruling appetite is his god."

Sua cuique quum sit ănĭmi cogitātio,
Colorque proprius. PHÆD.

—"Since each man has a turn of thinking of his own, and a tone peculiar to himself." See *Quot homines*, &c., and *Trahit sua*, &c.

Sua cuique vita obscūra est.—"Every man's life is in darkness to himself." No man is a competent judge of his own conduct.

Sua cuique voluptas.—"Every man has his own pleasure." "Every man to his liking." See *Trahit sua*, &c.

Sua mūnĕra mittit cum hamo. *Prov.*—"He sends his presents with a hook attached." He is angling for a return with interest. "He throws a sprat to catch a herring."

Sua quisque exempla debet æquo ănĭmo pati. PHÆD.—"Every one is bound to bear patiently the consequences of his own example."

Sua regīna regi placet, Juno Jovi. PLAUT.—"The king is pleased with his queen, Jupiter with his Juno." "Every Jack has his Jill." See *Asinus asino*, &c., *Pares cum*, &c., and *Simile gaudet*, &c.

Suam quisque homo rem mĕmĭnit.—"Every man is mindful of his own interests."

——*Suave est ex magno tollĕre acervo.* HOR.—"It is a pleasant thing to take from a great heap." Said satirically of a miser who takes from an immense heap the little that he will venture to use.

Suave, mari magno, turbantĭbus æquŏra ventis,
E terrâ magnum altĕrius spectāre labōrem. LUCRET.

—"It is a pleasant thing from the shore to behold the dangers of another upon the mighty ocean, when the winds are lashing the main." As Rochefoucauld says, "In the adversity of our best friends we often find something which does not displease us."

Suavĭtas sermōnum atque morum haudquăquam mediŏcre condimentum amicĭtiæ. Cic.—"Mildness of address and manner is by no means an unimportant seasoning to friendship."

Suavĭter in modo, fortĭter in re.—"Gentle in manner, resolute in deed." Motto of Earl Newborough.

Sub fine or ***finem.***—"Towards the end."

Sub hoc signo vinces. See *In hoc*, &c.

Sub inĭtio.—"Towards the beginning."

——***Sub Jove frigido.*** Hor.—"Under the cold sky."

Sub Jove pars durat, pauci tentŏria ponunt. Ovid.—"Some endure the open air, a few pitch tents."

Sub marmŏre ĕtiam atque auro servĭtus hăbĭtat. Sen.—"Even under marble and golden roofs dwells slavery." Slavery to the dominion of vice, sorrow, and discontent.

Sub omni lăpĭde scorpius dormit. *Prov.*—"Beneath every stone a scorpion lies asleep." A warning to act in all things with caution and deliberation.

Sub pœnâ. *Law Lat.*—"Under a penalty." The title of a writ issued for summoning witnesses.

Sub rosâ.—"Under the rose." See *Est rosa*, &c.

Sub silentio.—"In silence." The matter passed *sub silentio*—*i. e.* without any notice being taken of it, without being canvassed at all.

Sŭbĭta amicĭtia rarò sine pœnitentiâ cŏlĭtur.—"Sudden friendships are rarely contracted without repentance."

Sŭbĭto crevit, fungi instar, in divitias maxĭmas.—"He has suddenly started up, like a mushroom, into immense wealth."

Sublātâ causâ tollĭtur effectus. *Law Max.*—"The cause removed, the effect is removed." The cause removed, the effect must cease. See *Cessante causâ*, &c.

Sublātam ex ŏcŭlis quærĭmus invĭdi. Hor.—See *Virtutem incolumem*, &c.

Sublīmi fĕriam sīdĕra vertĭce. Hor.—"I shall tower to the stars with exalted head." Seriously said by Horace in a spirit of poetic rapture: but often quoted merely in burlesque.

Substantia prior et dignior est accidente. *Law Max.*—"The substance is prior to and of more weight than the accident." A judgment, for instance, solemnly pronounced, shall not be arrested for a defect in point of form.

Succedāneum.—"A substitute."

Successus ad perniciem multos devŏcat. PHÆD.—"Success leads many astray to their ruin."

Successus improbōrum plures allĭcit. PHÆD.—"The success of the wicked is a temptation to many."

Succōsior est virgo quæ serpyllum quam quæ moschum olet.—"The damsel is more tempting who smells of wild thyme than she who is scented with musk." A mediæval proverb.

Succurrendum parti maxĭmè laboranti. CELSUS.—"We should assist the part which has the most to endure."

Sudor Anglĭcus.—"The English sweat." The sweating sickness was so called.

Suffĭcit huic tŭmŭlus, cui non suffĕcĕrit orbis.—"This tomb now suffices for him, for whom the world did not suffice." The import of an epitaph for the tomb of Alexander the Great.

Suggestio falsi.—"The suggestion of a falsehood."

Sui amans, sine rivāli.—"A lover of himself, without a rival." Cicero says this of Pompey.

Sui cuique mores fingunt fortūnam. CORN. NEPOS.—"Every man's fortune is shaped by his own manners." So the English proverb, "Manners make the man."

Sui gĕnĕris.—"Of its own kind." Of its own genus or class, as distinguished from any other.

Sui juris. *Law Term.*—"Of his own right." Not dependent on the will or control of another.

Sum quod eris, fui quod es.—"I am what you will be, I was what you are." A lesson to the living on the tombs of the dead.

Sume călămum, tempĕra, et scribe velōcĭter.—"Take your pen, observe my words, and write quickly." The words of the Venerable Bede, addressed on his death-bed to his secretary.

——*Sume superbiam*
Quæsītam mĕrĭtis.—— HOR.

—"Assume the pride won by your deserts."

Sūmĭte in exemplum pĕcŭdes ratiōne carentes. OVID.—"Take as an example the beasts devoid of reason."

Sūmĭte mātĕriam vestris, qui scribĭtis, æquam
Vīrĭbus, et versāte diu, quid ferre recūsent,
Quid văleant hŭmĕri.—— HOR.

—"Ye who write, make choice of a subject suited to your abilities, and weigh in your mind what your powers are unable, and what they are able, to perform."

Summa perfectio attingi non potest. CIC.—"Consummate perfection cannot be attained."

——*Summa petit livor.* OVID.—"Envy strikes high." Envy takes a lofty flight.

Summa sedes non capit duos. *Prov.*—"The highest seat will not admit of two." See *Nulla fides*, &c.

Summam nec mĕtuas diem, nec optes. MART.—"Neither fear nor wish for your last day."

Summis nārĭbus olfăcĕre. *Prov.*—"To smell with the tip of the nose." To pass an opinion on a matter after a slight examination only.

Summum bonum.—"The chief good." The great object for which it is worth our while to live. Some philosophers among the ancients held pleasure to be the *Summum bonum*, others virtue.

Summum crede nefas ănĭmam præferre pudōri,
Et propter vitam vivendi perdĕre causas. JUV.

—"Consider it to be the greatest of infamy to prefer life to honour, and, for the sake of living, to lose the object of living."

Summum jus sæpe summa injūria est. CIC.—"Extreme justice is often extreme injustice." Applied to the enforcement of legal penalties to the very letter, without having regard to equity or the circumstances of the case. This was a favourite maxim with the Emperor Justinian. See *Jus summum*, &c.

Sumptus censum ne sŭpĕret. PLAUT.—"Do not let your expenses outrun your income." "Cut your coat according to your cloth." See *Messe tenus*, &c.

Sunt bona mixta malis, sunt mala mixta bonis.—"Good is mixed with evil, and evil with good."

Sunt bona, sunt quædam mediŏcria, sunt mala plura
Quæ legis.—— MART.
—"Of those which you will read, some are good, some middling, and more are bad." The character given by Martial of his Epigrams.

——*Sunt certi denĭque fines,*
Quos ultra citrăque nequit consistĕre rectum. HOR.
—See *Est modus*, &c.

Sunt delicta tamen, quibus ignōvisse velīmus. HOR.—"There are some faults, however, which we are ready to pardon."

Sunt ibi, si vivunt, nostrâ quoque consĭta quondam,
Sed non et nostrâ poma legenda manu. OVID.
—"There, too, if they are still alive, are apples, once planted with my hand, but not destined to be gathered by it." Said by Ovid, when in banishment, of his gardens in the vicinity of Rome.

——*Sunt Jovis omnia plena.* VIRG.—"All things are full of Jove." See *Dei plena*, &c.

Sunt lăcrymæ rerum, et mentem mortālia tangunt. VIRG.—"Tears are due to wretchedness, and mortal woes touch the heart."

Sunt plerumque regum voluntātes vehementes, et inter se contrāriæ. TACIT.—"The desires of monarchs are generally impetuous and inconsistent."

Sunt quædam vitia, quæ nemo est quin libenter fugiat. CIC. —"There are certain vices which every man would most gladly avoid."

——*Sunt quædam vitiōrum elementa.* JUV.—"There are certain first elements of vice." See *Nemo repente*, &c.

Sunt sŭpĕris sua jura.—— OVID.—"The gods of heaven have their own laws." Often quoted to show that even the highest powers are subject to certain laws.

Sunt tamen inter se commūnia sacra poētis;
Diversum quamvis quisque sequāmur iter. OVID.
—"Yet with poets there are certain common ties; although we each pursue our respective path."

Sunt verba et voces, quibus hunc lenīre dolōrem
Possis, et magnam morbi depōnĕre partem. HOR.
—"There are words and maxims by which you may miti-

gate your pain, and in a great measure overcome the disease." See *Fervet avaritiâ*, &c.

Suo jumento malum accersĕre. Prov.—"To fetch mischief upon one's own beast." To bring misfortunes upon one's self.

Suo Marte.—"By his own prowess." He performed it *suo Marte*,—by his own skill and ability.

Suo sibi gladio hunc jŭgŭlo. TER.—"With his own sword do I stab this man." I defeat him with his own weapons; by his own arguments. See *Suâ confessione*, &c.

Suos līběros neglĭgit, et ad eōrum arbĭtrium lĭbīdĭnemque vīvĕre sinit. CIC.—"He neglects his children, and lets them live according to their own will and pleasure."

Super subjectam matĕriam. Law Phrase.—"Upon the matter submitted." A solicitor is not responsible for his acts when founded *super subjectam materiam*, *i. e.* on the statement submitted to him by his client, which has turned out to be false.

——*Superanda omnis fortūna ferendo est.* VIRG.—See *Quicquid erit*, &c.

——*Sŭpĕrat quŏniam fortūna, sequāmur;*
Quoque vocat vertāmus iter.—— VIRG.
—"Since fortune compels us, let us follow; and whither she calls, let us direct our course."

Superbi hŏmĭnes in convīviis stulti sunt.—"Proud men in their cups become fools." Wine, like death, is a leveller of distinctions.

Supersĕdeas. Law Lat.—"You may supersede." You may set aside or annul. The title of a writ to stay proceedings in any case.

Superstĭtio, in quâ inest inānis timor Dei; relĭgio quæ Dei cultu pio continētur. CIC.—"Superstition is a senseless fear of God; religion, the pious worship of God."

Supparasitāri amīco. PLAUT.—"To toady one's friend."

Suppressio veri.—"A suppression of the truth." The withholding, or telling a part only of, the truth. See *Suggestio falsi.*

Suprēmum vale.—"A last farewell."

Suprēmumque vale——
Vix dixit.—— OVID.
—"And hardly could he bid the last farewell."

Surdo fābŭlam narras. — "You tell your story to a deaf man;"—to one who does not listen to you.

—— *Surgit amāri ălĭquid.* LUCR. — "Something bitter arises." See *Medio de*, &c.

Sursum corda.—"Lift up your hearts." *Lament.* iii. 41.

Sus erat in prĕtio.—— OVID.—"Pigs were in request."

Sus Minervam. *Prov.*—"A pig (teaching) Minerva."

Suspectum semper invisumque dominantĭbus qui proxĭmus destinaretur. TACIT.—"He who is the next heir is always suspected and hated by those who hold the supreme power."

Suspendătur per collum. *Law Lat.*—"Let him be hanged by the neck." The judge's order for the execution of a criminal, usually written *Sus. per coll.*

Suspensos pedes ponĕre. QUINT.—"To walk on tiptoe."

Sustĭne et abstĭne.—"Bear and forbear." A maxim of Epictetus.

Sustĭneas ut onus, nitendum vertĭce pleno est;
At flecti nervos si patiāre, cadet. OVID.
—"To sustain a burden, you must strive with the head fully erect; should you suffer the muscles to bend, it will fail."

Suum cuique.—"His own to every one." Let each have his own.

Suum cuique decus postĕrĭtas rependet.—"Posterity will give to every man his due."

Suum cuique incommŏdum ferendum est, potius quam de altĕrius commŏdis detrahendum. CIC.—"Every man should bear his own grievances, rather than abridge the comforts of another."

Suum cuique pulchrum. *Prov.*—"Every man's own is beautiful." "Every man thinks his own geese swans." See *Quisquis amat*, &c.

Suum cuique tribuĕre, ea demum summa justitia est. CIC.—"To give to every man his due, that in fact is supreme justice."

Suus cuique mos. TER.—"Every man has his way."

Sylosontis chlamys. *Prov.*—"The scarf of Syloson." Syloson gave to king Darius a rich scarf or mantle, and in return received the sovereignty of Samos. Hence, this term was applied to the gifts of those who "Throw a sprat to catch a herring."

——*Sylvas inter reptāre salūbres,*
Cūrantem quicquid dignum săpiente bonōque est. Hor.
—"To stroll among the healthful groves, meditating on whatever is worthy of the wise and the good."

T.

——*Tabesne cadāvĕra solvat,*
An rogus, haud refert.—— Lucan.
—"Whether corruption dissolve the carcase, or whether the funeral pile, it matters not."

Tābŭla in naufrăgio.—"A plank in a shipwreck." A last resource. The benefit secured by a posterior mortgagee by getting in an outstanding term, and thus gaining precedence over a prior mortgagee. A phrase used till recently in the courts of Equity.

Tābŭla rasa.—"A smoothed" or "planed tablet." This expression is used by metaphysicians to indicate the state of the human mind before it has received any impressions. The ancients used tablets covered with wax, on which they wrote with an iron instrument called a *stylus*, one end of which was broad and flat, for obliterating what had been written by smoothing the wax. Hence the expression.

Tacent, satis laudant. Ter.—"In being silent, they give sufficient praise." The silence of the censorious may be considered as so much praise.

Tacĭta bona est mŭlier semper quam loquens. Plaut.—"A silent woman is always better than a talkative one."

Tacĭtæ magis et occultæ inimīcitiæ timendæ sunt, quam indictæ et opertæ. Cic.—"Enmity unavowed and concealed is more to be feared than when open and declared."

——*Tacĭtum vivit sub pectŏre vulnus.* Virg.—"The secret wound still lives within his breast." The sense of injury still remains.

——*Tacĭtus pasci si corvus posset, habēret*
Plus dapis, et rixæ multo minus invidiæque. Hor.
—"If the crow could have only fed in silence, he would have had more to eat, and much less contention and envy." In allusion to the Fable of the Fox and the Crow.

——*Tædet cœli convexa tuēri.* VIRG.—"I am weary of looking upon the canopy of heaven."

Tædium vitæ.—"Weariness of life." *Ennui.* The state of the man who has had every desire gratified, but who can satisfy none.

——*Tale tuum carmen nobis, divīne poēta,*
Quale sopor fessis.—— VIRG.
—"Thy song is to us, divine poet, as sleep to the weary." These words are sometimes used sarcastically in reference to poets whose lines "remind one, not in vain, of sleep."

Tales sunt hŏmĭnum mentes, quali pater ipse
Jŭpĭter auctifĕrâ lustravit lumine terras.
—"The minds of men are according as father Jupiter shed light upon various lands with his fertilizing light." A translation by Cicero from Homer's Odyssey, B. xviii. ll. 135, 136; quoted by St. Augustin.

Tam consentientĭbus mihi sensĭbus nemo est in terris. CIC.—"There is not a man in the world whose sentiments so perfectly agree with my own."

Tam deest avāro quod habet, quam quod non habet. SYR.—"The miser is as much in want of that which he possesses as of that which he does not possess." Because he has not the courage to make use of it.

Tam ficti pravique tenax quam nuncia veri. VIRG.—"As ready to propagate falsehood and calumny, as to proclaim the truth."

Tam frictum ego illum reddam, quam frictum est cicer. PLAUT.—"I 'll have him parched as well as ever pea was parched."

Tam Marte quam Minervâ. *Prov.*—"As much by Mars as by Minerva." As much by courage as by wisdom.

Tam Marti quam Mercurio.—"As much for Mars as for Mercury." Equally qualified for war and for diplomacy.

Tam sæpe nostrum dĕcĭpi Fabullum, quid
Mirāris, Aule? Semper bonus homo tiro est. MART.
—"Why wonder, Aulus, that our friend Fabullus is so often deceived? The virtuous man is always a novice."

——*Tamen cantābĭtis, Arcădes, inquit,*
Montĭbus hæc vestris: soli cantāre perīti
Arcădes. O mihi tum quam mollĭter ossa quiescant,
Vestra meos olim si fistŭla dicat amōres! VIRG.

—"And yet you, Arcadians, will sing these woes of mine upon your hills,—Arcadians, alone skilled in song. Oh! how softly will my bones repose, if your pipe in times to come shall sing my loves!"

——*Tamen me*
Cum magnis vixisse invīta fatēbĭtur usque
Invidia.—— HOR.

—"Nevertheless, even envy, however unwilling, will have to admit that I have lived among the great."

Tandem pocŭlum mœrōris exhausit. CIC.—"He has exhausted at last the cup of grief." He has drained the cup of sorrow to the very dregs.

Tangĕre ulcus. TER.—"To touch a sore." To reöpen a wound. Figuratively, to renew one's grief.

Tanquam Argīvum clypĕum abstŭlĕrit, ita gloriātur.—"He boasts as though he had gained an Argive shield." Both among the Greeks and Romans it was considered disgraceful to lose the shield in battle, and equally meritorious to gain one. See *Relictâ non bene*, &c.

Tanquam in spĕcŭlum.—"As though in a mirror." A theatrical motto.

Tanquam nōbĭlis.—"As though noble." Noble by courtesy.

Tanquam ungues dĭgĭtosque suos. *Prov.*—"As well as his own nails and fingers." He knows the matter as well as if it were "at his fingers' ends."

——*Tanta est discordia fratrum.* OVID.—"So great is the discord of brothers." The quarrels of kinsmen are generally the most inveterate. See *Acerrima proximorum*, &c.

——*Tanta est quærendi cura decōris.* JUV.—"So great is their care in seeking to adorn their persons."

Tanta vis probitātis est ut eam vel in iis, quos nunquam vīdĭmus, vel, quod magis est, in hoste etiam diligāmus. CIC.—"There is so great a power in honesty, that we love it even in those whom we have never seen, or, what is still more, in an enemy even."

——*Tantæne ănĭmis cœlestĭbus iræ?* VIRG.—"Can such wrath exist in heavenly minds?"

Tantălus a labris sĭtiens fugientia captat
Flumĭna.—— HOR.

—"Tantalus, athirst, catches at the water which recedes from his lips."

Tanti eris ăliis, quanti tibi fuĕris. Cic.—"You will be of as much value to others as you are to yourself."

Tanti est quanti est fungus pŭtĭdus. Plaut.—"He is worth just as much as a rotten mushroom."

Tanti quantum hăbeas sis.—"You will be valued at what you are worth."

Tanto hŏmĭni fidus, tantæ virtūtis amātor.—"Faithful to such a man, a lover of virtue so great."

Tanto in mœrōre jacet, ut ab illo recreāri nullo modo possit. Cic.—"He is so prostrated by excessive grief, that he cannot, by any effort, be diverted from it."

——*Tanto major famæ sitis est, quam*
Virtūtis.—— Juv.

—"So much greater is the thirst for fame than for virtue." See *Quis enim*, &c.

Tantum bona valent, quantum vendi possunt. Coke.—"Things are worth just as much as they will sell for." "The worth of a thing is what it will bring."

Tantum cibi et potiōnis adhibendum est, ut reficiantur vires, non ut opprimantur. Cic.—"Just so much meat and drink should be used as to reïnvigorate our powers, not to oppress them."

Tantum de medio sumptis accēdit honōris. Hor.—"So much honour is due to subjects taken from middle life." The poet alludes to theatrical representations, the subject of which is drawn from those common occurrences which interest every one, and find sympathy in the breast of all below the rank of kings and heroes.

Tantum inter densas, umbrōsa cacūmĭna, fagos
Assĭdue vĕniēbat ; ibi hæc incondĭta solus
Montĭbus et sylvis stŭdio jactābat ināni. Virg.

—"Only among the dense beeches, lofty and umbrageous, did he constantly come; there in solitude with unavailing fondness did he utter to the mountains and woods these untutored lines."

Tantum magna suo debet Verōna Catullo,
Quantum parva suo Mantua Virgĭlio. Mart.

—"As much does great Verona owe to her Catullus, as little Mantua is indebted to her Virgil."

Tantum quantum.—"Just as much as."

Tantum religio pŏtuit suadēre malōrum. Lucr.—"To deeds

so dreadful could religion prompt." Said with reference to the sacrifice of Iphigenia by her father Agamemnon. See *Quantum religio*, &c.

Tantum se fortūnæ permittunt, etiam ut natūram dediscant. QUINT. CURT.—"They so entirely devote themselves to the pursuit of fortune, that their very nature is changed."

——*Tantum sĕries junctūrăque pollet.* HOR.—"Of such consequence are system and connexion." Two indispensable features in a book which proposes to treat of one subject.

——*Tantumne ab re tuā est otii tibi,*
Aliēna ut cures, eăque nihil quæ ad te attĭnent? TER.
—"Have you so much leisure from your own affairs, that you can attend to those of others, those which don't concern you?" This passage is followed by the famous one, "*Homo sum*," &c., which see.

Tantus amor florum, et generandi gloria mellis. VIRG.—"Such is their love of flowers, and their pride in producing honey." In allusion to the habits of bees.

Tantus amor laudum, tantæ est victōria curæ. VIRG.—"Such is the love of praise, so great the desire for victory."

Tarda sit illa dies, et nostro sērior ævo. OVID.—"May that day be slow to come, and deferred beyond our times!" A wish expressed for the prolongation of the life of Augustus.

Tarda solet magnis rebus inesse fides. OVID.—"Confidence is wont to be slowly given to great undertakings." Look for instance at the ridicule which was showered on Winser, who first proposed to light the streets with gas.

Tarda venit dictis diffĭcĭlisque fides. OVID.—"Credence is given to his words tardily and with difficulty."

Tarde benefĭcĕre nolle est; vel tarde velle nolentis est. SEN.—"To be slow in conferring a favour is to grudge it; even to be slow in consenting is to seem to grudge it."

——*Tarde, quæ crēdĭta lædunt,*
Crēdĭmus.—— OVID.
—"We are slow to believe what, if believed, would cause us sorrow." "The wish is father to the thought."

——*Tardo amīco nihil est quicquam inīquius.* PLAUT.—"There is nothing more vexing than a tardy friend." See *Gratia ab*, &c.

Taurum tollet qui vĭtŭlum sustŭlĕrit. *Prov.*—"He who has

carried the calf will be able to carry the ox." The force of habit or custom.

Te Deum laudāmus.—"We praise thee, O God." The beginning of the Doxology, or hymn of St. Ambrose.

Te putat ille suæ captum nidōre culīnæ;
Nec male conjectat.—— Juv.
—"He looks upon you as captivated by the savoury smell from his kitchen. Nor does he conjecture amiss."

Teque piācula nulla resolvent. Hor.—"No atonement will absolve you."

Te sine, nil altum mens inchŏat.—— Virg.—"Without thy aid, my mind can compass nothing great."

Te vĕniente die, te decedente canēbat. Virg.—"Thee did he sing as day approached, thee as it departed." A punster has thus rendered it :—

"At morning he sang the praises of *tea*,
The praises of *tea* too at ev'ning sang he."

Tecum hăbĭta. Pers.—"Live with yourself." "Keep within compass." Don't exceed your means.

Tecum vīvĕre amem, tecum ŏbeam libens. Hor.—"With thee I could wish to live, with thee I could cheerfully die."

——*Tĕgĭmen direpta leōni*
Pellis erat.—— Ovid.
—"A skin stripped from the lion was his covering."

Teipsum non alens, canes alis. *Prov.*—"Unable to keep yourself, you are keeping dogs." Said to a needy person who finds money to spend on superfluities.

Tēlĕphus et Peleus, cum pauper et exul uterque,
Prōjĭcit ampullas, et sesquipedālia verba,
Si curat cor spectantis tetigisse querēla. Hor.
—"Telephus and Peleus, when they are both in poverty and exile, lay aside their bombastic expressions and their words half a yard long, when it is their object to move the heart of their hearers by their complaint."

——*Telum imbelle sine ictu.* Virg.—"A feeble dart, devoid of force." Applied figuratively to a weak and valueless argument.

Temĕrĭtas est florentis ætātis, prudentia senescentis. Cic.—"Rashness belongs to vigorous youth, prudence to old age."

Temĕrĭtas nunquam cum prudentiâ commiscetur. Cic.—"Rashness is never united with prudence."

Temperantia est ratiōnis in libīdĭnem atque in ălios non rectos impĕtus ănĭmi firma et moderāta dominātio. Cic.—"Temperance is the firm and temperate dominion of reason over our passions and the other unlawful impulses of the mind."

Temperantia sedat appetitiōnes et effĭcit ut hæ rectæ ratiōni păreant. Cic.—"Temperance allays the appetites and makes them obedient to reason."

——*Temperātæ suaves sunt argutiæ,*
Immŏdĭcæ offendunt.—— Phæd.

—"Witticisms well-timed are pleasing; out of place they disgust."

Tempestas minātur antĕquam surgat.
Crepant ædifĭcia antĕquam corrŭant. Sen.

—"The tempest threatens before it bursts upon us. Houses creak before they fall." As Campbell says,

"Coming events cast their shadows before."

Tempestāte contentiōnis, serēnĭtas carĭtātis obumbrātur.—"Amid the storms of contention the serenity of Christian charity is obscured."

Templa quam dilecta!—"Temples, how beloved!" From *Psalm* lxxxiv. 1. Motto of the Duke of Buckingham. A pun on the family name, Temple.

Tempŏra labuntur, tăcĭtisque senescĭmus annis;
Et fugiunt fræno non rĕmorante dies. Ovid.

—"Time glides on, and with noiseless years we reach old age; the days flee away with no rein to check them."

Tempŏra mutantur, nos et mutāmur in illis.—"Times change, and we change with them." See *Omnia mutantur*, &c.

Tempora si fuĕrint nubĭla, solus eris. Ovid.—See *Donec eris*, &c.

Tempŏra sic fŭgiunt părĭter, părĭterque sequuntur,
Et nova sunt semper. Nam quod fuit ante, relictum est;
Fitque quod haud fuĕrat; momentaque cuncta novantur.
Ovid.

—"Thus do the moments ever fly on, and ever follow, and are for ever renewed. For the moment which was before is past, and that which was not is now; every moment is replaced by another."

Tempŏre crevit amor, qui nunc est summus, habendi:
Vix ultra, quo jam progrĕdiātur, habet. Ovid.
—"With time increased that love of acquiring which is now at its height; and hardly is there a further point to which it can proceed."

Tempŏre dūcĭtur longo fortasse cicātrix;
Horrent admŏtas vulnĕra cruda manus. Ovid.
—"A wound may, perhaps, in course of time be closed; but, when fresh, it shudders at the approach of the hand." Applicable also to the wounds of the heart.

Tempŏre fēlici multi numerantur amīci;
Si fortūna perit, nullus amicus erit. Ovid.
—"In happy times we reckon many friends; if fortune fails, no friend will be left." See *Ubi opes*, &c.

Tempŏri parendum.—"We must go with the times." A favourite maxim of the Emperor Theodosius II.

Tempŏris ars medicīna fere est.—— Ovid.—"The healing art is mostly a work of time."

Tempŏris illius cŏlui faveque poētas. Ovid.—"I have honoured and cherished the poets of those days."

Tempus abīre tibi est, ne——
Rideat et pulset lascīva decentiùs ætas. Hor.
—"It is time for you to be gone, lest that age, which plays the wanton with more propriety, should ridicule and drive you off the stage." Addressed to an aged sensualist. See *Lusisti satis*, &c.

Tempus ănĭma rei.—"Time is the soul of business."

Tempus edax rerum.—— Hor.—"Time, the devourer of all things."

Tempus erit, quo vos spĕcŭlum vidisse pigēbit. Ovid.—"The time will come when you will look in your mirror with regret."

Tempus est quædam pars æternitātis. Cic.—"Time is a certain part of eternity." Moments constitute eternity.

Tempus fugit.—"Time flies."

Tempus omnia revēlat.—"Time reveals all things."

Tendon Achillis.—"The tendon of Achilles." The tendon which passes from the muscle of the calf to the heel. The fable was that Achilles was held by his mother Thetis by this part, when she dipped him in the river Styx, to render him invulnerable in the other parts of his body.

—*Tĕnĕros ănĭmos aliēna opprōbria sæpe*
Absterrent vitiis.— HOR.
—"The disgrace of others often deters tender minds from vice."

—*Tenet insānābĭle multos*
Scribendi cacoēthes.— JUV.
—"An incurable itch for writing possesses many."

—*Tentenda via est quâ me quoque possim*
Tollĕre humo, victorque virûm volitāre per ora. VIRG.
—"I too must attempt a way by which I may raise myself from the ground, and triumphantly hover about the lips of men."

—*Teres atque rotundus.* HOR.—"A man polished and round." See *Quisnam igitur*, &c.

Terra antiqua, potens armis atque ūbĕre glebæ. VIRG.—"An ancient land, powerful in arms and in the richness of the soil." Said with reference to ancient Italy.

Terra firma.—"Dry land," in contra-distinction to sea.

Terra incognĭta.—"An unknown land." When a man goes, as we say, "out of his depth," he is said to venture on a "*terra incognita*."

Terra malos hŏmĭnes nunc ēdŭcat, atque pusillos. JUV.—"The earth now supports many bad and weak men." The complaint of every age.

Terra salūtĭfĕras herbas, eădemque nocentes
Nutrit, et urticæ proxĭma sæpe rosa est. OVID.
—"The earth produces both wholesome and deleterious plants, and the rose is often close to the nettle."

Terræ filius.—"A son of the earth." An Oxford student, who in former times was apppointed to recite a satirical poem at the University Acts, was so called. A satirical work against the Jacobite tendencies of that university, by Nicholas Amhurst, (London, 1726,) bears this name.

—*Terræ*
Pingue solum primis extemplo e mensĭbus anni
Fortes invertant tauri.— VIRG.
—"Let your stout oxen turn up the rich soil from the very earliest months of the year."

Terram cœlo miscent.—"They mingle heaven and earth." They create utter confusion.

Terret, lustrat, agit. Proserpĭna, Luna, Diana.
Ima, Suprēma, Feras. Sceptro, Fulgōre, Sagittâ.
—In reading these lines, which express the triple characters and attributes of Diana, we must take each word in conjunction with the third that follows. It will then read thus—

Terret Proserpina ima sceptro.
Lustrat Luna suprema fulgore.
Agit Diana feras sagittâ.

"Proserpine terrifies the realms below with her sceptre.
Luna illumines the realms above with her splendour.
Diana chases the wild beasts with her arrows."

Tertium quid.—"A third something." Produced by the union or collision of two opposite forces.

Tertius e cœlo cĕcĭdit Cato.—— Juv.—"A third Cato has dropt from heaven!" Sometimes used ironically.

——*Tetrum ante omnia vultum.* Juv.—"A countenance hideous beyond conception."

Thesaurus carbōnes erant. Prov.—"The treasure turned out charcoal." Said of speculations which end in loss. Among the ancients charcoal was strewed in the trench which was made as the dividing line between the fields of different owners. This, when covered up, would serve to show the boundaries for ages.

—— *Thesēâ pectŏra juncta fide.* Ovid.—"Hearts united in a Thesean attachment." In allusion to the friendship between Theseus and Pirithöus, king of the Lapithæ.

Thus aulĭcum. *Prov.*—"Court incense." The flatteries and promises of courtiers.

Tibi adversus me non compĕtit hæc actio. Law Phrase.—"You have no right of action against me in this matter." A legal plea, by the defendant, in exception.

Tibi nullum perīcŭlum esse perspĭcio, quod quidem sejunctum sit ab omnium intĕrĭtu. Cic.—"I can see no danger to which you are exposed, apart from that which threatens the destruction of us all."

——*Tibi, qui turpi secernis honestum.* Hor.—"To thee who can distinguish right from wrong."

——*Tibi, Tantăle, nullæ*
Deprenduntur aquæ, quæque immĭnet effŭgit arbos. Ovid.

—"By thee, Tantalus, no waters are reached, and the tree which overhangs thee starts away." See *Tantalus a*, &c.

Tibi tanto sumptui esse, mihi molestum est. PLAUT.—"It gives me concern to put you to such expense."

Tigrĭdis evīta sodalitātem. Prov.—"Shun the companionship of the tiger."

——*Tigris agit rabĭdâ cum tĭgrĭde pacem*
Perpĕtuam, sævis inter se convĕnit ursis. JUV.
—"The ferocious tiger always agrees with his fellow, the bear consorts with the bear."

——*Tĭmeo Dănăos, et dona ferentes.* VIRG.—"I fear the Greeks, even when they bring presents." Kindness proffered by an enemy is to be suspected.

Timidi est optāre necem.—"It is the act of a coward to wish for death." "Cowards haste to die, the brave live on."

Timidi mater non flet. Prov.—"The mother of the coward does not weep." Because he will take care to keep out of danger.

Timidi nunquam statuerunt trophæum. Prov.—"The timid never erected a trophy." Similar to our saying, "Faint heart never won fair lady."

Timidus Plutus. Prov.—"Plutus is full of fears." Riches are a cause of anxiety.

Timidus se vocat cautum, parcum sordĭdus. SYR.—"The coward calls himself cautious, the miser thrifty." We palliate our faults by glossing them with the names of the neighbouring virtues.

——*Timor unus erat; făcies non una timōris.* OVID.—"Their fear was the same; but not so the symptoms of their fear."

Tolle jocos—non est jocus esse malignum.—"Away with such jokes, there is no joke in being spiteful." A warning against ill-natured sarcasms. See *Sint sales*, &c.

Tolle moras, semper nŏcuit differre parātis. LUCAN.—"Away with delay," &c. See *Semper nocuit*, &c.

——*Tolle perīclum,*
Jam vaga prosĭliet frænis natūra remōtis. HOR.
—"Take away the danger, and vagrant nature will soon leap beyond bounds, when restraints are removed."

Tollenti onus auxiliāre, deponenti nequāquam. Prov.—"Assist him who is ready to carry the burden, not him who declines it."

Tollĕre nōdōsam nescit medicīna podăgram. OVID.—"Medicine knows not how to cure the nodous gout."

Tollĭmur in cœlum curvāto gurgĭte, et ĭdem
Subductâ ad Manes imos descendĭmus undâ. VIRG.
—"We are raised to the skies on the swelling wave, and again, by its subsiding, descend to the lowest depths of the abyss."

——*Tolluntur in altum*
Ut lapsu graviōre ruant.—— CLAUD.
—"They are raised aloft, that they may fall with a more signal ruin." See *Celsæ graviore*, &c.

Torqueat hunc æris mūtua summa sui. OVID.—"Let the borrowed sum of money be his torment."

Torquet ab obscœnis jam nunc sermōnĭbus aurem;
Mox etiam pectus præceptis format amīcis,
Asperitātis et invĭdiæ corrector et iræ. HOR.
—"The poet keeps from the child's ear all obscene discourse; and then in time he forms his heart with friendly precepts, the corrector of his rudeness, envy, and passion."

——*Torrens dicendi cōpia multis,*
Et sua mortĭfĕra est facundia.—— JUV.
—"To many the copious fluency of speech and their very eloquence is fatal." It was so with Cicero.

Tot căpĭta, tot sensus. TER.—"So many heads, so many ideas." "So many men, so many minds."

Tot părĭter pelves, tot tintinnābŭla dicas
Pulsāri.—— JUV.
—"You would say that so many basons were being beaten, so many bells ringing at once."

Tot tantisque rebus urgĕmur et premĭmur, ut nullam alleviatiōnem quisquam non stultissĭmus sperāre dēbĕat. CIC.—"We are embarrassed and overwhelmed by so many and weighty matters, that no man, who is not the greatest fool, can hope for any remission."

Tota hujus mundi concordia ex discordiis constat. SEN.—"The whole concord of this world consists in discords."

Tota jacet Babylon; destruxit tecta Luthĕrus,
Calvīnus muros, sed fundāmenta Socīnus.
—"All Babylon lies prostrate; Luther destroyed the roof,

Calvin the walls, but Socinus the foundations." A Socinian boast, on the disasters brought on the Romish Church by the Reformation.

Tŏtĭdem verbis.—"In so many words." He expressed himself *totidem verbis*—in just so many words as I have used, and no more.

Tŏties quŏties. Law Term.—"As often, so often." As often as the offence is committed, so often will the penalty be enforced. Also applied to a lease, granted by a lessee who derives immediately from a bishop, to a second lessee, in which the first binds himself to renew to his sub-lessee as often as the bishop shall renew to him. This is called a *Toties quoties* lease.

Totis diēbus, Afer, hæc mihi narras,
Et tĕneo melius ista, quam meum nomen. MART.
—"You are telling me this, Afer, every day, and I know these things better than I do my own name."

Totius autem injustitiæ nulla capitālior est, quam eōrum qui quum maxĭme fallunt, id agunt, ut viri boni esse videantur. CIC.—"But of all injustice, there is none more heinous than the acts of those who, when they most deceive us, act so as to be taken for good men."

Toto cœlo.—"By the whole heavens." As widely as the extent of the heavens. Signifying the greatest possible difference.

Totum mundum agit histrio.—"The player appears in every character."

Totus in toto, et totus in quâlibet parte.—"Whole in its entirety, and whole in every part." The definition given by the ancient schoolmen of the human mind.

Totus mundus agit histriōnem.—"All the world acts the player." "All the world 's a stage, and all the men and women merely players."—*Shaksp.*

Tradĭtus, non victus.—Betrayed, not conquered."

Trahit hŏmĭnes suis illĕcĕbris ad verum decus virtus. CIC.—"Virtue by her charms allures man to true honour."

——*Trahit ipse furōris*
Impĕtus, et visum est lenti quæsîsse nocentem. LUCAN.
—"The violence of their rage hurries them on, and to inquire who is guilty seems to them a waste of time." Applied to those who in the moment of fanatical or civic

frenzy are ready to slaughter all supposed foes who come in their reach. Witness the Massacre of St. Bartholomew, and the first French Revolution.

—*Trahit sua quemque voluptas.* VIRG.—"Each man is led by his own tastes."

Transeat in exemplum.—"Let it stand as an example." Let it pass into a precedent.

Trĕpĭde concursans, occupāta in ōtio. PHÆD.—"Hurriedly running to and fro, busily engaged in idleness."

Tres mihi convivæ prope dissentire videntur,
Poscentes vario multum diversa palāto.
Quid dem? Quid non dem?— HOR.
—"Three guests can scarcely be found to agree, requiring very different dishes with varying palates. What shall I give them? what shall I not give?"

Tria juncta in uno.—"Three joined in one." Sometimes applied to the Trinity, but more frequently to a political coalition.

Tria sunt quæ præstāre debet orātor, ut dŏceat, mŏveat, delectet. QUINTIL.—"There are three things which an orator should excel in,—instructing, moving, and pleasing."

—*Tribus Anticyris caput insanabile.*— HOR.—"A head incurable by the three Anticyræ even." The three places known by this name were famous for the growth of hellebore, which was used for the cure of melancholy madness.

—*Trinăcria quondam*
Italiæ pars una fuit, sed pontus et æstus
Mutavĕre situm.— CLAUD.
—"Trinacria was once a part of Italy, but the sea and the tides have changed its state." In allusion to a tradition that Sicily (called *Trinacria* from its three corners) was once a part of Italy.

Trinōda necessĭtas.—"A threefold necessity." A threefold tax among the Saxons was so called; being levied for the repair of bridges, the maintenance of garrisons, and the repelling of invaders. No person was exempted from it.

Triste lupus stăbŭlis, mātūris frūgĭbus imbres,
Arbŏrĭbus venti, nobis Amaryllĭdis iræ. VIRG.
—"The wolf is fatal to the flocks, showers to ripened corn, winds to the trees, the wrath of Amaryllis to me."

——*Tristia mæstum*
Vultum verba decent, irātum plena minārum. HOR.
—"Grave words befit a sorrowful countenance, those full of menace an angry one."

Tristis eris, si solus eris.—— OVID.—"You will be sad if you are alone."

Troja fuit. LUCAN.—"Troy was." Aptly applied to one fallen from his high estate. See *Fuit Ilium.*

Tros Tyriusve mihi nullo discrīmĭne agĕtur. VIRG.—"Trojan or Tyrian, it shall make no difference to me."

Trūdĭtur dies die. HOR.—"One day treads on the heels of another."

Trux tactu herba.—"A herb rough to be handled."

Tu autem.—"But thou." A hint to a person to leave off or be gone. The words "*Tu autem, Domine, miserere nostri,*" ("But thou, O Lord, have mercy upon us,") were used by the preacher at the end of his discourse, and hence were considered as a notice that service was concluded.

——*Tu dic mecum quo pignŏre certes.* VIRG.—"Tell me for what stake you will contend." Say what you will bet.

Tu doces.—"Thou tea-chest." A punning motto, said to have been placed by a facetious Cantab on his tea-caddy.

——*Tu, dum tua navis in alto est,*
Hoc age ne mutāta retrorsum te ferat aura. HOR.
—"Do you, while your bark is on the sea, be on your guard, lest a changing breeze bear you back again."

——*Tu fallāci nĭmium ne crede lucernæ.* OVID.—"Do not trust too much to the deceiving lamp." In judging of female beauty.

Tu fortis sis ănĭmo, et tua moderātio, constantia, eōrum infāmet injūriam. CIC.—"Do you be resolute in mind, and your patient and firm endurance will stamp with infamy the injuries they have inflicted on you."

——*Tu mihi magnus Apollo.* VIRG.—(Slightly altered.) "Thou [shalt be] my great Apollo." You shall be my oracle.

——*Tu mihi solus eras.* OVID.—"You were my only one." Said by a mother on losing her only child.

Tu ne quæsiĕris, scire nefas, quem mihi, quem tibi.

Finem Di dĕdĕrint, Leuconoë, nec Babylōnios
Tentāris nūmĕros.—— Hor.
—"Do not inquire, Leuconoë, for we are not permitted to know, how long a term of life the gods have granted to you, or to me; neither consult the Chaldæan tables."—The tables of the judicial astrologers.

Tu pol si sapis, quod scis nescis. Ter.—"You, by Jove, if you are wise, do not know what you do know." You will hold your tongue about it.

Tu pueros somno fraudas, tradisque magistris;
Ut sŭbeant tĕnĕræ verbĕra sæva manus. Ovid.
—"'Tis thou who dost defraud boys of their sleep, and dost hand them over to their masters, that their tender hands may suffer the cruel stripes." An address to the morning.

Tu, quamcunque Deus tibi fortunāvĕrit horam,
Gratâ sume manu; nec dulcia differ in annum,
Ut quocunque loco fuĕris, vixisse libenter
Te dicas.—— Hor.
—"Whatever happy moments God may have granted you, receive them with a thankful hand, and defer not the comforts of life to another year; that, in whatever place you are, you may say you have lived with satisfaction."

Tu quid ego, et populus mecum, desīdĕret, audi. Hor.—"Hear what I, and the public too, desire." Addressed to dramatic writers, who ought to consult the taste of the public.

Tu quidem ex ore oratiōnem mihi ērĭpis. Plaut.—"You really are taking the words out of my mouth."

Tu quoque.—"You too." A retort in the same words is called a *Tu quoque.* "You're another."

Tu quoque, Brute!—"You too, Brutus!" The expression used by Julius Cæsar on seeing his supposed friend, Brutus, in the number of his assassins. It is sometimes represented as "*Et tu, Brute!*"

Tu quoque ne prŏpĕra; mĕlius tua fīlia nubet. Ovid.—"Be not in haste: your daughter will make a better match."

Tu recte vivis, si curas esse quod audis. Hor.—"You live well if you make it your care to be what you seem."

Tu semper ora, Tu prōtĕge, Tuque labōra.—"Do you always pray for the rest, do you protect the rest, and do you labour for the rest." Quoted by Bacon, as illustrative of the grounds of tenure by frankalmoigne, knight-service, and socage.

Tu si ănĭmum vicisti, pŏtius quam ănĭmus te, est quod gaudeas. Plaut.—"If you have conquered your inclination, rather than your inclination you, there is something for you to rejoice at."

Tua ratio existimētur acūta, meum consilium necessārium. Cic.—"Your judgment may be considered acute, yet my advice may be necessary."

——*Tua res ăgĭtur, păries cūm proxĭmus ardet.* Hor.—"Your own property is at stake, when your neighbour's house is on fire." See *Proximus a*, &c., and *Proximus ardet*, &c.

Tui observantissĭmus.—"Yours most obediently."

Tum cornix plenâ pluviam vocat imprŏba voce,
Et sola in siccâ secum spatiātur arēnâ. Virg.
—"Then the prating crow, with loud note, invites the rain, and solitary stalks by herself on the dry sand." One of the symptoms of rain mentioned by Virgil.

Tum dēnĭque hŏmĭnes nostra intellĭgĭmus bona
Cum quæ in potestāte habuĭmus, ea amīsĭmus. Plaut.
—"We men know our blessings, only when we have lost what we once enjoyed."

Tum ĕquĭdem in senectâ hoc dĕpŭto miserrĭmum, sentīre eâ ætāte se odiōsum altĕri.—"For my part I think that to a person advanced in years it must be a most unfortunate thing to feel conscious that at that time of life he is hated by another."

Tum excĭdit omnis constantia, et mors non dubia ŏcŭlos cœpit obdūcĕre. Petron. Arbiter.—"Then did all our courage fail, and certain death began to stare us in the face."

Tunc et aves tutas movēre per aĕra pennas;
Et lepus impăvĭdus mĕdiis errāvit in agris;
Nec sua crēdŭlĭtas piscem suspendĕrat hamo
Cuncta sine insĭdiis, nullamque timentia fraudem,
Plēnăque pacis erant.—— Ovid
—"Then did the birds wing their way in safety in the air, and the hare without fear range over the fields; not then had its own credulity suspended the fish from the hook. Every place was without treachery, in dread of nc

injury, and full of peace." A description of the Golden Age.

Tune impūne hæc făcias? Tune hic hŏmĭnes adolescentŭlos Impĕrītos rerum, eductos lībĕrè, in fraudem illĭcis Sollicitando? et pollicitando eōrum ănĭmos lactas?—— Ter. —"Are you to be acting this way with impunity? are you to be luring here into snares, young men unacquainted with the world, and liberally brought up, by tempting them, and to be playing upon their fancies by making promises?"

Tŭnĭca pallio prŏpior. *Prov.*—"My shirt is nearer than my coat." "Near is my shirt, but nearer is my skin." "Charity begins at home."

Tuo tibi judicio est utendum; virtūtis et vitiōrum grave ipsius conscientiæ pondus est; quâ sublātâ jacent omnia. Cic.—"In your own guidance you must be directed by your own judgment; the influence of conscience is great in weighing your own virtues and vices; take this away and all is at an end."

——*Tuque, O! dŭbiis ne dĕfice rebus.* Virg.—"And thou, oh! do not abandon me in my doubtful fortunes."

Turba gravis paci, plăcĭdæque inimĭca quiēti. Mart.—"A multitude hostile to peace, and a foe to quiet ease."

Turba Remi sĕquĭtur fortūnam, ut semper, et odit Damnātos.—— Juv. —"The mob of Remus follows Fortune, as mobs always do, and hates those she has condemned."

Turdus ipse sibi malum cacat. *Prov.*—"The thrush sows misfortunes for itself." A foolish man "makes a rod for his own back." It was said that the thrush feeds on the seeds of the mistletoe, and, sowing them with its excrements, provides the bird-lime with which it is caught.

Turpe est ălĭud loqui, aliud sentīre; quanto turpius aliud scrībĕre, aliud sentīre! Sen.—"It is base to say one thing and to think another; how much more base to write one thing and to think another!" The latter, being more deliberate, and its effects more lasting, is in every way more pernicious.

Turpe est diffĭcĭles habēre nugas,
Et stultus labor est ineptiārum. Mart.
—"It is disgraceful to make difficulties of trifles, and labour on frivolities is folly."

Turpe est laudāri ab illaudātis.—"It is base to be praised by those who are undeserving of praise,"—whose censure is really praise. See *Laudari a*, &c.

Turpe est viro id in quo quotĭdie versātur ignorāre.—"It is a shame for any man to be ignorant of that in which he is daily engaged."

Turpe quidem dictu, sed si modo vera fatēmur,
Vulgus amicitias utilitāte probat. OVID.
—"It is a shocking thing to be owned, but, if we must confess the truth, the multitude esteems friendship according to interest."

Turpe senex miles, turpe senīlis amor. OVID.—"For an old man to be a soldier is shocking, amorousness in an old man is shocking."

Turpe, vir et mŭlier, juncti modo, prōtĭnus hostes. OVID.—"'Tis a shocking thing for a man and woman, just united, to be enemies at once."

Turpes amōres conciliāre.—"To form low attachments."

——***Turpi fregērunt sæcŭla luxu***
Dīvĭtiæ molles.—— JUV.
—"Enervating wealth has corrupted the age by vicious luxury."

Turpis est qui alto sole in lecto dormiens jacet, qui vigilāre mĕdiâ die incĭpit, qui officia lucis noctisque pervertit. SEN.—"It is disgraceful to be lying asleep when the sun is on high; to awake at mid-day, and to turn day into night, and night into day."

Turpis et rīdĭcula res est elementārius senex; jŭvĕni parandum, seni utendum est. SEN.—"An old man learning his rudiments is a disgraceful and ridiculous object; it is for the youth to acquire, the old man to apply."

Turpis in reum omnis exprobrātio.—"All reproach cast upon a person unconvicted is unwarrantable."

Turpissĭma est jactūra quæ fit per negligentiam. SEN.—"That loss is the most disgraceful which arises from neglect."

Turpĭter obtĭcuit, sublāto jure nocendi. HOR.—"The right of abusing taken away, it disgracefully became silent." Said of the abuses of the Chorus, in the Old Comedy, but susceptible of a general application.

Turpius ejicĭtur quam non admittĭtur hospes. OVID.—"It is more disgraceful to expel a guest than not to admit him."

Turtŭrâ loquācior. *Prov.*—" More noisy than a turtle-dove."

Tussis ferīna.—" A barking cough."

——*Tuta est hŏmĭnum tenuĭtas;*
Magnæ perīclo sunt opes obnoxiæ. PHÆD.
—" Poverty is safe; great riches are liable to danger."

Tuta frequensque via est per amicum fallĕre nomen:
Tuta frequens licet sit via, crimen habet. OVID.
—" Secure and much frequented is the path for deceiving under the name of friendship; secure and much frequented though that path be, it is to be condemned."

Tuta petant alii. Fortūna miserrĭma tuta est;
Nam timor eventûs detĕriŏris abest. OVID.
—" Let others seek safety. The most wretched fate affords its security; for all fear of worse fortune is withdrawn."

Tuta scĕlĕra esse possunt, non secūra. SEN.—" The wicked may be safe, but not secure." Not free from care.

Tuta timens. VIRG.—" Fearing even safety."

Tute hoc intristi, tibi omne est exedendum. TER.—" You yourself have hashed up all this, so you must swallow it."

Tutius errātur ex parte mitiŏri. *Law Max.*—" It is safest to err on the side of mercy."

——*Tutos pete, nāvĭta, portus;*
Ventus ab occāsu grandĭne mixtus erit. OVID.
—" Seek, mariner, the safety of the harbour; from the west there will be a wind mingled with hail."

Tutum silentii præmium.—" The reward of silence is sure." " Least said soonest mended."

Tutus ille non est quem omnes odĕrunt.—" He is not safe who is hated by all."

Tuum tibi narro somnium. *Prov.*—" I'll tell you your own dreams." An answer which we may aptly give to those who pretend to know more about our affairs than we do ourselves.

U.

Ubĕrĭbus semper lăcrymis, semperque parātis
In statiōne suâ, atque expectantĭbus illam
Quo jŭbeat manāre modo.—— JUV.

— "With tears always in abundance, always at command in their place, and ready to flow as she may bid them."

Uberrĭma fides.—"Boundless confidence." Implicit faith.

Ubi amici, ibi opes. Prov.—"Where there are friends there is wealth." Similar to our saying, "It is better to have friends without money than money without friends."

Ubi aut qualis est tua mens? potesne dīcĕre? Cic.—"Where is your mind, or what is its nature? Can you tell?"

Ubi bene, ibi patria. Prov.—"Where I am well off, there is my country." The motto of the unpatriotic and selfish man.

Ubi idem et maxĭmus et honestissĭmus amor est, ălĭquando præstat morte jungi quam vitâ distrăhi. Valer. Maxim. —"Where there exists the greatest and most genuine love, it is sometimes better to be united in death than separated in life."

Ubi inĕrit amor, condimentum cuivis plăcitūrum credo. Plaut. —"Where love is an ingredient, the seasoning, I believe, will please any one."

——*Ubi jam vălĭdis quassātum est vīrĭbus ævi*
Corpus, et obtūsis cĕcĭdĕrunt vīrĭbus artus,
Claudĭcat ingenium, delīrat linguăque mensque. Lucr.

—"When the body is shaken by the mighty power of time, and the limbs fail, their strength being blunted, the genius halts, and both mind and tongue are at fault."

Ubi jus, ibi remĕdium. Law Max.—"Where there is a right, there is a remedy."

Ubi jus incertum, ibi jus nullum. Law Max.—"Where the law is uncertain, there is no law."

Ubi major pars est, ibi est totum. Law Max.—"Where the greater part is, there is the whole." In deliberative assemblies, the vote of the majority binds the whole.

Ubi mel, ibi apes. Plaut.—"Where there is honey, there will be bees." Where there is attraction, there will be no want of admirers.

Ubi mens plūrĭma, ibi mĭnĭma fortūna. Prov.—"Where there is most mind, there is least money." See *Fortuna nimium*, &c.

——*Ubi non est pudor,*
Nec cura juris, sanctĭtas, piĕtas, fides,
Instăbĭle regnum est.——— Sen.

—"Where there is not modesty, respect for the laws, religion, piety, and faith, the government is insecure."

Ubi opes ibi amīci.—"Where there is wealth, there will there be friends."

Ubi quis dolet, ibi et manum frequens habet. *Prov.*—"Where a man feels the pain, there will he often place his hand."

——*Ubi summus imperātor non adest ad exercĭtum,*
Citius quod non facto 'st usus fit, quam quod facto 'st opus.
PLAUT.

—"When the commander in chief is not with the army, that is sooner done which ought not to be done than that which ought to be done."

Ubi supra.—"Where mentioned above."

Ubi timor adest, sapientia adesse nequit. LACTANTIUS.—"Where fear is present, wisdom cannot be present."

Ubi tres medĭci, duo athei.—"Where there are three physicians, there are two atheists." A mediæval proverb.

Ubi vanus ănĭmus, aurâ captus frivŏlâ,
Arrĭpuit insolentem sibi fidūciam,
Făcĭle ad derisum stulta lĕvĭtas dūcĭtur. PHÆD.

—"When a weak mind, beguiled by frivolous applause, has once given way to insolent self-sufficiency, its foolish vanity is easily exposed to ridicule."

Ubi vulnerătus est cubĭtus brăchium est infirmum. *Prov.*—"Where the elbow is wounded the arm is powerless."

Ubicunque ars ostentātur, vērĭtas abesse vidētur.—"Wherever art is displayed, truth seems to be wanting."

Udum et mollĕ lutum es, nunc, nunc prŏperandus, et acri
Fingendus sine fine rotâ.—— PERS.

—"You are now clay, moist and pliant; at once and unintermittingly you must be fashioned on the rapid wheel." "Youth and white paper take any impression."

Ulcĕra ănĭmi sananda magis quam corpŏris.—"The wounds of the mind need healing more than those of the body."

Ultĕrius ne tende ŏdiis.—— VIRG.—"Proceed no further with thy hatred." The appeal of Turnus to Æneas.

Ultĭma ratio regum.—"The last argument of kings." This motto was engraved on the French cannon by order of Louis XIV.

——*Ultĭma semper*

Expectanda dies hŏmĭni, dicīque beātus
Ante ŏbĭtum nemo suprēmăque fūnĕra debet. Ovid.
—"The last day of life must always be awaited by man, and no one should be pronounced happy before his death and his last obsequies." Similar to the famous reply of Solon to Crœsus, the wealthy king of Lydia.

Ultĭma Thule. Virg.—"Remotest Thule." The extremity of the earth, as known to the Romans. Supposed to have been the Faroe Islands. See *Venient annis*, &c.

Ultra vires nihil aggrĕdiendum. *Prov.*—"We should attempt nothing beyond our strength."

Ulŭlas Athēnas portas. *Prov.*—"You are carrying owls to Athens." Similar to our saying, "You are carrying coals to Newcastle." Owls abounded at Athens.

Umbra pro corpŏre. *Prov.*—"The shadow for the body." The shadow instead of the substance.

Umbram suam mĕtuĕre.—"To be afraid of his own shadow."

Una dies ăpĕrit, confĭcit una dies. Auson.—"In one day it blossoms, in one decays."

Una dies intĕreat inter maxĭmam cīvĭtātem ac nullam. Sen. —"One day may make all the difference between the greatest city and none at all." Said in reference to the ruin which may be at all times impending over the fortunes of mankind.

Una domus non alit duos canes. *Prov.*—"One house cannot keep two dogs." See *Canes socium*, &c.

Una eădemque manus vulnus opemque ferat.—"Let one and the same hand bring both wound and remedy." Adapted from Ovid.

Una salus victis nullam sperāre salūtem. Virg.—"The only safety for the conquered is to hope for no safety." Their only hope is in the bravery prompted by despair.

Unâ voce.—"With one voice." Unanimously.

Unde hăbeas quærit nemo; sed oportet habēre. Juv.—"Whence your wealth comes, nobody inquires; but wealth you must have."

Unde tibi frontem lībertātemque parentis,
Cum făcias pĕjora senex?—— Juv.
—"Whence do you derive the air and authority of a parent, when you, who are old, commit greater faults?"

Ungentem pungit, pungentem rustĭcus ungit. *Prov.*—"A

clown will show harshness to one who anoints him, but will anoint the man who is harsh to him." A man of low mind is apt to treat kindness with insult, but to fawn upon those who treat him as their inferior.

Unguĭbus et rostro. *Prov.*—"With nails and beak." With all one's powers. "Tooth and nail."

Unguis in ulcĕre. Cic.—"A nail in the wound." Words addressed by Cicero to Catiline the conspirator, who, when his country was already wounded by factions, fixed his talons in the wound, to keep it open.

——*Uni æquus virtūti, atque ejus amīcis.* Hor.—"Tolerant to virtue alone and to her friends." Said of Lucilius, who satirized the foibles of the great of his time. The first three words form the motto of the Earl of Mansfield.

Uni navi ne committas omnia. *Prov.*—"Venture not all in one bottom."

Unĭco digitŭlo scalpit caput. *Prov.*—"He scratches his head with one little finger." Said of brainless and effeminate men, as this was a habit with the fops of Greece and Rome.

Unigenĭtus.—The bull issued by pope Clement XI. in 1713, against the doctrines of the Jansenists, is known by this name, from its beginning "*Unigenitus Dei Filius,*"—"The only-begotten Son of God."

Unīus dementia dementes effĭcit multos. *Prov.*—"The madness of one makes many mad." "One fool makes many."

Universus hic mundus una cīvĭtas hŏmĭnum recte existimātur. Cic.—"The whole world is rightly deemed one city of mankind." See *Non sum uni*, &c., and *Socrates quidem*, &c.

——*Uno avulso, non dĕfĭcit alter.* Virg.—"One removed, another is not wanting."

——*Uno ore omnes omnia*
Bona dicĕre, et laudāre fortūnas meas,
Qui gnatum habērem tali ingĕnio præditum. Ter.
—"Everybody, with one voice, began to say all kinds of flattering things, and to extol my good fortune in having a son endowed with such a disposition."

Unus homo nobis cunctando rēstĭtuit rem;
Non pōnēbat enim rūmōres ante salūtem. *Fragm. of* Ennius.
—"One man, by delay, saved the state; for he cared less for what was said than for the public welfare." Said in praise of Fabius Cunctator, or the Delayer.

Unus in hoc populo nemo est, qui forte Latinè
Quælĭbet e medio reddĕre verba queat. OVID.
—"There is no one in all this people who can by any chance translate into Latin words in common use."

Unus Pellæo jŭvĕni non suffĭcit orbis;
Æstuat infēlix angusto līmĭte mundi. JUV.
—"One globe does not suffice for the youth of Pella; the unhappy man frets at the narrow limits of the world." Said of Alexander the Great.

——*Unus utrīque*
Error; sed văriis illūdit partĭbus.—— HOR.
—"There is the same error on both sides, only the illusion takes different directions." Different men pursue the same illusion, though by different paths.

Unus vir nullus vir. Prov.—"One man is no man."

Unusquisque abundat sensu suo.—"Every person abounds in his own sense." Is wise in his own conceit.

——*Urātur vestis amōre tuæ.* OVID.—"Let him be inflamed by love of your very dress."

Urbe silent totâ; vitreōque madentia rore
Tempŏra noctis eunt.—— OVID.
—"'Tis silence throughout the city; damp with the glistening dew, the hours of night glide on."

Urbem lătĕrĭtiam invēnit, marmŏream relīquit. SUET.—"He found a city of bricks, he left a city of marble." This, Augustus said, he did for Rome.

Urbem quam dicunt Romam, Melibœe, putāvi,
Stultus ego, huic nostræ sĭmĭlem.—— VIRG.
—"The city, Melibœus, which they call Rome, I in my simplicity imagined to be like this of ours."

——*Urbi pater est, urbīque marītus.* JUV.—"He is a father to the city and a husband to the city." Facetiously quoted with reference to a man of intrigue.

Urbs ŏrĭtur, (quis tunc hoc ulli crēdĕre posset?)
Victōrem terris impŏsitūra pedem. OVID.
—"A city arises (who then could have believed this tale from any one?) destined one day to place her conquering foot on all lands."

Urit grata protervĭtas,
Et vultus nĭmium lūbrĭcus aspĭci. HOR.

—"Her pleasing coquetry inflames me, and her features too dazzling for my gaze."

Urit matūrè urtīca vera. Prov.—"The real nettle stings early." A vindictive disposition is early seen.

——*Urtīcæ proxima sæpe rosa est.* Ovid.—"The nettle is often next to the rose."

Usque ad aras.—"To the very altars." To the last extremity.

Usque ad nauseam.—"Even to sickness." Properly a medical phrase, but often used as meaning, "Till we are quite sick and tired of it."

Usque ad sidera tellus.—"Earth exalts itself to the stars."

Usque adeōne mori mĭsĕrum est?—— Virg.—"Is it then so very dreadful to die?"

——*Usque adeōne*
Scire tuum nihil est, nisi te scire hoc sciat alter? Pers.
—"Is then your knowledge nothing worth, unless others know that you possess it?" Is not the knowledge you have acquired a source of comfort to you, without reference to the opinions of others?

Usu perītus harĭolo velōcior
Vulgo esse fertur.—— Phæd.
—"One taught by experience is proverbially said to be more quick-witted than a wizard."

Usus est tyrannus.—"Custom is a tyrant."

Usus promptum facit. Prov.—"Practice makes perfect."

Ut acerbum est, pro bene factis cum mali messem metas. Plaut.
—"How hard it is, when, for services done, you reap a harvest of evil."

Ut ager, quamvis fertĭlis, sine cultūrâ fructuōsus esse non potest, sic sine doctrīnâ ănĭmus. Sen.—"As a soil, although rich, cannot be productive without culture, so the mind without learning cannot be fruitful."

——*Ut amēris, amābĭlis esto.* Ovid.—"That you may be loved, be loveable." See *Sit procul*, &c.

Ut canis e Nilo. Prov.—"Like the dog at the Nile." Dogs, in drinking at the Nile, Phædrus says, are obliged to be on their guard against the crocodiles, and therefore lap as they run. Hence this proverb is applied to persons of desultory and careless habits. After Marc Antony ran away from the battle of Actium, it was said of him that,

Ut canes in Ægypto, bibit et fugit, "Like the dogs in Egypt, he drank and ran away."

Ut cuique hŏmĭni res parăta est, firmi amīci sunt ; si res lassa labat,
Itĭdem amīci collabascunt.—— PLAUT.
—"According as wealth is obtained by each man, so are his friends sure; if his prospects fade, his friends fade with them."

Ut desint vires, tamen est laudanda voluntas. OVID.—"Though the power is wanting, yet the will deserves praise."

Ut ejus modestiam cognōvi, gravis tibi nullâ in re erit. CIC. —"As I am well acquainted with his modesty, he will in no way be troublesome to you."

——*Ut hŏmĭnes sunt, ita morem geras ;*
Vita quam sit brevis, simul cŏgĭta. PLAUT.
—"As men are, so must you treat them. At the same time reflect how short life is."

Ut homo est, ita morem geras. TER.—"As a man is, so must you treat him."

Ut id ostendĕrem, quod te isti făcĭlem putant,
Id non fiĕri ex verâ vitâ, neque ădeo ex æquo et bono,
Sed ex assentando, indulgendo, et largiendo. TER.
—"That I may convince you that they consider you a kind-hearted man, not for your real life, nor indeed for your virtue and justice; but from your humouring, indulging, and pampering them."

Ut in vitâ, sic in studiis, pulcherrĭmum et humanissĭmum existĭmo sevĕrĭtātem cōmĭtātemque miscēre, ne illa in tristĭtiam, hæc in pĕtulantiam procēdat. PLINY *the Younger.*—"As in our lives, so in our pursuits, I deem it most becoming and most proper so to unite gravity with cheerfulness, that the former may not degenerate into melancholy, nor the latter into licentiousness."

Ut jŭgŭlent hŏmĭnes, surgunt de nocte latrōnes. HOR.—"Robbers rise by night that they may cut the throats of others." We sometimes hear of "stabbing a man in the dark.'

Ut lupus ovem amat. Prov.—"As the wolf loves the sheep."

Ut metus ad omnes, pœna ad paucos pervenīret. Law Max.—"That fear may reach all, punishment but few." A maxim of the Criminal Law, and the object of all laws.

Ut navem, ut ædificium idem dĕstruit facillĭme qui construxit; sic hŏmĭnem eădem optĭme, quæ conglŭtinăvit, natūra dissolvit. Cic.—"As he most easily destroys a ship or a house who has constructed it, so does that nature most becomingly effect man's dissolution which first put him together." He speaks of the natural decay which returns man to his "native earth."

——*Ut nec pes, nec caput uni*
Reddătur formæ.—— Hor.
—"So that neither the head nor foot shall correspond to the same figure." Applicable to a literary production or a picture of an incongruous character, of which we can make "neither head nor tail."

Ut nemo in sese tentat descendĕre, nemo!
Sed præcēdenti spectātur mantĭca tergo. Pers.
—"How is it that no man tries to search into himself? not a man but fixes his eye on the wallet upon the back of him who goes before." The Fable is here alluded to, which describes men as walking in a line, each having a wallet containing his faults on his back, while those of his neighbour are in another slung before. See *Peras imposuit*, &c.

Ut ōtium in ūtĭle vertĕrem negōtium.—"That I might turn my leisure into useful occupation."

Ut plăceas, debes immĕmor esse tui. Ovid.—"To please, you ought to be forgetful of yourself."

Ut plerumque solent, naso suspendis acūto
Ignōtos. Hor.
—"As is the way with most, you turn up your nose at those of obscure birth."

Ut populus, sic sacerdos. *Prov.*—"Like priest, like people." Quoted by St. Bernard, who preached the Second Crusade.

Ut puĕris placeas, et declamātio fias. Juv.—"To amuse children, and be the subject of a theme." "To point a moral and adorn a tale."—*Johnson.* See *I demens*, &c.

Ut *queant laxis resonare fibris*
Mira gestōrum famŭli tuōrum,
Solve pollūti labii reātum.
—"That thy servants may be able to sing thy wondrous deeds to the loosened strings, release them from the stain of polluted guilt." These lines, from the Hymn of John

the Baptist, contain the names originally given to the notes in Music, *Ut, Re, Mi, Fa, Sol, La.* They are said to have been given by Guido, a Benedictine monk of Arezzo, in the eleventh century. The note *Si* was afterwards added by a musician named Le Maire.

Ut quimus, quando ut vŏlŭmus non licet. TER.—"As we can, when we cannot as we wish."

Ut quisque suum vult esse, ita est. TER.—"As every person wishes his child to be, so he is." The mind of the child is so plastic, that it will admit of any training on the part of the parent. See *Udum et*, &c.

Ut rei servīre suave est! PLAUT.—"How delightful it is to keep one's money!"

Ut ridentĭbus arrīdent, ita flentĭbus adflent,
Humāni vultus.—— HOR.

—"The human countenance, as it smiles on those who smile, so does it weep with those who weep."

Ut sæpe summa ingĕnia in occulto latent! PLAUT.—"How often are the greatest geniuses buried in obscurity!"

Ut sementem fĕcĕris, ita et metes. CIC.—"As you sow, so shall you reap." "As you make your bed, so you must lie on it."

Ut servi volunt esse herum, ita solet esse;
Bonis boni sunt; imprŏbi cui malus fuit. PLAUT.

—"As servants would have their master to be, such is he wont to be. Masters are good to the good, severe to him who is bad."

Ut solent poētæ. PLINY *the Younger.*—"As it usually is with poets."—*i. e.* living on a scanty diet.

Ut solet accĭpĭter trĕpĭdas agitāre columbas. OVID.—"As the hawk is wont to pursue the trembling doves."

Ut sunt humāna, nihil est perpĕtuum. PLAUT.—"As human affairs go, nothing is everlasting."

Ut supra.—"As above stated."

Ut sylvæ fŏliis pronos mutantur in annos,
Prima cadunt; ita verbōrum vetus intĕrit ætas,
Et jŭvĕnum ritu florent modò nata vigentque.
Dēbēmus morti nos nostrăque —— HOR.

—"As, in the woods, the leaves are changed with each fleeting year, and the earliest fall the first; in like manner do words perish with old age, and those of more recent birth flourish and thrive like men in the time of youth. We and our works are doomed to death."

Ut tamen hoc ita sit, munus tua grande voluntas
Ad me pervēnit, consulitūrque boni. OVID.
—"But though it is so, your good wishes have come as a great boon to me, and are taken in good part."

Ut tu fortūnam, sic nos te, Celse, ferēmus. HOR.—"As you bear with your fortunes, Celsus, so shall we bear with you."

Ut tute es, item omnes censes esse. PLAUT.—"As you are yourself, you take all others to be."

Utātur motu ănĭmi, qui uti rătiōne non potest.—"Let him be guided by impulse who cannot be guided by reason."

Utcunque in alto ventus est, exin velum vertĭtur. PLAUT.—"Whichever way the wind is at sea, in that direction the sail is shifted."

Utendum est ætāte; cito pede lābĭtur ætas. OVID.—"We must make use of time; time flies with rapid foot."

Uterque bonus belli pacisque minister.—"Skilled equally in the administration of peace or of war."

Uti possidētis.—"As you now possess." A term in diplomacy, meaning that, at the termination of a war, each party is to retain whatever territory he may have gained in the contest. Its opposite is the *Status quo*, which see.

Utile dulci.—"The useful with the agreeable." See *Omne tulit*, &c.

Utĭlĭtas juvandi.—"The advantage of assisting others."

Utĭlĭtas lăteat: quod non profitēbere fiet. OVID.—"Let your object lie concealed: that will come to pass which you shall not avow."

Utiliumque sagax rerum, et divīna futuri. HOR.—"Skilled in wise suggestions, and prophetic of the future."

Utĭnam tam facĭlè vera invenīre possem, quam falsa convincĕre! CIC.—"Would that I could as easily find out the truth, as I can detect what is false!"

Utĭnam vĕtĕres mores, vĕtĕres parsimoniæ
Pŏtius majōri honōri hic essent, quam mores mali. PLAUT
—"I only wish that the old-fashioned ways and the old-fashioned thriftiness were in greater esteem here, than these bad ways."

Utĭtur anatĭnâ fortūnâ cum exit ex aquâ, aret.—"He has the good fortune of a duck, as soon as he comes out of the water he is dry." Said of those fortunate men who always "fall on their legs." An adaptation from Plautus.

Utĭtur, in re non dubiâ, testĭbus non necessārĭis. CIC.—"He employs unnecessary proofs in a matter on which there is no doubt."

Utque ălios industria, ita hunc ignāvia ad famam protŭlĕrat. TACIT.—"As industrious efforts have advanced others, so did this man attain celebrity by indolence."

Utrum horum mavis accĭpe.—"Take which you will of the two."

Utrumque vitium est, et omnĭbus crēdĕre et nulli. SEN.—"It is equally a fault to confide in all, and in none."

Uvăque conspectâ livōrem ducit ab uvâ. JUV.—"And grape contracts paleness from the grape which it has faced."

Uxōrem fato credat obesse suo. OVID.—"He may think that his wife is an obstacle to his success."

Uxōrem malam ŏbŏlo non ĕmĕrem.—"I would not give a doit for a bad wife."

——*Uxōrem, Posthŭme, ducis?*
Dic quâ Tīsĭphŏnē, quĭbus exăgĭtāre colŭbris. JUV.
—"What, Posthumus, marry a wife? by what Fury, say, by what serpents, are you driven to madness?"

——*Uxōri nubĕre nolo meæ.* MART.—"I will not be married to a wife." I will not have a wife who shall be my master. The verb *nubo* was only used in reference to the female sex. The man *marries*, the woman *is married*.

V.

V. P. for *Vitâ patris*, which see.

Vacāre culpâ magnum est solātium. CIC.—"It is a great solace to be free from fault."

Vacuus cantat coram latrōne viātor. JUV.—"The penniless traveller sings in the presence of robbers."

Vade in pace.—"Go in peace." According to some authorities, perpetual solitary imprisonment was thus called in the middle ages. It is generally, however, considered to have been applied to a more terrible punishment. See *In pace*.

Vade mecum.—"Go with me." A work which from its utility and portability is the constant companion of the man of business, or the traveller, is sometimes called his *Vade mecum.*

Væ mĭsĕro mihi! quantâ de spe decĭdi! TER.—"Woe unto wretched me! from what hopes have I fallen!"

Væ victis!—"Woe to the conquered!" We learn from Livy and Festus that this was the exclamation of Brennus the Gaul, when he threatened extermination to the Romans.

Vale, vale, cave ne tĭtŭbes, mandātăque frangas. HOR.—"Farewell! farewell! take care lest you stumble, and miscarry with my commands."

——*Vāleant mendācia vatum.* OVID.—"Farewell to the fictions of the poets."

——*Văleas, anus optĭma, dixi:*
Quod sŭpĕrest ævi, molle sit omne tui. OVID.
—"'Farewell, most worthy dame,' said I, 'tranquil be the remainder of your days.'"

Văleat quantum vălēre potest.—"Let it have weight, so far as it may." Often quoted, *Valeat quantum.*

——*Văleat res lūdĭcra, si me*
Palma negāta macrum, donāta redūcit opimum. HOR.
—"Adieu to the levities of verse, if the denial of applause is to reduce me to meagreness, and I am to be dependent on its bestowal for happiness."

Valēre malo quam dives esse. CIC.—"I would rather be in good health than rich."

Valet anchŏra virtus.—"Virtue is a sheet-anchor." Motto of Viscount Gardner.

——*Valet ima summis*
Mutāre, et insignem attĕnuat Deus,
Obscūra promens.—— HOR.
—"The Deity is able to make exchange between the highest and the lowest, abasing the exalted, and advancing the obscure."

Valĭdius est natūræ testimōnium quam doctrīnæ argumentum. ST. AMBROSE.—"The testimony of nature is of greater weight than the arguments of learning."

Valor ecclesiastĭcus.—"The ecclesiastical value."

Vana quoque ad veros accessit fama timōres. LUCAN.—"Idle rumours, too, were added to well-founded fears."

Vare, redde legiōnes!—"Varus, give me back my legions!" The words of Augustus Cæsar, on hearing of the defeat and slaughter of the Roman army, under Quintilius Varus, by the German chieftain Arminius.

——*Varium et mutābĭle semper*
Fœmĭna.—— VIRG.
—"Woman is ever changeable and capricious."

Vastius insurgens dĕcĭmæ ruit impĕtus undæ. OVID.—"The swell of the tenth wave, rising more impetuously than the rest, rushes onward." See *Qui venit*, &c.

Vectīgālia nervi sunt reipublĭcæ. CIC.—"Taxes are the sinews of the state."

Vĕhĕmens in utramque partem, aut largitāte nimiâ aut parsimōniâ. TER.—"Ready to run to either extreme, of excessive liberality or parsimony."

Vehĭmur in altum.—"We are launching into the deep."

——*Veiosque habitante Camillo,*
Illic Roma fuit.—— LUCAN.
—"Camillus dwelling at Veii, Rome was there." Camillus was so highly esteemed at Rome, that it was said, "Where Camillus is there is Rome."

Vel cæco appāreat. *Prov.*—"It would be evident to a blind man even."

Vel capillus habet umbram suam. PUB. SYR.—"Even a hair has its shadow."

Velim mehercŭle cum istis errāre, quam cum ăliis rectè sentīre.—"By Hercules, I would rather be in the wrong with these men than think aright with the others." See *Malo cum Platone*, &c.

Velim ut velles. PLAUT.—"I would wish as you would wish."

Velis et remis.—"With sails and oars." With all possible expedition.

Velle licet, potīri non licet.—"You may wish, but you may not enjoy." You may "look and long."

Velle suum cuiquam, nec voto vīvĭtur uno. PERS.—"Every man has his own fancy, and the tastes of all are not alike."

Vellem in amicitiâ sic errārēmus, et isti
Errōri nomen virtus posuisset honestum. HOR.
—"Would that in our friendships we committed the same mistake, and that virtue would designate such mistakes by an honourable name." The poet wishes that men were as

considerate to their friends as to their mistresses, and equally indulgent to their failings.

Velōcem tardus assequĭtur. *Prov.*—"The slow overtakes the swift." In allusion to the Fable of the Hare and the Tortoise. "The race is not always to the swift."

——*Velōcius ac cĭtius nos*
Corrumpunt vitiōrum exempla domestĭca, magnis
Cum sŭbeant ănĭmos auctōrĭbus.—— Juv.

—"The examples of vice which we witness at home more surely and more quickly corrupt us; for they insinuate themselves into our minds under the sanction of high authority."

Velōcius quam aspărăgi coquantur.—"Before you could cook a bundle of asparagus." A Roman proverb denoting an extremely short space of time. Suetonius tells us that it was frequently in the mouth of Augustus Cæsar.

Velox consilium sĕquĭtur pœnitentia. Syr.—"Repentance follows precipitate counsels."

——*Vĕlut inter ignes*
Luna minōres. Hor.

—"Like the moon amid the lesser lights."

——*Velut si*
Egrĕgio inspersos reprĕndas corpŏre nævos. Hor.

—"As if you were to condemn moles scattered over a beautiful skin."

Velŭti in spĕcŭlum.—"As though in a mirror." A theatrical motto.

Venālis popŭlus, venālis cūria patrum.—"The people venal, the house of senators venal." The state of Rome in the times of its decadence.

Vēnātor sĕquĭtur fŭgientia, capta relinquit;
Semper et inventis ultĕriōra petit. Ovid.

—"The huntsman follows the prey that flies, that which is caught he leaves behind: and he is ever on the search for still more than he has found."

——*Vendentem thus et odōres,*
Et piper, et quicquid chartis amicītur ineptis. Hor.

—"A seller of frankincense, perfumes, and pepper, and anything wrapped in worthless paper." To the use of such persons he says are consigned the productions of worthless writers.

Vendĭdit hic auro patriam.—— VIRG.—"He sold his country for gold."

Venēnum in auro bibĭtur. SEN.—"Poison is drunk out of gold." A risk not so likely to be incurred by those who drink out of less costly vessels.

Venerāri parentes lībĕros decet.—"It is the duty of children to reverence their parents."

Vēnĕrit insĭtio; fac ramum ramus adoptet. OVID.—"The time for grafting is now come; make branch adopt branch."

Veni, Creātor Spirĭtus.—"Come, Holy Ghost, Creator, come."

Veni Gotham, ubi multos
Si non omnes vidi stultos. *Drunken Barnaby's Journal.*
"Thence to Gotham, where, sure am I,
If though not *all* fools, saw I *many.*"

The men of Gotham, in Nottinghamshire, seem to have been proverbial in the Middle Ages for their stupidity, and to have been generally known as the "Wise men of Gotham." See *Ray's Proverbs*, p. 218.

Veni, Sancte Spirĭtus.—"Come, Holy Ghost." The name given to a mass of the Roman Catholic Church, to invoke the assistance of the Holy Spirit.

Veni, vidi, vici.—"I came, I saw, I conquered." The brief despatch in which Julius Cæsar announced to the senate his victory over Pharnaces.

Vēnia necessĭtāti datur. CIC.—"Pardon is granted to necessity." Similar to our saying that "Necessity has no laws."

——*Vēniat manus, auxĭlio quæ*
Sit mihi.—— HOR.
—"May there come a hand to give me aid."

——*Vēnient annis*
Sæcŭla seris, quibus Oceănus
Vincŭla rerum laxet, et ingens
Pateat tellus, Tiphysque novos
Dētĕgat orbes; nec sit terris
Ultĭma Thule. SEN.
—"After the lapse of years, ages will come in which Ocean shall relax his chains around the world, and a vast continent shall appear, and Tiphys shall explore new regions, and Thule shall be no longer the utmost verge of earth." Considered by Lord Bacon to be a prophecy of the discovery of America. See *Ultima Thule.*

——*Vĕnienti occurrĭte morbo.* PERS.—"Meet the coming disease." See *Neglecta*, &c. and *Principiis obsta*, &c.

Vĕniet tempus quo ista quæ nunc latent in lucem dies extrăhet, et longiōris ævi diligentia. Vĕniet tempus quo postĕri nostri tam aperta nos nescisse mirabuntur. CIC.—"The day will come, when time and the diligence of later ages will bring to light things which now lie concealed. The day will come when our posterity will wonder that we were ignorant of things so evident."

Venīre facias. *Law Term.*—"You are to cause to come together." A judicial writ, whereby the sheriff is commanded to cause a jury to appear, in order to try a cause.

Venīte, exultēmus Dŏmĭno.—"Oh come, let us sing unto the Lord." The beginning of the 95th Psalm.

——*Vĕniunt a dote sagittæ.* JUV.—"The darts come from her dowry."

Plutus, not Cupid, touched his sordid heart,
And 'twas her dower that winged the unerring dart.
Gifford.

Venter famēlĭcus aurĭcŭlis caret.—"A hungry belly has no ears." It is proof against advice or expostulation. A saying of Cato the Elder.

Venter non habet aures. *Prov.*—"The belly has no ears."

Ventis secundis.—"With a fair wind." With prosperous gales. Motto of Lord Hood.

Ventis verba fundis.—"You pour forth words to the winds." You talk to no purpose.

Ventum ad suprēmum est.—— VIRG.—"Matters have come to the last extremity."

Ver erat æternum ; plăcĭdique tepentĭbus auris
Mulcēbant Zĕphyri natos sine sēmĭne flores. OVID.
—"Then it was ever spring; and the gentle Zephyrs, with their soothing breezes, cherished flowers that grew unsown." The state of the earth in the Golden Age.

Ver non semper viret.—"The spring does not always flourish." Or, by an heraldic pun, "Vernon always flourishes." Motto of Lord Vernon.

Ver pingit vario gemmantia prata colōre.—"The spring decks the blooming fields with various colours."

Vera dico, sed nequicquam, quoniam non vis crēdĕre.—"I speak the truth, but in vain, since you will not believe me."

Vera gloria radīces agit, atque etiam propagātur; ficta omnia celĕrĭter, tanquam floscŭli, decĭdunt; nec simulātum potest quidquam esse diuturnum. CIC.—"True glory strikes root, and even spreads; all false pretensions fade speedily, like flowers; nor indeed can any counterfeit be lasting." Carlyle says, "No lie you can speak or act but it will come, after longer or shorter circulation, like a bill drawn on Nature's reality, and be presented there for payment—with the answer, No effects."

——*Vera incessu pătuit Dea.*—— VIRG.—"She stood revealed a goddess truly in her gait."

Vera redit făcies, dissimulāta perit. PETRON. ARBITER.—"Our natural countenance returns, the assumed one passes away." Hypocrisy will finally be detected.

Verba ănĭmi proferre et vitam impendĕre vero. JUV.—"To give utterance to the sentiments of the heart, and to stake one's life for the truth."

Verba dat omnis amans.—— OVID.—"Every lover gives fair words."

Verba de præsenti. *Law Term.*—"Promise made on the instant as a pledge for the future."

Verba fides sĕquĭtur.—— OVID.—"Fulfilment attends his words." No sooner said than done.

——*Verba fiunt mortuo.* TER.—"You are talking to a dead man." You are talking to one who will not heed you.

Verba ligant hŏmĭnes, taurōrum cornua fūnes.—"Words bind men, ropes the horns of bulls."

Verba nitent phalĕris; at nullas verba medullas
Intus habent. PALINGENIUS.

—"His words shine forth in fine compliments, without sincerity." Mere sound devoid of meaning.

Verba placent et vox, et quod corrumpĕre non est,
Quoque minor spes est, hoc magis ille cupit. OVID.

—"Her words charm him, her voice, and her incorruptible chastity; and the less hope there is, the more intensely does he desire." Said of Lucretia.

Verba togæ sequĕris, junctūra callĭdus acri,
Ore teres mŏdĭco, pallentes rādĕre mores
Doctus, et ingĕnuo culpam defīgĕre ludo. PERS.

—"You employ the language of the toga, skilful at judicious combination, with suitable style well rounded, expert at lashing depraved morals, and inflicting censure with subtle raillery." The character of a just and considerate satirist.

> Confined to common life, thy numbers flow,
> And neither soar too high, nor sink too low;
> There strength and ease in graceful union meet,
> Though polished, subtle, and though poignant, sweet;
> Yet powerful to abash the front of crime,
> And crimson error's cheek with sportive rhyme.
>
> *Gifford.*

Verbăque provīsam rem non invīta sequentur. Hor.—"Words will not fail the subject when it is well considered."

Verbātim et literātim.—"To the word and to the letter." Like the word *seriatim*, neither of these words is really Latin, having been coined probably in the Middle Ages. The correct Latin would be, *Ad verbum et ad literam.*

Verbo tenus.—"In name at least."

Verbōrum paupertas, imo egestas. Sen.—"A poverty, or rather an utter want, of expression."

——*Verbōsa ac grandis epistŏla venit*
A Capreis.—— Juv.

—"A verbose and grandiloquent epistle comes from Capreæ." Said of the haughty mandates issued by the Emperor Tiberius from his palace at Capreæ. Now used to mark a lofty tone upon slender pretensions.

Verbum sat săpienti. *Prov.*—"A word to the wise is sufficient."

——*Verbum verbo reddĕre, fidus*
Interpres.—— Hor.

—"To render word for word, as a faithful interpreter."

Vere calor redit ossĭbus.—— Virg.—"In Spring the flame of desire returns to the bones."

Verè magnum, habēre in se fragĭlĭtātem hŏmĭnis, secūrĭtātem dei. Sen.—"It is true greatness to have the frailty of a man, the equanimity of a god."

Vĕrĕcundāri nēmĭnem apud mensam decet. Plaut.—"At table no one should be bashful."

Vĕrĕcundia inūtĭlis viro egenti. *Prov.*—"Bashfulness is useless to a man in want." A man in distress cannot afford to be governed by rigid notions of etiquette.

Vĕrēcundia mulĭĕrem, non color fucātus, ornat.—"Modesty, not rouge, adorns a woman."

Verĭtas, a quocunque dīcĭtur, à Deo est.—"Truth, by whomsoever spoken, comes from God." Truth is of the Divine essence. "God is truth."

Verĭtas nihil verētur nisi abscondi.—"Truth fears nothing but concealment." Truth seeks publicity.

Verĭtas odium parit.—"Truth produces hatred."

Verĭtas sermo est simplex. AMMIAN.—"Truth is simple in its language," requiring neither study nor art.

Verĭtas vel mendācio corrumpĭtur vel silentio. AMMIAN.—"Truth is violated by falsehood, or by silence." Silence is, in some cases, as bad as a falsehood uttered.

Verĭtas vincit. *Law.*—"Truth conquers." Motto of the Scotch Earl Marechal.

Vērĭtas visu et morâ, falsa festinatiōne et incertis valescunt. TACIT.—"Truth is established by scrutiny and deliberation; falsehood thrives by precipitation and uncertainty."

Vērĭtātis simplex orātio est. SEN.—"The language of truth is simple." She stands in need of no meretricious arts.

Veros amīcos reparāre diffĭcĭle est. SEN.—"It is a difficult thing to replace true friends."

——*Versāte diu quid ferre recūsent,*
Quid vălеant, hŭmĕri.—— HOR.—See *Sumite materiam*, &c.

——*Versus ĭnŏpes rerum, nugæque canōræ.* HOR.—"Lines devoid of meaning; harmonious trifles." These words have been applied to the Opera.

"What though our songs to wit have no pretence,
The fiddle-stick shall scrape them into sense."

Vertentem sese frustrà sectābĕre canthum,
Cum rota postĕrior curras, et in axe secundo. PERS.
—"You will in vain endeavour to overtake the felly that revolves before you, since, as you run, you are the hind wheel, and on the second axle."

"Thou, like the hindmost chariot-wheels, art curst,
Still to be near, but never to be first." *Dryden.*

Vertĭtur in tĕnĕram căriem, rimisque dehiscit,
Si qua diu sŏlĭtis cymba vacārit aquis. OVID.
—"If a bark has been long out of the water to which it

had been accustomed, it turns to crumbling rottenness, and gapes wide with leaks."

——*Verum decepta avĭdĭtas,*
Et quem tenēbat ore, demīsit cibum,
Nec quem pĕtēbat adeo pŏtuit adtingĕre. PHÆD.
—"His greediness however was deceived; he not only dropped the food which he was holding in his mouth, but was after all unable to reach that at which he grasped." From the Fable of the Dog and the Shadow.

Verum est illud, quod vulgo dĭcĭtur, mendăcem mĕmŏrem esse oportet. QUINT.—"There is truth in the common saying, that a liar should have a good memory."

Verum est verbum, quod memorātur, ubi amīci ĭbĭdem sunt opes. PLAUT.—"It is a true proverb that is quoted, 'Where there are friends, there are riches.'"

Verum illud est, vulgo quod dici solet,
Omnes sibi malle melius esse quam altĕri. TER.
—"The common saying is true, that we all wish matters to go better with ourselves than with another."

Verum opĕre in longo fas est obrepĕre somnum. HOR.—"But in a long work it is allowable sometimes to be overcome by sleep." Occasional negligence may be pardoned in a long work, which in a brief one would be reprehensible.

Verum putas haud ægrè, quod valdè expĕtis.—"You have no difficulty in believing that to be true which you anxiously desire." "The wish is father to the thought."

Verùm ubi plura nitent in carmĭne, non ego paucis
Offendar măcŭlis.—— HOR.
—"But where many beauties shine in a poem, I will not be offended with a few blemishes." See *Non ego*, &c.

Verus amīcus est is qui est tanquam alter īdem. CIC.—"A true friend is he who is, as it were, another self."

——*Vesāna cupīdo,*
Plurĭma cum tenuit, plura tenēre cupit.
—"Unreasoning cupidity, the more it has the more it desires to have."

Vestĭbŭlum domûs ornamentum est. *Prov.*—"The hall is the ornament of a house." First impressions are of the greatest importance.

Vestīgia nulla retrorsum.—"No stepping back again." Retreat must not be thought of. An adaptation from Horace The motto of the Earl of Buckinghamshire.

Vestis virum facit. *Prov.*—"The garment makes the man." It is so in the opinion of the vulgar.

Vestri, jūdĭces, hoc maxĭme intĕrest, non ex lĕvitāte testium causas hŏmĭnum ponderāri. Cic.—"To you, O judges, it is of the greatest moment, that the interests of men should not be dealt with upon slight testimony."

——*Vetābo, qui Cĕrĕris sacrum*
Vulgārit arcānæ, sub ĭsdem
Sĭt trăbĭbus, frăgĭlemve mecum
Solvat phasēlum.—— Hor.

—"I will forbid the man, who shall have divulged the sacred rites of mysterious Ceres, to be under the same roof with me, or to sail with me in the same fragile bark." From fear of the vengeance of an offended deity.

Vĕtĕra extollĭmus recentium incuriōsi. Tacit.—"We extol things that are ancient, heedless of those of later date." See *Ætas parentum*, &c., and *Laudator*, &c.

Vĕtĕra quæ nunc sunt fuĕrunt olim nova.—"Things which are now old, were once new."

Vĕtĕrem injūriam ferendo, invītas novam.—"By submitting to an old injury, you lay yourself open to a fresh one." Even patience must have its limits. See *Post folia*, &c.

Veterum id dictum est, Felīcĭter is sapit, qui perīcŭlo aliēno sapit.—"It is an old saying, that he is happy in his wisdom, who is wise at the expense of another." From an interpolated scene in the *Mercator* of Plautus, probably written by Hermolaüs Barbarus.

Vetustas pro lege semper habētur. *Law Max.*—"Ancient custom is always regarded as law." It is the basis of our common law.

Vexāta quæstio.—"A disputed question." A moot point.

Vi et armis.—"By force and arms." By main force, not by sanction of the law.

Via crucis via lucis.—"The path of the cross the path of light." A mediæval saying, and an heraldic motto.

Via media.—"The middle way."

Via trita est tutissĭma Coke.—"The beaten path is the safest."

Via trita, via tuta.—"The beaten path is the safe path." Motto of Earl Normanton.

——*Viamque insiste domandi,*
Dum făcĭles ănĭmi jŭvĕnum, dum mōbĭlis ætas. VIRG.
—"Enter upon a course of training while their disposition in youth is tractable, while their age is pliant." See *Udum.*

Viam qui nescit quâ devĕniat ad mare,
Eum oportet amnem quærĕre cŏmĭtem sibi. PLAUT.
—"He who knows not his way to the sea, should take a river as his guide." A prolonged route which is certain to lead to our object is better than a short but doubtful one.

Vice gerens.—"Acting in the place of." A vicegerent, or deputy.

Vice regis.—"In the king's behalf." Acting as viceroy.

Vice versâ.—"The terms being reversed." Or "reversely." Dr. Parr used to say it ought to be "*Versâ vice,*" referring to *Ulpian. Dig.* 43. 29. III.

Vicistis cochleam tarditāte. PLAUT.—"You have surpassed a snail in slowness."

Victor volentes per popŭlos dat jura.—"A conqueror gives laws to a submissive people."

Victoria concordiâ crescit.—"Victory increases by concord." Motto of Earl Normanton, and Lord Amherst.

Victoria, et per victoriam vita.—"Victory, and through victory life."

Victoria, et pro victoriâ vita.—"Victory, and for victory life." A toast for heroes.

Victoriâ pax non pactiōne parienda est. CIC.—"Peace is to be secured by victory, not by negotiation."

Victrix causa Diis placuit, sed victa Catōni.—"The conquering cause was pleasing to the gods, the conquered one to Cato." An extravagant compliment paid by Lucan to the heroic patriotism of Cato of Utica.

Victrix fortūnæ săpientia.—— JUV.—"Wisdom conquers fortune." By prudence we may sometimes get the better of fortune.

Victūrosque Dei celant, ut vīvĕre durent,
Felix esse mori.—— LUCAN.
—"And the gods conceal, from those destined to live, how sweet it is to die, that they may continue to live."

***Victus** cultusque corpŏris ad vălētūdĭnem rĕfĕrantur et ad vires, non ad voluptātem.* Cic.—"Let the food and clothing of the body bear reference to health and strength, not to mere gratification."

Vide licet.—"You may see." "Namely." Denoted in English books by the contracted form, *viz.*

Vide ne, fūnĭcŭlum nimis intendendo, aliquando abrumpas.—"Take care, lest by stretching the rope too tight you break it at last."

Vide ut supra.—"See as above." "See the preceding passage."

Vĭdeo et gaudeo.—See *Videsne qui,* &c.

——*Vĭdeo meliōra probōque,*
Deteriōra sequor.—— Ovid.
—"I perceive the better course, and applaud it; but I follow the worse." The words of a person hurried on by passion against the dictates of reason.

Vides, ut altâ stet nive candĭdum
Soracte, nec jam sustĭneant onus
Silvæ laborantes.—— Hor.
—"You see how Soracte stands white with deep snow, nor can the bending woods any longer support the weight."

Videsne qui venit?—"Do you see who is coming?" To which the answer is, *Video et gaudeo,* "I see and am glad." *Love's Labour's Lost,* act v. sc. i.

Vidēte, quæso, quid potest pecūnia. Plaut.—"See, prithee, what money can effect."

Vidi ego naufrăgiumque, viros et in æquŏre mergi;
Et, Nunquam, dixi, justior unda fuit. Ovid.
—"I myself have seen a shipwreck, and men drowned in the sea; and I said, 'Never were the waves more just in their retribution.'"

Vidit et ĕrŭbuit lympha pŭdīca Deum.—"The modest water saw its God and blushed." A line on the miracle at Cana in Galilee, most probably composed by Richard Crashaw. Dryden has had the credit of having composed a similar line when a school-boy at Westminster:—

"The conscious water saw its God and blush'd."

If so, he was probably indebted to Crashaw for the thought. It is, however, a matter of doubt whether the line of Crashaw did not originally read, "*Nympha pudica,*" "The modest nymph."

Vigilantibus, non dormientibus, subvĕniunt jura. Law Max.—"The laws assist the watchful, not those who sleep." The law assists those only who take due care to preserve their rights.

Vigilāri decet hŏmĭnem, qui vult sua tempŏri confĭcĕre offĭcia. Plaut.—"It behoves him to be vigilant who wishes to do his duty in good time."

Vigilāte et orāte.—"Watch and pray." Motto of Lord Castlemaine.

Vigor ætātis fluit ut flos veris.—"The vigour of manhood passes away like a flower of spring."

Vile donum, vilis gratia. Prov.—"A small gift, small thanks."

Vilescunt dignitātes cum tenentur ab indignis. Sall.—"High offices become valueless when held by unworthy persons."

Vilis sæpe cadus nobĭle nectar habet. Prov.—"Full oft does an humble cask contain generous nectar." A repulsive exterior may conceal excellent qualities.

Vilius argentum est auro, virtūtibus aurum. Hor.—"Silver is of less value than gold, gold than virtue."

Villārum culmĭna fumant. Vir.—"The tops of the cottages send forth their smoke."

Vim vi repellĕre omnia jura clamant. Law Max.—"All laws declare that we may repel force by force."

Vina parant ănĭmos, făciuntque calōribus aptos :
Cura fugit multo dīluĭturque mero. Ovid.
—"Wine composes the feelings and makes them ready to be inflamed: care flies and is drowned in plenteous draughts."

Vince ănĭmos, iramque tuam, qui cætĕra vincis. Ovid.—"You, who conquer other difficulties, go conquer your own feelings and your anger."

Vincit amor patriæ. Virg.—"The love of our country conquers all other considerations." "The noblest motive is the public good." Motto of the Irish Viscount Molesworth, and Lord Muncaster.

Vincit omnia verĭtas.—"Truth conquers all things." However veiled by hypocrisy or by fraud, truth will generally come to light. Motto of the Baron Kinsale.

Vincit qui se vincit.—"He is indeed a conqueror who conquers himself." Motto of Lord Howard of Walden.

Vincŭla da linguæ, vel tibi vincla dabit.—"Put a curb on your tongue, or it will put a curb on you." An indiscreet tongue is very likely to bring us into trouble.

Vindictam mandasse sat est; plus nōmĭnis horror
Quam tuus ensis aget; mĭnuit præsentia famam. LUCAN.
—"'Tis enough to have commanded vengeance; more will the dread of your name effect than your sword; your presence detracts from your fame."

Vino diffugiunt mordāces curæ.—"Cankering cares are dispelled by wine." An adaptation from Horace.

——*Vino tortus et irâ.* HOR.—"Excited by wine and anger."

Vinum bonum lætifĭcat cor hŏmĭnis.—"Good wine maketh glad the heart of man." See *Psalm* civ. 15.

Vinum purum potum, puer, infundĭto.
A summo ad imum more majōrum bibunto.
Decem cyăthi summa potio sunto. LIPSIUS.
—"Unmix'd be our wine, and pure let it flow,
As our fathers ordain'd, from the high to the low,
Let our bumpers, while jovial we give out the toast,
In gay compotation, be ten at the most."

Violenta nemo impĕria contĭnuit diu;
Moderāta durant. SEN.
—"No one has long held power exercised with violence; moderation insures continuance."

Vipĕra Cappădŏcem nŏcĭtūra momordit: at illa,
Gustāto periit sanguĭne Cappădŏcis.
—"A baneful viper bit a Cappadocian; but having tasted the Cappadocian's blood it died." A translation from the *Anthologia Græca.* The people of Cappadocia were of a dull disposition, and addicted to every vice.

Vir bonus dicendi perītus.—"A good man skilled in the art of speaking." The ancient definition of an orator.

——*Vir bonus est quis?*
Qui consulta patrum, qui leges juraque servat. HOR.
—"Who is a good man? He who obeys the decrees of the senators, he who respects the laws and ordinances."

Vir bonus et săpiens dignis ait esse parātum,
Nec tamen ignōrat quid distant æra lupīnis. HOR.
—"A good and a wise man declares himself ready to assist the deserving; he is not ignorant, however, of the dif-

ference between money and lupines." He is able to distinguish between the meritorious and the undeserving. Lupines were used for money on the stage.

Vir est maxĭmæ escæ. PLAUT.—"He is a man of a most capacious appetite."

Vir pietāte gravis.—— VIRG.—"A man respected for his piety."

Vir săpiens forti mĕlior.—"A wise man is better than a valiant one."

Vir săpiens omnia quæ in vitam humānam incurrunt fert libenter, ut pareat legi natūræ. SEN.—"A wise man bears willingly all those events which are the lot of human life, that he may obey the law of nature."

Vir sapit qui pauca loquĭtur.—"The man is wise who says but little."

——*Vires acquīrit eundo.* VIRG.—"She acquires strength as she goes." The poet speaks of Fame, or Rumour.

Virescit vulnĕre virtus.—"Virtue flourishes from a wound." Motto of the Earl of Galloway.

Viri infelicis procul amīci. SEN.—"The friends of the unfortunate man are at a distance."

Viris fortĭbus non opus est mœnĭbus.—"Brave men have no need of walls."

Virtus agrestiōres ad se ănĭmos allĭcit. CIC.—"Virtue allures to herself even the most uncultivated minds."

Virtus ariĕte fortior.—"Virtue is stronger than a battering-ram." Motto of the Earl of Abingdon.

Virtus est mĕdium vitiōrum, et utrinque reductum. HOR.—"Virtue is the mean between two vices, and equally removed from either." The *golden* mean.

Virtus est una altissĭmis defixa radicĭbus, quæ nunquam ullâ vi lăbĕfactāri potest. CIC.—"Virtue is a thing which having once struck deep root, can never be shaken by any power."

Virtus est vitium fugĕre, et săpientia prima
Stultitiâ caruisse.—— HOR.

—"It is virtue to fly from vice, and the first step of wisdom is to be exempt from folly." Temptation is better avoided than combated.

Virtus hŏmĭnem jungit Deo. CIC.—"Virtue unites man with God."

Virtus in actiōne consistit.—"Virtue consists in action." Motto of Lord Craven.

Virtus in arduis.—"Virtue," or "Valour in danger." Adapted from Horace.

——*Virtus laudātur et alget.* Juv.—"Virtue is praised and starves."

Virtus mille scuta.—"Virtue is as good as a thousand shields." Motto of the Earl of Effingham.

Virtus non advĕnit a natūrâ, neque a doctrīnâ, sed a nūmĭne divīno. Sen.—"Virtue proceeds not from nature, nor from education, but from the Deity."

Virtus non est virtus nisi compărem habet ălĭquem, in quo superando vim suam ostendat. Cic.—"Virtue is not really virtue unless it has some associate, in excelling whom it may display its strength."

Virtus probāta florēbit.—"Approved virtue will flourish." Motto of Earl Bandon.

Virtus, reclūdens immĕrĭtis mori
Cœlum, negātâ tentat iter viâ;
Cœtusque vulgāres, et udam
Spernit humum fŭgiente pennâ. Hor.

—"Virtue, throwing open heaven to those who deserve not to die, directs her course by paths hitherto denied, and spurns with rapid wing the grovelling crowds and the foggy earth."

Virtus repulsæ nescia sordĭdæ
Intāminātis fulget honōrĭbus;
Nec sumit aut ponit secūres
Arbitrio populāris auræ. Hor.

—"Virtue, which knows no base repulse, shines with untarnished honours; she neither receives nor resigns the emblems of authority at the will of popular caprice."

"Virtue repulsed, yet knows not to repine,
But shall with unattainted honour shine." *Swift.*

Virtus requiēi nescia sordidæ.—"Virtue which knows not mean repose." Motto of the Earl of Dysart.

Virtus sine rătiōne constāre non potest. Pliny *the Younger.* —"Without reason, virtue cannot subsist."

Virtus sola nobilitat.—"Virtue alone ennobles." Motto of Lord Walscourt.

Virtus sub cruce crescit, ad æthĕra tendens.—"Virtue grows under the cross, and tends towards heaven." Motto of the Earl of Charleville.

Virtus vincit invidiam.—"Virtue subdues envy." Motto of Marquis Cornwallis.

Virtūte ambīre oportet, non favitōrĭbus.
Sat habet favitōrum semper qui rectè facit. PLAUT.
—"By merit, not by patrons, ought we to seek our ends. He who does well has always patrons enough."

Virtūte non astūtiâ.—"By virtue, not by cunning." Motto of Viscount Pery.

Virtūte, non verbis.—"By virtue, not by words." Motto of the Earl of Kerry, and of the Marquis of Lansdowne.

Virtūte quies.—"In virtue there is tranquillity." Virtue confers peace of mind. Motto of Lord Mulgrave.

Virtūtem doctrīna paret, naturāne donet? HOR.—"Does study produce virtue, or does nature bestow it on us?"

Virtūtem incolŭmem ōdĭmus,
Sublātam ex ŏcŭlis quærĭmus invĭdi. HOR.
—"We hate virtue when present, but gaze after her with regret when she has passed from our sight."

——*Virtūtem verba putes, ut*
Lucum ligna?—— HOR.
—"Do you consider virtue to consist merely of words, as a grove consists of trees?"

Virtūtes ita copulātæ connexæque sunt, ut omnes omnium partĭcĭpes sint, nec aliâ ab aliâ possit separāri. CIC.—"The virtues are so closely joined and connected that they all partake of the qualities of each other, nor can they be separated."

Virtūti nihil obstat et armis.—"Nothing can resist valour and arms." Motto of the Earl of Aldborough.

Virtūti non armis fido.—"I trust to virtue, not to arms." Motto of the Earl of Wilton.

——*Virtūtĭbus obstat*
Res angusta domi.—— JUV.
—"Straitened means stand in the way of virtues" of the more active exercise of charitable virtues.

Virtūtis avōrum præmium.—"The reward of the valour of my forefathers." Motto of Lord Templeton.

Virtūtis ergo.—"For the sake of virtue."

Virtūtis expers verbis jactans gloriam
Ignōtos fallit, notis est derīsui. PHÆDRUS.
—"A dastard who brags of his prowess, and is devoid of courage, imposes on strangers, but is the jest of those who know him."

Virtūtis fortūna comes.—"Fortune is the companion of virtue." Motto of Lords Newhaven and Harberton.

Virtūtis laus omnis in actiōne consistit. CIC.—"All the merit of virtue depends upon the activity with which it is exercised." See *Paulum sepultæ*, &c.

——*Virtūtis uberrĭmum alimentum*
Est honos.
—"Honour is the chief support of virtue."

Virtūtisque viam dēsĕrit arduæ. HOR.—"And he deserts the arduous path of virtue."

Virtūtum omnium fundamentum piĕtas.—"Piety is the foundation of all the virtues."

Virtūtum primam esse puta compescĕre linguam;
Proxĭmus ille Deo est qui scit ratiōne tacēre. CATO.
—"Think it the first of virtues to restrain the tongue; he approaches nearest to a god who knows when it is best to be silent."

Virum bonum nec pretio, nec grātiâ, nec perīcŭlo a viâ recti dedūci oportet. AD HERENN.—"A good man ought not to be drawn from the path of rectitude by wealth, by favour, or by danger."

Virum imprŏbum vel mus mordeat. *Prov.*—"A mouse even may bite the wicked man." Said of those who are paralyzed by a bad conscience.

Vis comĭca.—"Comic power," or "talent."

Vis consĭli expers mole ruit suâ;
Vim temperātam Dî quoque prōvĕhunt
In majus; īdem odēre vires
Omne nefas ănĭmo moventes. HOR.
—"Force, without judgment, falls by its own weight; moreover, the gods promote well-regulated force to further advantage: but they detest force that meditates every crime."

Vis inertiæ.—"The power of inertness." The tendency of every body to remain at rest, and consequently to resist motion. Used figuratively for indolence or mental inertness.

——*Vis recte vivĕre? Quis non?*
Si virtus hoc una potest dare; fortis omissis
Hoc age delĭciis. HOR.
—"Would you live happily? Who would not? If virtue alone can confer this, discard pleasures, and strenuously pursue it."

Vis unīta fortior.—"Power is strengthened by union." Motto of the Earl of Mountcashel.

Viscus merus vestra est blandĭtia. PLAUT.—"Your coaxing is so much bird-lime."

Visu carentem magna pars veri latet. SEN.—"A great part of the truth lies concealed from him who wants discernment."

Visum visu.—"To see and be seen," or "Face to face." Whence most probably the French word *vis-à-vis*.

——*Vitâ*
Cedat, uti conviva satur.—— HOR.
—"Let him withdraw from life, like a guest well filled." See *Cur non*, &c.

Vita enim mortuōrum in memoriâ vivōrum est pŏsĭta. CIC.—"The life of the dead is retained in the memory of the living."

Vita hŏmĭnis sine lĭtĕris mors est.—"The life of a man without letters is death."

Vita laudābĭlis boni viri, honesta ergo quŏniam laudābĭlis. CIC.—"The life of the good man is praiseworthy, and being praiseworthy must be honourable."

Vitâ patris.—"In his father's lifetime." Often written *v. p.*

Vita turpis ne morti quidem honestæ locum relinquit. CIC.—"A life of shame leaves no room even for an honourable death." See *Qualis vita*, &c.

Vitæ est ăvĭdus, quisquis non vult
Mundo secum pereunte mori. SEN.
—"He is greedy of life who is unwilling to die when the world is perishing around him."

——*Vitæ*
Percĭpit humānos ŏdium, lucisque videndæ,
Ut sibi consciscant mœrenti pectŏre lethum. LUCRET.
—"Hatred of life, and of beholding the light, seizes upon

men, to make them with sorrowing breast inflict death upon themselves."

——*Vitæ post-scēnia celant.* LUCRET.—"They conceal the secret actions of their lives." The *Post-scenium* was the part of the theatre behind the scenes, containing the robing-room; hence it is here used in the plural, to signify secret actions hidden from the eyes of the world.

Vitæ signum pulsus est. *Med. Aphor.*—"The pulse is the sign of life."

Vitæ summa brevis spem nos vetat inchoāre longam. HOR.—"The short span of life forbids us to encourage prolonged hope."

Vitæ via virtus.—"Virtue is the way of life." Motto of the Earl of Portarlington.

——*Vitam impendĕre vero.* JUV.—"To lay down one's life for the truth." See *Ille igitur*, &c.

Vitam regit fortūna, non săpientia. CIC.—"Fortune governs this life, and not wisdom."

——*Vitanda est imprŏba Siren*
Desĭdia.—— HOR.
—"Sloth, that seductive Syren, is to be shunned."

Vitāret cœlum Phaëton, si vīvĕret; et quos
Optārat stulté, tangĕre nollet equos. OVID.
—"If Phaëton were living he would shun the skies, and would be loth to touch the horses for which, in his folly, he wished."

——*Vitāri dēnĭque culpam,*
Non laudem mĕrui.—— HOR.
—"I have avoided error, not merited praise."

Vitia hŏmĭnum atque fraudes damnis, ignomĭniis, vincŭlis, verbĕrĭbus, exĭliis, morte mulctantur. CIC.—"The vices and frauds of men are punished with fines, ignominy, chains, stripes, exile, and death."

Vitia nobis sub virtūtum nōmĭne obrĕpunt. SEN.—"Vices creep upon us, under the name of virtues." Thus, avarice will palm itself off under the name of economy.

Vitia otii negōtio discutienda sunt. SEN.—"The evils of sloth are only to be shaken off by attending to business."

Vitiant artus ægræ contāgia mentis. OVID.—"The diseases of the mind contagiously impair the bodily powers."

Vitiis nemo sine nascĭtur; optĭmus ille
Qui mĭnĭmis urgētur. Hor.
—"No man is born without faults; he is the best who is burthened with fewest."

Vitiis suis pervidendis cæcus est homo, in aliēnis perspĭcax.—"Man is blind to his own faults, but quick at perceiving those of others." He readily sees "the mote in his brother's eye."

Vitium capiunt ni moveantur aquæ.—"Water becomes putrid if kept stagnant."

——*Vitium commūne omnium est,*
Quod nimium ad rem in senectâ attenti sumus. Ter.
—"It is a fault common to us all, that in old age we become too attached to worldly interests."

Vitium exemplo princĭpis inolescit.—"Vice, through the example of the prince, becomes fashionable."

Vitium fuit, nunc mos est, assentātio. Syr.—"Flattery, which was formerly a vice, is now a fashion."

Vivâ voce.—"By the living voice." By oral testimony.

Vivat; et absentem, quoniam sic fata tulērunt,
Vivat, et auxĭlio sublēvet usque suo. Ovid.
—"May he live on; and since the Fates have thus decreed, may he live ever to relieve me, far, far away, by his aid."

Vivat rex.—"Long live the king." *Vivat regīna.*—"Long live the queen." *Vivant rex et regīna.*—"Long live the king and queen."

Vive memor lethi.—— Pers.—"Live mindful of death."

Vive sine invĭdiâ, mollesque inglōrius annos
Exĭge; amicĭtias et tibi junge pares. Ovid.
—"Live without envy; pass in obscurity thy tranquil years, and in friendship attach thy equals to thyself."

Vive valēque.—"Live and fare well." "Health and happiness."

——*Vivendi rectè qui prōrŏgat horam*
Rustĭcus expectat dum defluat amnis.—— Hor.
—"He who postpones the hour of living well, is like the peasant who waits until the river shall cease to flow." See *Rusticus expectat*, &c.

Vivendum est ĭgĭtur, ut eâ libĕrālĭtāte utāmur, quæ prosit ami-

cis, noceat nĕmĭni. Cic.—"We must make it our care then to exercise such liberality as may benefit our friends and injure no one."

Vivendum est rectè, cum propter plūrĭma, tunc his
Præcĭpuè causis, ut linguas mancipiōrum
Contemnas: nam lingua mali pars pessĭma servi. Juv.
—"You should lead a correct life for many reasons, but especially for this, that you may defy the tongues of your domestics; for the tongue is the worst part of a bad servant."

Vivĕre sat, vincĕre.—"To conquer is to live enough." Motto of the Earl of Sefton.

Vīvĕre si rectè nescis, dĕcēde perītis. Hor.—"If you know not how to live aright, make way for those who do."
"Learn to live well, or fairly make your will." *Pope.*

Vīvĭda vis ănĭmi. Lucret.—"The strong force of the mind." The active powers of the understanding.

Vīvĭmus aliēnâ fiduciâ. Pliny *the Elder.*—"We live by trusting one another."

Vīvĭmus in postĕris.—"We live in our posterity." See *Vita enim, &c.*

Vīvĭt adhuc, vitamque tibi dĕbēre fatētur. Ovid.—"He lives still, and acknowledges that he owes his life to you."

Vīvit post funĕra virtus.—"Virtue survives the grave." Motto of the Irish Earl of Shannon.

Vīvĭte felices, quibus est fortūna peracta
Jam sua!—— Virg.
—"Live happily, ye whose destinies are already fulfilled!" Struggling onward, I can behold those without envy who have successfully terminated their labours.

——*Vīvĭte fortes,*
Fortiaque adversis oppōnĭte pectŏra rebus. Hor.
—"Live as brave men, and bravely breast adversity."

Vīvĭtur exĭguo mĕlius: natūra beātis
Omnĭbus esse dedit, si quis cognōvĕrit uti. Claud.
—"Men live best upon a little: nature has granted to all to be happy, if they did but know how to use her gifts."

Vīvĭtur parvo bene, cui paternum
Splendet in mensâ tĕnui salīnum;
Nec leves somnos timor aut cupīdo
Sordĭdus aufert. Hor.

—"He lives happily on a little whose paternal salt-cellar shines on his frugal board; nor does fear or sordid covetousness disturb his quiet repose."

——*Vivo et regno, simul ista relīqui,*
Quæ vos ad cœlum fertis rumōre secundo. Hor.
—"I live and am a king, as soon as I have quitted those scenes which you extol to the skies in such high terms."

Vivunt ii qui ex corpŏrum vincŭlis, tanquam e carcĕre, evolārunt. Cic.—"Those live who have escaped from the fetters of the body, as though from a prison." Who are not chained down by fleshly lusts.

Vivunt in Vĕnĕrem frondes, etiam nemus omne per altum
Felix arbor amat; nutant ad mūtua palmæ
Fœdĕra, pŏpŭleo suspīrat pŏpŭlus ictu,
Et plătăni plătănis, alnōque assībĭlat alnus. Claud.
—"The leaves live but to love, and, throughout the whole lofty grove the happy trees indulge their loves; palm, as it nods to palm, confirms their ties; the poplar sighs for the poplar's embrace; plane whispers to plane, alder to alder." Ancient intimation of the Sexual System of Linnæus.

Vix a te vīdeor posse tenēre manus. Ovid.—"I hardly seem to be able to keep my hands off you."

——*Vix dĕcĭmus quisque est, qui ipsus sese nŏvĕrit.* Plaut.
—"There is hardly one man in ten who knows himself."

Vix duo tresve mihi de tot sŭperestis, amīci.
Cætĕra Fortūnæ, non mea turba, fuit. Ovid.
—"Out of so many friends, scarcely two or three of you are now left to me. The rest of the crowd belonged to Fortune, not to me."

Vix ea nostra voco. Ovid.—"I scarcely call these things our own." Motto of Lord Sundridge and the Earl of Warwick.

Vix ĕquĭdem credo, sed et insultāre jacenti
Te mihi, nec verbis parcĕre, fama refert. Ovid.
—"For my part I hardly believe it, but rumour says that you insult me now prostrate, and are not sparing of your reproaches."

Vix mihi credĕtis, sed crēdīte, Troja manēret,
Præceptis Priămi si foret usa sui. Ovid.
—"You will hardly believe me, yet may believe me;

Troy would have been still standing if she had followed the advice of her Priam."

Vix tamen ĕrĭpiam, pŏsĭto pavōne, velis quin
Hoc pŏtiŭs, quam gallīnâ tergĕre palātum,
Rara avis, et pictâ pandat spectācŭla caudâ. HOR.
—" Were a peacock placed on table, I should scarcely be able to prevail on you not to eat of it instead of a pullet, merely because it is a rare bird and makes a show with its gaudy tail."

Vixêre fortes ante Agamemnŏna
Multi ; sed omnes illăcrymābiles
Urgentur, ignōtique longâ
Nocte, carent quia vate sacro. HOR.
—" Many brave men lived before Agamemnon ; but all of them, unlamented and unknown, are whelmed in endless night, having found no sacred bard."

——*Vocat in certāmĭna Divos.* VIRG.—" He calls the gods to arms."

——*Volat ambĭguis*
Mobĭlis alis hora, nec ulli
Præstat velox Fortūna fidem. SEN.
—" The fleeting hour speeds on with doubtful wing, nor does hastening fortune keep faith with any one."

Volenti non fit injūria. *Law Max.*—" No injury is done to a consenting party." This applies only to those who are by law considered responsible for their actions.

——*Volitāre per ora virûm.* VIRG.—" To hover on the lips of men." See *Tentanda*, &c.

Volo, non vălеo.—" I am willing but unable." Motto of the Earl of Carlisle.

Voluntas non potest cogi.—" The will cannot be forced."
" He that complies against his will,
Is of the same opinion still."—*Hudibras* II. 3. 547.

Voluptas est malōrum esca : quod eâ non minus hŏmĭnes
Quam hamo capiuntur pisces. PLAUT.
—" Pleasure is the bait of misfortune ; for by it men are caught just as fishes are by the hook."

——*Voluptātes commendat rārior usus.* JUV.—" Pleasures sparingly enjoyed have a higher relish."

Voluptāti mœror sequĭtur.—" Sorrow follows indulgence."

Voluptāti obsĕquens. TER.—" Devoted to pleasure."

Voluptātibus se constringendum dare.—"To resign himself to the enthralment of pleasure."

Vos, procul! O procul! este profāni! VIRG.—See *Procul*, &c.

Vos săpĕre et solos aio bene vīvĕre, quorum
Conspĭcitur nĭtĭdis fundāta pecūnia villis. HOR.
—"I say that you alone are wise and live well, whose wealth is conspicuous in the elegance of your villas."

Vos valēte!—"Fare ye well!"

Vos valēte et plaudĭte. TER.—"Farewell, and give your applause." This expression, or the words *Plausum date*, "Grant applause," was used at the conclusion of the Latin Comedies.

Vota vita mea.—"My life is devoted." Motto of the Earl of Westmeath.

Vox audita perit, litĕra scripta manet.—"The word that is heard passes away, the letter that is written remains." See *Litera scripta*, &c.

Vox clamantis in deserto.—"The voice of one crying in the wilderness." See *John* i. 23.

Vox erat in cursu, cum me mea prōdĭdit umbra. OVID.—"She was in the middle of her speech, when my shadow betrayed me."

Vox erat in cursu; vultum dubitantis habēbam. OVID.—"She was in the middle of her speech; I had the look of one in doubt"

Vox et prætĕrea nihil.—"A voice and nothing more." A mere sound; fine words without meaning. Said originally of the nightingale. From the Greek.

——*Vox faucĭbus hæsit.* VIRG.—"His voice cleaved to his throat" He was dumb through amazement and dread.

Vox popŭli vox Dei.—"The voice of the people is the voice of God." A maxim of the opponents of the *Jus divinum* of kings. The origin of it is not known, but it is quoted as a proverb by William of Malmesbury, who lived in the early part of the twelfth century.

Vox stellārum.—"The voice of the stars." A favourite title with the old Almanacs.

Vulgāre amīci nomen, sed rara est fides. PHÆD.—"The title of friend is common, but fidelity is rare."

Vulgāto corpŏre mulier. LIVY.—"An abandoned woman."

——*Vulgo audio*
Dici, diem adimĕre ægritudĭnem homĭnibus. TER.
—"I hear it often said that time assuages human sorrow."

Vulgus amicĭtias utilitāte probat. OVID.—"The multitude estimate friends by the advantages to be derived from them."

Vulgus consuetūdĭnem pro lege habet.—"It is a common error to consider usage as law."

Vulgus ex vĕrĭtāte pauca, ex opiniōne multa, æstĭmat. CIC.—"The populace judge of few things on truthful grounds, of many from prejudice."

Vulnĕra nisi sint tacta tractātăque sanāri non possunt. LIV.—"Unless wounds are handled and dressed they cannot be healed."

Vulnus alit venis, et cæco carpĭtur igni. VIRG.—"She nourishes the poison in her veins, and is consumed by a secret flame." Said of Dido's secret passion for Æneas.

Vultus ănĭmi janua et tabŭla. CIC.—"The countenance is the very portal and portrait of the mind." So *Ecclus.* xix. 29, "A man is known by the eye, and the face discovers wisdom."

Vultus est index ănĭmi. *Prov.*—"The countenance is the index of the mind." The opinion of Lavater and the physiognomists.

Z.

Zonam perdĭdit. HOR.—"He has lost his purse." He is in desperate or distressed circumstances.

APPENDIX

A divitibus omnia magnificè fiunt.—"Everything is done magnificently by the rich."

A solis ortu usque ad occăsum.—"From sunrise to sunset."

Ab inŏpiâ ad virtūtem obsepta est via. TER.—"The road to virtue is obstructed by poverty." See *Res angusta*, &c.

Abi in malam rem.—"Be off, and ill may it fare with you." "Go to the deuce."

Abiit, excessit, evāsit, erūpit. CIC.—"He has departed, fled, escaped, disappeared." Cicero's description of the abrupt flight of the guilt-stricken Catiline.

Absit invidia.—"All offence apart."

Absit omen.—"May it not prove ominous."

Actis ævum implet, non segnĭbus annis.—"He fills up life with deeds, not with long years of indolence." An adaptation from the Elegy to Livia Augusta, generally attributed to Pedo Albinovanus.

Ad amussim.—"According to line and rule." Exactly.

Ad nauseam.—"So as even to create disgust."

Ad ostentātiōnem opum.—"To show off his wealth."

Ad rem.—"To the purpose."

Admonēre volŭmus, non mordēre; prodesse, non lædēre; consulĕre morbis hŏmĭnum, non officĕre. ERAS.—"Our object is, to admonish, not to carp; to improve, not to wound; to think of remedies for the diseases of mankind, not to obstruct their cure."

Ægritūdo anĭmi, sine ullâ rerum expectātiōne meliōre.—"Despondency unmitigated by the prospect of better fortune."

Agunt, non cogunt.—"They lead, not drive."

Ah! quam dulce est meminisse!—"Ah! how great are the delights of memory!"

——*Alii taurīnis follĭbus auras*
Accipiunt redduntque. VIRG.

—"Others draw in and eject the air from bellows made of bulls' hide." The Cyclops working their bellows.

Alĭquis in omnĭbus, nullus in singŭlis. SCAL.—"Somebody in all, nobody in each." Jack of all trades, master of none!

Alter altĕrius auxilio eget. SALL.—"One requires the aid of the other."

Alter ego.—"A second self." A bosom friend.

Amĭci qui diu abfuĕrunt, in mutuos ruunt amplexus.—"Friends who have been long separated rush into each other's embraces."

Amor laudis et patriæ pro stipendio est.—"Love of praise and of our country are their own reward." In the consciousness of having acted rightly.

Amōre nihil mollius, nihil violentius.—"Nothing is more tender, nothing more violent, than love."

An ideo tantum vĕnĕras ut exīres? MART.—"Did you then come only to go away again?" See *Cur in*, &c.

Anathĕma maran-ātha.—"May he be cursed, and may the Lord at his coming take vengeance on him." See 1 *Cor.* xvi. 22. The first word is Greek, the second Syriac.

Angustâ utĭtur fortūnâ. CIC.—"He is in narrow circumstances." His means are small.

Angusta via est quæ ducit ad vitam.—"Narrow is the way which leadeth to life." *Matt.* vii. 14.

Animal implūme bipes.—"A two-legged animal without feathers." Said to have been Plato's definition of man.

Anĭmus non defĭcit æquus.—"A well-regulated mind is not wanting." Motto of Lord Gwydyr, taken from Horace, Ep. 1. 12. 30.

Annus inceptus habĕtur pro complĕto. *Law Max.*—"A year entered on is reckoned as completed."

Aqua pumpāgĭnis.—A cant expression with medical men for "spring water." The second word, we need hardly say, is dog Latin.

Aquæ guttæ saxa excăvant.—"Dropping water hollows out rocks." See *Stillicidi casus*, &c.

Arcădes ambo. VIRG.—"Both Arcadians,"—used ironically to signify "a pair well-matched" or "Birds of a feather." See *Par nobile fratrum.*

Astra castra, numen lumen.—"The stars are my camp, the

Deity my light." A verbal quibble, the motto of the Earl of Balcarras.

Astrictus necessitāte. CIC.—"Compelled by necessity."

At spes non fracta.—"But my hope is not broken." Motto of the Earl of Hopetoun.

Aurea mediocrĭtas.—"The golden mean" between great wealth and poverty. See *Auream quisquis*, &c.

Auspicium meliōris ævi.—"A presage of better times." Motto of the Duke of St. Alban's.

Aut vincĕre aut mori.—"To conquer or to die." Motto of the late Duke of Kent.

Avi numerantur avōrum. VIRG.—"I boast of a long train of ancestors." Motto of Lord Grantley. See *Genus immortale*, &c.

Avīto viret honōre.—"He flourishes with ancestral honours." Motto of the Earl of Bute.

B.

Basis virtūtum constantia.—"Steadiness is the basis of all the virtues." Motto of the Viscount Hereford.

Bellum internecīnum.—"A war of extermination."

Bene nati, bene vestiti, et mediŏcrĭter docti.—"Well born, well clothed, and moderately learned." The qualifications required of a Fellow, by the statutes of All Souls College, Oxford.

Bonum magis carendo quàm fruendo cernĭtur. Prov.—"We appreciate more sensibly the good which we have not, than that which we have."

C.

Cacoēthes loquendi.—"An itch for speaking."

——*Cælia ridens*
Est Venus, incēdens Juno, Minerva loquens.
—"Cælia laughing, is beauteous as Venus; walking, majestic as Juno; speaking, wise as Minerva."

Cætĕris pārĭbus.—"Other things being equal." Being equal in other respects.

Casta morĭbus et intĕgra pudōre. MART.—"Of chaste morals and irreproachable modesty."

Cave ab homĭne unīus libri.—"Beware of the man of one book." He is the most likely to have mastered it thoroughly. See *Homo unius*, &c.

Cedat amor rebus, res age, tutus eris. OVID.—"Let love give way to business, attend to business and you will be safe." See *Qui finem*, &c.

Clamōrem ad sidĕra mittunt. STATIUS.—"They send their shouts to the stars." The welkin rings with their cries.

Cœlĭtŭs mihi vires.—"My strength is from heaven." Motto of Viscount Ranelagh.

Commūne quodcumque est lucri. PHÆD.—"A windfall is common property." The law of the road, that when two persons make a lucky "find" they go halves.

Compendia, dispendia. *Prov.*—"A short cut is a losing cut." "The longest way about is the shortest way home."

Conando Græci Trojâ potīti sunt.—"By trying, the Greeks became masters of Troy." A translation from Theocritus. See Ἐς Τροίαν, &c.

Conscius libidĭnum. CIC.—"A partner in his debaucheries."

Consĕquĭtur quodcunque petit.—"He attains whatever he aims at." Motto of the Marquis of Headfort.

Consilium ne sperne meum, tibi fausta parantur.—"Despise not my advice, auspicious days await you."

Consuetūdo malōrum bonos mores contamĭnat.—"The companionship of the wicked corrupts good morals." See Φθείρουσιν, &c.

Contempsi gladium Catilīnæ, non pertimescam tuos. CIC.—"I have despised the sword of Catiline, I shall not dread yours."

Contractāta jure, contrārio jure pereunt. *Law. Max.*—"Privileges established by one law are abrogated by the provisions of an opposite law."

Cooperante diabŏlo.—"With the assistance of the devil."

Cōpia verbōrum.—"A copious stock of words."

Cor et mentem colĕre nītimur.—"We endeavour to improve the heart and the mind." Motto over the entrance of a school at Marquise, between Calais and Boulogne.

Cor unum, via una.—"One heart, one way." Motto of the Marquis of Exeter

Cruci dum spiro fido.—"While I breathe I put my trust in the cross." Motto of Viscount Galway.

Cujus gloriæ neque profuit quisquam laudando; nec vituperando quisquam nocuit.—"Whose glory no praises could enhance, no censure injure."

Cum permissu superiōrum.—"With permission of the superior authorities."

Cur omnium fit culpa paucōrum scelus?—"Why should the wickedness of a few be deemed the guilt of all?"

Curiōsa felicitas. PETR. ARB.—"Studied happiness," or *artful artlessness* of style.

D.

De bonis non. *Law Term.*—"Of goods not (administered)," *administratis* being understood. Where all the personalty of an intestate has not been administered to, and a new administrator is appointed, he is technically known as an "administrator *de bonis non.*"

Decŏri decus addit avīto.—"He adds new lustre to the honours of his forefathers." Motto of the Scotch Earl of Kellie.

Dejectâ arbŏre quivis ligna collĭgit. *Prov.*—"When the tree is down, every one gathers wood." See Δρυὸς πεσούσης, &c.

Deo adjuvante, non timendum.—"God assisting, there is nothing to be feared." Motto of Earl Fitzwilliam.

Detur digniōri.—"Let it be given to the most worthy."

Deus ex machĭnâ. *Prov.*—"A god from the clouds." An expression implying unexpected aid in an emergency. In allusion to the mode in which, in the Greek and Roman theatres, the divinities were launched on the stage by the aid of mechanism. See *Nec Deus*, &c., and Θεὸς ἐκ μηχανῆς.

Disjecta membra.—"The scattered limbs." See *Disjecti membra poetæ.*

Disputandi prurītus ecclesiārum scabies.—"The itch of disputation will prove the scab of the church." A favourite saying of Sir Henry Wotton, inscribed on his tomb at Eton.

Domĭne, dirĭge nos.—"O Lord! direct us." The motto of the city of London.

Domĭni pudet, non servitūtis. SEN.—"I am ashamed of my master, not of my servitude."

Domĭnus providēbit.—"The Lord will provide." Motto of the Earl of Glasgow. See *Gen.* xxii. 8.

Dotātæ uxōres mactant malo et damno viros. PLAUT.—"Well-dowered wives involve their husbands in misfortune and ruin."

Ducit amor patriæ.—"The love of my country leads me on." Motto of Baron Milford.

Dulce sodalitium. MART.—"A happy association." A sweet society.

E.

E fungis nati hŏmĭnes.—"Men sprung from mushrooms." Upstarts.

Erĭmus, fortasse, quando illi non erunt.—"We shall perhaps survive, after they have ceased to exist."

Et decus et pretium recti.—"At once the ornament and the reward of virtue." Motto of the Duke of Grafton.

Et nos quoque tela sparsĭmus.—"We too have flung our darts." Motto of Earl Moira.

Ex aliēno tergŏre lata secantur lora. *Prov.*—"Broad thongs are cut from another man's leather."

Ex sese. CIC.—"From himself." He has risen by his own industry.

Excessit medicīna malum.—"The remedy has done more than the disease."

Excessus in jure reprobātur. *Law Max.*—"Excess is condemned in the law." See *Jus summum*, &c.

——*Eximius præstanti corpŏre taurus.* VIRG.—"A bull excelling in beauty."

Exĭtus acta probat.—"The result proves the deed." "All's well that ends well."

Expectans expectāvi.—"I waited patiently." The beginning of the fortieth Psalm.

Experientia stultōrum magistra. *Prov.*—"Experience is the teacher of fools." They can only be taught by suffering.

F.

Facĭlè consilia damus ălīis.—"We easily bestow advice on others."

Făcĭle primus.—"By far the first."

Fax mentis incendium gloriæ.—"The flame of glory is the torch of the mind." Motto of the Earl of Granard.

Fidei commissum. Law Term.—"Entrusted to faith." In the Roman law a species of testamentary disposition, in reliance on the good faith of the heir.

Fides carbonāria.—"The coal-heaver's faith," or "belief." A comparatively modern expression, said to have originated in the following circumstance: A coal-porter, being asked what he believed, made answer, "What the Church believes;" and on being asked what the Church believed, replied, "What I believe." According to some of the French authorities, it means, "A simple, blind, unreasoning faith."

Fidus Achātes. VIRG.—"The faithful Achates." A character in the Æneid, somewhat indistinctly drawn, but always at the side of Æneas in his numerous perils and misfortunes. Hence a faithful friend is sometimes called a *Fidus Achates*, but the phrase is more commonly used in an ironical sense.

Fidus et audax.—"Faithful and intrepid." Motto of the Earl of Lismore.

Finis ecce labōrum!—"Behold the end of my toils!"

Flecti, non frangi.—"To bend, not to break." Motto of Viscount Palmerston.

Flumĭna rapĭdè subsīdunt.—"Swollen rivers subside rapidly."

Forte scutum salus ducum.—"A strong shield is the safety of leaders." Motto of Earl Fortescue.

Fortis sub forte fatiscet.—"Even a brave man will succumb to fortune." Motto of the Earl of Upper Ossory.

Fortĭter, fidelĭter, felicĭter.—"Boldly, faithfully, successfully." Motto of Viscount Monk and Lord Hutchinson.

Fortūna multis parcĕre in pœnam solet. LABES.—"Fortune spares many only to punish them."

Fortūna sua è cujusque fingĭtur mōrĭbus.—"Every man's fortune is shaped by his own conduct."

Fratres dilĭgĭte, et matris consilia ne aspernamĭni.—"Love your brethren, and despise not your mother's counsel."

Fraus latet in generālĭbus. Law Max.—"In generalities fraud lies concealed."

——*Fremunt immāni turbĭne venti.* Ovid.—"The winds rage in a tremendous storm."

Frons dŏmĭni plus prodest quàm occipĭtium.—"The forehead of the master is more useful than his hindhead." A proverb quoted by Cato and Pliny the Elder. The eye and thought of the master are necessary to the success of his business.

Fures clamōrem. Prov.—"Thieves raising the hue and cry," that they have been robbed. See *Clodius accusat*, &c.

G.

Gaudet tentāmĭne virtus. Luc.—"Virtue rejoices in temptation." Motto of the Earl of Dartmouth.

Gula plures occĭdit quam glădius, estque fomes omnium malōrum. Fr. Patricius, *Bishop of Gaëta.*—"The gullet kills more than the sword, and is the fuel that kindles all evils."

H.

Habet Deus suas horas et moras.—"God has his hours and his delays."

Historiæ decus est, et quasi anĭma, ut cum eventis causæ copulentur. Bacon *de Aug. Scien.*—"It is the beauty and, as it were, the soul, of history, that events are duly connected with their causes."

——*Hoc genus omne.* Hor.—"All that class of men." Generally used in a contemptuous sense.

Honor est a Nilo.—"Honour is from the Nile." Dr. Burney's celebrated anagram upon the name of Horatio Nelson.

Hostes magis assidui quàm graves.—"Enemies rather assiduous than powerful."

Hostis honōri invidia.—"An enemy's envy is an honour." Motto of the Earl of Harborough.

I.

Ilĭas malōrum. Cic.—"A whole Iliad of woes." See Ἰλιὰς ναι ἡ

Imminente lunâ. HOR.—"By the light of the moon."

Impĕrio regit unus æquo. HOR.—"He alone rules all with justice." Motto of Sir Robert Gunning.

In articŭlo mortis.—"At the point of death."

In ferrum pro libertāte ruĕbant.—"For liberty they rushed upon the sword." Motto of the Earl of Leicester.

In hoc signo spes mea.—"In this sign is my hope." Motto of Viscount Taaffe.

In me consumpsit vires fortūna nocendo.—"Fortune has exhausted on me her power in the injury which she has done me."

In pretio pretium nunc est; dat census honōres,
Census amicitias; pauper ubique jacet. OVID.
—"Money now is the only thing prized; wealth alone gives honours, wealth gives friendships; the poor man is everywhere despised."

In statu pupillāri.—"In the condition of a pupil." All students at the University, under the degree of Master of Arts, are *in statu pupillari.*

Incultum ac derelictum solum.—"An uncultivated and neglected soil."

Indignante invidiâ florēbit justus.—"In spite of envy the just man will flourish." Motto of the Earl of Glendore.

Inepta patris lenĭtas, et facilĭtas prava.—"The foolish lenity and mischievous indulgence of a father."

Ingĕnia gravia et solemnia, ac mutāri nescia, plus plerumque habent dignitātis quàm felicitātis. BACON *de Augmen. Scien.*—"Men whose minds are stern, solemn, and inflexible enjoy, in general, more dignity than happiness."

Ingentes virtūtes ingentia vitia. LIVY.—"Great virtues often lead to great vices."

Ingrātus est, qui beneficium se accepisse negat quod accĕpit; ingrātus, qui dissimŭlat; ingrātus, qui non reddit; ingrātissimus omnium, qui oblītus est. CIC.—"He is ungrateful who denies that he has received a kindness when he has received it; ungrateful who conceals the fact that he has received it; ungrateful who does not return it; but the most ungrateful of all is he who forgets it."

Inque brevi spatio mutantur sæcla animantûm,
. . quasi cursōres vitaï lampăda tradunt. LUCRET.
"And in a short space of time the tribes of living crea-

tures are changed (by successive generations), and, like the racers, deliver the torch of life (from hand to hand)." In allusion to the torch-race at the festival of Vulcan at Athens, when the runners handed a lighted torch from one to another, and he who carried the torch lighted to the end of the course was proclaimed victor. See Λαμπάδια, &c.

Insĭtâ homin*ĭ*bus lib*ī*d*ĭ*ne alendi de industriâ rum*ō*res.—"The natural propensity of mankind to propagate reports with eagerness."

Instar omnium.—"Equal to all the others." *Plato est mihi instar omnium.* CIC.

Intamin*ā*tis hon*ō*r*ĭ*bus. HOR.—"With unspotted honours." Motto of Lord St. Helens.

Inv*ī*tum sequ*ĭ*tur honos.—"Honour follows him even against his will." Motto of the Marquis of Donegal.

Iram qui vincit, hostem sup*ĕ*rat max*ĭ*mum.—"He who controls his anger subdues his greatest enemy."

J.

Jacta est alea.—"The die is cast." The words of Cæsar on passing the Rubicon.

Jej*ū*nus venter non audit verba libenter.—"A hungry belly has no ears." A mediæval Leonine proverb.

Judic*ā*ta res pro verit*ā*te acc*ĭ*pitur. *Law Max.*—"An award that has been made is received as a just precedent."

Jus omnium in omnia, et consequenter bellum omnium in omnes.—"Where all men have a right to all things, the consequence is war of all men with all men." The natural state of man, as described by Hobbes.

Justum ab injustis pet*ĕ*re insipientia est. PLAUT.—"It is folly to expect justice at the hands of the unjust."

K.

Kudos.—"Praise," "glory," or "fame." From the Greek κῦδος, which has almost become a dictionary word in the English language.

L.

Labor ipse voluptas.—"Even labour itself is a pleasure." Motto of Lord King.

Laborāre est orāre. Prov.—"To labour is to pray." To the same effect as the proverb that says, "The gods help those who help themselves." See *Qui laborat*, &c. (App.)

Lachrymâ nil citius arescit. CIC.—"Nothing dries up sooner than a tear."

Lateat scintillŭla forsan.—"Perchance a small spark may lie concealed." The motto of the Royal Humane Society.

Latrantes ride; te tua fama manet.—"Laugh at cynics; your well-earned fame awaits you."

Lentus in dicendo, et pene frigĭdus orātor. CIC.—"An orator tedious in delivery and almost freezing."

——*Levius fit patientiâ*
Quicquid corrigĕre est nefas. HOR.
—"Misfortunes which we cannot prevent are mitigated by resignation." "What can't be cured must be endured," says the old proverb.

Libĕra me ab hŏmĭne malo, a meipso. ST. AUGUSTIN.—"Deliver me from the evil man, even from myself."

Lingua, Tropus, Ratio, Numĕrus, Tonus, Angŭlus, Astra,
Rus, Nemus, Arma, Faber, Vulnĕra, Lana, Rates.
—Literally, "Tongue, trope, reason, number, tone, angle, stars; country, grove, arms, workman, wounds, wool, ships." In the first line the ancients summed up the *artes ingenuæ* or *liberales;* the ingenuous arts, which might be practised, according to their notions, without disgrace, by freemen: "Language, Rhetoric, Logic, Arithmetic, Music, Geometry, and Astronomy." In the latter line were included the mechanical arts, practised only by slaves: "Agriculture, propagation of Trees, manufacture of Arms, Carpenter's work, Medicine, Weaving, and Ship-building."

Lucernam olet. Prov.—"It smells of the lamp." It is a studied composition.

Lusus anĭmo debent aliquando dari,
Ad cogitandum melior ut redeat sibi. PHÆDRUS.
—"The mind ought occasionally to be indulged with re-

laxation, that it may, with increased vigour, return to study."

M.

Malitia supplet ætātem. Law Max.—"Malice supplies the want of age." Children at a certain age are to bear the punishment of their actions if malice prepense can be shown.

Malo mori quàm fædāri.—"I had rather die than be disgraced." The motto of the Earl of Athlone.

Malum est mulier, sed necessārium malum.—"Woman is an evil, but a necessary evil."

——*Manifesta phrenēsis,*
Ut locŭples moriāris, egenti vīvĕre fato. Juv.
—"It is evident madness to live in penury that you may die rich."

Manus hæc inimīca tyrannis.—"This hand is hostile to tyrants." Motto of the Earl of Carysfort.

Maxĭmum miracŭlum homo sapiens.—"A wise man is (now-a-days) the greatest of prodigies."

——*Meâ*
Virtūte me involvo. Hor.
—"I wrap myself in my own virtue." As the philosopher in his cloak.

Medicīna mortuōrum sera est. Quintil.—"Medicine is too late for the dead."

Medĭcus non dat quod pătiens vult, sed quod ipse bonum scit.—"A physician does not prescribe what his patient wishes, but what he himself knows to be good."

Meliōrĭbus auspiciis.—"Under more favourable auspices."

——*Melius fuĕrat non scribĕre, namque tacēre*
Tutum semper erit.
—"It had been better not to write, for silence is always safe."

Mens sana in corpŏre sano. Juv.—"A sound mind in a sound body."

Miles, Mercātor, Stultus, Marītus, Amātor.—"Soldier, Merchant, Fool, Husband, Lover." An ancient line, assigning a character to each finger, beginning with the thumb. It seems intended for an Hexameter, but has a false quantity.

——*Militāri non sine gloriā.* Hor.—"I too have fought, not without glory." He alludes to his skirmishes in the wars of love. See *Militat omnis*, &c.

Multa bibens ac multa vorans.—"Drinking much and devouring much."

Murus ahēneus conscientia sana.—"A clear conscience is a wall of brass." Motto of the Earl of Scarborough.

Mutāre vel timēre sperno.—"I scorn either to change or to fear." Motto of the Duke of Beaufort.

N.

Nec plăcĭdā contentus quiēte est.—"Nor is he contented in soft repose." Motto of the Earl of Peterborough, adapted from Virgil.

Nec prece nec pretio.—"Neither by entreaty nor by bribe." Motto of Viscount Bateman.

Nec quærĕre nec spernĕre honōrem.—"Neither to hunt after nor to despise honours." Motto of Viscount Bolingbroke.

Nec rege nec popŭlo sed utrōque.—"Neither for king nor people, but for both." Motto of Lord Rolle.

Nec temĕrè, nec timĭdè.—"Neither rashly nor timidly." Motto of the Earl of Darlington and Viscount Bulkeley.

Nemo est tam senex, qui se annum non putet posse vivĕre. Cic.—"No man is so old that he does not think he may yet live a year."

Nescio quid curtæ semper abest rei. Hor.—"Something is ever wanting to render our fortunes complete."

Nihil per saltum.—"Nothing is done with a leap." A part of Bacon's maxim, *Nihil facit natura per saltum.* All the operations of nature are gradual.

Nihil simĭle est idem.—"Nothing that is like is the same." Things that are similar are not identical.

Nil molītur ineptè. Hor.—"He attempts nothing injudiciously."

——*Nil nisi carmĭna desunt.* Virg.—"Nothing is wanting but a song."

Nimīrum hic ego sum. Hor.—"Here I am." In this opinion, in this way of thinkiug, I take my stand.

Nimium nec laudāre nec lædĕre.—"Neither to praise nor to censure too much."

Nobilitātis virtus, non stemma, character.—"Virtue, not pedigree, should characterize nobility." Motto of the Marquis of Westminster.

Nomināti̇m.—"By name."

Non anĭmi curas demunt montes auri et superba atria.—"Neither heaps of gold nor superb halls can remove the cares of the mind."

Non est disputandum.—"It is not to be disputed." There is no disputing.

Non est usus ullius rei consociandus cum imprŏbo. PHÆD.—"In all our dealings we should shun association with a dishonest man."

Non est venātor quivis per cornua flator.—"Not every one is a huntsman that blows a horn." A mediæval Leonine proverb.

Non genĕrant aquĭlæ columbas.—"Eagles do not produce pigeons." Motto of the late Earl Rodney, adapted from Horace.

Non indĭget calcārĭbus.—"He needs no spur." Said by De Foe of the Devil. From the remark of Isocrates concerning Ephorus, that he needed the spur in his compositions.

Non mî aurum posco, nec mî pretium.—"I seek not gold, nor am I to be bought."

Non numĕro hæc judicantur sed pondĕre. CIC.—"These things are not to be estimated by their number, but by their importance."

Non plus aurum tibi quàm monedŭlæ committēbant.—CIC.—"They would no more trust gold to you than they would to a jackdaw." A proverbial expression in allusion to the thievish propensities of that bird.

Non pros. Law Term.—A contraction of "*non prosequitur.*" "He does not prosecute." A judgment entered against the plaintiff, in a suit where he does not appear to prosecute, is so called. See *Nolle prosequi.*

Non versiōnes sed eversiōnes.—"Not versions but eversions." Said by St. Jerome of the Latin Versions of the Scriptures used in his day.

Nosce teipsum.—"Know thyself" See *E cœlo descendit,* and Γνῶθι σεαυτόν.

Nullius boni jucunda possessio sine socio.—"Of no blessing can the enjoyment be perfect, unless it be shared with a friend."

Nullum quod tetĭgit non ornāvit.—"He attempted nothing that he did not embellish." From Dr. Johnson's epitaph on Goldsmith.

Nullum tam impŭdens mendācium est ut teste căreat. PLINY *the Elder.*—"There is no lie so bare-faced as to be at a loss for a voucher."

Nunc aut nunquam.—"Now or never." Motto of the Earl of Kilmorey.

Nunquam non parātus.—"Never unprepared." Motto of the Marquis of Annandale.

Nuper idoneus. HOR.—"Lately fit for." Or, some time ago I was equal to this.

O.

O amāri dies! O flebĭles noctes!—"Oh! agonizing days! Oh! nights of tears!"

O dea certè. VIRG.—"O surely a divinity."
"O goddess, for no less you seem."

O mors, ero mors tua.—"O death, I will be thy death." Motto of a Society called *the Black Society.*

Occupāri in multis et magnis negōtiis.—"To be engaged in various and important affairs."

Ocŭlum non curābit sine toto capĭte,
Nec caput sine toto corpŏre,
Nec totum corpus sine anĭmâ.
—"The physician cannot cure the eye while the head is diseased, nor the head while the bodily system is deranged, nor the body while the mind is ill at ease."

Omnia bona bonis.—"All things are good to good men." Motto of Lord Wenman.

Omnia venālia nummo.—"All things are to be bought with money." Everything has its price.

Omnis sors ferendo superanda est.—"Every lot is to be overcome by endurance."

Ora et labōra.—"Pray and work." Motto of the Earl of Dalhousie. See *Laborare,* &c.

Ore rotundo.—"With round mouth," i. e. with a full-sounding, or eloquent mouth.

P.

Parvi sunt foris arma, nisi est consilium domi. CIC.—"Arms are worth little abroad, if there is not wisdom at home."

Patientia læsa fit furor.—"Patience abused becomes fury."

Patĭtur qui vincit.—"He suffers who conquers." Motto of Lord Kinnaird. No victory is to be obtained without some inconvenience.

Patria cara, carior libertas.—"Dear is my country, but dearer is liberty." Motto of the Earl of Radnor.

Pauci dignoscĕre possunt
Vera bona, atque illis multum diversa. JUV.
—"Few men can discriminate between things which are really good, and those which are of a very different nature."

Paulo post futūrum.—"A little after the future." The name of one of the Greek tenses facetiously translated, used ironically to signify something remotely distant, or postponed to an indefinite period.

Paupertas durum onus misĕris mortālĭbus.—"Poverty is a cruel burden to miserable man."

Paupertātis pudor et fuga.—"The shame and dread of poverty."

Per angusta ad augusta.—"Through difficulties to grandeur." Motto of the Earl of Massarene.

Per ardua libĕri.—"Through difficulties we obtain freedom." Motto of Lord Camelford.

Per mare, per terras.—"By sea and land." Motto of Baron Macdonald.

Pericŭlum fortitūdĭne evāsi.—"I have escaped danger by fortitude." Motto of Lord Hartland.

Perĭmus licĭtis.—"We perish by things permitted." A favourite saying of Sir Matthew Hale. Those vices are the most insidious of which the law takes no positive cognizance.

Plausu petis clarescĕre vulgi.—"You seek celebrity through the plaudits of the mob."

Plus è medĭco quàm è morbo pericŭli.—"There is more to be feared from the physician than from the disease."

Porro unum est necessārium.—"Moreover one thing is needful." Motto of the Duke of Wellington and Marquis Wellesley.

Post prœlia prœmia.—"After battle rewards." Motto of the Lord Rossmore.

Post tot naufragia tutus.—"Safe after so many shipwrecks."

Postrēmus in pugnâ, primus in fugâ.—"The last to fight, the first to fly."

Prima virtus est vitio carēre. QUINTIL.—"The beginning of excellence is to be free from error."

Pro qualitāte tempŏris.—"According to the nature of the emergency."

Pro rege et patriâ.—"For my king and country." Motto of the Earl of Leven.

Pro rege et popŭlo.—"For the king and the people." Motto of Lord De Dunstanville.

Pro rege, lege, grege.—"For the king, the law, and the people." Motto of Lord Brougham.

Procēras dejĭcit arbŏres procella vehĕmens.—"A violent storm uproots lofty trees."

Prodesse quàm conspĭci.—"To do good rather than be conspicuous." Motto of Lord Somers.

Puellis idoneus. HOR.—"A ladies' man."

Q.

Quæ amissa salva.—"What was lost is safe." Motto of the Earl of Kintore.

Qualis rex, talis grex.—"As the king is, so are his subjects."

Qui labŏrat orat. ST. AUGUSTIN.—"He who labours prays." See *Laborare*, &c.

Qui me amat, amat et canem meum. *Prov.*—"Who loves me, loves my dog." Quoted by Saint Bernard.

Qui stat, vĭdeat ne cadat.—"Let him who stands take heed lest he fall." See 1 *Cor.* x. 12.

Qui uti scit, ei bona.—"He should possess wealth who knows how to use it."

Quicquid sibi imperāvit anĭmus, obtinuit. SEN.—"Whatever the mind enjoins on itself as an object, it attains."

Quid est dignĭtas indigno, nisi circŭlus aureus in nārĭbus suis? SILVIANUS.—"What is honour to the unworthy, but a golden ring in a swine's snout?"

Quid obserătis aurĭbus fundis preces? HOR.—"Why persist in your importunity to ears that are closed?"

Quis erit innŏcens, si clam vel palam accusāre sufficiat?—"Who would be innocent, if mere accusation, secret or open, could convict?"

Quis non invĕniet turbâ quod amāret in illâ? OVID.—"Who can fail to find in such a medley something to please him?"

Quis separābit nos?—"Who shall separate us?"

Quod ab initio non valet, tractu tempŏris convalescĕre non potest. Law Max.—"That which is invalid from the first, cannot be made valid by lapse of time."

Quod est inconveniens et contra ratiōnem non est permissum in lege. Law Max.—"Whatever is inconsistent with itself and contrary to reason is not permitted by law."

Quod fiĕri non dĕbuit, factum valet. COKE.—"That which ought not to have been done, when done holds good." A marriage, for instance, at an illegal age.

Quod stultè suscĭpitur, impiè gĕrĭtur, mĭsĕre fīnītur.—"What is foolishly conceived, is wickedly executed, and has a wretched termination."

R.

Rectè et suavĭter.—"Uprightly and mildly." Motto of Lord Scarsdale.

Relicta sunt cuncta neglecta apud illum.—"Everything in his house is left neglected." Everything lies in disorder.

Res notæ, atque ad omnes pervulgātæ.—"Things well known, and spoken of universally."

——*Ripa irremeābilis undæ.* VIRG.—"The bank of the stream never to be repassed."

S.

Salārium non dat multis salem.—"To many salary does not give salt." In many official situations the salary is not equal to the expense.

Sapientia vino obumbrātur. PLINY *the Elder.*—"Wisdom

is obscured by wine." "When the wine's in, the wit's out."

——*Scenis decōra alta futūris.* VIRG.—"Lofty ornaments for future scenic magnificence."

Se causam clamat, crimenque, caputque malōrum. VIRG.—"She exclaims that she is the cause, that hers is the crime, and that she is the author of their woes."

Secundis dubiisque rectus.—"Unshaken in prosperous or in adverse fortune." Motto of Viscount Duncan.

Sed nunc non erat his locus. HOR.—"But at present there is no place for these." These matters are not wanted.

Sedet æternumque sedēbit. VIRG.—"He sits and will sit for ever."

Semper fidēlis.—"Always faithful." Motto of Lord Onslow.

Semper habens Pylăden alĭquem qui curet Oresten.—"Always having a Pylades (a friend) to take care of Orestes."

Sequor, nec infĕrior.—"I follow, but not inferior." Motto of Lord Crewe.

Serpentes avĭbus geminentur, tigrĭbus agni. HOR.—"As though serpents should couple with birds, lambs with tigers." You may as well expect the most opposite things in nature to be reconciled, as that such a thing can happen.

Servāta fides cinĕri.—"Faithful to the memory of my ancestors." Motto of Lord Harrowby.

Si hic esses, alĭter sentīres.—"If you stood in my circumstances, you would think otherwise."

Si jus violandum, regnandi gratiâ violandum est.—"If justice may ever be violated, it may be violated for the sake of empire."

Si natūra negat, facit indignātio versum. JUV.—"If nature refuses indignation will prompt a verse."

——*Si volet usus,*
Quem penes arbitrium est et jus et norma loquendi. HOR.—"If it is the will of custom, with which rests the direction, and law, and rule of speech." See *Mortalia facta*, &c.

Sibi parat malum qui altĕri parat.—"He meditates evil for himself who meditates it for another."

Sic in orig.—For *Sic in originali.* "So in the original."

Sic ruit ad celĕbres cultissĭma fœmĭna ludos. OVID.—"Thus

do the women in their best attire eagerly flock to the games."

Siccis omnia nam dura Deus proposuit; neque
Mordāces alĭter diffugiunt solicitūdĭnes. HOR.
—"The god (Bacchus) makes everything grievous to those who love not wine; nor can corroding cares be dispelled by other means."

Sicut in stagno genĕrantur vermes, sic in otiōso malæ cogitātiōnes.—"As worms are generated in a stagnant pool, so are evil thoughts in the mind of him who is unemployed."

Similitūdo morum parit amicitiam.—"A congeniality of manners and disposition begets friendship."

Sola Deo salus.—"Safety is in God alone." Motto of Lord Rokeby.

Sola nobilĭtas virtus.—"Virtue is the only nobility." Motto of the Marquis of Abercorn, adapted from Juvenal.

Solet agi sincerĭtas ad perniciem. PHÆD.—"Sincerity is used to our destruction." Sincerity and candour may expose us to the arts of the overreaching.

Spectēmur agendo.—"Let us make our character known by our actions." Motto of Viscount Clifden.

Spero meliōra.—"I hope for better things." Motto of Viscount Stormont.

Spes alit exŭles.—"Hope supports the exile."

Spes servat afflictos.—"Hope sustains the unfortunate."

Spirĭtus promptus, caro autem infirma.—"The spirit is willing, but the flesh is weak." See *Matt.* xxvi. 41. Virtuous resolutions are often formed without the requisite firmness to carry them into execution.

Squamis astantĭbus Hydri. CIC.—"The scales of the Hydra bristling up."

Stare loco nescit, micat aurĭbus, et tremit artus,
Collectumque premens volvit sub nārĭbus ignem. VIRG.
—"He cannot stand still, he pricks up his ears, he trembles in every limb, and rolls the collected fire compressed within his nostrils." Description of a spirited horse.

Studiis et rebus honestis.—"By honourable pursuits and actions." Motto of Lord Ashburton.

Suffĭcit ad id, natūra quod poscit. SEN.—"It suffices for what nature requires."

Super abyssum ambŭlans.—"Treading on an abyss." Applied to a man who is on unsafe ground, and in danger of sinking into the gulf of ruin.

Suspendens omnia naso. HOR.—"Turning everything to ridicule."

Suum quemque scelus agĭtat. CIC.—"Every man has his besetting sin."

T.

Tale quale.—"Such as it is."

Tandem fit surcŭlus arbor.—"A twig in time becomes a tree." Motto of the Marquis of Waterford.

Tardè sed tutè.—"Slowly but surely."

Tectior et occultior cupidĭtas. CIC.—"Avariciousness close and concealed."

Termĭnus a quo.—"The limits" or "bounds from which." In metaphysics, the place at which any motion commences is so called, and stands in contradistinction to the other extreme, called the *Terminus ad quem.* A bastard is, in law, a *Terminus a quo,* i. e. the first of his family, the source from which it originates.

Torpent mihi membra. HOR.—"My limbs are enfeebled," become languid.

——*Trudit gemmas, et frondes explĭcat omnes.* VIRG.—"It puts forth buds and unfolds all its leaves." Description of the vine bursting into leaf.

Tu ne cede malis, sed contra audentior ito. VIRG.—"Yield not to misfortune, but, on the contrary, meet it with greater spirit." The first four words form the motto of Lord Milton.

Turbĭne raptus ingĕnii.—"Impelled by the impetuosity of his genius."

Turpe est in patriâ peregrināri, et in iis rebus quæ ad patriam pertĭnent hospĭtem esse. MANUT.—"It is disgraceful to be as a stranger in one's own country, and to be unacquainted with matters relating to it."

GREEK QUOTATIONS

A

Ἁ οἱ φίλοι τοῖς βασιλεῦσιν οὐ θαῤῥοῦσι παραινεῖν, ταῦτα ἐν τοῖς βιβλίοις γέγραπται. PLUTARCH.—"The advice which their friends have not the courage to give to kings is found written in books." The words of Demetrius Phalereus to King Ptolemy.

Ἀγαθὴ δ' ἔρις ἥδε βροτοῖσι. HESIOD.—"Emulation is good for mankind."

Ἀγαθοὶ δ' ἀριδάκρυες ἄνδρες. *Prov.*—"Men prone to tears are good."

Ἄγει δε πρὸς φῶς τὴν ἀλήθειαν χρόνος. *Prov.*—"Time brings the truth to light."

Ἀγνώστῳ Θεῷ.—"To the unknown God." The inscription on the altar at Athens mentioned by St. Paul, *Acts* xvii. 23.

Ἀγροίκου μὴ καταφρόνει ῥήτορος.—"Despise not a rustic orator."

Ἀγὼν πρόφασιν οὐκ ἐπιδέχεται, οὔτε φιλία.—"War and friendship admit of no excuses."

Ἀδύνατον πολλὰ τεχνώμενον ἄνθρωπον πάντα καλῶς ποιεῖν. XENOPH.—"It is impossible for a man who attempts many things to do them all well."

Ἀεὶ κολοιὸς παρὰ κολοιῷ ἵζάνει. *Prov.*—"A jackdaw always perches near a jackdaw." "Birds of a feather flock together."

Ἀεὶ τᾶν ποσὶν ὄντα παρατρεχόμεσθα μάταιοι,
Κεῖνο ποθοῦντες ὅπερ μακρὸν ἄπωθεν ἔφυ. PINDAR.
—"In our folly we are always passing by what lies at our feet, and desiring that which is at a great distance."

Ἀετὸν ἵπτασθαι διδάσκεις. *Prov.*—"You are teaching an eagle to fly." "You teach your grandam to suck eggs." See *Aquilam volare*, &c.

Ἀετοῦ γῆρας, κορύδου νεότης.—"The old age of the eagle is better than the youth of the sparrow." Respecting the κορύδος, see 'Εν ἀμούσοις, &c.

Ἀθανάτους μὲν πρῶτα θεοὺς, νόμῳ ὡς διάκειται,
Τίμα.—— PYTHAGORAS.
—"First of all, honour the immortal gods, as by law enjoined."

——**Αἱ δὲ σάρκες αἱ κεναὶ φρενῶν**
Ἀγάλματ' ἀγορᾶς εἰσι. EURIPIDES.
—"Flesh destitute of mind is like the statues in the market-place."

Αἵ τε γὰρ συμφοραὶ ποιοῦσι μακρολόγους. APPIAN.—"Misfortunes make us verbose."

Αἰδὼς μὲν γὰρ ὄλωλεν, ἀναιδείη δὲ καὶ ὕβρις
Νικήσασα δίκην, γῆν κατὰ πᾶσαν ἔχει. THEOGNIS.
—"Shame has perished; impudence and insolence, prevailing over justice, possess the whole land."

Αἰεὶ δ' ἀμβολιεργὸς ἀνὴρ ἄτῃσι παλαίει. HESIOD.—"The man who procrastinates is ever struggling with misfortunes." See Δεῖ ἀμέλλητον, &c.

Αἰὲν ἀριστεύειν καὶ ὑπείροχον ἔμμεναι ἄλλων. HOMER.—"Always to excel and to be superior to others."

Αἱροῦντες ᾑρήμεθα.—"We who went to catch are ourselves caught." "The biter bit."

Ἀκέφαλος μῦθος.—"A story without a head."

Ἀκίνητα κινεῖς.—"You move what should not be moved."

Ἄκουε τοῦ τέσσαρα ὦτα ἔχοντος.—"Listen to him who has four ears." Listen to him who shows himself ready to be instructed by others. A saying of Zenodotus, the Stoic philosopher.

Ἀκούσατ' ἀνθρώποισι τὰς μὲν ἐκ θεῶν
Τύχας δοθείσας ἔστ' ἀναγκαῖον φέρειν. SOPHOCLES.
—"Listen: the fortunes which the gods impose we must of necessity endure." See Τὰς γάρ, &c.

Ἄκρον λάβε, καὶ μέσον ἕξεις. *Prov.*—"Seize the end, and you will hold the middle." Those who would make sure of their object must entertain high aspirations.

Ἅλας ἄγων καθεύδεις.—"You sleep with salt on board." Said of those who are careless in danger; as in case of a leak a cargo of salt would be liquefied and wasted, even if it did not sink the ship.

Ἀλλ' οἱ γὰρ ἀθυμοῦντες ἄνδρες οὔποτε
Τρόπαιον ἐστήσαντο. EUPOLIS.
—"Men without spirit never yet erected a trophy." So our proverb, "Faint heart never won fair lady." See *Timidi nunquam*, &c.

Ἀλλὰ κέρδει καὶ σοφία δέδεται. PINDAR.—"For wisdom even is overpowered by self-interest."

Ἀλλ' ὅμως κρεῖσσον τῶν οἰκτιρμῶν φθόνος.—"Envy is better worth having than compassion."

Ἀλλ' οὐκ αὖθις ἀλώπηξ πάγαις.—"A fox is not (caught) twice in the same snare." See Γέρων ἀλώπηξ, &c.

Ἄλλοι κάμον, ἄλλοι ὤναντο.—"Some toil, others reap."

Ἄλλων ἰατρὸς, αὐτὸς ἕλκεσι βρύων.—"The physician of others, himself overrun with ulcers." Quoted by Plutarch.

Ἅλμη οὐκ ἔνεστιν αὐτῷ.—"There is no salt in him."

Ἅμα δὲ κιθῶνι ἐκδυομένῳ συνεκδύεται καὶ τὴν αἰδῶ γυνή.—"When a woman puts off her garments she puts off her modesty as well." The words of Gyges to king Candaules, as related by Herodotus.

Αμφοῖν *φίλοιν ὄντοιν, ὅσιον προτιμᾶν τὴν ἀλήθειαν.* ARISTOTLE.—"Though both [Plato and truth] are dear to me, it is right to prefer truth." See *Amicus Plato*, &c.

Αμφότεροι *κλῶπες, καὶ ὁ δεξάμενος, καὶ ὁ κλέψας.* PHOCYLIDES.—"Both are thieves, the receiver as much as the stealer."

'Ανάγκῃ *οὐδὲ θεοὶ μάχονται.* *Prov.*—"Not even the gods can fight against necessity." "Necessity has no law."

'Αναφαίρετον *κτῆμ' ἐστὶ παιδεία βροτοῖς.*—"Learning is a possession of which man cannot be deprived."

Ανδρες *γὰρ πόλις, καὶ οὐ τείχη, οὐδὲ νῆες ἀνδρῶν κεναί.*—"It is men that make a city, and not walls, or ships unmanned." The words of Nicias in Thucydides.

Ανδρων *ἡρώων τέκνα πήματα.* *Prov.*—"The children of heroes are so many nuisances." So our old proverb, "Many a good cow hath but a bad calf."

'Ανὴρ *ὁ φεύγων καὶ πάλιν μαχήσεται.*—"The man who flies shall fight again." This line is generally thought to have been made by or for Demosthenes, as his best defence for running away and leaving his shield behind him at the battle of Chæronea. The famous lines of Sir John Mennes, in the *Deliciæ Musarum*, are no doubt derived from this,—

> "He that fights and runs away
> May live to fight another day."

Ανθρακες *ὁ θησαυρός.* *Prov.*—"The treasure turns out coals." The words of a disappointed man. See *Thesaurus*, &c.

Ανθρωπος *ἀνθρώπῳ δαιμόνιον.*—"Man is to man a god." That is, to those whom he assists. In the exercise of benevolence we approach nearest to the Deity. See *Homo homini*, &c.

Ανθρωπος *οὐκ ἔχων εἰπεῖν ὄνομα πάππου, ἀλλ' οὐδὲ πατρὸς, ὡς φάσι.* SYNESIUS.—"A man who is not able so much as to tell the name of his grandsire, or of his father even, as the saying is."

'Ανοος *ὁ μακρός.* *Prov.*—"A tall man is a fool." Aristotle (*in Physiogn.*) confirms this dictum. We may be certain, therefore, that *he* was not a tall man.

'Αξία *ἡ κύων τοῦ βρώματος.* SUID.—"The dog is worthy of its food." So our proverb, "'Tis an ill dog that deserves not a crust."

Απασα *δὲ χθὼν ἀνδρὶ γενναίῳ πατρίς.* *Prov.*—"To the brave man every land is a native country." He is a citizen of the world. See *Omne solum*, &c.

Απαντα *τοῖς καλοῖσιν ἀνδράσιν πρέπει.*—"Everything is becoming to the noble." See *Omnia bonos*, &c.

Απληστος *πίθος.* *Prov.*—"A cask that will never fill." An endless task. This saying, quoted by Lucian, is an allusion to the pierced vessel of the Danaides.

Απορία *ψαλτοῦ βήξ.* *Prov.*—"The musician slurs his mistake with a cough."

Ἀργυράγχην πάσχει. PLUT.—"He has got the silver quinsy." A satirical expression applied to the excuses made by Demosthenes, whose silence in a certain cause was supposed to have been purchased, and who alleged a quinsy as the pretext for not pleading: the word is formed in imitation of κυνάγχη, "a quinsy."

Ἄριστον μὲν ὕδωρ. PINDAR.—"Water is the best of all things." A motto for tee-totallers.

Ἀρχὰ πολιτείας ἁπάσης νέων τροφά.—"The foundation of every state is its education of its youth." A saying of Diogenes, quoted by Stobæus.

Ἀρχὴ ἄνδρα δείκνυται.—"Rule shows the man." A saying attributed to Bias, Solon, Pittacus, and others. See *Magistratus*, &c.

——Ἀρχὴ ἥμισυ παντός. HESIOD.—"The beginning is half of the whole." "Well begun is half done." See *Dimidium facti*, &c.

Αὐτὸ δὲ τὸ σιγᾶν ὁμολογοῦντος ἐστί σου. EURIP.—"Your silence is as good as consent." "Silence gives consent."

Ἀφοβία μεγίστη τὸ φοβεῖσθαι τοὺς νόμους. SYNES.—"It is the greatest security from fear to fear the laws."

Ἀφορᾷν οὖν δεῖ εἰς τὸν νοῦν, καὶ μὴ εἰς τὴν ὄψιν.—"We must look to the mind, and not to the outward appearance." The words of Æsop to his master.

B.

Βάρος τι καὶ τὸ δ' ἐστιν, αἰνεῖσθαι λίαν. *Prov.*—"It is a sort of encumbrance to be praised overmuch."

Βριάρευς φαίνεται, ὢν λαγώς. *Prov.*—"He appears to be a Briareus when he is but a hare." Said of a cowardly vapourer.

Βροτοῖς ἅπασι κατθανεῖν ὀφείλεται. EURIPIDES.—"To die is a debt due by all mortals."

Βροτοῖς ἅπασιν ἡ συνείδησις θεός. MENANDER.—"Conscience to all mortals is a god."

Βρῶμα θεῶν.—"Food for the gods." Nero said this of mushrooms, because it was by their agency that his mother, Agrippina, killed his predecessor, the Emperor Claudius.

Γ.

Γαμεῖν ὁ μέλλων εἰς μετάνοιαν ἔρχεται. *Prov.*—"He who is about to marry is on the road to repentance."

Γάμος γὰρ ἀνθρώποισιν εὐκταῖον κακόν.—"Wedlock is an ill which men eagerly embrace." A fragment from an ancient poet.

Γέλως ἄκαιρος ἐν βροτοῖς δεινὸν κακόν.—"Ill-timed laughter in men is a sad evil." A fragment from an ancient poet.

Γέροντα τὸν νοῦν σάρκα δ' ἡβῶσαν φέρει. ÆSCHYLUS.—"He has an aged mind in a youthful body."

Γέρων ἀλώπηξ οὐχ ἁλίσκεται πάγῃ,
Γέρων δὲ καὶ μῦς οὐχ ἁλίσκεται πάγῃ. *Prov.*
—"An old fox is not to be caught with a springe, nor is an old mouse to be taken with a trap."

Γῆν ὁρῶ.—"I see land." A nautical expression, but used by Diogenes when just coming to the end of a voluminous and wearisome book, in which he had found himself "quite at sea."

Γηράσκω δ' ἀεὶ πολλὰ διδασκόμενος.—"The older I grow, the more I learn." A saying of Solon the Athenian. "We live and learn."

Γλαῦκας εἰς Ἀθήνας. *Prov.*—"Owls to Athens." Similar to our proverb, "To carry coals to Newcastle;"—owls being numerous in the vicinity of Athens.

Γλῶσσα διπλῆ.—"A double tongue."

Γνῶθι σεαυτόν.—"Know thyself." This precept was inscribed in gold letters over the portico of the Temple at Delphi. It has been ascribed to Pythagoras, Chilo, Thales, Cleobulus, Bias, and Socrates. It has also been ascribed to Phemonoë, a mythical Greek poetess of the ante-Homeric period. Juvenal says, *Sat.* xi. ver. 27, that this precept descended from heaven:—

——*E cœlo descendit* γνῶθι σεαυτόν.

Γυναικὶ μὴ πίστευε, μήδ' ἂν ἀποθάνῃ.—"Believe not a woman, though she be at the point of death." Or, "Trust not a woman even when she is dead," in allusion to the step-mother whose corpse fell upon her step-son and killed him. See *Erasmus*, Chil. ii. Cent. x. 21.

Γυνὴ τὸ συνολόν ἐστι δαπανηρὸν φύσει. *Prov.*—"Woman, take her all in all, is extravagant by nature."

Δ.

Δεῖ ἀμέλλητον εἶναι τὴν πρὸς τὰ καλὰ ὁρμην. LUCIAN.—"There must be no procrastination in an honourable enterprise." A precept of Nigrinus, the Platonic philosopher. See *Αἰεὶ δ' ἀμβολιεργός*, &c.

Δίδου μοι τὴν σήμερον, καὶ λάμβανε τὴν αὔριον.—"Give me to-day, and take to-morrow." A current proverb, censured by Chrysostom.

Δὶς κράμβη θάνατος.—"Cabbage, twice over, is death." A proverb quoted by a Scholiast on Juvenal, upon the line, "*Occidit miseros crambe repetita magistros.*" It would appear by this that the Greeks did not set the same value upon cabbage as the elder Cato and Pliny the Naturalist did, who gave it the very highest rank among vegetables.

Δὶς πρὸς τὸν αὐτὸν αἰσχρὸν προσκρούειν λίθον.—"It is disgraceful to stumble twice against the same stone."

Δοκεῖ δέ μοι χαλεπώτερον εἶναι εὑρεῖν ἄνδρα τ' ἀγαθὰ καλῶς φέροντα, ἢ

τὰ κακά. XENOPHON.—"I look upon it as more difficult to find a man who bears prosperity well than one who bears misfortune well."

Δός τι, καὶ λάβε τι. *Prov.*—"Give and take."

Δός που στῶ καὶ τὴν γῆν κινήσω.—"Give me where to stand, and I will move the earth." The proud boast of the mathematician Archimedes, in reference to his discovery of the mechanical power of the lever.

Δρυὸς πεσούσης πᾶς ἀνὴρ ξυλεύεται. MEN.—"When an oak falls, every one gathers wood."

Δῶρα πείθειν καὶ θεοὺς λόγος. EURIP.—"Gifts persuade even the gods, as the proverb says."

Δῶρα θεοὺς πείθει, δῶρ' αἰδοίους βασιλῆας.—"Gifts prevail upon the gods, gifts prevail upon venerated kings."

E.

Ἐγγύα, πάρεστι δ' ἄτη.—"Be surety, and evil is at hand." A saying attributed to Chilo the Lacedæmonian, or, according to Ausonius, to the philosopher Thales. See *Sponde*, &c.

Ἐγὼ γὰρ εἰμὶ τῶν ἐμῶν ἐμος μόνος. APOLLOD.—"For I am the only one of my friends that I can rely upon." So Terence says, "*Nam ego meorum solus sum meus.*"

Εγὼ δὲ νομίζω τὸ μὲν μηδενὸς δεῖσθαι θεῖον εἶναι, τὸ δὲ ὡς ἐλαχίστων ἐγγυτάτον τοῦ θείου.—"To want nothing I consider divine, and the less a man wants the nearer does he approach divinity." The words of Socrates as quoted by Xenophon.

Ἐγὼ δὲ ᾤμην τὴν παιδιὰν ἄνεσιν τε εἶναι τῆς ψυχῆς, καὶ ἀνάπαυσιν τῶν φροντίδων. *The Emperor* JULIAN.—"I considered play to be a holiday to the mind, a relaxation from thought."

Εἰ γάρ κεν καὶ σμικρὸν ἐπὶ σμικρῷ καταθεῖο,
Καὶ θάμα τοῦτ' ἔρδοις, τάχα κεν μέγα καὶ τὸ γένοιτο. HESIOD.
—"For if you add little to little, and do so repeatedly, it will very quickly become much." So our old proverb, "Many a little makes a mickle."

Εἰ δὲ θεὸν ἀνήρ τις ἔλπεται λαθέμεν
Ἐρδων, ἁμαρτάνει. PINDAR.
—"If any man hopes that his deeds will be hidden from God, he deceives himself."

Εἴ κε πάθοι τά κ' ἔρεξε δίκη ἰθεῖα γένοιτο. Quoted by Aristotle.—"It is nothing but strict justice if a man suffers from his own deeds."

Εἰ μὲν γὰρ πλουτῇς πόλλοι φίλοι, ἢν δὲ πένηαι
Παῦροι, κ' οὐκεθ' ὁμῶς αὐτὸς ἀνὴρ ἀγαθός. THEOGNIS.
—"If you are rich you will have many friends; but if you are poor you will have but few, and will no longer be the good man you were before."

Εἴ τι ἀγαθὸν θέλεις, παρὰ σεαυτοῦ λάβε. ARRIAN.—"If you wish for any blessing, look for it to yourself." Like the Latin, *Nec te quæsiveris extra.*

Εἷς ἀνὴρ, οὐδεὶς ἀνήρ. *Prov.*—"One man is no man." We enjoy life by the help and society of others.

Εἰς τὸ πῦρ ἐκ τοῦ καπνοῦ. LUCIAN.—"Out of the smoke into the fire." Or, as we say, "Out of the frying-pan," &c.

Ἐκ παντὸς ξύλου κίων ἂν γένηται. *Prov.*—"A pillar may be made of any wood." Ordinary talents will serve for ordinary employments.

Ἐκ τοῦ ὁρᾶν γίγνεται τὸ ἐρᾶν. *Prov.*—"From seeing comes loving;" or, to preserve the jingle, "From seeing comes sighing." A play on the resemblance of the words ὁρᾶν and ἐρᾶν.

Ἐκ τοῦ φοβεροῦ κατ' ὀλίγον ὑπονοστεῖ πρὸς τὸ εὐκαταφρόνητον. LONGINUS.—"Little by little we recede from the terrible to the contemptible." To this, probably through the writings of Tom Paine, Napoleon would seem to have been indebted for his celebrated saying, "Du sublime au ridicule il n'y a qu'un pas." (There is but one step from the sublime to the ridiculous.)

Ἐκ τῶν γὰρ αἰσχρῶν λημμάτων τοὺς πλείονας
Ἀτωμένους ἴδοις ἂν ἢ σεσωσμένους. SOPHOCLES.
—"You will see more ruined than saved by money ill gotten." See Μὴ κακά, &c.

Ἐκ τῶν ὀνύχων τὸν λέοντα γινώσκειν. *Prov.*—"To judge of the lion from his claws." To form a conception of anything great from seeing only a small portion of it. See *Ex ungue leonem.*

Ἕκαστος διὰ τὰ πράγματα σεμνός ἐστι καὶ ταπεινός. APOLLOD.—"Every man is arrogant or humble, according to his fortunes."

Ἐλέφας μῦν οὐχ ἁλίσκει. *Prov.*—"The elephant does not catch mice." See *Aquila non capit,* &c., and Ὁ Ἰνδός, &c.

Ἐλπίδες ἐν ζώοισιν, ἀνέλπιστοι δὲ θανόντες.—"While there is life there is hope, when we are dead there is none."

Ἐμοῦ θανόντος γαῖα μιχθήτω πυρί.—"When I am dead, may earth be mingled with fire." This line, from one of the Greek tragedians, was quoted before Nero, who immediately added, "Immo, ἐμοῦ ζῶντος," "Aye, and while I am living, too." The sentiment is similar to "*Après moi le deluge,*" a saying which has been often attributed to Prince Metternich, but of which the real author was Madame de Pompadour. See *Notes and Queries,* vol. iii. p. 299, 397.

Ἐμποδίζει τὸν λόγον ὁ φόβος. DEMADES.—"Fear is a check upon speech."

Ἐν ἀμούσοις καὶ κόρυδος φθέγγεται. *Prov.*—"With those who know no melody the sparrow even is musical." The *Corydus* was a lark with a very inferior note, found near Athens.

Ἐν ἐλπίσιν χρὴ τοὺς σοφοὺς ἔχειν βίον. EURIPIDES.—"The wise should possess their lives in hope." See *Nil desperandum,* &c.

'Εν νύκτι βουλή. *Prov.*—"In the night there is counsel." Similar to our saying, "I will sleep upon it." The French have it *La nuit porte conseil.* See *In nocte*, &c., Οὐ χρὴ, &c.

'Εν οἴνῳ ἀλήθεια. *Prov.*—"In wine there is truth." See *In vino veritas.*

Εν ὄλβῳ ὄλβια πάντα. THEOCR.—"With a fortunate man all things are fortunate."

'Εν ὄρφνῃ δραπέτης μέγα σθένει. EURIP.—"When it is dark, the coward is very valiant."

'Εν πενθοῦσι γελᾷν. *Prov.*—"To laugh among those who weep."

'Εν τῷ φρονεῖν γὰρ μηδὲν, ἥδιστος βίος. SOPHOCL.—"To know nothing is the happiest life." "Fools and children lead merry lives," says the old proverb.

Ένεστι κἀν μύρμηκι κἀν σέρφῳ χολή. *Prov.*—"The ant and the worm even have their wrath." See *Habet et*, &c.

Έννους τὰ καινὰ τοῖς πάλαι τεκμαίρεται. SOPHOCL.—"A wise man gathers from the past what is to come."

Εξω βελῶν καθῆσθαι.—"To keep out of shot," i. e., out of danger.

'Επαίρεται γὰρ μεῖζον, ἵνα μεῖζον πέσῃ. MENANDER.—"He is raised the higher that he may fall the heavier." Or, as Shakspeare says, "Raised up on high to be hurled down below." See *Celsæ graviore*, &c.

Επὶ σαυτῷ τὴν σελήνην καθέλκεις. *Prov.*—"You are drawing down the moon upon yourself." Of similar meaning to our saying, "You are making a rod for your own back."

Έρδοι τις, ἣν ἕκαστος εἰδείη τεχνήν. *Prov.*—"Let each betake himself to the pursuit which he understands." See *Ne sutor*, &c.

'Ες Τροίαν πειρώμεναι ἦλθον 'Αχαιοί. THEOC.—"By trying, the Greeks got to Troy." See *Conando*, &c. (App.)

Έτερόν τι ἐστὶ τῷ νῷ θεωρεῖν, καὶ τοῖς τοῦ σώματος ἀπατηλοῖς ὄμμασιν. EUNAPIUS.—"It is one thing to perceive with the mind, and another to see with the eyes of the body, so apt to deceive."

Εὐδαίμων ὁ μηδὲν ὀφείλων. *Prov.*—"Happy is he who owes nothing." "Out of debt out of danger."

Εὕδοντι κύρτος αἱρεῖ. *Prov.*—"The net of the sleeper catches fish." God's blessings come unseen.

Εὕρηκα.—"I have found it." The exclamation of Archimedes the philosopher, when he discovered the means of ascertaining the purity of the golden crown made for King Hiero, from the space which it should occupy in water. It is sometimes used in an ironical sense.

Εὕρηκα ὃ οὐκ ἐζήτουν.—"I have found what I did not seek." I have got more than I bargained for.

Εὐτυχία πολύφιλος. *Prov.*—"Success has many friends."

Εχει τε γὰρ ὄλβιος οὐ μείονα φθόνον. PINDAR.—"The successful man is attended with no small envy."

Ἐχθρὸς γάρ μοι κεῖνος ὁμῶς Ἀΐδαο πύλῃσιν,
Ὅς χ' ἕτερον μὲν κεύθῃ ἐνὶ φρεσίν, ἄλλο δὲ βάζῃ. HOMER.
—"Hateful to me as the gates of hell is he who conceals one thing in his mind, and utters another."

Ἐχθρῶν ἄδωρα δῶρα κοὐκ ὀνήσιμα. SOPH.—"The gifts of enemies are not gifts, and are worthless."

Z.

Ζεῖ χύτρα, ζῇ φιλία.—"The pot boils, and friendship thrives." See *Fervet olla*, &c.

Ζεῦ βασιλεῦ, τὰ μὲν ἐσθλὰ καὶ εὐχομένοις καὶ ἀνεύκτοις
Ἄμμι δίδου· τὰ δὲ δεινὰ καὶ εὐχομένοις ἀπαλέξοις.
—"Father Jove, grant us good, whether we pray for it or not; and avert from us evil, even though we pray for it." A prayer, by an unknown poet, highly commended by Plato.
"Unask'd, what good thou knowest, grant,
What ill, though ask'd, deny." POPE'S *Universal Prayer*.

Ζηλωτὸς, ὅστις ηὐτύχησεν εἰς τέκνα. EURIP.—"The man is to be envied who has been fortunate with his children."

Ζωὴ καὶ ψυχή.—"My life and soul." Words of endearment, mentioned by Juvenal and Martial as used by the courtesans and demireps of imperial Rome.

Ζῶμεν οὐχ ὡς θέλομεν, ἀλλ' ὡς δυνάμεθα.—"We live, not as we would but as we can."

H.

Ἡ γλῶσσ' ὀμώμοχ', ἡ δὲ φρὴν ἀνώμοτος. EURIP.—"My tongue has sworn, but my mind is unsworn." The words of Medea.

Ἢ ἥκιστα, ἢ ἥδιστα.—"As little as possible, or as pleasant as possible." Said by Æsop to Solon of the language necessary to be used by courtiers.

Ἡ σοφίας πήγη διὰ βιβλίων ῥέει.—"The fountain of wisdom flows through books."

Ἢ τὰν ἢ ἐπὶ τάν.—"Either this or upon this." The words of a Spartan mother on presenting her son with a shield, enjoining him either to bring it back from battle or to be brought home, slain, upon it.

Ἥδιστον ἄκουσμα ἔπαινος. XENOPHON.—"The sweetest of all sounds is praise."

Ἧλιξ ἥλικα τέρπει.—"Like pleases like." A proverb quoted by Pliny and Aristotle. See Ὅμοιοι, &c.

Θ.

Θάνατος ἀπροφάσιστος. EURIP.—"Death will hear of no excuse."

Θεὸς ἐκ μηχανῆς. LUCIAN.—"A god from the clouds." See *Deus ex machinâ.* (App.)

Θεὸς ἡ ἀναίδεια. *Prov.*—"Impudence is a goddess."

Θεῷ δουλεύειν οὐκ ἐλευθερίας μόνον, ἀλλὰ καὶ βασιλείας ἄμεινον. PHILO JUDÆUS.—"To serve God is better, not only than liberty, but even than a kingdom." It has been remarked that these words are very similar to those in the Book of Common Prayer, in the collect for Peace,—"Whose service is perfect freedom."

I.

Ἰατρὲ, θεράπευσον σεαυτόν.—"Physician, heal thyself." See *Luke* iv. 23.

Ἴδμεν ψεύδεα πολλὰ λέγειν ἐτύμοισιν ὁμοῖα,
Ἴδμεν δ', εὖτ' ἐθέλωμεν, ἀληθέα μυθήσασθαι. HESIOD.
—"We know how to utter many fictions similar to truths, and we know, when we choose, how to convey the truth in fables."

Ἱερὸν ἡ συμβουλή ἐστιν.—"Counsel is a divine thing."

Ἰλιὰς κακῶν. *Prov.*—"An Iliad of woes."

Ἵππῳ γηράσκοντι τὰ μείονα κύκλ' ἐπίβαλλε.—"Impose lighter tasks on the aged courser." See *Solve senescentem,* &c.

Ἰχθὺς ἐκ τῆς κεφαλῆς ὄζειν ἄρχεται. *Prov.*—"Fish begins to stink at the head." The corruption of a state is first discernible in the higher classes.

K.

Καδμεία νίκη.—"A Cadmæan victory." A victory in which the conqueror suffered as much as the conquered.

Καὶ γὰρ καὶ μέλιτος τὸ πλέον ἐστὶ χολή.—"For even honey in excess becomes gall." See Πᾶν γὰρ, &c.

Καί ἐστι καὶ ὁ ἄρχων πολέως μέρος, καὶ οἱ ἀρχόμενοι παραπλησίως. MAX. TYRIUS.—"The ruler is as much a part of the state as those who are ruled." He must equally obey the laws.

Καὶ πτωχὸς πτωχῷ φθονέει. HESIOD.—"Even a beggar is envied by a beggar." "'Tis one beggar's woe to see another by the door go." "Two of a trade," &c.

——**Καιροῖο λαβώμεθα, ὃν προσιόντα**
Ἔστιν ἑλεῖν, ζητεῖν δὲ παραθρέξαντα, μάταιον. GREG. NAZ.
—"Let us seize opportunity; for as it comes we may catch it, but when it has passed 'tis vain to seek it."

Καιρὸν γνῶθι.—"Know your opportunity." A saying of Pittacus, one of the Seven Wise Men of Greece.

Καιρῷ λατρεύειν, μηδ' ἀντιπνέειν ἀνέμοισι. *Prov.*—"To go with the times, and not to blow against the winds."

Κακὰ *κέρδεα ἶσ' ἄτῃσι.* HESIOD.—"Evil gains are as bad as a loss." "Ill-gotten goods seldom prosper." See *Μὴ κακά*, &c.

Κακοῖς *ὁμιλῶν, κ' αὐτὸς ἐκβήσῃ κακός.* MENANDER.—"If you associate with the wicked, you will become wicked yourself." See *Φθείρουσιν ἤθη*, &c.

Κακοῦ *κόρακος κακὸν ᾠόν. Prov.*—"Bad crow, bad egg." See *Mala gallina*, &c., *Nec imbellem*, &c.

Καλῶς *ἀκούειν μᾶλλον ἢ πλουτεῖν θέλε.* MENANDER.—"Wish rather to be well spoken of than to be rich."

Κάμηλος *καὶ ψωριῶσα πολλῶν ὄνων ἀνατίθεται φορτία. Prov.*—"The camel, even when mangy, bears the burdens of many asses."

Κατ' *ἐξοχήν.*—"Pre-eminently," or, as the French say, *Par excellence.*

Κατατήκει *ὁ χρόνος, καὶ γηράσκει πάντα.* ARISTOTLE.—"Time wears away, and everything grows old."

Κατόπιν *ἑορτῆς ἥκεις.*—"You are come after the feast."

Κλαίει *ὁ νικήσας ὁ δὲ νικηθεὶς ἀπόλωλεν.*—"The conqueror mourns, but the conquered is undone." See *Flet victus*, &c., *Καδμεία νίκη.*

Κοινὰ *πάθη πάντων· ὁ βίος τρόχος, ἄστατος ὄλβος.* PHOCYLIDES.—"Misfortunes are common to all; life is a wheel, and prosperity unstable."

Κοινὰ *τὰ τῶν φίλων. Prov.*—"The goods of friends are in common." A saying attributed to Pythagoras.

Κούφη *γῆ τοῦτον καλύπτοι.*—"May the earth be light upon him." A common epitaph with the Greeks. See *Sit tibi terra*, &c.

Κρεῖσσον, *ἄριστον ἐόντα κακὸν γένος, ἠὲ κάκιστον*
Ἔμμεναι εὐγενέτην. GREG. NAZ.
—"It is better to be the best of a low family, than the worst of a noble one."

Κρεῖσσον *τοι σοφίη καὶ μεγάλης ἀρετῆς.* THEOGNIS.—"Wisdom is better even than great valour."

Κρείττων *ἡ πρόνοια τῆς μεταμελείας.* DION. HALIC.—"Precaution is better than repentance."

Κρῆτες *ἀεὶ ψεῦσται, κακὰ θηρία, γαστέρες ἀργαί.*—"The Cretans are always liars, evil beasts, slow bellies." An hexameter line quoted by St. Paul in his *Epistle to Titus*, i. 12, from "a prophet" of the Cretans, supposed to have been the poet Epimenides.

Κῦδος.—"Glory," or "applause." "Kudos" has almost become a dictionary word in our language.

Κυμινοπρίστης.—"A splitter of cummin." A stingy miserable "skinflint" was thus called by the Athenians; and the word is used in a similar sense by Theocritus and Athenæus. The name "*cymini sector*," was however applied by the Romans to a person nicely scrupulous, and the Emperor Antoninus Pius was thus called for his diligence in inquiring into the merits of the causes that came before him. Lord Bacon gives the name "*cymini sectores*" to learned triflers.

——Κύνος ὄμματ' ἔχων. HOMER.—"Having the eyes of a dog," i. e. an impudent face.

Κύριε ἐλέησον.—"Lord, have mercy upon us." See *Kyrie eleison.*

Λ.

Λαγὼς καθεύδων.—"A sleeping hare." One who sleeps with his eyes open. Like our saying, "Catch a weasel asleep."

Λαμπάδια ἔχοντες διαδώσουσιν ἀλλήλοις. PLATO.—"Those who have lamps will pass them to others."

Λάμπις ἐρωτηθεὶς πῶς ἐκτήσατο τὸν πλοῦτον, οὐ χαλεπῶς, ἔφη, τον μέγαν, τὸν δὲ βραχὺν ἐπιπόνως καὶ βραδέως. PLUTARCH.—"Lampis being asked how he had made his money, replied, '*Much* without difficulty, but a *little* slowly and laboriously.'"

Λάῳ μὴ πίστευε, πολύτροπός ἐστιν ὅμιλος.—"Trust not the populace, the multitude is versatile."

Λίθος κυλινδόμενος τὸ φῦκος οὐ ποιεῖ. *Prov.*—"A rolling stone gathers no moss."

Λίμος δὲ πολλῶν γίγνεται διδάσκαλος. *Prov.*—"Hunger is the teacher of many." See *Magister artis*, &c.

——Λοιδορεῖσθαι δ' οὐ πρέπει
Ἄνδρας ποιητάς, ὥσπερ ἀρτοπώλιδας. ARISTOPHANES.
—"It does not become poets to abuse one another, like old wives who sell cakes."

Λύχνου ἀρθέντος, γυνὴ πᾶσα ἡ αὐτή. *Prov.*—"When the light is out every woman is alike." Like the French "*La nuit tous les chats sont gris.*"

M.

Μάντις δ' ἄριστος ὅστις εἰκάζει καλῶς.—"He is the best prophet who makes the best guesses."

Μέγα βιβλίον μέγα κακόν. CALLIM.—"A great book is a great evil."

Μεγάλη πόλις μεγάλη ἐρημία. *Prov.*—"A great city is a great solitude." To those who have no friends in it. The sentiment is finely expanded by Byron (*Childe Harold*, c. ii. st. 26).

Μεγάλην παράκαιρος ἡδονὴ τίκτει βλάβην·
Ἐξ ἡδονῆς γὰρ φύεται τὸ δυστυχεῖν. MENANDER.
—"Ill-timed pleasure produces great evil; for misfortune springs from pleasure."

Μετὰ πόλεμον ἡ συμμαχία. *Prov.*—"After the war, aid." Similar to our proverb, "After death, the doctor."

Μέτρον ἄριστον.—"Moderation is best." A saying of the philosopher Cleobulus.

Μέτρῳ ὕδωρ πίνοντες, ἀμέτρως μάζαν ἔδοντες. *Prov.*—"They drink their water by measure, but eat their cake without." Said of people who are "penny-wise and pound-foolish."

Μὴ εἰς τὴν αὔριον ἀναβάλλου· ἡ γὰρ αὔριον οὐδέ ποτε λαμβάνει τέλος. ST. CHRYSOSTOM.—"Put not off till to-morrow; for to-morrow admits no fulfilment." As we say, "To-morrow never comes."

Μὴ ἐπιλαθώμεθα τῆς ζάλης ἐν τῇ γαλήνῃ, μηδὲ τῆς ἀῤῥωστίας ἐν τῷ καιρῷ τῆς ὑγιείας. GREG. NAZ.—"Let us not forget the tempest in the calm, or sickness in the moments of health."

Μὴ γένοιτο.—"God forbid." *Rom.* iii. 31, *atque alibi.*

Μὴ κακὰ κερδαίνειν· κακὰ κέρδεα ἶσ' ἄτῃσιν. HESIOD.—"Make not evil gains; evil gains are equal to a loss." See Ἐκ τῶν, &c.

Μὴ κίνει Καμαρίναν.—"Do not disturb Camarina." An injunction of Apollo respecting a pestiferous marsh. "Let sleeping dogs lie."

Μὴ κίνει κακὸν εὖ κείμενον. *Prov.*—"Disturb not an evil that is well placed."

Μὴ παιδὶ μάχαιραν. *Prov.*—"Do not give a sword to a child."

Μὴ πῦρ ἐπὶ πῦρ. *Prov.*—"Add not fire to fire."

Μή τι καινόν;—"Any news?" See *Acts* xvii. 21.

Μηδὲν ἄγαν.—"Not too much of anything." A saying ascribed by Pliny the Elder and Clemens Alexandrinus to Chilon the Lacedæmonian; but by other authorities to Solon, to Thales, and to Stratodemus of Tegea. See *Ne quid nimis.*

Μηδὲν ἄγαν· καιρῷ πάντα πρόσεστι καλά.—"Not too much of anything; everything is good at the proper time." An ancient inscription by Sodanius the son of Eperatus.

Μῆνιν ἄειδε, θεά, Πηληϊάδεω Ἀχιλῆος
Οὐλομένην, ἣ μυρί' Ἀχαιοῖς ἄλγε' ἔθηκε. HOMER.
—"Sing, O goddess, the destructive wrath of Achilles, Peleus' son, which wrought for the Greeks innumerable woes." The beginning of Homer's Iliad.

Μήτηρ τῆς ἐνδείας ἡ ἀεργία. IGNATIUS.—"Idleness is the mother of want."

Μία γάρ ἐστι πρὸς τύχην ἀσφάλεια, τὸ μὴ τοσαυτάκις αὐτὴν πειρᾶσαι.—"One way of making sure against fortune is not to try her too often." A saying of Diocles of Carystus, quoted by Seneca.

Μία χελιδὼν ἔαρ οὐ ποιεῖ. *Prov.*—"One swallow does not make the spring."

Μιᾶς γὰρ χειρὸς ἀσθενὴς μάχη. EURIP.—"The battle is weak that is waged with one hand." "Two to one is odds."

Μικρὰ πρόφασίς ἐστι τοῦ πρᾶξαι κακῶς.—"A slight pretence suffices for doing evil."

Μικρὸν κακὸν, μέγα ἀγαθόν. *Prov.*—"A small evil is a great good."

Μισῶ σοφιστὴν ὅστις οὐκ αὑτῷ σοφός.—"I hate the wise man who is not wise for himself."

Μόνος ὁ σοφὸς ἐλεύθερος, καὶ πᾶς ἄφρων δοῦλος.—"The wise man alone is free; every fool is a slave." A maxim of the Stoics, quoted by Cicero.

N.

Ναυηγοὺς οἴκτειρον, ἐπεὶ πλόος ἐστὶν ἄδηλος. PHOCYLID.—"Pity the shipwrecked sailor, for a life at sea is full of uncertainty."

Νεκρὸν ἰατρεύειν καὶ γέροντα νουθετεῖν ταὐτόν. *Prov.*—"You might as well physic the dead as advise an old man."

Νέος ἔμπειρος οὐκ ἐστί· πλῆθος γὰρ χρόνου ποιήσει τὴν ἐμπειρίαν. ARISTOTLE.—"Youth has no experience; for it is length of years that gives experience."

Νήπιος ὃς τὰ ἕτοιμα λιπὼν τ' ἀνέτοιμα διώκει. HESIOD.—"He is a fool who leaves a certainty to pursue an uncertainty."

Ξ.

Ξενίων δέ τε θύμος ἄριστος. *Prov.*—"In hospitality it is the spirit that is the chief thing." "Welcome is the best cheer."

Ξύλον ἀγκύλον οὐδέποτ' ὀρθόν. *Prov.*—"Wood that grows warped never can be straightened."

Ξὺν τῷ δικαίῳ γὰρ μέγ' ἔξεστι φρονεῖν. SOPHOCLES.—"In a just cause we may assume confidence."

Ξυρεῖν ἐπιχειρεῖν λέοντα. PLATO.—"To attempt to shave a lion." A task not to be lightly undertaken.

O.

Ὁ ἄνθρωπος εὐεργετὸς πεφυκώς. ANTONINUS.—"Man is born to do good."

Ὁ βίος ἀνθρώποις λογισμοῦ καὶ ἀριθμοῦ δεῖται πάνυ. EPICHARMUS.—"The life of man stands much in need of calculation and number."

Ὁ γὰρ διαιτητὴς τὸ ἐπιεικὲς ὁρᾷ, ὁ δὲ δικαστὴς τὸν νόμον. ARISTOTLE.—"The arbitrator looks to equity, the judge to law."

Ὁ γὰρ θεος βλέπει σε, πλησίον παρών,
Ὃς τοῖς δικαίοις ἥδεται, κ' οὐ τἀδίκοις. MENANDER.
—"For God beholds thee, being near at hand, who is pleased with just deeds, and not with unjust."

Ὁ δ' ὄλβος οὐ βέβαιος, ἀλλ' ἐφήμερος. EURIPIDES.—"Happiness is not lasting, but only for a day."

Ο ἐλαχίστων δεόμενος ἔγγιστα θεῶν.—"He who wants the least is nearest the gods." A saying of Socrates, quoted by Xenophon. See Ἐγὼ δὲ νομίζω, &c.

Ο Ἰνδὸς ἐλέφας τὴν μυῖαν οὐκ ἀλεγίζει. PHALARIS.—"The Indian elephant heedeth not the fly."

Ὁ πᾶς πρέπει ἐννέπειν τὰ δίκαια χρόνος. SOPHOCL.—"Any time is the proper one for saying what is just."

Ο σοφὸς ἐν αὑτῷ περιφέρει τὴν οὐσίαν. MENANDER.—"The wise man carries with him his wealth." See the Fable of "Simonides preserved by the gods." *Phædrus.* b. v. f. 21. See *Omnia mea*, &c.

Ο σοφὸς οὐδὲν πράττει τοῦ εὐδοκιμεῖν χάριν.—"The wise man does nothing for the purpose of being well thought of." He practises virtue for its own sake.

Ο φεύγων μύλον ἄλφιτα φεύγει. *Prov.*—"He who shuns the mill-stone shuns the meal." "No mill no meal." See *Qui vitat molam*, &c.

Ο χοῖρος ἥδεται κόπροις καὶ βορβόρῳ.—"The swine delights in dung and filth." A line quoted by Clemens Alexandrinus.

Οἱ αὐτοὶ περὶ τῶν αὐτῶν τοῖς αὐτοῖς τὰ αὐτά.—"The same persons saying the same things to the same persons, about the same things." A proverbial saying quoted by Grangæus, a commentator on Juvenal, illustrative of the drudgery of the pedagogue. Observe the declension of αὐτὸς, in the Nominative, Genitive, Dative, and Accusative cases. See Δὶς κράμβη, &c.

Οἱ γὰρ κακοί, κακίους ἐπαινούμενοι. PHILOSTRATUS.—"The bad, when praised, become still worse."

Οἱ γὰρ πνέοντες μεγάλα, τοὺς κρείσσους λόγους
Πικρῶς φέρουσι τῶν ἐλασσόνων ὕπο. EURIPID.
—"Those who have high notions dislike a better reason given by an inferior."

Οἱ γὰρ πολλοὶ μᾶλλον ὀρέγονται τοῦ κέρδους, ἢ τῆς τιμῆς. ARISTOTLE.—"The multitude are more desirous of gain than of honour."

Οἱ διψῶντες σιωπῇ πίνουσι. *Prov.*—"Those who are thirsty drink in silence." People who are in earnest make few professions.

Οἱ πλείονες κακοί.—"Most people are bad." A saying of Bias the philosopher, one of the Seven Wise Men of Greece.

Οἱ πολλοί.—"The many." The multitude.

Οἵη δὴ φύλλων γενεὴ τοιήδε καὶ ἀνδρῶν. HOMER.—"The generations of men are as leaves."

Οἴκοι λέοντες, ἐν μάχῃ δ' ἀλώπεκες. ARISTOPH.—"Lions at home, but foxes in battle."

Οἴνου κατιόντος ἐπιπλέουσιν ἔπη. HERODOT.—"When the wine sinks, the words swim." *Fecundi calices quem non fecēre disertum?* HOR.

——Οἷοι νῦν βροτοί εἰσι. HOMER.—"Such as men are now-a-days."

Οἷος ὁ βίος, τοῖος ὁ λόγος. *Prov.*—"As the life is, so will be the language." Like the Scotch proverb, "What can you have from a hog but a grunt?" "Out of the abundance of the heart," &c.

Ὄμμα γὰρ
Δόμων νομίζω δεσπότου παρουσίαν. ÆSCHYLUS.
—"For I take the presence of the master to be the eye of the house." See Οὐδὲν οὕτω πιαίνει, &c.

Ὅμοιον ὁμοίῳ φίλον. *Prov.*—"Like loves like." Similar to our proverb, "Birds of a feather flock together." See Ἧλιξ, &c.

Ὁμοιότης τῆς φιλότητος μήτηρ. *Prov.*—"Likeness is the mother of love."

Ὃν οἱ θεοὶ φιλοῦσιν ἀποθνήσκει νέος.—"He whom the gods love, dies young." A fragment of Menander. See *Quem di diligunt*, &c.

Ὄνον γένεσθαι κρεῖττον, ἢ τοὺς χείρονας
Ὁρᾷν ἑαυτοῦ ζῶντας ἐπιφανέστερον. MENANDER.
—"Better to be born an ass, than to see worse men than oneself living in a more exalted station."

Ὄνος ἐν πιθήκοις. *Prov.*—"An ass among apes." See *Asinus inter*, &c.

Ὄνου οὐρὰ ἠθμὸν οὐ ποιεῖ. *Prov.*—"An ass's tail will not make a sieve." So our proverb, "You cannot make a silk purse out of a sow's ear."

Ὄνου πόκας ζητεῖς.—"You are seeking wool from an ass."

Ὄνῳ τις ἔλεγε μῦθον· ὁ δὲ τὰ ὦτα ἐκίνει.—"Some one related a fable to an ass, and he—wagged his ears." "Throw not your pearls before swine."

Ὅρα τέλος μακροῦ βίου.—"Regard the end of a long life." The words of Solon to Crœsus. See *Respice finem*.

Ὄρος ὄρει οὐ μίγνυται. *Prov.*—"Mountain will not mingle with mountain." See *Mons cum monte*, &c.

Ὁρῶ γὰρ τῶν ἀνθρώπων οὐδένα ἀναμάρτητον διατελοῦντα. XENOPH.
—"For I find no man always free from faults."

Ὃς δ' ἂν πλεῖστ' ἔχῃ, σοφώτατος. EURIP.—"He that possesses the most is the wisest."

Ὅς τε πολὺ γλυκίων μέλιτος καταλειβομένοιο. HOMER.—"Sweeter it is by far than flowing honey." Said of the so-called pleasures of revenge.

Ὅταν γὰρ ἐξ ἁπάντων συνεισφέρηται, ἑκάστῳ κοῦφον γίνεται τὸ ἐπίταγμα. ST. CHRYSOSTOM.—"When all contribute, the proportion of each is lightly borne."

Ὅταν δὲ δαίμων ἀνδρὶ πορσύνῃ κακά,
Τὸν νοῦν ἔβλαψε πρῶτον.——
—"When a divinity would bring ruin on a man, he first deprives him of his senses." A fragment of Euripides, quoted by Athenagoras. See *At dæmon*, &c., *Quem Jupiter*, &c., and *Quos Deus*, &c.

Οὐ γὰρ ἂν γένοιτο φρόνημα εὐγενὲς ἐν ἀνδράσιν ἀπορουμένοις τῶν καθ' ἡμέραν ἀναγκαίων. DION. HALICARN.—"No generous thoughts can suggest themselves to men in want of the daily necessaries of life." See *Ab inopiâ*, &c. (App.)

Οὐ γαρ ἄν ποτε τρέφειν δύναιτ' ἂν μία λόχμη κλέπτας δύω. ARISTOPH.—"One thicket could never find support for two thieves."

Οὐ γάρ ἐστι πικρῶς ἐξετάσαι τί πέπρακται τοῖς ἄλλοις, ἂν μὴ παρ' ὑμῶν αὐτῶν πρῶτον ὑπάρξῃ τὰ δέοντα. DEMOSTH.—"You must not severely scrutinize the actions of others, unless you have first done your duty yourselves."

Οὐ γάρ πώ τις ἑὸν γόνον αὐτὸς ἀνέγνω. HOMER.—"For no man yet living has been certain of his own offspring." Somewhat similar to our proverb, "'Tis a wise child that knows his own father."

Οὐ γὰρ τὰ ὀνόματα πίστις τῶν πραγμάτων ἐστί, τὰ δὲ πράγματα καὶ τῶν ὀνομάτων. DIO CHRYSOST.—"It is not names that gain credit for things, but things for names."

Οὐ γνῶσις ἀλλὰ πρᾶξις.—"Not theory but practice."

Οὐ λέγειν δεινός, ἀλλὰ σιγᾶν ἀδύνατος. EPICHARMUS.—"Not clever at speaking, but unable to hold his tongue."

Οὐ λόγων δεῖται 'Ελλὰς ἀλλ' ἔργων.—"Greece stands in need, not of words, but deeds."

Οὐδὲ 'Ηρακλῆς πρὸς δύο. *Prov.*—"Not even Hercules against two." See *Ne Hercules*, &c.

Οὐ παντὸς ἀνδρὸς εἰς Κόρινθον ἔσθ' ὁ πλοῦς.—"It is not every man's lot to make a voyage to Corinth." See *Non cuivis homini*, &c.

Οὐ φιλεῖ συγγίνεσθαι φαντασία τε καὶ ἀλήθεια. SYNES.—"Appearances and reality do not always agree."

Οὐ χρὴ παννύχιον εὕδειν βουληφόρον ἄνδρα. HOMER.—"A man in authority must not pass all the night in sleep."

Οὐδ' εἴ μοι δέκα μὲν γλῶσσαι δέκα δὲ στόματ' εἶεν. HOMER.—"Not if I had ten tongues and ten mouths."

Οὐδ' ἔτι μιν παῖδες ποτὶ γούνασι παππάζουσιν. HOMER.—"No more do his children cling to his knees and call him father." See *Gray's Elegy in a Country Churchyard*, St. 6.

———Οὐδὲ γὰρ ὁ Ζεὺς
Οὔθ' ὕων πάντας ἁνδάνει οὔτ' ἀνέχων. THEOGN.
—"For not even Jove can please all, whether he rains or whether he lets it alone."

Οὐδεὶς δίχα ἀπωλείας καὶ ζημίας κακός ἐστι. EPICTETUS.—"No one is wicked without loss and punishment." The punishment at least of an evil conscience. See *Prima et*, &c.

Οὐδεὶς ἐπλούτησε ταχέως δίκαιος ὤν. MENANDER.—"No just man ever became rich all at once."

Οὐδὲν γὰρ τοῦ πάσχειν εὑρετικώτερον. GREG. NAZIANZEN.—"For there is nothing more inventive than suffering.' "Necessity is the mother of invention."

Οὐδὲν οὕτω πιαίνει τὸν ἵππον ὡς βασιλέως ὀφθαλμός. PLUTARCH.—"Nothing fattens the horse so much as the master's eye."

Οὐδὲν πρὸς ἔπος.—"Nothing to do with the subject." See *Nihil ad versum.*

Οὐκ ἂν γένοιτο χωρὶς ἐσθλὰ καὶ κακὰ,
  'Αλλ' ἔστι τις σύγκρασις, ὥστ' ἔχειν καλῶς.
—"There cannot be good without evil, but there is a mixture, in order that things may go well." A quotation from Euripides by Plutarch. See *Nemo est,* &c.

Οὐκ ἂν πριαίμην τοῦτο τετρημένον χαλκοῦ.—"I would not buy it for a brass farthing with a hole in it." An expression of contempt.

Οὐκ ὠνοῦμαι μυρίων δραχμῶν μεταμέλειαν.—"I shall not buy repentance at the price of ten thousand drachmæ." The answer of Demosthenes to the extravagant demands of Lais, the courtesan, for her favours.

Οὔποτε ποιήσεις τὸν καρκίνον ὀρθὰ βαδίζειν. ARISTOPH.—"You can never bring a crab to walk straight." "What is bred in the bone will never be out of the flesh."

Οὔτε πάντα, οὔτε πάντῃ, οὔτε παρὰ πάντων. *Prov.*—"Neither every thing, nor every where, nor from every body." In taking, as well as giving, consider your motives on every occasion. See *Quid de quoque,* &c.

Οὗτός ἐστι γαλεώτης γέρων. MENANDER.—"A shrewd old fox this!"

Οὕτως, οὐ πάντεσσι θεὸς χαρίεντα δίδωσιν
  'Ανδράσιν.———— HOMER.
—"God does not bestow good gifts on all persons." See *Non omnia,* &c.

Οὕτω χρὴ ποιεῖν, ὅπως ἕκαστός τις ἑαυτῷ ξυνείσεται τῆς νίκης αἰτιώτατος ὤν. XENOPH.—"We must so exert ourselves that each may consider himself as the chief contributor to the victory."

————Οὐχ εὕδει Διὸς
'Οφθαλμός· ἐγγὺς δ' ἐστι καὶ παρὼν πόνῳ.
—"The eye of God sleeps not: whatever we do, he is present and at hand." A fragment quoted by Stobæus.

Οχλος ἀσταθμητότατον πρᾶγμα τῶν ἁπάντων καὶ ἀσυνετώτατον. DEMOSTHENES.—"The multitude is the most unstable of all things and the most destitute of sense." See *Mobilium,* &c.

Οψὲ θεῶν ἀλέουσι μύλοι, ἀλέουσι δὲ λεπτά. *Prov.*—"The mill of the gods grinds late, but it grinds fine." Severe retribution will overtake us at last.

Π.

Παθήματα μαθήματα.—"Sufferings are lessons." So the Latin, *nocumenta documenta:* and our proverb, "Bought wit is the best." See Τὰ δέ μοι, &c.

Παθὼν δέ τε νήπιος ἔγνω. HESIOD.—"Even the fool knows from

experience." Like our proverb, "Experience is the mistress of fools."

Πᾶν γὰρ τὸ πολὺ πολέμιον τῇ φύσει. HIPPOCRATES.—"Everything in excess is adverse to nature." See Καὶ γὰρ, &c., and *Ne quid nimis.*

Πᾶν τὸ σκληρὸν χαλεπῶς μαλάττεται. PLUTARCH.—"Everything that has once hardened receives impressions with difficulty." Said with reference to youthful minds. See *Udum*, &c.

Πάντα ἀναῤῥίπτειν κύβον. *Prov.*—"To hazard every throw."

Πάντα λίθον κίνει.—"Turn every stone."

Πάντα μὲν καθαρὰ τοῖς καθαροῖς. *Tit.* i. 15.—"To the pure all things are pure."

Πάντας γ' ἐφέλκων, οἷα μαγνήτης λίθος. *Prov.*—"Attracting all, like a loadstone."

Πάντων δὲ μάλιστ' αἰσχύνεο σαυτόν.—"But most of all respect thyself." A precept from the Golden Verses of the Pythagoreans.

Oft-times nothing profits more
Than self-esteem, grounded on just and right
Well managed. MILTON.

Παραμυθίαν φέρει τὸ κοινωνοὺς εἶναι τῶν συμφορῶν. DIO CHRYSOSTOM.—"To have partners in misfortune is some comfort." See *Haud ignara*, &c., and *Solamen miseris*, &c.

Πᾶς ἐστὶ νόμος εὕρημα μὲν καὶ δῶρον θεῶν. DEMOSTH.—"Every law is a gift and invention of the gods."

Πᾶσιν γὰρ εὖ φρονοῦσι συμμαχεῖ τύχη.—"Good fortune ever fights on the side of prudence." Fragment of an ancient Greek poet. See *Audentes fortuna*, &c.

Πειθὼ μὲν γὰρ ὄνειαρ, ἔρις δ' ἔριν ἀντιφυτεύει. PHOCYLIDES.—"Conciliation is profitable, but strife begets strife."

Πένης τὴν γυναῖκα πλουσίαν λαβὼν, ἔχει δέσποιναν, οὐ γυναῖκ' ἔτι.—"A poor man who takes a rich wife has a ruler, not a wife." The words of Alexandrides, as quoted by Stobæus.

Πειρῶ τύχης ἄγνοιαν εὐχερῶς φέρειν. *Prov.*—"Endeavour to bear the ignorance of fortune with patience."

Πῆμα κακὸς γείτων, ὅσσον τ' ἀγαθὸς μέγ' ὄνειαρ. HESIOD.—"A bad neighbour is as great an evil as a good one is a blessing."

Πίστει χρήματ' ὄλεσσα, ἀπιστίῃ δ' ἐσάωσα. THEOGN.—"By trusting I lost money, and by distrusting I saved it."

Πλάνη βίον τίθησι σωφρονέστερον. *Prov.*—"Travelling renders life more modest." Those who have travelled are less likely to be conceited than those who have never left their own country. "Home-keeping youth hath ever homely wits." SHAKSPEARE.

Πλούτῳ δ' ἀρετὴ καὶ κῦδος ὀπηδεῖ. HESIOD.—"Virtue and glory attend upon wealth." See *Et genus*, &c.

Πλοῦτος ὁ τῆς ψυχῆς πλοῦτος μόνος ἐστὶν ἀληθής.—"The wealth of the mind is the only true wealth."

Πολλὰ μεταξὺ πέλει κύλικος καὶ χείλεος ἄκρου. *Prov.*—"Many things happen between the cup and the lip," or, as we say, "There's many a slip between the cup and the lip." See *Multa cadunt*, &c.

Πολλαὶ μὲν θνητοῖς γλῶτται, μία δ' ἀθανάτοισιν.—"The inhabitants of earth have many tongues, those of heaven but one." A translation of *Multæ terricolis*, &c., which see.

Πολλάκι καὶ ξύμπασα πόλις κακοῦ ἀνδρὸς ἐπαυρεῖ. Hesiod.—"Full oft does a whole city suffer from one bad man."

Πολλάκι καὶ κηπωρὸς ἀνὴρ μάλα καίριον εἶπεν.—"Full oft has even a labouring man spoken very much to the purpose." Otherwise read, Πολλάκι τοι καὶ μωρὸς ἀνὴρ κατακαίριον εἶπε, "Often has a fool spoken to the purpose."

Πολλὰς ἂν εὕροις μηχανάς, γυνὴ γὰρ εἶ. Eurip.—"You can discover many a contrivance, for you are a woman."

Πολλάκις δοκεῖ τὸ φυλάξαι τἀγαθὰ τοῦ κτήσασθαι χαλεπώτερον εἶναι. Demosthenes.—"It often seems more difficult to preserve a blessing than to obtain it."

Πολλάκις, ὦ Πολύφαμε, τὰ μὴ καλὰ καλὰ πέφανται. Theocritus.—"Often, O Polyphemus, does that which is not fair appear fair (in the eyes of love)." See *Decipit frons*, &c.

——Amatorem quod amicæ
Turpia decipiunt cæcum vitia, aut etiam ipsa hæc
Delectant; veluti Balbinum polypus Hagnæ. Hor.

Πολλοὶ δὲ πολλοὺς ηὔξησαν ἤδη καὶ ἰδιώτας καὶ πόλεις, ὑφ' ὧν αὐξηθέντων τὰ μέγιστα κακὰ ἔπαθον. Xenophon.—"Many a one before now has been the making of both persons and cities, from whom, when they have waxed strong, he has received the greatest of injuries."

Πολλοὶ θριοβόλοι, παῦροι δέ τε μάντιες ἄνδρες.—"There are many soothsayers, but few prophets."

Πολλοὶ μαθηταὶ κρείττονες διδασκάλων.—"Many scholars are better than their teachers." Quoted by Cicero from an unknown poet.

Πολλοὶ τραπέζης, οὐκ ἀληθείας, φίλοι. *Prov.*—"Many are friends of the table, not of truth."

Πολλῷ τοι πλέονας λιμοῦ κόρος ὤλεσεν ἄνδρας. Theognis.—"Satiety has killed far more than famine." See *Plures crapula*, &c.

Πολλῶν ἡ γλῶττα προτρέχει τῆς διανοίας. Isocr.—"In many the tongue outruns the discretion."

Πολιὰ χρόνου μήνυτις, οὐ φρονήσεως. *Prov.*—"White hairs are a proof of age, not of wisdom."

Πολλῶν ἰατρῶν εἴσοδός μ' ἀπώλεσεν. *Prov.*—"The visits of many physicians have destroyed me." An Epitaph.

Πομφόλυξ ὁ ἄνθρωπος. *Prov.*—"Man is a bubble."

Προμηθεύς ἐστι μετὰ τὰ πράγματα.—"He is quite a Prometheus, after the matter is over." Said of a person who is for shutting the door when the steed is stolen. Cited by Lucian from some comic poet.

Προπέτεια πολλοῖς ἐστὶν αἰτία κακῶν.—"Precipitation is the cause of misfortune to many."

Πρῶτον ἀγαθὸν ἀναμαρτία, δεύτερον δὲ αἰσχύνη. DEMADES.—"The first of all virtues is Innocence, Modesty the second."

Πτωχοῦ πήρα οὐ πίμπλαται.—"The beggar's pouch is never filled.

Πῦρ σιδήρῳ μὴ σκαλεύειν. *Prov.*—"Stir not the fire with a sword." See *Ignem ne*, &c. Do not provoke an angry man; do not make bad worse.

Ρ.

Ῥᾷον βίον ζῇς, ἂν γυναῖκα μὴ τρέφῃς. *Prov.*—"You will pass your life more easily if you have not to maintain a wife."

Ῥᾷστον ἁπάντων ἐστὶν αὑτὸν ἐξαπατῆσαι· ὁ γὰρ βούλεται, τοῦθ' ἕκαστος καὶ οἴεται. DEMOSTH.—"It is the easiest thing in the world for a man to deceive himself, for whatever he wishes, that he thinks." "The wish is father to the thought." *Facilè homines quod volunt, credunt.* CÆS.

Ῥέγχει παρούσης τῆς τύχης τὰ πράγματα. *Prov.*—"Affairs sleep soundly when fortune is present." Akin to our saying, "Get a good name and go to sleep."

Ῥῆμα παρὰ καιρὸν ῥηθὲν ἀνατρέπει βίον. *Prov.*—"A word unseasonably spoken may mar the course of a whole life."

Σ.

Σκηνὴ πᾶς ὁ βίος, καὶ παίγνιον· ἢ μάθε παίζειν,
Τὴν σπουδὴν μεταθείς, ἢ φέρε τὰς ὀδύνας.
"Life is a stage, a play: so learn thy part,
All cares removed, or rend with griefs thy heart."
From the Greek Anthology.

Σκιομαχία.—"A fighting with shadows." Much ado about nothing

Σκληρόν σοι πρὸς κέντρα λακτίζειν.—"It is hard for thee to kick against the pricks." See *Acts* xxvi. 14. This was a current proverb before it was applied by our Lord to St. Paul. It bears reference to the pointed goads with which oxen were driven. See *Si stimulos*, &c.

Σολοικισμός.—"A solecism." This, though a single word, was a proverbial expression among the Athenians. The people of Soli, a city of Cilicia, were originally a colony from Athens, but in process of time lost the Attic purity of speech and became noted for the corruptness of their dialect. Hence a grammatical impropriety came to be called a "Solecism." The story is sometimes told with reference to the people of Soli in Cyprus.

Σοφὴν δὲ μισῶ. Μὴ γὰρ ἔν γ' ἐμοῖς δόμοις
Εἴη φρονοῦσα πλεῖον, ἢ γυναῖκα χρῆν. EURIPIDES.
—"I hate a learned woman. May there be no woman in my house who knows more than a woman ought to know."

Σπεῦδε βραδέως. *Prov.*—The same as *Festina lente;* a favourite saying of Augustus Cæsar.

Στιγμὴ χρόνου πᾶς ὁ βίος ἐστι. Ζῆν καὶ οὐ παραζῆν προσήκει. PLUTARCH.—"The whole of life is but a moment of time. It behoves us then to live and not to miss the object of life."

Στόμα ἔοικε τάφῳ, ὅσα γὰρ ἂν λάβοι τὸ στόμα διαφθείρει καὶ φυλάττει. ARTEMIDORUS.—"The mouth of man is like the tomb, for whatever it receives it destroys and keeps close within."

Στύλος γὰρ οἴκου παῖδές εἰσιν ἄῤῥενες. *Prov.*—"Male children are the pillar of a house."

Συκίνη μάχαιρα. *Prov.*—"A sword made of the fig-tree." A wooden sword. In reference to frivolous arguments, which may easily be refuted.

Σύμβουλος οὐδεὶς ἐστι βελτίων χρόνου. *Prov.*—"There is no better counsellor than time."

Συνειδὸς ἀγαθὸν φιλεῖ παῤῥησιάζεσθαι. PAUSANIAS.—"A good conscience is wont to speak out."

Συντριβῇ προηγεῖται ὕβρις.—"Insolence is a prelude to destruction." A proverb quoted by Gregory Nazianzen. "Pride goeth before a fall."

Σώματα πολλὰ τρέφειν, καὶ δώματα πολλ' ἀνεγείρειν,
Ἀτραπὸς εἰς πενίην ἐστιν ἑτοιμοτάτη.
—"To feed many persons and to build many houses is the readiest way to poverty."

T.

Τὰ δάνεια δούλους τοὺς ἐλευθέρους ποιεῖ. *Prov.*—"Debts turn freemen into slaves."

Τὰ δέ μοι παθήματα, ἐόντα ἄχαριτα, μαθήματα γεγόνε. HERODOT.—"My misfortunes, disagreeable as they were, have proved a lesson to me." The words of Crœsus to Cyrus. See *Παθήματα*, &c.

Τὰ δεινὰ κέρδη πημονὰς ἐργάζεται. SOPHOCLES, *Antig.* 326.—"Ill-gotten gains are productive of evil." Otherwise read, *Τὰ δειλὰ κέρδη*, &c.—"Mean gains," &c. See *Μὴ κακὰ κερδαίνειν*, &c.

Τὰ μεγάλα τῶν πραγμάτων, μεγάλων δεῖται κατασκευῶν. HELIODOR.—"Great undertakings require great preparations."

Τὰ πολλὰ τοῦ πολέμου, γνώμῃ καὶ χρημάτων περιουσίᾳ κρατοῦνται. THUCYD.—"Most things in war depend for success on counsel and abundance of money."

Τὰ σκληρὰ μαλθακῶς λέγειν.—"To say harsh things in soothing language." To use the language of euphemism.

Τὰ χρήματ' ἀνθρώποισι τιμιώτατα,
Δύναμίν τε πλείστην τῶν ἐν ἀνθρώποις ἔχει. EURIPIDES.
—"Wealth is of all things the most esteemed by men, and has the greatest power of all things in the world."

——Τας γὰρ ἐκ
Θεῶν ἀνάγκας, θνητὸν ὄντα δεῖ φέρειν. EURIPIDES.
—"For he who is mortal must put up with the fate imposed by the gods." See "Ακουσον· &c.

Ταυτόματον ἡμῶν καλλίω βουλεύεται. *Prov.*—"Chance (often) contrives better than we ourselves."

Τέλος ὁρᾶν μάκρου βίου.—"To see the end of a long life." The wish of Chilon, one of the Seven Wise Men of Greece.

Τέτταρας δακτύλους θάνατον οἱ πλέοντες ἀπέχουσιν.—"Those who go to sea are only four inches from death." A saying of Anacharsis, the Scythian philosopher.

I nunc et ventis animam committe, dolato
Confisus ligno, digitis à morte remotus
Quatuor, aut septem, si sit latissima tæda. JUV.

Τῇ χειρὶ δεῖ σπείρειν, ἀλλὰ μὴ ὅλῳ τῷ θυλάκῳ. *Prov.*—"We must sow with the hand and not with the whole sack."

Τηλοῦ ναιόντες φίλοι οὐκ εἰσὶ φίλοι. *Prov.*—"Friends who live at a distance are not friends." "Seldom seen, soon forgotten."

——Τὴν γὰρ 'Απόλλων
'Αμφότερον μάντιν τ' ἀγαθὸν καὶ ἄπιστον ἔθηκε. TRYPHIODORUS.
—"For Apollo had made her to be a true prophetess, and yet not to be believed." Said of Cassandra.

Τὴν δὲ μάλιστα γαμεῖν, ἥτις σέθεν ἔγγυθι ναίει. HESIOD.—"Marry a woman who lives near you, in preference to others." One with whose mind you are acquainted.

Τὴν παρεοῦσαν ἄμελγε, τί τὸν φεύγοντα διώκεις. THEOCR.—"Milk the cow that is at hand; why pursue the one that flies?" "A bird in the hand," &c.

Τῆς λανθανούσης μουσικῆς οὐδεὶς λόγος. *Prov.*—"Music not heard is held in no esteem." Suetonius translates it "*Occultæ musicæ nullus est respectus.*" See *Paulum sepultæ*, &c.

Τῆς σῆς λατρείας τὴν ἐμὴν δυσπραξίαν
Σαφῶς ἐπίστασ', οὐκ ἂν ἀλλάξαιμ' ἐγώ. ÆSCHYLUS.
—"Know for certain, that I would not change my sufferings for your servitude." The words of Prometheus to Mercury.

Τῆς φύσεως γραμματεὺς ἦν, τὸν κάλαμον ἀποβρέχων εἰς νοῦν.—"He was the interpreter of nature, dipping his pen in his mind."

Τί γὰρ ἂν μεῖζον τοῦδ' ἐπὶ θνατοῖς
Παθὸς ἐξεύροις,
Ἢ τέκνα θανοντ' ἐσιδέσθαι. EURIPIDES.

—"What greater affliction can you find among mankind, than to look upon one's dead children?"

Τί δὲ καὶ ἔστιν ὅλως τὸ ἀείμνηστον; ὅλον κενόν. ANTONINUS.—"And yet after all what is posthumous fame? Altogether vanity."

"What is the end of fame? Tis but to fill
A certain portion of uncertain paper." BYRON.

Τί κοινὸν κυνὶ καὶ βαλανείῳ.—"What has a dog to do with a bath?"

Τί τυφλῷ καὶ κατόπτρῳ. *Prov.*—"What has a blind man to do with a mirror?" What have people to do with that which they cannot use?

Τὸ ἀργύριόν ἐστιν αἷμα καὶ ψυχὴ βροτοῖς. ANTIPHANES.—"Money is the very blood and life of mortals."

Τὸ γὰρ κακίας ἐλεύθερον, καὶ ὑποφορᾶσθαι κακίαν ἀργότερον. GREG. NAZ.—"He who is free from vice himself is the slower to suspect vice in others."

Τὸ γὰρ σπάνιον τίμιον, τὸ δὲ ὕδωρ εὐωνότατον ἄριστον ὄν, ὡς ἔφη Πίνδαρος. PLATO.—"That which is rare is dear, but water is to be had at the cheapest rate, though it is, as Pindar said, the best of all things."

Τὸ γὰρ τρέφον με, τοῦτ' ἐγὼ κρίνω θεόν. *Prov.*—"That which maintains me I regard as a god."

Τὸ γὰρ ψευδὲς ὄνειδος οὐ περαιτέρω τῆς ἀκοῆς ἀφικνεῖται. ÆSCHINES.—"An undeserved reproach goes no farther than the ears."

Τὸ καλόν.—"What is handsome." The noble and beautiful.

Τὸ ὅλον.—"The whole."

Τὸ μηδὲν εἰκῇ, πανταχοῦ 'στι χρήσιμον. *Prov.*—"The admonition, 'nothing rashly,' is everywhere useful."

Τὸ μὲν ἀληθὲς πικρόν ἐστι καὶ ἀηδὲς τοῖς ἀνοήτοις· τὸ δὲ ψεῦδος γλυκὺ καὶ προσηνές. DIO CHRYSOST.—"The truth is bitter and disagreeable to fools; while falsehood is sweet and soothing."

Τὸ μὲν τελευτῆσαι, πάντων ἡ πεπρωμένη κατέκρινε, τὸ δὲ καλῶς ἀποθανεῖν ἴδιον τοῖς σπουδαίοις. ISOCRATES.—"To die Fate has appointed to all, but to die honourably is peculiar to the good."

Τὸ μὴ πιστεύειν τοῖς πονηροῖς σωφρονέστερον τοῦ προπιστεύσαντας κατηγορεῖν. DION. HALIC.—"It is more prudent not to trust the wicked than to trust them first and then censure them."

Τὸ πρέπον.—"What is becoming, or decorous."

Τό γε λοιδορῆσαι θεοῖς, ἐχθρὰ σοφία. PINDAR.—"To reproach the gods is wisdom misapplied."

Τοῖς δὲ κακῶς ῥέξασι δίκης τέλος οὐχὶ χρονιστόν. ORPHEUS.—"Justice is not long in overtaking those who do ill." See *Rarò antecedentem*, &c.

Τοῖς σίτου ἀποροῦσι σπουδάζονται οἱ ὄροβοι. *Prov.*—"Chick-peas are sought after by those who have no corn."

Τοῖς τοι δικαίοις χὡ βραχὺς νικᾷ μέγαν. SOPH.—"Where the cause is just even the small conquers the great."

Τὸν *δὲ ἀποιχόμενον μνήμῃ τιμᾶτε, μὴ δάκρυσιν.* DIO CHRYSOSTOM.—"Him who is dead and gone, honour with your remembrance, not with your tears."

Τὸν *Κολοφῶνα ἐπέθηκεν.* *Prov.*—"He has put the Colophon to it." The cavalry of the city of Colophon in Asia Minor was so excellent, that it was thought to assure the victory to the side on which it fought. Hence this proverb, according to most authorities, is similar in meaning to our saying, "He has put a clincher to it." But the Scholiast on the Theætetus of Plato gives a different explanation; he says, that in the council of the twelve Ionian cities, Colophon had the casting vote, whence the proverb. In the early periods of printing, before the introduction of title pages, the designation was applied to the final paragraph of a volume, which generally contained the printer's name, date, &c.

Τότε *γὰρ χρή, κἂν ἄδηλον ᾖ τὸ μέλλον, αἱρεῖσθαι κινδυνεύειν, ὅταν τὸ τὴν ἡσύχιαν ἄγειν φανερῶς χεῖρον ᾖ.* ARISTIDES *the Rhetorician.*—"When it is clear that to live in peace is the less desirable course, we must make up our minds to face danger, however uncertain the result may be."

Τοῦ *ἀριστεύειν ἕνεκα.*—"In order to excel." A punning motto attached to the crest of Lord Henniker.

Τοῦ *δ' ἀπὸ γλώσσης μέλιτος γλυκίων ῥέεν αὐδή.* HOMER.—"Words flowed from his tongue sweeter than honey." Said of the eloquence of Nestor.

——**Τοῦ** *γὰρ καὶ γένος ἐσμέν.*—"For we are also his offspring." Quoted by St. Paul in his address to the Athenians, *Acts* xvii. 28, as being the words of "certain of their poets."

Τοῦτ' *ἐν ψυχῇ λόγοι, ὅπερ κάλλος ἐν σώματι.* ARISTIDES *the Rhetorician.*—"Language is to the mind what beauty is to the body."

Τρισκαιδεκαπηχύς.—"A thirteen-cubit-high man." "A long-lubber-gawky," as Polwhele translates it.

Τύραννος *τυράννῳ συγκατεργάζεται.* HERODOT.—"One tyrant helps another." "Fellow-feeling makes us wondrous kind."

Τύχη *δ' ἀρετῆς ἀναίτιος.* SYNES.—"Fortune is not the cause of worth." Worth is independent of fortune.

Τῶν *ἀνθρώπων οἱ πονηροὶ εὐεργετούμενοι μᾶλλον ἀδικεῖν παροξύνονται.* PLANUDES.—"Wicked men, when benefited, are the more encouraged to do wrong."

Τῶν *γὰρ πενήτων εἴσιν οἱ λόγοι κένοι.* *Prov.*—"Poor men's words have little weight."

Τῶν *εὐτυχούντων πάντες εἰσὶ συγγενεῖς.* *Prov.*—"All persons claim relationship with the fortunate."

Τῶν *πονηρῶν σπερμάτων ἄξια τὰ γεώργια.* NICEPHORUS GREGORAS.—"The produce of bad seed is worthy of it." See *Mala gallina*, &c., Κακοῦ κόρακος, &c.

Τῶν *πόνων πωλοῦσιν ἡμὶν πάντ' ἀγαθὰ θεοί.* EPICHARM.—"The gods

sell us all good things for labour." See *Nil sine magno, &c.*
Τῆς δ' ἀρετῆς ἱδρῶτα θεοὶ προπάροιθεν ἔθηκαν.—HESIOD.

Τῶν ὤτων ἔχω τὸν λύκον, οὔτ' ἔχειν, οὔτ' ἀφεῖναι δύναμαι. *Prov.*—"I have got a wolf by the ears, I can neither hold him nor let go." See *Auribus teneo, &c.*

Υ.

Ὕδραν τέμνεις.—"You are wounding a Hydra." A monstrous snake, which, as soon as Hercules cut off one of its eight heads, received two others in its place.

Ὑγίεια καὶ νοῦς ἐσθλὰ τῷ βίῳ δύο. *Prov.*—"Health and understanding are the two great blessings of life."

Ὕπνος τὰ μικρὰ τοῦ θανάτου μυστήρια. *Prov.*—"Sleep is the *lesser mysteries* of death." Sleep is to death what the lesser Eleusinian mysteries were to the greater.

Ὑπὸ παντὶ λίθῳ σκόρπιος εὕδει. *Prov.*—"Beneath every stone a scorpion sleeps." It was commonly used, according to Erasmus, in reference to captious and envious persons, who were ready to find fault with everything said or done to them; sometimes with reference to hidden dangers: *Latet anguis in herbâ.*

Ὕστερον πρότερον.—See *Hysteron proteron.*

Φ.

Φάγωμεν καὶ πίωμεν· αὔριον γὰρ ἀποθνήσκομεν.—"Let us eat and drink, for to-morrow we die." The doctrine of the Epicureans and others who did not believe in the resurrection, as stated by St. Paul, 1 *Cor.* xv. 32.

Φανήσομαί σοι, &c. See Ὤδινεν ὄρος, &c.

Φείδεο τῶν κτεάνων.—"Husband thy resources."

Φήμη γάρ τε κακὴ πέλεται· κούφη μὲν ἀεῖραι
'Ρεῖα μάλ', ἀργαλέη δὲ φέρειν—— HESIOD.
—"There is evil (as well as good) report; it is very light and easy to lift, but very difficult to carry."

Φθείρουσιν ἤθη χρησθ' ὁμιλίαι κακαί. MENAN.—"Evil communications corrupt good manners." Quoted as a precept by St. Paul, 1 *Cor.* xv. 33. See *Corrumpunt bonos, &c.*

Φθονέεσθαι κρέσσον ἐστὶν ἢ οἰκτείρεσθαι. HERODOT.—"It is better to be envied than pitied."

Φίλος με βλάπτων, οὐδὲν ἐχθροῦ διαφέρει. *Prov.*—"A friend who injures me (by injudicious conduct) is not unlike an enemy."

Φοβοῦ τὸ γῆρας, οὐ γὰρ ἔρχεται μόνον. *Prov.*—"Dread old age, for it does not come alone."

Φρέατα ἀντλούμενα βελτίω γίνεται. BASIL.—"Drawn wells have the sweetest water." The intellect is improved by use.

Φρονεῖν γαρ οἱ ταχεῖς, οὐκ ἀσφαλεῖς. SOPHOCLES.—"Those who are quick to decide are unsafe."

Φύεται μὲν ἐκ τῶν τυχόντων πολλάκις τὰ μέγιστα τῶν πραγμάτων. POLYB.—"The greatest events often arise from accidents."

Φυέται ἐκ πολυορκίας ψευδορκία καὶ ἀσέβεια. PHILO JUDÆUS.—"From a habit of taking oaths arise perjury and impiety."

X.

Χαλεπὰ τὰ καλά. *Prov.*—"What is good is difficult." A rebuke addressed by Plato to the Sophists of Athens, who pretended to show to their youthful disciples a short cut or *royal road* to wisdom and learning.

Χαριεντισμὸς πᾶς ἐν σπουδῇ καὶ κακοῖς γινόμενος ἄωρον πρᾶγμα καὶ πολεμιώτατον ἐλέῳ. ISOCRATES.—"All affectation of gracefulness in serious matters or in adversity is altogether unseasonable and most adverse to compassion."

Χάρις ἀμεταμέλητος. THEOPHRASTUS.—"Graciousness knows no repentance." "Good deeds are never ill-bestowed."

Χάρις χάριν τίκτει. SOPHOCL.—"Grace begets grace." So our proverb, "One good turn asks another."

Χεὶρ χεῖρα νίπτει, δάκτυλός τε δάκτυλον. *Prov.*—"Hand washes hand, and finger finger." Men must assist each other.

Χειρῶν δεῖ τῷ πολέμῳ, καὶ οὐκ ὀνομάτων πολλῶν. SYNES.—"We want hands in war, and not many names."

Χελιδὼν ἔαρ οὐ ποιεῖ. ARISTOT.—"One swallow does not make a spring."

Χρήματ' ἀνηρ. PINDAR.—"Money makes the man."

Χρήματα γὰρ ψυχὴ πέλεται δειλοῖσι βροτοῖσι. HESIOD.—"With us wretched mortals money is life."

Χρόνῳ τὰ πάντα γίγνεται καὶ κρίνεται. *Prov.*—"By time everything is done and judged."

Χρυσὸς ὁ ἀφανὴς τύραννος. GREG. NAZ.—"Gold is an unseen tyrant."

Χωρὶς ὑγιείας ἄβιος βίος, βίος ἀβίωτος.—"Without health life is not life, life is lifeless." A saying of Ariphron the Sicyonian.

Ψ.

Ψύχης ἰατρεῖον.—"A repository of medicine for the mind." Said of a library.

Ω.

Ω μὴ εἷς καὶ ὁ αὐτός ἐστιν ἀεὶ τοῦ βίου σκοπὸς, οὗτος εἷς καὶ ὁ αὐτὸς δι' ὅλου τοῦ βίου εἶναι οὐ δύναται. ANTONINUS.—"He who does not keep one and the same object in view through life, cannot be one and the same person throughout life."

Ὡ ὀλίγον οὐχ ἱκανόν, ἀλλὰ τούτῳ γε οὐδὲν ἱκανόν.—"Nothing will content him who is not content with a little." A saying of the philosopher Epicurus, quoted by Ælian.

Ὤδινεν ὄρος, Ζεὺς δ' ἐφοβεῖτο, τὸ δ' ἔτεκεν μῦν.—"The mountain was in labour, and Jove was in dread—but it was delivered of a mouse." Athenæus tells us that these were the words of Tachos, king of Egypt, on first seeing his ally, Agesilaus, who was of diminutive stature. The reply of the Spartan was, Φανήσομαί σοι πότε καὶ λέων. "Some day I shall appear in your eyes a lion." See *Parturiunt montes*, &c.

Ὡς ἡδὺ τὸν σωθέντα μεμνῆσθαι πόνου. EURIPIDES.—"How pleasant it is for him who has been preserved to remember his toil!" *Dulce est meminisse laborum actorum.*

Ὡς μικρὰ τὰ σφάλλοντα, καὶ μί' ἡμέρα
Τὰ μὲν καθεῖλεν ὑψόθεν, τὰ δ' ἦρ' ἄνω. EURIPIDES.
—"How small things overthrow us! even a single day levels what is exalted, and raises aloft what lies low."

Ὡς οὐδὲν ἡ μάθησις, ἂν μὴ νοῦς παρῇ. *Prov.*—"How vain is learning, unless understanding be united with it!"

Ὡς τρὶς κακοδαίμων, ὅστις ὢν πένης γαμεῖ. *Prov.*—"How thrice-wretched is he who marries when he is poor!

Ὥσπερ οἱ ἰατροὶ ἀεὶ τὰ ὄργανα καὶ σιδήρια πρόχειρα ἔχουσι πρὸς τὰ αἰφνίδια τῶν θεραπευμάτων, οὕτω τὰ δόγματα σὺ ἕτοιμα ἔχε. ANTONINUS.—"As surgeons always have their implements and instruments at hand for an operation on an emergency, so do you have your precepts in readiness."

THE END.

LONDON: PRINTED BY WILLIAM CLOWES AND SONS, LIMITED,
STAMFORD STREET AND CHARING CROSS.

INDEX VERBORUM

TO

BOHN'S DICTIONARY

OF

LATIN QUOTATIONS

WITH A SUPPLEMENTARY INDEX TO THE

GREEK QUOTATIONS.

IN WHICH THE QUANTITIES AND ACCENTS ARE MARKED.

LONDON: GEORGE BELL AND SONS, YORK STREET,
COVENT GARDEN.
1891.

INDEX TO THE LATIN QUOTATIONS.

THE Quotations being alphabetically arranged in the volume, it has been thought unnecessary to repeat the initial words in this Index. All the other words, however, or at least those which are most likely to be recollected, are carefully entered.

A.

B.

D.

E.

F.

G.

H.

I.

J.

L.

M.

O.

P.

Q.

S.

T.

U.

V.

Z.

INDEX TO THE GREEK QUOTATIONS.

A.

E.

Z.

H.

Θ.

I.

K.

Λ.

M.

Π.

P.

Σ.

T.

Y.

Φ.

X.

Ψ.

Ω.

LONDON: PRINTED BY WILLIAM CLOWES AND SONS, LIMITED,
STAMFORD STREET AND CHARING CROSS.

CATALOGUE OF

BOHN'S LIBRARIES.

736 *Volumes*, £158 9*s*.

The Publishers are now issuing the Libraries in a NEW AND MORE ATTRACTIVE STYLE OF BINDING. The original bindings endeared to many book-lovers by association will still be kept in stock, but henceforth all orders will be executed in the New binding, unless the contrary is expressly stated.

New Volumes of Standard Works in the various branches of Literature are constantly being added to this Series, which is already unsurpassed in respect to the number, variety, and cheapness of the Works contained in it. The Publishers beg to announce the following Volumes as recently issued or now in preparation:—

Johnson's Lives of the Poets. Edited by Mrs. Napier. 3 Vols. [*See p. 6*

The Works of Flavius Josephus. Whiston's Translation. Revised by Rev. A. R. Shilleto, M.A. With Topographical and Geographical Notes by Colonel Sir C. W. Wilson, K.C.B. 5 volumes. [*See p. 6*

North's Lives of the Norths. Edited by Rev. Dr. Jessopp. 3 vols. [*See p. 7*

Goethe's Faust. Part I. The Original Text, with Hayward's Translation and Notes, carefully revised, with an Introduction and Bibliography, by C. A. Buchheim, Ph.D., Professor of German Language and Literature at King's College London. [*In the Press*

Arthur Young's Tour in Ireland. Edited by A. W. Hutton, Librarian National Liberal Club. [*Preparing*

Ricardo on the Principles of Political Economy and Taxation. Edited with Notes by E. C. K. Gonner, M.A., Lecturer, University College, Liverpool. [*In the press*

Schopenhauer's Essays. Selected and Translated. By E. Belfort Bax. [*In the press*

Edgeworth's Stories for Children. With 8 Illustrations by L. Speed. [*See p. 4*

Racine's Plays. Second and Concluding Volume. Translated by R. B Boswell. [*See p. 7*

Hoffmann's Works. Translated by Lieut.-Colonel Ewing. Vol. II. [*In the press*

Bohn's Handbooks of Games. New enlarged edition. In 2 vols. *See p. 21*

Vol. I.—Table Games, by Major-General Drayson, R.A., R. F. Green, and 'Berkeley.'
II.—Card Games, by Dr. W. Pole, F.R.S., R. F. Green, 'Berkeley, and Baxter Wray.

Bohn's Handbooks of Athletic Sports. [*3 vols. ready.* *See p. 21*

By Hon. and Rev. E. Lyttelton, H. W. Wilberforce, Julian Marshall, Major Spens, Rev. J. A. Arnan Tait, W. T. Linskill, W. B. Woodgate, E. F. Knight, Martin Cobbett, Douglas Adams, Harry Vassall, C. W. Alcock, E. T. Sachs, H. H. Griffin, R. G. Allanson-Winn, Walter Armstrong, H. A. Colmore Dunn, C. Phillipps-Wolley, F. S. Creswell, A. F. Jenkin.

For BOHN'S SELECT LIBRARY, see p. 23.

February, 1891.

BOHN'S LIBRARIES.

STANDARD LIBRARY.

336 *Vols. at 3s. 6d. each, excepting those marked otherwise.* (59*l.* 10*s.* 6*d.*)

ADDISON'S Works. Notes of Bishop Hurd. Short Memoir, Portrait, and 8 Plates of Medals. 6 vols.

This is the most complete edition of Addison's Works issued.

ALFIERI'S Tragedies. In English Verse. With Notes, Arguments, and Introduction, by E. A. Bowring, C.B. 2 vols.

AMERICAN POETRY. — *See Poetry of America.*

BACON'S Moral and Historical Works, including Essays, Apophthegms, Wisdom of the Ancients, New Atlantis, Henry VII., Henry VIII., Elizabeth, Henry Prince of Wales, History of Great Britain, Julius Cæsar, and Augustus Cæsar. With Critical and Biographical Introduction and Notes by J. Devey, M.A. Portrait.

— *See also Philosophical Library.*

BALLADS AND SONGS of the Peasantry of England, from Oral Recitation, private MSS., Broadsides, &c. Edit. by R. Bell.

BEAUMONT AND FLETCHER. Selections. With Notes and Introduction by Leigh Hunt.

BECKMANN (J.) History of Inventions, Discoveries, and Origins. With Portraits of Beckmann and James Watt. 2 vols.

BELL (Robert).—*See Ballads, Chaucer, Green.*

BOSWELL'S Life of Johnson, with the TOUR in the HEBRIDES and JOHNSONIANA. New Edition, with Notes and Appendices, by the Rev. A. Napier, M.A., Trinity College, Cambridge, Vicar of Holkham, Editor of the Cambridge Edition of the 'Theological Works of Barrow.' With Frontispiece to each vol. 6 vols.

BREMER'S (Frederika) Works. Trans. by M. Howitt. Portrait. 4 vols.

BRINK (B. ten). Early English Literature (to Wiclif). By Bernhard ten Brink. Trans. by Prof. H. M. Kennedy.

BROWNE'S (Sir Thomas) Works. Edit. by S. Wilkin, with Dr. Johnson's Life of Browne. Portrait. 3 vols.

BURKE'S Works. 6 vols.

— **Speeches on the Impeachment** of Warren Hastings; and Letters. 2 vols.

— **Life.** By Sir J. Prior. Portrait.

BURNS (Robert). Life of. By J. G. Lockhart, D.C.L. A new and enlarged edition. With Notes and Appendices by W. Scott Douglas. Portrait.

BUTLER'S (Bp.) Analogy of Religion, Natural and Revealed, to the Constitution and Course of Nature; with Two Dissertations on Identity and Virtue, and Fifteen Sermons. With Introductions, Notes, and Memoir. Portrait.

CAMOËN'S Lusiad, or the Discovery of India. An Epic Poem. Trans. from the Portuguese, with Dissertation, Historical Sketch, and Life, by W. J. Mickle. 5th edition.

CARAFAS (The) of Maddaloni. Naples under Spanish Dominion. Trans. from the German of Alfred de Reumont. Portrait of Massaniello.

CARREL. The Counter-Revolution in England for the Re-establishment of Popery under Charles II. and James II., by Armand Carrel; with Fox's History of James II. and Lord Lonsdale's Memoir of James II. Portrait of Carrel.

CARRUTHERS. — *See Pope, in Illustrated Library.*

CARY'S Dante. The Vision of Hell, Purgatory, and Paradise. Trans. by Rev. H. F. Cary, M.A. With Life, Chronological View of his Age, Notes, and Index of Proper Names. Portrait.

This is the authentic edition, containing Mr. Cary's last corrections, with additional notes.

CELLINI (Benvenuto). Memoirs of, by himself. With Notes of G. P. Carpani. Trans. by T. Roscoe. Portrait.

CERVANTES' Galatea. A Pastoral Romance. Trans. by G. W. J. Gyll.

— **Exemplary Novels.** Trans. by W. K. Kelly.

— **Don Quixote de la Mancha.** Motteux's Translation revised. With Lockhart's Life and Notes. 2 vols.

CHAUCER'S Poetical Works. With Poems formerly attributed to him. With a Memoir, Introduction, Notes, and a Glossary, by R. Bell. Improved edition, with Preliminary Essay by Rev. W. W. Skeat, M.A. Portrait. 4 vols.

CLASSIC TALES, containing Rasselas, Vicar of Wakefield, Gulliver's Travels, and The Sentimental Journey.

COLERIDGE'S (S. T.) Friend. A Series of Essays on Morals, Politics, and Religion. Portrait.

— **Aids to Reflection. Confessions** of an Inquiring Spirit; and Essays on Faith and the Common Prayer-book. New Edition, revised.

— **Table-Talk and Omniana.** By T. Ashe, B.A.

— **Lectures on Shakespeare and** other Poets. Edit. by T. Ashe, B.A.

Containing the lectures taken down in 1811-12 by J. P. Collier, and those delivered at Bristol in 1813.

— **Biographia Literaria; or, Biographical** Sketches of my Literary Life and Opinions; with Two Lay Sermons.

— **Miscellanies, Æsthetic and** Literary; to which is added, THE THEORY OF LIFE. Collected and arranged by T. Ashe, B.A.

COMMINES.—*See Philip.*

CONDÈ'S History of the Dominion of the Arabs in Spain. Trans. by Mrs. Foster. Portrait of Abderahmen ben Moavia. 3 vols.

COWPER'S Complete Works, Poems, Correspondence, and Translations. Edit. with Memoir by R. Southey. 45 Engravings. 8 vols.

COXE'S Memoirs of the Duke of Marlborough. With his original Correspondence, from family records at Blenheim. Revised edition. Portraits. 3 vols.

*** An Atlas of the plans of Marlborough's campaigns, 4to. 10s. 6d.

COXE'S History of the House of Austria. From the Foundation of the Monarchy by Rhodolph of Hapsburgh to the Death of Leopold II., 1218-1792. By Archdn. Coxe. With Continuation from the Accession of Francis I. to the Revolution of 1848. 4 Portraits. 4 vols.

CUNNINGHAM'S Lives of the most Eminent British Painters. With Notes and 16 fresh Lives by Mrs. Heaton. 3 vols.

DEFOE'S Novels and Miscellaneous Works. With Prefaces and Notes, including those attributed to Sir W. Scott. Portrait. 7 vols.

DE LOLME'S Constitution of England, in which it is compared both with the Republican form of Government and the other Monarchies of Europe. Edit., with Life and Notes, by J. Macgregor.

DUNLOP'S History of Fiction. New Edition, revised. By Henry Wilson. 2 vols., 5s. each.

EDGEWORTH'S Stories for Children. With 8 Illustrations by L. Speed.

ELZE'S Shakespeare.—*See Shakespeare*

EMERSON'S Works. 3 vols.

Vol. I.—Essays, Lectures, and Poems.

Vol. II.—English Traits, Nature, and Conduct of Life.

Vol. III.—Society and Solitude—Letters and Social Aims—Miscellaneous Papers (hitherto uncollected)—May-Day, &c.

FOSTER'S (John) Life and Correspondence. Edit. by J. E. Ryland. Portrait. 2 vols.

— **Lectures at Broadmead Chapel.** Edit. by J. E. Ryland. 2 vols.

— **Critical Essays contributed to** the 'Eclectic Review.' Edit. by J. E. Ryland. 2 vols.

— **Essays: On Decision of Charac**ter; on a Man's writing Memoirs of Himself; on the epithet Romantic; on the aversion of Men of Taste to Evangelical Religion.

— **Essays on the Evils of Popular** Ignorance, and a Discourse on the Propagation of Christianity in India.

— **Essay on the Improvemen of** Time, with Notes of Sermons and other Pieces.

— **Fosteriana:** selected from periodical papers, edit. by H. G. Bohn.

FOX (Rt. Hon. C. J.)—*See Carrel.*

GIBBON'S Decline and Fall of the Roman Empire. Complete and unabridged, with variorum Notes; including those of Guizot, Wenck, Niebuhr, Hugo, Neander, and others. 7 vols. 2 Maps and Portrait.

GOETHE'S Works. Trans. into English by E. A. Bowring, C.B., Anna Swanwick, Sir Walter Scott, &c. &c. 14 vols.

Vols. I. and II.—Autobiography and Annals. Portrait.

Vol. III.—Faust. Complete.

Vol. IV.—Novels and Tales: containing Elective Affinities, Sorrows of Werther, The German Emigrants, The Good Women, and a Nouvelette.

Vol. V.—Wilhelm Meister's Apprenticeship.

Vol. VI.—Conversations with Eckerman and Soret.

Vol. VII.—Poems and Ballads in the original Metres, including Hermann and Dorothea.

Vol. VIII.—Götz von Berlichingen, Torquato Tasso, Egmont, Iphigenia, Clavigo, Wayward Lover, and Fellow Culprits.

Vol. IX.—Wilhelm Meister's Travels. Complete Edition.

Vol. X.—Tour in Italy. Two Parts. And Second Residence in Rome.

Vol. XI.—Miscellaneous Travels, Letters from Switzerland, Campaign in France, Siege of Mainz, and Rhine Tour.

Vol. XII.—Early and Miscellaneous Letters, including Letters to his Mother, with Biography and Notes.

Vol. XIII.—Correspondence with Zelter.

Vol. XIV.—Reineke Fox, West-Eastern Divan and Achilleid. Translated in original metres by A. Rogers.

—— **Correspondence with Schiller.** 2 vols.—*See Schiller.*

—— **Faust.**—*See Collegiate Series.*

GOLDSMITH'S Works. 5 vols.

Vol. I.—Life, Vicar of Wakefield, Essays, and Letters.

Vol. II.—Poems, Plays, Bee, Cock Lane Ghost.

Vol. III.—The Citizen of the World, Polite Learning in Europe.

Vol. IV.—Biographies, Criticisms, Later Essays.

Vol. V.—Prefaces, Natural History, Letters, Goody Two-Shoes, Index.

GREENE, MARLOWE, and BEN JONSON (Poems of). With Notes and Memoirs by R. Bell.

GREGORY'S (Dr.) The Evidences, Doctrines, and Duties of the Christian Religion.

GRIMM'S Household Tales. With the Original Notes. Trans. by Mrs. A. Hunt. Introduction by Andrew Lang, M.A. 2 vols.

GUIZOT'S History of Representative Government in Europe. Trans. by A. R. Scoble.

—— **English Revolution of 1640.** From the Accession of Charles I. to his Death. Trans. by W. Hazlitt. Portrait.

—— **History of Civilisation.** From the Roman Empire to the French Revolution. Trans. by W. Hazlitt. Portraits. 3 vols.

HALL'S (Rev. Robert) Works and Remains. Memoir by Dr. Gregory and Essay by J. Foster. Portrait.

HAUFF'S Tales. The Caravan—The Sheikh of Alexandria—The Inn in the Spessart. Translated by Prof. S. Mendel.

HAWTHORNE'S Tales. 3 vols.

Vol. I.—Twice-told Tales, and the Snow Image.

Vol. II.—Scarlet Letter, and the House with Seven Gables.

Vol. III.—Transformation, and Blithedale Romance.

HAZLITT'S (W.) Works. 7 vols.

—— **Table-Talk.**

—— **The Literature of the Age of** Elizabeth and Characters of Shakespeare's Plays.

—— **English Poets and English Comic** Writers.

—— **The Plain Speaker.** Opinions on Books, Men, and Things.

—— **Round Table.** Conversations of James Northcote, R.A.; Characteristics.

—— **Sketches and Essays,** and Winterslow.

—— **Spirit of the Age;** or, Contemporary Portraits. New Edition, by W. Carew Hazlitt.

HEINE'S Poems. Translated in the original Metres, with Life by E. A. Bowring, C.B.

—— **Travel-Pictures.** The Tour in the Harz, Norderney, and Book of Ideas, together with the Romantic School. Trans. by F. Storr. With Maps and Appendices.

HOFFMANN'S Works. The Serapion Brethren. Vol. I. Trans. by Lt.-Col. Ewing. [*Vol. II. in the press.*

HOOPER'S (G.) Waterloo: The Downfall of the First Napoleon: a History of the Campaign of 1815. By George Hooper. With Maps and Plans. New Edition, revised.

HUGO'S (Victor) Dramatic Works: Hernani—Ruy Blas—The King's Diversion. Translated by Mrs. Newton Crosland and F. L. Slous.

— **Poems,** chiefly Lyrical. Collected by H. L. Williams.

HUNGARY: its History and Revolution, with Memoir of Kossuth. Portrait.

HUTCHINSON (Colonel). Memoirs of. By his Widow, with her Autobiography, and the Siege of Lathom House. Portrait.

IRVING'S (Washington) Complete Works. 15 vols.

— **Life and Letters.** By his Nephew, Pierre E. Irving. With Index and a Portrait. 2 vols.

JAMES'S (G. P. R.) Life of Richard Cœur de Lion. Portraits of Richard and Philip Augustus. 2 vols.

— **Louis XIV.** Portraits. 2 vols.

JAMESON (Mrs.) Shakespeare's Heroines. Characteristics of Women. By Mrs. Jameson.

JEAN PAUL.—*See Richter.*

JOHNSON'S Lives of the Poets. Edited, with Notes, by Mrs. Alexander Napier. And an Introduction by Professor J. W. Hales, M.A. [illegible] vols.

JONSON (Ben). Poems of.—*See Greene.*

JOSEPHUS (Flavius), The Works of. Whiston's Translation. Revised by Rev. A. R. Shilleto, M.A. With Topographical and Geographical Notes by Colonel Sir C. W. Wilson, K.C.B. 5 vols.

JUNIUS'S Letters. With Woodfall's Notes. An Essay on the Authorship. Facsimiles of Handwriting. 2 vols.

LA FONTAINE'S Fables. In English Verse, with Essay on the Fabulists. By Elizur Wright.

LAMARTINE'S The Girondists, or Personal Memoirs of the Patriots of the French Revolution. Trans. by H. T. Ryde. Portraits of Robespierre, Madame Roland, and Charlotte Corday. 3 vols.

— **The Restoration of Monarchy** in France (a Sequel to The Girondists). 5 Portraits. 4 vols.

— **The French Revolution of 1848.** Portraits.

LAMB'S (Charles) Elia and Eliana. Complete Edition. Portrait.

LAMB'S (Charles) Specimens of English Dramatic Poets of the time of Elizabeth. With Notes and the Extracts from the Garrick Plays.

— **Talfourd's Letters of Charles** Lamb. New Edition, by W. Carew Hazlitt. 2 vols.

LANZI'S History of Painting in Italy, from the Period of the Revival of the Fine Arts to the End of the 18th Century. With Memoir and Portraits. Trans. by T. Roscoe. 3 vols.

LAPPENBERG'S England under the Anglo-Saxon Kings. Trans. by B. Thorpe, F.S.A. 2 vols.

LESSING'S Dramatic Works. Complete. By E. Bell, M.A. With Memoir by H. Zimmern. Portrait. 2 vols.

— **Laokoon, Dramatic Notes, and** Representation of Death by the Ancients. Trans. by E. C. Beasley and Helen Zimmern. Frontispiece.

LOCKE'S Philosophical Works, containing Human Understanding, Controversy with Bishop of Worcester, Malebranche's Opinions, Natural Philosophy, Reading and Study. With Introduction, Analysis, and Notes, by J. A. St. John. Portrait. 2 vols.

— **Life and Letters,** with Extracts from his Common-place Books. By Lord King.

LOCKHART (J. G.)—*See Burns.*

LUTHER'S Table-Talk. Trans. by W. Hazlitt. With Life by A. Chalmers, and LUTHER'S CATECHISM. Portrait after Cranach.

— **Autobiography.**—*See Michelet.*

MACHIAVELLI'S History of Florence, THE PRINCE, Savonarola, Historical Tracts, and Memoir. Portrait.

MARLOWE. Poems of.—*See Greene.*

MARTINEAU'S (Harriet) History of England (including History of the Peace) from 1800-1846. 5 vols.

MENZEL'S History of Germany, from the Earliest Period to the Crimean War. Portraits. 3 vols.

MICHELET'S Autobiography of Luther. Trans. by W. Hazlitt. With Notes.

— **The French Revolution to the** Flight of the King in 1791. Frontispiece.

MIGNET'S The French Revolution, from 1789 to 1814. Portrait of Napoleon.

MILTON'S Prose Works. With Preface, Preliminary Remarks by J. A. St. John, and Index. 5 vols. Portraits.

—— Poetical Works. With 120 Wood Engravings. 2 vols.

MITFORD'S (Miss) Our Village. Sketches of Rural Character and Scenery. 2 Engravings. 2 vols.

MOLIÈRE'S Dramatic Works. In English Prose, by C. H. Wall. With a Life and a Portrait. 3 vols.

'It is not too much to say that we have here probably as good a translation of Molière as can be given.'—*Academy.*

MONTAGU. Letters and Works of Lady Mary Wortley Montagu. Lord Wharncliffe's Third Edition. Edited by W. Moy Thomas. New and revised edition. With steel plates. 2 vols. 5*s.* each.

MONTESQUIEU'S Spirit of Laws. Revised Edition, with D'Alembert's Analysis, Notes, and Memoir. 2 vols.

NEANDER (Dr. A.) History of the Christian Religion and Church. Trans. by J. Torrey. With Short Memoir. 10 vols.

—— Life of Jesus Christ, in its Historical Connexion and Development.

—— The Planting and Training of the Christian Church by the Apostles. With the Antignosticus, or Spirit of Tertullian. Trans. by J. E. Ryland. 2 vols.

—— Lectures on the History of Christian Dogmas. Trans. by J. E. Ryland. 2 vols.

—— Memorials of Christian Life in the Early and Middle Ages; including Light in Dark Places. Trans. by J. E. Ryland.

NORTH'S Lives of the Right Hon. Francis North, Baron Guildford, the Hon. Sir Dudley North, and the Hon. and Rev. Dr. John North. By the Hon. Roger North. Edited by A. Jessopp, D.D. With 3 Portraits. 3 vols. 3*s.* 6*d.* each.

'Lovers of good literature will rejoice at the appearance of a new, handy, and complete edition of so justly famous a book, and will congratulate themselves that it has found so competent and skilful an editor as Dr. Jessopp.'—*Times.*

OCKLEY (S.) History of the Saracens and their Conquests in Syria, Persia, and Egypt. Comprising the Lives of Mohammed and his Successors to the Death of Abdalmelik, the Eleventh Caliph. By Simon Ockley, B.D., Portrait of Mohammed.

PASCAL'S Thoughts. Translated from the Text of M. Auguste Molinier by C. Kegan Paul. 3rd edition.

PERCY'S Reliques of Ancient English Poetry, consisting of Ballads, Songs, and other Pieces of our earlier Poets, with some few of later date. With Essay on Ancient Minstrels, and Glossary. 2 vols.

PHILIP DE COMMINES. Memoirs of. Containing the Histories of Louis XI. and Charles VIII., and Charles the Bold, Duke of Burgundy. With the History of Louis XI., by Jean de Troyes. Translated, with a Life and Notes, by A. R. Scoble. Portraits. 2 vols.

PLUTARCH'S LIVES. Translated, with Notes and Life, by A. Stewart, M.A., late Fellow of Trinity College, Cambridge, and G. Long, M.A. 4 vols.

POETRY OF AMERICA. Selections from One Hundred Poets, from 1776 to 1876. With Introductory Review, and Specimens of Negro Melody, by W. J. Linton. Portrait of W. Whitman.

RACINE'S (Jean) Dramatic Works. A metrical English version, with Biographical notice. By R. Bruce Boswell, M.A. Oxon. 2 vols.

RANKE (L.) History of the Popes, their Church and State, and their Conflicts with Protestantism in the 16th and 17th Centuries. Trans. by E. Foster. Portraits. 3 vols.

—— History of Servia. Trans. by Mrs. Kerr. To which is added, The Slave Provinces of Turkey, by Cyprien Robert.

—— History of the Latin and Teutonic Nations. 1494-1514. Trans. by P. A. Ashworth, translator of Dr. Gneist's 'History of the English Constitution.'

REUMONT (Alfred de). —*See Carafas.*

REYNOLDS' (Sir J.) Literary Works. With Memoir and Remarks by H. W. Beechy. 2 vols.

RICHTER (Jean Paul). Levana, a Treatise on Education; together with the Autobiography, and a short Memoir.

—— Flower, Fruit, and Thorn Pieces, or the Wedded Life, Death, and Marriage of Siebenkaes. Translated by Alex. Ewing. The only complete English translation.

ROSCOE'S (W.) Life of Leo X., with Notes, Historical Documents, and Dissertation on Lucretia Borgia. 3 Portraits. 2 vols.

—— Lorenzo de' Medici, called 'The Magnificent,' with Copyright Notes, Poems, Letters, &c. With Memoir of Roscoe and Portrait of Lorenzo.

RUSSIA, History of, from the earliest Period to the Crimean War. By W. K. Kelly. 3 Portraits. 2 vols.

SCHILLER'S Works. 7 vols.
Vol. I.—History of the Thirty Years' War. Rev. A. J. W. Morrison, M.A. Portrait.
Vol. II.—History of the Revolt in the Netherlands, the Trials of Counts Egmont and Horn, the Siege of Antwerp, and the Disturbance of France preceding the Reign of Henry IV. Translated by Rev. A. J. W. Morrison and L. Dora Schmitz.
Vol. III.—Don Carlos. R. D. Boylan —Mary Stuart. Mellish — Maid of Orleans. Anna Swanwick—Bride of Messina. A. Lodge, M.A. Together with the Use of the Chorus in Tragedy (a short Essay). Engravings.
These Dramas are all translated in metre.
Vol. IV.—Robbers—Fiesco—Love and Intrigue—Demetrius—Ghost Seer—Sport of Divinity.
The Dramas in this volume are in prose.
Vol. V.—Poems. E. A. Bowring, C.B.
Vol. VI.—Essays, Æsthetical and Philosophical, including the Dissertation on the Connexion between the Animal and Spiritual in Man.
Vol. VII. — Wallenstein's Camp. J. Churchill. — Piccolomini and Death of Wallenstein. S. T. Coleridge. —William Tell. Sir Theodore Martin, K.C.B., LL.D.

SCHILLER and GOETHE. Correspondence between, from A.D. 1794-1805. Trans. by L. Dora Schmitz. 2 vols.

SCHLEGEL (F.) Lectures on the Philosophy of Life and the Philosophy of Language. Trans. by A. J. W. Morrison.

— **The History of Literature,** Ancient and Modern.

— **The Philosophy of History.** With Memoir and Portrait. Trans. by J. B. Robertson.

— **Modern History,** with the Lectures entitled Cæsar and Alexander, and The Beginning of our History. Translated by L. Purcell and R. H. Whitelock.

— **Æsthetic and Miscellaneous** Works, containing Letters on Christian Art, Essay on Gothic Architecture, Remarks on the Romance Poetry of the Middle Ages, on Shakspeare, the Limits of the Beautiful, and on the Language and Wisdom of the Indians. By E. J. Millington.

SCHLEGEL (A. W.) Dramatic Art and Literature. By J. Black. With Memoir by Rev. A. J. W. Morrison. Portrait.

SCHUMANN (Robert), His Life and Works. By A. Reissmann. Trans. by A. L. Alger.

— **Early Letters.** Translated by May Herbert. With Preface by Sir G. Grove.

SHAKESPEARE'S Dramatic Art. The History and Character of Shakspeare's Plays. By Dr. H. Ulrici. Trans. by L. Dora Schmitz. 2 vols.

SHAKESPEARE (William). A Literary Biography by Karl Elze, Ph.D., LL.D. Translated by L. Dora Schmitz. 5*s*.

SHERIDAN'S Dramatic Works. With Memoir Portrait (after Reynolds).

SKEAT (Rev. W. W.)—*See Chaucer.*

SISMONDI'S History of the Literature of the South of Europe. Trans. by T. Roscoe. Portraits. 2 vols.

SMITH'S (Adam) Theory of Moral Sentiments; with Essay on the First Formation of Languages, and Critical Memoir by Dugald Stewart.

— *See Economic Library.*

SMYTH'S (Professor) Lectures on Modern History; from the Irruption of the Northern Nations to the close of the American Revolution. 2 vols.

— **Lectures on the French Revolu**tion. With Index. 2 vols.

SOUTHEY.—*See Cowper, Wesley, and (Illustrated Library) Nelson.*

STURM'S Morning Communings with God, or Devotional Meditations for Every Day. Trans. by W. Johnstone, M.A.

SULLY. Memoirs of the Duke of, Prime Minister to Henry the Great. With Notes and Historical Introduction. 4 Portraits. 4 vols.

TAYLOR'S (Bishop Jeremy) Holy Living and Dying, with Prayers, containing the Whole Duty of a Christian and the parts of Devotion fitted to all Occasions. Portrait.

TEN BRINK.—*See Brink.*

THIERRY'S Conquest of England by the Normans; its Causes, and its Consequences in England and the Continent. By W. Hazlitt. With short Memoir. 2 Portraits. 2 vols.

ULRICI (Dr.)—*See Shakespeare.*

VASARI. Lives of the most Eminent Painters, Sculptors, and Architects. By Mrs. J. Foster, with selected Notes. Portrait. 6 vols., Vol. VI. being an additional Volume of Notes by Dr. J. P. Richter.

WERNER'S Templars in Cyprus. Trans. by E. A. M. Lewis.

WESLEY, the Life of, and the Rise and Progress of Methodism. By Robert Southey. Portrait. 5*s*.

WHEATLEY. A Rational Illustration of the Book of Common Prayer, being the Substance of everything Liturgical in all former Ritualist Commentators upon the subject. Frontispiece.

YOUNG (Arthur) Travels in France. Edited by Miss Betham Edwards. With a Portrait.

HISTORICAL LIBRARY.

22 Volumes at 5s. each. (5*l.* 10*s. per set.*)

EVELYN'S Diary and Correspondence, with the Private Correspondence of Charles I. and Sir Edward Nicholas, and between Sir Edward Hyde (Earl of Clarendon) and Sir Richard Browne. Edited from the Original MSS. by W. Bray, F.A.S. 4 vols. 45 Engravings (after Vandyke, Lely, Kneller, and Jamieson, &c.).

N.B.—This edition contains 130 letters from Evelyn and his wife, printed by permission, and contained in no other edition.

PEPYS' Diary and Correspondence. With Life and Notes, by Lord Braybrooke. 4 vols. With Appendix containing additional Letters, an Index, and 31 Engravings (after Vandyke, Sir P. Lely, Holbein, Kneller, &c.).

N.B.—This is a reprint of Lord Braybrooke's fourth and last edition, containing all his latest notes and corrections, the copyright of the publishers.

JESSE'S Memoirs of the Court of England under the Stuarts, including the Protectorate. 3 vols. With Index and 42 Portraits (after Vandyke, Lely, &c.).

—— Memoirs of the Pretenders and their Adherents. 6 Portraits.

NUGENT'S (Lord) Memorials of Hampden, his Party and Times. With Memoir. 12 Portraits (after Vandyke and others).

STRICKLAND'S (Agnes) Lives of the Queens of England from the Norman Conquest. From authentic Documents, public and private. 6 Portraits. 6 vols.

—— Life of Mary Queen of Scots. 2 Portraits. 2 vols.

—— Lives of the Tudor and Stuart Princesses. With 2 Portraits.

PHILOSOPHICAL LIBRARY.

16 *Vols. at* 5*s. each, excepting those marked otherwise.* (3*l.* 14*s. per set.*)

BACON'S Novum Organum and Advancement of Learning. With Notes by J. Devey, M.A.

BAX. A Handbook of the History of Philosophy, for the use of Students. By E. Belfort Bax, Editor of Kant's 'Prolegomena.'

COMTE'S Philosophy of the Sciences. An Exposition of the Principles of the *Cours de Philosophie Positive.* By G. H. Lewes, Author of 'The Life of Goethe.'

DRAPER (Dr. J. W.) A History of the Intellectual Development of Europe. 2 vols.

HEGEL'S Philosophy of History. By J. Sibree, M.A.

KANT'S Critique of Pure Reason. By J. M. D. Meiklejohn.

—— Prolegomena and Metaphysical Foundations of Natural Science, with Biography and Memoir by E. Belfort Bax. Portrait.

LOGIC, or the Science of Inference. A Popular Manual. By J. Devey.

MILLER (Professor). History Philosophically Illustrated, from the Fall of the Roman Empire to the French Revolution. With Memoir. 4 vols. 3*s.* 6*d.* each.

SCHOPENHAUER on the Fourfold Root of the Principle of Sufficient Reason, and on the Will in Nature. Trans. from the German.

—— Essays. Selected and Translated by E. Belfort Bax. [*In the press.*

SPINOZA'S Chief Works. Trans. with Introduction by R. H. M. Elwes. 2 vols.

Vol. I.—Tractatus Theologico-Politicus —Political Treatise.

Vol. II.—Improvement o the Understanding—Ethics—Letters.

THEOLOGICAL LIBRARY.

15 *Vols. at 5s. each (except Chillingworth, 3s. 6d.).* (3*l.* 13*s.* 6*d. per set.*)

BLEEK. Introduction to the Old Testament. By Friedrich Bleek. Trans. under the supervision of Rev. E. Venables, Residentiary Canon of Lincoln. 2 vols.

CHILLINGWORTH'S Religion of Protestants. 3*s.* 6*d.*

EUSEBIUS. Ecclesiastical History of Eusebius Pamphilius, Bishop of Cæsarea. Trans. by Rev. C. F. Cruse, M.A. With Notes, Life, and Chronological Tables.

EVAGRIUS. History of the Church. —*See Theodoret.*

HARDWICK. History of the Articles of Religion; to which is added a Series of Documents from A.D. 1536 to A.D. 1615. Ed. by Rev. F. Proctor.

HENRY'S (Matthew) Exposition of the Book of Psalms. Numerous Woodcuts.

PEARSON (John, D.D.) Exposition of the Creed. Edit. by E. Walford, M.A. With Notes, Analysis, and Indexes.

PHILO-JUDÆUS, Works of. The Contemporary of Josephus. Trans. by C. D. Yonge. 4 vols.

PHILOSTORGIUS. Ecclesiastical History of.—*See Sozomen.*

SOCRATES' Ecclesiastical History. Comprising a History of the Church from Constantine, A.D. 305, to the 38th year of Theodosius II. With Short Account of the Author, and selected Notes.

SOZOMEN'S Ecclesiastical History. A.D. 324-440. With Notes, Prefatory Remarks by Valesius, and Short Memoir. Together with the ECCLESIASTICAL HISTORY OF PHILOSTORGIUS, as epitomised by Photius. Trans. by Rev. E. Walford, M.A. With Notes and brief Life.

THEODORET and EVAGRIUS. Histories of the Church from A.D. 332 to the Death of Theodore of Mopsuestia, A.D. 427; and from A.D. 431 to A.D. 544. With Memoirs.

WIESELER'S (Karl) Chronological Synopsis of the Four Gospels. Trans. by Rev. Canon Venables.

ANTIQUARIAN LIBRARY.

35 *Vols. at 5s. each.* (8*l.* 15*s. per set.*)

ANGLO-SAXON CHRONICLE. —*See Bede.*

ASSER'S Life of Alfred.—*See Six O. E. Chronicles.*

BEDE'S (Venerable) Ecclesiastical History of England. Together with the ANGLO-SAXON CHRONICLE. With Notes, Short Life, Analysis, and Map. Edit. by J. A. Giles, D.C.L.

BOETHIUS'S Consolation of Philosophy. King Alfred's Anglo-Saxon Version of. With an English Translation on opposite pages, Notes, Introduction, and Glossary, by Rev. S. Fox, M.A. To which is added the Anglo-Saxon Version of the METRES OF BOETHIUS, with a free Translation by Martin F. Tupper, D.C.L.

BRAND'S Popular Antiquities of England, Scotland, and Ireland. Illustrating the Origin of our Vulgar and Provincial Customs, Ceremonies, and Superstitions. By Sir Henry Ellis, K.H., F.R.S. Frontispiece. 3 vols.

CHRONICLES of the CRUSADES. Contemporary Narratives of Richard Cœur de Lion, by Richard of Devizes and Geoffrey de Vinsauf; and of the Crusade at Saint Louis, by Lord John de Joinville. With Short Notes. Illuminated Frontispiece from an old MS.

DYER'S (T. F. T.) British Popular Customs, Present and Past. An Account of the various Games and Customs associated with different Days of the Year in the British Isles, arranged according to the Calendar. By the Rev. T. F. Thiselton Dyer, M.A.

EARLY TRAVELS IN PALESTINE. Comprising the Narratives of Arculf, Willibald, Bernard, Sæwulf, Sigurd, Benjamin of Tudela, Sir John Maundeville, De la Brocquière, and Maundrell; all unabridged. With Introduction and Notes by Thomas Wright. Map of Jerusalem.

ELLIS (G.) Specimens of Early English Metrical Romances, relating to Arthur, Merlin, Guy of Warwick, Richard Cœur de Lion, Charlemagne, Roland, &c. &c. With Historical Introduction by J. O. Halliwell, F.R.S. Illuminated Frontispiece from an old MS.

ETHELWERD, Chronicle of.—*See Six O. E. Chronicles.*

FLORENCE OF WORCESTER'S Chronicle, with the Two Continuations: comprising Annals of English History from the Departure of the Romans to the Reign of Edward I. Trans., with Notes, by Thomas Forester, M.A.

GEOFFREY OF MONMOUTH. Chronicle of.—*See Six O. E. Chronicles.*

GESTA ROMANORUM, or Entertaining Moral Stories invented by the Monks. Trans. with Notes by the Rev. Charles Swan. Edit. by W. Hooper, M.A.

GILDAS. Chronicle of.—*See Six O. E. Chronicles.*

GIRALDUS CAMBRENSIS' Historical Works. Containing Topography of Ireland, and History of the Conqnest of Ireland, by Th. Forester, M.A. Itinerary through Wales, and Description of Wales, by Sir R. Colt Hoare.

HENRY OF HUNTINGDON'S History of the English, from the Roman Invasion to the Accession of Henry II.; with the Acts of King Stephen, and the Letter to Walter. By T. Forester, M.A. Frontispiece from an old MS.

INGULPH'S Chronicles of the Abbey of Croyland, with the CONTINUATION by Peter of Blois and others. Trans. with Notes by H. T. Riley, B.A.

KEIGHTLEY'S (Thomas) Fairy Mythology, illustrative of the Romance and Superstition of Various Countries. Frontispiece by Cruikshank.

LEPSIUS'S Letters from Egypt, Ethiopia, and the Peninsula of Sinai; to which are added, Extracts from his Chronology of the Egyptians, with reference to the Exodus of the Israelites. By L. and J. B. Horner. Maps and Coloured View of Mount Barkal.

MALLET'S Northern Antiquities, or an Historical Account of the Manners, Customs, Religions, and Literature of the Ancient Scandinavians. Trans. by Bishop Percy. With Translation of the PROSE EDDA, and Notes by J. A. Blackwell. Also an Abstract of the 'Eyrbyggia Saga' by Sir Walter Scott. With Glossary and Coloured Frontispiece.

MARCO POLO'S Travels; with Notes and Introduction. Edit. by T. Wright.

MATTHEW PARIS'S English History, from 1235 to 1273. By Rev. J. A. Giles, D.C.L. With Frontispiece. 3 vols.—*See also Roger of Wendover.*

MATTHEW OF WESTMINSTER'S Flowers of History, especially such as relate to the affairs of Britain, from the beginning of the World to A.D. 1307. By C. D. Yonge. 2 vols.

NENNIUS. Chronicle of.—*See Six O. E. Chronicles.*

ORDERICUS VITALIS' Ecclesiastical History of England and Normandy. With Notes, Introduction of Guizot, and the Critical Notice of M. Delille, by T. Forester, M.A. To which is added the CHRONICLE OF St. EVROULT. With General and Chronological Indexes. 4 vols.

PAULI'S (Dr. R.) Life of Alfred the Great. To which is appended Alfred's ANGLO-SAXON VERSION OF OROSIUS. With literal Translation interpaged, Notes, and an ANGLO-SAXON GRAMMAR and Glossary, by B. Thorpe. Frontispiece.

RICHARD OF CIRENCESTER. Chronicle of.—*See Six O. E. Chronicles.*

ROGER DE HOVEDEN'S Annals of English History, comprising the History of England and of other Countries of Europe from A.D. 732 to A.D. 1201. With Notes by H. T. Riley, B.A. 2 vols.

ROGER OF WENDOVER'S Flowers of History, comprising the History of England from the Descent of the Saxons to A.D. 1235, formerly ascribed to Matthew Paris. With Notes and Index by J. A. Giles, D.C.L. 2 vols.

SIX OLD ENGLISH CHRONICLES: viz., Asser's Life of Alfred and the Chronicles of Ethelwerd, Gildas, Nennius, Geoffrey of Monmouth, and Richard of Cirencester. Edit., with Notes, by J. A. Giles, D.C.L. Portrait of Alfred.

WILLIAM OF MALMESBURY'S Chronicle of the Kings of England, from the Earliest Period to King Stephen. By Rev. J. Sharpe. With Notes by J. A. Giles, D.C.L. Frontispiece.

YULE-TIDE STORIES. A Collection of Scandinavian and North German Popular Tales and Traditions, from the Swedish, Danish, and German. Edit. by B. Thorpe.

ILLUSTRATED LIBRARY.

80 Vols. at 5s. each, excepting those marked otherwise. (19*l.* 17*s.* 6*d. per set.*)

ALLEN'S (Joseph, R.N.) Battles of the British Navy. Revised edition, with Indexes of Names and Events, and 57 Portraits and Plans. 2 vols.

ANDERSEN'S Danish Fairy Tales. By Caroline Peachey. With Short Life and 120 Wood Engravings.

ARIOSTO'S Orlando Furioso. In English Verse by W. S. Rose. With Notes and Short Memoir. Portrait after Titian, and 24 Steel Engravings. 2 vols.

BECHSTEIN'S Cage and Chamber Birds: their Natural History, Habits, &c. Together with SWEET'S BRITISH WARBLERS. 43 Coloured Plates and Woodcuts.

BONOMI'S Nineveh and its Palaces. The Discoveries of Botta and Layard applied to the Elucidation of Holy Writ. 7 Plates and 294 Woodcuts.

BUTLER'S Hudibras, with Variorum Notes and Biography. Portrait and 28 Illustrations.

CATTERMOLE'S Evenings at Haddon Hall. Romantic Tales of the Olden Times. With 24 Steel Engravings after Cattermole.

CHINA, Pictorial, Descriptive, and Historical, with some account of Ava and the Burmese, Siam, and Anam. Map, and nearly 100 Illustrations.

CRAIK'S (G. L.) Pursuit of Knowledge under Difficulties. Illustrated by Anecdotes and Memoirs. Numerous Woodcut Portraits.

CRUIKSHANK'S Three Courses and a Dessert; comprising three Sets of Tales, West Country, Irish, and Legal; and a Mélange. With 50 Illustrations by Cruikshank.

—— **Punch and Judy.** The Dialogue of the Puppet Show; an Account of its Origin, &c. 24 Illustrations and Coloured Plates by Cruikshank.

DANTE, in English Verse, by I. C. Wright, M.A. With Introduction and Memoir. Portrait and 34 Steel Engravings after Flaxman.

DIDRON'S Christian Iconography; a History of Christian Art in the Middle Ages. By the late A. N. Didron. Trans. by E. J. Millington, and completed, with Additions and Appendices, by Margaret Stokes. 2 vols. With numerous Illustrations.

Vol. I. The History of the Nimbus, the Aureole, and the Glory; Representations of the Persons of the Trinity.

Vol. II. The Trinity; Angels; Devils The Soul; The Christian Scheme. Appendices.

DYER (Dr. T. H.) Pompeii: its Buildings and Antiquities. An Account of the City, with full Description of the Remains and Recent Excavations, and an Itinerary for Visitors. By T. H. Dyer, LL.D. Nearly 300 Wood Engravings, Map, and Plan. 7*s.* 6*d.*

—— **Rome:** History of the City, with Introduction on recent Excavations. 8 Engravings, Frontispiece, and 2 Maps.

GIL BLAS. The Adventures of. From the French of Lesage by Smollett. 24 Engravings after Smirke, and 10 Etchings by Cruikshank. 612 pages. 6*s.*

GRIMM'S Gammer Grethel; or, German Fairy Tales and Popular Stories, containing 42 Fairy Tales. By Edgar Taylor. Numerous Woodcuts after Cruikshank and Ludwig Grimm. 3*s.* 6*d.*

HOLBEIN'S Dance of Death and Bible Cuts. Upwards of 150 Subjects, engraved in facsimile, with Introduction and Descriptions by the late Francis Douce and Dr. Dibdin.

INDIA, Pictorial, Descriptive, and Historical, from the Earliest Times. 100 Engravings on Wood and Map.

JESSE'S Anecdotes of Dogs. With 40 Woodcuts after Harvey, Bewick, and others; and 34 Steel Engravings after Cooper and Landseer.

KING'S (C. W.) Natural History of Precious Stones and Metals. Illustrations. 6*s.*

KRUMMACHER'S Parables. 40 Illustrations.

LODGE'S Portraits of Illustrious Personages of Great Britain, with Biographical and Historical Memoirs. 240 Portraits engraved on Steel, with the respective Biographies unabridged. Complete in 8 vols.

LONGFELLOW'S Poetical Works, including his Translations and Notes. 24 full-page Woodcuts by Birket Foster and others, and a Portrait.

— Without the Illustrations, 3*s*. 6*d*.

— **Prose Works.** With 16 full-page Woodcuts by Birket Foster and others.

LOUDON'S (Mrs.) Entertaining Naturalist. Popular Descriptions, Tales, and Anecdotes, of more than 500 Animals. Numerous Woodcuts.

MARRYAT'S (Capt., R.N.) Masterman Ready; or, the Wreck of the *Pacific*. (Written for Young People.) With 93 Woodcuts. 3*s*. 6*d*.

— **Mission; or, Scenes in Africa.** (Written for Young People.) Illustrated by Gilbert and Dalziel. 3*s*. 6*d*.

— **Pirate and Three Cutters.** (Written for Young People.) With a Memoir. 8 Steel Engravings after Clarkson Stanfield, R.A. 3*s*. 6*d*.

— **Privateersman.** Adventures by Sea and Land One Hundred Years Ago. (Written for Young People.) 8 Steel Engravings. 3*s*. 6*d*.

— **Settlers in Canada.** (Written for Young People.) 10 Engravings by Gilbert and Dalziel. 3*s*. 6*d*.

— **Poor Jack.** (Written for Young People.) With 16 Illustrations after Clarkson Stanfield, R.A. 3*s*. 6*d*.

— **Midshipman Easy.** With 8 full-page Illustrations. Small post 8vo. 3*s*. 6*d*.

— **Peter Simple.** With 8 full-page Illustrations. Small post 8vo. 3*s*. 6*d*.

MAXWELL'S Victories of Wellington and the British Armies. Frontispiece and 4 Portraits.

MICHAEL ANGELO and RAPHAEL, Their Lives and Works. By Duppa and Quatremère de Quincy. Portraits and Engravings, including the Last Judgment, and Cartoons.

MILLER'S History of the Anglo-Saxons, from the Earliest Period to the Norman Conquest. Portrait of Alfred, Map of Saxon Britain, and 12 Steel Engravings.

MUDIE'S History of British Birds. Revised by W. C. L. Martin. 52 Figures of Birds and 7 coloured Plates of Eggs. 2 vols.

NAVAL and MILITARY HEROES of Great Britain; a Record of British Valour on every Day in the year, from William the Conqueror to the Battle of Inkermann. By Major Johns, R.M., and Lieut. P. H. Nicolas, R.M. Indexes. 24 Portraits after Holbein, Reynolds, &c. 6*s*.

NICOLINI'S History of the Jesuits: their Origin, Progress, Doctrines, and Designs. 8 Portraits.

PETRARCH'S Sonnets, Triumphs, and other Poems, in English Verse. With Life by Thomas Campbell. Portrait and 15 Steel Engravings.

PICKERING'S History of the Races of Man, and their Geographical Distribution; with AN ANALYTICAL SYNOPSIS OF THE NATURAL HISTORY OF MAN. By Dr. Hall. Map of the World and 12 coloured Plates.

PICTORIAL HANDBOOK OF Modern Geography on a Popular Plan. Compiled from the best Authorities, English and Foreign, by H. G. Bohn. 150 Woodcuts and 51 coloured Maps.

— Without the Maps, 3*s*. 6*d*.

POPE'S Poetical Works, including Translations. Edit., with Notes, by R. Carruthers. 2 vols.

— **Homer's Iliad,** with Introduction and Notes by Rev. J. S. Watson, M.A. With Flaxman's Designs.

— **Homer's Odyssey,** with the BATTLE OF FROGS AND MICE, Hymns, &c., by other translators including Chapman. Introduction and Notes by J. S. Watson, M.A. With Flaxman's Designs.

— **Life,** including many of his Letters. By R. Carruthers. Numerous Illustrations.

POTTERY AND PORCELAIN, and other objects of Vertu. Comprising an Illustrated Catalogue of the Bernal Collection, with the prices and names of the Possessors. Also an Introductory Lecture on Pottery and Porcelain, and an Engraved List of all Marks and Monograms. By H. G. Bohn. Numerous Woodcuts.

— With coloured Illustrations, 10*s*. 6*d*.

PROUT'S (Father) Reliques. Edited by Rev. F. Mahony. Copyright edition, with the Author's last corrections and additions. 21 Etchings by D. Maclise, R.A. Nearly 600 pages.

RECREATIONS IN SHOOTING. With some Account of the Game found in the British Isles, and Directions for the Management of Dog and Gun. By 'Craven.' 62 Woodcuts and 9 Steel Engravings after A. Cooper, R.A.

RENNIE. Insect Architecture. Revised by Rev. J. G. Wood, M.A. 186 Woodcuts.

ROBINSON CRUSOE. With Memoir of Defoe, 12 Steel Engravings and 74 Woodcuts after Stothard and Harvey.

—— Without the Engravings, 3*s.* 6*d.*

ROME IN THE NINETEENTH CENTURY. An Account in 1817 of the Ruins of the Ancient City, and Monuments of Modern Times. By C. A. Eaton. 34 Steel Engravings. 2 vols.

SHARPE (S.) The History of Egypt, from the Earliest Times till the Conquest by the Arabs, A.D. 640. 2 Maps and upwards of 400 Woodcuts. 2 vols.

SOUTHEY'S Life of Nelson. With Additional Notes, Facsimiles of Nelson's Writing, Portraits, Plans, and 50 Engravings, after Birket Foster, &c.

STARLING'S (Miss) Noble Deeds of Women; or, Examples of Female Courage, Fortitude, and Virtue. With 14 Steel Portraits.

STUART and REVETT'S Antiquities of Athens, and other Monuments of Greece; with Glossary of Terms used in Grecian Architecture. 71 Steel Plates and numerous Woodcuts.

SWEET'S British Warblers. 5*s.*—*See Bechstein.*

TALES OF THE GENII; or, the Delightful Lessons of Horam, the Son of Asmar. Trans. by Sir C. Morrell. Numerous Woodcuts.

TASSO'S Jerusalem Delivered. In English Spenserian Verse, with Life, by J. H. Wiffen. With 8 Engravings and 24 Woodcuts.

WALKER'S Manly Exercises; containing Skating, Riding, Driving, Hunting, Shooting, Sailing, Rowing, Swimming, &c. 44 Engravings and numerous Woodcuts.

WALTON'S Complete Angler, or the Contemplative Man's Recreation, by Izaak Walton and Charles Cotton. With Memoirs and Notes by E. Jesse. Also an Account of Fishing Stations, Tackle, &c., by H. G. Bohn. Portrait and 203 Woodcuts, and 26 Engravings on Steel.

—— **Lives of Donne, Wotton, Hooker,** &c., with Notes. A New Edition, revised by A. H. Bullen, with a Memoir of Izaak Walton by William Dowling. 6 Portraits, 6 Autograph Signatures, &c.

WELLINGTON, Life of. From the Materials of Maxwell. 18 Steel Engravings.

—— **Victories of.**—*See Maxwell.*

WESTROPP (H. M.) A Handbook of Archæology, Egyptian, Greek, Etruscan, Roman. By H. M. Westropp. Numerous Illustrations.

WHITE'S Natural History of Selborne, with Observations on various Parts of Nature, and the Naturalists' Calendar. Sir W. Jardine. Edit., with Notes and Memoir, by E. Jesse. 40 Portraits and coloured Plates.

CLASSICAL LIBRARY.

TRANSLATIONS FROM THE GREEK AND LATIN.

103 *Vols. at* 5*s. each, excepting those marked otherwise.* (25*l.* 4*s.* 6*d. per set.*)

ACHILLES TATIUS. — *See Greek Romances.*

ÆSCHYLUS, The Dramas of. In English Verse by Anna Swanwick. 4th edition.

—— **The Tragedies of.** In Prose, with Notes and Introduction, by T. A. Buckley, B.A. Portrait. 3*s.* 6*d.*

AMMIANUS MARCELLINUS. History of Rome during the Reigns of Constantius, Julian, Jovianus, Valentinian, and Valens, by C. D. Yonge, B.A. Double volume. 7*s.* 6*d.*

ANTONINUS (M. Aurelius), The Thoughts of. Translated, with Notes. Biographical Sketch, and Essay on the Philosophy, by George Long, M.A. 3*s.* 6*d.* Fine Paper edition on hand-made paper. 6*s.*

APOLLONIUS RHODIUS. 'The Argonautica.' Translated by E. P. Coleridge.

APULEIUS, The Works of. Comprising the Golden Ass, God of Socrates, Florida, and Discourse of Magic, &c. Frontispiece.

ARISTOPHANES' Comedies. Trans., with Notes and Extracts from Frere's and other Metrical Versions, by W. J. Hickie. Portrait. 2 vols.

ARISTOTLE'S Nicomachean Ethics. Trans., with Notes, Analytical Introduction, and Questions for Students, by Ven. Archdn. Browne.

— **Politics and Economics.** Trans., with Notes, Analyses, and Index, by E. Walford, M.A., and an Essay and Life by Dr. Gillies.

— **Metaphysics.** Trans., with Notes, Analysis, and Examination Questions, by Rev. John H. M'Mahon, M.A.

— **History of Animals.** In Ten Books. Trans., with Notes and Index, by R. Cresswell, M.A.

— **Organon**; or, Logical Treatises, and the Introduction of Porphyry. With Notes, Analysis, and Introduction, by Rev. O. F. Owen, M.A. 2 vols. 3*s*. 6*d*. each.

— **Rhetoric and Poetics.** Trans., with Hobbes' Analysis, Exam. Questions, and Notes, by T. Buckley, B.A. Portrait.

ATHENÆUS. The Deipnosophists. Trans. by C. D. Yonge, B.A. With an Appendix of Poetical Fragments. 3 vols.

ATLAS of Classical Geography. 22 large Coloured Maps. With a complete Index. Imp. 8vo. 7*s*. 6*d*.

BION.—*See Theocritus.*

CÆSAR. Commentaries on the Gallic and Civil Wars, with the Supplementary Books attributed to Hirtius, including the complete Alexandrian, African, and Spanish Wars. Portrait.

CATULLUS, Tibullus, and the Vigil of Venus. Trans. with Notes and Biographical Introduction. To which are added, Metrical Versions by Lamb, Grainger, and others. Frontispiece.

CICERO'S Orations. Trans. by C. D. Yonge, B.A. 4 vols.

— **On Oratory and Orators.** With Letters to Quintus and Brutus. Trans., with Notes, by Rev. J. S. Watson, M.A.

— **On the Nature of the Gods,** Divination, Fate, Laws, a Republic, Consulship. Trans. by C. D. Yonge, B.A.

— **Academics,** De Finibus, and Tusculan Questions. By C. D. Yonge, B.A. With Sketch of the Greek Philosophers mentioned by Cicero.

CICERO'S Works.—*Continued.*

— **Offices**; or, Moral Duties. Cato Major, an Essay on Old Age; Lælius, an Essay on Friendship; Scipio's Dream; Paradoxes; Letter to Quintus on Magistrates. Trans., with Notes, by C. R. Edmonds. Portrait. 3*s*. 6*d*.

DEMOSTHENES' Orations. Trans., with Notes, Arguments, a Chronological Abstract, and Appendices, by C. Rann Kennedy. 5 vols. (One, 3*s*. 6*d*; four, 5*s*.)

DICTIONARY of LATIN and GREEK Quotations; including Proverbs, Maxims, Mottoes, Law Terms and Phrases. With the Quantities marked, and English Translations. With Index Verborum (622 pages).

— Index Verborum to the above, with the *Quantities* and Accents marked (56 pages), limp cloth. 1*s*.

DIOGENES LAERTIUS. Lives and Opinions of the Ancient Philosophers. Trans., with Notes, by C. D. Yonge, B.A.

EPICTETUS. The Discourses of. With the Encheiridion and Fragments. With Notes, Life, and View of his Philosophy, by George Long, M.A.

EURIPIDES. Trans. by T. A. Buckley, B.A. Portrait. 2 vols.

GREEK ANTHOLOGY. In English Prose by G. Burges, M.A. With Metrical Versions by Bland, Merivale, and others.

GREEK ROMANCES of Heliodorus, Longus, and Achilles Tatius; viz., The Adventures of Theagenes and Chariclea; Amours of Daphnis and Chloe; and Loves of Clitopho and Leucippe. Trans., with Notes, by Rev R. Smith, M.A.

HELIODORUS.—*See Greek Romances.*

HERODOTUS. Literally trans. by Rev. Henry Cary, M.A. Portrait.

HESIOD, CALLIMACHUS, and Theognis. In Prose, with Notes and Biographical Notices by Rev. J. Banks, M.A. Together with the Metrical Versions of Hesiod, by Elton; Callimachus, by Tytler; and Theognis, by Frere.

HOMER'S Iliad. In English Prose, with Notes by T. A. Buckley, B.A. Portrait.

— **Odyssey,** Hymns, Epigrams, and Battle of the Frogs and Mice. In English Prose, with Notes and Memoir by T. A. Buckley, B.A.

HORACE. In Prose by Smart, with Notes selected by T. A. Buckley, B.A. Portrait. 3*s*. 6*d*.

JULIAN THE EMPEROR. Containing Gregory Nazianzen's Two Invectives and Libanius' Monody, with Julian's Theosophical Works. By the Rev. C. W. King, M.A.

JUSTIN, CORNELIUS NEPOS, and Eutropius. Trans., with Notes, by Rev. J. S. Watson, M.A.

JUVENAL, PERSIUS, SULPICIA, and Lucilius. In Prose, with Notes, Chronological Tables, Arguments, by L. Evans, M.A. To which is added the Metrical Version of Juvenal and Persius by Gifford. Frontispiece.

LIVY. The History of Rome. Trans. by Dr. Spillan and others. 4 vols. Portrait.

LONGUS. Daphnis and Chloe.—*See Greek Romances.*

LUCAN'S Pharsalia. In Prose, with Notes by H. T. Riley.

LUCIAN'S Dialogues of the Gods, of the Sea Gods, and of the Dead. Trans. by Howard Williams, M.A.

LUCRETIUS. In Prose, with Notes and Biographical Introduction by Rev. J. S. Watson, M.A. To which is added the Metrical Version by J. M. Good.

MARTIAL'S Epigrams, complete. In Prose, with Verse Translations selected from English Poets, and other sources. Dble. vol. (670 pages). 7*s.* 6*d.*

MOSCHUS.—*See Theocritus.*

OVID'S Works, complete. In Prose, with Notes and Introduction. 3 vols.

PAUSANIAS' Description of Greece. Trans., with Notes and Index, by Rev. A. R. Shilleto, M.A., sometime Scholar of Trinity College, Cambridge. 2 vols.

PHALARIS. Bentley's Dissertations upon the Epistles of Phalaris, Themistocles, Socrates, Euripides, and the Fables of Æsop. With Introduction and Notes by Prof. W. Wagner, Ph.D.

PINDAR. In Prose, with Introduction and Notes by Dawson W. Turner. Together with the Metrical Version by Abraham Moore. Portrait.

PLATO'S Works. Trans. by Rev. H. Cary, H. Davis, and G. Burges. 6 vols.

—— Dialogues. A Summary and Analysis of. With Analytical Index to the Greek text of modern editions and to the above translations, by A. Day, LL.D.

PLAUTUS'S Comedies. In Prose, with Notes by H. T. Riley, B.A. 2 vols.

PLINY'S Natural History. Trans., with Notes, by J. Bostock, M.D., F.R.S., and H. T. Riley, B.A. 6 vols.

PLINY. The Letters of Pliny the Younger. Melmoth's Translation, revised, with Notes and short Life, by Rev. F. C. T. Bosanquet, M.A.

PLUTARCH'S Morals. Theosophical Essays. Trans. by Rev. C. W. King, M.A.

—— Ethical Essays. Trans. by Rev. A. R. Shilleto, M.A.

—— Lives. *See page 7.*

PROPERTIUS, The Elegies of. With Notes, translated by Rev. P. J. F. Gantillon, M.A., with metrical versions of Select Elegies by Nott and Elton. 3*s.* 6*d.*

QUINTILIAN'S Institutes of Oratory. Trans., by Rev. J. S. Watson, M.A. 2 vols.

SALLUST, FLORUS, and VELLEIUS Paterculus. Trans., with Notes and Biographical Notices, by J. S. Watson, M.A.

SENECA DE BENEFICIIS. Translated by Aubrey Stewart, M.A. 3*s.* 6*d.*

SENECA'S Minor Essays. Translated by A. Stewart, M.A.

SOPHOCLES. The Tragedies of. In Prose, with Notes, Arguments, and Introduction. Portrait.

STRABO'S Geography. Trans., with Notes, by W. Falconer, M.A., and H. C. Hamilton. Copious Index, giving Ancient and Modern Names. 3 vols.

SUETONIUS' Lives of the Twelve Cæsars and Lives of the Grammarians. The Translation of Thomson, revised, with Notes, by T. Forester.

TACITUS. The Works of. Trans., with Notes. 2 vols.

TERENCE and PHÆDRUS. In English Prose, with Notes and Arguments, by H. T. Riley, B.A. To which is added Smart's Metrical Version of Phædrus. With Frontispiece.

THEOCRITUS, BION, MOSCHUS, and Tyrtæus. In Prose, with Notes and Arguments, by Rev. J. Banks, M.A. To which are appended the METRICAL VERSIONS of Chapman. Portrait of Theocritus.

THUCYDIDES. The Peloponnesian War. Trans., with Notes, by Rev. H. Dale. Portrait. 2 vols. 3*s.* 6*d.* each.

TYRTÆUS.—*See Theocritus.*

VIRGIL. The Works of. In Prose, with Notes by Davidson. Revised, with additional Notes and Biographical Notice, by T. A. Buckley, B.A. Portrait. 3*s.* 6*d.*

XENOPHON'S Works. Trans., with Notes, by J. S. Watson, M.A., and Rev. H. Dale. Portrait. In 3 vols.

COLLEGIATE SERIES.

10 *Vols. at* 5*s. each.* (2*l.* 10*s. per set.*)

DANTE. The Inferno. Prose Trans., with the Text of the Original on the same page, and Explanatory Notes, by John A. Carlyle, M.D. Portrait.

—— **The Purgatorio.** Prose Trans., with the Original on the same page, and Explanatory Notes, by W. S. Dugdale.

DOBREE'S Adversaria. (Notes on the Greek and Latin Classics.) Edited by the late Prof. Wagner. 2 vols.

DONALDSON (Dr.) The Theatre of the Greeks. With Supplementary Treatise on the Language, Metres, and Prosody of the Greek Dramatists. Numerous Illustrations and 3 Plans. By J. W. Donaldson, D.D.

GOETHE'S Faust. Part I. German Text, with Hayward's Prose Translation and Notes. Revised, with Introduction and Bibliography, by Dr. C. A. Buchheim. [*In the Press.*

KEIGHTLEY'S (Thomas) Mythology of Ancient Greece and Italy. Revised by Dr. Leonhard Schmitz. 12 Plates.

HERODOTUS, Notes on. Original and Selected from the best Commentators. By D. W. Turner, M.A. Coloured Map.

—— **Analysis and Summary of,** with a Synchronistical Table of Events—Tables of Weights, Measures, Money, and Distances—an Outline of the History and Geography—and the Dates completed from Gaisford, Baehr, &c. By J. T. Wheeler.

NEW TESTAMENT (The) in Greek. Griesbach's Text, with the Readings of Mill and Scholz, and Parallel References. Also a Critical Introduction and Chronological Tables. Two Fac-similes of Greek Manuscripts. 650 pages. 3*s.* 6*d.*

—— or bound up with a Greek and English Lexicon to the New Testament (250 pages additional, making in all 900). 5*s.*

The Lexicon separately, 2*s.*

THUCYDIDES. An Analysis and Summary of. With Chronological Table of Events, &c., by J. T. Wheeler.

SCIENTIFIC LIBRARY.

50 *Vols. at* 5*s. each, excepting those marked otherwise.* (13*l.* 6*s.* 0*d. per set.*)

AGASSIZ and GOULD. Outline of Comparative Physiology. Enlarged by Dr. Wright. With Index and 300 Illustrative Woodcuts.

BOLLEY'S Manual of Technical Analysis; a Guide for the Testing and Valuation of the various Natural and Artificial Substances employed in the Arts and Domestic Economy, founded on the work of Dr. Bolley. Edit. by Dr. Paul. 100 Woodcuts.

BRIDGEWATER TREATISES.

—— **Bell (Sir Charles) on the Hand;** its Mechanism and Vital Endowments, as evincing Design. Preceded by an Account of the Author's Discoveries in the Nervous System by A. Shaw. Numerous Woodcuts.

—— **Kirby on the History, Habits,** and Instincts of Animals. With Notes by T. Rymer Jones. 100 Woodcuts. 2 vols.

—— **Buckland's Geology and Mineralogy.** With Additions by Prof. Owen, Prof. Phillips, and R. Brown. Memoir of Buckland. Portrait. 2 vols. 15*s.* Vol. I. Text. Vol. II. 90 large plates with letter-press.

BRIDGEWATER TREATISES. *Continued.*

—— **Chalmers on the Adaptation of** External Nature to the Moral and Intellectual Constitution of Man. With Memoir by Rev. Dr. Cumming. Portrait.

—— **Prout's Treatise on Chemistry,** Meteorology, and the Function of Digestion, with reference to Natural Theology. Edit. by Dr. J. W. Griffith. 2 Maps.

—— **Roget's Animal and Vegetable** Physiology. 463 Woodcuts. 2 vols. 6*s* each.

—— **Kidd on the Adaptation of External** Nature to the Physical Condition of Man. 3*s.* 6*d.*

CARPENTER'S (Dr. W. B.) Zoology. A Systematic View of the Structure, Habits, Instincts, and Uses of the principal Families of the Animal Kingdom, and of the chief Forms of Fossil Remains. Revised by W. S. Dallas, F.L.S. Numerous Woodcuts. 2 vols. 6*s.* each.

—— **Mechanical Philosophy, Astronomy,** and Horology. A Popular Exposition. 181 Woodcuts.

CARPENTER'S Works.—*Continued.*

— **Vegetable Physiology and Systematic Botany.** A complete Introduction to the Knowledge of Plants. Revised by E. Lankester, M.D., &c. Numerous Woodcuts. 6*s.*

— **Animal Physiology.** Revised Edition. 300 Woodcuts. 6*s.*

CHEVREUL on Colour. Containing the Principles of Harmony and Contrast of Colours, and their Application to the Arts; including Painting, Decoration, Tapestries, Carpets, Mosaics, Glazing, Staining, Calico Printing, Letterpress Printing, Map Colouring, Dress, Landscape and Flower Gardening, &c. Trans. by C. Martel. Several Plates.

— With an additional series of 16 Plates in Colours, 7*s.* 6*d.*

ENNEMOSER'S History of Magic. Trans. by W. Howitt. With an Appendix of the most remarkable and best authenticated Stories of Apparitions, Dreams, Second Sight, Table-Turning, and Spirit-Rapping, &c. 2 vols.

HIND'S Introduction to Astronomy. With Vocabulary of the Terms in present use. Numerous Woodcuts. 3*s.* 6*d.*

HOGG'S (Jabez) Elements of Experimental and Natural Philosophy. Being an Easy Introduction to the Study of Mechanics, Pneumatics, Hydrostatics, Hydraulics, Acoustics, Optics, Caloric, Electricity, Voltaism, and Magnetism. 400 Woodcuts.

HUMBOLDT'S Cosmos; or, Sketch of a Physical Description of the Universe. Trans. by E. C. Otté, B. H. Paul, and W. S. Dallas, F.L.S. Portrait. 5 vols. 3*s.* 6*d.* each, excepting vol. v., 5*s.*

— **Personal Narrative of his Travels** in America during the years 1799–1804. Trans., with Notes, by T. Ross. 3 vols.

— **Views of Nature; or, Contemplations** of the Sublime Phenomena of Creation, with Scientific Illustrations. Trans. by E. C. Otté.

HUNT'S (Robert) Poetry of Science; or, Studies of the Physical Phenomena of Nature. By Robert Hunt, Professor at the School of Mines.

JOYCE'S Scientific Dialogues. A Familiar Introduction to the Arts and Sciences. For Schools and Young People. Numerous Woodcuts.

JOYCE'S Introduction to the Arts and Sciences, for Schools and Young People. Divided into Lessons with Examination Questions. Woodcuts. 3*s.* 6*d.*

JUKES-BROWNE'S Student's Handbook of Physical Geology. By A. J. Jukes-Browne, of the Geological Survey of England. With numerous Diagrams and Illustrations, 6*s.*

— **The Student's Handbook of** Historical Geology. By A. J. Jukes-Brown, B.A., F.G.S., of the Geological Survey of England and Wales. With numerous Diagrams and Illustrations. 6*s.*

— **The Building of the British** Islands. A Study in Geographical Evolution. By A J. Jukes-Browne, F.G.S. 7*s.* 6*d.*

KNIGHT'S (Charles) Knowledge is Power. A Popular Manual of Political Economy.

LILLY. Introduction to Astrology. With a Grammar of Astrology and Tables for calculating Nativities, by Zadkiel.

MANTELL'S (Dr.) Geological Ex-cursions through the Isle of Wight and along the Dorset Coast. Numerous Woodcuts and Geological Map.

— **Petrifactions and their Teach-**ings. Handbook to the Organic Remains in the British Museum. Numerous Woodcuts. 6*s.*

— **Wonders of Geology; or, a** Familiar Exposition of Geological Phenomena. A coloured Geological Map of England, Plates, and 200 Woodcuts. 2 vols. 7*s.* 6*d.* each.

SCHOUW'S Earth, Plants, and Man. Popular Pictures of Nature. And Kobell's Sketches from the Mineral Kingdom. Trans. by A. Henfrey, F.R.S. Coloured Map of the Geography of Plants.

SMITH'S (Pye) Geology and Scrip-ture; or, the Relation between the Scriptures and Geological Science. With Memoir.

STANLEY'S Classified Synopsis of the Principal Painters of the Dutch and Flemish Schools, including an Account of some of the early German Masters. By George Stanley.

STAUNTON'S Chess Works. —*See page* 21.

STÖCKHARDT'S Experimental Chemistry. A Handbook for the Study of the Science by simple Experiments. Edit. by C. W. Heaton, F.C.S. Numerous Woodcuts.

URE'S (Dr. A.) Cotton Manufacture of Great Britain, systematically investigated; with an Introductory View of its Comparative State in Foreign Countries. Revised by P. L. Simmonds. 150 Illustrations. 2 vols.

— **Philosophy of Manufactures,** or an Exposition of the Scientific, Moral, and Commercial Economy of the Factory System of Great Britain. Revised by P. L. Simmonds. Numerous Figures. 800 pages. 7*s.* 6*d.*

ECONOMICS AND FINANCE.

GILBART'S History, Principles, and Practice of Banking. Revised to 1881 by A. S. Michie, of the Royal Bank of Scotland. Portrait of Gilbart. 2 vols. 10*s*.

RICARDO on the Principles of Political Economy and Taxation. Edited by E. C. K Gonner, M.A., Lecturer, University College, Liverpool. *In the press.*

SMITH (Adam). The Wealth of Nations. An Inquiry into the Nature and Causes of. Edited by E. Belfort Bax. 2 vols. 7*s*.

REFERENCE LIBRARY.

32 *Volumes at Various Prices.* (8*l*. 18*s*. *per set.*)

BLAIR'S Chronological Tables. Comprehending the Chronology and History of the World, from the Earliest Times to the Russian Treaty of Peace, April 1856. By J. W. Rosse. 800 pages. 10*s*.

—— Index of Dates. Comprehending the principal Facts in the Chronology and History of the World, from the Earliest to the Present, alphabetically arranged; being a complete Index to the foregoing. By J. W. Rosse. 2 vols. 5*s*. each.

BOHN'S Dictionary of Quotations from the English Poets. 4th and cheaper Edition. 6*s*.

BOND'S Handy-book of Rules and Tables for Verifying Dates with the Christian Era. 4th Edition. 5*s*.

BUCHANAN'S Dictionary of Science and Technical Terms used in Philosophy, Literature, Professions, Commerce, Arts, and Trades. By W. H. Buchanan, with Supplement. Edited by Jas. A. Smith. 6*s*.

CHRONICLES OF THE TOMBS. A Select Collection of Epitaphs, with Essay on Epitaphs and Observations on Sepulchral Antiquities. By T. J. Pettigrew, F.R.S., F.S.A. 5*s*.

CLARK'S (Hugh) Introduction to Heraldry. Revised by J. R. Planché. 5*s*. 950 Illustrations.

—— *With the Illustrations coloured*, 15*s*.

COINS, Manual of.—*See Humphreys.*

COOPER'S Biographical Dictionary. Containing concise notices of upwards of 15,000 eminent persons of all ages and countries. 2 vols. 5*s*. each.

DATES, Index of.—*See Blair.*

DICTIONARY of Obsolete and Provincial English. Containing Words from English Writers previous to the 19th Century. By Thomas Wright, M.A., F.S.A., &c. 2 vols. 5*s*. each.

EPIGRAMMATISTS (The). A Selection from the Epigrammatic Literature of Ancient, Mediæval, and Modern Times. With Introduction, Notes, Observations, Illustrations, an Appendix on Works connected with Epigrammatic Literature, by Rev. H. Dodd, M.A. 6*s*.

GAMES, Handbook of. Edited by Henry G. Bohn. Numerous Diagrams. 5*s*. (*See also page* 21.)

HENFREY'S Guide to English Coins. Revised Edition, by C. F. Keary, M.A., F.S.A. With an Historical Introduction. 6*s*.

HUMPHREYS' Coin Collectors' Manual. An Historical Account of the Progress of Coinage from the Earliest Time, by H. N. Humphreys. 140 Illustrations. 2 vols. 5*s*. each.

LOWNDES' Bibliographer's Manual of English Literature. Containing an Account of Rare and Curious Books published in or relating to Great Britain and Ireland, from the Invention of Printing, with Biographical Notices and Prices, by W. T. Lowndes. Parts I.-X. (A to Z), 3*s*. 6*d*. each. Part XI. (Appendix Vol.), 5*s*. Or the 11 parts in 4 vols., half morocco, 2*l*. 2*s*. Also in 6 vols. cloth, 5*s*. each.

MEDICINE, Handbook of Domestic, Popularly Arranged. By Dr. H. Davies. 700 pages. 5*s*.

NOTED NAMES OF FICTION. Dictionary of. Including also Familiar Pseudonyms, Surnames bestowed on Eminent Men, &c. By W. A. Wheeler, M.A. 5*s*.

POLITICAL CYCLOPÆDIA. A Dictionary of Political, Constitutional, Statistical, and Forensic Knowledge; forming a Work of Reference on subjects of Civil Administration, Political Economy, Finance, Commerce, Laws, and Social Relations. 4 vols. 3*s*. 6*d*. each.

PROVERBS, Handbook of. Containing an entire Republication of Ray's Collection, with Additions from Foreign Languages and Sayings, Sentences, Maxims, and Phrases. 5s.

—— A Polyglot of Foreign. Comprising French, Italian, German, Dutch, Spanish, Portuguese, and Danish. With English Translations. 5s.

SYNONYMS and ANTONYMS; or, Kindred Words and their Opposites, Collected and Contrasted by Ven. C. J. Smith, M.A. 5s.

WRIGHT (Th.)—*See Dictionary.*

NOVELISTS' LIBRARY.

13 *Volumes at* 3s. 6d. *each, excepting those marked otherwise.* (2l. 8s. 6d. *per set.*)

BJORNSON'S Arne and the Fisher Lassie. Translated from the Norse with an Introduction by W. H. Low, M.A.

BURNEY'S Evelina; or, a Young Lady's Entrance into the World. By F. Burney (Mme. D'Arblay). With Introduction and Notes by A. R. Ellis, Author of 'Sylvestra,' &c.

—— Cecilia. With Introduction and Notes by A. R. Ellis. 2 vols.

DE STAËL. Corinne or Italy. By Madame de Staël. Translated by Emily Baldwin and Paulina Driver.

EBERS' Egyptian Princess. Trans. by Emma Buchheim.

FIELDING'S Joseph Andrews and his Friend Mr. Abraham Adams. With Roscoe's Biography. *Cruikshank's Illustrations.*

—— Amelia. Roscoe's Edition, revised. *Cruikshank's Illustrations.* 5s.

—— History of Tom Jones, a Foundling. Roscoe's Edition. *Cruikshank's Illustrations.* 2 vols.

GROSSI'S Marco Visconti. Trans. by A. F. D.

MANZONI. The Betrothed: being a Translation of 'I Promessi Sposi.' Numerous Woodcuts. 1 vol. 5s.

STOWE (Mrs. H. B.) Uncle Tom's Cabin; or, Life among the Lowly. 8 full-page Illustrations.

ARTISTS' LIBRARY.

9 *Volumes at Various Prices.* (2l. 8s. 6d. *per set.*)

BELL (Sir Charles). The Anatomy and Philosophy of Expression, as Connected with the Fine Arts. 5s. Illustrated.

DEMMIN. History of Arms and Armour from the Earliest Period. By Auguste Demmin. Trans. by C. C. Black, M.A., Assistant Keeper, S. K. Museum. 1900 Illustrations. 7s. 6d.

FAIRHOLT'S Costume in England. Third Edition. Enlarged and Revised by the Hon. H. A. Dillon, F.S.A. With more than 700 Engravings. 2 vols. 5s. each.

Vol. I. History. Vol. II. Glossary.

FLAXMAN. Lectures on Sculpture. With Three Addresses to the R.A. by Sir R. Westmacott, R.A., and Memoir of Flaxman. Portrait and 53 Plates. 6s.

HEATON'S Concise History of Painting. New Edition, revised by W. Cosmo Monkhouse. 5s.

LECTURES ON PAINTING by the Royal Academicians, Barry, Opie, Fuseli. With Introductory Essay and Notes by R. Wornum. Portrait of Fuseli. 5s.

LEONARDO DA VINCI'S Treatise on Painting. Trans. by J. F. Rigaud, R.A. With a Life and an Account of his Works by J. W. Brown. Numerous Plates. 5s.

PLANCHÉ'S History of British Costume, from the Earliest Time to the 19th Century. By J. R. Planché. 400 Illustrations. 5s.

LIBRARY OF SPORTS AND GAMES.

10 Volumes at 3s. 6d. and 5s. each. (2l. 6s. 0d. per set.)

BOHN'S Handbooks of Athletic Sports. With numerous Illustrations. In 7 vols. 3s. 6d. each.

Vol. I.—Cricket, by Hon. and Rev. E. Lyttelton; Lawn Tennis, by H. W. W. Wilberforce; Tennis, Rackets, and Fives, by Julian Marshall, Major Spens, and J. A. Tait; Golf, by W. T. Linskill; Hockey, by F. S. Creswell.

Vol. II.—Rowing and Sculling, by W. B. Woodgate; Sailing, by E. F. Knight; Swimming, by M. and J. R. Cobbett.

Vol. III.—Boxing, by R. G. Allanson-Winn; Single Stick and Sword Exercise, by R. G. Allanson-Winn and C. Phillipps-Wolley: Wrestling, by Walter Armstrong; Fencing, by H. A. Colmore Dunn.

Vol. IV.—Skating, by Douglas Adams; Rugby Football, by Harry Vassall: Association Football, by C. W. Alcock. [*In the press.*

Vol. V. — Cycling and Athletics, by H. H. Griffin; Rounders, Field Ball, Baseball, Bowls, Quoits, Skittles, &c., by J. M. Walker, M.A., Assistant Master Bedford Grammar School. [*In the press.*

Vol. VI.—Gymnastics, by A. F. Jenkin; Clubs and Dumb-bells, by G. T. B. Cobbett and A. F. Jenkin. [*In the press.*

Vol. VII.—Riding, Driving, and Stable Management. By W. A. Kerr, V.C., and other writers. [*Preparing.*

BOHN'S Handbooks of Games. New Edition, entirely rewritten. 2 volumes. 3s. 6d. each.

Vol. I. TABLE GAMES.

Contents:—Billiards, with Pool, Pyramids, and Snooker, by Major-Gen. A. W. Drayson, F.R.A.S., with a preface by W. J. Peall—Bagatelle, by 'Berkeley'—Chess, by R. F. Green—Draughts, Backgammon, Dominoes, Solitaire, Reversi, Go Bang, Rouge et noir, Roulette, E.O., Hazard, Faro, by 'Berkeley.'

Vol. II. CARD GAMES.

Contents:—Whist, by Dr. William Pole, F.R.S., Author of 'The Philosophy of Whist, &c.'—Solo Whist, by R. F. Green; Piquet, Ecarté, Euchre, Bézique, and Cribbage, by 'Berkeley;' Poker, Loo, Vingt-et-un, Napoleon, Newmarket, Rouge et Noir, Pope Joan, Speculation, &c. &c., by Baxter-Wray.

CHESS CONGRESS of 1862. A collection of the games played. Edited by J. Löwenthal. New edition, 5s.

MORPHY'S Games of Chess, being the Matches and best Games played by the American Champion, with explanatory and analytical Notes by J. Löwenthal. With short Memoir and Portrait of Morphy. 5s.

STAUNTON'S Chess-Player's Hand-book. A Popular and Scientific Introduction to the Game, with numerous Diagrams. 5s.

— Chess Praxis. A Supplement to the Chess-player's Handbook. Containing the most important modern Improvements in the Openings; Code of Chess Laws; and a Selection of Morphy's Games. Annotated. 636 pages. Diagrams. 5s.

— Chess-Player's Companion. Comprising a Treatise on Odds, Collection of Match Games, including the French Match with M. St. Amant, and a Selection of Original Problems. Diagrams and Coloured Frontispiece. 5s.

— Chess Tournament of 1851. A Collection of Games played at this celebrated assemblage. With Introduction and Notes. Numerous Diagrams. [illegible]

BOHN'S CHEAP SERIES.

Price 1s. each.

A Series of Complete Stories or Essays, mostly reprinted from Vols. in Bohn's Libraries, and neatly bound in stiff paper cover, with cut edges, suitable for Railway Reading.

ASCHAM (Roger). Scholemaster. By Professor Mayor.

CARPENTER (Dr. W. B.). Physiology of Temperance and Total Abstinence.

EMERSON. England and English Characteristics. Lectures on the Race, Ability, Manners, Truth, Character, Wealth, Religion, &c. &c.

— **Nature**: An Essay. To which are added Orations, Lectures, and Addresses.

— **Representative Men**: Seven Lectures on PLATO, SWEDENBORG, MONTAIGNE, SHAKESPEARE, NAPOLEON, and GOETHE.

— **Twenty Essays on Various Subjects.**

— **The Conduct of Life.**

FRANKLIN (Benjamin). Autobiography. Edited by J. Sparks.

HAWTHORNE (Nathaniel). Twice-told Tales. Two Vols. in One.

— **Snow Image,** and Other Tales.

— **Scarlet Letter.**

— **House with the Seven Gables.**

— **Transformation**; or the Marble Fawn. Two Parts.

HAZLITT (W.). Table-talk: Essays on Men and Manners. Three Parts.

— **Plain Speaker**: Opinions on Books, Men, and Things. Three Parts.

— **Lectures on the English Comic** Writers.

— **Lectures on the English Poets.**

— **Lectures on the Characters of** Shakespeare's Plays.

— **Lectures on the Literature of** the Age of Elizabeth, chiefly Dramatic.

IRVING (Washington). Lives of Successors of Mohammed.

— **Life of Goldsmith.**

— **Sketch-book.**

— **Tales of a Traveller.**

— **Tour on the Prairies.**

— **Conquests of Granada and** Spain. Two Parts.

— **Life and Voyages of Columbus.** Two Parts.

— **Companions of Columbus**: Their Voyages and Discoveries.

— **Adventures of Captain Bonne**-ville in the Rocky Mountains and the Far West.

— **Knickerbocker's History of New** York, from the beginning of the World to the End of the Dutch Dynasty.

— **Tales of the Alhambra.**

— **Conquest of Florida under Her**-nando de Soto.

— **Abbotsford & Newstead Abbey.**

— **Salmagundi**; or, The Whim-Whams and Opinions of LAUNCELOT LANGSTAFF, Esq.

— **Bracebridge Hall**; or, The Humourists.

— **Astoria**; or, Anecdotes of an Enterprise beyond the Rocky Mountains.

— **Wolfert's Roost,** and other Tales.

LAMB (Charles). Essays of Elia. With a Portrait.

— **Last Essays of Elia.**

— **Eliana.** With Biographical Sketch.

MARRYAT (Captain). Pirate and the Three Cutters. With a Memoir of the Author.

Bohn's Select Library of Standard Works.

Price 1s. in paper covers, and 1s. 6d. in cloth.

1. BACON'S ESSAYS. With Introduction and Notes.
2. LESSING'S LAOKOON. Beasley's Translation, revised, with Introduction, Notes, &c., by Edward Bell, M.A. With Frontispiece.
3. DANTE'S INFERNO. Translated, with Notes, by Rev. H. F. Cary.
4. GOETHE'S FAUST. Part I. Translated, with Introduction, by Anna Swanwick.
5. GOETHE'S BOYHOOD. Being Part I. of the Autobiography. Translated by J. Oxenford.
6. SCHILLER'S MARY STUART and THE MAID OF ORLEANS. Translated by J. Mellish and Anna Swanwick.
7. THE QUEEN'S ENGLISH. By the late Dean Alford.
8. LIFE AND LABOURS OF THE LATE THOMAS BRASSEY. By Sir A. Helps, K.C.B.
9. PLATO'S DIALOGUES: The Apology—Crito—Phaedo—Protagoras. With Introductions.
10. MOLIÈRE'S PLAYS: The Miser—Tartuffe—The Shopkeeper turned Gentleman. Translated by C. H. Walt, M.A. With brief Memoir.
11. GOETHE'S REINEKE FOX, in English Hexameters. By A. Rogers.
12. OLIVER GOLDSMITH'S PLAYS.
13. LESSING'S PLAYS: Nathan the Wise—Minna von Barnhelm.
14. PLAUTUS'S COMEDIES: Trinummus — Menaechmi — Aulularia — Captivi.
15. WATERLOO DAYS. By C. A. Eaton. With Preface and Notes by Edward Bell.
16. DEMOSTHENES—ON THE CROWN. Translated by C. Rann Kennedy.
17. THE VICAR OF WAKEFIELD.
18. OLIVER CROMWELL. By Dr. Reinhold Pauli.
19. THE PERFECT LIFE. By Dr. Channing. Edited by his nephew, Rev. W. H. Channing.
20. LADIES IN PARLIAMENT, HORACE AT ATHENS, and other pieces, by Sir George Otto Trevelyan, Bart.
21. DEFOE'S THE PLAGUE IN LONDON.
22. IRVING'S LIFE OF MAHOMET.
23. HORACE'S ODES, by various hands. [*Out of Print.*
24. BURKE'S ESSAY ON 'THE SUBLIME AND BEAUTIFUL.' With Short Memoir.
25. HAUFF'S CARAVAN.
26. SHERIDAN'S PLAYS.
27. DANTE'S PURGATORIO. Translated by Cary.
28. HARVEY'S TREATISE ON THE CIRCULATION OF THE BLOOD
29. CICERO'S FRIENDSHIP AND OLD AGE.
30. DANTE'S PARADISO. Translated by Cary.

THE NEW WEBSTER.

AN ENTIRELY NEW EDITION,
Thoroughly Revised, considerably Enlarged, and reset in new type from beginning to end.

2118 PAGES. 3500 ILLUSTRATIONS.

PRICES: *Cloth, £1 11s. 6d.; Sheep, £2 2s.;*
Half Russia, £2 5s.: Calf, £2 8s.

Editorial work upon this revision has been in active progress for over **10 years.**

Not less than **100** editorial labourers have been engaged upon it.

Over **60,000*l*.** was expended in its preparation before the first copy was printed.

Webster is the Standard in our Postal Telegraph Department.

Webster is the Standard in the U.S. Government Printing Office.

The *Times* said of the last edition: 'It has all along kept a leading position.'

The *Quarterly Review* said: 'Certainly the best practical dictionary extant.'

The *Lord Chief Justice of England* said: 'I have looked, so that I may not go wrong, at WEBSTER'S DICTIONARY, a work of the greatest learning, research, and ability.'

The *Chief Justice of the U.S.A.* said: 'I have used and relied on WEBSTER'S UNABRIDGED DICTIONARY for many years, and entirely concur in the general commendation it has received.'

The only Authorised and Complete Edition.

LONDON: GEORGE BELL AND SONS.

Lightning Source UK Ltd.
Milton Keynes UK
UKHW010630020421
381430UK00001B/157